D1603661

Archer Chu
1995.

New Testament Greek Syntax

Greek Syntax

AN ILLUSTRATED MANUAL

Wesley J. Perschbacher

NEW TESTAMENT GREEK SYNTAX

AN ILLUSTRATED MANUAL

WESLEY J. PERSCHBACHER

Moody Press
Chicago

CONTENTS

Introduction	vii
Abbreviations	xi
Glossary	xiii
Basic Bibliography	xxi
Adjectives	1
Select Bibliography for Adjectives	22
Adverbs	23
Select Bibliography for Adverbs	30
Articles	31
Select Bibliography for Articles	70
Conjunctions	73
Select Bibliography for Conjunctions	94
Negatives	97
Select Bibliography for Negatives	110
Nouns and Cases	111
Select Bibliography for Nouns and Cases	169
Particles	171
Select Bibliography for Particles	184
Prepositions	185
Select Bibliography for Prepositions	233
Pronouns	235
Select Bibliography for Pronouns	260
Finite Verbs	261
Indicative Mood	261
Voice	264
Tense	278
Present Tense	279
Future Tense	290
Imperfect Tense	298
Aorist Tense	303
Perfect Tense	310
Pluperfect Tense	314
Select Bibliography for the Indicative Mood	316
Subjunctive Mood	319
Voice	330
Tense	340
Present Tense	340
Aorist tense	342
Select Bibliography for the Subjunctive Mood	343

Imperative Mood   345
    Voice   351
    Tense   357
        Present Tense   357
        Aorist Tense   358
    Select Bibliography for the Imperative Mood   360
Optative Mood   361
    Voice   363
    Tense   364
        Present Tense   364
        Aorist Tense   364
    Select Bibliography for the Optative Mood   366
Infinitives   367
    Voice   374
    Tense   378
        Present Tense   378
        Aorist Tense   379
        Perfect Tense   379
        Future Tense   380
    Substantive Accusatives   380
    Select Bibliography for Infinitives   382
Participles   383
    Adjectival   383
    Substantival   387
    Adverbial   397
    Verbal   403
        Voice   411
        Tense   420
    Select Bibliography for Participles   424
Scripture Index   425
Subject Index   443

INTRODUCTION

Syntax refers to the structure and relationship of words, phrases, or clauses within a given sentence or paragraph. It is also called "exegetical grammar" by some grammarians, because syntax is a branch of grammar.

"One picture is worth a thousand words" describes the intention of this manual of Greek syntax—to paint verbal pictures of Greek syntax and grammar. More than 3,000 New Testament verses are used in this volume. When a given verse is used more than once, at least two principles are used in reference to that verse so that duplication of verses and principles should not occur. Some Greek grammars give long, detailed definitions and explanations, with few examples or illustrations, and the examples that are given often refer to a New Testament text rather than quoting the text itself. Other grammars may articulate more extensively with principles and exceptions to rules. The design of this book is to state a principle clearly but briefly and then to illustrate the principle with a series of examples from the New Testament. The goal is to assist the student of the Greek New Testament to develop his or her ability and skill at reading and understanding the Greek text by providing a definitive, detailed, comprehensive, but not exhaustive, manual filled with New Testament examples that illustrate the main varieties of functions of any given Greek term (word, phrase, or clause).

How to Use this Book: *New Testament Greek Syntax* is structured according to outline form. Grammatical and syntactical principles are grouped according to the various parts of speech in an alphabetic arrangement from "adjectives" to "verbs." A principle is stated and is followed by several New Testament Greek examples, with the verse reference in parentheses and the English translation directly below the Greek text. The words that are the focus of the specific principle are in bold type in both the Greek and English. The English translation of the Greek text is the author's own and is not designed to follow any published English translation. Frequently in the English translation an omission within the Greek is indicated by brackets. This ellipsis may include an English term only or both Greek and English terms. The order of the examples provided usually (but not always) follow this pattern: singular, plural; nom., gen., dat., acc., voc.; masc., fem., neut.; 1st pers., 2d pers., 3d pers.

The Greek text used is generic in respect to five Greek editions—GNT, NA, WH, TR & MT (see the following section on abbreviations). Any variation within these Greek editions will be so indicated in a footnote. Two exceptions: the movable nu (ν) and the movable sigma (ς) are placed in parentheses when the various Greek texts are not in agreement.

Often the categories presented are an obvious feature of the Greek text. For example, the first and second attributive adjectives as well as the articular substantive adjectives are clearly marked by the article in relation to the adjective and noun. However, when the article is not present, the adjective may be attributive, predicate, substantive, or adverbial. These various options test the perception and skill of the New Testament Greek student in understanding the Greek text. Regular and consistent exposure to the Greek New Testament will enhance the ability of the student to refine this skill.

Reference to the *glossary* may be helpful for terms that are new or unfamiliar. Checking the *subject index* for references to a particular topic of study will help locate places where that topic is addressed in other sections. This will help show how a given topic relates to other topics. The *Scripture index* may be used when one is studying a particular passage and desires grammatical insight. Study in other grammars is encouraged in conjunction with this manual, since they will complement this text. The *select bibliography* at the end of each section will point you to helpful reference material to supplement your use of this volume.

A basic rule of thumb is to be noted. The function of a term (word, phrase, clause, or sentence) will be determined by three factors: the meaning of the term; the form (or parsing) of the term; and the context in which the term is found. All three factors must be carefully and consistently considered in order to obtain the correct use or function of the term in question.

The Five-case System Versus the Eight-case System:

1. The five-case system identifies the cases as nominative, genitive, dative, accusative, and vocative. The eight-case system identifies them as nominative, genitive, ablative, dative, locative, instrumental, accusative, and vocative. The five case system combines the ablative with the genitive, and the instrumental and locative with the dative.

2. The five-case system defines *case* in terms of form, each case having a different and distinct form. The eight-case system defines *case* in terms of function, each case having a specific function. However, function is determined by context as well as by case and rarely by case alone. Ernest De Witt Burton has stated the following in reference to verbal forms, but the application to case forms is apropos: "It is important that the nature of the relation between form and function be clearly held in mind. It is by no means . . . that each form has but one function, and that each function can be discharged by but one form. . . . We find that a given form . . . performs various distinct functions."[1]

3. Grammarians differ on this question. Some hold to a five-case system (e.g., F. W. Blass, J. Harold Greenlee, C. F. D. Moule, James Hope Moulton, Nigel Turner, J. W. Wenham) and others to the eight-case system (e.g., J. A. Brooks and C. L. Winbery, Wm. D. Chamberlain, H. E. Dana and J. R. Mantey, A. T. Robertson, Ray Summers). Thus, it is important to be aware of both systems in the study of New Testament Greek.

4. Of even greater practical significance is the fact that virtually all lexicons, concordances, and analytical helps follow the five-case system.

5. This volume follows the five-case system. These case forms and their functions will be considered under the treatment of nouns.

---

[1] Ernest De Witt Burton, *Syntax of the Moods and Tenses in New Testament Greek* (Edinburgh: T & T Clark, 1955), 1-2.

I wish to express appreciation to those who have assisted me in the completion of this volume. My son Dan has given me valuable technical help on the computer when my lack of skill and ability left me frustrated. My colleagues at Moody Bible Institute, Dr. Brent Garrison and Dr. Jay Fernlund, have encouraged me in this entire endeavor, often asking about the progress I was making. Scot Martin, an instructor with MBI External Studies, has reviewed and critiqued this book, giving valuable advice and suggestions along the way. Lowell Yoder, a former student and a practicing lawyer, has exhibited great enthusiasm as he also critiqued and corrected the manuscript from two points of view—as a student and as a lawyer. My daughter Ruth Morton has worked on the Scripture and subject indexes when the pressures of meeting deadlines for the completion of this book seemed more than what I could accomplish on my own. My wife, Selma, has shown great patience and support when the demands of completing this project kept me from giving proper attention to her. Joe O'Day and Dave DeWit of Moody Press have given me the support needed to make this volume a reality. Of course, the input and feedback of both my former teachers and my students over the past years have contributed to the development and completion of this work.

I am well aware of the weaknesses, incompleteness, and fallibility of this manual. Any errors that remain after the careful process of editing are fully my responsibility. If those who desire to know the words of the New Testament as they were given in the Greek language find this book beneficial to their understanding of God's Word, I will have succeeded in my task. May God's people be enriched by the use of this volume.

ABBREVIATIONS

acc.	accusative case
act.	active voice
adj.	adjective; adjectival
adv.	adverb; adverbial
aor.	aorist tense; aoristic
cf.	compare
dat.	dative case
dep.	deponent
Eph.	Ephesians
fem.	feminine gender
fut.	future tense
Gal.	Galatians
gen.	genitive case
GNT	*The Greek New Testament*. 4th ed. Edited by Aland et al. United Bible Societies, 1993.
Heb.	Hebrews
imper.	imperative mood
impf.	imperfect tense
indecl.	indeclinable, having a fixed form
indic.	indicative mood
infin.	infinitive
masc.	masculine gender
Matt.	Matthew
mid.	middle voice
MT	*The Greek New Testament According to the Majority Text*. Edited by Zane C. Hodges and L. Farstad. Nashville: Nelson, 1982.
NA	*Novum Testamentum Graece*. 26th ed. Edited by Nestle-Aland et al. Stuttgart, Germany, 1979.
neut.	neuter gender
nom.	nominative case
NT	New Testament
opt.	optative mood
OT	Old Testament
part.	particle
pass.	passive voice
perf.	perfect tense
pers.	person
Phil.	Philippians
Philem.	Philemon

plupf.	pluperfect tense
prep.	preposition
pres.	present tense
pron.	pronoun
ptc.	participle
Rev.	Revelation
Rom.	Romans
sing.	singular
subj.	subjunctive mood
TR	*Textus Receptus, The Received Text of the Greek New Testament*
TRb	TR, Beza's text, 1598.
TRs	TR, Stephens' text, 1550.
voc.	vocative case
WH	*The New Testament in the Original Greek.* Edited by Westcott and Hort, 1881.
1 Cor.	1 Corinthians
2 Cor.	2 Corinthians
1 Thess.	1 Thessalonians
2 Thess.	2 Thessalonians
1 Tim.	1 Timothy
2 Tim.	2 Timothy

GLOSSARY

Ablative case. The case of separation, source, or origin.

Absolute. A word or phrase standing independently and having no grammatical relationship or a subordinate relationship with the main sentence.

Accusative case. The accusative case is most often used as the direct object of a verb. In English, it is called the objective case. The idea of the case is extension, limitation, goal, or motion toward.

Active case. The subject of the verb performs the action of the verb.

Adjective/adjectival. A word, phrase, or clause modifying a substantive.

Adverb/adverbial. A word, phrase, or clause modifying a verb, adjective, or another adverb.

Adverbial participle. The participle may function as an adverb in a dependent clause. The adverbial function depends on the context and is not inherent in the participle itself.

Adversative. Indicates contrast or antithesis.

Ambiguity/ambiguous. A word or phrase that has more than one form, meaning, or function.

Anaphoric/anaphora. The use of the definite article with a substantive to refer back to a corresponding anarthrous word in the preceding context.

Anarthrous substantive. A word without an article.

Antecedent. 1) A substantive to which a pronoun refers is called an antecedent. 2) A temporal relationship indicating an action having taken place prior to the action of the main verb.

Antonym. A word that is opposite in meaning to another word.

Aorist/aoristic. The action of a verb considered undefined as to durative or completed action. It states a simple fact.

Apodosis. The conclusion of a conditional sentence, i.e., the "then . . ." clause of an "if . . . then . . ." sentence.

Apposition/appositive. A word, phrase, or clause following a substantive, which explains or gives further information about the substantive.

Arthrous substantive. A word with an article.

Articular substantive. A word with an article.

Ascensive. Intensive or increasing the basic meaning of a conjunction.

Aspect. Describes the kind of action of the verb, whether durative action with present and imperfect tenses; completed action with perfect or pluperfect tenses; or undefined action with aorist and future tenses.

Asyndeton. The omission of coordinating conjunctions that would usually join words, clauses, or sentences together.

Attributive adjective. An adjective or participle that qualifies another noun or substantive.

Cardinal numbers. Numbers indicating sequence— one, two, three, etc.

Case. Indicates inflected endings of nouns, adjectives, pronouns, articles, and participles.

Casus pendens. The subject of the sentence is isolated from the rest of the sentence. Psalm 18:30, "God, his way is perfect."

Causal clause. An adverbial clause expressing a causal relationship to the main verb.

Causative verb. A transitive verb that causes the action.

Chiasmus. An arrangement of a text in an a-b-c-c-b-a structure; that is, a series of two or more items is repeated in reverse order.

> A. The Sabbath
>> B. was made for man
>> B. and not man
> A. for the Sabbath.

Circumstantial participle. An additional thought that affects the main verbal action as an adverbial clause, e.g., causal, conditional, or temporal.

Cognate. Words having a common origin or meaning, e.g., truth, true, truly, truthful.

Cognate accusative. An accusative noun that contains the same idea or root form as the verb and indicates emphasis.

Collective noun. A noun that is singular in form but referring to a group of individuals or things.

Comparative degree. Adjectives and adverbs that express relative quantity, quality, or intensity.

Complement/complementary. A word that completes the meaning of another word, e.g., a predicate nominative.

Complementary infinitive. An infinitive required to complete the meaning of a verb, adjective, or an adverb.

Complex sentence. A sentence composed of one main clause and one or more subordinate or dependent clauses.

Compound sentence. A sentence composed of two or more main or independent clauses.

Compound verb. A verb combined with a preposition.

Conative action. Attempted or contemplated, but incompleted action; synonym of tendential.

Concessive participle. The participle may function as the protasis of a concessive sentence, e.g., even if, although.

Concord. Agreement of person, gender, and number among grammatical parts of speech within a sentence.

Condition/conditional clause. An adverbial clause that expresses an "if" clause, followed by a "then" clause.

Conditional participle. A participle that functions as the protasis of a conditional sentence.

Conjugation. An orderly arrangement of inflected forms of verbs, based on person, gender, number, tense, voice, and mood.

Conjunction. A part of speech that joins words, phrases, clauses, and sentences.

Conjunctive participle. A participle that accompanies the action of the main verb and is translated as a finite verb and is connected to the main verb by "and."

Consecutive clause. A clause expressing result.

Constative. The use of the aorist to summarize action that took place over a period of time; synonymous with "historical."

Coordinate conjunction. Links two or more grammatical units of equal rank.

Copula. A linking word, such as a conjunction or a verb of being. The Greek verb εἰμί (or its various forms) links the subject and complement.

Coronis. A mark that looks like an apostrophe and which points out crasis, a contracted syllable, e.g., κἀκεῖθεν = καὶ ἐκεῖθεν.

Customary action. Action that is repeated, habitual, or customary.

Crasis. The merging of a word with a following word by the omission and contraction of vowels, e.g., καὶ ἐγώ = κἀγώ.

Culminative. The conclusion or the end of an action is in focus; synonymous with "effective"

Dative case. The case of personal interest often expressed in an indirect object relationship.

Declinable/decline(d)/declension. An orderly arrangement of inflected adjectives, nouns, pronouns, and participles, based on case, gender, and number.

Deliberative. A real or rhetorical question.

Dependent clause. A subordinate clause.

Deponent. A verb with a middle or passive form but an active function.

Diaresis. A mark (") over the second of two consecutive vowels (distinguishing two vowels), which may otherwise be perceived as a diphthong.

Diphthong. Two vowels pronounced with one sound, e.g., οἱ, αἱ.

Direct discourse. Quotation of the exact words of a speaker or writer.

Direct object. A substantive that is directly affected by the action of the verb.

Disjunctive. Two words, phrases, or clauses that are mutually exclusive, **"either/or."**

Distributive term. Each member of a group is considered individually.

Dramatic. A present or future event expressed in the aorist tense for emphasis.

Durative. Another name for linear, progressive, continuing, or repetitive action.

Ecbatic clause. A result clause.

Effective. Emphasizing the completion or culmination of an action.

Elative. A function of an adjective or adverb that expresses a very high degree of intensity, quality, or quantity apart from expressing comparison.

Elision. The elimination of a vowel for euphonic reasons, e.g., διὰ ἀληθείας = δι᾽ ἀληθείας.

Ellipsis or **elliptical**. A word or group of words omitted in the text but implicitly understood. Information that is implicit in the original language often has to become explicit in the English translation.

Enclitic. A word so closely linked to a preceding word that it has no accent of its own.

Epexegetic. A grammatical function that is explanatory.

Equative verb. A copula, linking verb, joining a subject and complement.

Euphemism. A softened word or expression substituted for another word or expression that might be harsh, unpleasant, or offensive.

Exceptive clause. A conditional clause beginning with "except" or "unless."

Explicit. Something clearly stated; e.g., the pronoun "I" being clearly stated in the phrase ἐγὼ ἀκούω, **I hear**. *See* Implicit.

Final clause. Another term for a clause expressing purpose.

Finite verb. A verb that limits the subject in relation to number and person.

Future/futuristic. A tense expressing a future action or state of being.

Gender. A grammatical distinction between masculine, feminine, and neuter. It is not necessarily synonymous with biological gender.

Generic. This term refers to classes or groups of individuals or things.

Genitive case. Expresses possession, relationship, or description.

Genitive absolute. Consists of a genitive substantive and a genitive participle functioning as an adverbial clause. The substantive functions as the subject of the participle.

Gnomic. Indicating a maxim, generalization, or timeless truth.

Historical aorist. An event expressed in the simple past tense.

Historical present. A past event viewed as a present event for vividness and dramatic effect.

Hortatory clause. An exhortation or encouragement to action or some state of being.

Hyperbole. An exaggeration for the purpose of emphasis, not deception.

Hypotactic conjunction. A subordinating conjunction that introduces a dependent clause.

Idiom. A grammatical construction or expression that is peculiar or unique to a given language and often cannot easily be translated literally and still be understood.

Imperative/imperatival. Expresses a command or exhortation.

Imperfect tense. Expresses incomplete action taking place in past time.

Impersonal verb. A verb expressing action but with no personal subject, e.g., **it is better**.

Implicit. Something understood or assumed but not actually stated; e.g., the pronoun "I" is implicit in the verb, ἀκούω, **I hear**.

Improper preposition. Prepositions that are not used to form compound verbs. Prepositions that are used to form compound verbs are called proper prepositions.

Inceptive. Indicates action that begins to take place. Synonymous with "ingressive."

Indeclinable. A noun with no case inflection; i.e., it has only one form for all cases.

Independent nominative. A noun in the nominative case independent of any grammatical relationships in the completed sentence.

Indicative mood. A verb stating a fact (true or false) or asking a question.

Indirect discourse. Words of a speaker or writer reported indirectly, usually in a rephrased construction.

Indirect object. A person or thing indirectly affected by the action of a verb. It is usually found in Greek in the dative case.

Inferential. Introduces a deduction from a previous statement.

Infinitive. A verbal noun that includes characteristics of both verbs and nouns.

Inflection. Indicating a suffix and/or prefix that identifies a grammatical change in regards to case, gender, number, person, tense, voice, and mood.

Ingressive. The beginning of an action. Synonymous with "inceptive."

Instrumental. Expressing means or agency.

Intensive. With reference to the perfect tense, completed action focusing on the existence of the results of that action.

Interrogative. Introduces a question.

Intransitive. A verb that does not have a direct object.

Iterative. Repeated action or action occurring at intervals.

Koine Greek. The common Greek language spoken during NT times.

Linear action. Continuing action or action in progress.

Linking verb. A copula or equative verb.

Main clause. An independent clause.

Majority Text. The text of the majority of Greek manuscripts, abbreviated MT.

Metaphor. Someone or something said to be someone or something else for comparative reasons.

Metonymy. One word used for another, specifically the whole used for a part.

Middle voice. A Greek voice whose verbal action in some way is performed by and refers back to the subject of the verb.

Modal participle. Expresses the manner in which the action of the main verb takes place.

Modifier. A word that describes or in some way limits another word.

Mood. The manner in which action is described, e.g., indicative, subjunctive, imperative, or optative.

Nominative case. The naming case. A substantive most often used as the subject of a sentence.

Noun. Name of a person, place, thing, action, event, or quality.

Number. Indicating whether a word is singular or plural.

Object complement. A word or phrase completing the meaning of a direct object.

Objective genitive. A noun of action followed by a genitive noun expressing the object of the action.

Oblique cases. All case forms except the nominative and vocative.

Optative mood. Expressing a wish, desire, or prayer.

Ordinal number. A series of numbers expressing priority or position, e.g., first, second, third, etc.

Paradigm. An example of a declension or conjugation, showing a word in all its inflected forms.

Paraphrase. A restatement of a passage in words other than those of the original writer.

Paratactic conjunctions. Coordinating conjunctions that join two words, phrases, or clauses.

Parse or **parsing**. Identifying the inflectional elements of a word: noun/declension/ pronoun/adjective—case, number, gender; verb—person, number, tense, voice, mood; infinitive—tense, voice; participle—case, number, gender, tense, voice.

Participle. A verbal noun or adjective that has characteristics of both nouns or adjectives and verbs.

Particle. An uninflected unit of speech not found among the other parts of speech (not an adjective, adverb, article, conjunction, negative, noun, preposition, pronoun, or verb). Some grammarians do not distinguish between conjunctions and particles.

Partitive. The genitive noun indicates the whole of something from which a part is taken.

Passive voice. The subject of the verb receives the action of the verb.

Perfect tense. A verb expressing completed action.

Periphrastic. A clause consisting of an equative verb and a participle used instead of a simple verb.

Person. There are three persons in Greek and English, 1st (I/we), 2d (you[sing/pl.]), 3d (he, she, it/they).

Phrase. A group of two or more words that function as a unified whole, a substantive (subject or object) or a modifier of a clause.

Pleonastic. Redundant use of words.

Pluperfect tense. Represents an action as completed with the results existing at some point in past time.

Positive degree. A basic form of an adjective or adverb not expressing comparison; e.g., "good" is positive, "better" is comparative.

Post-positive. Following the word modified.

Potential. Expressing possibility, probability, or capability.

Predicate accusative. An accusative noun or pronoun functions as a complement of a passive participle in the accusative case, usually after verbs of calling or after the infinitive ἔναι or γενέσθαι when the subject of the infinitive is accusative.

Predicate adjective. The complement of a linking or passive verb.

Predicate nominative. The complement of an equative or linking verb or verb of being, such as εἰμί or γίνομαι.

Predicate noun. The complement of a linking or passive verb.

Predicate participle. Follows a linking verb and makes an assertion about the subject of the sentence.

Predicate position. When the article does not immediately precede the adjective or pronoun it goes with.

Predictive future. Action stated as taking place in the future.

Pre-positive. Preceding the word modified. Take care not to confuse with preposition.

Preposition. A word showing some relationship between its object and another word in the sentence.

Prescriptive. The future third person may be used to prescribe what should or should not be true or done.

Proclitic. A word linked so closely to a following word that it has no accent of its own.

Progressive. Action in progress in past, present, or future tenses.

Prohibitive. Future, imperative, or subjunctive verb preceded by a negative and forbidding a certain action or state of being.

Pronoun. A word that takes the place of a noun.

Protasis. The "if" or condition in a conditional sentence.

Punctiliar. A verbal aspect that is undefined as to duration or completion.

Purpose. An adverbial or dependent clause expressing purpose; a final or telic clause introduced by "in order that."

Reciprocal. Expressing mutual or interchangeable action; e.g., "They love each other."

Recitative. When the conjunction ὅτι introduces direct discourse and is equivalent to quotation marks.

Redundant. The use of additional and unneccessary words.

Reflexive pronoun. A pronoun that refers back to the subject of the verb.

Reflexive action. Action referring back to the subject of the verb.

Sentence. A grammatical unit that expresses a complete thought.

Stative. A verb indicating a state of being rather than action.

Subjective genitive. A noun of action is followed by a genitive noun that indicates the subject of the action.

Subjunctive. The mood of probability expressing a measure of uncertainty.

Subordinate clause. A clause that is dependent on the main verb.

Substantive. A word or group of words equivalent to a noun.

Substantival participle. Like the adjective, the participle may function in the place of a noun or other substantive. As substantive, it may function as the subject, direct object, indirect object of the main verb, object of preposition, and rarely as a vocative.

Superlative. Forms of adjectives and adverbs that express an unsurpassed degree of intensity, quality, or quantity in comparative terms.

Synonym. A word that is similar or the same in meaning as another word.

Syntax. The relationship of words, phrases, and clauses to each other within a given sentence.

Telic. Another word for purpose.

Temporal. Expressing a relationship of time; antecedent, contemporaneous simultaneous, or subsequent time in relationship to the main verb.

Tendential. Attempted but incompleted action; synonymous with "conative."

Tense. The time of action is indicated in the indicative mood. However, tense in Greek primarily refers to kind of action: incomplete, complete, or undefined.

Textual criticism. The science that studies manuscripts to determine the original text of ancient documents.

Transitive. A verb that requires a direct object to complete its meaning.

Translation. Transferring the speech or writings of one language into another language.

Transliteration. The writing or spelling of a word in one language with the equivalent letters or letter sound of another language.

Variant reading. A term used in textual criticism referring to differences in the wording of a biblical passage based on one or more variations in ancient manuscripts.

Verb. A word expressing action or a state of being.

Verbal noun or **adjective**. A name given to the nonfinite verbs, such as infinitive and participle.

Vocative case. Denoting a person or person addressed. The vocative is grammatically unrelated to the sentence but points out the audience that is being spoken to.

Voice. Indicates whether the subject of the verb performs the action or receives the action or some combination of the two. Three voices occur in Greek: active, middle, and passive.

Volitive. An aspect of the future tense expressing will, command, or request.

BASIC BIBLIOGRAPHY

Intermediate Grammars

Brooks, J. A., and C. L. Winbery. *Syntax of New Testament Greek*. Washington, D.C.: University Press of America, 1978.

Chamberlain, William Douglas. *An Exegetical Grammar of the Greek New Testament*. Grand Rapids, Mich.: Baker, 1941.

Dana, Harvey Eugene, and Julius R. Mantey. *A Manual Grammar of the Greek New Testament*. New York: Macmillan, 1957.

Funk, Robert W. *A Beginning Intermediate Grammar of Hellenistic Greek*. 3 vols. Society of Biblical Literature, 1973.

Green, Samuel G. *Handbook to the Grammar of the Greek Testament*. London: Religious Tract Society, 1907.

Greenlee, J. Harold. *A Concise Exegetical Grammar of the New Testament Greek*. Grand Rapids, Mich.: Eerdmans, 1963.

Hewett, James Allen. *New Testament Greek: A Beginning and Intermediate Grammar*. Peabody, Mass.: Hendrickson, 1986.

LaSor, William Sanford. *Handbook of New Testament Greek: An Inductive Approach Based on the Greek Text of Acts*. 2 vols. Grand Rapids: Eerdmans, 1973.

MacDonald, William G. *Greek Enchiridion: A Concise Handbook of Grammar for Translation and Exegesis*. Peabody, Mass.: Hendrickson, 1986.

Porter, Stanley E. *Idioms of the Greek New Testament*. Sheffield, England: JSOT Press, 1992.

Robertson, A. T., and W. Hersey Davis. *A New Short Grammar of the Greek Testament*. New York: Harper, 1933.

Wallace, Daniel B. *Exegetical Syntax of the Greek New Testament*. Grand Rapids: Zondervan, 1995.

Williams, Philip R. *Grammar Notes on the Noun and the Verb and Certain Other Items*. Tacoma, Wash.: Northwest Baptist Seminary, 1976.

Young, Richard A. *Intermediate New Testament Greek: A Linguistic and Exegetical Approach*. Nashville, Tenn.: Broadman & Holman, 1994.

Advanced Grammars

Abbott, Edwin A. *Johannine Grammar*. London: Adam & Charles Black, 1906.

Buttman, Alexander. *Grammar of the New Testament Greek*. Translated by J. H. Thayer. Andover: Warren F. Draper, 1876.

Blass, Friedrich William, and A. de Brunner. Translated by Robert W. Funk. *Greek Grammar of the New Testament and Other Early Christian Literature*. Chicago: Univ. of Chicago, 1961.

Moule, C. F. D. *An Idiom-Book of New Testament Greek*. Cambridge: Cambridge Univ., 1968.

Moulton, James Hope. *Grammar of New Testament Greek*. Edinburgh: T & T Clark, 1908.

Moulton, James Hope, and W. F. Howard. *Grammar of New Testament Greek*. Edinburgh: T & T Clark, 1920.

Moulton, James Hope, and Nigel Turner. *Grammar of New Testament Greek: Syntax*. Edinburgh: T & T Clark, 1963.

_____. *Grammar of New Testament Greek: Style*. Edinburgh: T & T Clark, 1976.

Robertson, A. T. *Grammar of the Greek New Testament in the Light of Historical Research*. Nashville, Tenn.: Broadman, 1934.

Turner, Nigel. *Grammatical Insights into the New Testament*. Edinburgh: T & T Clark, 1965.

Winer, George Benedict. *A Grammar of the Idiom of the New Testament*. 7th ed. Translated by J. Henry Thayer. Edited by Gottlieb Lunemann. Andover: Warren F. Draper, 1869.

Zerwick, Maximilian, S. J. *Biblical Greek Illustrated by Examples*. Translated by Joseph Smith, S.J. Rome: Scripta Pontificii Instituti Biblici, 1963.

ADJECTIVES

Forms. The adjective follows the pattern of the noun declensions and agrees with the substantive it modifies in case, gender, and number. Most adjectives have three sets of endings corresponding to the three genders: masc., fem., neut., given in that order below.

first and second declension adjectives
ἀγαθός, ἀγαθή, ἀγαθόν
ἄλλος, ἄλλη, ἄλλο
ἅγιος, ἁγία, ἅγιον

third declension adjectives
μέγας, μεγάλη, μέγα
πᾶς, πᾶσα, πᾶν
πολύς, πολλή, πολύ

Other adjectives have two sets of endings or terminations. The masculine and feminine genders have the same form, which is listed first below; the neuter is listed second.
αἰώνιος, αἰώνιον
μείζων, μεῖζον
πλείων, πλεῖον
ἀληθής, ἀληθές

Functions. The adjective describes, distinguishes, or qualifies another adjective, a noun, a pronoun, or another substantive. The adjective thus performs in several different functions: attributive, predicate, substantival, comparatival, adverbial, and numerals.

I. **Attributive Adjective**. The attributive adjective modifies, restricts, or ascribes a quality or quantity to a substantive and is found with or without the article. The attributive always follows an article if an article occurs in the construction. This function occurs in both the singular and plural numbers, in all three genders, and in all five cases.

A. With the article (articular or arthrous).
1. First attributive position (article-adjective-noun). The articular adjective in this construction has more emphasis than the noun. The following New Testament examples are given as illustrations of this category in all four cases (the vocative case never has the article), with an uneven mixture of singular and plural as well as of the three genders.

1

    a. Nom. sing. masc.

      οὗτός ἐστιν ὁ **ἀληθινὸς θεός** (1 John 5:20)

      this one is **the true God**

    b. Gen. sing. fem.

      ἐπιλαβοῦ **τῆς αἰωνίου ζωῆς** (1 Tim. 6:12)

      lay hold **of eternal life**

    c. Dat. pl. masc.

      ὡς νῦν ἀπεκαλύφθη τοῖς **ἁγίοις ἀποστόλοις** αὐτοῦ (Eph. 3:5)

      as now it has been revealed to his **holy apostles**

    d. Acc. pl. neut.

      ὅπως ἴδωσιν ὑμῶν **τὰ καλὰ ἔργα** (Matt. 5:16)

      in order that they may see your **good works**

2. Second attributive position (article-noun-article-adjective). Both the substantive and adjective are articular, with the adjective always following the substantive and having equal emphasis with the substantive.

    a. Nom. sing. masc.

      Ἐγώ εἰμι ὁ **ποιμὴν ὁ καλός** (John 10:11)

      I am **the good shepherd**

    b. Gen. sing. fem.

      τῶν ἁγίων λειτουργὸς καὶ **τῆς σκηνῆς τῆς ἀληθινῆς**, ἣν ἔπηξεν ὁ κύριος (Heb. 8:2)

      a minister of the holy things and **of the true tabernacle**, that the Lord set up

    c. Acc. sing. fem.

      ἄλλα δὲ ἔπεσεν ἐπὶ **τὴν γῆν τὴν καλήν** (Matt. 13:8)

      and other [seed] fell on **the good soil**

    d. Dat. pl. neut.

      καὶ **τοῖς πνεύμασι(ν) τοῖς ἀκαθάρτοις** ἐπιτάσσει (Mark 1:27)

      he even gives orders **to the unclean spirits**

3. Third attributive position (anarthrous noun-article-adjective).

    a. The best illustration of this position uses a possessive pronoun. Acc. sing. fem.

      εἰρήνην ἀφίημι ὑμῖν, **εἰρήνην τὴν ἐμὴν** δίδωμι ὑμῖν (John 14:27)

      I am leaving peace with you, **peace [that is] mine** I give to you

    b. The other possibilities of this position appear to function as adjectival substantives in apposition to the noun

      (1) Nom. sing. fem.

        Ἔπεσεν ἔπεσε(ν) **Βαβυλὼν ἡ μεγάλη** (Rev. 18:2)

        Babylon the great has fallen has fallen

(2) Acc. sing. masc.

ἀσπάσασθε Ἐπαίνετον τὸν ἀγαπητόν μου (Rom. 16:5)

greet **Epenetus [who is] my dear friend**

(3) Gen. pl. fem.

τῶν τε σεβομένων Ἑλλήνων πλῆθος πολύ, **γυναικῶν** τε **τῶν πρώτων** οὐκ ὀλίγαι (Acts 17:4)[1]

and of the worshiping Greeks a large number, and **of the women who were chief** not a few

(4) Dat. sing. masc.

ὁ πρεσβύτερος **Γαίῳ τῷ ἀγαπητῷ**, ὃν ἐγὼ ἀγαπῶ ἐν ἀληθείᾳ (3 John 1)

the elder **to Gaius my dear friend**, whom I love in truth

4. Irregular or exceptional adjectives. Certain adjectives, while in a predicate position, function as attributives modifying articular substantives. These include ὅλος, η, ον and πᾶς, πᾶσα, πᾶν. πολύς, πολλή, πολύ is also somewhat irregular.

a. ὅλος, η, ον, is found only in the singular.

(1) Nom. sing. fem.

καὶ ἐπίστευσεν αὐτὸς καὶ **ἡ οἰκία αὐτοῦ ὅλη** (John 4:53)

and he himself believed and **his entire household**

(2) Gen. sing. fem.

καὶ ἀγαπήσεις κύριον τὸν θεόν **σου ἐξ ὅλης τῆς καρδίας** σου (Mark 12:30)

and you shall love the Lord your God **with your whole heart**

(3) Dat. sing. masc.

ἡ πίστις ὑμῶν καταγγέλλεται ἐν **ὅλῳ τῷ κόσμῳ** (Rom. 1:8)

your faith is being announced **in the whole world**

(4) Acc. sing. masc.

καὶ ἀπῆλθεν ἡ ἀκοὴ αὐτοῦ εἰς **ὅλην τὴν Συρίαν** (Matt. 4:24)

and his fame went out **into all Syria**

b. πᾶς, πᾶσα, πᾶν often modify an articular substantive that is in apposition to the adjective (πᾶς).

(1) Nom. sing. fem.

πᾶσα ἡ πόλις ἐξῆλθεν εἰς ὑπάντησιν τῷ Ἰησοῦ (Matt. 8:34)[2]

all the city went out to meet Jesus

(2) Dat. sing. masc.

λέγω γὰρ ... **παντὶ τῷ ὄντι** ἐν ὑμῖν (Rom. 12:3)

for I say ... **to everyone who is** among you

---

[1] Acts 17:4 text is from GNT, NA & WH: TR & MT have πολὺ πλῆθος.

[2] Matt. 8:34 text is from GNT, NA & WH: TR & MT have συνάντησιν τῷ Ἰησοῦ.

4 Articular Attributive Adjectives

(3) Gen. pl. neut.

ἔσεσθε μισούμενοι **ὑπὸ πάντων τῶν ἐθνῶν** διὰ τὸ ὄνομά μου (Matt. 24:9)

you shall be hated **by all the nations** because of my name

(4) Acc. pl. masc.

δεῖ γὰρ αὐτὸν βασιλεύειν ἄχρι οὗ θῇ **πάντας τοὺς ἐχθροὺς** ὑπὸ τοὺς πόδας αὐτοῦ (1 Cor. 15:25)[3]

for he must reign until he has placed **all enemies** under his feet

c. πολύς, πολλή, πολύ is found over 92 percent of the time without the article and about 8 percent of the time with the article.

(1) The anarthrous is used as an attributive, substantive, adverb, comparative, and predicate.

(a) Attributive

πολλοὶ προφῆται καὶ δίκαιοι ἐπεθύμησαν ἰδεῖν ἃ βλέπετε (Matt. 13:17)

many prophets and righteous [people] have desired to see what you see

(b) Substantive

πολλοὺς γὰρ ἐθεράπευσεν, ὥστε ἐπιπίπτειν αὐτῷ, ἵνα αὐτοῦ ἅψωνται (Mark 3:10)

for he healed **many [people]** so that they eagerly approached him, in order that they might touch him

(c) Adverb

οὐκέτι **πολλὰ** λαλήσω μεθ᾽ ὑμῶν (John 14:30)[4]

I will no longer speak **much** with you

(d) Comparative

καὶ τὰ ἔργα σου τὰ ἔσχατα **πλείονα** τῶν πρώτων (Rev. 2:19)[5]

and your last works [εἰσιν/ἐστιν, are] **more than** the first

(e) Predicate

ὁ μισθὸς ὑμῶν **πολὺς** ἐν τῷ οὐρανῷ (Luke 6:23)

your reward [ἐστιν, is] **great** in heaven

(2) The articular is used as 1st and 2d attributive and as a substantive.

(1) First attributive (8 times)

τότε ἤρξατο ὀνειδίζειν τὰς πόλεις ἐν αἷς ἐγένοντο **αἱ πλεῖσται** δυνάμεις αὐτοῦ (Matt. 11:20)

then he began to rebuke the cities in which **most of** his **miracles** took place

---

[3] 1 Cor. 15:25 text is from GNT, NA & WH: TR & MT have ἄχρις οὗ ἂν θῇ.
[4] John 14:30 text is from GNT, NA, WH TR*b* & WH: TR*s* has οὐκ ἔτι.
[5] Rev. 2:19 text is from GNT, NA, MT & WH: TR has καὶ τὰ ἔσχατα.

    (2) Second attributive (once)
οὗ χάριν λέγω σοι, ἀφέωνται **αἱ ἁμαρτίαι** αὐτῆς **αἱ πολλαί,**
ὅτι ἠγάπησεν πολύ (Luke 7:47)
on account of this I tell you her **many sins** have been
forgiven, because she loved much
    (3) Substantive (23 times)
καθὼς γέγραπται, ὁ **τὸ πολὺ** οὐκ ἐπλεόνασεν· καὶ ὁ **τὸ ὀλίγον**
οὐκ ἠλαττόνησεν (2 Cor. 8:15)
even as it is written, "the one who [gathered] **much** did not
have more than enough; and the one who [gathered] **little**
did not have too little"

B. Without the article (anarthrous).
  1. Most anarthrous adjectives are postpositive, following the noun modified.
    a. Nom. sing. masc.
πῶς δύναται **ἄνθρωπος ἁμαρτωλὸς** τοιαῦτα σημεῖα ποιεῖν;
(John 9:16)
how is **a sinful man** able to perform such miracles?
    b. Gen. sing. fem.
ἵνα . . . κληρονόμοι γενηθῶμεν κατ᾽ ἐλπίδα **ζωῆς αἰωνίου**
(Titus 3:7)[6]
that . . . we might become heirs according to the hope **of eternal life**
    c. Dat. sing. neut.
ὡς ἔχρισεν αὐτὸν ὁ θεὸς **πνεύματι ἁγίῳ** (Acts 10:38)
how God anointed him **with the Holy Spirit**
    d. Acc. pl. masc.
οὕτως πᾶν δένδρον ἀγαθὸν **καρποὺς καλοὺς** ποιεῖ (Matt. 7:17)
thus every healthy tree produces **good fruit**
    e. Voc. sing. masc.
Διδάσκαλε ἀγαθέ, τί ποιήσω ἵνα ζωὴν αἰώνιον κληρονομήσω;
(Mark 10:17)
Good teacher, what shall I do in order that I may inherit eternal life?
  2. Adjectives that precede the substantive are pre-positive.
    a. Anarthrous adjectives that precede the modified substantive often
have some degree of emphasis or indicate chiasmus (see Glossary).
    (1) Nom. sing. masc.
καλὸς ἔσῃ **διάκονος** Χριστοῦ Ἰησοῦ (1 Tim. 4:6)[7]
you shall be **a good minister** of Christ Jesus

---

[6] Titus 3:7 text is from GNT, NA & WH: TR & MT have κληρονόμοι γενώμεθα.
[7] 1 Tim. 4:6 text is from GNT, NAS & WH: TR & MT have Ἰησοῦ Χριστοῦ.

(2) Gen. pl. neut.
μανθανέτωσαν δὲ καὶ οἱ ἡμέτεροι **καλῶν ἔργων** προΐτασθαι
(Titus 3:14)
but let our people also learn to maintain **good works**
(3) Dat. pl. fem.
τὸ δὲ **ἀνίπτοις χερσὶν** φαγεῖν οὐ κοινοῖ τὸν ἄνθρωπον
(Matt. 15:20)
but to eat **with unwashed hands** does not defile a person
(4) Acc. sing. masc.
σὺ τίς εἶ ὁ κρίνων **ἀλλότριον οἰκέτην**; (Rom. 14:4)
who are you who judges **another man's servant?**
(5) Voc. sing. masc.
Ὦ **ἀνόητοι Γαλάται,** τίς ὑμᾶς ἐβάσκανεν . . . ; (Gal. 3:1)
O **foolish Galatians,** who bewitched you . . . ?

b. A few adjectives (e.g., ἄλλος, ἕτερος) normally precede the modified
substantive without indicating emphasis or chiasmus.
(1) Nom. sing. masc.
ἠκολούθει δὲ τῷ Ἰησοῦ Σίμων Πέτρος καὶ **ἄλλος μαθητής**
(John 18:15)[8]
and Simon Peter and **another disciple** were following Jesus
(2) Gen. sing. fem.
δι᾿ **ἄλλης ὁδοῦ** ἀνεχώρησαν εἰς τὴν χώραν αὐτῶν (Matt. 2:12)
by another way they departed into their country
(3) Dat. pl. fem.
καὶ ἤρξαντο λαλεῖν **ἑτέραις γλώσσαις** (Acts 2:4)
and they began to speak **in other languages**
(4) Acc. sing. masc.
καὶ εἶδον **ἄλλον ἄγγελον** (Rev. 7:2)
and I saw **another angel**

3. Two or more anarthrous adjectives with one substantive.
a. Adjective-noun-adjective construction
Voc. sing. masc.
ὁ κύριος αὐτοῦ εἶπεν αὐτῷ **πονηρὲ δοῦλε** καὶ **ὀκνηρέ** (Matt. 25:26)
his lord said to him, **wicked** and **lazy servant**
b. Adjective-adjective-noun construction
Dat. sing. masc.
μόνῳ σοφῷ θεῷ διὰ Ἰησοῦ Χριστοῦ (Rom. 16:27)
to the only wise God through Jesus Christ

---

[8] John 18:15 text is from GNT, NA, TR*b* & WH: TR*s* & MT have ὁ before ἄλλος.

c. Noun-adjective-adjective-adjective construction
　Acc. pl. fem.
　ἐμπίπτουσιν εἰς πείρασμον καὶ παγίδα καὶ ἐπιθυμίας πολλὰς
　ἀνοήτους καὶ βλαβεράς (1 Tim. 6:9)
　they fall into temptation and a trap and **many kinds of foolish** and
　harmful lusts
4. One anarthrous adjective, two or more substantives.
　a. Adjective-nouns
　　Nom. sing. masc.
　　εἷς θεὸς καὶ πατὴρ πάντων (Eph. 4:6)
　　One God and **Father** of all
　b. Noun-adjective-noun
　　Acc. pl. neut.
　　δώσουσιν σημεῖα μεγάλα καὶ τέρατα (Matt. 24:24)
　　they shall provide **great signs** and **wonders**

II. **Predicate Adjective.** The predicate adjective makes a statement or assertion about, or indicates some quality or characteristic of the subject. The predicate function of the adjective occurs with a form of εἰμί, γίνομαι, ὑπάρχω, a passive verb form, an ellipsis (implied) of an equative verb form, and occasionally with μένω. The predicate adjective occurs with all three persons, both numbers, all tenses and moods, as well as with the infinitive and participles. The predicate adjective is always anarthrous rather than articular.

A. It is found in the nominative case with forms of εἰμί in all tenses (except the aorist, perfect, and pluperfect since εἰμί does not occur in these tenses), moods, infinitives, and participles. Voice is not a factor here inasmuch as εἰμί has no voice.
　1. Present indicative
　　a. 1 pers. sing.
　　　οὐκ εἰμὶ ἱκανὸς καλεῖσθαι ἀπόστολος (1 Cor. 15:9)
　　　I am not worthy to be called an apostle
　　b. 2 pers. sing.
　　　Διδάσκαλε, οἴδαμεν ὅτι ἀληθὴς εἶ (Matt. 22:16)
　　　Teacher, we know that **you are genuine**
　2. Future indicative
　　a. 3 pers. sing.
　　　Εἴ τις θέλει πρῶτος εἶναι, ἔσται πάντων ἔσχατος (Mark 9:35)
　　　if anyone wants to be first, **he shall be last** of all

    b. 1 pers. pl.

      οἴδαμεν ὅτι ἐὰν φανερωθῇ **ὅμοιοι** αὐτῷ **ἐσόμεθα** (1 John 3:2)[9]

      we know that if he is manifested **we shall be like** him

3. Imperfect indicative

    a. 2 pers. pl.

      ὅτε γὰρ δοῦλοι ἦτε τῆς ἁμαρτίας, **ἐλεύθεροι** ἦτε τῇ δικαιοσύνῃ (Rom. 6:20)

      for when you were servants of sin **you were free** from righteousness

    b. 3 pers. pl.

      ἦσαν γὰρ οἱ ἐρχόμενοι καὶ οἱ ὑπάγοντες **πολλοί** (Mark 6:31)

      for those who were coming and going **were many**

4. Elliptical equative verb

    a. 3 pers. sing.

      ἄξιος ὁ ἐργάτης τοῦ μισθοῦ αὐτοῦ (1 Tim. 5:18)

      the worker **[ἔστιν, is] worthy** of his wages

    b. 3 pers. pl.

      'ἀλλ' εἰ καὶ πάσχοιτε διὰ δικαιοσύνην, **μακάριοι** (1 Peter 3:14)

      but if you also suffer for righteousness, **[ἐστέ, you are] blessed**

    c. Anarthrous noun and adjective

      (1) Nom. sing. masc.

          Ἰησοῦς δὲ **πλήρης** πνεύματος ἁγίου ὑπέστρεψεν ἀπὸ τοῦ Ἰορδάνου (Luke 4:1)[10]

          now **Jesus, [who was] filled** with the Holy Spirit, departed from the Jordan

      (2) Nom. sing. fem.

          ἔρημός ἐστιν ὁ τόπος καὶ ἤδη **ὥρα πολλή** (Mark 6:35)

          the place is deserted and [the] hour [ἔστιν, is] already **late**

5. Present subjunctive

    a. 3 pers. sing.

      ἀλλ' ἵνα ᾖ **ἁγία** καὶ **ἄμωμος** (Eph. 5:27)

      but that **she should be holy** and **blameless**

    b. 2 pers. pl.

      ἵνα ἦτε **τέλειοι** καὶ **ὁλόκληροι** (James 1:4)

      in order that **you may be perfect** and **complete**

6. Present imperative

    a. 3 pers. sing.

      γνωστὸν ἔστω πᾶσιν ὑμῖν καὶ παντὶ τῷ λαῷ Ἰσραήλ (Acts 4:10)

      let it be known to you all and to all the people of Israel

---

[9] 1 John 3:2 text is from GNT, NA & WH: TR & MT have οἴδαμεν δὲ ὅτι.

[10] Luke 4:1 text is from GNT, NA & WH: TR & MT have πνεύματος ἁγίου πλήρης.

b. 2 pers. sing.

ὕπαγε εἰς εἰρήνην, καὶ ἴσθι ὑγιὴς ἀπὸ τῆς μάστιγός σου
(Mark 5:3)

Go in peace and **be whole [healed]** from your illness

7. Present optative of εἰμί is found only in 3 pers. sing. in the NT.

εἰσῆλθεν δὲ διαλογισμὸς ἐν αὐτοῖς, τὸ τίς ἂν εἴη μείζων αὐτῶν
(Luke 9:46)

and a discussion came up among them, namely, who **should be the greatest** of them

8. Present infinitive
δι᾽ ἧς ἐμαρτυρήθη εἶναι δίκαιος (Heb. 11:4)

by which it was testified **he was righteous**

9. Present participle
ὅτι δι᾽ ὑμᾶς ἐπτώχευσεν πλούσιος ὤν (2 Cor. 8:9)

for **even though he was rich** he became poor for us

B. The predicate adjective is found in the NT in the nominative case, with forms of γίνομαι in all tenses (except imperfect), moods (except optative), infinitives, and participles. As γίνομαι is a deponent form, the voice is functionally active even when it has a distinct passive form, as in the aorist tense. γίνομαι sometimes functions as an equative verb or verb of being, and thus would appropriately have a predicate adjective.

1. 3 pers. sing. pres. mid./pass. dep. indic.
καὶ ἄκαρπος γίνεται (Matt. 13:22)
and **it becomes unfruitful**

2. 1 pers. pl. pres. mid./pass. dep. subj.
μὴ γινώμεθα κενόδοξοι (Gal. 5:26)
let us not be conceited

3. 2 pers. pl. pres. mid./pass. dep. imper.
καὶ εὐχάριστοι γίνεσθε (Col. 3:15)
and **be grateful**

4. 3 pers. sing. fut. mid. dep. indic.
ἑκάστου τὸ ἔργον φανερὸν γενήσεται (1 Cor. 3:13)
the work of each person **shall be made known**

5. 3 pers. sing. 2 aor. mid. dep. indic.
τὰ δὲ ἱμάτια αὐτοῦ ἐγένετο λευκὰ ὡς τὸ φῶς (Matt. 17:2)
and his garments **became white** as the light

6. 2 pers. pl. 2 aor. mid. dep. subj.
ἵνα γένησθε ἄμεμπτοι καὶ ἀκέραιοι (Phil. 2:15)
in order that **you may be faultless** and **innocent**

7. 3 pers. sing. 2 aor. mid. dep. imper.
εἴ τις δοκεῖ σοφὸς εἶναι ἐν ὑμῖν ἐν τῷ αἰῶνι τούτῳ, μωρὸς γενέσθω,
ἵνα γένηται σοφός (1 Cor. 3:18)
if anyone among you thinks [himself] to be wise in this world, **let him
become foolish** in order that he may become wise

8. 2 aor. mid. dep. infin.
ἀλλ᾽ ὃς ἐὰν θέλῃ ἐν ὑμῖν μέγας γενέσθαι ἔσται ὑμῶν διάκονος
(Matt. 20:26)[11]
but whoever wants **to be great** among you shall be your servant

9. Nom. sing. masc. 2 aor. mid. dep. ptc.
ὅτι δόκιμος γενόμενος λήμψεται τὸν στέφανον τῆς ζωῆς
(James 1:12)[12]
for **when he is approved** he shall receive the crown of life

10. 3 pers. sing. aor. pass. dep. indic.
καὶ ἡ χάρις αὐτοῦ ἡ εἰς ἐμὲ οὐ κενὴ ἐγενήθη (1 Cor. 15:10)
and his grace that [οὖσα, was] in me **was not in vain**

11. 2 pers. pl. aor. pass. dep. imper.
καὶ αὐτοὶ ἅγιοι ἐν πάσῃ ἀναστροφῇ γενήθητε (1 Peter 1:15)
you yourselves also **be holy** in all [your] conduct

12. 3 pers. sing. perf. act. indic.
ὥστε ὁ νόμος παιδαγωγὸς ἡμῶν γέγονεν εἰς Χριστόν (Gal. 3:24)
so that the law **has been** our **tutor** unto Christ

C. μένω is a stative verb and functions like εἰμι in certain contexts, and thus
takes a predicate adjective.
1. 3 pers. sing. pres. act. indic.
εἰ ἀπιστοῦμεν, ἐκεῖνος πιστὸς μένει (2 Tim. 2:13)
if we are unfaithful, **that one remains faithful**
2. 3 pers. sing. pres. act. imper.
μενέτω ἄγαμος ἢ τῷ ἀνδρὶ καταλλαγήτω (1 Cor. 7:11)
let her remain unmarried or be reconciled to her husband

D. ὑπάρχω functions as an equative verb at times with a predicate adjective.
1. 3 pers. pl. pres. act. subj.
ἐὰν ἀδελφὸς ἢ ἀδελφὴ γυμνοὶ ὑπάρχωσι(ν) (James 2:15)[13]
if a brother or sister **should be naked**

---

[11] Matt. 20:26 text is from GNT, NA & MT: WH has ὃς ἄν; TR has γενέσθαι ἔστω.
[12] James 1:12 text is from GNT, NA & WH: TR & MT have λήψεται.
[13] James 2:15 text is from GNT, NA & WH: TR & MT have ἐὰν δέ.

2. Pres. act. infin.

   τὰ δοκοῦντα μέλη τοῦ σώματος ἀσθενέστερα ὑπάρχειν
   ἀναγκαῖά ἐστιν (1 Cor. 12:22)

   the members of the body that seem **to be weaker** are necessary

3. Nom. sing. masc. pres. act. ptc.

   ὁ γὰρ μικρότερος ἐν πᾶσιν ὑμῖν ὑπάρχων, οὗτός ἐστιν μέγας
   (Luke 9:48)[14]

   for **the one who is least** among you all, this one is the greatest

E. Intransitive passive verbs often require a predicate adjective.

1. 3 pers. sing. pres. pass. indic.

   ἥτις λέγεται Ἅγια (Heb. 9:2)[15]

   which **is called the Holy of holies**

2. 3 pers. sing. fut. pass. indic.

   οὗτος μέγας κληθήσεται ἐν τῇ βασιλείᾳ τῶν οὐρανῶν (Matt. 5:19)

   this one **shall be called great** in the kingdom of heaven

3. 3 pers. sing. aor. pass. indic.

   οὐδεὶς ἄξιος εὑρέθη ἀνοῖξαι τὸ βιβλίον (Rev. 5:4)[16]

   no one **was found worthy** to open the book

4. 2 pers. pl. aor. pass. subj.

   μήποτε καὶ θεομάχοι εὑρεθῆτε (Acts 5:39)

   lest **you also should be found fighting God**

5. pres. pass. infin.

   οὐκ εἰμὶ ἱκανὸς καλεῖσθαι ἀπόστολος (1 Cor. 15:9)

   I am not worthy **to be called an apostle**

6. Nom. sing. masc. pres. pass. ptc.

   καὶ ὁ καθήμενος ἐπ' αὐτὸν καλούμενος πιστὸς καὶ ἀληθινός
   (Rev. 19:11)

   and the one who is sitting on it **is called faithful** and **true**

7. Nom. sing. fem. pres. pass. ptc.

   οὗτός ἐστιν ἡ δύναμις τοῦ θεοῦ ἡ καλουμένη μεγάλη
   (Acts 8:10)[17]

   this is the power of God, **which is called great**

---

[14] Luke 9:48 text is from GNT, NA & WH: TR & MT have ἔσται μέγας.

[15] Heb. 9:2 text is from GNT, NA, WH, MT & TRb: TRs has ἁγία.

[16] Rev. 5:4 text is from GNT, NA, MT & WH: TR adds καὶ ἀναγνῶναι after ἀνοῖξαι.

[17] Acts 8:10 text is from GNT, NA & WH: TR & MT omit καλουμένη.

F. The predicate adjectives in the oblique cases (gen., dat., and acc.) with explicit verbs are limited to infinitives and participles.
  1. In the genitive case
    a. The genitive absolute construction with the participle of εἰμί may at times have a predicate genitive.
      ἔτι ἁμαρτωλῶν ὄντων ἡμῶν Χριστὸς ὑπὲρ ἡμῶν ἀπέθανεν (Rom. 5:8)
      while we were yet **sinful** Christ died for us
    b. A passive participle may require a predicate adjective.
      ἑκατοντάρχης ἐκ σπείρης τῆς καλουμένης Ἰταλικῆς (Acts 10:1)
      a captain of the cohort **that is called Italian**
  2. In the dative case, present participle of εἰμί
    πάντα συνεργεῖ εἰς ἀγαθόν, τοῖς κατὰ πρόθεσιν κλητοῖς οὖσιν (Rom. 8:28)
    he (God) works all things together for good **to those who are called** according to [His] purpose
  3. In the accusative case
    a. Present participle of εἰμι
      Ἰησοῦν, πιστὸν ὄντα τῷ ποιήσαντι αὐτόν (Heb. 3:1-2)
      Jesus, **who was faithful** to the one who appointed him
    b. Passive participle of λέγω
      ὃν ἐτίθουν καθ᾽ ἡμέραν πρὸς τὴν θύραν τοῦ ἱεροῦ τὴν λεγομένην Ὡραίαν (Acts 3:2)
      whom they daily set at the door of the temple **that is called Beautiful**
    c. Present infinitive of εἰμί
      Εἰ κεκρίκατέ με πιστὴν τῷ κυρίῳ εἶναι (Acts 16:15)
      if you have considered me **to be faithful** to the Lord
    d. 2 aor. mid. dep. infin. of γίνομαι
      τοῦτον ὁ θεὸς ἤγειρε(ν) ἐν τῇ τρίτῃ ἡμέρᾳ καὶ ἔδωκεν αὐτὸν ἐμφανῆ γενέσθαι (Acts 10:40)[18]
      God raised him on the third day and granted him **to be visible**
    e. The accusative object complement is a subset of the predicate accusative making an assertion about the direct object noun or pronoun
      (1) Pres. act. indic.
        τί μέ λέγεις ἀγαθόν; (Luke 18:19)
        why do you call **me good**?

---

[18] Acts 10:40 text is GNT & NA: WH, TR & MT omit ἐν.

(2) Aor. mid. dep. indic.
ὅτι **πιστόν** με ἡγήσατο (1 Tim. 1:12)
for he considered **me [to be] faithful**

(3) Aor. act. imper.
ποιήσατε τὸ δένδρον **καλὸν** καὶ τὸν καρπὸν αὐτοῦ **καλόν**
(Matt. 12:33)
make **the tree good** and its **fruit good**

(4) Pres. act. ptc.
τὴν ἀναστροφὴν ὑμῶν ἐν τοῖς ἔθνεσιν ἔχοντες **καλήν**
(1 Peter 2:12)
having your **conduct right** among the Gentiles

(5) Aor. act. ptc.
ὁ ποιήσας με ὑγιῆ (John 5:11)
the one who made **me whole**

f. The predicate accusative often occurs with anarthrous noun adjective constructions.

(1) Aor. act. imper.
ποιήσατε οὖν **καρποὺς ἀξίους** τῆς μετανοίας (Luke 3:8)
produce then **fruits [that are] worthy** of repentance

(2) Aor. act. indic.
εἶδεν **ἄνθρωπον τυφλὸν** ἐκ γενετῆς (John 9:1)
he saw **a man [who was] blind** from birth

(3) Pres. act. indic.
τί με λέγεις **ἀγαθόν**; οὐδεὶς ἀγαθὸς εἰ μὴ εἷς ὁ θεός
(Mark 10:18)
why do you call **me good**? No one [ἐστιν, is] good except one, God

(4) Pres. act. ptc.
ἔχοντες δὲ **χαρίσματα** κατὰ τὴν χάριν τὴν δοθεῖσαν ὑμῖν
διάφορα (Rom. 12:6)
and having **gifts [that are] different** according to the grace given to us

G. Anarthrous noun and adjective constructions may function as predicates. Most anarthrous noun and adjective combinations are attributive. However, the following examples illustrate the predicate function of the adjective in an anarthrous construction, even though there is no equative verb.

1. Noun-adjective construction
   a. Nom. sing. masc.
   Παῦλος δοῦλος Χριστοῦ Ἰησοῦ, **κλητὸς** ἀπόστολος (Rom. 1:1)
   Paul, a servant of Christ Jesus, **[who was] called** an apostle

  b. Nom. pl. neut.

ἵνα γένησθε . . . **τέκνα** θεοῦ **ἄμωμα** (Phil. 2:15)[19]

in order that you may be . . . **children** of God **[who are] blameless**

  c. Acc. pl. neut.

τέκνα ἔχων **πιστά** (Titus 1:6)

having **children [who are] faithful**

  d. Acc. sing. fem.

παραστῆσαι τὰ **σώματα** ὑμῶν **θυσίαν** ζῶσαν **ἁγίαν** τῷ θεῷ **εὐάρεστον** (Rom. 12:1)

present your bodies a living sacrifice, **[which is] holy, acceptable** to God

2. Adjective-noun-adjective construction in an equative clause

  a. Nom. sing. masc.

οὐδεὶς **προφήτης δεκτός** ἐστιν ἐν τῇ πατρίδι αὐτοῦ (Luke 4:24)

no prophet is acceptable in his hometown

  b. Nom. sing. fem.

πᾶσα γραφὴ θεόπνευστος καὶ **ὠφέλιμος** πρὸς διδασκαλίαν (2 Tim. 3:16)

all Scripture [ἐστίν, is] God breathed and **profitable** for teaching

  c. Nom. sing. neut.

ὅτι **πᾶν κτίσμα** θεοῦ **καλόν** (1 Tim. 4:4)

for **every creation** of God **[ἐστίν, is] good**

  d. Acc. sing. masc.

ἵνα παραστήσωμεν **πάντα ἄνθρωπον τέλειον** ἐν Χριστῷ (Col. 1:28)

in order that we may present **every man perfect** in Christ

  e. Acc. pl. neut.

πνευματικὰς θυσίας εὐπροσδέκτους τῷ θεῷ διὰ Ἰησοῦ Χριστοῦ (1 Peter 2:5)

spiritual sacrifices [that are] acceptable to God through Jesus Christ

3. Adjective-adjective-noun-adjective construction

Acc. pl. neut.

παραλαμβάνει μεθ᾽ ἑαυτοῦ **ἑπτὰ ἕτερα πνεύματα πονηρότερα** ἑαυτοῦ (Matt. 12:45)

he takes with him **seven other spirits [who are] more wicked than** himself

4. Adjective-adjective construction—one adjective functions as a substantive, the other as predicate.

  a. Nom. sing. masc.

οὐδεὶς ἀγαθὸς εἰ μὴ εἷς ὁ θεός (Mark 10:18)

no one [ἐστιν, is] good except one, God

---

[19] Phil. 2:15 text is from GNT, NA & WH: TR*s* has ἀμώματα; TR*b* & MT have ἀμώμητα.

b. Nom. sing. neut.
οὐδὲν ἄξιον θανάτου ἐστὶν πεπραγμένον αὐτῷ (Luke 23:15)
nothing [that is] worthy of death has been done by him
c. Nom. pl. masc.
πολλοὶ γάρ εἰσιν κλητοί, ὀλίγοι δὲ ἐκλεκτοί (Matt. 22:14)
for **many are called**, but few [εἰσίν, **are**] **chosen**
d. Nom. pl. fem. and nom. pl. masc.
πέντε δὲ ἐξ αὐτῶν ἦσαν μωραὶ καὶ πέντε φρόνιμοι (Matt. 25:2)
but **five** of them **were foolish** and **five** [ἦσαν, **were**] **wise**
e. Nom. pl. neut.
πάντα γὰρ δυνατὰ παρὰ τῷ θεῷ (Mark 10:27)
for **all things** [ἐστιν/εἰσιν, **are**] **possible** with God
f. Acc. sing. masc. as predicate
οὗτος δὲ οὐδὲν ἄτοπον ἔπραξεν (Luke 23:41)
but this man did **nothing [that was] amiss**

III. **Substantive Adjectives.** The adjective often functions as a substantive, with or without the article.

A. Articular adjectival substantives
1. Nom. sing. masc. as subject of main verb
ὅτι ὁ δίκαιος ἐκ πίστεως ζήσεται (Gal. 3:11)
for **the just** shall live by faith
2. Gen. sing. neut. as object of preposition
καὶ ὑμεῖς χρῖσμα ἔχετε ἀπὸ τοῦ ἁγίου (1 John 2:20)
and you yourselves have an anointing **from the holy one**
3. Dat. pl. fem. as indirect object
λέγω δὲ τοῖς ἀγάμοις καὶ ταῖς χήραις (1 Cor. 7:8)
but I speak **to the unmarried** and to the widows
4. Acc. sing. masc. as direct object of finite verb
ἢ γὰρ τὸν ἕνα μισήσει καὶ τὸν ἕτερον ἀγαπήσει (Matt. 6:24)
for either he will hate **the one** and will love **the other**

B. Anarthrous adjectival substantives
1. Nom. sing. masc. as appositional
Χριστὸς ἅπαξ περὶ ἁμαρτιῶν ἔπαθεν, δίκαιος ὑπὲρ ἀδίκων (1 Peter 3:18)
Christ died once for sins, **the just one** for the unjust ones
2. Dat. pl. masc. as indirect object
καὶ δώσει τὸν ἀμπελῶνα ἄλλοις (Mark 12:9)
and he will give the vineyard **to others**

3. Acc. sing. neut. as direct object
   ἡ ἀγάπη τῷ πλησίον **κακὸν** οὐκ ἐργάζεται (Rom. 13:10)
   love does not work **evil** to [one's] neighbor
4. Voc. sing, masc. in address
   ἀγαπητέ, μὴ μιμοῦ τὸ **κακὸν** ἀλλὰ τὸ **ἀγαθόν** (3 John 11)
   dear friend, do not imitate the evil but the good
5. Gen. sing. masc. as object of preposition
   ὅτι πάντες εἰδήσουσί(ν) με **ἀπὸ μικροῦ ἕως μεγάλου** αὐτῶν
   (Heb. 8:11)[20]
   for all shall know me **from the least to the greatest** of them

IV. **Comparative, Superlative, and Elative Adjectives**. Adjectives may be considered in four degrees of force: positive (μέγας, great); comparative (generally used for two persons or things; μείζων, greater); superlative (generally used for three or more persons or things; μειζότερος, greatest); and elative (very great).

A. A positive adjective.
   1. A positive adjective makes no comparison, but stands alone.
      a. Articular substantive
         ἀποστυγοῦντες **τὸ πονηρόν**, κολλώμενοι **τῷ ἀγαθῷ** (Rom. 12:9)
         hate **the evil**, cling **to the good**
      b. Anarthrous predicate
         ὁ νόμος **πνευματικός** ἐστιν (Rom. 7:14)
         the law is **spiritual**
      c. Object complement (a second accusative that completes the meaning of the direct object).
         ἐγὼ ἦλθον ἵνα ζωὴν ἔχωσιν καὶ **περισσὸν** ἔχωσιν (John 10:10)
         I came in order that they might have life and [that] they might have **[it] in abundance**
   2. A positive adjective may be used as a comparative.
      a. With a dative of degree of difference
         ὁ θεὸς οὕτως ἀμφιέννυσιν, οὐ **πολλῷ μᾶλλον** ὑμᾶς; (Matt. 6:30)
         does not God thus clothe you **with much more**? (Yes!)
      b. with ἤ
         καλόν σοί ἐστιν μονόφθαλμον εἰς τὴν ζωὴν εἰσελθεῖν **ἢ** δύο ὀφθαλμοὺς ἔχοντα βληθῆναι εἰς τὴν γέενναν τοῦ πυρός (Matt. 18:9)
         for you to enter into life one-eyed is **better than**, having two eyes, to be cast into the Gehenna of fire

---

[20] Heb. 8:11 text is from GNT, NA & WH: TR & MT have ἀπὸ μικροῦ αὐτῶν.

3. A positive adjective may be used as a superlative.
   a. First attributive position
      αὕτη ἐστὶ(ν) ἡ μεγάλη καὶ πρώτη ἐντολή (Matt. 22:38)[21]
      this is **the greatest** and **most important command**
   b. Substantive object of preposition
      ᾧ προσεῖχον πάντες ἀπὸ μικροῦ ἕως μεγάλου (Acts 8:10)
      to whom all gave heed, **from the smallest to the greatest**

B. Comparative adjectives.
   1. A comparative adjective is sometimes used as a positive.
      a. Attributive position
         μήτε δὲ ἡλίου μήτε ἄστρων ἐπιφαινόντων ἐπὶ πλείονας ἡμέρας
         (Acts 27:20)
         but when neither the sun nor the stars appeared **for many days**
      b. Object complement
         Ἀθηναῖοι δὲ πάντες καὶ οἱ ἐπιδημοῦντες ξένοι εἰς οὐδὲν ἕτερον
         ηὐκαίρουν ἢ λέγειν τι ἢ ἀκούειν τι καινότερον (Acts 17:21)[22]
         and all the Athenians and the visiting strangers were customarily
         spending time either to say something or hear **something novel**
   2. A comparative adjective may function as a comparative in several ways.
      a. Attributive with παρά
         πλείονος γὰρ οὗτος δόξης παρὰ Μωϋσῆν ἠξίωται (Heb. 3:3)[23]
         for this man was counted worthy **of more glory than Moses**
      b. Attributive with genitive of comparison
         μείζονα ταύτης ἀγάπην οὐδεὶς ἔχει (John 15:13)
         no one has **greater love than this**
      c. Attributive with ἤ
         Ἰησοῦς πλείονας μαθητὰς ποιεῖ καὶ βαπτίζει ἢ Ἰωάννης
         (John 4:1)[24]
         Jesus is making and baptizing **more disciples than John**
      d. Predicate adjective with ὑπέρ
         ζῶν γὰρ ὁ λόγος τοῦ θεοῦ καὶ ἐνεργὴς καὶ τομώτερος ὑπὲρ πᾶσαν
         μάχαιραν δίστομον (Heb. 4:12)
         for the word of God [ἐστιν, is] living and effective and **sharper than
         every two-edged sword**

---

[21] Matt. 22:38 text is from GNT, NA & WH: TR & MT have πρώτη καὶ μεγάλη ἐντολή.
[22] Acts 17:21 text is from GNT & NA: WH, TR & MT have εὐκαίρουν ἢ λέγειν τι καὶ ἀκούειν καινότερον.
[23] Heb. 3:3 text is from GNT & NA: TR & MT have δόξης οὗτος; TR has Μωσῆν; MT has Μωϋσῆν; WH has Μωυσῆν.
[24] John 4:1 text is from GNT, NA, TR & MT: WH has Ἰωάνης.

  e. Substantive use of adjective
      ὁ μείζων δουλεύσει τῷ ἐλάσσονι (Rom. 9:12)
      the older shall serve **the younger**
3. A comparative adjective may occasionally be used as a superlative.
  a. Second attributive position
      ζηλοῦτε δὲ τὰ χαρίσματα τὰ μείζονα (1 Cor. 12:31)
      but you are seeking **the most spectacular gifts**
  b. Substantive as predicate nominative
      οὗτός ἐστιν ὁ μείζων ἐν τῇ βασιλείᾳ τῶν οὐρανῶν (Matt. 18:4)
      this one is **the greatest** in the kingdom of heaven
  c. Elliptical verb with predicate adjective
      μείζων δὲ τούτων ἡ ἀγάπη (1 Cor. 13:13)
      but love [ἐστιν, is] **the greatest of these**
4. A comparative adjective may be used as an elative.
  a. Accusative plural masculine
      ἄνδρες Ἀθηναῖοι, κατὰ πάντα ὡς δεισιδαιμονεστέρους ὑμᾶς θεωρῶ
      (Acts 17:22)
      Athenian men, I notice you as being **very religious** in all things
  b. Accusative singular neuter
      ὃ μικρότερον μέν ἐστιν πάντων τῶν σπερμάτων (Matt. 13:32)
      which is indeed **very small** among all seeds

C. Superlative adjectives.
  1. A superlative may be used as a comparative.
    a. Adverbial use
        καὶ ὁ ἄλλος μαθητὴς προέδραμεν τάχιον τοῦ Πέτρου καὶ ἦλθεν
        πρῶτος εἰς τὸ μνημεῖον (John 20:4)
        and the other disciple ran ahead faster than Peter and came **first** to the
        tomb
    b. First attributive position
        τὸν μὲν **πρῶτον λόγον** ἐποιησάμην περὶ πάντων . . . (Acts 1:1)
        indeed **the first account** I made about all things . . .
  2. A superlative adjective may be used as a superlative, but this is
      not its main use; rather it is rare. It is used most often as an elative.
    a. Second attributive position
        Ἰησοῦ υἱὲ **τοῦ θεοῦ τοῦ ὑψίστου** (Luke 8:28)
        Jesus, son **of the most high God**
    b. Substantive with genitive of comparison
        Ἐγὼ γάρ εἰμι ὁ **ἐλάχιστος τῶν ἀποστόλων** (1 Cor. 15:9)
        for I am the **least significant of the apostles**

   c. First attributive position
     ἤρξατο ὀνειδίζειν τὰς πόλεις ἐν αἷς ἐγένοντο **αἱ πλεῖσται**
     δυνάμεις αὐτοῦ (Matt. 11:20)
     he began to reproach the cities in which **most of his miracles** were
     done
3. A superlative used as an elative, its most frequent use.
   a. Attributive object of preposition
     μετάγεται **ὑπὸ ἐλαχίστου πηδαλίου** (James 3:4)
     [ships] are turned **by a very small rudder**
   b. Second attributive position
     ἐφ᾽ ὅσον ἐποιήσατε ἑνὶ τούτων **τῶν ἀδελφῶν μου τῶν ἐλαχίστων**
     ἐμοὶ ἐποιήσατε (Matt. 25:40)
     inasmuch as you did [it] to one **of the very insignificant of my**
     brothers, you did [it] to me
   c. Predicate nominative of passive verb
     ἐλάχιστος κληθήσεται ἐν τῇ βαειλείᾳ τῶν οὐρανῶν (Matt. 5:19)
     he shall be called **very insignificant** in the kingdom of heaven
   d. Attributive as subject
     καὶ συνάγεται πρὸς αὐτὸν **ὄχλος πλεῖστος** (Mark 4:1)
     and **a very large crowd** was gathered to him

V. **Adverbial Adjectives.** Some adjectives function as an adverb modifying a verb
rather than a noun. The form is sometimes found in the nominative, genitive, and
dative cases, but most often in the accusative case. It is often the neuter
accusative of the following adjectives, as well as others: ἴδιον, λοιπόν, μικρόν,
μόνον, ὀλίγον, πολλά, πολύ, πρῶτον.

  A. In the nominative case.
     εὑρέθη Ἰησοῦς **μόνος** (Luke 9:36)[25]
     Jesus was found **alone**

  B. In the dative case.
   1. πάντα δὲ ταῦτα ἐνεργεῖ τὸ ἓν καὶ τὸ αὐτὸ πνεῦμα, διαιροῦν **ἰδίᾳ**
     ἑκάστῳ καθὼς βούλεται (1 Cor. 12:11)
     but the one and the same Spirit produces all these things, dividing
     to each person **individually** even as He wills
   2. ἐγνωρίσθη μοι τὸ μυστήριον, καθὼς προέγραψα **ἐν ὀλίγῳ** (Eph. 3:3)[26]
     the mystery was made known to me, even as I wrote before **briefly**

---

[25] Luke 9:36 text is from GNT, NA & WH: TR & MT have ὁ Ἰησοῦς.
[26] Eph. 3:3 text is from GNT, NA & WH: TR & MT have ἐγνώρισε(ν).

C. In the genitive case.

τοῦ λοιποῦ, κόπους μοι μηδεὶς παρεχέτω (Gal. 6:17)

from now on, let no one cause me troubles

D. In the accusative case.
   1. Feminine ἰδίαν with preposition
      ἀνέβη εἰς τὸ ὄρος κατ᾽ ἰδίαν προσεύξασθαι (Matt. 14:23)
      he went up into the mountain **privately** to pray
   2. λοιπόν as an adverb of time
      λοιπὸν ἀπόκειταί μοι ὁ τῆς δικαιοσύνης στέφανος (2 Tim. 4:8)
      for the future the crown of righteousness is reserved for me
   3. μικρόν as an adverb of time
      τεκνία, ἔτι μικρὸν μεθ᾽ ὑμῶν εἰμι (John 13:33)
      little children, yet **a little while** I am with you
   4. μόνον as an adverb of manner
      ἐξήχηται ὁ λόγος τοῦ κυρίου οὐ μόνον ἐν τῇ Μακεδονίᾳ (1 Thess. 1:8)
      the word of the Lord went out **not only** in Macedonia
   5. ὀλίγον as an adverb of manner
      ᾧ δὲ ὀλίγον ἀφίεται, ὀλίγον ἀγαπᾷ (Luke 7:47b)
      but to whom a little is forgiven, he loves **a little**
   6. πολλά as an adverb of manner
      ἀσπάζεται ὑμᾶς ἐν κυρίῳ πολλὰ Ἀκύλας καὶ Πρίσκα (1 Cor. 16:19)[27]
      Aquila and Priscilla greet you **earnestly** in the Lord
   7. πολύ as an adverb of manner
      ἀφέωνται αἱ ἁμαρτίαι αὐτῆς αἱ πολλαί, ὅτι ἠγάπησε(ν) πολύ
      (Luke 7:47a)
      her many sins are forgiven, because she loved **greatly**
   8. πρῶτον as an adverb of manner
      ἡ δὲ ἄνωθεν σοφία πρῶτον μὲν ἁγνή ἐστιν (James 3:17)
      but the wisdom from above is **first** pure

VI. **Numerals are a special group of adjectives.** They are classified as cardinals, ordinals, and adverbials. The cardinal numeral is any number used in counting (e.g., εἷς, **one**; δύο, **two**; τρεῖς, **three**; δώδεκα, **twelve**; etc.); ordinals indicate an order, succession, or series of numbers (πρῶτος, **first**; δεύτερος, **second**; τρίτος, **third**; etc.); adverbial numerals indicate frequency (e.g., ἅπαξ, **once**; δίς, **twice**; τρίς, **thrice** or **three times**; etc.). Cardinals and ordinals function as attributives and substantives. All numerals are adjectives except the numbers

---

[27] 1 Cor. 16:19 text is from GNT, NA & WH: TR & MT have ἀσπάζονται and Πρίσκιλλα.

χιλιάς, **thousand**; μυριάς, **myriad** or **ten thousand**; and their compounds, which are nouns. Cardinal numerals from 1 to 4 are declinable, from 5 to 100 all are indeclinable, and from 200 and up all are declinable.

A. Attributive numerals.
1. Articular numerals
    a. First attributive position
        οἱ γὰρ πάντες ἐκ **τοῦ ἑνὸς ἄρτου** μετέχομεν (1 Cor. 10:17)
        for we all partake of **the one loaf**
    b. Second attributive position
        καὶ ὁ θάνατος καὶ ὁ ᾅδης ἐβλήθησαν εἰς τὴν λίμνην τοῦ πυρός.
        οὗτος ὁ **θάνατος** ὁ δεύτερός ἐστιν (Rev. 20:14)[28]
        both death and Hades were thrown into the lake of fire. This is
        the second death
2. Anarthrous numerals
    a. Numerals most often precede the noun modified.
        γέγραπται ὅτι **δύο ἀνθρώπων** ἡ μαρτυρία ἀληθής ἐστιν (John 8:17)
        it is written that the testimony **of two men** is true
    b. Postposition (following the noun) numerals often indicate some
        measure of emphasis, chiasmus or stylistic pattern.
        κύριος ὁ θεὸς ἡμῶν **κύριος εἷς** ἐστιν (Mark 12:29)
        the Lord our God is **one Lord**

B. Substantive numerals.
1. Articular numerals
    ἀναιρεῖ **τὸ πρῶτον** ἵνα **τὸ δεύτερον** στήσῃ (Heb. 10:9)
    he takes away **the first** in order that he may establish **the second**
2. Anarthrous numerals
    καὶ ἐποίησεν **δώδεκα** (Mark 3:14)
    and he appointed **twelve**

C. The numeral εἷς may be used as an indefinite article.
1. As an attributive to the subject
    ἰδοὺ **ἄρχων εἷς** ἐλθὼν προσεκύνει αὐτῷ (Matt. 9:18)[29]
    behold **a ruler** came and worshiped him
2. As an attributive to the direct object
    καὶ εἶδον **ἕνα ἄγγελον** ἑστῶτα ἐν τῷ ἡλίῳ (Rev. 19:17)
    and I saw **an angel** standing in the sun

---

[28] Rev. 20:14 text is from GNT, NA & WH: TR has οὗτός ἐστιν ὁ δεύτερος θάνατος; MT has Ἅιδης.
[29] Matt. 9:18 text is from GNT, NA, MT & TRb: TRs omits εἷς; WH has προσελθών.

D. The cardinal εἷς may be used in place of the ordinal πρῶτος.
  1. First attributive position
     ἡ οὐαὶ ἡ μία ἀπῆλθεν (Rev. 9:12)
     the first woe (woe number one) has passed
  2. Substantive numerals
     τῇ δὲ μιᾷ τῶν σαββάτων ὄρθρου βαθέως ἐπὶ τὸ μνῆμα ἦλθον
     (Luke 24:1)[30]
     and **on the first day** of the week, very early in the morning, they came to
     the tomb

E. The numerals may be used in a distributive sense.
  1. When the numeral is doubled
     καὶ προσκαλεῖται τοὺς δώδεκα καὶ ἤρξατο αὐτοὺς ἀποστέλλωιν
     δύο δύο (Mark 6:7)
     and he summoned the twelve and began to send them out **two by two**
  2. With certain prepositions
     a. With ἀνά
        κατακλίνατε αὐτοὺς κλισίας ὡσεὶ ἀνὰ πεντήκοντα (Luke 9:14)[31]
        make them sit down in groups of about **fifty apiece**
     b. With κατά
        ἐξηγεῖτο καθ᾽ ἓν ἕκαστον ὧν ἐποίησεν ὁ θεὸς ἐν τοῖς ἔθνεσι(ν) διὰ
        τῆς διακονίας αὐτοῦ (Acts 21:19)
        he related **one by one [in detail]** the things that God did among the
        Gentiles through his ministry

Select Bibliography for Adjectives

Kilpatrick, G. D. "The Order of Some Noun and Adjective Phrases in the New
    Testament." *Novum Testamentum* 5 (July 1962): 111-14.
Porter, Stanley E. "The Adjectival Attributive Genitive in the New Testament: A
    Grammatical Study." *Trinity Journal* 4, no. 1 (1983): 3-17.
Roberts, J. W. "Note on the Adjective after ΠΑΣ in 2 Timothy 3:16." *Expository Times*
    7 (1964): 359, 650-75, 1076-77.
Wallace, Daniel B. "The Relation of Adjective to Noun in Anarthrous Constructions
    in the New Testament." *Novum Testamentum* 26 (April 1984): 128-67.
_____. "The Relation of Adjective to Noun in Anarthrous Constructions in the
    New Testament." Th.M. Thesis. Dallas Theological Seminary (May 1979).

---

[30] Luke 24:1 text is from GNT & NA & WH: TR & MT have βαθέος ἦλθον ἐπὶ τὸ μνῆμα; MT have βαθέως; WH has ἦλθαν ἐπὶ τὸ μνῆμα.
[31] Luke 9:14 text is from GNT, NA & WH: TR & MT omit ὡσεί.

ADVERBS

Forms. Adverbs are found with a variety of forms and do not fall into easy classifications. A clear distinction between adverbs, conjunctions, prepositions, and particles is hard to describe, as the adverbs are fixed case forms of various adjectives, numerals, participles, prepositional phrases, pronouns, or substantives. Adverbs are never inflected; the spelling always remains the same, with the exception of the movable ς (sigma), as with οὕτω(ς). There are more than 250 adverbs in the Greek NT. Approximately 100 of these have an -ως ending and are mostly adverbs of manner. Another 100 have the following endings (in descending frequency): -θεν, -ι, -α, -ε, -ω, -ον, -ου. Negative adverbs will be considered under the fifth section on Negatives (pp. 97-110).

Functions. Adverbs usually answer the questions, How? When? Where? Why? and How often? or How much? Some of the more frequent adverbs are as follows:

How? Adverbs of manner: οὕτως, **thus, so**; καλῶς, **well, beautifully**; ὁμοίως, **likewise, similarly**; ἀληθῶς, **truly**; ταχέως, **quickly**

When? Adverbs of time: τότε, **then**; νῦν, **now**; ἤδη, **already**; σήμερον, **today**; πάλιν, **again**

Where? Adverbs of place: ἐκεῖ, **there**; ἔξω, **outside**; ὧδε, **here**; ἐκεῖθεν, **from there**; ποῦ, **somewhere**

Interrogative adverbs: πῶς, **how?**; ποῦ, **where?**; πόθεν, **from where?**; πότε, **when?**

How often? Numerical adverbs: ἅπαξ, **once**; τρίς, **thrice, three times**; δίς, **twice**; ἑπτάκις, **seven times**

How much? Adverbs of degree, or to what degree; comparative or superlative adverbs: λίαν, **very**; μάλιστα, **most of all, especially**; μᾶλλον, **more, rather**; σφόδρα, **extremely, greatly**

I. **An adverb usually modifies the verb closest to it**. When an adverb is sandwiched between two verbs, the following rule is the general guideline. Adverbs of time and manner often precede the word modified and adverbs of place often follow the word modified.

A. Adverb of time preceding the verb.
ἀλέκτορα **φωνῆσαι** τρὶς **ἀπαρνήσῃ** με (Matt. 26:34)
before the cock **crows you will deny** me **three times**

B. Adverb of manner preceding the verb.
ἐβουλήθη **λάθρα ἀπολῦσαι** αὐτήν (Matt. 1:19)
he desired to divorce her **secretly**

23

24   Adverbs Modifying Verbs, Adjectives, and Adverbs

C. Adverb of place following the verb.
καὶ προβὰς ἐκεῖθεν, εἶδεν ἄλλους δύο ἀδελφούς (Matt. 4:21)
and **when he went on from there, he saw** two other brothers

II. **In addition to modifying verbs, adjectives, and adverbs, the following classifications occur**: attributive adverbs functioning as adjectives; substantive adverbs functioning as nouns; predicate adverbs with equative, passive, or elliptical verbs; comparative use of adverbs; and special uses of adverbs. Some adverbs are called particles and sometimes function as improper prepositions or as conjunctions.

A. Modifying verbs or verb phrases.
1. Adverb of manner
νῦν οἶδα ἀληθῶς ὅτι ἐξαπέστειλεν ὁ κύριος τὸν ἄγγελον αὐτοῦ (Acts 12:11)
now **I know truly** that the Lord sent forth his angel
2. Adverb of place/location
ἀλλ' ἡ τελεία ἀγάπη ἔξω βάλλει τὸν φόβον (1 John 4:18)
but perfect love **casts out** fear
3. Adverb of time
υἱός μου εἶ σύ, ἐγὼ σήμερον γεγέννηκά σε (Heb. 1:5)
you are my son, **today I have begotten** you
4. Interrogative adverb
μνημόνευε οὖν πόθεν πέπτωκας (Rev. 2:5)
remember then **from what place you have fallen**
5. Numerical adverb
ἀπόκειται τοῖς ἀνθρώποις ἅπαξ ἀποθανεῖν (Heb. 9:27)
it is destined for men **to die once**
6. Adverb of degree, elative adv.
ὁ δὲ Ἡρῴδης ἰδὼν τὸν Ἰησοῦν ἐχάρη λίαν (Luke 23:8)[1]
and when Herod saw Jesus, **he rejoiced greatly**

B. Modifying adjectives.
1. Adverb of manner
ὁμολογουμένως μέγα ἐστὶν τὸ τῆς εὐσεβείας μυστήριον (1 Tim. 3:16)
the mystery of godliness is **confessedly great**
2. Adverb of place/location
πάντα ταῦτα τὰ πονηρὰ ἔσωθεν ἐκπορεύεται καὶ κοινοῖ τὸν ἄνθρωπον (Mark 7:23)
all these evil things within go out and defile the person

---

[1] Luke 23:8 text is from GNT, NA, WH & MT: TR has Ἡρώδης.

3. Adverb of time
   ἕτοιμοι ἀεὶ πρὸς ἀπολογίαν παντὶ τῷ αἰτοῦντι ὑμᾶς (1 Peter 3:15)
   [ἔστε, be] **always ready** for a defense to everyone who asks you
4. Interrogative adverb
   πῶς δύσκολόν ἐστιν εἰς τὴν βασιλείαν τοῦ θεοῦ εἰσελθεῖν
   (Mark 10:24)
   how difficult it is to enter into the kingdom of God
5. Numerical adverb
   οὐ λέγω σοι ἕως ἑπτάκις ἀλλὰ ἕως **ἑβδομηκοντάκις ἑπτά** (Matt. 18:22)
   I do not tell you until seven times but until **seventy seven times** (not seventy
   times seven; cf. Gen. 4:24)
6. Adverb of degree
   ἦν γὰρ **πλούσιος σφόδρα** (Luke 23:24)
   for he was **extremely rich**

C. Qualifying an adverb. Two adverbs together highlight and emphasize each
   other.
   1. Adverb of manner
      ὁμοίως καθὼς ἐγένετο ἐν ταῖς ἡμέραις Λώτ (Luke 17:28)[2]
      in like manner as it was in the days of Lot
   2. Adverb of place/location
      Σὺ κάθου **ὧδε καλῶς** (James 2:3)
      You sit **here in a good place**
   3. Adverb of time
      καὶ **νῦν** ἐν τῷ κόσμῳ ἐστὶν **ἤδη** (1 John 4:3)
      even **now already** he is in the world
   4. Interrogative adverb
      πῶς δυσκόλως οἱ τὰ χρήματα ἔχοντες εἰς τὴν βασιλείαν τοῦ θεοῦ
      εἰσελεύσονται (Mark 10:23)
      how difficultly those who have riches shall enter into the kingdom of God
   5. Numerical adverb
      ἔτι **ἅπαξ** ἐγὼ σείσω οὐ μόνον τὴν γῆν ἀλλὰ καὶ τὸν οὐρανόν
      (Heb. 12:26)[3]
      yet once I will shake not only the earth but the heaven also
   6. Adverb of degree
      ἥδιστα οὖν **μᾶλλον** καυχήσομαι ἐν ταῖς ἀσθενείαις μου (2 Cor. 12:9)
      therefore I will boast **rather all the more gladly** in my weaknesses

---

[2] Luke 17:28 text is from GNT, NA & WH: TR & MT have καὶ ὡς for καθώς.

[3] Heb. 12:26 text is from GNT, NA & WH: TR & MT have σείω.

D. Attributive adverbs functioning as adjectives.
  1. First attributive position (article-adverb-noun)
    a. Adverb of manner
      χήρας τίμα **τὰς ὄντως χήρας** (1 Tim. 5:3)
      honor widows [who are] **truly widows**
    b. Adverb of place/location
      ἡ δὲ **ἄνωθεν σοφία** πρῶτον μὲν ἀγνή ἐστιν (James 3:17)
      but **the wisdom from above** is first pure
    c. Adverb of time
      μαρτύρομαι ὑμῖν **ἐν τῇ σήμερον ἡμέρᾳ** ὅτι καθαρός εἰμι ἀπὸ τοῦ
      αἵματος πάντων (Acts 20:26)
      I testify to you **on this very day** that I am clean from the blood of all
      people
    d. Adverb of degree
      ἦν γὰρ **μέγας σφόδρα** (Mark 16:4)
      for it was **very large**
  2. Second attributive position (article-noun-article-adverb)
    adverb of place/location
    καὶ **τὴν αὐλὴν τὴν ἔξωθεν** τοῦ ναοῦ ἔκβαλε ἔξωθεν (Rev. 11:2)
    and leave out **the outer court** of the temple
  3. Anarthrous attributive adverb
    a. Adverb of manner
      ἴδε **ἀληθῶς Ἰσραηλίτης** ἐν ᾧ δόλος οὐκ ἔστιν (John 1:47)
      here is **truly an Israelite** in whom deceit does not exist
    b. Adverb of place/location
      ἀνοίξαντες δὲ **ἔσω οὐδένα** εὕρομεν (Acts 5:23)
      and when we opened [it] we found **no one inside**
    c. Adverb of time
      Κρῆτες **ἀεὶ ψεῦσται** (Titus 1:12)
      the Cretans [εἰσίν, are] **always liars**

E. Substantive adverbs functioning as nouns.
  1. Articular adverbs
    a. Adverb of manner
      καὶ πάντες δὲ οἱ προφῆται **ἀπὸ** Σαμουὴλ καὶ **τῶν καθεξῆς**
      (Acts 3:24)
      and all the prophets **from** Samuel and **his successors**
    b. Adverb of place/location
      ἄφρονες, οὐχ ὁ ποιήσης **τὸ ἔξωθεν** καὶ **τὸ ἔσωθεν** ἐποίησε(ν);
      (Luke 11:40)
      foolish ones, did not he who made **the outside** make **the inside** also?

    c. Adverb of time
       μὴ οὖν μεριμνήσητε **εἰς τὴν αὔριον** (Matt. 6:34)
       do not worry then **for tomorrow**
  2. Anarthrous adverbs
    a. Interrogative adverb
       ἕως πότε μεθ' ὑμῶν ἔσομαι; (Matt. 17:17)
       how long shall I be with you?
    b. Numerical adverb
       τοῦτο δὲ ἐγένετο **ἐπὶ τρίς** (Acts 10:16; 11:10)
       and this took place **yet a third time**
    c. Adverb of place/location
       τὸ καταπέτασμα τοῦ ναοῦ ἐσχίσθη **ἀπ' ἄνωθεν ἕως κάτω εἰς δύο**
       (Matt. 27:51)
       the veil of the temple was torn in two **from the top to the bottom**
    d. Adverb of time
       ἀλλ' **ἕως σήμερον** ἡνίκα ἂν ἀναγινώσκηται Μωϋσῆς (2 Cor. 3:15)[4]
       but **until today** whenever Moses is read

F. Predicate adverbs.
  1. With equative verb εἰμί
    a. Adverb of manner
       ἀλλὰ καθὼς **ἐστιν ἀληθῶς** λόγον θεοῦ (1 Thess. 2:13)
       but even as **it is truly** the word of God
    b. Adverb of place/location
       ὅπου γάρ ἐστιν ὁ θησαυρός σου, **ἐκεῖ ἔσται** καὶ ἡ καρδία σου
       (Matt. 6:21)
       for where your treasure is, your heart **will be there** also
    c. Adverb of time
       ὁ καιρὸς γὰρ **ἐγγύς ἐστιν** (Rev. 22:10)
       for the time **is near**
    d. Interrogative adverb
       τὸ βάπτισμα τὸ Ἰωάννου **πόθεν ἦν**; (Matt. 21:25)
       the baptism that [ὄντα, was] of John **was from where**?

---

[4] 2 Cor. 3:15 text is from GNT & NA: WH has Μωυσῆς; TR has ἀναγινώσκεται Μωσῆς; MT has ἡνίκα ἀναγινώσκεται Μωϋσῆς.

   2. With γίνομαι
      a. Adverb of manner
         Ἐὰν δὲ ἔλθῃ Τιμόθεος, βλέπετε ἵνα ἀφόβως γένηται πρὸς ὑμᾶς
         (1 Cor. 16:10)
         and if Timothy comes, see that **he is without fear** among you
      b. Three adverbs together
         ὡς ὁσίως καὶ δικαίως καὶ ἀμέμπτως ὑμῖν τοῖς πιστεύουσιν
         ἐγενήθημεν (1 Thess. 2:10)
         how **devoutly** and **uprightly** and **blamelessly we were** among you who
         believe
   3. With passive verb
      Adverb of place/location
      ἐγενήθητε ἐγγὺς ἐν τῷ αἵματι τοῦ Χριστοῦ (Eph. 2:13)
      you were made near by the blood of Christ
   4. With elliptical verb
      a. Adverb of place/location
         ὁ κύριος ἐγγύς (Phil. 4:5)
         the Lord [**ἐστίν, is**] **near**
      b. Adverb of time
         Σήμερον χειμών (Matt. 16:3)
         stormy weather [**ἔσται, will be**] **today**
      c. Interrogative adverb
         εἰ ὅλον τὸ σῶμα ὀφθαλμός ποῦ ἡ ἀκοή; (1 Cor. 12:17)
         if the whole body [**ἐστιν, is**] an eye, **where** [**ἐστίν, is**] **the hearing**?
      d. With ἔχω, functioning as a stative verb
         ἀλλὰ καὶ ἀποθανεῖν εἰς Ἰερουσαλὴμ ἑτοίμως ἔχω ὑπὲρ τοῦ ὀνόματος
         τοῦ κυρίου Ἰησοῦ (Acts 21:13)[5]
         but **I am ready** also to die in Jerusalem for the name of the Lord Jesus

G. Comparative use of adverbs.
   1. Comparative adverb
      a. Adverb of manner with οὕτως and καθώς
         καθὼς καὶ ὁ κύριος ἐχαρίσατο ὑμῖν **οὕτως** καὶ ὑμεῖς (Col. 3:13)
         even as also the Lord forgave you, **so** also [do] you
      b. Adverb of time as predicate of elliptical ἐστίν
         νῦν γὰρ **ἐγγύτερον** ἡμῶν ἡ σωτηρία ἢ ὅτε ἐπιστεύσαμεν
         (Rom. 13:11)
         for now our salvation [**ἐστίν, is**] **nearer than** when we believed

---

[5] Acts 21:13 text is from GNT, NA, WH & MT: TR has Ἱερουσαλήμ.

2. Superlative adverbs
  a. Adverb of manner as elative
    ὡς καὶ σὺ **κάλλιον** ἐπιγινώσκεις (Acts 25:10)
    as you also know **very well**
  b. Superlative of manner as superlative
    ἵνα **ὡς τάχιστα** ἔλθωσιν πρὸς αὐτόν (Acts 17:15)
    that they should come to him **as quickly as possible**

H. Special uses of adverbs.
  1. Imperatival adverb of place
    a. Singular δεῦρο
      καὶ **δεῦρο** ἀκολούθει μοι (Matt. 19:21)
      and **come** follow me
    b. δεῦτε as plural of δεῦρο
      δεῦτε ὀπίσω μου, καὶ ποιήσω ὑμᾶς γενέσθαι ἁλιεῖς ἀνθρώπων
      (Mark 1:17)
      come after me, and I will make you to become fishers of men
  2. Adverb of language. Several adverbs occur with the meaning **in the language** (of a country or people): Ἑβραϊστί, Ἑλληνιστί, Ἰουδαϊκῶς, Λυκαονιστί, and Ῥωμαϊστί.
    καὶ ἦν γεγραμμένον **Ἑβραϊστί, Ῥωμαϊστί, Ἑλληνιστί** (John 19:20)[6]
    and it was written **in Hebrew, in Latin, in Greek**
  3. Exclamatory adverb
    εὖγε, ἀγαθὲ δοῦλε, ὅτι ἐν ἐλαχίστῳ πιστὸς ἐγένου (Luke 19:17)
    well done, good servant, for you were faithful in the least thing
  4. Special use of ἔχω with the adverb
    a. ἔχω functions in a sense similar to an equative verb.
      (1) Dat. sing. masc. pres. act. ptc
        οἳ ἀποδώσουσιν λόγον τῷ **ἑτοίμως ἔχοντι** κρῖναι ζῶντας καὶ νεκρούς (1 Peter 4:5)
        who will give account **to him who is ready** to judge the living and the dead
      (2) Acc. pl. masc. pres. act. ptc.
        καὶ προσήνεγκαν αὐτῷ **πάντας τοὺς κακῶς ἔχοντας** (Matt. 4:24)
        and they brought to him **all who were sick**

---

[6] John 19:20 text is from GNT & NA: WH has Ἑβραϊστί; TR & MT have Ἑλληνιστί, Ῥωμαϊστί.

(3) 3 pers. pl. fut. act. indic.

ἐπὶ ἀρρώστους χεῖρας ἐπιθήσουσιν, καὶ **καλῶς ἕξουσιν**
(Mark 16:18)

they shall lay hands on the infirm and **they shall be well**

(4) 3 pers. sing. pres. act. indic.

ὅτι τὸ θυγάτριόν μου **ἐσχάτως ἔχει** (Mark 5:23)

for my daughter **is extremely ill**

b. Comparative adverb

ἐπύθετο οὖν τὴν ὥραν παρ' αὐτῶν ἐν ᾗ **κομψότερον ἔσχεν**
(John 4:52)[7]

he then inquired from them the hour in which **he got better**

J. Some adverbs function in more than one way: as an adverb and as an improper preposition with a genitive object; or as an adverb and conjunction. Some of the more frequent of these are: improper prepositions, ἔμπροσθεν, ἔξω, ὀπίσω, χωρίς; conjunctions, ὅπως, πλήν ὡς.

1. Adverb as improper preposition with genitive object

ἔξω τῆς πύλης ἔπαθεν (Heb. 13:12)

he suffered **outside the gate**

2. Adverb as conjunction

ὅπως χάριτι θεοῦ ὑπὲρ πάντος γεύσηται θανάτου (Heb. 2:9)

so that by God's grace he should taste death for everyone

Select Bibliography for Adverbs

Boyer, James L. "Adverbial Clauses: Statistical Studies." *Grace Theological Journal* 11, no. 1 (1991): 71-96.

Davies, David P. "The Position of Adverbs in Luke," In *Studies in NT Language and Text: Essays in Honour of George D. Kilpatrick on the Occasion of His 65th Birthday*, edited by J. K. Elliott. Leiden: E. J. Brill (1976): 106-21.

Jung, Min-Young. "The Position of Adverbs in Biblical Greek." Master's thesis, Univ. of Texas at Arlington, 1985.

Wu, Michael Yick Kuen. "The Position of Adverbs in Matthew." Master's thesis, Dallas Theological Seminary, 1983.

---

[7] John 4:52 text is from GNT, NA & WH: TR & MT have παρ' αὐτῶν τὴν ὥραν.

ARTICLES

The article was originally a demonstrative pronoun. In Homer's work the pronominal use predominates, but in Classical and Hellenistic Greek the articular use is prominent. Thus, the basic function of the article is to stress the identity of a person, a class, or a quality. Some grammarians indicate that the presence of the article denotes definiteness. However, proper names as well as other substantives are definite even without the article.

Forms. The article agrees with its substantive in gender, number, and case. One must be careful to distinguish the article from the relative pronoun inasmuch as specific articles have only the rough breathing (ὁ, οἱ, ἡ, αἱ), whereas the parallel relative pronouns have both the rough breathing and the accent (ὅ, οἵ, ἥ, αἵ).

A. Distinctions between the nom. sing. masc. article ὁ and the nom. sing. neut. relative pronoun ὅ.
1. Nom. sing. masc. article ὁ
   ἵνα γένηται ὡς ὁ διδάσκαλος αὐτοῦ καὶ ὁ δοῦλος ὡς ὁ κύριος αὐτοῦ
   (Matt. 10:25)
   that he should be as his teacher and **the** servant as his master
2. Nom. sing. neut. relative pron. ὅ
   οὐδὲν γάρ ἐστιν κεκαλυμμένον ὃ οὐκ ἀποκαλυφθήσεται καὶ κρυπτὸν ὃ οὐ γνωσθήσεται (Matt. 10:26)
   for nothing is hidden **that** will not be revealed nor secret **that** will not be known
3. Acc. sing. neut. relative pron. ὅ
   ὃ λέγω ὑμῖν ἐν τῇ σκοτίᾳ εἴπατε ἐν τῷ φωτί, καὶ ὃ εἰς τὸ οὖς ἀκούετε κηρύξατε ἐπὶ τῶν δωμάτων (Matt. 10:27)
   what I tell you in the darkness, speak in the light, and **what** you hear in the ear, proclaim upon the rooftops

B. Distinctions between the nom. pl. masc. article οἱ and the nom. pl. masc. relative pronoun οἵ.
   ἀλλ' εἰσὶν ἐξ ὑμῶν τινες οἳ οὐ πιστεύουσιν. ᾔδει γὰρ ἐξ ἀρχῆς ὁ Ἰησοῦς τίνες εἰσὶν οἱ μὴ πιστεύοντες (John 6:64)
   but there are some of you **who** do not believe. For Jesus knew from the beginning who they were **who** did not believe

C. Distinctions between the nom. sing. fem. article ἡ and the nom. sing. fem. relative pronoun ἥ.
1. Nom. sing. fem. article ἡ
   ἡ δὲ Μάρθα περιεσπᾶτο περὶ πολλὴν διακονίαν (Luke 10:40)
   but **Martha** was distracted with much preparation [for a meal]

2. Nom. sing. fem. relative pron. ἥ

    καὶ τῇνδε ἦν ἀδελφὴ καλουμένη Μαριάμ, ἣ καὶ παρακαθεσθεῖσα
    πρὸς τοὺς τοῦ κυρίου ἤκουεν τὸν λόγον αὐτοῦ (Luke 10:39)
    and she had a sister named Mary, **who** also while sitting at the feet of the Lord
    was listening to his word

D. Distinctions between the nom. pl. fem. art. αἱ and the nom. pl. fem. relative
   pronoun αἵ.

    αἳ ὅτε ἦν ἐν τῇ Γαλιλαίᾳ ἠκολούθουν αὐτῷ καὶ διηκόνουν αὐτῷ,
    καὶ ἄλλαι πολλαὶ αἱ συναναβᾶσαι αὐτῷ εἰς Ἱεροσόλυμα (Mark 15:41)[1]
    who, when he was in Galilee, were following him and ministering to him, and
    many others **who** went up with him to Jerusalem

Functions. The Greek article has a wide range of applications to NT words, as
indicated in the following classifications. The article is used with adjectives, adverbs,
other articles, conjunctions, nouns, particles, prepositions, pronouns, finite verbs,
infinitives, and participles. The reason for the use or nonuse of the article in the
Greek NT is determined by the context.

I. **Articular adjectives**.

   A. The article may be used with an adjective or numeral in an attributive sense.
      1. First attributive position, article-adjective-noun. The articular adjective
         receives emphasis.
         a. Adjectives
           (1) Nom. sing. fem.
              ἀλλ᾽ ἡ τελεία ἀγάπη ἔξω βάλλει τὸν φόβον (1 John 4:18)
              but **perfect love** casts out fear
           (2) Gen. sing. masc.
              ἐμάθετε ἀπὸ Ἐπαφρᾶ **τοῦ ἀγαπητοῦ συνδούλου** ἡμῶν (Col. 1:7)
              you learned from Epaphras our **beloved fellow servant**
           (3) Dat. sing. fem.
              ἀναστήσεται ἐν τῇ ἀναστάσει **ἐν τῇ ἐσχάτῃ ἡμέρᾳ** (John 11:24)
              he shall rise in the resurrection **in the last day**
           (4) Acc. sing. masc.
              δέξασθε **τὸν ἔμφυτον λόγον** τὸν δυνάμενον σῶσαι τὰς ψυχὰς
              ὑμῶν (James 1:21)
              receive **the implanted word,** which is able to save your souls

---

[1] Mark 15:41 text is from GNT, NA, WH & MT: TR has Ἱεροσόλυμα.

b. Numerals
   (1) Nom. pl. masc.
      οἱ ἑπτὰ ἀστέρες ἄγγελοι τῶν ἑπτὰ ἐκκλησιῶν εἰσιν (Rev. 1:20)
      the seven stars are the messengers of the seven churches
   (2) Gen. sing. neut.
      ἤκουσα τοῦ δευτέρου ζῴου λέγοντος (Rev. 6:3)
      I heard **the second living creature** say
   (3) Dat. pl. fem.
      Ἰωάννης ταῖς ἑπτὰ ἐκκλησίαις ταῖς ἐν τῇ Ἀσίᾳ (Rev. 1:4)
      John **to the seven churches** that [οὖσαις, are] in Asia
   (4) Acc. sing. masc.
      τὸν μὲν πρῶτον λόγον ἐποιησάμην περὶ πάντων (Acts 1:1)
      I made **the first discourse** concerning all things

2. Second attributive position, article-noun-article-adjective. As both noun and adjective, each have an article; they receive equal emphasis. The articular adjective functions appositionally.
   a. Adjectives
      (1) Nom. sing. neut.
         ἦν τὸ φῶς τὸ ἀληθινόν, ὃ φωτίζει πάντα ἄνθρωπον (John 1:9)
         he was **the true light**, which sheds light on every person
      (2) Gen. sing. masc.
         ὅς ἐστιν εἰκὼν τοῦ θεοῦ τοῦ ἀοράτου (Col. 1:15)
         who is the image **of the invisible God**
      (3) Dat. sing. neut.
         ἐπετίμησε(ν) τῷ πνεύματι τῷ ἀκαθάρτῳ
         (Mark 9:25)
         he repeatedly commands **the unclean spirits**
      (4) Acc. sing. masc.
         τὸν υἱὸν αὐτοῦ τὸν μονογενῆ ἀπέσταλκεν ὁ θεὸς εἰς τὸν κόσμον
         (1 John 4:9)
         God has sent his **only son** into the world
   b. Numerals
      (1) Nom. sing. fem.
         ἡ οὐαὶ ἡ δευτέρα ἀπῆλθεν· ἰδού, ἡ οὐαὶ ἡ τρίτη ἔρχεται ταχύ
         (Rev. 11:14)
         the second woe is past; behold, **the third woe** is coming quickly
      (2) Gen. sing. masc.
         ὁ νικῶν οὐ μὴ ἀδικηθῇ ἐκ τοῦ θανάτου τοῦ δευτέρου
         (Rev. 2:11)
         the one who overcomes shall not be hurt **by the second death**

(3) Dat. sing. masc.

ἐν δὲ τῷ μηνὶ τῷ ἕκτῳ ἀπεστάλη ὁ ἄγγελος Γαβριήλ (Luke 1:26)
and **in the sixth month** the angel Gabriel was sent

(4) Acc. sing. fem.

καὶ εἶδον ὅτε ἤνοιξεν **τὴν σφραγῖδα τὴν ἕκτην** (Rev. 6:12)
and I looked when he opened **the sixth seal**

3. Third attributive position, noun-article-adjective. This adjective functions appositionally and most often follows a proper noun.

   a. Nom. sing. fem.

   καὶ **Βαβυλὼν ἡ μεγάλη** ἐμνήσθη ἐνώπιον τοῦ θεοῦ (Rev. 16:19)
   and **Babylon the great** was remembered before God

   b. Gen. pl. fem.

   τῶν τε σεβομένων Ἑλλήνων πλῆθος πολύ, **γυναικῶν τε τῶν πρώτων** οὐκ ὀλίγαι (Acts 17:4)[2]
   and of the worshiping Greeks a large number, and **of the women who were chief** not a few

   c. Dat. sing. masc.

   ὁ πρεσβύτερος **Γαΐῳ τῷ ἀγαπητῷ** ὃν ἐγὼ ἀγαπῶ ἐν ἀληθείᾳ
   (3 John 1)
   the elder **to Gaius my beloved friend,** whom I myself love in truth

   d. Acc. sing. fem.

   κατῴκησεν εἰς **Καφαρναοὺμ τὴν παραθαλασσίαν** (Matt. 4:13)[3]
   he resided **in Capernaum beside the sea**

4. Certain adjectives, such as ὅλος, πᾶς, are often used with an attributive sense in the predicate position.

   a. Nom. sing. masc.

   πᾶς ὁ πιστεύων ἐπ᾽ αὐτῷ οὐ καταισχυνθήσεται (Rom. 10:11)
   everyone who believes on him shall not be put to shame

   b. Gen. sing. masc.

   οὐ περὶ τῶν ἡμετέρων δὲ μόνον ἀλλὰ καὶ **περὶ ὅλου τοῦ κόσμου**
   (1 John 2:2)
   and not concerning ours only but also **concerning the whole world**

   c. Dat. sing. fem.

   οἱ δὲ ἐξελθόντες διεφήμισαν αὐτὸν ἐν **ὅλῃ τῇ γῇ ἐκείνῃ**
   (Matt. 9:31)
   and they went out and made him known **in all that country**

---

[2] Acts 17:4 text is from GNT, NA & WH: TR & MT have πολὺ πλῆθος.
[3] Matt. 4:13 text is from GNT, NA & WH: TR & MT have Καπερναούμ.

d. Acc. pl. masc.

καὶ ἀποστείλας ἀνεῖλεν **πάντας τοὺς παῖδας** τοὺς ἐν Βηθλέεμ (Matt. 2:16)

and he sent to destroy **all the male children** who [ὄντα, were] in Bethlehem

B. The article is used with an adjective or numeral to make it a substantive.
  1. Adjectives as substantives
    a. Nom. pl. masc.

    μακάριοι **οἱ ἐλεήμονες,** ὅτι αὐτοὶ ἐλεηθήσονται (Matt. 5:7)

    the merciful [εἰσιν, are] blessed, for they shall be shown mercy
    b. Gen. pl. masc.

    καὶ ἀνέβη ὁ καπνὸς τῶν θυμιαμάτων, ταῖς προσευχαῖς **τῶν ἁγίων** (Rev. 8:4)

    and the smoke of the incense ascended with the prayers **of the saints**
    c. Dat. pl. fem.

    καὶ ἦν **ἐν ταῖς ἐρήμοις** ἕως ἡμέρας ἀναδείξεως αὐτοῦ πρὸς τὸν Ἰσραήλ (Luke 1:80)

    and he was **in the deserted places** until the days of his manifestation to Israel
    d. Acc. sing. neut.

    ἀγαπητέ, μὴ μιμοῦ **τὸ κακὸν** ἀλλὰ **τὸ ἀγαθόν** (3 John 11)

    beloved friend, do not imitate **the evil** but **the good**
  2. Numerals as substantives
    a. Nom. sing. neut.

    τὸ δέκατον τῆς πόλεως ἔπεσεν (Rev. 11:13)

    and **the tenth [part]** of the city fell
    b. Gen. sing. fem.

    εἴρηκεν γάρ που **περὶ τῆς ἑβδόμης** (Heb. 4:4)

    for it has been said somewhere **concerning the seventh [day]**
    c. Acc. sing. neut.

    ὁ κύριος ἅπαξ λαὸν ἐκ γῆς Αἰγύπτου σώσας **τὸ δεύτερον** τοὺς μὴ πιστεύσαντας ἀπώλεσεν (Jude 5)[4]

    the Lord once having saved the people out of the land of Egypt **the second time** destroyed those who did not believe

---

[4] Jude 5 text is from GNT & NA: WH has κύριος λαόν: TR & MT omit ἅπαξ here.

d. Dat. sing. fem.

τῇ δὲ μιᾷ τῶν σαββάτων Μαρία ἡ Μαγδαληνὴ ἔρχεται πρωῒ
σκοτίας ἔτι οὔσης εἰς τὸ μνημεῖον (John 20:1)

now **on the first [day]** of the week Mary Magdalene came very early
to the tomb while it was yet dark

II. **The article with adverbs.**

A. First attributive position adverb functioning like an adjective.
1. Nom. sing. masc.
ἀλλ᾽ εἰ καὶ **ὁ ἔξω ἡμῶν ἄνθρωπος** διαφθείρεται (2 Cor. 4:16)
but even if **our outer man** is perishing
2. Gen. sing. fem.
ἄχρι γὰρ **τῆς σήμερον ἡμέρας** τὸ αὐτὸ κάλυμμα ἐπὶ τῇ ἀναγνώσει
τῆς παλαιᾶς διαθήκης μένει (2 Cor. 3:14)
for **until this very day** the same veil remains at the reading of the
old covenant
3. Dat. sing. fem.
τὸ δὲ Ἁγὰρ . . . συστοιχεῖ δὲ **τῇ νῦν Ἰερουσαλήμ** (Gal. 4:25)[5]
now Hagar . . . corresponds **to the present Jerusalem**
4. Acc. sing. masc.
συνήδομαι γὰρ τῷ νόμῳ τοῦ θεοῦ **κατὰ τὸν ἔσω ἄνθρωπον** (Rom. 7:22)
for I agree with the law of God **according to the inner man**

B. Only one second attributive position adverb is noted.
Acc. sing. fem.
καὶ **τὴν αὐλὴν τὴν ἔξωθεν** τοῦ λαοῦ ἔκβαλε (Rev. 11:2)
and leave out **the outer court** of the temple

C. The article with the adverb may also function as a substantive.
1. Nom. sing. fem.
ἡ γὰρ **αὔριον** μεριμνήσει ἑαυτῆς (Matt. 6:34)[6]
for **tomorrow** will worry about itself
2. Gen. pl. masc.
δεῖ δὲ καὶ μαρτυρίαν καλὴν ἔχειν ἀπὸ **τῶν ἔξωθεν** (1 Tim. 3:7)[7]
and he also must have a good testimony **from those outside**

---

[5] Gal. 4:25 text is from GNT & NA: WH has τὸ δὲ Ἅγαρ and συνστοιχεῖ; TR has τὸ γὰρ Ἅγαρ and Ἱερουσαλήμ; MT has τὸ γὰρ Ἁγάρ.

[6] Matt. 6:34 text is from GNT & NA: TR & MT have τὰ ἑαυτῆς; WH has αὑτῆς.

[7] 1 Tim. 3:7 text is from GNT, NA & WH: TR & MT have δεῖ δὲ αὐτὸν καί.

3. Dat. sing. fem.
τῇ ἐπαύριον βλέπει τὸν Ἰησοῦν ἐρχόμενον πρὸς αὐτόν (John 1:29)[8]
on the next day he saw Jesus coming to him
4. Acc. sing. masc.
ἀγαπήσεις τὸν πλησίον σου (Matt. 5:43)
you shall love your **neighbor**

III. **The article may be used with another article or singly in various ways**.

A. Two articles in conjunction with each other.
1. The first article may indicate an ellipsis, derived from the context.
a. Nom. sing. neut.
ὅτι τὸ τῆς δόξης καὶ τὸ τοῦ θεοῦ πνεῦμα ἐφ᾽ ὑμᾶς ἀναπαύεται (1 Peter 4:14)
for **the [πνεῦμα, Spirit] of glory** and **the Spirit of God** is resting upon you
b. Nom. sing. masc.
ὁ λόγος γὰρ ὁ τοῦ σταυροῦ τοῖς μὲν ἀπολλυμένοις μωρία ἐστίν (1 Cor. 1:18)
for the word, **which [ὤν, is] of the** cross, is foolishness to those who are perishing
c. Nom. pl. neut.
τίς γὰρ οἶδεν ἀνθρώπων τὰ τοῦ ἀνθρώπου εἰ μὴ τὸ πνεῦμα τοῦ ἀνθρώπου τὸ ἐν αὐτῷ (1 Cor. 2:11)
for who among men knows **the things [ὄντα, that] belong to** a man except the spirit of the man that [ὄν, is] in him
2. The first article is an object of a preposition with an implied noun, and the second article indicates a genitive of relationship.
Gen. sing. fem.
Δαυὶδ δὲ ἐγέννησεν τὸν Σολομῶνα ἐκ τῆς τοῦ Οὐρίου (Matt. 1:6)[9]
and David begat Solomon of **the [γυναῖκος, wife] of** Uriah (or **of her who had been the wife of** Uriah)

---

[8] John 1:29 text is from GNT, NA, WH & MT: TR has βλέπει ὁ Ἰωάννης.
[9] Matt. 1:6 text is from GNT & NA: WH has Δαυείδ; TR & MT have Δαβίδ δὲ ὁ βασιλεύς; TR has Σολομῶντα; WH & MT have Σολομῶνα.

3. The first article may be in apposition to a noun and the second article indicates possession, relationship, or description.
   a. Dat. sing. fem.
   ἐν πίστει ζῶ τῇ τοῦ υἱοῦ τοῦ θεοῦ τοῦ ἀγαπήσαντός με καὶ παραδόντος ἑαυτὸν ὑπὲρ ἐμοῦ (Gal. 2:20)
   I live by faithfulness **that [οὔσῃ, belongs] to the son** of God who loved me and gave himself for me
   b. Acc. sing. masc.
   Ἰάκωβον τὸν τοῦ Ζεβεδαίου καὶ Ἰωάννην τὸν ἀδελφὸν αὐτοῦ (Matt. 4:21)[10]
   James **the [υἱὸν, son] of Zebedee** and John his brother
4. The first article may be substantival, followed by an article indicating possession.
   Acc. pl. neut.
   ὁ ἄγαμος μεριμνᾷ τὰ τοῦ κυρίου πῶς ἀρέσῃ τῷ κυρίῳ (1 Cor. 7:32)
   the unmarried man is concerned **about the things [ὄντα, that] belong to the Lord**, how he may please the Lord

B. The independent neuter article may introduce a citation or indirect discourse, a phrase, clause, or entire sentence.
   1. Nom. sing. neut
   τὸ εἰ δύνῃ, πάντα δυνατὰ τῷ πιστεύοντι (Mark 9:23)[11]
   if you can! all things are possible to the one who believes
   2. Dat. sing. neut.
   ὁ γὰρ πᾶς νόμος ἐν ἑνὶ λόγῳ πεπλήρωται, ἐν τῷ Ἀγαπήσεις τὸν πλησίον σου ὡς σεαυτόν (Gal. 5:14)[12]
   for the entire law is fulfilled in one word, **namely in this**, you shall love your neighbor as yourself
   3. Acc. sing. neut.
   καθὼς παρελάβετε παρ' ἡμῶν τὸ πῶς δεῖ ὑμᾶς περιπατεῖν καὶ ἀρέσκειν θεῷ (1 Thess. 4:1)
   even as you received from us **how you ought to walk** and please God

IV. **The article with conjunctions.**

A. Granville Sharp's rule: "When the copulative καί connects two nouns of the same case (viz., either substantive or adjective, or participle of personal

---

[10] Matt. 4:21 text is from GNT, NA, TR & MT: WH has Ἰωάνην.
[11] Mark 9:23 text is from GNT, NA & WH: TR & MT have τὸ εἰ δύνασαι πιστεῦσαι.
[12] Gal. 5:14 text is from GNT, NA & WH: TR has πληροῦται and ἑαυτόν; MT has πληροῦται and σεαυτόν.

description, respecting office, dignity, affinity or connection, and attributes, properties or qualities, good or ill), if the article ὁ, or any of its cases, precedes the first of the said nouns or participles, and is not repeated before the second noun or participle, the latter always relates to the same person that is expressed or described by the first noun or participle; i.e., it denotes a further description of the first-named person." This rule applies only to substantives. Specific examples of this phenomenon are given with nouns, adjectives, and participles.

1. Nouns
   a. Gen. sing. masc.

      κατὰ τὸ θέλημα **τοῦ θεοῦ καὶ πατρὸς ἡμῶν** (Gal. 1:4)

      according to the will **of our God and Father**
   b. Nom. sing. masc.

      εὐλογητὸς **ὁ θεὸς καὶ πατὴρ** τοῦ κυρίου ἡμῶν Ἰησοῦ Χριστοῦ, **ὁ πατὴρ** τῶν οἰκτιρμῶν **καὶ θεὸς** πάσης παρακλήσεως (2 Cor. 1:3)

      blessed [ἐστιν, is] **the God and Father** of our Lord Jesus Christ, **the Father** of mercies **and God** of all encouragement
   c. Dat. sing. masc.

      θρησκεία καθαρὰ καὶ ἀμίαντος παρὰ **τῷ θεῷ καὶ πατρὶ** αὕτη ἐστίν (James 1:27)

      this is pure and undefiled worship of **God and Father**
   d. Acc. sing. masc.

      κατανοήσατε **τὸν ἀπόστολον καὶ ἀρχιερέα** τῆς ὁμολογίας ἡμῶν (Heb. 3:1)

      consider **the apostle and high priest** of our confession
2. Adjectives
   a. Nom. sing. masc.

      καὶ εἰ ὁ δίκαιος μόλις σῴζεται, **ὁ ἀσεβὴς καὶ ἁμαρτωλὸς** ποῦ φανεῖται; (1 Peter 4:18)

      and if the righteous are saved with difficulty, where shall **the ungodly and sinner** appear?
   b. Dat. sing. masc. (an adjective and a noun)

      Παῦλος δέσμιος Χριστοῦ Ἰησοῦ καὶ Τιμόθεος ὁ ἀδελφὸς **Φιλήμονι τῷ ἀγαπητῷ καὶ συνεργῷ** ἡμῶν (Philem. 1)

      Paul a prisoner of Christ Jesus and Timothy my brother **to Philemon**, our **dear friend and fellow worker**
   c. Acc. sing. masc.

      ὑμεῖς δὲ **τὸν ἅγιον καὶ δίκαιον** ἠρνήσασθε (Acts 3:14)

      but you yourselves denied **the holy and just one**

3. Participles
   a. Nom. sing. masc.
      μακάριος ὁ γρηγορῶν καὶ τηρῶν τὰ ἱμάτια αὐτοῦ (Rev. 16:15)
      blessed [ἐστιν, is] **the one who watches and keeps** his garments
   b. Gen. sing. masc.
      κατὰ δύναμιν θεοῦ, τοῦ σώσαντος ἡμᾶς καὶ καλέσαντος κλήσει
      ἁγίᾳ (2 Tim. 1:8-9)
      according to the power of God **who saved us and called** [us] with a holy
      calling
   c. Dat. sing. masc.
      καὶ ὑπὲρ πάντων ἀπέθανεν ἵνα οἱ ζῶντες μηκέτι ἑαυτοῖς ζῶσιν
      ἀλλὰ τῷ ὑπὲρ αὐτῶν ἀποθανόντι καὶ ἐγερθέντι (2 Cor. 5:15)
      and he died for all [people] that those who live should no longer
      live for themselves but **for the one who died** for them **and was raised**
   d. Acc. sing. masc.
      τοὺς δι' αὐτοῦ πιστοὺς εἰς θεὸν τὸν ἐγείραντα αὐτὸν ἐκ νεκρῶν
      καὶ δόξαν αὐτῷ δόντα (1 Peter 1:21)
      who by him believe in God, **who raised** him from the dead **and gave**
      him glory

B. Exceptions to Granville Sharp's rule.
   1. Proper nouns/names may be found in the article-noun-καί-noun
      construction. However, with proper names, the article will apply to the
      second noun as well as to the first, without confusion of identity of
      persons or places.
      a. Gen. sing. masc.
         θεωροῦντες δὲ τὴν τοῦ Πέτρου παρρησίαν καὶ Ἰωάννου
         (Acts 4:13)[13]
         and while they saw the boldness **of Peter and John**
      b. Gen. sing. fem.
         καὶ ἠκολούθησαν αὐτῷ ὄχλοι πολλοὶ ἀπὸ τῆς Γαλιλαίας καὶ
         Δεκαπόλεως καὶ Ἱεροσολύμων καὶ Ἰουδαίας καὶ πέραν τοῦ
         Ἰορδάνου (Matt. 4:25)
         and large crowds followed him **from Galilee and Decapolis and
         Jerusalem and Judea** and across the Jordan

---

[13] Acts 4:13 text is from GNT, NA, TR & MT: WH has Ἰωάνου.

c. Acc. sing. masc.

παραλαμβάνει ὁ Ἰησοῦς τὸν Πέτρον καὶ Ἰάκωβον καὶ Ἰωάννην
(Matt. 17:1)[14]

Jesus took along **Peter and James and John**

d. Acc. sing. fem.

τοῖς κατὰ τὴν Ἀντιόχειαν καὶ Συρίαν καὶ Κιλικίαν ἀδελφοῖς
τοῖς ἐξ ἐθνῶν χαίρειν (Acts 15:23)

to the brothers **in Antioch and Syria and Cilicia** who [οὖσιν, are]
of the Gentiles, greetings

2. Granville Sharp's rule does not apply to impersonal nouns. There is a
   unifying principle with the article, in which the plurality of nouns shares
   something in common, yet each noun is distinct in some way from the
   other.

   a. Nom. sing. neut.

   τί τὸ πλάτος καὶ μῆκος καὶ ὕψος καὶ βάθος (Eph. 3:18)

   what [ἐστιν, is] **the breadth and length and height and depth**

   b. Gen. sing. fem.

   οἶδα γὰρ ὅτι τοῦτό μοι ἀποβήσεται εἰς σωτηρίαν διὰ τῆς ὑμῶν
   δεήσεως καὶ ἐπιχορηγίας τοῦ πνεύματος Ἰησοῦ Χριστοῦ (Phil. 1:19)

   for I know that this will turn out for me to [be] salvation through **your
   prayer and the supply** of the Spirit of Jesus Christ

   c. Dat. sing. fem.

   τοῦτον τῇ ὡρισμένῃ βουλῇ καὶ προγνώσει τοῦ θεοῦ ἔκδοτον
   (Acts 2:23)

   this one [was] delivered up **by the determinate counsel and
   foreknowledge** of God

   d. Acc. sing. fem.

   ἄξιόν ἐστιν τὸ ἀρνίον τὸ ἐσφαγμένον λαβεῖν τὴν δύναμιν καὶ
   πλοῦτον καὶ σοφίαν καὶ ἰσχὺν καὶ τιμὴν καὶ δόξαν καὶ εὐλογίαν
   (Rev. 5:12)

   worthy is the lamb that was slain to receive **the power and riches and
   wisdom and might and honor and glory and blessing**

3. Two articular subjects joined by καί with a singular verb indicate a special
   unity, the nature of which is determined by the context.

   a. Nom. sing. masc.

   αὐτὸς δὲ ὁ θεὸς καὶ πατὴρ ἡμῶν καὶ ὁ κύριος ἡμῶν Ἰησοῦς
   κατευθύναι τὴν ὁδὸν ἡμῶν πρὸς ὑμᾶς (1 Thess. 3:11)

   now, **God Himself,** even our Father, **and our Lord Jesus direct** our
   journey to you

---

[14] Matt. 17:1 text is from GNT, NA, TR & MT: WH has Ἰωάνου.

b. Nom. sing. fem.
ἡ χάρις καὶ ἡ ἀλήθεια διὰ Ἰησοῦ Χριστοῦ ἐγένετο (John 1:17)
grace and truth came through Jesus Christ

4. Two singular articular substantives joined by καί with a plural verb indicat
distinction of function within a unity, determined by the context.
   a. Nom. sing. masc.
   ὁ φυτεύων δὲ καὶ ὁ ποτίζων ἓν εἰσιν (1 Cor. 3:8)
   but **the one who plants and the one who waters are** one
   b. Nom. sing. pron. and articular noun
   ἐγὼ καὶ ὁ πατὴρ ἕν ἐσμεν (John 10:30)
   I and the Father, we are one

5. Two articular plural nouns joined by καί indicate a specific distinction
between the two groups.
   a. Nom. pl. masc.
   οἱ ἀπόστολοι καὶ οἱ πρεσβύτεροι ἀδελφοὶ τοῖς κατὰ τὴν
   Ἀντιόχειαν καὶ Συρίαν καὶ Κιλικίαν ἀδελφοῖς τοῖς ἐξ ἐθνῶν
   (Acts 15:23)[15]
   the apostles and the elder brothers to the brothers in Antioch and
   Syria and Cilicia who [οὖσιν, are] of the Gentiles
   b. Gen. pl. masc.
   παρεδέχθησαν ἀπὸ τῆς ἐκκλησίας καὶ **τῶν ἀποστόλων καὶ τῶν
   πρεσβυτέρων** (Acts 15:4)[16]
   they were received by the church and **the apostles and the elders**
   c. Dat. pl. masc.
   τότε ἔδοξε **τοῖς ἀποστόλοις καὶ τοῖς πρεσβυτέροις** σὺν ὅλῃ τῇ
   ἐκκλησίᾳ (Acts 15:22)
   then it seemed good **to the apostles and to the elders** with the whol
   church
   d. Acc. pl. masc.
   καὶ ἐλθὼν εἰς τὸν οἶκον συγκαλεῖ **τοὺς φίλους καὶ τοὺς γείτονα**
   (Luke 15:6)[17]
   and when he entered his house he called together **his friends and
   neighbors**

6. Two plural nouns joined by καί with only the first noun articular indicat
some distinction between the two nouns, but both are considered as some

---

[15] Acts 15:23 text is from BNT, NA & WH; TR & MT have οἱ πρεσβύτεροι καὶ οἱ ἀδελφοί.
[16] Acts 15:4 text is from GNT, NA & WH; TR & MT have ἀπεδέχθησαν ὑπὸ.
[17] Luke 15:6 text is from GNT, NA TR & MT; WH has συνκαλεῖ.

kind of unit that the context will determine.[18]

   a. Nom. pl. masc. (identical groups)

μακάριοι **οἱ πεινῶντες καὶ διψῶντες** τὴν δικαιοσύνην (Matt. 5:6)
blessed [εἰσιν, are] **those who hunger and thirst** after righteousness

   b. Gen. pl. masc. & fem. (distinct groups)

πολλοὶ μὲν οὖν ἐξ αὐτῶν ἐπίστευσαν, καὶ **τῶν Ἑλληνίδων γυναικῶν τῶν εὐσχημόνων καὶ ἀνδρῶν** οὐκ ὀλίγοι (Acts 17:12)
then indeed many of them believed, both **of the honorable Grecian women and [the] men**

   c. Dat. pl. masc. (identical groups)

ὅμοιοί εἰσιν παιδίοις **τοῖς** ἐν ἀγορᾷ **καθημένοις καὶ προσφωνοῦσιν** ἀλλήλοις (Luke 7:32)
they are like children **who sit** in the market place **and call** to one another

   d. Acc. pl. neut. (distinct groups)

ἔταξαν ἀναβαίνειν Παῦλον καὶ Βαρναβᾶν καί τινας ἄλλους ἐξ αὐτῶν πρὸς **τοὺς ἀποστόλους καὶ πρεσβυτέρους** εἰς Ἰερουσαλὴμ περὶ τοῦ ζητήματος τούτου (Acts 15:2)[19]
they ordered Paul and Barnabas and some other members of them to go up **to the apostles and elders** in Jerusalem concerning this question

V. **The article with nouns.** This is the most frequent use of the article.

  A. The article with proper nouns. Proper nouns are definite in themselves and may or may not take the article. The article with proper nouns is difficult to classify by rules. However, the articular use in the Greek language is prevalent.

   1. Names of people with the article

    a. Gen. sing. masc.

καὶ αὕτη ἐστὶν ἡ μαρτυρία **τοῦ Ἰωάννου** (John 1:19)[20]
and this is the testimony **of John**

---

[18] Daniel Wallace distinguishes five semantic categories: two entirely distinct groups, though united (Matt. 2:4; 3:7; 16:1, 6, 11, 12, 21; 20:18; 26:47; 27:3, 12, 41; Mark 15:1; Luke 9:22; 22:52; John 7:45; Acts 17:12; 23:7); two overlapping groups (Luke 14:21; Rev. 21:8); the first-named group a sub-set of the second (Matt. 5:20; 9:11; 12:38; Mark 2:16; Luke 5:30; 6:35; 14:3); the second-named group a sub-set of the first (Mark 2:16; 1 Cor. 5:10; 1 Tim. 5:8; 3 John 5); and the groups may be entirely identical (Matt. 5:6; 11:28; 21:15; Mark 12:40; Luke 7:32; 8:21; 11:28; 12:4; 18:9; 20:46; John 1:40; 11:31, 45; 20:29; Rom. 16:7; 2 Cor. 12:21; Gal. 1:7; Eph. 1:1; Phil. 3:3; Col. 1:2; 1 Thess. 5:12; 2 Tim. 3:6; Titus 1:15; 1 Peter 2:18; 2 Peter 2:10; Rev. 1:3; 12:17; 18:9). "The Semantic Range of the Article-Noun-καί-Noun Plural Construction in the New Testament." *Grace Theological Journal* 4, no. 1 (1983): 59-84.

[19] Acts 15:2 text is from GNT, NA, WH & MT: TR has Ἰερουσαλήμ.

[20] John 1:19 text is from GNT, NA, TR & MT: WH has Ἰωάνου.

    b. Nom. sing. masc.

      τότε ὁ Ἰησοῦς ἀνήχθη εἰς τὴν ἔρημον ὑπὸ τοῦ πνεύματος (Matt. 4:1)

      then **Jesus** was led by the Spirit into the wilderness

    c. Dat. sing. masc.

      ὁ Φῆστος δέ . . . τῷ Παύλῳ εἶπεν (Acts 25:9)

      and Festus . . . said **to Paul**

    d. Acc. sing. masc.

      ὅστις ποιμανεῖ τὸν λαόν μου τὸν Ἰσραήλ (Matt. 2:6)

      who shall shepherd **my people Israel**

2. Names of places with the article

    a. Nom. sing. fem.

      ἡ δὲ ἄνω Ἰερουσαλὴμ ἐλευθέρα ἐστίν (Gal. 4:26)[21]

      but **the Jerusalem** above is free

    b. Gen. sing. fem.

      ἔπειτα ἦλθον εἰς τὰ κλίματα τῆς Συρίας καὶ τῆς Κιλικίας (Gal. 1:21)

      then I went into the regions **of Syria** and **Cilicia**

    c. Acc. sing. masc.

      τότε παραγίνεται ὁ Ἰησοῦς ἀπὸ τῆς Γαλιλαίας ἐπὶ τὸν Ἰορδάνην

      (Matt. 3:13)

      then Jesus came from Galilee **to the Jordan [River]**

    d. Dat. sing. fem.

      ποιεῖτε αὐτὸ εἰς πάντας τοὺς ἀδελφοὺς τοὺς ἐν ὅλῃ τῇ

      Μακεδονίᾳ (1 Thess. 4:10)

      you do this to all the brothers who [ὄντα, are] **in all Macedonia**

3. The article is often used to identify the case of an indeclinable proper noun.

    a. Nom. sing. fem.

      καὶ ἐπλήσθη πνεύματος ἁγίου ἡ Ἐλισάβετ (Luke 1:41)

      and **Elisabeth** was filled with the Holy Spirit

    b. Gen. sing. masc.

      ἵνα εἰς τὰ ἔθνη ἡ εὐλογία τοῦ Ἀβραὰμ γένηται (Gal. 3:14)

      that the blessing **of Abraham** might come to the Gentiles

    c. Dat. sing. masc.

      ἄγγελος κυρίου φαίνεται κατ᾽ ὄναρ τῷ Ἰωσήφ (Matt. 2:13)

      an angel of the Lord appeared in a dream **to Joseph**

    d. Acc. sing. masc.

      Ἀβραὰμ ἐγέννησεν τὸν Ἰσαάκ, Ἰσαὰκ δὲ ἐγέννησεν τὸν Ἰακώβ

      (Matt. 1:2)

      Abraham begat **Isaac**, and Isaac begat **Jacob**

---

[21] Gal. 4:26 text is from GNT, NA, WH & MT: TR has Ἰερουσαλήμ.

B. The article is used with common nouns of people, places, things, and ideas.
  1. The article is often used with monadic nouns, i.e., referring to one of a kind.
    a. Nom. sing. masc.
       ὁ δὲ Μιχαὴλ ὁ ἀρχάγγελος (Jude 9)
       but Michael **the archangel**
    b. Gen. sing. fem.
       ὁ ὢν ἐκ τῆς γῆς ἐκ τῆς γῆς ἐστιν καὶ ἐκ τῆς γῆς λαλεῖ (John 3:31)
       the one who is **of the earth** is **from the earth** and speaks **of the earth**
    c. Dat. sing. masc.
       εὐχαριστῶ τῷ θεῷ μου πάντοτε περὶ ὑμῶν (1 Cor. 1:4)
       I thank my **God** always for you
    d. Acc. sing. masc.
       οὕτω(ς) γὰρ ἠγάπησεν ὁ θεὸς τὸν κόσμον (John 3:16)
       for God so loved **the world**
  2. The article may illustrate Apollonius' Canon. Apollonius of Dyscolus was
     a second century A.D. Greek grammarian who stated that, usually when a
     noun is modified by another noun in the genitive case, both nouns will have
     the article prefixed to them or neither will have the article. When both nouns
     are anarthrous, usually they are both mutually definite or both indefinite or
     both qualitative.
    a. Nom. pl. neut.
      (1) Articular
          ἐν τούτῳ φανερά ἐστιν τὰ τέκνα τοῦ θεοῦ (1 John 3:10)
          by this **the children of God** are manifest
      (2) Anarthrous
          ἀγαπητοί, νῦν τέκνα θεοῦ ἐσμεν (1 John 3:2)
          dear friends, now we are **children of God**
    b. Dat. sing. fem. and nom. sing. fem.
       χάριτι δὲ θεοῦ εἰμι ὅ εἰμι . . . ἀλλὰ περισσότερον αὐτῶν πάντων
       ἐκοπίασα, οὐκ ἐγὼ δὲ ἀλλὰ ἡ χάρις τοῦ θεοῦ ἡ σὺν ἐμοί
       (1 Cor. 15:10)
       but **by the grace of God** I am what I am . . . but I worked harder than
       all of them, yet not I, but **the grace of God**, which [οὖσῃ, was] with me
  3. Exceptions to Apollonius' Canon.
    a. When the genitive noun is a proper noun, the article may be absent when
       the proper noun precedes or follows the articular noun and also when
       it is bracketed between the article and the noun.
      (1) Nom. sing. neut.
          καὶ τὸ αἷμα Ἰησοῦ τοῦ υἱοῦ αὐτοῦ καθαρίζει ἡμᾶς ἀπὸ πάσης
          ἁμαρτίας (1 John 1:7)
          and **the blood of Jesus** his son cleanses us from every sin

(2) Acc. sing. neut.

εἰς τί οὖν ἐβαπτίσθητε; οἱ δὲ εἶπαν Εἰς τὸ Ἰωάννου βάπτισμα (Acts 19:3)[22]

unto what then were you baptized? and they said, "**unto the baptism of John**"

b. The first noun may be anarthrous because it is the complement of an equative verb.

(1) With εἰμί

ὅτι θρόνος ἐστὶν τοῦ θεοῦ (Matt. 5:34)

because **it is the throne of God**

(2) With γίνομαι

ὅπως γένησθε υἱοὶ τοῦ πατρὸς ὑμῶν τοῦ ἐν οὐρανοῖς (Matt. 5:45)

so that **you may be sons of your father** who [ὄντος, is] in heaven

(3) With ὑπάρχω

γένος οὖν ὑπάρχοντες τοῦ θεοῦ (Acts 17:29)

since then **we are the offspring of God**

(4) With elliptical verb

οὐ τὰ τέκνα τῆς σαρκὸς ταῦτα τέκνα τοῦ θεοῦ (Rom. 9:8)

these children of the flesh [ἐστιν/εἰσιν, are] not **the children of God**

(5) With passive verb

εὑρισκόμεθα δὲ καὶ ψευδομάρτυρες τοῦ θεοῦ (1 Cor. 15:15)

but **we** also **are being found false witnesses of God**

c. The first noun may reflect the Hebrew idiom in the construct state (see Glossary), especially with a quotation from or reference to the OT.

ὃς καί ἐστιν ἐν δεξιᾷ τοῦ θεοῦ (Rom. 8:34)

who also is **at the right hand of God**

d. The vocative case never has the article.

τί ἐμοὶ καὶ σοί, Ἰησοῦ υἱὲ τοῦ θεοῦ τοῦ ὑψίστου; (Luke 8:28)

what to me and you, Jesus **son of the most high God**?

e. Indeclinable proper names are usually anarthrous in the genitive case.

Ἐγώ εἰμι ὁ θεὸς Ἀβραὰμ καὶ ὁ θεὸς Ἰσαὰκ καὶ ὁ θεὸς Ἰακώβ (Matt. 22:32)

I am **the God of Abraham** and **the God of Isaac** and **the God of Jacob**

f. The object of a preposition is often anarthrous.

δι' οὗ ἐκλήθητε εἰς κοινωνίαν τοῦ υἱοῦ αὐτοῦ (1 Cor. 1:9)

by whom you were called **into the fellowship** of his son

---

[22] Acts 19:3 text is from GNT, NA, TR & MT: WH has Ἰωάνου.

g. A noun in apposition may be anarthrous.
οὗτος οὐκ ἐκβάλλει τὰ δαιμόνια εἰ μὴ ἐν τῷ Βεελζεβοὺλ ἄρχοντι
τῶν δαιμονίων (Matt. 12:24)
this man does not cast out demons except **by Beelzebul the ruler**
of the demons
h. πᾶς modifies an anarthrous noun when it means **every**.
ἵνα σταθῆτε τέλειοι καὶ πεπληροφορημένοι ἐν παντὶ θελήματι τοῦ
θεοῦ (Col. 4:12)[23]
that you may stand perfect and assured **in every part of God's will**
i. The genitive of κύριος is often anarthrous.
πᾶς γὰρ ὃς ἂν ἐπικαλέσηται τὸ ὄνομα κυρίου σωθήσεται
(Rom. 10:13)
for everyone who shall call on **the name of the Lord** shall be saved
j. A noun may be modified by an anarthrous adjective with an articular
noun as in the following:
(1) With a cardinal numeral
εὐκοπώτερον δέ ἐστιν τὸν οὐρανὸν καὶ τὴν γῆν παρελθεῖν ἢ
τοῦ νόμου μίαν κεραίαν πεσεῖν (Luke 16:17)
but it is easier for heaven and earth to pass away than for **one tittle
of the law** to fall
(2) With πᾶς
ὅς ἐστιν ἡ κεφαλὴ πάσης ἀρχῆς καὶ ἐξουσίας (Col. 2:10)
who is **the head of all rule and authority**
(3) With πολύς modifying ὄχλος and πλῆθος
(a) With πλῆθος
ἠκολούθει δὲ αὐτῷ πολὺ πλῆθος τοῦ λαοῦ (Luke 23:27)
and **a large crowd of people** were following him
(b) With ὄχλος
πολύς τε ὄχλος τῶν ἱερέων ὑπήκουον τῇ πίστει (Acts 6:7)
and **a large number of the priests** was obedient to the faith
(4) With ἱκανός modifying ὄχλος
καὶ ὄχλος τῆς πόλεως ἱκανὸς ἦν σὺν αὐτῇ (Luke 7:12)
and **a considerable crowd from the city** was with her
(5) With πόσος modifying an anarthrous noun
πόσοι μίσθιοι τοῦ πατρός μου περισσεύονται ἄρτων
(Luke 15:17)
how many hired servants of my father have an abundance of bread

[23] Col. 4:12 text is from GNT, NA & WH: TR & MT have στῆτε and πεπληρωμένοι.

4. The article may function as a pronoun.
  a. As a demonstrative pronoun
    (1) Nom. sing. fem.
        τί τὸ ὄφελος, ἀδελφοί μου, ἐὰν πίστιν λέγῃ τις ἔχειν ἔργα δὲ
        μὴ ἔχῃ; μὴ δύναται ἡ πίστις σῶσαι αὐτόν; (James 2:14)[24]
        what is the profit, my brothers, if a person claims to have faith but
        does not have works? is **that faith** able to save him?
    (2) Nom. pl. masc.
        οἱ δὲ τοῦ Χριστοῦ (Gal. 5:24)
        but **those** [ὄντες, who] belong to Christ
    (3) Gen. sing. masc.
        τοῦ γὰρ καὶ γένος ἐσμέν (Acts 17:28)
        for we also are offspring **of that one**
    (4) Acc. sing. masc.
        πόθεν οὖν ἔχεις τὸ ὕδωρ τὸ ζῶν; (John 4:11)[25]
        from where then do you have **that living water?**
  b. The article may function as a possessive pronoun for relationships.
    (1) Nom. sing. masc.
        Παῦλος ἀπόστολος Χριστοῦ Ἰησοῦ . . . καὶ Τιμόθεος
        ὁ ἀδελφός (2 Cor. 1:1)[26]
        Paul an apostle of Christ Jesus . . . and Timothy **my/our brother**
    (2) Gen. sing. masc.
        ἐγερθεὶς δὲ ὁ Ἰωσὴφ ἀπὸ τοῦ ὕπνου ἐποίησεν ὡς προσέταξεν
        αὐτῷ ὁ ἄγγελος κυρίου (Matt. 1:24)[27]
        and when Joseph awoke **from his sleep** he did as the angel of
        the Lord instructed him
    (3) Dat. sing. neut.
        ὑμᾶς δὲ ὁ κύριος πλεονάσαι καὶ περισσεῦσαι τῇ ἀγάπῃ εἰς
        ἀλλήλους (1 Thess. 3:12)
        but the Lord make you to increase and abound **in your love**
        toward one another
    (4) Acc. pl. fem.
        καὶ ἡμεῖς ὀφείλομεν ὑπὲρ τῶν ἀδελφῶν τὰς ψυχὰς θεῖναι
        (1 John 3:16)[28]
        we ourselves also ought to lay down **our lives** for the brothers

---

[24] Here the pronominal use is closely related to the anaphoric use.
[25] Here again the pronominal use is closely related to the anaphoric use.
[26] 2 Cor. 1:1 text is from GNT, NA & WH: TR & MT have Ἰησοῦ Χριστοῦ.
[27] Matt. 1:24 text is from GNT, NA & WH: TR & MT have διεγερθείς.
[28] 1 John 3:16 text is from GNT, NA & WH: TR & MT have τιθέναι.

5. In an equative clause, the article sometimes indicates the subject and sometimes the predicate.
   a. The articular substantive indicates the subject when the anarthrous noun is not a proper noun.
      (1) With an implicit or elliptical verb
         θεὸς ὁ δικαιῶν (Rom. 8:33)
         the one who justifies [ἐστιν, is] God
      (2) With an explicit verb
         καὶ θεὸς ἦν ὁ λόγος (John 1:1)
         and **the Word was God**
   b. The articular noun may be the predicate of an equative verb when a pronoun is the subject.
      (1) Nom. sing. fem.
         καὶ αὕτη ἐστὶν ἡ ἐπαγγελία ἥ αὐτὸς ἐπηγείλατο ἡμῖν, τὴν ζωὴν τὴν αἰώνιον (1 John 2:25)
         and **this is the promise** that he himself promised us, eternal life
      (2) Nom. sing. masc.
         οὗτος ἐστιν ὁ υἱός μου ὁ ἀγαπητός (Matt. 3:17)
         this is my beloved son
6. The article may introduce an epexegetical or appositional phrase to the previous noun or pronoun.
   a. Nom. sing. masc.
      Ἀβραὰμ **ὁ πατὴρ ἡμῶν** οὐκ ἐξ ἔργων ἐδικαιώθη . . . ; (James 2:21)
      was not **Abraham our father** justified by works . . . ?
   b. Gen. sing. fem.
      καὶ αὐτός ἐστιν ἡ κεφαλὴ **τοῦ σώματος τῆς ἐκκλησίας** (Col. 1:18)
      and he himself is the head of **the body, [which is] the church**
   c. Dat. sing. masc.
      ἱλάσθητί μοι **τῷ ἁμαρτωλῷ** (Luke 18:13)
      be merciful **to me a sinner**
   d. Acc. sing. masc.
      κύριον τὸν θεόν σου προσκυνήσεις (Matt. 4:10)
      you shall worship **the Lord your God**
7. The article may be anaphoric, i.e., referring to a noun in the previous context, or to someone or something that is already familiar. The first noun may or may not have the article.
   a. Nom. sing. fem.
      τί τὸ ὄφελος ἀδελφοί μου, ἐὰν **πίστιν** λέγῃ τις ἔχειν ἔργα δὲ μὴ ἔχῃ; μὴ δύναται **ἡ πίστις** σῶσαι αὐτόν; (James 2:14)
      what [ἐστιν, is] the benefit, my brothers, if someone claims to have **faith** but does not have works? is **that faith** able to save him?

b. Gen. sing. masc.

τοῦ δὲ Ἰησοῦ γεννηθέντος ἐν Βηθλεὲμ τῆς Ἰουδαίας
(Matt. 2:1; cf. 1:16)

now when **Jesus** was born in Bethlehem in Judea

c. Dat. sing. neut.

ἐὰν δὲ ἐν τῷ φωτὶ περιπατῶμεν ὡς αὐτός ἐστιν ἐν τῷ φωτί
(1 John 1:7; cf. 1:5 ὁ θεὸς φῶς)

but if we walk **in the light** as he himself is **in the light**

d. Acc. pl. fem.

μετὰ δὲ τὰς δύο ἡμέρας ἐξῆλθεν ἐκεῖθεν (John 4:43; cf. 4:40)

now after **two days** he went out from there

8. The article may be kataphoric and thus point out a specific subject or object,
which is clearly identified by the following relative clause.

a. Nom. sing. masc.

εἴπερ εἷς ὁ θεὸς ὃς δικαιώσει περιτομὴν ἐκ πίστεως καὶ
ἀκροβυστίαν διὰ τῆς πίστεως (Rom. 3:30)[29]

since [**ἐστιν, there is**] one God who shall justify the circumcised by faith
and the uncircumcised by the same faith

b. Acc. sing. fem.

οἶδα γὰρ **τὴν προθυμίαν** ὑμῶν ἣν ὑπὲρ ὑμῶν **καυχῶμαι** Μακεδόσιν
(2 Cor. 9:2)

for I know **your readiness, which I boast** about you to the Macedonians

c. Gen. sing. fem.

ἀρξάμενος ἀπὸ τοῦ βαπτίσματος Ἰωάννου ἕως τῆς ἡμέρας ἧς
ἀνελήμφθη ἀφ᾽ ἡμῶν (Acts 1:22)[30]

beginning from the baptism of John **until the day in which he was
taken up** from us

d. Dat. sing. fem.

ὁ κύριος Ἰησοῦς ἐν τῇ νυκτὶ ᾗ **παρεδίδετο** ἔλαβεν ἄρτον
(1 Cor. 11:23)[31]

the Lord Jesus **in the night in which he was betrayed** took bread

9. The article is used to identify a generic class or group of individuals or
things. The singular indicates a representative of the entire class, and the
plural refers to all of the members in a class.

a. Gen. pl. masc.

οὕτως λαμψάτω τὸ φῶς ὑμῶν **ἔμπροσθεν τῶν ἀνθρώπων** (Matt. 5:16)

in this way let your light shine **before people**

---

[29] Rom. 3:30 text is from GNT, NA & WH: TR & MT have ἐπείπερ.

[30] Acts 1:22 text is from GNT & NA: WH has Ἰωάνου: TR & MT have ἀνελήφθη.

[31] 1 Cor. 11:23 text is from GNT, NA & WH: TR & MT have παρεδίδοτο.

b. Nom. sing. masc.

ὁ κλέπτης οὐκ ἔρχεται εἰ μὴ ἵνα κλέψῃ καὶ θύσῃ καὶ ἀπολέσῃ (John 10:10)

the thief does not come except to steal and kill and destroy

c. Dat. pl. masc.

πολυμερῶς καὶ πολυτρόπως πάλαι ὁ θεὸς λαλήσας **τοῖς πατράσιν** ἐν τοῖς προφήταις (Heb. 1:1)

at many times and various ways God long ago spoke **to the fathers** by the prophets

d. Acc. sing. masc.

δεῖ γὰρ **τὸν ἐπίσκοπον** ἀνέγκλητον εἶναι (Titus 1:7)

for **the overseer** must be unimpeachable

10. The article may point out a specific subject or object.

a. Nom. sing. fem.

ἢ δοκεῖτε ὅτι κενῶς **ἡ γραφὴ** λέγει (James 4:5)

or do you think that **the Scripture** says in vain

b. Gen. pl. neut.

καὶ πῶς ἐπεστρέψατε πρὸς τὸν θεὸν **ἀπὸ τῶν εἰδώλων** (1 Thess. 1:9)

and how you turned to God **from idols**

c. Dat. sing. fem.

ταῖς δώδεκα φυλαῖς ταῖς **ἐν τῇ διασπορᾷ** (James 1:1)

to the twelve tribes that [οὖσαις, are] **in the dispersion**

d. Acc. sing. & pl. masc.

μὴ νομίσητε ὅτι ἦλθον καταλῦσαι **τὸν νόμον** ἢ **τοὺς προφήτας** (Matt. 5:17)

do not think that I came to destroy **the law** or **the prophets**

11. The article with certain nouns gives a distributive sense to the term.

a. Gen. sing. neut.

εἰς δὲ τὴν δευτέραν ἅπαξ **τοῦ ἐνιαυτοῦ** μόνος ὁ ἀρχιερεύς (Heb. 9:7)

but into the second the high priest [went] alone once **a year**

b. Acc. sing. fem.

συμφωνήσας δὲ μετὰ τῶν ἐργατῶν ἐκ δηναρίου **τὴν ἡμέραν** ἀπέστειλεν αὐτοὺς εἰς τὸν ἀμπελῶνα αὐτοῦ (Matt. 20:2)

and when he agreed with the workers for a denarius **per day** he sent them into his vineyard

12. The repetition of the article with a plurality of subjects and a singular verb indicates a single unit of thought. The two or more subjects are joined together in a close association by the singular verb.

a. Nom. pl. masc.

αὐτὸς **ἐνέβη** εἰς πλοῖον καὶ **οἱ μαθηταὶ** αὐτοῦ (Luke 8:22)

he and his **disciples entered** into the boat

b. Nom. sing. fem. and pl. masc.
μετὰ τοῦτο **κατέβη** εἰς Καφθρμαοὺμ αὐτὸς καὶ **ἡ μήτηρ αὐτοῦ** καὶ **οἱ ἀδελφοὶ αὐτοῦ** καὶ **οἱ μαθηταὶ αὐτοῦ** (John 2:12)
after this he and **his mother** and **his brothers** and **his disciples** **went down** to Capernaum
c. Nom. sing. masc. and fem.
ἀνέστη τε ὁ βασιλεὺς καὶ ὁ ἡγεμὼν ἥ τε Βερνίκη καὶ οἱ συγκαθήμενοι αὐτοῖς (Acts 26:30)
the king and **the governor** and **Bernice** and those sitting with them **stood up**
d. Nom. sing. and pl. masc.
ἐκλήθη δὲ καὶ ὁ **Ἰησοῦς** καὶ οἱ **μαθηταὶ** αὐτοῦ εἰς τὸν γάμον (John 2:2)
now both **Jesus** and his **disciples were invited** to the wedding
13. Colwell's Rule.
a. Definite predicate nouns following an equative verb normally take the article (90 percent of the time).
(1) Nom. sing. masc.
ναὶ κύριε, ἐγὼ πεπίστευκα ὅτι **σὺ εἶ ὁ Χριστὸς** ὁ υἱὸς τοῦ θεοῦ (John 11:27)
yes, Lord, I have believed that **you are the Christ**, the son of God
(2) Nom. sing. masc.
σὺ οὖν εἶ ὁ υἱὸς τοῦ θεοῦ; (Luke 22:70)
are you then **the son** of God?
b. Predicate nouns preceding the verb normally do not have the article.
(1) Nom. sing. masc.
Βασιλεύς εἰμι τῶν Ἰουδαίων (John 19:21)
I am the king of the Jews
(2) Nom. sing. fem. and nom. pl. masc.
ὁ δὲ ἐχθρὸς ὁ σπείρας αὐτά ἐστιν ὁ διάβολος, ὁ δὲ θερισμὸς **συντέλεια** αἰῶνός ἐστιν, οἱ δὲ θερισταὶ **ἄγγελοί εἰσιν** (Matt. 13:39)
and the enemy who sowed them is the devil and the harvest **is the end** of the age and the reapers **are the angels**
14. An articular substantive in the nominative case may be used in a vocative sense.
a. Nom. sing. masc.
καὶ ἔλεγον, Χαῖρε, ὁ **βασιλεὺς** τῶν Ἰουδαίων (John 19:3)
and they said, Greetings, **king** of the Jews
b. Nom. pl. masc.
οἱ **ἄνδρες**, ἀγαπᾶτε τὰς γυναῖκας καὶ μὴ πικραίνεσθε πρὸς αὐτάς (Col. 3:19)
husbands, love your wives and do not be bitter against them

c. Nom. pl. neut.

τὰ τέκνα, ὑπακούετε τοῖς γονεῦσιν ὑμῶν (Eph. 6:1)
children, obey your parents

VI. **The article with certain particles** functions as a pronoun.

A. With μέν . . . δέ as an alternate pronoun, translated **he, they,** or **some**.
1. Nom. pl. masc.
καὶ οἱ μὲν ἐπείθοντο τοῖς λεγομένοις, οἱ δὲ ἠπίστουν
(Acts 28:24)
and **some** were persuaded by the things spoken, **but others** disbelieved
2. Nom. pl. and sing. masc.
οἱ μὲν γὰρ χωρὶς ὁρκωμοσίας εἰσὶν ἱερεῖς γεγονότες, ὁ δὲ
μετὰ ὁρκωμοσίας (Heb. 7:20-21)
for **some** were made priests without an oath, **but he** with an oath
3. Acc. pl. masc.
καὶ αὐτὸς ἔδωκεν τοὺς μὲν ἀποστόλους, τοὺς δὲ προφάτας, τοὺς
δὲ εὐαγγελιστάς (Eph. 4:11)
and he gave **some** apostles **and some** prophets **and some** evangelists

B. Sometimes only one of the two particle members is present.
1. οἱ δέ without οἱ μέν
τότε ἐνέπτυσαν εἰς τὸ πρόσωπον αὐτοῦ καὶ ἐκολάφισαν αὐτόν,
οἱ δὲ ἐράπισαν (Matt. 26:67)[32]
then they spit in his face and mistreated him, **and some** slapped [him]
2. οἱ μέν without οἱ δέ
οἱ μὲν οὖν ἀπολυθέντες κατῆλθον εἰς Ἀντιόχειαν
(Acts15:30)[33]
so, when **they** were dismissed, they went down to Antioch.
3. ὁ δέ without ὁ μέν (used frequently in narrative to indicate a change in
the one who is speaking)
ὁ δὲ εἶπεν αὐτοῖς (John 4:32)
but he said to them
4. ὁ μέν without ὁ δέ
ὁ μὲν οὖν παραλαβὼν αὐτὸν ἤγαγεν πρὸς τὸν χιλίαρχον
(Acts 23:18)
he indeed then took him and led [him] to the chief captain

---

[32] Matt. 26:67 text is from GNT, NA & WH: TR & MT have ἐρράπισαν.
[33] Acts 15:30 text is from GNT, NA & WH: TR & MT have ἦλθον.

VII. **The article with prepositions.**

A. The article preceding the preposition often functions as a pronoun with an elliptical or implied participle.
   1. Nom. sing. masc.
      ὅτι μείζων ἐστὶν ὁ ἐν ὑμῖν ἢ ὁ ἐν τῷ κόσμῳ (1 John 4:4)
      because **the one [ὤν, who is] in you** is greater than **the one [ὤν, who is] in the world**
   2. Gen. sing. masc.
      ὅπως γένησθε υἱοὶ τοῦ πατρὸς ὑμῶν τοῦ ἐν οὐρανοῖς (Matt. 5:16)
      so that you may be sons of your father **who [ὄντος, is] in heaven**
   3. Dat. pl. fem.
      ἤμην δὲ ἀγνοούμενος τῷ προσώπῳ ταῖς ἐκκλησίαις τῆς Ἰουδαίας ταῖς ἐν Χριστῷ (Gal. 1:22)
      but I was unknown by face to the churches of Judea **that [οὔσαις, are] in Christ**
   4. Acc. pl. neut.
      καὶ λέγων τὰ περὶ τῆς βασιλείας τοῦ θεοῦ (Acts 1:3)
      and speaking **the things [ὄντα, that] concern the kingdom** of God

B. The articular prepositional attribute is found in three different word order positions in all the cases; the differences are stylistic rather than substantive.
   1. First attributive position, nom. sing. fem.
      ἡ δὲ ἐκ πίστεως δικαιοσύνη (Rom. 10:6)
      but **the righteousness [that is] of faith**
   2. Second attributive position, gen. sing. fem.
      τῆς δικαιοσύνης τῆς ἐκ πίστεως[34]
      the righteousness that [is] of faith
   3. Third attributive position, acc. sing. fem.
      δικαιοσύνην δὲ τὴν ἐκ πίστεως (Rom. 9:30)
      but **righteousness that [is] of faith**

VIII. **The article with pronouns.** The article is found with a number of pronouns but not with all of them.

A. With demonstrative pronouns (ἐκεῖνος and οὗτος) in a predicate position but with an attributive sense.

---

[34] Rom. 10:5 uses different words but the same position is found. τὴν δικαιοσύνην τὴν ἐκ τοῦ νόμου, the righteousness that [is] of the law. GNT, NA, TR & MT: WH has ἐκ νόμου.

1. Nom. sing. masc.
μὴ γὰρ οἰέσθω ὁ **ἄνθρωπος ἐκεῖνος** ὅτι λήμψεταί τι παρὰ τοῦ κυρίου (James 1:7)[35]
for do not let **that person** expect that he shall receive anything from the Lord

2. Gen. sing. fem.
καὶ ἐγένετο τὸ ῥῆγμα **τῆς οἰκίας ἐκείνης** μέγα (Luke 6:49)
and the ruin **of that house** was great

3. Dat. sing. masc.
Κύριε, εἰ **ἐν τῷ χρόνῳ τούτῳ** ἀποκαθιστάνεις τὴν βασιλείαν τῷ Ἰσραήλ; (Acts 1:6)
Lord, will you **at this time** restore the kingdom to Israel?

4. Acc. sing. fem.
καὶ **ταύτην τὴν φωνὴν** ἡμεῖς ἠκούσαμεν ἐξ οὐρανοῦ ἐνεχθεῖσαν (2 Peter 1:18)
and we ourselves heard **this voice** that came from heaven

B. With personal pronouns in the genitive and an articular noun in any case. The article is usually present.

1. Gen. sing. masc.
ὃ προεπηγγείλατο **διὰ τῶν προφητῶν αὐτοῦ** ἐν γραφαῖς ἁγίαις (Rom. 1:2)
which he promised beforehand **through his prophets** in holy scriptures

2. Nom. sing. neut.
ὅτι **τὸ εὐαγγέλλιον ἡμῶν** οὐκ ἐγενήθη εἰς ὑμᾶς ἐν λόγῳ μόνον ἀλλὰ καὶ ἐν δυνάμει καὶ ἐν πνεύματι ἁγίῳ (1 Thess. 1:5)
for **our gospel** did not come to you in word only but also in power and in the Holy Spirit

3. Dat. sing. fem.
ἐπιχορηγήσατε **ἐν τῇ πίστει ὑμῶν** τὴν ἀρετήν (2 Peter 1:5)
provide moral goodness **to your faith**

4. Acc. pl. masc.
καὶ πάντα ὑπέταξεν **ὑπὸ τοὺς πόδας αὐτοῦ** (Eph. 1:22)
and he subjected all things **under his feet**

---

[35] James 1:7 text is from GNT, NA & WH: TR & MT have λήψεται.

C. With intensive pronoun.
  1. In the predicate position, pronoun-article-noun, meaning **itself, himself**
    a. Nom. sing. masc.
      αὐτὸς δὲ ὁ Ἰωάννης εἶχεν τὸ ἔνδυμα αὐτοῦ ἀπὸ τριχῶν
      καμήλου (Matt. 3:4)[36]
      now **John himself** had his clothing from camel's hair
    b. Gen. sing. fem.
      Δημητρίῳ μεμαρτύρηται ὑπὸ πάντων καὶ **ὑπὸ αὐτῆς τῆς**
      ἀληθείας (3 John 12)[37]
      Demetrius has been witnessed to by all and **by the truth itself**
    c. Dat. sing. fem.
      τὸ γὰρ ἅγιον πνεῦμα διδάξει ὑμᾶς **ἐν αὐτῇ τῇ ὥρᾳ** ἃ δεῖ εἰπεῖν
      (Luke 12:12)
      for the Holy Spirit will teach you **in that very hour** what you must say
    d. Acc. sing. fem.
      σκιὰν γὰρ ἔχων ὁ νόμος τῶν μελλόντων ἀγαθῶν, οὐκ **αὐτὴν τὴν**
      εἰκόνα τῶν πραγμάτων (Heb. 10:1)
      for the law having a shadow of the coming good things, not **the image itself** of the things
  2. Intensive pronoun as a substantive
    a. Nom. sing. masc.
      Ἰησοῦς Χριστὸς ἐχθὲς καὶ σήμερον **ὁ αὐτὸς** καὶ εἰς τοὺς αἰῶνας
      (Heb. 13:8)
      Jesus Christ **the same** yesterday, today, and forever
    b. Gen. pl. neut.
      καὶ αὐτὸς παραπλησίως μετέσχεν **τῶν αὐτῶν** (Heb. 2:14)
      he himself also in the same manner partook **of the same**
    c. Acc. sing. neut.
      παρακαλεῖσθε, **τὸ αὐτὸ** φρονεῖτε εἰρηνεύετε (2 Cor. 13:11)
      be encouraged, think **the same thing**, live in peace
  3. The intensive pronoun in the first attributive position means **the same**
    a. Nom. sing. masc.
      καὶ διαιρέσεις διακονιῶν εἰσιν, καὶ **ὁ αὐτὸς** κύριος (1 Cor. 12:5)
      and there are differences of ministry but **the same Lord**
    b. Gen. sing. neut.
      ἐκ **τοῦ αὐτοῦ** στόματος ἐξέρχεται εὐλογία καὶ κατάρα
      (James 3:10)
      blessing and cursing come **out of the same mouth**

---

[36] Matt. 3:4 text is from GNT, NA, TR & MT: WH has Ἰωάνου.
[37] 3 John 12 text is from GNT, NA, WH & MT: TR has ὑπ' before αὐτῆς.

c. Dat. sing. masc. and fem.

ἵνα . . . ἦτε δὲ κατηρτισμένοι **ἐν τῷ αὐτῷ νοῒ** καὶ
ἐν τῇ αὐτῇ γνώμῃ (1 Cor. 1:10)

but that you may be made complete **with the same attitude** and **with the same purpose**

d. Acc. pl. neut.

ἔχοντες δὲ **τὸ αὐτὸ πνεῦμα** τῆς πίστεως (2 Cor. 4:13)

and having **the same spirit** of faith

4. The intensive pronoun in the second attributive position

a. Gen. sing. fem.

μετὰ Ἰσαὰκ καὶ Ἰακὼβ τῶν συγκληρονόμων **τῆς ἐπαγγελίας τῆς αὐτῆς** (Heb. 11:9)

with Isaac and Jacob the joint heirs **of the same promise**

b. Dat. sing. fem.

καὶ ποιμένες ἦσαν **ἐν τῇ χώρᾳ τῇ αὐτῇ** ἀγραυλοῦντες (Luke 2:8)

and shepherds were lodging **in the same country**

D. The article is used with the possessive pronoun.

1. In the first attributive position

a. Nom. sing. fem.

ἡ ἐμὴ διδαχὴ οὐκ ἔστιν ἐμὴ ἀλλὰ τοῦ πέμψαντός με (John 7:16)

my doctrine is not mine but belongs to the one who sent me

b. Gen. sing. fem.

ἵνα τὸ καύχημα ὑμῶν περισσεύῃ ἐν Χριστῷ Ἰησοῦ ἐν ἐμοὶ **διὰ τῆς ἐμῆς παρουσίας** πάλιν πρὸς ὑμᾶς (Phil. 1:26)

in order that your boasting may abound in Christ Jesus in me **through my coming** again to you

c. Dat. sing. fem.

ἐγὼ Παῦλος ἔγραψα **τῇ ἐμῇ χειρί** (Philem. 19)

I Paul wrote [it] **with my own hand**

d. Acc. sing. fem.

σπουδάσω δὲ καὶ ἑκάστοτε ἔχειν ὑμᾶς **μετὰ τὴν ἐμὴν ἔξοδον** τὴν τούτων μνήμην ποιεῖσθαι (2 Peter 1:15)

but I also will make every effort that **after my exodus** you will have memory of these things

2. In the second attributive position (a stylistic preference of John)

a. Nom. sing. fem.

καὶ **ἡ κοινωνία** δὲ **ἡ ἡμετέρα** μετὰ τοῦ πατρὸς καὶ μετὰ τοῦ υἱοῦ αὐτοῦ (1 John 1:3)

and **our fellowship** also [ἐστιν, is] with the Father and with his son

b. Gen. pl. neut.

   ἀλλὰ ὑμεῖς οὐ πιστεύετε, ὅτι οὐκ ἐστὲ **ἐκ τῶν προβάτων τῶν ἐμῶν** (John 10:26)[38]

   but you yourselves do not believe, because you are not **of my sheep**

c. Dat. sing. masc.

   καὶ **ἐν τῷ νόμῳ** δὲ **τῷ ὑμετέρῳ** γέγραπται ὅτι δύο ἀνθρώπων ἡ μαρτυρία ἀληθής ἐστιν (John 8:17)

   but also **in your law** it is written that the testimony of two men is true

d. Acc. sing. neut.

   ὅτι οὐ ζητῶ **τὸ θέλημα τὸ ἐμὸν** ἀλλὰ τὸ θέλημα τοῦ πέμψαντός με (John 5:30)

   for I do not seek **my own will** but the will of the one who sent me

3. Possessive pronoun as a substantive

a. Nom. pl. neut.

   καὶ **τὰ ἐμὰ πάντα** σά ἐστιν καὶ **τὰ σὰ** ἐμά (John 17:10)

   and **all my things** are yours and **your things** [ἐστιν, are] mine

b. Gen. pl. fem.

   καὶ αὐτὸς ἱλασμός ἐστιν περὶ τῶν ἁμαρτιῶν ἡμῶν, οὐ περὶ τῶν **ἡμετέρων** δὲ μόνον ἀλλὰ καὶ περὶ ὅλου τοῦ κόσμου (1 John 2:2)

   and he himself is the propitiation for our sins, and not **for ours** only but also for the whole world

c. Acc. pl. neut.

   ἐγὼ εἰμι ὁ ποιμὴν ὁ καλὸς καὶ γινώσκω **τὰ ἐμὰ** καὶ γινώσκουσί με **τὰ ἐμά** (John 10:14)

   I am the good shepherd and I know **my own [sheep]** and my own [sheep] know me

d. Dat. sing. neut.

   οὐκ ἔξεστί(ν) μοι ὃ θέλω ποιῆσαι **ἐν τοῖς ἐμοῖς;** (Matt. 20:15)[39]

   is it unlawful for me to do what I want **with my own things?**

E. The article with the third person reflexive pronoun (ἑαυτῆς, etc.) is used as a possessive pronoun in the oblique cases.

   1. Gen. pl. neut.

      αἱ δὲ φρόνιμοι ἔλαβον ἔλαιον ἐν τοῖς ἀγγείοις μετὰ **τῶν λαμπάδων ἑαυτῶν** (Matt. 25:4)[40]

      but the wise women took oil in their containers **with their own lamps**

---

[38] John 10:26 text is from GNT, NA & WH; TR & MT have ἀλλ' and οὐ γάρ for ὅτι οὐκ.

[39] Matt. 20:15 text is from GNT, NA & WH; TR & MT have ποιῆσαι ὃ θέλω.

[40] Matt. 25:4 text is from GNT, NA & WH; TR & MT have αὐτῶν after ἀγγείοις and MT has αὐτῶν in place of ἑαυτῶν.

2. Dat. pl. neut.

οὕτως οὖν πᾶς ἐξ ὑμῶν ὃς οὐκ ἀποτάσσεται **πᾶσι(ν)** τοῖς ἑαυτοῦ
ὑπάρχουσιν οὐ δύναται εἶναί μου μαθητής (Luke 14:33)[41]

so then everyone of you who will not renounce **all his possessions** is not
able to be my disciple

3. Acc. pl. fem.

εὐδοκοῦμεν μεταδοῦναι ὑμῖν οὐ μόνον τὸ εὐαγγέλιον τοῦ θεοῦ
ἀλλὰ καὶ **τὰς ἑαυτῶν ψυχάς** (1 Thess. 2:8)

we were pleased to impart to you not only the gospel of God but also
our own lives

IX. **The article with verbs.**

A. With an equative or elliptical verb (εἰμί, γίνομαι).

1. The articular noun or substantive is normally the subject of the verb and
the anarthrous noun or adjective is the complement. The article points out
the subject.

a. Nom. sing. masc. and nom. sing. neut.

ὁ θεὸς φῶς ἐστιν καὶ σκοτία ἐν αὐτῷ οὐκ ἔστιν οὐδεμία
(1 John 1:5)

God is light and darkness does not exist in him whatsoever

b. Nom. sing. masc.

μάρτυς γάρ μού **ἐστιν ὁ θεός** (Rom. 1:9)

for **God is** my **witness**

c. Nom. sing. masc and nom. sing. fem.

ὁ θεὸς ἀγάπη ἐστίν (1 John 4:8)

God is love

d. Nom. sing. masc.

εἰ **ὁ θεὸς πατὴρ** ὑμῶν **ἦν**, ἠγαπᾶτε ἂν ἐμέ (John 8:42)

if **God were** your **father**, you would have loved me

2. When two articular substantives are joined by an equative or elliptical verb,
they are interchangeable. However, the first articular substantive is
normally considered as the subject and the second substantive as the
predicate.

a. Nom. sing. fem.

πᾶς ὁ ποιῶν τὴν ἁμαρτίαν καὶ τὴν ἀνομίαν ποιεῖ, καὶ **ἡ ἁμαρτία**
ἐστὶν ἡ ἀνομία (1 John 3:4)

everyone who practices sin also practices lawlessness, for **sin is**
lawlessness

---

[41] Luke 14:33 text is from GNT, NA & WH: TR & MT have μου εἶναι.

     b. Nom. sing. masc. and neut.
       ὁ δὲ **κύριος τὸ πνεῦμά ἐστιν** (2 Cor. 3:17)
       and **the Lord is the Spirit**

     c. Nom. sing. masc.
       ὁ δὲ **ἀγρός ἐστιν ὁ κόσμος** (Matt. 13:38)
       and **the field is the world**

     d. Nom. sing. neut. fem. and masc.
       τὸ δὲ **κέντρον** τοῦ θανάτου ἡ **ἁμαρτία**, ἡ δὲ **δύναμις** τῆς ἁμαρτίας ὁ **νόμος** (1 Cor. 15:56)
       and **the sting** of death [ἐστιν, is] **sin**, and **the power** of sin [ἐστιν, is] **the law**

   3. When the subject is a pronoun or a proper name, the predicate may be articular.
     a. Demonstrative pron.
       οὗτος γάρ ἐστιν ὁ **νόμος** καὶ οἱ **προφῆται** (Matt. 7:12)
       for **this** is **the law** and **the prophets**

     b. Personal pron.
       ἐγώ εἰμι ὁ **ἄρτος ὁ ζῶν** ὁ ἐκ τοῦ οὐρανοῦ καταβάς (John 6:51)
       I am **the living bread** that descended from heaven

     c. Proper name
       πᾶς ὁ πιστεύων ὅτι **Ἰησοῦς** ἐστιν ὁ **Χριστὸς** ἐκ τοῦ θεοῦ γεγέννηται (1 John 5:1)
       everyone who believes that **Jesus** is **the Christ** has been born of God

     d. Plural personal pron.
       ὑμεῖς ἐστε τὸ **φῶς** τοῦ κόσμου (Matt. 5:14)
       you are **the light** of the world

B. The article with infinitives. "The articular infinitive singles out the act as a particular occurrence while the anarthrous infinitive employs the act as descriptive."[42]
   1. With the infinitive as the object of a preposition
     a. Gen. sing. neut.
       πρὸ τοῦ δὲ **ἐλθεῖν** τὴν πίστιν ὑπὸ νόμον ἐφρουρούμεθα (Gal. 3:23)
       but **before** faith **came** we were confined under the law

     b. Dat. sing. neut.
       καὶ ἐθαύμαζον **ἐν τῷ χρονίζειν** ἐν τῷ ναῷ αὐτόν (Luke 1:21)
       and they were wondering **while** he **lingered** in the temple

---

[42] Dana and Mantey, *A Manual Grammar of the Greek New Testament*, 138.

   c. Acc. sing. neut.

οἷς καὶ παρέστησεν ἑαυτὸν ζῶντα μετὰ τὸ παθεῖν αὐτὸν ἐν πολλοῖς τεκμηρίοις (Acts 1:3)

to whom also he presented himself alive **after he suffered** by many convincing proofs

2. With subject infinitive of impersonal (elliptical) verb

ἐμοὶ γὰρ τὸ ζῆν Χριστὸς καὶ τὸ ἀποθανεῖν κέρδος (Phil. 1:21)[43]

for me **to live** [ἐστιν, is] Christ and **to die** [ἐστιν, is] gain

3. With purpose infinitive

τότε παραγίνεται ὁ Ἰησοῦς ἀπὸ τῆς Γαλιλαίας ἐπὶ τὸν Ἰορδάνην πρὸς τὸν Ἰωάννην τοῦ βαπτισθῆναι ὑπ᾽ αὐτοῦ (Matt. 3:13)[44]

then Jesus came from Galilee to the Jordan to John **to be baptized** by him

4. With infinitive as complement of a noun or adjective

   a. Complement of noun

ὅτι ὁ καιρὸς τοῦ ἄρξασθαι τὸ κρίμα ἀπὸ τοῦ οἴκου τοῦ θεοῦ (1 Peter 4:17)

for [ἐστιν, it is] **the time to begin** the judgment from the house of God

   b. Complement of adjective

ἔστω δὲ πᾶς ἄνθρωπος ταχὺς εἰς τὸ ἀκοῦσαι, βραδὺς εἰς τὸ λαλῆσαι (James 1:19)[45]

but let every man be **swift to hear, slow to speak**

5. Articular infinitive as appositional to a noun

ἁγιασμῷ . . . τὸ μὴ ὑπερβαίνειν καὶ πλεονεκτεῖν ἐν τῷ πράγματι τὸν ἀδελφὸν αὐτοῦ (1 Thess. 4:6)

sanctification . . . that no one should transgress and **defraud** his brother in this matter

C. The article with participles.

1. Attributive participles

   a. First attributive position

    (1) Nom. sing. masc.

καθὼς ἀπέστειλέν με ὁ ζῶν πατὴρ κἀγὼ ζῶ διὰ τὸν πατέρα (John 6:57)

even as **the living Father** sent me and I live because of the Father

---

[43] Phil. 1:21 text is from GNT, NA & MT: Wh & TR have ζῆν.

[44] Matt. 3:13 text is from GNT, NA, TR & MT: WH has Ἰωάνην.

[45] James 1:19 text is from GNT, NA & WH: TR & MT omit δέ.

(2) Gen. sing. masc.

ἠκρίβωσεν παρ' αὐτῶν τὸν χρόνον **τοῦ γαινομένου ἀστέρος**
(Matt. 2:7)

he inquired carefully from them the time **of the appearing star**

(3) Dat. sing. fem.

καίπερ εἰδότας καὶ ἐστηριγμένους ἐν **τῇ παρούσῃ ἀληθείᾳ**
(2 Peter 1:12)

even though you know and have been confirmed **in the present truth**

(4) Acc. sing. fem.

τελείως ἐλπίσατε ἐπὶ **τὴν φερομένην** ὑμῖν χάριν ἐν
ἀποκαλύψει Ἰησοῦ Χριστοῦ (1 Peter 1:13)

set your hope completely on **the grace being brought** to you at the
revelation of Jesus Christ

b. Second attributive position or appositional participle to articular noun
is equivalent to a relative clause.

(1) Gen. sing. masc.

περὶ **τοῦ υἱοῦ** αὐτοῦ **τοῦ γενομένου** ἐκ σπέρματος Δαυίδ
(Rom. 1:3)[46]

concerning his **son who came** from the seed of David

(2) Dat. sing. fem.

τῇ ἐκκλησίᾳ τοῦ θεοῦ **τῇ οὔσῃ** ἐν Κορίνθῳ (1 Cor. 1:2)
to the church of God **that is** in Corinth

(3) Nom. sing. neut.

γνωρίζω γὰρ ὑμῖν, ἀδελφοί, **τὸ εὐαγγέλιον τὸ εὐαγγελισθὲν**
ὑπ' ἐμοῦ ὅτι οὐκ ἔστιν κατὰ ἄνθρωπον (Gal. 1:11)

for I make known to you, brothers, **the gospel that was preached**
by me, that it is not according to man

(4) Acc. sing. fem.

διὰ **τὴν ἐλπίδα τὴν ἀποκειμένην** ὑμῖν ἐν τοῖς οὐρανοῖς
(Col. 1:5)

because of **the hope that is reserved** for you in heaven

2. Substantive participles

a. Nom. sing. masc.

ὁ διώκων ἡμᾶς ποτε νῦν εὐαγγελίζεται τὴν πίστιν (Gal. 1:23)

the one who once persecuted us now proclaims the faith

b. Acc. sing. masc.

ἀλλὰ **κατὰ τὸν καλέσαντα** ὑμᾶς ἅγιον (1 Peter 1:15)

but **according as the one who called** you [is] holy

---

[46] Rom. 1:3 text is from GNT & NA: TR & MT have Δαβίδ; WH has Δαυείδ.

c. Gen. pl. masc.

πρὸς ὑποτύπωσιν **τῶν μελλόντων** πιστεύειν ἐπ᾽ αὐτῷ εἰς ζωὴν
αἰώνιον (1 Tim. 1:16)

for an example **of those who will** believe on him unto eternal life

d. Dat. pl. masc.

διδόντος ἐκδίκησιν **τοῖς μὴ εἰδόσιν** θεὸν καὶ **τοῖς μὴ
ὑπακούουσιν** τῷ εὐαγγελίῳ τοῦ κυρίου ἡμῶν Ἰησοῦ (2 Thess. 1:8)

who will impart vengeance **on those who do not know** God and **on
those who do not obey** the gospel of our Lord Jesus

e. The substantive participle is another way of expressing a relative
clause.

(1) Nom. sing. masc. relative pron.

πᾶς οὖν **ὅστις ἀκούει** μου τοὺς λόγους τούτους . . . (Matt. 7:24)

therefore, **everyone who hears** these words of mine . . .

(2) Nom. sing. masc. participle

καὶ **πᾶς ὁ ἀκούων** μου τοὺς λόγους τούτους . . . (Matt. 7:26)

and **everyone who hears** these words of mine . . .

3. Articular participles in apposition to noun(s)

a. Gen. sing. masc.

Ἰησοῦ Χριστοῦ **τοῦ ἀποθανόντος** ὑπὲρ ἡμῶν (1 Thess. 5:9-10)
Jesus Christ, who died for us

b. Nom. sing. masc.

εἷς ἐστιν ὁ **νομοθέτης** καὶ **κριτής, ὁ δυνάμενος** σῶσαι καὶ
ἀπολέσαι (James 4:12)[47]

one is **the lawgiver** and **judge, who is able** to save and destroy

c. Dat. sing. masc.

οὐχ ὡς ἀνθρώποις ἀρέσκοντες ἀλλὰ **θεῷ τῷ δοκιμάζοντι**
τὰς καρδίας ἡμῶν (1 Thess. 2:4)[48]

not as trying to please men but **God, who examines** our hearts

d. Acc. sing. fem.

χάριν τὴν δοθεῖσαν ἡμῖν ἐν Χριστῷ πρὸ χρόνων αἰωνίων
(2 Tim. 1:9)

grace that was imparted to us in Christ Jesus before eternal times

4. Articular participles in apposition to pronouns

a. Nom. pl. masc.

ὅτι **ἡμεῖς οἱ ζῶντες οἱ περιλειπόμενοι** εἰς τὴν παρουσίαν
τοῦ κυρίου (1 Thess. 4:15)

that **we who are alive [and] remain** unto the coming of the Lord

[47] James 4:12 text is from GNT & NA: WH omits ὁ before νομοθέτης; TR & MT omit καὶ κριτής.
[48] 1 Thess. 2:4 text is from GNT, NA & WH: TR & MT has τῷ before θεῷ.

   b. Dat. pl. masc.
   ὡς ὁσίως καὶ δικαίως καὶ ἀμέμπτως ὑμῖν τοῖς πιστεύουσιν
   ἐγενήθημεν (1 Thess. 2:10)
   how devoutly and uprightly and blamelessly we were **among you who
   believe**
   c. Acc. pl. masc.
   εἰς ὑμᾶς τοὺς ἐν δυνάμει θεοῦ φρουρουμένους διὰ πίστεως
   (1 Peter 1:4-5)
   for **you who are being kept** by the power of God through faith
5. Articular participles used as address in place of vocative
   a. Nom. sing. masc.
   ὁ οὖν διδάσκων ἕτερον σεαυτὸν οὐ διδάσκεις; ὁ κηρύσσων μὴ
   κλέπτειν κλέπτεις; (Rom. 2:21)
   you then **who teaches** another, do you not teach yourself? **you who
   preaches** not to steal, do you steal?
   b. Nom. pl. masc.
   λέγετέ μοι, οἱ ὑπὸ νόμον θέλοντες εἶναι, τὸν νόμον οὐκ
   ἀκούετε; (Gal. 4:21)
   tell me, **you who want** to be under law, do you not hear the law?
6. Articular participles used in apposition to vocative noun
   Nom. sing. masc.
   διὸ ἀναπολόγητος εἶ, ὦ ἄνθρωπε πᾶς ὁ κρίνων (Rom. 2:1)
   wherefore you are without excuse, O **man, everyone who judges**

X. **Greek has no indefinite article.** However, the indefinite idea may be expressed by
   the cardinal numeral εἷς, μία, ἕν, or the indefinite pronoun τις, τι, as well as by
   the anarthrous noun.

   A. Cardinal numeral.
      1. Nom. sing. fem.
         καὶ προσῆλθεν αὐτῷ μία παιδίσκη (Matt. 26:69)
         and **a young girl** came to him
      2. Nom. sing. masc.
         καὶ προσελθὼν εἷς γραμματεὺς εἶπεν αὐτῷ, Διδάσκαλε, ἀκολουθήσω
         σοι (Matt. 8:19)
         and **a scribe** approached and said to him, Teacher, I will follow you
      3. Acc. sing. fem.
         εὐκοπώτερον δέ ἐστιν τὸν οὐρανὸν καὶ τὴν γῆν παρελθεῖν ἢ τοῦ
         νόμου μίαν κεραίαν πεσεῖν (Luke 16:17)
         but it is easier for heaven and earth to pass away than for **a tittle** of the
         law to fall

4. Acc. sing. fem.

καὶ ἰδὼν **συκῆν μίαν** ἐπὶ τῆς ὁδοῦ (Matt. 21:19)

and when he saw **a fig tree** by the road

B. Indefinite pronoun.

1. Nom. sing. masc.

ἄνθρωπός τις κατέβαινεν ἀπὸ Ἰερουσαλὴμ εἰς Ἰεριχὼ καὶ λῃσταῖς περιέπεσεν (Luke 10:30)[49]

a man went down from Jerusalem to Jericho and encountered bandits

2. Acc. pl. masc.

ἔταξαν ἀναβαίνειν Παῦλον καὶ Βαρναβᾶν καὶ **τινας ἄλλους** ἐξ αὐτῶν πρὸς τοὺς ἀποστόλους καὶ πρεσβυτέρους εἰς Ἰερουσαλήμ (Acts 15:2)[50]

they appointed Paul and Barnabas and **some others** of them to go up to the apostles and elders in Jerusalem

XI. **The nonuse or absence of the article** is much more frequent than the use or presence of the article in the NT. Moulton points out the importance of this: "For exegesis, there are few of the finer points of Greek which need more constant attention than this omission of the article when the writer would lay stress on the quality or character of the object."[51] The term "omission of the article" suggests that the article should be present, which is not necessarily true; therefore, this manual uses the term "nonuse" instead. However, there are three possible functions of a substantive without the article: definite, indefinite, and qualitative.

A. The anarthrous substantive may be definite.

1. Vocative forms are definite but have no article.

γράφω ὑμῖν, **τεκνία**, ὅτι ἀφέωνται ὑμῖν αἱ ἁμαρτίαι διὰ τὸ ὄνομα αὐτοῦ (1 John 2:12)

I write to you, **children**, that your sins have been forgiven because of his name

2. The adjective as a substantive object of a preposition may be anarthrous, indicating both definiteness and quality.

Acc. pl. masc.

ὅτι τὸν ἥλιον αὐτοῦ ἀνατέλλει ἐπὶ **πονηροὺς** καὶ **ἀγαθοὺς** καὶ βρέχει ἐπὶ **δικαίους** καὶ **ἀδίκους** (Matt. 5:45)

for he causes his sun to shine **upon the evil** and **the good,** and he causes it to rain **upon the just** and **the unjust**

---

[49] Luke 10:30 text is from GNT, NA, WH & MT; TR has Ἰερουσαλήμ.

[50] Acts 15:2 text is from GNT, NA & MT; WH & TR has Βαρνάβαν; TR has Ἰερουσαλήμ.

[51] James H. Moulton, *A Grammar of New Testament Greek* (Edinburgh: T & T Clark, 1957), 1:83.

3. The noun may be the predicate or complement of an equative verb.
Nom. sing. masc., neut., and fem.

ἐγὼ δὲ λέγω ὑμῖν μὴ ὀμόσαι ὅλως· μήτε ἐν τῷ οὐρανῷ, ὅτι **θρόνος ἐστὶν** τοῦ θεοῦ, μήτε ἐν τῇ γῇ, ὅτι **ὑποπόδιόν ἐστιν** τῶν ποδῶν αὐτοῦ, μήτε εἰς Ἱεροσόλυμα, ὅτι **πόλις ἐστὶν** τοῦ μεγάλου βασιλέως (Matt. 5:34-35)[52]

but I tell you not to swear at all: neither by heaven, for **it is the throne** of God; neither by the earth, for **it is the footstool** of his feet; neither by Jerusalem, for **it is the city** of the great king

4. Proper names, with or without the article, are always definite.

Ἰακὼβ δὲ ἐγέννησεν τὸν **Ἰωσὴφ** τὸν ἄνδρα **Μαρίας** (Matt. 1:16)

and **Jacob** begot **Joseph** the husband **of Mary**

5. Definiteness may be expressed by an adjoining genitive or possessive pronoun, which shows by the information it gives that the noun it modifies or describes is definite.

   a. Personal pronoun as a possessive

   εἰ ὁ θεὸς **πατὴρ ὑμῶν** ἦν, ἠγαπᾶτε ἂν ἐμέ (John 8:42)

   if God were **your father**, you would have loved me

   b. Adjoining genitive noun

   καὶ ἦν **χεὶρ κυρίου** μετ᾽ αὐτῶν (Acts 11:21)

   and **the hand of the Lord** was with them

6. Colwell's Rule: Definite predicate anarthrous nouns normally precede the verb (87 percent of the time).[53]

   a. ἐγώ εἰμι **τὸ φῶς** τοῦ κόσμου (John 8:12)

   I am the light of the world

   b. ὅταν ἐν τῷ κόσμῳ ὦ, **φῶς εἰμι** τοῦ κόσμου (John 9:5)

   as long as I am in the world, **I am the light** of the world

7. Nouns in salutations, titles, lists, and proverbs are normally anarthrous.

   a. Salutations or greetings

   χάρις ὑμῖν καὶ εἰρήνη ἀπὸ **θεοῦ πατρὸς** ἡμῶν καὶ **κυρίου Ἰησοῦ Χριστοῦ** (2 Cor. 1:2)

   grace to you and peace from **God** our **father** and **the Lord Jesus Christ**

   b. Titles

   Βίβλος γενέσεως Ἰησοῦ Χριστοῦ υἱοῦ Δαυὶδ υἱοῦ Ἀβραάμ (Matt. 1:1)[54]

   The book of the ancestry of Jesus Christ son of David son of Abraham

---

[52] Matt. 5:34-35 text is from GNT, NA, TR & MT: WH has Ἱεροσόλυμα.

[53] E. C. Colwell. "A Definite Rule for the Use of the Article in the Greek New Testament." *Journal of Biblical Literature* 52 (1933): 12-21.

[54] Matt. 1:1 text is from GNT & NA: WH has Δαυείδ; TR & MT have Δαβίδ.

c. Lists

Πέτρος ἀπόστολος Ἰησοῦ Χριστοῦ ἐκλεκτοῖς παρεπιδήμοις διασπορᾶς Πόντου, Γαλατίας, Καππαδοκίας, Ἀσίας καὶ Βιθυνίας (1 Peter 1:1)

Peter, an apostle of Jesus Christ, to the elect sojourners of the dispersion **in Pontus, Galatia, Cappadocia, Asia,** and **Bithynia**

d. Proverbs

ὅτι ἀγάπη καλύπτει πλῆθος ἁμαρτιῶν (1 Peter 4:8)[55]

for **love** covers a multitude of sins

8. Apollonius' Canon, without the article.

χάριτι δὲ θεοῦ εἰμι ὅ εἰμι (1 Cor. 15:10*a*; cf. ἡ χάρις τοῦ θεοῦ, 15:10*b*)

but **by the grace of God** I am what I am

9. Idiomatic prepositional phrases often have no article.

καὶ ἐν οἰκίᾳ οὐκ ἔμενεν ἀλλ' ἐν τοῖς μνήμασιν (Luke 8:27)

and he was not living **at home** but among the tombs

10. The second substantive in Granville Sharp's construction is definite and anarthrous.

ὁ ἀγαπήσας ἡμᾶς καὶ δοὺς παράκλησιν αἰωνίαν καὶ ἐλπίδα ἀγαθὴν ἐν χάριτι (2 Thess. 2:16)

the one who loved us and **gave** eternal consolation and good hope in grace

11. Ordinal numerals are often anarthrous, yet definite.

ὥρα ἦν ὡς ἕκτη (John 4:6)[56]

the hour was about **the sixth**

12. Monadic (one of a kind) nouns do not require the article and yet are definite.

καὶ ἔσονται σημεῖα ἐν ἡλίῳ καὶ σελήνῃ καὶ ἄστροις (Luke 21:25)[57]

and there shall be signs **in the sun** and **the moon** and **the stars**

13. When an indeclinable noun is found in an oblique case, and the prepositional possession or appositional phrase makes the case of the noun clear, the article is not necessary.

a. Gen. sing. masc.

καὶ δώσει αὐτῷ κύριος ὁ θεὸς τὸν θρόνον Δαυὶδ τοῦ πατρὸς αὐτοῦ (Luke 1:32)[58]

and the Lord God will give him the throne **of David** his father

---

[55] 1 Peter 4:8 text is from GNT, NA & WH: TR & MT have καλύψει; TR*b* has ἡ ἀγάπη.
[56] John 4:6 text is from GNT, NA & WH: TR & MT have ὡσεί for ὡς.
[57] Luke 21:25 text is from GNT, NA & WH: TR & MT have ἔσται.
[58] Luke 1:32 text is from GNT & NA: WH has Δαυείδ; TR & MT have Δαβίδ.

b. Dat. sing. masc.

ἀλλ’ ἐν Ἰσαὰκ κληθήσεταί σοι σπέρμα (Rom. 9:7)

but your seed shall be called **in Isaac**

c. Acc. sing. masc.

τὶ οὖν ἐροῦμεν εὑρηκέναι Ἀβραὰμ τὸν προπάτορα ἡμῶν κατὰ σάρκα; (Rom. 4:1)[59]

what then shall we say [that] **Abraham** our forefather according to the flesh has found?

14. Anarthrous nouns modified by πᾶς or ὅλος refer to the whole class.

πᾶν οὖν δένδρον μὴ ποιοῦν καρπὸν καλὸν ἐκκόπτεται καὶ εἰς πῦρ βάλλεται (Matt. 3:10)

so then **every tree** not bearing good fruit is cut down and cast into the fire

B. Indefinite nouns are always anarthrous in Greek, though obviously not all anarthrous nouns are indefinite, as the above and following sections show. Indefinite substantives are without specific indication of identity.

1. Nom. sing. masc.

ἐγένετο **ἄνθρωπος** ἀπεσταλμένος παρὰ θεοῦ (John 1:6)

a man was sent from God

2. Gen. sing. fem.

καὶ ἐθαύμαζον ὅτι μετὰ **γυναικὸς** ἐλάλει (John 4:27)[60]

and they were wondering because he was speaking with **a woman**

3. Dat. pl. masc.

κινδύνοις ποταμῶν, **κινδύνοις** ληστῶν (2 Cor. 11:26)

in perils of rivers, **in perils** of robbers

4. Acc. pl. masc.

ἔταξαν ἀναβαίνειν Παῦλον καὶ Βαρναβᾶν καὶ **τινας ἄλλους** ἐξ αὐτῶν πρὸς τοὺς ἀποστόλους καὶ πρεσβυτέρους εἰς Ἰερουσαλὴμ περὶ τοῦ ζητήματος τούτου (Acts 15:2)[61]

they ordered Paul and Barnabas and **some others** of them to go up to the apostles and elders in Jerusalem concerning this question

C. Qualitative substantives are always anarthrous in Greek and focus on the attribute, characteristic, or quality of the person or object named. Qualitativeness and definiteness are not mutually exclusive. Thus, one must carefully determine from the context which emphasis or emphases the author intended.

---

[59] Rom. 4:1 text is from GNT & NA: WH omits εὑρηκέναι: TR & MT have Ἀβραὰμ τὸν πατέρα ἡμῶν εὑρηκέναι.

[60] John 4:27 text is from GNT, NA & WH: TR & MT have ἐθαύμασαν.

[61] Acts 15:2 text is from GNT, NA & MT: WH & TR have Βαρνάβαν; TR has Ἱερουσαλήμ.

1. The substantive may be the predicate complement of an equative verb, when the subject is a pronoun (whether stated or implied), proper name, or an articular substantive.

   a. Nom. pl. masc. implicit pron.

   ὅπως **γένησθε υἱοὶ** τοῦ πατρὸς ὑμῶν τοῦ ἐν οὐρανοῖς (Matt. 5:45)
   so that **you may be sons** of your father who [ὄντος, is] in heaven

   b. Nom. sing. fem. implicit pron.

   χήρα καταλεγέσθω μὴ ἔλαττον ἐτῶν ἑξήκοντα γεγονυῖα, **ἑνὸς ἀνδρὸς γυνή** (1 Tim. 5:9)
   let not a widow be enrolled being less than sixty years [old], [if she is]
   a one husband kind of wife

   c. Nom. pl. neut. explicit pron.

   ὅσοι δὲ ἔλαβον αὐτὸν ἔδωκεν αὐτοῖς ἐξουσίαν **τέκνα** θεοῦ **γενέσθαι** (John 1:12)
   but as many as received him, he gave them authority **to become children** of God

2. Qualitative nouns in prepositional phrase are often anarthrous.

   a. Gen. and dat. sing. masc.

   καὶ ὅσοι **ἐν νόμῳ** ἥμαρτον, **διὰ νόμου** κριθήσονται (Rom. 2:12)
   and as many as have sinned **in law** shall be judged **by law**

   b. Dat. sing. fem.

   αἰτείτω δὲ **ἐν πίστει** (James 1:6)
   but let him ask **in faith**

   c. Acc. sing. fem.

   ἀλλὰ συνέκλεισεν ἡ γραφὴ τὰ πάντα **ὑπὸ ἁμαρτίαν** (Gal. 3:22)
   but the Scripture shut up all things **under sin**

3. Anarthrous nouns are often limited by a qualifying genitive.

   a. Nom. sing. fem.

   διὰ γὰρ νόμου **ἐπίγνωσις ἁμαρτίας** (Rom. 3:20)
   for through law [ἐστιν, is] **knowlege of sin**

   b. Gen. sing. masc.

   διὰ ποίου νόμου; τῶν ἔργων; οὐχί, ἀλλὰ διὰ **νόμου πίστεως** (Rom.3:27)
   by what law? of works? no, but by **the law of faith**

   c. Acc. pl. neut.

   ἀλλὰ παραστήσατε . . . τὰ μέλη ὑμῶν **ὅπλα δικαιοσύνης** (Rom. 6:13)
   but yield . . . your members **[as] instruments of righteousness**

4. The subject of a finite verb may be qualitative.
   a. Nom. sing. fem. and masc.
      ἄχρι γὰρ νόμου **ἁμαρτία** ἦν ἐν κόσμῳ, **ἁμαρτία** δὲ οὐκ
      ἐλλογεῖται μὴ ὄντος νόμου (Rom. 5:13)
      for until the law, **sin** was in the world; but **sin** is not imputed when
      law does not exist
   b. Nom. sing. fem.
      νυνὶ δὲ μένει **πίστις, ἐλπίς, ἀγάπη**, τὰ τρία ταῦτα· μείζων δὲ
      τούτων ἡ ἀγάπη (1 Cor. 13:13)
      but now **faith, hope, love** remain, these three, but the greatest of these
      [ἐστιν, is] love
5. The object complement of an accusative substantive will be qualitative.
   a. Acc. pl. masc.
      ἀλλὰ παρακάλει ὡς πατέρα, νεωτέρους ὡς **ἀδελφούς** (1 Tim. 5:1)
      but, as a father, encourage the younger men as **brothers**
   b. Acc. pl. masc.
      Δεῦτε ὀπίσω μου, καὶ ποιήσω ὑμᾶς **ἁλιεῖς** ἀνθρώπων (Matt. 4:19)
      come after me, and I will make you **fishers** of men

Select Bibliography for Articles

Blum, E. A. "Studies in Problem Areas of the Greek Article." Master's thesis, Dallas Theological Seminary, 1961.
Colwell, E. C. "A Definite Rule for the Use of the Article in the Greek New Testament." *Journal of Biblical Literature* 52 (1933): 12-21.
Dixon, Paul Stephen. "The Significance of the Anarthrous Predicate Nominative in John." Master's thesis, Dallas Theological Seminary, 1975.
Fee, Gordon D. "The Use of the Definite Article with Personal Names in the Gospel of John." *New Testament Studies* 17, no. 2 (1970-1971): 168-83.
Funk, Robert W. "The Syntax of the Greek Article: Its Importance for Critical Pauline Problems." Ph.D. diss., Vanderbilt Univ., 1953.
Greenlee, J. Harold. "The Greek Definite Article." *Bible Translator* 1 (1950): 162-65.
Harner, Philip B. "Qualitative Anarthrous Predicate Nouns." *Journal of Biblical Literature* 92 (March 1973): 75-87.

Harris, Murray J. *Jesus as God*, Appendix 1. Grand Rapids, Mich.: Baker, 1992.

_____. "Titus 2:13 and the Deity of Christ." In *Pauline Studies*, edited by Donald A. Hagner and Murray J. Harris. Grand Rapids, Mich.: Eerdmans, 1980.

Hedges, David Wm. "Apollonius' Canon and Anarthrous Constructions in Pauline Literature." Master's thesis, Grace Theological Seminary, 1983.

Hillstrom, Leonard N. "A Selective Study of the Greek Article in the New Testament." Master's thesis, Western Conservative Baptist Seminary, 1967.

Hoerber, Robert G. "God Be Merciful to Me a Sinner, A Note on Luke 18:13." *Concordia Theological Monthly* 33 (May 1962): 283-86.

Householder, Fred W. *The Syntax of Apollonius Dyscolus*. Amsterdam Studies in the Theory and History of Linguistic Science, Series III, vol. 23. Amsterdam: John Benjamins B.V., 1981.

Hull, Sanford D. "Exceptions to Apollonius' Canon in the New Testament: A Grammatical Study." *Trinity Journal* n.s. (1986): 3-16.

Jones, John. *An Examination of the Greek Article in Three Parts*. London: Longman Rees, Orme, Brown, & Green, 1827.

Kuehne, C. "The Greek Article and the Doctrine of Christ's Deity." *Journal of Theology* 13 (September 1973): 12-28; 13 (December 1973): 14-30; 14 (March 1974): 11-20; 14 (June 1974): 16-25; 14 (September 1974): 21-33; 14 (December 1974): 8-19; 15 (January 1975): 8-22.

McGhee, H. William. "The Greek Article and the Abstract Noun." Master's thesis, Tennessee Temple Univ., 1985.

Metzger, B. M. "The Jehovah's Witnesses and Jesus Christ." *Theology Today* (1953): 65-89.

Middleton, T. F. *The Doctrine of the Greek Article Applied to the Criticism and Illustration of the New Testament*. 2d ed. London: Rivington, 1841.

Mowery, Robert L. "The Articular Prepositional Attributes in the Pauline Corpus." *Biblica* 71 (1990): 85-92.

Nelson, Dotson M., Jr. "The Articular and Anarthrous Predicate Nominative in the Greek New Testament." Th.D. diss., Southern Baptist Theological Seminary, 1944.

Nevius, Richard C. "The Use of the Definite Article with 'Jesus' in the Fourth Gospel." *New Testament Studies* 12 (1965-1966): 81-85.

O'Rourke, John J. "The Article as Pronoun in the Synoptic Gospels." *Catholic Biblical Quarterly* 37, no. 4 (1975): 492-99.

_____. "Paul's Use of the Article as a Pronoun." *Catholic Biblical Quarterly* 34 (1972): 59-65.

Peck, Lester Duane. "An Investigation of the Articular and the Anarthrous πνεῦμα in the Gospels and Acts." Th.M. thesis, Dallas Theological Seminary, 1968.

Perry, Alfred M. "Translating the Greek Article." *Journal of Biblical Literature* 68 (1949): 329-39.

Rider, Glenn W. "An Investigation of the Granville Sharp Phenomenon and Plurals." Master's thesis, Grace Theological Seminary, 1980.

Roberts, J. W. "Exegetical Helps: the Greek Noun with and without the Article." *Restoration Quarterly* 14, no. 1 (1971): 28-47.

Robertson, A. T. "The Greek Article and the Deity of Christ." *Expositor* 8th series, no. 21 (1921): 182-88.

Sharp, Granville. *Remarks on the Uses of the Definitive Article in the Greek Text of the New Testament; Containing Many New Proofs of the Divinity of Christ, from Passages Which Are Wrongly Translated in the Common English Version.* 1st American ed. Philadelphia: Hopkins, 1807.

Slaten, Arthur W. Qualitative Nouns in the Pauline Epistles and their Translation in the Revised Version. Chicago: Univ. of Chicago, 1918.

_____. "The Qualitative Use of νόμος in the Pauline Epistles." *American Journal of Theology* 23 (1919): 213-19.

Teeple, H. M. "The Greek Article with Personal Names in the Synoptic Gospels." *New Testament Studies* 19 (1972-1973): 302-17.

Walker, William Henry. "The Importance of the Greek Article in the Epistle to the Romans." Th.M. thesis, Dallas Theological Seminary, 1939.

Wallace, Daniel B. "The Relation of Adjective to Noun in Anarthrous Constructions in the New Testament." *Novum Testamentum* 26 (April 1984): 128-67.

_____. "The Semantic Range of the Article-Noun-Kai-Noun Plural Construction in the New Testament." *Grace Theological Journal* 3, no. 2 (1982): 163-75.

_____. "Selected Notes on the Syntax of New Testament Greek." Class notes.

Wuest, Kenneth S. "The Greek Article in New Testament Interpretation." *Bibliotheca Sacra* 118, no. 469 (1961): 27-34.

CONJUNCTIONS

Forms. Conjunctions are words that connect other words, phrases, clauses, and sentences. The forms of conjunctions generally do not change; i.e., conjunctions are not inflected. However, crasis and elision affect the forms of several conjunctions and particles.

I. **Crasis** is the merging of one word with an immediately following word by the omission and contraction of vowels. The contraction is indicated by the breathing mark from the second word, which is called a coronis. Crasis affects only the conjunction καί when followed by the pronouns ἐγώ and ἐκεῖνος, the adverbs ἐκεῖ and ἐκεῖθεν and the particle ἐάν.

A. The personal pronoun κἀγώ is the equivalent of καὶ ἐγώ.
   1. Nom. sing. masc.
      καθὼς ἐμὲ ἀπέστειλας εἰς τὸν κόσμον, **κἀγὼ** ἀπέστειλα αὐτοὺς εἰς τὸν κόσμον (John 17:18)
      as you sent me into the world, **I also** sent them into the world
   2. Dat. sing. masc.
      ὤφθη **κἀμοί**. ἐγὼ γάρ εἰμι ὁ ἐλάχιστος τῶν ἀποστόλων (1 Cor. 15:8-9)
      he appeared **to me also**. for I myself am the least of the apostles
   3. Acc. sing. masc.
      κἀμὲ οἴδατε καὶ οἴδατε πόθεν εἰμί (John 7:28)
      you **both** know **me** and know whence I am [where I came from]

B. The demonstrative pronoun κἀκεῖνος is the equivalent of καὶ ἐκεῖνος.
   1. Nom. sing. masc.
      τὰ ἔργα ἃ ἐγὼ ποιῶ **κἀκεῖνος** ποιήσει (John 14:12)
      the works that I myself do, **that one also** will do
   2. Acc. sing masc.
      οἱ δὲ **κἀκεῖνον** δείραντες καὶ ἀτιμάσαντες ἐξαπέστειλαν κενόν (Luke 20:11)
      and they beat **that one also** and dishonored [him] and sent [him] away empty
   3. Nom. pl. masc.
      καὶ γάρ ἐσμεν εὐηγγελισμένοι καθάπερ **κἀκεῖνοι** (Heb. 4:2)
      for indeed we have had good news preached, even as **they also**
   4. Acc. pl. masc.
      κἀκείνους κατέλιπεν αὐτοῦ (Acts 18:19)
      and he left **them** there

73

5. Acc. pl. neut.
   κἀκεῖνα δεῖ με ἀγαγεῖν (John 10:16)[1]
   I must bring **them also**
6. Nom. pl. neut.
   κἀκεῖνα κοινοῖ τὸν ἄνθρωπον (Matt. 15:18)
   and these things defile the person

C. Crasis with adverbs ἐκεῖ and ἐκεῖθεν.
   1. κἀκεῖ is the equivalent of καὶ ἐκεῖ.
      ἐξῆλθεν καὶ ἀπῆλθεν εἰς ἔρημον τόπον **κἀκεῖ** προσηύχετο (Mark 1:35)
      he went out and departed into a deserted place, **and** he began praying **there**
   2. κἀκεῖθεν is the equivalent of καὶ ἐκεῖθεν.
      κἀκεῖθεν ἀπέπλευσαν εἰς Ἀντιόχειαν (Acts 14:26)
      and from there they sailed to Antioch

D. κἄν is the equivalent of καὶ and the particle ἐάν.
   κἄν δέῃ με σὺν σοὶ ἀποθανεῖν, οὐ μή σε ἀπαρνήσομαι (Matt. 26:35)
   even if I must die with you, I will never deny you

II. **Elision** is the omission of the final short vowel of a word that is followed by another word beginning with a vowel. The omission is indicated by an apostrophe and affects two conjunctions, ἀλλά and δέ.

A. ἀλλ᾽ is the equivalent of ἀλλά.
   οὐχ ὅτι ἡμεῖς ἠγαπήκαμεν τὸν θεὸν **ἀλλ᾽** ὅτι αὐτὸς ἠγάπησεν ἡμᾶς
   (1 John 4:10)
   not that we loved God, **but** that he himself loved us

B. δ᾽ is the equivalent of δέ, usually preceding ἄν, and once preceeding αὐτό.
   1. ὃς **δ᾽ ἄν** πίῃ ἐκ τοῦ ὕδατος οὗ ἐγὼ δώσω αὐτῷ οὐ μὴ διψήσει εἰς τὸν αἰῶνα (John 4:14)[2]
      but whoever will drink of the water that I will give him shall never thirst forever

---

[1] John 10:16 text is from GNT, NA & WH: TR & MT have με δεῖ.
[2] John 4:14 text is from GNT, NA & WH: TR & MT have διψήσῃ.

2. τὸ δ' αὐτὸ καὶ οἱ λῃσταὶ οἱ συσταυρωθέντες σὺν αὐτῷ ὠνείδιζον αὐτόν (Matt. 27:44)[3]
   and at the same time also the robbers who were crucified with him were heaping insults on him

III. **Accenting** of enclitic conjunctions εἰ and ὡς.

A. εἰ is accented when followed immediately by another enclitic.
   1. Nom. sing. masc.
      Εἴ τις ἔχει οὖς, ἀκουσάτω (Rev. 13:9)
      If anyone has ears, let him hear
   2. Acc. sing. neut.
      ἀφίετε **εἴ** τι ἔχετε κατά τινος· ἵνα καὶ ὁ πατὴρ ὑμῶν ὁ ἐν τοῖς οὐρανοῖς ἀφῇ ὑμῖν τὰ παραπτώματα ὑμῶν (Mark 11:25)
      if you have **anything** against someone, forgive, in order that your Father who [ὤν, is] in heaven may also forgive you your transgressions
   3. Gen. sing. masc.
      καὶ **εἴ** τινός τι ἐσυκοφάντησα, ἀποδίδωμι τετραπλοῦν (Luke 19:8)
      and, **if** I extorted anything **from anyone,** I will pay back fourfold
   4. Acc. sing. masc.
      ἐβάπτισα δὲ καὶ τὸν Στεφανᾶ οἶκον· λοιπὸν οὐκ οἶδα **εἴ** τινα ἄλλον ἐβάπτισα (1 Cor. 1:16)
      and I baptized also the household of Stephanus; furthermore I do not know **if** I baptized **any** other

B. ὡς is accented when followed immediately by another enclitic.
   ἢ μὴ χρῄζομεν, **ὥς** τινες, συστατικῶν ἐπιστολῶν πρὸς ὑμᾶς, ἢ ἐξ ὑμῶν συστατικῶν; (2 Cor. 3:1)[4]
   do we need, **as some,** letters of introduction to you or [ἐπιστολῶν, letters] of introduction from you?

IV. **Position in the sentence.** Conjunctions generally are positioned at the beginning of the sentence or clause they are joining to the preceding sentence or clause. However, several conjunctions are postpositive; that is, they come after the first word in the sentence or clause (not necessarily immediately after). in the sentence

---

[3] Matt. 27:44 text is from GNT & NA: WH has συνσταυρωθέντες; TR omits σύν and has αὐτῷ for αὐτόν; MT omits σύν.
[4] 2 Cor. 3:1 is from GNT, NA & WH: TR & MT have εἰ μή instead of ἢ μή.

A. ἄρα is sometimes postpositive and sometimes initial when it is joined with another conjunction (e.g., οὖν or καί) or found in the apodosis (conclusion) of a conditional sentence.
   1. Postpositive
      οὐδὲν **ἄρα** νῦν κατάκριμα τοῖς ἐν Χριστῷ Ἰησοῦ (Rom. 8:1)
      so then [ἐστιν, there is] now no condemnation for those [οὖσιν, who are] in Christ Jesus
   2. Initial
      ἄρα οὖν τὰ τῆς εἰρήνης διώκωμεν καὶ τὰ τῆς οἰκοδόμης τῆς εἰς ἀλλήλους (Rom. 14:19)
      so then let us pursue the things of peace and the things that edify one another

B. γάρ is always postpositive.
   νῦν **γὰρ** ἐγγύτερον ἡμῶν ἡ σωτηρία, ἢ ὅτε ἐπιστεύσαμεν (Rom. 13:11)
   for now our salvation is nearer than when we began to believe

C. δέ is always postpositive, but not always second in position.
   1. Second position
      τὸ **δὲ** ῥῆμα κυρίου μένει εἰς τὸν αἰῶνα (1 Peter 1:25)
      but the word of the Lord continues forever
   2. Third position
      ἐν αὐτῇ **δὲ** τῇ οἰκίᾳ μένετε (Luke 10:7)
      but remain in the same house
   3. Fourth position
      οὐ περὶ τούτων **δὲ** ἐρωτῶ μόνον (John 17:20)
      but I do not request only for these
   4. Fifth position
      οὐ περὶ τῶν ἡμετέρων **δὲ** μόνον ἀλλὰ καὶ περὶ ὅλου τοῦ κόσμου (1 John 2:2)
      and not for ours only but also for the whole world

D. οὖν is always postpositive.
   τότε **οὖν** παρέδωκεν αὐτὸν αὐτοῖς ἵνα σταυρωθῇ (John 19:16)
   then he, **therefore,** delivered him to them in order that he might be crucified

E. τε is a postpositive enclitic (without accent) conjunction/particle.
   πέποιθάς **τε** σεαυτὸν ὁδηγὸν εἶναι τυφλῶν, φῶς τῶν ἐν σκότει (Rom. 2:19)
   and so you have persuaded yourself to be a guide of the blind, a light of those [ὄντων, who are] in darkness

Functions. A conjunction is a connecting word that joins words, phrases, clauses, sentences, and paragraphs. Conjunctions function in a variety of ways. However, the following conjunctions are categorized according to their primary functions, with secondary functions following. There are two main classes of conjunctions, coordinating and subordinating conjunctions. Not all conjunctions are illustrated below; only those that occur fifty or more times in the NT.

I. **Coordinating (paratactic) conjunctions** join two words, phrases, clauses, and sentences. When they introduce clauses, they are grammatically independent clauses.

A. Adversative conjunctions. The following illustrations are not exhaustive but illustrative of the most frequent.
   1. ἀλλά, a strong adversative
      a. Introduces a contrast after a negative
         θεὸς δὲ **οὐκ** ἔστιν νεκρῶν **ἀλλὰ** ζώντων (Luke 20:38)
         but He is **not** God of the dead **but** of the living
      b. In an emphatic sense
         εἰ γὰρ σύμφυτοι γεγόναμεν τῷ ὁμοιώματι τοῦ θανάτου αὐτοῦ,
         ἀλλὰ καὶ τῆς ἀναστάσεως ἐσόμεθα (Rom. 6:5)
         for if we have been planted together in the likeness of his death,
         certainly also we shall be [in the likeness] of his resurrection
      c. With imperative
         ἡ θυγάτηρ μου ἄρτι ἐτελεύτησεν· **ἀλλὰ** ἐλθὼν ἐπίθες τὴν χεῖρά
         σου ἐπ᾽ αὐτήν, καὶ ζήσεται (Matt. 9:18)
         my daughter just now died; **now** come and place your hand upon her
         and she shall live
      d. Joined with καί
         ἀλλὰ καὶ καυχώμεθα ἐν ταῖς θλίψεσιν (Rom. 5:3)
         but let us **also** boast in tribulations
   2. δέ, adversative (but not as strong as ἀλλά) and connective
      a. To indicate a contrast
         αἱ ἀλώπεκες φωλεοὺς ἔχουσιν καὶ τὰ πετεινὰ τοῦ οὐρανοῦ
         κατασκηνώσεις, ὁ **δὲ** υἱὸς τοῦ ἀνθρώπου οὐκ ἔχει ποῦ τὴν
         κεφαλὴν κλίνῃ (Matt. 8:20)
         the foxes have dens and the birds of the sky have nests, **but** the son of
         man does not have [a place] where he might lay his head
      b. To indicate a connective, often with a change of subject
         Ἀβραὰμ ἐγέννησεν τὸν Ἰσαάκ, Ἰσαὰκ **δὲ** ἐγέννησεν τὸν Ἰακώβ
         (Matt. 1:2)
         Abraham begot Isaac, **and** Isaac begot Jacob

c. After a negative
    ἵνα μὴ νωθροὶ γένησθε, μιμηταὶ δὲ τῶν διὰ πίστεως καὶ
    μακροθυμίας κληρονομούντων τὰς ἐπαγγελίας (Heb. 6:12)
    do not be lazy, **but rather** be imitators of those who through faith and
    patience inherit the promises
d. Emphatic
    καὶ πάντες δὲ οἱ προφῆται . . . ἐλάλησαν . . . τὰς ἡμέρας ταύτας
    (Acts 3:24)
    and **in fact** all the prophets . . . spoke . . . of these days

B. Connectives
    1. καί, as a connective, usually joins two or more of the same grammatical
        kind (adjectives, adverbs, nouns, verbs, infinitives, participles, prepositions,
        phrases, clauses, and sentences); it is also adverbial, adversative,
        appositional, and emphatic.
        a. Connective of words, phrases, and clauses of the same grammatical rank
            (1) Adjectives
                 σοφοῖς τε καὶ ἀνοήτοις ὀφειλέτης εἰμί (Rom. 1:14)
                 I am debtor **both to the wise and unwise**
            (2) Adverbs
                 ἵνα ἡ ἀγάπη ὑμῶν ἔτι μᾶλλον καὶ μᾶλλον περισσεύῃ ἐν
                 ἐπιγνώσει καὶ πάσῃ αἰσθήσει (Phil. 1:9)
                 that your love may abound yet **more and more** in knowledge and all
                 insight
            (3) Nouns
                 καὶ αὐτὸς προελεύσεται ἐνώπιον αὐτοῦ ἐν πνεύματι καὶ
                 δυνάμει Ἠλίου (Luke 1:17)[5]
                 and he shall go before him **in the spirit and power** of Elijah
            (4) Prepositions
                 ἵνα . . . δὲ κατηρτισμένοι ἐν τῷ αὐτῷ νοῒ καὶ ἐν τῇ αὐτῇ
                 γνώμῃ (1 Cor. 1:10)
                 but that you may be knit together **with the same attitude and with
                 the same purpose**
            (5) Pronouns
                 τόν ποτέ σοι ἄχρηστον νυνὶ δὲ καὶ σοὶ καὶ ἐμοὶ εὔχρηστον
                 (Philem. 11)
                 who once [ὄντα, was] useless to you but now also [is] useful
                 both to you and to me

---

[5] Luke 1:17 text is from GNT, NA, TR*b* & MT: WH has Ἠλεία; TR*s* has Ἠλίου.

(6) Verbs and verb clauses

τέξεται δὲ υἱόν, **καὶ καλέσεις** τὸ ὄνομα αὐτοῦ Ἰησοῦν
(Matt. 1:21)

and **she shall bear** a son, **and you shall call** his name Jesus

(7) Infinitives

ἤρξατο ὁ Ἰησοῦς **ποιεῖν** τε **καὶ διδάσκειν** (Acts 1:1)
Jesus began **both to do and to teach**

(8) Participles and clauses

τινές εἰσιν οἱ **ταράσσοντες** ὑμᾶς **καὶ θέλοντες** μεταστρέψαι
τὸ εὐαγγέλιον τοῦ Χριστοῦ (Gal. 1:7)

there are some **who trouble** you **and want** to pervert the gospel of
Christ

(9) Clauses and sentences

καὶ ἐποίησεν δώδεκα ἵνα ὦσιν μετ᾽ αὐτοῦ καὶ ἵνα ἀποστέλλῃ
αὐτοὺς κηρύσσειν (Mark 3:14)

and he appointed twelve **that they might be with him and that he
might send them out to preach**

(10) Redundant καί and verb

ἀπεκρίθη Ἰησοῦς **καὶ εἶπεν** αὐτοῖς (John 8:14)
Jesus **replied** to them

b. Adverbial καί, translated **also, likewise, even**

(1) Often with pronouns

ἀληθῶς **καὶ σὺ** ἐξ αὐτῶν εἶ (Matt. 26:73)
truly **you also** are [one] of them

(2) Often with adverbs, such as καθώς and οὕτως

(a) With καθώς

καθὼς καὶ ὁ Χριστὸς ἠγάπησεν τὴν ἐκκλησίαν (Eph. 5:25)
even as Christ **also** loved the church

(b) With οὕτως

οὕτως καὶ ἡ χάρις βασιλεύσῃ διὰ δικαιοσύνης εἰς
ζωὴν αἰώνιον (Rom. 5:21)

so also grace might reign through righteousness unto eternal life

(3) As ascensive, meaning **even**

ὑμῶν δὲ **καὶ** αἱ τρίχες τῆς κεφαλῆς πᾶσαι ἠριθμημέναι εἰσίν
(Matt. 10:30)

but **even** all the hairs of your head are numbered

(4) καί . . . καί, translated **both . . . and**, or **even . . . and**. In this
construction the first καί is adverbial and the second is connective.

θεὸς γάρ ἐστιν ὁ ἐνεργῶν ἐν ὑμῖν **καὶ** τὸ θέλειν **καὶ** τὸ
ἐνεργεῖν ὑπὲρ τῆς εὐδοκίας (Phil. 2:13)

for the one who is working in you **both** to will **and** to perform
for his good pleasure is God

(5) The Granville Sharp rule. One singular articular substantive and one
anarthrous substantive joined by καί refer to the same person. This
is true only of personal singular substantives (excluding proper
names), not of plural or impersonal terms.

προσδεχόμενοι τὴν μακαρίαν ἐλπίδα καὶ ἐπιφάνειαν τῆς
δόξης **τοῦ μεγάλου θεοῦ καὶ σωτῆρος** ἡμῶν Ἰησοῦ Χριστοῦ
(Titus 2:13)

awaiting the blessed hope and appearance of the glory **of our great
God and savior** Jesus Christ

c. καί as appositional or explaining a previous word or clause

ἀπήγγειλαν πάντα **καὶ** τὰ τῶν δαιμονιζομένων (Matt. 8:33)

they reported everything, **namely** the things concerning those who
were demonized

d. καί as adversative

(1) **but**

πολλοὶ προφῆται **καὶ** δίκαιοι ἐπεθύμησαν . . . ἀκοῦσαι ἃ
ἀκούετε **καὶ** οὐκ ἤκουσαν (Matt. 13:17)

many prophets and righteous men desired . . . to hear what you
hear **but** did not hear

(2) **and yet**

μακάριοι οἱ μὴ ἰδόντες **καὶ** πιστεύσαντες (John 20:29)

blessed [εἰσιν, are] those who have not seen **and yet** have believed

e. Emphatic καί, translated **indeed, verily, in fact**

(1) With γάρ

καὶ γὰρ ἐν ἑνὶ πνεύματι ἡμεῖς πάντες εἰς ἓν σῶμα
ἐβαπτίσθημεν (1 Cor. 12:13)

for indeed by one Spirit we all were baptized into one body

(2) With δέ

ὁ δὲ Παῦλος ἔφη, Ἐγὼ δὲ **καὶ** γεγέννημαι (Acts 22:28)

and Paul said, **but** I myself **verily** was born [free]

2. Postpositive and enclitic τε

a. Connecting phrases or clauses

χάρις **τε** μεγάλη ἦν ἐπὶ πάντας αὐτούς (Acts 4:33)

and much grace was upon them all

   b. τε . . . τε, translated **both** . . . **and**

εἰς τοῦτο γὰρ ὤφθην σοι, προχειρίσασθαί σε ὑπηρέτην καὶ
μάρτυρα ὧν τε εἶδες ὧν τε ὀφθήσομαί σοι (Acts 26:16)
for this purpose I appeared to you, to appoint you a minister and
a witness **both** of what you saw **and** of what I will show you

   c. τε καί, translated **both** . . . **and**

Ἕλλησίν τε καὶ Βαρβάροις, σοφοῖς τε καὶ ἀνοήτοις, ὀφειλέτης
εἰμί (Rom. 1:14)
I am a debtor **both** to Greeks **and** Barbarians, **both** to wise **and** unwise

C. Disjunctive conjunctions, indicating a contrast or an alternative between words
or clauses.
  1. Disjunctive ἤ
    a. Mutually exclusive ἤ

μενέτω ἄγαμος ἤ τῷ ἀνδρὶ καταλλαγήτω (1 Cor. 7:11)
let her remain unmarried **or** be reconciled to her husband

    b. Mutually exclusive ἤ . . . ἤ, translated **either** . . . **or**

οὐδεὶς οἰκέτης δύναται δυσὶ κυρίοις δουλεύειν· ἢ γὰρ τὸν ἕνα
μισήσει καὶ τὸν ἕτερον ἀγαπήσει, ἢ ἑνὸς ἀνθέξεται καὶ τοῦ
ἑτέρου καταφρονήσει (Luke 16:13)
no servant is able to serve two lords; for **either** he will hate the one and
love the other, **or** he will be devoted to one and will despise the other

    c. In negative statements, translated **nor**

οὐχ ὅτι ἤδη ἔλαβον, ἢ ἤδη τετελείωμαι (Phil. 3:12)
not that I already received **nor** have I already been perfected

    d. Indicating comparison when used with a comparative adjective or
adverb, translated **than**
      (1) With comparative adjective

Ἰησοῦς **πλείονας** μαθητὰς ποιεῖ καὶ βαπτίζει **ἤ** Ἰωάννης
(John 4:1)[6]
Jesus makes and baptizes **more** disciples **than** John

      (2) With comparative adverb

χαίρει ἐπ᾽ αὐτῷ **μᾶλλον ἤ** ἐπὶ τοῖς ἐνενήκοντα ἐννέα τοῖς
μὴ πεπλανημένοις (Matt. 18:13)
he rejoices over it **more than** over the ninety-nine who did not
wander away

---

[6] John 4:1 text is from GNT, NA, TR & MT: WH has Ἰωάνης.

  e. Indicating time with πρίν, translated **before**
  πρὶν ἢ συνελθεῖν αὐτοὺς εὑρέθη ἐν γαστρὶ ἔχουσα ἐκ πνεύματος
  ἁγίου (Matt. 1:18)
  before they lived together she was found [to be] pregnant by the Holy
  Spirit

2. εἴτε . . . εἴτε, translated **whether . . . or**
  a. With subjunctive mood
  ἵνα **εἴτε** γρηγορῶμεν **εἴτε** καθεύδωμεν ἅμα σὺν αὐτῷ ζήσωμεν
  (1 Thess. 5:10)
  that **whether** we are awake **or** sleep, we shall live together with Him
  b. With indicative mood
  εἴτε γλῶσσαι, παύσονται· **εἴτε** γνῶσις, καταργηθήσεται
  (1 Cor. 13:8)
  whether tongues, they shall cease; **whether** knowledge, it shall be
  done away
  c. After a verb
  ἄρα οὖν, ἀδελφοί, στήκετε, καὶ κρατεῖτε τὰς παραδόσεις ἃς
  ἐδιδάχθητε **εἴτε** διὰ λόγου **εἴτε** δι᾽ ἐπιστολῆς ἡμῶν (2 Thess. 2:15)
  so then, brothers, stand firm and hold fast the traditions that you
  were taught, **whether** by word **or** by our epistle

D. Inferential conjunctions, indicating a result from what has preceded.
  1. ἄρα, postpositive
  a. Translated **so, then, consequently**
  οὐδὲν **ἄρα** νῦν κατάκριμα τοῖς ἐν Χριστῷ Ἰησοῦ (Rom. 8:1)
  [ἐστίν, there is] **consequently** now no condemnation to those [οὖσιν,
  who are] in Christ Jesus
  b. In questions
  τίς **ἄρα** μείζων ἐστὶν ἐν τῇ βασιλείᾳ τῶν οὐρανῶν; (Matt. 18:1)
  who **then** is the greatest in the kingdom of heaven?
  c. In the apodosis (conclusion) of conditional sentences, indicating the
  result
  εἰ γὰρ διὰ νόμου δικαιοσύνη, **ἄρα** Χριστὸς δωρεὰν ἀπέθανεν
  (Gal. 2:21)
  for **if** righteousness [ἐστιν, exists] through law, **then** Christ died for
  no purpose
  2. διό and διόπερ, translated **therefore, for this reason**
  a. **διὸ** οὐδὲ ἐμαυτὸν ἠξίωσα πρὸς σὲ ἐλθεῖν (Luke 7:7)
  therefore, neither did I count myself worthy to come to you

b. **διόπερ** εἰ βρῶμα σκανδαλίζει τὸν ἀδελφόν μου, οὐ μὴ φάγω κρέα εἰς τὸν αἰῶνα (1 Cor. 8:13)
therefore, if meat offends my brother, I will never eat meat forever

3. οὖν, postpositive, translated **therefore, consequently, then**

a. In statements
ὑμῖν **οὖν** ἡ τιμὴ τοῖς πιστεύουσιν (1 Peter 2:7)
therefore, the preciousness [ἐστιν, is] to you who believe

b. In commands and invitations
μετανοήσατε **οὖν** καὶ ἐπιστρέψατε (Acts 3:19)
repent **therefore** and convert

c. In questions
εἶπον οὖν αὐτῷ, τί **οὖν** ποιεῖς σὺ σημεῖον (John 6:30)
they said then to him, "what sign **then** will you perform"

E. γάρ, postpositive.

1. Explanatory, translated **for**
ἐλεύσομαι δὲ πρὸς ὑμᾶς ὅταν Μακεδονίαν διέλθω· Μακεδονίαν **γὰρ** διέρχομαι (1 Cor. 16:5)
but I will come to you when I pass through Macedonia; **for** I am going to pass through Macedonia

2. Illative **γάρ**, expressing a reason or ground for the statement
τέξεται δὲ υἱόν, καὶ καλέσεις τὸ ὄνομα αὐτοῦ Ἰησοῦν· αὐτὸς **γὰρ** σώσει τὸν λαὸν αὐτοῦ ἀπὸ τῶν ἁμαρτιῶν αὐτῶν (Matt. 1:21)
and she will give birth to a son, and you shall call his name Jesus; **for** he himself shall save his people from their sins

3. Emphatic, translated **indeed, certainly**
καὶ νῦν λάθρα ἡμᾶς ἐκβάλλουσιν; οὐ **γάρ**, ἀλλὰ ἐλθόντες αὐτοὶ ἡμᾶς ἐξαγαγέτωσαν (Acts 16:37)
and now secretly are they going to thrust us out? **certainly not**! rather let them personally come and bring us out

II. **Subordinating (hypotactic) conjunctions** introduce grammatically dependent clauses that express various ideas: purpose, result, cause, condition, comparison, concession, temporal, and location. These conjunctions function in many ways; they are categorized below according to their primary function, with secondary functions following.

A. Purpose conjunctions indicate intention or design.

1. ἵνα with the subjunctive mood

a. ἵνα functions primarily as a purpose conjunction.

(1) Affirmative purpose

τί οὖν ποιεῖς σὺ σημεῖον, ἵνα **ἴδωμεν** καὶ **πιστεύσωμέν** σοι; (John 6:30)

what sign then will you perform, **in order that we may see** and **believe** you?

(2) Negative purpose, ἵνα μή

τεκνία μου, ταῦτα γράφω ὑμῖν **ἵνα μὴ ἁμάρτητε** (1 John 2:1)

my little children, I am writing these things to you **in order that you may not sin**

b. ἵνα sometimes introduces a result clause.

οὔτε οὗτος ἥμαρτεν οὔτε οἱ γονεῖς αὐτοῦ, ἀλλ᾽ ἵνα φανερωθῇ τὰ ἔργα τοῦ θεοῦ ἐν αὐτῷ (John 9:3)

neither did this man sin nor his parents, but **as a result** the works of God shall be made known by him

c. ἵνα sometimes introduces a substantive clause.

(1) Introducing a subject clause of an impersonal verb

συμφέρει γάρ σοι ἵνα ἀπόληται ἓν τῶν μελῶν σου καὶ μὴ ὅλον τὸ σῶμά σου βληθῇ εἰς γέενναν (Matt. 5:29)

for **that** one of your members should perish and your entire body should not be cast into Gehenna **is profitable** for you

(2) Introducing an object clause of indirect discourse

εἰς ὃ καὶ **προσευχόμεθα** πάντοτε περὶ ὑμῶν, ἵνα ὑμᾶς ἀξιώσῃ τῆς κλήσεως ὁ θεὸς ἡμῶν (2 Thess. 1:11)

for this purpose **we** also **pray** always for you, **that** our God would count you worthy of [this] calling

(3) Introducing an appositional clause

καὶ **αὕτη** ἐστὶν ἡ ἀγάπη ἵνα περιπατῶμεν κατὰ τὰς ἐντολὰς αὐτοῦ (2 John 6)

and **this** is love, **that** we should walk according to his command

(4) Introducing a clause modifying an adjective

πιστός ἐστιν καὶ **δίκαιος**, ἵνα ἀφῇ ἡμῖν τὰς ἁμαρτίας καὶ καθαρίσῃ ἡμᾶς ἀπὸ πάσης ἀδικίας (1 John 1:9)

he is **faithful** and **just to** forgive our sins and cleanse us from all unrighteousness

d. ἵνα sometimes introduces an imperatival clause, which is an independent clause.

ἡ δὲ γυνὴ ἵνα φοβῆται τὸν ἄνδρα (Eph. 5:33)

and **let** the wife respect her husband

e. ἵνα with τί becomes an interrogative with the indicative and means **why? for what reason?**
ἱνατί γὰρ ἡ ἐλευθερία μου κρίνεται ὑπὸ ἄλλης συνειδήσεως;
(1 Cor. 10:29)
for **why** is my freedom judged by the conscience of another?

2. ὅπως with the subjunctive

a. Introducing purpose
ἐπὰν δὲ εὕρητε, ἀπαγγείλατέ μοι, **ὅπως κἀγὼ ἐλθὼν προσκυνήσω** αὐτῷ (Matt. 2:8)
and when you find [him] report to me, **in order that** I also may go and worship him

b. Introducing an object clause of indirect discourse
οἵτινες . . . προσηύξαντο περὶ αὐτῶν **ὅπως λάβωσιν** πνεῦμα ἅγιον (Acts 8:15)
who . . . prayed for them, **that** they might receive the Holy Spirit

c. Introducing a negative result clause
μεταξὺ ἡμῶν καὶ ὑμῶν χάσμα μέγα ἐστήρικται, **ὅπως** οἱ θέλοντες διαβῆναι ἔνθεν πρὸς ὑμᾶς **μὴ** δύνωνται (Luke 16:26)[7]
between us and you a great chasm has been fixed **so that** those who want to pass over from here to you are **not** able

B. Result ὥστε, indicating an outcome, effect, or consequence.

1. With the indicative denoting actual result
οὕτω(ς) γὰρ ἠγάπησεν ὁ θεὸς τὸν κόσμον, **ὥστε** τὸν υἱὸν τὸν μονογενῆ **ἔδωκεν** (John 3:16)
for in this way God loved the world, **with the result that he gave** his only son

2. With the infinitive indicating actual result
συνήχθησαν πολλοί, **ὥστε μηκέτι χωρεῖν** (Mark 2:2)
many were assembled together, **so that there was no more room**

3. Sometimes the infinitive indicates intention, rather than actual result. This is determined by the context.
συμβούλιον ἔλαβον πάντες οἱ ἀρχιερεῖς καὶ οἱ πρεσβύτεροι τοῦ λαοῦ κατὰ τοῦ Ἰησοῦ **ὥστε θανατῶσαι** αὐτόν (Matt. 27:1)
all the chief priests and the elders of the people took counsel against Jesus **so that they might put** him **to death**

---

[7] Luke 16:26 text is from GNT, NA, WH & MT: TR has ἐντεῦθεν for ἔνθεν.

4. Sometimes ὥστε introduces an independent clause with the indicative or imperative, translated **therefore, for this reason**.
   a. With the indicative
      ὥστε εἴ τις ἐν Χριστῷ, καινὴ κτίσις (2 Cor. 5:17)
      therefore, if anyone [ἐστιν, is] in Christ, [ἐστιν, he is] a new creation
   b. With the imperative
      ὥστε παρακαλεῖτε ἀλλήλους ἐν τοῖς λόγοις τούτοις (1 Thess. 4:18)
      therefore, encourage one another with these words

C. Causal conjunctions express a cause or reason for an effect.
   1. ὅτι, primarily as a causal conjunction, but serving other functions as well
      a. Introducing a causal clause
         ὅτι οὐκ εἰμὶ χείρ, οὐκ εἰμὶ ἐκ τοῦ σώματος (1 Cor. 12:15)
         because I am not a hand, I do not belong to the body
      b. Introducing an object clause after verbs of perception (physical and mental), sense, speaking, or affirmation, translated **that**.
         μαρτύρομαι δὲ πάλιν παντὶ ἀνθρώπῳ περιτεμνομένῳ, ὅτι ὀφειλέτης ἐστὶν ὅλον τὸν νόμον ποιῆσαι (Gal. 5:3)
         and I testify again to every circumcised man, **that** he is a debtor to perform the entire law
      c. Introducing an epexegetical (explanatory) clause after a demonstrative pronoun
         αὕτη δέ ἐστιν ἡ κρίσις, ὅτι τὸ φῶς ἐλήλυθεν εἰς τὸν κόσμον (John 3:19)
         and **this** is the judgment, **that** light has come into the world
      d. Recitative ὅτι, introducing direct discourse, functioning as quotation marks and thus not translated
         πρὸς ὃν ἐλαλήθη ὅτι ἐν Ἰσαὰκ κληθήσεταί σοι σπέρμα (Heb. 11:18)
         to whom it was spoken, "your seed shall be called in Isaac"
   2. ἐπεί (also ἐπειδή, ἐπειδήπερ)
      a. Translated **because, since, for**
         τῷ γὰρ Ἀβραὰμ ἐπαγγειλάμενος ὁ θεός, ἐπεὶ κατ' οὐδενὸς εἶχεν μείζονος ὀμόσαι, ὤμοσεν καθ' ἑαυτοῦ (Heb. 6:13)
         for when God made the promise to Abraham, **since** he could swear by no one greater, he swore by himself

  b. Translated **for otherwise, else**
  εἰ δὲ χάριτι, οὐκέτι ἐξ ἔργων, ἐπεὶ ἡ χάρις οὐκέτι γίνεται χάρις
  (Rom. 11:6)
  but if [ἐστιν, it is] by grace, [ἐστιν, it is] no longer of works, **else** grace
  is no longer grace

D. Comparative conjunctions express a comparison between two words,
   phrases, or clauses.
   1. ὡς, with various possible translations
      a. Expressing manner or similarity
         (1) Manner, translated **in the way**
             ἵνα φανερώσω αὐτὸ ὡς δεῖ με λαλῆσαι (Col. 4:4)
             that I might make it known **in the way** I must speak
         (2) ὡς . . . οὕτως, indicating similarity, translated **like**
             ἡμέρα κυρίου ὡς κλέπτης ἐν νυκτὶ οὕτως ἔρχεται
             (1 Thess. 5:2)
             the day of the Lord will **so** come **like** a thief in the night
      b. Introducing direct discourse, translated **that**, similar to ὅτι
         μάρτυς γάρ μού ἐστιν ὁ θεός . . . ὡς ἀδιαλείπτως μνείαν ὑμῶν
         ποιοῦμαι (Rom. 1:9)
         for God is my witness . . . **that** I make continuous mention of you
      c. Introducing indirect discourse, translated **how**
         καὶ αὐτοὶ ἐξηγοῦντο τὰ ἐν τῇ ὁδῷ καὶ ὡς ἐγνώσθη αὐτοῖς ἐν
         τῇ κλάσει τοῦ ἄρτου (Luke 24:35)
         and they related the things along the road and **how** he was made
         known to them by the breaking of bread
      d. As a temporal conjunction
         (1) With aorist tense, translated **when, after**
             ὡς δὲ ἐγεύσατο ὁ ἀρχιτρίκλινος τὸ ὕδωρ οἶνον γεγενημένον
             . . . φωνεῖ τὸν νυμφίον ὁ ἀρχιτρίκλινος (John 2:9)
             and **when** the master of the feast tasted the water that had
             become wine . . . the master of the feast called the bridegroom
         (2) With present tense, translated **while, as long as, as**
             ἄρα οὖν ὡς καιρὸν ἔχομεν, ἐργαζώμεθα τὸ ἀγαθὸν πρὸς
             πάντας (Gal. 6:10)
             so then, **as** we have time, let us perform good to all people
         (3) With imperfect tense, translated **while**
             καὶ ὡς ἀτενίζοντες ἦσαν εἰς τὸν οὐρανὸν πορευομένου
             αὐτοῦ (Acts 1:10)
             and **while** they were watching him go into heaven

    (4) With subjunctive mood, translated **when, as soon as**

        τὰ δὲ λοιπὰ ὡς ἂν ἔλθω διατάξομαι (1 Cor. 11:34)

        and the other things I will set in order **as soon as** I come

    (5) With superlative, translated **as quickly as possible**

        καὶ λαβόντες ἐντολὴν πρὸς τὸν Σιλᾶν καὶ τὸν Τιμόθεον ἵνα ὡς τάχιστα ἔλθωσι(ν) πρὸς αὐτὸν ἐξῄεσαν (Acts 17:15)[8]

        and when they received a command to Silas and Timothy that they should come to him **as quickly as possible**, they departed

e. With numerals indicating an approximated number, translated **about, approximately**, similar to ὡσεί.

    ὅτι θυγάτηρ μονογενὴς ἦν αὐτῷ ὡς ἐτῶν δώδεκα (Luke 8:42)

    for she was his only daughter, **about** twelve years old

f. Indicating cause or reason

    ὡς πάντα ἡμῖν τῆς θείας δυνάμεως αὐτοῦ τὰ πρὸς ζωὴν καὶ εὐσέβειαν δεδωρημένης (2 Peter 1:3)

    because his divine power has given to us all things that pertain to life and godliness

g. Indicating result, translated **so that**

    ὡς ὤμοσα ἐν τῇ ὀργῇ μου (Heb. 3:11)

    so that I swore in my anger

h. In exclamations, translated **how**

    ὡς ἀνεξεραύνητα τὰ κρίματα αὐτοῦ καὶ ἀνεξιχνίαστοι αἱ ὁδοὶ αὐτοῦ (Rom. 11:33)[9]

    how inscrutable [ἐστιν, are] his judgments and incomprehensible his ways

2. ὡσεί

    a. Similar to comparative ὡς, translated **as, like**

       καὶ ὡσεὶ περιβόλαιον ἑλίξεις αὐτούς (Heb. 1:12)

       and **like** a cloak you will roll them up

    b. With numerals and measures, translated **about, approximately**

       καὶ αὐτὸς ἀπεσπάσθη ἀπ᾽ αὐτῶν ὡσεὶ λίθου βολήν (Luke 22:41)

       and he was withdrawn from them **about** a stone's throw

3. ὥσπερ, translated **just as**

    καὶ ἔκραξε(ν) φωνῇ μεγάλῃ ὥσπερ λέων μυκᾶται (Rev. 10:3)

    and he cried out with a loud voice **just as** a lion roars

---

[8] Acts 17:15 text is from GNT, NA & WH: TR & MT omit τόν before Τιμόθεον.

[9] Rom. 11:33 text is from GNT, NA & WH: TR & MT have ἀνεξερεύνητα.

4. ὥσπερεί, translated **even as, just as, as though**

ἔσχατον δὲ πάντων **ὥσπερεί** τῷ ἐκτρώματι ὤφθη κἀμοί (1 Cor. 15:8)

and last of all he appeared to me also **as though** to one born prematurely

E. Conditional conjunctions express the "if" clause followed by a "then" clause.
  1. εἰ with the indicative
      a. The first class condition implies a logical connection between the protasis and apodosis, or a simple condition. This condition sets forth the conclusion as true, if and only if the condition is true. The truth of the condition is not found in the form of the sentence but in the context. Any tense may be used in either the protasis or the apodosis. The following classifications are determined by the context.
         (1) The condition is obviously untrue.

   εἰ δὲ **Χριστὸς οὐκ ἐγήγερται**, ματαία ἡ πίστις ὑμῶν
   (1 Cor. 15:17)

   but **if Christ has not been raised**, your faith [ἐστιν, is] vain

         (2) The condition is true, either in fact or in the conception of the speaker or writer.

   Εἰ υἱὸς εἶ τοῦ θεοῦ, εἰπὲ ἵνα οἱ λίθοι οὗτοι ἄρτοι γένωνται
   (Matt. 4:3)

   If you are God's son, command these stones to become bread

         (3) The condition is undetermined as to truth or falsity in the mind of the speaker or writer.

   εἰ δέ τις ὑμῶν **λείπεται σοφίας**, αἰτείτω παρὰ τοῦ διδόντος θεοῦ πᾶσιν ἁπλῶς (James 1:5)

   but **if anyone lacks wisdom**, let that one ask of the God who gives freely to everyone

      b. The second class condition, or contrary to fact, uses only past tenses in the apodosis, whereas the first class may use any tense. It is the apodosis that determines the second class condition, as it is always an indicative in the imperfect, aorist, or pluperfect tense, usually with ἄν. The negative of the protasis is almost always μή, and the negative of the apodosis is always οὐ or οὐδέ. It indicates a condition that in reality is not true, followed by a statement of what would have been true if the condition had been true.
         (1) The imperfect tense emphasizes the durative aspect of the past time.

   Εἰ ὁ θεὸς πατὴρ ὑμῶν **ἦν, ἠγαπᾶτε ἄν** ἐμέ (John 8:42)
   If God were your Father, **you would have loved** me

      (2) The aorist tense indicates undefined action (undefined as to
            complete or incomplete action).

            εἰ γὰρ **ἔγνωσαν, οὐκ ἄν** τὸν κύριον τῆς δόξης **ἐσταύρωσαν**
            (1 Cor. 2:8)

            for **if they knew, they would not have crucified** the Lord of glory

      (3) The pluperfect indicates completed action.

            εἰ **ᾔδει** ὁ οἰκοδεσπότης ποίᾳ φυλακῇ ὁ κλέπτης ἔρχεται,
            ἐγρηγόρησεν ἄν (Matt. 24:43)

            if the householder had known in what watch of the night the thief
            would come, **he would have watched**

    c. εἰ sometimes introduces indirect discourse, translated **whether, that**.

        εἰ ἁμαρτωλός ἐστιν οὐκ οἶδα (John 9:25)

        I do not know **whether** he is a sinner

    d. εἰ as an interrogative introduces direct or indirect questions.

        ἵνα ἡμῖν εἴπῃς εἰ σὺ εἶ ὁ Χριστὸς ὁ υἱὸς τοῦ θεοῦ (Matt. 26:63)

        that you tell us **whether** you are the Christ, the son of God

    e. εἰ may introduce an oath and thus indicate a strong negative.

        ὡς ὤμοσα ἐν τῇ ὀργῇ μου· **Εἰ εἰσελεύσονται** εἰς τὴν κατάπαυσίν
        μου (Heb. 3:11)

        as I swore in my anger, "**they shall not** enter into my rest"

2. ἐάν (formed by crasis from εἰ and ἄν), with the subjunctive, translated **if**.
    The third class condition in the protasis expresses the idea of being potential,
    contingent, uncertain, future, or undetermined. The concept of futurity is
    most prominent. Whether it is likely or unlikely to happen is determined by
    the context.

    a. A speaker or writer may express the same condition with ἐάν or εἰ.

      (1) With ἐάν and the subjunctive

            ἐὰν γὰρ **ἀγαπήσητε** τοὺς ἀγαπῶντας ὑμᾶς, τίνα μισθὸν ἔχετε;
            (Matt. 5:46)

            for **if you love** those who love you, what reward do you have?

      (2) With εἰ and the indicative

            καὶ **εἰ ἀγαπᾶτε** τοὺς ἀγαπῶντας ὑμᾶς, ποία ὑμῖν χάρις ἐστίν;
            (Luke 6:32)

            and **if you love** those who love you, what thanks is there for you?

    b. With the aorist tense

        ἐὰν μόνον ἅψωμαι τοῦ ἱματίου αὐτοῦ σωθήσομαι (Matt. 9:21)

        if only I may touch his clothing I shall be saved

c. With the present tense

ἐὰν δὲ καὶ ἀθλῇ τις, οὐ στεφανοῦται ἐὰν μὴ νομίμως ἀθλήσῃ (2 Tim. 2:5)

and **even if someone** also **competes in a game**, he is not crowned unless he competes according to the rules

d. ἐάν occasionally approaches the meaning of ὅταν, **when**.

κἀγὼ **ἐὰν** ὑψωθῶ ἐκ τῆς γῆς, πάντας ἑλκύσω πρὸς ἐμαυτόν (John 12:32)

and **when** I am lifted up from the earth, I will draw all people to myself

3. ἐάνπερ, translated **if indeed, if only**

καὶ τοῦτο ποιήσομεν, **ἐάνπερ** ἐπιτρέπῃ ὁ θεός (Heb. 6:3)

and we will do this **if indeed** God permits

F. Concessive conjunctions indicate a concession or grant that a certain thing is true.

1. With the indicative, εἰ καί, translated **even if, even though, although**

εἰ γὰρ **καὶ** τῇ σαρκὶ ἄπειμι, ἀλλὰ τῷ πνεύματι σὺν ὑμῖν εἰμι (Col. 2:5)

for **even if** I am absent in the flesh, yet I am with you in the spirit

2. With the subjunctive

a. κἄν, formed by crasis from καὶ ἐάν

(1) Translated **even if, even though**

ἀλλὰ **κἄν** τῷ ὄρει τούτῳ εἴπητε, Ἄρθητι καὶ βλήθητι εἰς τὴν θάλασσαν, (Matt. 21:21)

but **even if** you say to this mountain, be taken up and cast into the sea

(2) κἄν may also function as a conditional conjunction, translated **and if**.

κἄν ἁμαρτίας ᾖ πεποιηκώς, ἀφεθήσεται αὐτῷ (James 5:15)

and if he has committed sins, they shall be forgiven to him

b. ἐὰν καί or καὶ ἐάν, translated **even if, although**

(1) ἐὰν καί

ἐὰν καὶ προλημφθῇ ἄνθρωπος ἔν τινι παρατώματα ὑμεῖς οἱ πνευματικοὶ καταρτίζετε τὸν τοιοῦτον (Gal. 6:1)[10]

even if a person should be overtaken in some transgression, you who are spiritual, restore such a person

---

[10] Gal. 6:1 text is from GNT, NA & WH: TR & MT have προλημφθῇ.

(2) καὶ ἐάν
    καὶ ἐὰν κρίνω δὲ ἐγώ, ἡ κρίσις ἡ ἐμὴ ἀληθινή ἐστιν
    (John 8:16)[11]
    but **although I judge**, my judgment is true

G. Temporal conjunctions indicate a time frame within which something takes
    place.
    1. With the indicative
        a. ὅτε
            (1) With the imperfect, translated **while, as long as**
                καὶ γὰρ **ὅτε** ἦμεν πρὸς ὑμᾶς, τοῦτο παρηγγέλλομεν ὑμῖν
                (2 Thess. 3:10)
                for even **while** we were with you, we charged this to you
            (2) With the aorist, translated **when**
                νῦν γὰρ ἐγγύτερον ἡμῶν ἡ σωτηρία ἢ **ὅτε** ἐπιστεύσαμεν
                (Rom. 13:11)
                for now our salvation is nearer than **when** we believed
        b. ἕως
            (1) With the present indicative, translated **while, as long as**
                ἡμᾶς δεῖ ἐργάζεσθαι τὰ ἔργα τοῦ πέμψαντός με **ἕως** ἡμέρα
                ἐστίν (John 9:4)
                we must work the works of the one who sent me **as long as** it is
                day
            (2) With the aorist indicative, translated **until**
                καὶ οὐκ ἔγνωσαν **ἕως** ἦλθεν ὁ κατακλυσμὸς καὶ ἦρεν ἅπαντας
                (Matt. 24:39)
                and they did not know **until** the flood came and took them all
                away
        c. ὅταν is rarely used with the indicative and sometimes when ὅτε is
            normally expected.
            καὶ **ὅταν** ὀψὲ ἐγένετο, ἐξεπορεύοντο ἔξω τῆς πόλεως (Mark 11:19)
            and **when** evening came, they went out of the city
    2. With the subjunctive
        a. ἕως
            (1) With the aorist tense, translated **while**
                καθίσατε ὧδε **ἕως** προσεύξωμαι (Mark 14:32)
                sit here **while** I pray

---

[11] John 8:16 text is from GNT, NA & WH: TR & MT have ἀληθής.

    (2) With the aorist tense, translated **until**
       καὶ πορεύεται ἐπὶ τὸ ἀπολωλὸς ἕως εὕρῃ αὐτό (Luke 15:4)
       and he goes after the lost one **until** he finds it
  b. ὅταν
    (1) With the present tense, translated **whenever, as often as**
       χαίρομεν γὰρ **ὅταν** ἡμεῖς ἀσθενῶμεν, ὑμεῖς δὲ δυνατοὶ ἦτε
       (2 Cor. 13:9)
       for we rejoice **whenever** we are weak, but you are strong
    (2) With the aorist tense, translated **when**
       ὅταν δὲ ἔλθῃ ὁ υἱὸς τοῦ ἀνθρώπου ἐν τῇ δόξῃ αὐτοῦ
       (Matt. 25:31)
       but **when** the son of man shall come in his glory

H. Relative clauses may be introduced by ἐάν with the relative pronoun.
   αἴτησόν με ὃ ἐὰν θέλῃς καὶ δώσω σοι (Mark 6:22)
   ask me **whatever you want**, and I will give [it] to you

J. Local clauses with ὅπου ἐάν, translated **wherever**
   ἀκολουθήσω σοι ὅπου ἐὰν ἀπέρχῃ (Luke 9:57)
   I will follow you **wherever you go**

Select Bibliography for Conjunctions

Baima, John K. "Making Valid Conclusions from Greek Conditional Sentences."
    Master's thesis. Grace Theological Seminary, 1986.
Bird, C. H. "Some γάρ Clauses in St. Mark's Gospel." *Journal of Theological Studies*, n.s.
    4 (1953): 171-87.
Boyer, James L. "Third and Fourth Class Conditions." *Grace Theological Journal* 3, no.
    2 (1982): 163-75.
_____. "First Class Conditions: What Do They Mean?" *Grace Theological Journal*
    3, no. 1 (1981): 75-114.
_____. "Second Class Conditions in New Testament Greek." *Grace Theological*
    Journal 3, no. 1 (1982): 81-88.
_____. "Other Conditional Elements in New Testament Greek." *Grace*
    Theological Journal 4, no. 2 (1983): 173-88.
Cadoux, C. J. "The Imperatival Use of ἵνα in the New Testament." *Journal of*
    Theological Studies 42 (1941): 165-73.
Curry, W. B. "The Nature and Use of the ἵνα Clause in the New Testament." Doctoral
    diss., Southwestern Baptist Seminary, 1949.

Deer, D. S. "More about the Imperatival ἵνα." *Bible Translator* 24, no. 3 (1973): 328-29.

Denniston, J. D. *The Greek Particles.* 2d ed. Oxford: Clarendon, 1959.

Edwards, Richard A. "Narrative Implications of *Gar* in Matthew." *Catholic Biblical Quarterly* 52 (1990): 636-55.

Elliott, Wm. E. "Conditional Sentences in the New Testament." Th.D. diss., Grace Theological Seminary, May 1981.

George, A.R. "The Imperatival Use of ἵνα in the New Testament." *Journal of Theological Studies* 45 (1944): 56-60.

Gibbs, Duncan G. "The Third Class Condition in New Testament Usage." Th.M. thesis, Dallas Theological Seminary, 1979.

Greenlee, J.H. "ἵνα Substantive Clauses in the New Testament." *Asbury Seminarian* 2 (1947): 154-63.

_____. "'If' in the New Testament." *Bible Translator* 13, no. 1 (1962): 39-43.

Hoopert, Daniel A. "The Greek Conjunction ΚΑΙ Used with a Personal Pronoun. *OPTAT* 3, no. 2: 83-89.

Kujne, John H. "Greek Conditional Sentences." *Bible Translator* 13 (October 1962): 223-224.

Larsen, Iver. "Notes on the Function of γάρ, οὖν, μέν, δέ, καί, and τε in the Greek New Testament." *Notes on Translation* 5, no. 1: 35-47.

Ledgerwood III, L.W. "What Does the Greek First Class Conditional Imply? Grecean Methodology and the Testimony of the Ancient Greek Grammarians." *Grace Theological Journal* 12.1 (1992): 99-118.

Levinson, Stephen H. "Four Narrative Connectives in the Book of Acts." *Notes on Translation* (January 1979): 1-20.

Mantey, Julius R. "The Meaning of οὖν in John's Writings." Doctoral diss., Southern Baptist Theological Seminary, 1921.

_____. "Newly Discovered Meanings for οὖν." *Expositor 8th series*, no. 22 (1921): 205-14.

Marshall, A. "A Note on τε . . . καί." *Bible Translator* 5 (1954):182-83.

Meecham, H. G. "The Imperatival Use of ἵνα in the New Testament." *Journal of Theological Studies* 43 (1942): 179-80.

Morrice, W. G. "The Imperatival ἵνα." *Bible Translator* 23, no. 3 (1972): 326-30.

Muraoka, Takamitsy. "Purpose or Result? ΩΣΤΕ in Biblical Greek." *Novum Testamentum* 15 (July 1973): 205-19.

_____. "The Use of ΩΣ in the Greek Bible." *Novum Testamentum* 7 (1964): 51-72.

Poythress, Vern S. "The Use of the Intersentence Conjunctions ΔΕ, ΟΥΝ, ΚΑΙ, and Asyndeton in the Gospel of John." *Novum Testamentum* 26, no. 4 (1984): 312-40.

Pritchett, W. Kendrick. "The Conditional Sentence in Attic Greek." *American Journal of Philology* 76, no. 1 (1955): 1-17.

Roberts, J.W. "Some Aspects of Conditional Sentences in the Greek New Testament. *Bible Translator* 15, no. 2 (1964): 70-76.

Robertson, A. T. "The Causal Use of ἵνα." *Studies in Early Christianity*, edited by Shirley Jackson Case. New York: Century, 1928.

Robson, Edward Alfred. "KAI-Configuration in the Greek New Testament." Ph.D. diss., Syracuse University, 1979.

Thrall, Margaret. *Greek Particles in the New Testament*. Grand Rapids, Mich.: Eerdmans, 1962.

Titrud, Kermit. "The Abused KAI." M.A. thesis, Trinity Evangelical Divinity School, 1986.

_____. "The Overlooked KAI in the Greek New Testament." *Notes on Translation*, vol. 5, no. 1 (1991): 1-28.

Tune, Cecil L. "The Use of Conditional Sentences in Hebrews." Master's thesis, Dallas Theological Seminary, 1973.

Waters, Dan Riley. "Conditional Sentences in Romans." Master's thesis, Dallas Theological Seminary, 1976.

Young, Richard A. "A Classification of Conditional Sentences Based on Speech Act Theory." *Grace Theological Journal* 10, no. 1 (1989): 29-49.

NEGATIVES

Negatives are adjectives, adverbs, conjunctions, and particles that negate (deny, nullify) the sentence or some element within the sentence.

Forms.
I. Generally speaking, the negatives related to οὐ (οὐκ, οὐχ, οὐδαμῶς, οὐδέ, οὐδείς, οὐδέποτε, οὐδέπω, οὐκέτι, οὔτε, οὔπω, or οὐχί) are primarily used with the indicative mood.

II. The negatives related to μή (e.g., μηδέ, μηδείς, μηδέποτε, μηδέπω, μηκέτι, μήποτε, μήπω, μήτε, μήτι, or μήτιγε) are primarily used with the imperative, subjunctive and optative moods, as well as with the participle and infinitive.

Functions.
I. **οὐ** and other related negatives

  A. οὐ (οὐκ before a vowel or diphthong having a smooth breathing mark; οὐχ before a word with an initial vowel or diphthong having a rough breathing mark).

    1. οὐ is used with all indicative tenses to negate the verb.

      a. With present tense
        οὐκ εἰσὶν ἐκ τοῦ κόσμου καθὼς **ἐγὼ οὐκ εἰμὶ** ἐκ τοῦ κόσμου
        (John 17:14)
        they are not of the world even as **I am not** of the world

      b. With aorist tense
        ὁ υἱὸς τοῦ ἀνθρώπου **οὐκ ἦλθεν** διακονηθῆναι ἀλλὰ διακονῆσαι
        (Matt. 20:28)
        the son of man **did not come** to be served but to serve

      c. With perfect tense
        οὐκ ἐλήλυθα καλέσαι δικαίους ἀλλὰ ἁμαρτωλοὺς εἰς μετάνοιαν
        (Luke 5:32)
        I did not come to call righteous people but sinners to repentance

      d. With future tense
        (1) A negative command, prohibitive future
           ὁ δὲ Ἰησοῦς εἶπεν, τὸ **οὐ φονεύσεις, οὐ μοιχεύσεις, οὐ κλέψεις, οὐ ψευδομαρτυρήσεις** (Matt. 19:18)
           and Jesus said, **you shall not commit murder, you shall not commit adultery, you shall not steal, you shall not bear false witness**
        (2) As future prescriptive, indirect prohibition
           ἁμαρτία γὰρ ὑμῶν **οὐ κυριεύσει** (Rom. 6:14)
           for **sin shall not rule** over you

97

    (3) Negating a future event
        νὺξ γὰρ **οὐκ ἔσται** ἐκεῖ (Rev. 21:25)
        for night **shall not be** there

  e. With imperfect tense
      καὶ ἴσαι αἱ μαρτυρίαι **οὐκ ἦσαν** (Mark 14:56)
      and **the testimonies were not** in agreement

  f. With pluperfect tense
      καὶ **οὐκ ᾔδει** ὅτι ἀληθές ἐστιν τὸ γινόμενον διὰ τοῦ ἀγγέλου
      (Acts 12:9)
      and **he did not know** that the thing happening by means of the angel
      was true

  g. οὐκ with ἄν, potential indicative
      εἰ γὰρ ἔγνωσαν, **οὐκ ἂν** τὸν κύριον τῆς δόξης **ἐσταύρωσαν**
      (1 Cor. 2:8)
      for if they had known, **they would not have crucified** the Lord of glory

2. οὐ sometimes functions as an interrogative with the expectation or
    anticipation of an affirmative answer. This occurs in all tenses.

  a. With present indicative
      οὐ μνημονεύετε ὅτι ἔτι ὢν πρὸς ὑμᾶς ταῦτα ἔλεγον ὑμῖν;
      (2 Thess. 2:5)
      do you not remember that while I was yet with you I told you these
      things? (Yes!)

  b. With aorist indicative
      οὐ τῷ αὐτῷ πνεύματι **περιεπατήσαμεν**; (2 Cor. 12:18)
      did we not walk in the same spirit? (Yes!)

  c. With perfect indicative
      οὐ γέγραπται ὅτι ὁ οἶκός μου οἶκος προσευχῆς κληθήσεται πᾶσιν
      τοῖς ἔθνεσιν; (Mark 11:17)
      has it not been written that my house shall be called a house of prayer
      for all nations? (Yes!)

  d. With imperfect indicative
      οὐκ ἔδει λυθῆναι ἀπὸ τοῦ δεσμοῦ τούτου τῇ ἡμέρᾳ τοῦ σαββάτου;
      (Luke 13:16)
      ought she not to be set free from this bond on the Sabbath day? (Yes!)

  e. With future indicative
      οὐκ ἐροῦσιν ὅτι μαίνεσθε; (1 Cor. 14:23)
      will they not say that you are mad? (Yes!)

      f. With pluperfect indicative

         οὐκ ᾔδειτε ὅτι ἐν τοῖς τοῦ πατρός μου δεῖ εἶναί με; (Luke 2:49)

         did you not know that I must be among the things belonging to my Father? (Yes!)

  3. οὐ sometimes negates other parts of speech, such as adjectives, adverbs, conjunctions, prepositions, substantives, and participles. It normally precedes the word it modifies.

      a. With adjectives

         οὐ γὰρ ἄδικος ὁ θεὸς ἐπιλαθέσθαι τοῦ ἔργου ὑμῶν (Heb. 6:10)

         for God [ἐστιν, is] **not unrighteous** to forget your work

      b. With adverbs

         ὑμεῖς δὲ οὐχ οὕτως ἐμάθετε τὸν Χριστόν (Eph. 4:20)

         not in this way did you learn Christ

      c. With conjunctions

         οὐχ ὅτι ἐπιζητῶ τὸ δόμα (Phil. 4:17)

         not that I desire a gift

      d. With prepositions

         οὐκ εἰς κενὸν ἔδραμον οὐδὲ εἰς κενὸν ἐκοπίασα (Phil. 2:16)

         I ran **not in vain**, neither did I labor in vain

      e. With substantives

         καὶ ἡ πόλις οὐ χρείαν ἔχει τοῦ ἡλίου (Rev. 21:23)

         and the city has **no need** of the sun

      f. Occasionally with a participle, indicating emphasis

         οἱ οὐκ ἠλεημένοι, νῦν δὲ ἐλεηθέντες (1 Peter 2:10)

         who **had not received mercy**, but now have received mercy

  4. οὔ with accent means **no!**

    ἤτω δὲ ὑμῶν τὸ ναί ναί καὶ τὸ οὒ οὔ (James 5:12)

    but let your yes be yes, and [ἤτω, let] your **no** [be] **no!**

B. οὐχί is a strengthened form of οὐ.

  1. It is most often used as an interrogative in questions expecting an affirmative answer.

    τὸν ἄρτον ὃν κλῶμεν, οὐχὶ κοινωνία τοῦ σώματος τοῦ Χριστοῦ ἐστιν; (1 Cor. 10:16)

    the bread that we break, **is it not** the fellowship of the body of Christ? (Yes!)

2. οὐχί, as emphatic, means **not at all, by no means**.
   καὶ ἀποκριθεῖσα ἡ μήτηρ αὐτοῦ εἶπεν, **Οὐχί**, ἀλλὰ κληθήσεται
   Ἰωάννης (Luke 1:60)[1]
   and his mother answered, **by no means**, but he shall be named John
3. οὐχί sometimes means **not**
   καὶ ὑμεῖς καθαροί ἐστε, ἀλλ᾽ **οὐχὶ πάντες** (John 13:10)
   and you yourselves are clean, but **not all**

C. The combined negatives, οὐ μή, are emphatic and are found only with the
   future indicative and the aorist subjunctive.
   1. With future indicative
      καὶ **οὐ μὴ ἐξαλείψω** τὸ ὄνομα αὐτοῦ ἐκ τῆς βίβλου τῆς ζωῆς (Rev. 3:5)
      and **I will by no means blot out** his name from the book of life
   2. With aorist subjunctive
      καὶ ὁ πιστεύων ἐπ᾽ αὐτῷ **οὐ μὴ καταισχυνθῇ** (1 Peter 2:6)
      and the one who believes in him **shall not at all be ashamed**

D. The adjectives οὐδείς, οὐδεμία, οὐδέν mean **no**; as a substantive, they mean
   no one, nothing; as an emphatic adverb, they mean **in no respect, in no way**.
   1. As attributive adjective
      οὐδεὶς οἰκέτης δύναται δυσὶ κύριοις δουλεύειν (Luke 16:13)
      no slave is able to serve two owners
   2. As substantive adjective
      καὶ τὸν ἁγιασμόν, οὗ χωρὶς **οὐδεὶς** ὄψεται τὸν κύριον (Heb. 12:14)
      and sanctification, without which **no one** will see the Lord
   3. As emphatic adjective functioning as an adverb
      ὁ θεὸς φῶς ἐστιν καὶ σκοτία ἐν αὐτῷ οὐκ ἔστιν **οὐδεμία** (1 John 1:5)
      God is light and darkness is not in him **at all**

E. Conjunctions, οὐδέ and οὔτε.
   1. οὐδέ, a negative conjunction, usually follows another negative word
      and thus joins negative clauses.
      a. Used primarily with the indicative mood
         (1) With present tense
             ἐμβλέψατε εἰς τὰ πετεινὰ τοῦ οὐρανοῦ, ὅτι οὐ σπείρουσιν
             οὐδὲ θερίζουσιν οὐδὲ συνάγουσιν εἰς ἀπόθηκας (Matt. 6:26)
             consider the birds of the sky, for they do not sow, **neither
             do they reap, neither do they gather** into granaries

---

[1] Luke 1:60 text is from GNT, NA, TR & MT: WH has Ἰωάνης.

(2) With aorist tense

ὃς ἁμαρτίαν οὐκ ἐποίησεν **οὐδὲ εὑρέθη δόλος** ἐν τῷ στόματι αὐτοῦ (1 Peter 2:22)

who did not commit sin, **neither was deceit found** in his mouth

(3) Occasionally οὐδέ negates an infinitive (normally negated by μή) to indicate emphasis

ὁ μόνος ἔχων ἀθανασίαν φῶς οἰκῶν ἀπρόσιτον, ὃν εἶδεν οὐδεὶς ἀνθρώπων **οὐδὲ ἰδεῖν** δύναται (1 Tim. 6:16)

the only one having immortality inhabiting unapproachable light, whom no man has seen **nor** can **see**

(4) With future tense

οὐ πεινάσουσιν ἔτι **οὐδὲ διψήσουσιν** ἔτι (Rev. 7:16)

they shall not hunger any longer, **neither shall they thirst** any longer

b. Used sometimes to negate substantives

πᾶς ὁ ἀρνούμενος τὸν υἱόν, **οὐδὲ τὸν πατέρα** ἔχει (1 John 2:23)

everyone who denies the son, **neither** has **the Father**

c. Used occasionally to negate prepositional phrases

Παῦλος ἀπόστολος, οὐκ ἀπ᾽ ἀνθρώπων, **οὐδὲ δι᾽ ἀνθρώπου** (Gal. 1:1)

Paul an apostle, not from men, **nor by a man**

d. Used in questions expecting an affirmative answer

οὐδὲ φοβῇ σὺ τὸν θεόν, ὅτι ἐν τῷ αὐτῷ κρίματι εἶ; (Luke 23:40)

do you not fear God, since you are in the same condemnation? (Yes!)

2. οὔτε is often exchanged with οὐδέ in the Greek manuscripts and is thus considered here as a conjunction rather than as an adverb.

a. οὔτε is primarily found with another οὔτε in the same clause.

ἐν γὰρ Χριστῷ Ἰησοῦ **οὔτε περιτομή** τι ἰσχύει **οὔτε ἀκροβυστία** (Gal. 5:6)

for in Christ Jesus **neither circumcision nor uncircumcision** has any significance

b. οὔτε, like οὐδέ, is sometimes preceded by another negative.

οὐκ ἀφεθήσεται αὐτῷ **οὔτε** ἐν τούτῳ τῷ αἰῶνι **οὔτε** ἐν τῷ μέλλοντι (Matt. 12:32)

it will not be forgiven him, **neither** in this age **nor** in the coming one

F. Negative adverbs

1. οὐδαμῶς is an emphatic negative adverb.

καὶ σὺ Βηθλεέμ, γῆ Ἰούδα, **οὐδαμῶς** ἐλαχίστη εἶ ἐν τοῖς ἡγεμόσιν Ἰούδα (Matt. 2:6)

and you Bethlehem, land of Judah, **by no means** are you least among the rulers of Judah

2. οὐδέπω is a temporal adverb meaning **not yet, ever.**
   οὐδέπω γὰρ ᾔδεισαν τὴν γραφήν, ὅτι δεῖ αὐτὸν ἐκ νεκρῶν ἀναστῆναι
   (John 20:9)
   for they did **not yet** know the Scripture, that he must rise from the dead
3. οὐδέποτε is a temporal adverb meaning **never, not ever.**
   a. In a statement
      καὶ τὰς αὐτὰς πολλάκις προσφέρων θυσίας, αἵτινες **οὐδέποτε**
      δύνανται περιελεῖν ἁμαρτίας (Heb. 10:11)
      and offering the same sacrifices often, which are **never** able to take
      away sins
   b. As an interrogative adverb in questions expecting an affirmative answer
      οὐδέποτε ἀνέγνωτε ὅτι ἐκ στόματος νηπίων καὶ θηλαζόντων
      κατηρτίσω αἶνον; (Matt. 21:16)
      did you **never** read, "out of the mouth of infants and sucklings you
      prepared praise"?
4. οὐκέτι is a temporal adverb meaning **no more, no longer.**
   a. In a statement
      ὅπου δὲ ἄφεσις τούτων, **οὐκέτι** προσφορὰ περὶ ἁμαρτίας (Heb. 10:18)
      but where forgiveness of these things [ἐστιν, exists], an offering for sin
      no longer [ἐστιν, exists]
   b. With other negatives, emphatic
      ὁ δὲ Ἰησοῦς **οὐκέτι οὐδὲν ἀπεκρίθη** (Mark 15:5)
      but Jesus **no longer answered anything**
5. οὔπω is a temporal adverb meaning **not yet.**
   a. In a statement
      καὶ **οὔπω** ἐφανερώθη τί ἐσόμεθα (1 John 3:2)
      and it has **not yet** appeared what we shall be
   b. In questions expecting an affirmative answer
      οὔπω νοεῖτε, οὐδὲ μνημονεύετε τοὺς πέντε ἄρτους τῶν
      πεντακισχιλίων καὶ πόσους κοφίνους ἐλάβετε; (Matt. 16:9)
      do you not yet understand, neither remember the five loaves of the five
      thousand, and how many baskets did you take [up]?

II. **μή and other related negatives.**

A. μή is the basic or foundational particle from which all the forms of the related negatives originate.
   1. μή with the indicative
      a. μή is sometimes used as an interrogative when a negative answer is expected.
         (1) With the future tense
             μὴ λίθον ἐπιδώσεις αὐτῷ; (Matt. 7:9)
             will he give him a stone? (No!)
         (2) With the present tense
             μὴ δύνανται οἱ υἱοὶ τοῦ νυμφῶνος ἐν ᾧ ὁ νυμγίος μετ᾽ αὐτῶν ἐστιν νηστεύειν; (Mark 2:19)
             the sons of the bridegroom are **not able** to fast while the bridegroom is with them (are they)?
         (3) With the aorist tense
             μὴ Παῦλος ἐσταυρώθη ὑπὲρ ὑμῶν; (1 Cor. 1:13)
             was Paul **crucified** for you? (No!)
         (4) With an elliptical verb
             μὴ ἄδικος ὁ θεὸς ὁ ἐπιφέρων τὴν ὀργήν; (Rom. 3:5)
             [ἐστιν, is] God, who inflicts wrath, **unjust**? (No!)
         (5) With the perfect tense
             μὴ καὶ ὑμεῖς πεπλάνησθε; (John 7:47)
             have you also **been deceived**? (No!)
      b. With οὐ(κ), μή is the interrogative and οὐ(κ) negates the clause, causing an expected affirmative answer.
         μὴ οὐκ ἔχομεν ἐξουσίαν φαγεῖν καὶ πεῖν; (1 Cor. 9:4)
         do not we have a right to eat and drink? (Yes!)
      c. μή with the conditional εἰ (εἰ μή), meaning **if not, except**
         ὑπὲρ δὲ ἐμαυτοῦ οὐ καυχήσομαι εἰ μὴ ἐν ταῖς ἀσθενείαις (2 Cor. 12:5)
         but for myself I will not boast **except** in my weakness
   2. μή with the imperative. The prohibitive μή is found primarily in the present tense, with a few instances in the aorist tense.
      a. With the present tense, prohibiting an action or state of being of a general nature
         (1) Prohibiting an action
             μὴ μεριμνᾶτε τῇ ψυχῇ ὑμῶν τί φάγητε (Matt. 6:25)
             do not be anxious for your life [as to] what you shall eat

(2) Prohibiting a state of being

μὴ γίνεσθε φρόνιμοι παρ᾽ ἑαυτοῖς (Rom. 12:16)

do not become wise with yourselves [in your own estimation]

b. Present tense to prohibit the continuation of an action

μὴ ποιεῖτε τὸν οἶκον τοῦ πατρός μου οἶκον ἐμπορίου (John 2:16)

stop making my Father's house a house of business

c. When the aorist is used for the prohibitive, the aorist subjunctive is used all but eight times in the NT.

καὶ ὁ ἐν τῷ ἀγρῷ ὁμοίως μὴ ἐπιστρεψάτω εἰς τὰ ὀπίσω (Luke 17:31)

and **let** the one [ὤν, who is] in the field in the same manner **not turn back** to the things [ὤν, that are] behind

3. μή with the perfect indicative is an exception to the rule.

ὁ δὲ μὴ πιστεύων ἤδη κέκριται, ὅτι μὴ πεπίστευκεν εἰς τὸ ὄνομα τοῦ μονογενοῦς υἱοῦ τοῦ θεοῦ (John 3:18)

but the one who does not believe is already judged, because **he has not believed** in the name of the only son of God

4. μή with the optative, indicating a strong emphatic wish or prayer

ἁμαρτήσωμεν, ὅτι οὐκ ἐσμὲν ὑπὸ νόμον ἀλλὰ ὑπὸ χάριν; μὴ γένοιτο (Rom. 6:15)

shall we sin because we are not under law but under grace? **may it not be!**

5. μή with the subjunctive

a. The aorist prohibits an action from beginning.

(1) 3 pers. indirect prohibition

μή τις ὑμᾶς ἐξαπατήσῃ κατὰ μηδένα τρόπον (2 Thess. 2:3)

let no one deceive you in any way

(2) 2 pers. direct prohibition—this is similar to the future indicative with οὐ.

ὁ γὰρ εἰπών, Μὴ μοιχεύσῃς, εἶπε(ν) καί, Μὴ φονεύσῃς (James 2:11)

for the one who said, **"Do not commit adultery,"** said also, **"Do not commit murder"**

b. With the present tense

(1) After verbs of fear or warning

(a) With βλέπω, indicating a warning

βλέπετε μή τις ὑμᾶς πλανήσῃ (Mark 13:5)

beware, lest anyone deceive you

(b) With φοβέομαι, expressing fear

φοβοῦμαι γὰρ μή πως ἐλθὼν οὐχ οἵους θέλω εὕρω ὑμᾶς (2 Cor. 12:20)

for **I fear lest** when I come I will find you not as I wish

(2) Negative hortatory exhortation

    (a) 1 pers. pl. aor. tense

        μὴ σχίσωμεν αὐτόν (John 19:24)

        let us not divide it

    (b) 1 pers pl. pres. tense

        ἄρα οὖν **μὴ καθεύδωμεν** ὡς οἱ λοιποί ἀλλὰ γρηγορῶμεν

        καὶ νήφωμεν (1 Thess. 5:6)[2]

        so then **let us not sleep** as the rest, but let us watch and

        be sober

c. μή with conjunctions

    (1) With ἵνα

        (a) Indicating negative purpose

            οἱ πατέρες, μὴ ἐρεθίζετε τὰ τέκνα ὑμῶν, ἵνα μὴ ἀθυμῶσιν

            (Col. 3:21)

            parents, do not irritate your children, **lest they should be**

            discouraged

        (b) Indicating negative result

            οὗτοι ἔχουσι(ν) τὴν ἐξουσίαν κλεῖσαι τὸν οὐρανόν,

            ἵνα μὴ ὑετὸς βρέχῃ τὰς ἡμέρας τῆς προφητείας αὐτῶν

            (Rev. 11:6)[3]

            these have authority to shut up heaven **so that rain does not**

            fall during the days of their prophecy

        (c) Indicating a substantive clause

            [1] Functioning as a direct object of indirect discourse

                παρακαλῶ δὲ ὑμᾶς, ἀδελφοί, διὰ τοῦ ὀνόματος τοῦ

                κυρίου ἡμῶν Ἰησοῦ Χριστοῦ, **ἵνα** τὸ αὐτὸ λέγητε

                πάντες καὶ **μὴ ᾖ** ἐν ὑμῖν σχίσματα (1 Cor. 1:10)

                now I exhort you, brothers, through the name of our Lord

                Jesus Christ, **that** you all say the same thing and **[that]**

                there should be no schisms among you

            [2] ἵνα μή may introduce a clause in apposition to a pronoun.

                τοῦτο δέ ἐστι(ν) τὸ θέλημα τοῦ πέμψαντός με, **ἵνα** πᾶν

                ὃ δέδωκέ(ν) μοι **μὴ ἀπολέσω** (John 6:39)[4]

                and **this** is the will of the one who sent me, **that** everything

                he gave me **will not perish**

---

[2] 1 Thess. 5:6 text is from GNT, NA & WH: TR & MT have ὡς καί.

[3] Rev. 11:6 text is from GNT, NA & WH: TR has βρέχῃ ὑετὸς ἐν ἡμέρας αὐτῶν τῆς προφητείας; MT has τὸν οὐρανὸν ἐξουσίαν κλεῖσαι.

[4] John 6:39 text is from GNT, NA & WH: TR & MT have τοῦ πέμψαντός με πατρός.

[3] ἵνα μή may introduce a substantive clause functioning as the subject of an impersonal passive verb.

καὶ ἐδόθη αὐτοῖς **ἵνα μὴ ἀποκτείνωσιν** αὐτούς (Rev. 9:5)

and it was given to them **that they should not kill** them

  (2) With ὅπως, indicating negative purpose

      (a) With aorist tense

ὅπως μὴ καυχήσηται πᾶσα σὰρξ ἐνώπιον τοῦ θεοῦ (1 Cor. 1:29)[5]

in order that no flesh should boast before God

      (b) With present tense

ὅπως οἱ θέλοντες διαβῆναι ἔνθεν πρὸς ὑμᾶς **μὴ δύνωνται, μηδὲ** ἐκεῖθεν πρὸς ἡμᾶς **διαπερῶσιν** (Luke 16:26)[6]

so that those who want to cross over from her to you **are unable, neither can they cross over** from there to us

  (3) With ἐάν or ἄν

      (a) Third class negative conditional

ἀγαπητοί, **ἐὰν** ἡ καρδία ἡμῶν **μὴ καταγινώσκῃ,** παρρησίαν ἔχομεν πρὸς τὸν θεὸν (1 John 3:21)[7]

dear friends, **if our heart does not condemn** us, we have confidence with God

      (b) ἐὰν μή as an exceptive clause

ἐὰν γὰρ **μὴ ἀπέλθω,** ὁ παράκλητος οὐκ ἐλεύσεται πρὸς ὑμᾶς (John 16:7)

for **unless I depart,** the paraclete will not come to you

    d. ἄν μή with a relative pronoun

καὶ **ὃς ἂν μὴ ἔχῃ,** καὶ ὃ δοκεῖ ἔχειν ἀρθήσεται ἀπ᾽ αὐτοῦ (Luke 8:18)

and **whoever does not have,** even what he seems to have shall be taken away from him

  6. μή with the infinitive

    a. With an infinitive of indirect discourse

ἵνα παραγγείλῃς τισὶν **μὴ ἑτεροδιδασκαλεῖν** (1 Tim. 1:3)

that you might charge some **not to teach other doctrines**

    b. With an articular infinitive expressing negative purpose

καὶ κατεῖχον αὐτὸν **τοῦ μὴ πορεύεσθαι** ἀπ᾽ αὐτῶν (Luke 4:42)

and they detained him **so that he would not depart** from them

---

[5]   1 Cor. 1:29 text is from GNT, NA & WH: TR & MT have αὐτοῦ for τοῦ θεοῦ.

[6]   Luke 16:26 text is from GNT, NA, WH & MT: TR has ἐντεῦθεν and οἱ ἐκεῖθεν respectively for ἔνθεν and ἐκεῖθεν.

[7]   1 John 3:21 text is from GNT & NA: WH omits ἡμῶν: TR & MT have ἡμῶν μὴ καταγινώσκῃ ἡμῶν.

    c. With causal preposition διὰ τό
       καὶ διὰ τὸ μὴ ἔχειν ῥίζαν ἐξηράνθη (Mark 4:6)
       and **because it did not have** root it was withered
    d. With **ὥστε** as a negative result clause
       καθὼς τὸ μαρτύριον τοῦ Χριστοῦ ἐβεβαιώθη ἐν ὑμῖν, **ὥστε ὑμᾶς μὴ**
       ὑστερεῖσθαι ἐν μηδενὶ χαρίσματι (1 Cor. 1:6-7)
       even as the testimony of Christ was confirmed in you **so that you are**
       behind in no gift.
    e. As negated complement of a verb
       Ἔδει μέν, ὦ ἄνδρες, πειθαρχήσαντάς μοι **μὴ ἀνάγεσθαι** ἀπὸ τῆς
       Κρήτης (Acts 27:21)
       men, **you should** have obeyed me and **not to have set sail** from Crete
  7. **μή** with the participle. Most of these are found in the present tense.
    a. With a present participle
       ὁ **μὴ ὢν** μετ᾽ ἐμοῦ κατ᾽ ἐμοῦ ἐστι(ν), καὶ ὁ **μὴ συνάγων** μετ᾽ ἐμοῦ
       σκορπίζει (Matt. 12:30)
       the one who is not with me is against me, and **the one who does not**
       gather with me scatters
    b. With an aorist participle
       κατὰ πίστιν ἀπέθανον οὗτοι πάντες, **μὴ λαβόντες** τὰς ἐπαγγελίας
       (Heb. 11:13)
       these all died in faith, **not having received** the promises
    c. With a perfect participle
       πῶς οὗτος γράμματα οἶδε(ν) **μὴ μεμαθηκώς**; (John 7:15)
       how does this person know letters **without having learned**?

B. **μηδείς, μηδεμία, μηδέν**, adjectives
  1. As attributive adjective
    μή τις ὑμᾶς ἐξαπατήσῃ **κατὰ μηδένα τρόπον** (2 Thess. 2:3)
    let no one deceive you **by any means**
  2. As substantive
    a. Nom. sing. masc. (as subject of verb)
       μηδείς σου τῆς νεότητος **καταφρονείτω** (1 Tim. 4:12)
       let no one despise your youth
    b. Gen. sing. neut. (as noun complement)
       ἵνα περιπατῆτε εὐσχημόνως πρὸς τοὺς ἔξω καὶ **μηδενὸς χρείαν**
       ἔχητε (1 Thess. 4:12)
       that you may walk decently toward those outside, and [that] you may
       have **need of nothing**

    c. Dat sing. neut. (as object of preposition)

       ἵνα **ἐν μηδενὶ** ζημιωθῆτε ἐξ ἡμῶν (2 Cor. 7:9)

       that **in nothing** you may suffer loss by us

    d. Acc. sing. neut. (as object of preposition)

       πᾶν τὸ παρατιθέμενον ὑμῖν ἐσθίετε **μηδὲν ἀνακρίνοντες** διὰ τὴν συνείδησιν (1 Cor. 10:27)

       eat everything that is set before you, **asking nothing** because of conscience

    e. With the conjunction ἵνα

       (1) Appositional to pronoun, imperatival

          τοῦτο λέγω, **ἵνα μηδεὶς** ὑμᾶς **παραλογίζηται** ἐν πιθανολογίᾳ (Col. 2:4)

          I say this, **let no one deceive** you by persuasive words

       (2) Substantive clause (as direct object of indirect discourse)

          καὶ ἐπετίμησεν αὐτοῖς **ἵνα μηδενὶ λέγωσιν** περὶ αὐτοῦ (Mark 8:30)

          and he ordered them **that they should tell no one** about him

  3. As adverbial

    ἀκούομεν γάρ τινας περιπατοῦντας ἐν ὑμῖν ἀτάκτως **μηδὲν ἐργαζομένους** (2 Thess. 3:11)

    for we hear [that] some are walking [in a] disorderly [way] among you, **working not at all**

C. Negative adverbs

  1. μήποτε, negative purpose

    a. With present subjunctive

       ἐν τῇ ὁδῷ δὸς ἐργασίαν ἀπηλλάχθαι ἀπ᾽ αὐτοῦ, **μήποτε κατασύρῃ** σε πρὸς τὸν κριτήν (Luke 12:58)

       along the way give diligence to be set free from him, **lest he should drag** you to the judge

    b. With aorist subjunctive

       καὶ ἀπολῦσαι αὐτοὺς νήστεις οὐ θέλω, **μήποτε ἐκλυθῶσιν** ἐν τῇ ὁδῷ (Matt. 15:32)

       and I do not want to send them away hungry, **lest they become weary** on the road

  2. μηδαμῶς, adverb of manner

    ὁ δὲ Πέτρος εἶπεν, **Μηδαμῶς**, κύριε, ὅτι οὐδέποτε ἔφαγον πᾶν κοινόν (Acts 10:14)

    but Peter said, **by no means**, Lord, for I never ate anything common

3. μηδέποτε, temporal adverb

πάντοτε μανθάνοντα καὶ **μηδέποτε** εἰς ἐπίγνωσιν ἀληθείας ἐλθεῖν δυνάμενα (2 Tim. 3:7)

always learning and **never** able to come to the knowledge of truth

4. μηδέπω, temporal adverb

πίστει χρηματισθεὶς Νῶε περὶ τῶν **μηδέπω** βλεπομένων, εὐλαβηθεὶς κατεσκεύασεν κιβωτὸν εἰς σωτηρίαν τοῦ οἴκου αὐτοῦ (Heb. 11:7)

by faith after Noah was divinely instructed concerning the things **not yet** seen, being moved by fear, he prepared an ark for the salvation of his household

5. μηκέτι, temporal adverb

a. Introducing a negative hortatory exhortation, prohibiting continuation of action

μηκέτι οὖν ἀλλήλους **κρίνωμεν** (Rom. 14:13)

let us then **no longer repeatedly criticize** one another

b. With ἵνα, indicating negative purpose

ἵνα **μηκέτι** ὦμεν νήπιοι (Eph. 4:14)

in order that we should no longer be infants

c. Introducing a prohibition

ἔξελθε ἐξ αὐτοῦ καὶ **μηκέτι εἰσέλθῃς** εἰς αὐτόν (Mark 9:25)

come out of him, and **you shall no longer enter** into him

D. Negative conjunctions

1. μηδέ, with subjunctive

a. Negative hortatory exhortation

μηδὲ πορνεύωμεν, καθώς τινες αὐτῶν ἐπόρνευσαν (1 Cor. 10:8)

neither let us commit sexual promiscuity, even as some of them were promiscuous

b. Prohibitive aorist subjunctive after another negative

μὴ ἅψῃ **μηδὲ** γεύσῃ **μηδὲ** θίγῃς (Col. 2:21)

do not touch, **neither shall you taste, nor shall you handle**

2. μήτε, prohibitive aorist subjunctive preceded by another negative

ἐγὼ δὲ λέγω ὑμῖν μὴ ὀμόσαι ὅλως· **μήτε** ἐν τῷ οὐρανῷ, ὅτι θρόνος ἐστὶν τοῦ θεοῦ **μήτε** ἐν τῇ γῇ, ὅτι ὑποπόδιόν ἐστιν τῶν ποδῶν αὐτοῦ (Matt. 5:34-35)

but I tell you not to swear at all, **neither** by heaven, because it is the throne of God, **nor** by the earth, because it is the footstool of his feet

Select Bibliography for Negatives

Fernando, Andrew P. "Translation of Questions and Prohibitions in Greek." *Bible Translator* 27, no. 1 (January 1976): 138-42.

Jung, Min-Young. "The Position of Adverbs in Biblical Greek." Master's thesis, Univ. of Texas at Arlington, 1985.

Marshall, Alfred. "οὐ and μή in Questions." *Bible Translator* 4 (1953): 41-42

Moorhouse, Alfred Charles. *Studies in the Greek Negatives.* Cardiff: Univ. of Wales, 1959.

NOUNS AND CASES

Forms. A noun indicates a person, place, thing, event, idea, or emotion. Nouns may be common or proper, indicating a specific person or place. This distinction is also found in current editions of the Greek New Testament. Proper nouns are capitalized, whereas common nouns are not.

I. **Proper nouns or names** are either declinable (with inflected case endings) or indeclinable (only one form is used for all cases).

    A. Some declinable names follow the normal pattern of Greek noun declension (e.g., Χριστός, Χριστοῦ, Χριστῷ, Χριστόν, Χριστέ), but others have a unique pattern (e.g., Ἰησοῦς, Ἰησοῦ, Ἰησοῦ, Ἰησοῦν, Ἰησοῦ).

    B. Indeclinable names are often a transliteration (with or without some modification) of a name from a language other than Greek, whether Hebrew, Latin, Aramaic, or some other language. Thus, we have Ἰωσήφ, Ἀβραάμ, Βηθλεέμ, Ἰσραήλ, Ἰσαάκ, with only one form functioning for all cases. Sometimes the case is made evident by the use of an article, e.g., ὁ Ἰωσήφ, τοῦ Ἀβραάμ, τῷ Ἰσραήλ, τὸν Ἰσαάκ.

II. **Common nouns** generally are declinable; that is, they have inflected case endings.

    A. There are three declensions in Greek: first, second, and third declensions. The second declension is usually considered first in most grammars because most nouns are found in that declension. However, the numerical order will be followed here.

      1. First declension nouns follow five basic patterns. Most are feminine, some are masculine, none are neuter.

        a. When the stem ends in ε, ι, or ρ, the nominative singular or lexical form will end in long α, which will be retained throughout the declension, except for the genitive plural, which has the ω and the circumflex accent, a characteristic of all first declension nouns.

	sing.	pl.	meaning
nom.	ἁμαρτία	ἁμαρτίαι	**sin**
gen.	ἁμαρτίας	ἁμαρτιῶν	
dat.	ἁμαρτίᾳ	ἁμαρτίαις	
acc.	ἁμαρτίαν	ἁμαρτίας	

Notice that the gen. sing. and the acc. pl. have the same inflected form. The context and/or the article will determine its proper use.

111

b. An exception to the above class is found in a few words, of which
ἀλήθεια is the most prominent and frequent in the NT. The α following
ι is short in the nom. and acc. sing.; elsewhere the α is long.

	sing.	pl.	meaning
nom.	ἀλήθεια	(The form is not	**truth**
gen.	ἀληθείας	found in the pl.)	
dat.	ἀληθείᾳ		
acc.	ἀλήθειαν		

c. When the stem ends in σ, λλ, ζ, ξ, or ψ, the nominative singular ends
in short α, followed by the gen. and dat. forms, which have an η. The
acc. sing. utilizes the α, as do the plural forms, except for the gen.
pl.

nom.	γλῶσσα	γλῶσσαι	**tongue**
gen.	γλώσσης	γλωσσῶν	
dat.	γλώσσῃ	γλώσσαις	
acc.	γλῶσσαν	γλώσσας	

d. When the stem ends in any other letter, the nom. sing. ends with η,
which is then used throughout the singular.

nom.	γραφή	γραφαί	**writing**
gen.	γραφῆς	γραφῶν	
dat.	γραφῇ	γραφαῖς	
acc.	γραφήν	γραφάς	

e. Most masculine forms of the first declension have the nom. sing. ending
with ης, as follows:

nom.	προφήτης	προφῆται	**prophet**
gen.	προφήτου	προφητῶν	
dat.	προφήτῃ	προφήταις	
acc.	προφήτην	προφήτας	

2. Second declension nouns are primarily masculine nouns, along with a good
number of neuter nouns, but only a few feminine nouns.

a. Masculine nouns are found the most frequently.

nom.	ἄγγελος	ἄγγελοι	**messenger**
gen.	ἀγγέλου	ἀγγέλων	
dat.	ἀγγέλῳ	ἀγγέλοις	
acc.	ἄγγελον	ἀγγέλους	

b. Neuter nouns are formed like the masculine nouns except for the nom. and acc. forms. Note that the nom. and acc. forms of each number are identical.

	sing.	pl.	meaning
nom.	ἔργον	ἔργα	**work, deed**
gen.	ἔργου	ἔργων	
dat.	ἔργῳ	ἔργοις	
acc.	ἔργον	ἔργα	

c. Feminine nouns of this declension are rare and are declined exactly like the masculine nouns. Second declension feminine nouns are identifiable by the article ἡ.

nom.	ὁδός	ὁδοί	**way, road**
gen.	ὁδοῦ	ὁδῶν	
dat.	ὁδῷ	ὁδοῖς	
acc.	ὁδόν	ὁδούς	

3. The third declension (also called the consonant declension) contains nouns of all three genders and has five major classifications.

a. Liquid noun stems end in λ, μ, ν, or ρ. The dative plural has the movable ν. The following example is masculine.

nom.	(αἰών)	αἰῶνες	**age**
gen.	αἰῶνος	αἰώνων	
dat.	αἰῶνι	αἰῶσι(ν)	
acc.	αἰῶνα	αἰῶνας	

b. Mute noun stems have three variations, called palatal (or guttural), labial (using the lips), and dental (or lingual). The following three examples are feminine.

(1) The palatal stem ends in κ, γ, or χ. In the dative plural, the stem consonant is joined with σι and produces ξ.

nom.	γυνή	γυναῖκες	**woman, wife**
gen.	γυναικός	γυναικῶν	
dat.	γυναικί	γυναιξίν	
acc.	γυναῖκα	γυναῖκας	
voc.	γύναι		

(2) The labial stem ends in π, β, or φ.

nom.	ἐλπίς	(not found in	**hope**
gen.	ἐλπίδος	the pl.)	
dat.	ἐλπίδι		
acc.	ἐλπίδα		

(3) The dental stem ends in τ, δ, or θ. If it is joined with σι in the dat.
     pl. form, σι is left intact and the consonant ending is dropped.

	sing.	pl.	meaning
nom.	χάρις	(χάριτες)	**grace**
gen.	χάριτος	(χαρίτων)	
dat.	χάριτι	(χάρισιν)	
acc.	χάριν	χάριτας	

c. Syncopated nouns (so called because of the shifting of the regular
   accent) have various inflections.

(1)			
nom.	πατήρ	πατέρες	**father**
gen.	πατρός	πατέρων	
dat.	πατρί	πατράσι(ν)	
acc.	πατέρα	πατέρας	
voc.	πατέρ	πατέρες	

(2)			
nom.	ἀνήρ	ἄνδρες	**man, husband**
gen.	ἀνδρός	ἀνδρῶν	
dat.	ἀνδρί	ἀνδράσιν	
acc.	ἄνδρα	ἄνδραν	
voc.	ἄνερ	ἄνδρες	

(3)			
nom.	μήτηρ	(μητέρες)	**mother**
gen.	μητρός	(μητέρων)	
dat.	μητρί	(μητράσιν)	
acc.	μητέρα	μητέρας	
voc.	(μήτερ)	(μητέρες)	

(4)			
nom.	θυγάτηρ	θυγατέρες	**daughter**
gen.	θυγατρός	θυγατέρων	
dat.	θυγατρί	θυγατράσιν	
acc.	θυγατέρα	θυγατέρας	
voc.	θύγατερ	(θυγατέρες)	

d. Vowel stem nouns

   (1) masculine

nom.	βασιλεύς	βασιλεῖς	**king**
gen.	βασιλέως	βασιλέων	
dat.	βασιλεῖ	βασιλεῦσι(ν)	
acc.	βασιλέα	βασιλεῖς	
voc.	βασιλεῦ	(βασιλεῖς)	

	sing.	pl.	meaning
(2) feminine			
nom.	πόλις	πόλεις	**city**
gen.	πόλεως	πόλεων	
dat.	πόλει	πόλεσιν	
acc.	πόλιν	πόλεις	

e. Neuter nouns

(1) ες stem nouns

nom.	ἔθνος	ἔθνη	**nation, Gentile**
gen.	ἔθνους	ἐθνῶν	
dat.	ἔθνει	ἔθνεσι(ν)	
acc.	ἔθνος	ἔθνη	

(2) ατ stem nouns

nom.	αἷμα	αἵματα	**blood**
gen.	αἵματος	αἱμάτων	
dat.	αἵματι	(αἵμασιν)	
acc.	αἷμα	(αἵματα)	

B. Greek nouns display three qualities apart from declension: gender, number, and case.

1. Gender refers to masculine, feminine, and neuter and may be either biological or grammatical. Generally the significance of gender is grammatical rather than biological. However, often in family relationships, a term is both grammatical and biological when the context so indicates.

    a. Masc. and fem., **mother** and **father**

    τίμα τὸν πατέρα σου καὶ τὴν μητέρα (Eph. 6:2)

    honor **your father** and **your mother**

    b. Masc. and fem., **father, sons**, and **daughters**

    καὶ ἔσομαι ὑμῖν εἰς πατέρα καὶ ὑμεῖς ἔσεσθέ μοι εἰς υἱοὺς καὶ θυγατέρας (2 Cor. 6:18)

    and I shall be **your father** and you shall be **my sons** and **daughters**

    c. Masc. and fem., **brother, sister**, and **mother**

    αὐτός μου ἀδελφὸς καὶ ἀδελφὴ καὶ μήτηρ ἐστίν (Matt. 12:50)

    he is my **brother** and **sister** and **mother**

2. Number distinguishes between the singular (one person or thing) and plural (two or more persons or things). Concord is a term used to indicate agreement or grammatical harmony between various elements in a sentence, such as a subject and its verb. In other words, a singular subject normally has a singular verb, and a plural subject normally has a plural verb. However, there are several exceptions to this rule of concord.

a. It is a Greek idiom that the neuter plural substantive most often takes a singular verb, but not always.

   (1) Plural verb

   καὶ **ἐπαναστήσονται** τέκνα ἐπὶ γονεῖς καὶ θανατώσουσιν αὐτούς (Mark 13:12)

   and **children shall rise up** against parents, and they shall kill them.

   (2) Singular verb

   ἐν τούτῳ φανερά **ἐστι(ν)** τὰ **τέκνα** τοῦ θεοῦ καὶ τὰ τέκνα τοῦ διαβόλου (1 John 3:10)

   in this **the children** of God **are** manifest and the children of the devil

b. Collective nouns may have the verb in the singular or plural. Thus, they are translated according to sense rather than rigid rules of grammar.

   (1) Singular verb

   ἠκολούθει δὲ αὐτῷ **ὄχλος πολύς** (John 6:2)[1]

   and **a large crowd was following** him

   (2) Plural verb

   καὶ **πᾶς ὁ ὄχλος ἐζήτουν** ἅπτεσθαι αὐτοῦ (Luke 6:19)

   and **all the people were seeking** to touch him

   (3) Both singular and plural verbs used in the same sentence.

   ἀλλὰ ὁ **ὄχλος** οὗτος ὁ μὴ **γινώσκων** τὸν νόμον **ἐπάρατοί εἰσι(ν)** (John 7:49)[2]

   but **this people who do not know** the law **are** accursed

c. Something belonging to each person in a group may be singular in form and is called a distributive singular.

   (1) Nom. sing. neut.

   ἢ οὐκ οἴδατε ὅτι **τὸ σῶμα ὑμῶν** ναὸς τοῦ ἐν ὑμῖν ἁγίου πνεύματός ἐστιν (1 Cor. 6:19)

   or do you not know that **your body** is the temple of the Holy Spirit who [ὄντος, is] in you

   (2) Dat. sing. fem.

   εἰ δὲ ζῆλον πικρὸν ἔχετε καὶ ἐριθείαν ἐν **τῇ καρδίᾳ ὑμῶν** (James 3:14)

   but if you have bitter jealousy and selfish ambition **in your hearts**

---

[1] John 6:2 text is from GNT, NA & WH: TR & MT have καὶ ἠκολούθει.

[2] John 7:49 text is from GNT, NA & WH: TR & MT have ἀλλ' and ἐπικατάρατοί.

d. The generalizing plural consists of a plural actually referring to a
   singular subject.
   (1) τελευτήσαντος δὲ τοῦ Ἡρῴδου . . . τεθνήκασι(ν) γὰρ οἱ
       ζητοῦντες τὴν ψυχὴν τοῦ παιδίου (Matt. 2:19-20)
       now **when Herod was dead** . . . for **they who were seeking** the
       life of the child **are dead**
   (2) ἐγένετο τότε τὰ ἐγκαίνια ἐν τοῖς Ἱεροσολύμοις (John 10:22)
       then **the festival of rededication was** in Jerusalem
e. The epistolary plural is used by a writer referring to himself.
   (1) δι' οὗ ἐλάβομεν χάριν καὶ ἀποστολὴν εἰς ὑπακοὴν πίστεως
       ἐν πᾶσι(ν) τοῖς ἔθνεσιν ὑπὲρ τοῦ ὀνόματος αὐτοῦ (Rom. 1:5)
       through whom **we received** grace and apostleship for the
       obedience of faith among all the Gentiles for His name
   (2) προσεύχεσθε **περὶ ἡμῶν** . . . **παρακαλῶ** δὲ ὑμᾶς, ἀδελφοί,
       ἀνέχεσθε τοῦ λόγου τῆς παρακλήσεως (Heb. 13:18, 22)
       pray **for us** . . . but **I exhort** you, brothers, willingly listen to the
       word of encouragement
f. Coordinate singular nouns or a combination of one or more singular
   nouns plus one or more plural nouns connected by the conjunction
   καί are sometimes found with a singular verb and sometimes with
   a plural verb. Most often if the verb precedes the subjects, it will
   agree in person and number with the first subject. If the verb
   follows two or more subjects, it will be in the plural. Some
   variations of this follow.
   (1) Singular verb
       (a) Preceding nouns
           καὶ ἐξῆλθεν ὁ Ἰησοῦς καὶ οἱ μαθηταὶ αὐτοῦ εἰς τὰς
           κώμας Καισαρείας τῆς Φιλίππου (Mark 8:27)
           and **Jesus and** his **disciples went out** into the villages of
           Caesarea of Philip
       (b) Following nouns
           ὅτε δὲ ἡ χρηστότης καὶ ἡ φιλανθρωπία ἐπεφάνη τοῦ
           σωτῆρος ἡμῶν θεοῦ (Titus 3:4)
           but when **the kindness and philanthropy** of God our savior
           appeared
   (2) Plural verb
       (a) Following nouns
           ὁ οὐρανὸς καὶ ἡ γῆ παρελεύσονται (Mark 13:31)
           heaven and earth shall pass away

(b) Preceding nouns

ἐπέστησαν αὐτοῖς οἱ ἱερεῖς καὶ ὁ στρατηγὸς τοῦ ἱεροῦ
καὶ οἱ Σαδδουκαῖοι (Acts 4:1)
the priests and the captain of the temple **and the
Sadducees came** to them

Functions. The significance of the cases of substantives will receive prominence here
under nouns, although adjectives, adverbs, articles, pronouns, infinitives, and
participles also function as substantives. As noted earlier, the five case system will
be followed rather than the eight case system. Ablatives will be considered under
genitives. Locatives and instrumentals will be considered under datives. The
nominative, accusative, and vocative cases remain the same in both systems.

I. **The Nominative Case.** This is the naming case, pointing out the subject, predicate
noun, appositional noun, or person addressed.

A. The nominative case most often indicates the subject of the verb.
   1. A noun is unique in that it can only be the subject of a third person singular
      or plural verb. The first and second person singular and plural verbs always
      have an implied or explicit personal pronoun as their subject. The third
      person verbs may have an implied personal pronoun or an explicit pronoun
      (personal, relative, demonstrative, indefinite, or interrogative), as well as a
      noun, as their subject. The nouns with the third person verb will be
      illustrated in sections to follow.
      a. 1 pers. sing. verb with implicit pronoun, ἐγώ
         λέγει αὐτοῖς, **Σπλαγνίζομαι** ἐπὶ τὸν ὄχλον (Mark 8:1-2)
         he said to them, "**I have compassion** on the people"
      b. 1 pers. sing. verb with explicit pronoun, ἐγώ
         καὶ ἰδού **ἐγὼ** μεθ' ὑμῶν **εἰμι** πάσας τὰς ἡμέρας ἕως τῆς συντελείας
         τοῦ αἰῶνος (Matt. 28:20)
         and behold, **I am** with you all the days until the completion of the age
      c. 2 pers. sing. verb with implicit pronoun, σύ
         πεποιθὼς τῇ ὑπακοῇ σου ἔγραψά σοι, εἰδὼς ὅτι καὶ ὑπὲρ ἃ λέγω
         ποιήσεις (Philem. 21)
         I wrote to you because I have confidence in your obedience, knowing
         that **you will do** even beyond what I say
      d. 2 pers. sing. verb with explicit pronoun, σύ
         Σὺ εἶ ὁ βασιλεὺς τῶν Ἰουδαίων; (Mark 15:2)
         are you the king of the Jews?

e. 3 pers. sing. verb with implicit pronoun, αὐτός

Ἰδοὺ ἡ σκηνὴ τοῦ θεοῦ μετὰ τῶν ἀνθρώπων, καὶ **σκηνώσει** μετ᾽ αὐτῶν (Rev. 21:3)

behold, the tabernacle of God [ἐστιν, is] with men, and **he will dwell** with them

f. 3 pers. sing. verb with explicit pronoun, αὐτός

αὐτὸς γάρ **ἐστιν** ἡ εἰρήνη ἡμῶν (Eph. 2:14)

for **he is** our peace

g. 1 pers. pl. verb with implicit pronoun, ἡμεῖς

εἰ δὲ **ἀπεθάνομεν** σὺν Χριστῷ, **πιστεύομεν** ὅτι καὶ **συζήσομεν** αὐτῷ (Rom. 6:8)

but if **we died** with Christ, **we believe** that **we shall** also **live** with him

h. 1 pers. pl. verb with explicit pronoun, ἡμεῖς

Ἡμεῖς δὲ **ὀφείλομεν** εὐχαριστεῖν τῷ θεῷ πάντοτε περὶ ὑμῶν (2 Thess. 2:13)

but **we ought** to thank God always for you

i. 2 pers. pl. verb with implicit pronoun, ὑμεῖς

αἰτεῖτε καὶ δοθήσεται ὑμῖν, **ζητεῖτε** καὶ **εὑρήσετε** (Luke 11:9)

ask and it shall be given to you, **seek** and **you shall find**

j. 2 pers. pl. verb with explicit pronoun, ὑμεῖς

ὑμεῖς δὲ οὐχ οὕτως **ἐμάθετε** τὸν Χριστόν (Eph. 4:20)

but **you did** not in this way **learn** Christ

k. 3 pers. pl. verb with implicit pronoun, αὐτοί

καὶ **ἥξουσιν** ἀπὸ ἀνατολῶν καὶ δυσμῶν καὶ ἀπὸ βορρᾶ καὶ νότου καὶ **ἀνακλιθήσονται** ἐν τῇ βασιλείᾳ τοῦ θεοῦ (Luke 13:29)

and **they will come** from east and west and from north and south, and **they will recline [at a banquet]** in the kingdom of God

l. 3 pers. pl. verb with explicit pronoun, αὐτοί

καὶ **αὐτοὶ ἐνίκησαν** αὐτὸν διὰ τὸ αἷμα τοῦ ἀρνίου (Rev. 12:11)

and **they conquered** him because of the blood of the lamb

2. An anarthrous noun often is the subject of the 3 pers. finite verb.

a. Nom. sing. masc.

εἰ γὰρ πιστεύομεν ὅτι **Ἰησοῦς ἀπέθανεν** καὶ **ἀνέστη** (1 Thess. 4:14)

for if we believe that **Jesus died** and **rose again**

b. Nom. sing. fem.

γυνὴ δὲ ἐὰν **κομᾷ**, δόξα αὐτῇ ἐστιν (1 Cor. 11:15)

but if **a woman has long hair**, it is her glory

c. Nom. sing. neut.

καὶ **ἐξῆλθεν αἷμα** ἐκ τῆς ληνοῦ (Rev. 14:20)

and **blood came out** of the winepress

    d. Nom. pl. masc.

       ἐν ταύταις δὲ ταῖς ἡμέραις **κατῆλθον** ἀπὸ Ἰεροσολύμων **προφῆται**
       εἰς Ἀντιόχειαν (Acts 11:27)

       and in these days **prophets came down** from Jerusalem to Antioch

3. An articular noun most often is the subject of a 3 pers. finite verb.

    a. Nom. sing. masc.

       ὅτε δὲ ἦλθεν τὸ πλήρωμα τοῦ χρόνου, **ἐξαπέστειλεν ὁ θεὸς** τὸν υἱὸν
       αὐτοῦ (Gal. 4:4)

       but when the fullness of time came, **God sent forth** his son

    b. Nom. sing. fem.

       ἐν τούτῳ **τετελείωται ἡ ἀγάπη** μεθ᾽ ἡμῶν (1 John 4:17)

       in this, **love has been perfected** with us

    c. Nom. sing. neut.

       τὸ πνεῦμά ἐστιν τὸ ζῳοποιοῦν, **ἡ σὰρξ** οὐκ **ὠφελεῖ** οὐδέν (John 6:63)

       the spirit is the one who gives life, **the flesh profits** nothing

    d. Nom. pl. masc.

       τότε **συνῆκαν οἱ μαθηταὶ** ὅτι περὶ Ἰωάννου τοῦ βαπτιστοῦ εἶπεν
       αὐτοῖς (Matt. 17:13)[3]

       then **the disciples understood** that he spoke to them concerning John
       the Baptist

4. A noun phrase often functions as a subject of a 3 pers. finite verb. The
   noun may be modified by a genitive noun or pronoun or an attributive
   adjective.

    a. Nom. sing. masc.

       ἔφη αὐτῷ **ὁ κύριος** αὐτοῦ, Εὖ δοῦλε ἀγαθὲ καὶ πιστέ (Matt. 25:23)

       his lord said to him, Well [done]! good and faithful servant

    b. Nom. sing. fem.

       ἤγγικεν ἡ βασιλεία τοῦ θεοῦ· μετανοεῖτε, καὶ πιστεύετε ἐν τῷ
       εὐαγγελίῳ (Mark 1:15)

       the kingdom of God has come near; repent and believe in the gospel

    c. Nom. sing. neut.

       πάτερ ἡμῶν ὁ ἐν τοῖς οὐρανοῖς, **ἁγιασθήτω τὸ ὄνομά σου** (Matt. 6:9)

       our Father who [ὤν, is] in heaven, **let your name be sanctified**

    d. Nom. pl. fem.

       ὡς **ἐπλήσθησαν αἱ ἡμέραι** τῆς λειτουργίας αὐτοῦ ἀπῆλθεν, εἰς τὸν
       οἶκον αὐτοῦ (Luke 1:23)

       when **the days of his service were fulfilled**, he went away to his home

---

[3] Matt. 17:13 text is from GNT, NA, TR & MT: WH has Ἰωάνου.

e. Nom. sing. masc. with attributive adj.

ὁ ποιμὴν ὁ καλὸς τὴν ψυχὴν αὐτοῦ **τίθησιν** ὑπὲρ τῶν προβάτων
(John 10:11)

the good shepherd lays down his life for the sheep

5. The nominative noun or phrase frequently functions as the subject of a 3 pers. elliptical verb.

a. Nom. sing. masc.

τέλος γὰρ νόμου **Χριστὸς** εἰς δικαιοσύνην παντὶ τῷ πιστεύοντι
(Rom. 10:4)

for **Christ [ἐστιν, is]** the end of the law for righteousness to everyone who believes

b. Nom. sing. fem.

εἰ δὲ Χριστὸς οὐκ ἐγήγερται, ματαία **ἡ πίστις ὑμῶν** (1 Cor. 15:17)

but if Christ is not risen, **your faith [ἐστιν, is]** vain

c. Nom. sing. neut.

εἰ **ὅλον τὸ σῶμα** ὀφθαλμός, ποῦ ἡ ἀκοή; (1 Cor. 12:17)

if **the whole body [ἐστιν, is]** an eye, where [ἐστιν, is] the hearing?

d. Nom. pl. masc.

μακάριοι **οἱ ὀφθαλμοὶ οἱ βλέποντες** ἃ βλέπετε (Luke 10:23)

the eyes that see what you see [εἰσιν, are] blessed

6. The nominative may function as the subject of a participle or of both a participle and a 3 pers. finite verb.

a. Nom. sing. masc.

καὶ **ὀργισθεὶς ὁ κύριος** αὐτοῦ **παρέδωκεν** αὐτὸν τοῖς βασανισταῖς
(Matt. 18:34)

and **because he was angry his lord delivered** him to the tormentors

b. Nom. sing. fem.

προϊδοῦσα δὲ **ἡ γραφὴ** ὅτι ἐκ πίστεως δικαιοῖ τὰ ἔθνη ὁ θεός, **προευηγγελίσατο** τῷ Ἀβραάμ (Gal. 3:8)

and **because the scripture foresaw** that God justifies the nations by faith, **it proclaimed the gospel before** to Abraham

c. Nom. pl. neut.

καὶ **ἐξελθόντα τὰ πνεύματα τὰ ἀκάθαρτα εἰσῆλθον** εἰς τοὺς χοίρους
(Mark 5:13)

and **when the unclean spirits came out they entered** the swine

d. Nom. pl. masc.

ἰδόντες δὲ **οἱ ἀρχιερεῖς** . . . τὰ θαυμάσια ἃ ἐποίησεν
(Matt. 21:15)

but when **the chief priests** . . . **saw** the wonders which he performed

B. The nominative noun or noun phrase often functions as a predicate nominative (the complement of an equative, or linking, verb, or a verb of being, or a passive verb).

1. Of the equative verb εἰμι and its various finite forms

   a. Nom. sing. masc.

   ὁ υἱός μου ὁ ἀγαπητός οὗτός ἐστιν (2 Peter 1:17)[4]

   this **is my beloved son**

   b. Nom. sing. fem.

   πᾶν δὲ ὃ οὐκ ἐκ πίστεως ἁμαρτία ἐστίν (Rom. 14:23)

   and everything that [ἐστιν, is] not of faith **is sin**

   c. Nom. sing. neut.

   ἦν δὲ σάββατον ἐν ἐκείνῃ τῇ ἡμέρᾳ (John 5:9)

   now **it was the sabbath** on that day

   d. Nom. sing. masc.

   ἐγώ εἰμι ὁ ἄρτος ὁ ζῶν ὁ ἐκ τοῦ οὐρανοῦ καταβάς (John 6:51)

   I am the living bread that came down from heaven

2. Of an elliptical verb (εἰμι)

   a. Nom. sing. masc.

   τὰ γὰρ ὀψώνια τῆς ἁμαρτίας θάνατος (Rom. 6:23)

   for the wages of sin [ἐστιν, is] **death**

   b. Nom. sing. fem.

   οὐ πᾶσα σὰρξ ἡ αὐτὴ σάρξ (1 Cor. 15:39b)

   not all flesh [ἐστιν, is] **the same flesh**

   c. Nom. sing. neut.

   καὶ ἡ γλῶσσα πῦρ (James 3:6)

   and the tongue [ἐστιν, is] **a fire**

   d. Nom. sing. neut.

   πνεῦμα ὁ θεός (John 4:24)

   God [ἐστιν, is] **spirit**

3. Of the participle of εἰμι or ὑπάρχω

   a. Nom. sing. fem.

   ἀνὴρ μὲν γὰρ οὐκ ὀφείλει κατακαλύπτεσθαι τὴν κεφαλήν, εἰκὼν καὶ δόξα θεοῦ ὑπάρχων (1 Cor. 11:7)

   for man ought not to have his head covered, **since he is the image** and **glory** of God

---

[4] 1 Peter 1:17 text is from GNT, NA & WH: TR & MT have οὗτός ἐστιν ὁ υἱός μου ὁ ἀγαπητός.

b. Nom. pl. masc.

ἐλευθερίαν αὐτοῖς ἐπαγγελλόμενοι, αὐτοὶ **δοῦλοι ὑπάρχοντες** τῆς φθορᾶς (2 Peter 2:19)

while they promise them freedom, they **are servants** of corruption

c. Nom. sing. masc.

οὐδὲν διαφέρει δούλου, **κύριος** πάντων **ὤν** (Gal. 4:1)

he differs nothing from a servant, **even though he is owner** of all

d. Nom. pl. masc.

Ἰούδας τε καὶ Σίλας, καὶ αὐτοὶ **προφῆται ὄντες** (Acts 15:32)

both Judas and Silas, who also **were prophets**

4. Of the infinitive εἶναι

a. Nom. sing. masc.

εἴ τις δοκεῖ **προφήτης εἶναι** ἢ πνευματικός (1 Cor. 14:37)

if anyone thinks **to be a prophet** or spiritual

b. Nom. pl. masc.

καὶ γὰρ ὀφείλοντες **εἶναι διδάσκαλοι** διὰ τὸν χρόνον (Heb. 5:12)

for indeed you ought **to be teachers** because of the time

5. Of the verb γίνομαι

a. Nom. pl. masc.

πιστεύετε εἰς τὸ φῶς, ἵνα **υἱοὶ** φωτὸς **γένησθε** (John 12:36)

believe in the light **so that you may become sons** of light

b. Nom. sing. masc.

ἵνα **ἐλεήμων γένηται** καὶ **πιστὸς ἀρχιερεὺς** τὰ πρὸς τὸν θεόν (Heb. 2:17)

that **he should be a merciful** and **faithful high priest** in things pertaining to God

c. Nom. sing. fem.

εἰ δὲ χάριτι, οὐκέτι ἐξ ἔργων, ἐπεὶ ἡ χάρις οὐκέτι **γίνεται χάρις** (Rom. 11:6)

but if [ἐστιν, it is] by grace, [ἐστιν, it is] no longer of works; otherwise grace no longer **is grace**

6. Of a passive finite verb

a. Nom. sing. masc.

γέγραπται, ὁ οἶκός μου **οἶκος** προσευχῆς **κληθήσεται** (Matt. 21:13)

it is written, my house **shall be called a house** of prayer

b. Nom. sing. fem.

οὕτως καὶ ἡ καύχησις ἡμῶν ἡ ἐπὶ Τίτου **ἀλήθεια ἐγενήθη** (2 Cor. 7:14)

thus also our boasting, which [οὖσα, was] to Titus, **became truth**

   c. Nom. pl. masc.

    ἐκεῖ **κληθήσονται υἱοὶ** θεοῦ ζῶντος (Rom. 9:26)

    there **they shall be called sons** of the living God

  7. Of a passive participle

    Nom. sing. masc.

    οἶδα ὅτι Μεσσίας ἔρχεται, **ὁ λεγόμενος Χριστός** (John 4:25)

    I know that Messiah is coming, **who is called Christ**

  8. Of a passive infinitive

    Nom. sing. masc.

    οὐκ εἰμὶ ἱκανὸς **καλεῖσθαι ἀπόστολος** (1 Cor. 15:9)

    I am not worthy **to be called an apostle**

  9. Of a verbal adjective

    Nom. sing. masc.

    Παῦλος **κλητὸς ἀπόστολος** Χριστοῦ Ἰησοῦ διὰ θελήματος θεοῦ

    (1 Cor. 1:1)[5]

    Paul **called an apostle** of Christ Jesus by the will of God

 10. Of ἰδού or ἴδε[6]

    a. Nom. sing. masc.

      ἴδε **ὁ τόπος** ὅπου ἔθηκαν αὐτόν (Mark 16:6)

      here is the place where they laid him

    b. Nom. sing. fem. and nom. pl. masc.

      Ἴδε **ἡ μήτηρ μου** καὶ **οἱ ἀδελφοί μου** (Mark. 3:34)[7]

      here is my mother and **my brothers**

    c. Nom. pl. neut.

      Ἰδοὺ ἐγὼ καὶ **τὰ παιδία** ἅ μοι ἔδωκεν ὁ θεός (Heb. 2:13)

      Here I am and **the children** that God gave to me

C. Appositional nominative. The nominative noun in apposition to another
  nominative noun gives explanation, identification or further information about
  the first noun.

  1. Nom. sing. masc.

    Ἀβραὰμ **ὁ πατὴρ** ὑμῶν ἠγαλλιάσατο ἵνα ἴδῃ τὴν ἡμέραν τὴν ἐμήν

    (John 8:56)

    Abraham your **father** rejoiced to see my day

---

[5] "In the broadest sense, however, these verbals are participles, since they partake of both verb and adjective" (A. T. Robertson, A *Grammar of the Greek New Testament in the Light of Historical Research*, 1095). It would appear that κλητός functions here as a passive participle with ἀπόστολος as its predicate nominative.

[6] ἰδού is used with a noun without a finite verb, translated **here** or **there is (are)**, **here** or **there was (were)** (Arndt, Gingrich and Bauer, *A Greek-English Lexicon of the NT*, 371).

[7] ἰδού and ἴδε are often synonymous. See Matt. 12:49.

2. Nom. sing. fem.

καὶ αὕτη ἐστὶν ἡ **νίκη** ἡ νικήσασα τὸν κόσμον, **ἡ πίστις** ἡμῶν
(1 John 5:4)

and this is **the victory** that conquers the world, **our faith**

3. Nom. sing. neut.

ὁ δὲ **παράκλητος, τὸ πνεῦμα τὸ ἅγιον**, ὃ πέμψει ὁ πατὴρ ἐν τῷ ὀνόματί
μου (John 14:26)

but **the paraclete, the Holy Spirit**, whom the Father will send in my name

4. Nom. pl. masc.

καὶ προσπορεύονται αὐτῷ **Ἰάκωβος καὶ Ἰωάννης οἱ υἱοὶ** Ζεβεδαίου
(Mark 10:35)

now **James and John, the sons** of Zebedee, came to him

D. Nominative of address (used primarily with the article, the nominative may
   function the same as the vocative of address).
   1. With the article
      a. Nom. sing. masc.

         ὑμεῖς φωνεῖτέ με **ὁ διδάσκαλος** καὶ **ὁ κύριος** (John 13:13)[8]

         you call me **teacher** and **lord**

      b. Nom. pl. fem.

         αἱ γυναῖκες, ὑποτάσσεσθε τοῖς ἰδίοις ἀνδράσιν (Col. 3:18)[9]

         wives, submit yourselves to your own husbands

      c. Nom. sing. neut.

         ἔλεγεν γὰρ αὐτῷ, Ἔξελθε **τὸ πνεῦμα τὸ ἀκάθαρτον** ἐκ τοῦ
         ἀνθρώπου (Mark 5:8)

         for he said to him, **unclean spirit**, come out of the person

      d. Nom. pl. neut.

         τὰ τέκνα, ὑπακούετε τοῖς γονεῦσιν ὑμῶν (Eph. 6:1)

         children, obey your parents

      e. Nom. pl. masc.

         διὰ τοῦτο εὐφραίνεσθε, **οἱ οὐρανοὶ** καὶ οἱ ἐν αὐτοῖς σκηνοῦντες
         (Rev. 12:12)

         because of this rejoice, **you heavens** and you who dwell in them

   2. Without the article
      a. Nom. sing. fem.

         ὁ δὲ εἶπεν αὐτῇ, **θυγάτηρ**, ἡ πίστις σου σέσωκέν σε (Mark 5:34)

         and he said to her, **daughter**, your faith has saved you

---

[8] Some grammars (Dana and Mantey, Brooks and Winbery) call these nominatives in John 13:13 nominatives of appellation.

[9] Col. 3:18 text is from TR & MT: GNT, NA & WH omit ἰδίοις.

b. Nom. sing. masc.
   Ἐλέησον ἡμᾶς, **υἱὸς** Δαυίδ (Matt. 9:27)[10]
   have mercy on us, **son** of David
c. Nom. pl. fem.
   ὁ Ἰησοῦς εἶπεν, **θυγατέρες** Ἰερουσαλήμ, μὴ κλαίετε ἐπ' ἐμέ
   (Luke 23:28)
   Jesus said, **daughters** of Jerusalem, do not weep for me

E. Independent nominatives are without grammatical relationship to a complete
   sentence. This is found in various constructions.
   1. In the greetings of epistles
      a. Nom. sing. fem.
         χάρις ὑμῖν καὶ **εἰρήνη** ἀπὸ θεοῦ πατρὸς ἡμῶν (Philem. 3)
         grace to you and **peace** from God our Father
      b. Nom. sing masc.
         ὁ δὲ **θεὸς** τῆς εἰρήνης μετὰ πάντων ὑμῶν (Rom. 15:33)
         now **the God** of peace [be] with you all
      c. Nom. pl. masc.
         καὶ οἱ σὺν ἐμοὶ **πάντες ἀδελφοί**, ταῖς ἐκκλησίαις τῆς Γαλατίας
         (Gal. 1:2)
         and **all the brothers** with me, to the churches of Galatia
   2. As a hanging nominative (nominative pendens or pendent nominative),
      the nominative is introduced and then later is identified with the subject of
      a following clause or with an oblique case pronoun.
      a. Nom. sing. masc.
         ὁ **θεὸς ὁ ποιήσας** τὸν κόσμον καὶ πάντα τὰ ἐν αὐτῷ, **οὗτος** ... οὐκ
         ἐν χειροποιήτοις ναοῖς κατοικεῖ (Acts 17:24)
         God who made the world and everything in it, **this one** ... does not
         dwell in temples made by hands
      b. Nom. sing. masc.
         ἐγὼ καὶ ὁ **πατὴρ** ἕν ἐσμεν (John 10:30)
         I and **the Father, we are** one
      c. Nom. sing. neut.
         πᾶν ῥῆμα ἀργὸν, ὃ λαλήσουσιν οἱ ἄνθρωποι ἀποδώσουσιν περὶ
         αὐτοῦ λόγον ἐν ἡμέρᾳ κρίσεως (Matt. 12:36)
         every idle word that people shall speak, they shall give an account of
         it in the day of judgment

---

[10] Matt. 9:27 text is from GNT & NA: TR & MT have Δαβίδ; WH has Δαυείδ.

3. In doxologies
Nom. sing. fem.
λέγοντες, Ἀμήν, ἡ εὐλογία καὶ ἡ δόξα καὶ ἡ σοφία καὶ ἡ εὐχαριστία καὶ ἡ τιμὴ καὶ ἡ δύναμις καὶ ἡ ἰσχὺς τῷ θεῷ ἡμῶν εἰς τοὺς αἰῶνας τῶν αἰώνων (Rev. 7:12)
saying, Amen, **praise** and **glory** and **wisdom** and **gratitude** and **honor** and **power** and **strength** to our God for ever and ever

4. In the title of a book
Nom. sing. fem.
Ἀρχὴ τοῦ εὐαγγελίου Ἰησοῦ Χριστοῦ (Mark 1:1)
the beginning of the gospel of Jesus Christ

5. In exclamations
Nom. sing. neut.
Ὦ βάθος πλούτου καὶ σοφίας καὶ γνώσεως θεοῦ (Rom. 11:33)
O **the depth** of the riches and wisdom and knowledge of God

F. Adverbial nominative. This emphasizes an adverbial relationship rather than a strict nominative function.
1. Nom. sing. fem.
καὶ ἐπέταξεν αὐτοῖς ἀνακλῖναι πάντας **συμπόσια συμπόσια** ἐπὶ τῷ χλωρῷ χόρτῳ (Mark 6:39)[11]
and he ordered them to make all recline **in rows** on the green grass

2. Nom. pl. fem.
σπλαγχνίζομαι ἐπὶ τὸν ὄχλον, ὅτι ἤδη **ἡμέραι τρεῖς** προσμένουσίν μοι (Mark 8:2)[12]
I have compassion on the people, because they already have remained with me **three days**

II. **The genitive case.** The genitive case is difficult to define in a general overarching sense. It is often called the case of description and definition, but those are only two of its functions, which are more than any of the other cases. They include possession, relationship, subjective, and objective with nouns of action, direct object of certain verbs, apposition, partitive, adverbial functions of time and space, genitive absolute, complements of certain terms (nouns, adjectives, adverbs, and verbs), content, comparison, quality, predicate genitive, etc. The largest use of the genitive is with prepositions, which will be covered last. The classifications given are found otherwise in their order of frequency, from most frequent to least frequent.

---

[11] The repetition of the noun has a distributive sense.

[12] μένω sometimes functions like an equative verb, having a predicate nominative. This may be true of προσμένουσιν here.

A. Most frequent uses of the genitive.
   1. Genitive of possession indicates ownership, belonging to someone or something.
      a. The genitive points out the possessor of the object indicated by the other noun.
         (1) Gen. sing. masc.
             ἵνα ἐν τῷ ὀνόματι Ἰησοῦ πᾶν γόνυ κάμψῃ (Phil. 2:10)
             that at **the name of Jesus** every knee should bow
         (2) Gen. sing. fem.
             εὐδόκησεν ὁ θεὸς ὁ ἀφορίσας με ἐκ κοιλίας μητρός μου
             (Gal. 1:15)
             God was pleased, who set me apart from **my mother's womb**
         (3) Gen. sing. neut.
             ὃς ἐρρύσατο ἡμᾶς ἐκ τῆς ἐξουσίας τοῦ σκότους (Col. 1:13)
             who delivered us from **the power of darkness**
         (4) Gen. pl. masc.
             ἵνα ἡ πίστις ὑμῶν μὴ ᾖ ἐν σοφίᾳ ἀνθρώπων (1 Cor. 2:5)
             that your faith should not be in **the wisdom of men**
      b. The genitive sometimes functions as a predicate genitive of a form of εἰμι and denotes possession.
         (1) Finite verb
            (a) Gen. sing. masc.
                ἐμβὰς δὲ εἰς ἓν τῶν πλοίων, ὃ ἦν Σίμωνος (Luke 5:3)
                and having entered into one of the boats that **belonged to Simon**
            (b) Gen. sing. masc.
                ἕκαστος ὑμῶν λέγει, Ἐγὼ μέν εἰμι Παύλου, Ἐγὼ δὲ
                Ἀπολλῶ, Ἐγὼ δὲ Κηφᾶ, Ἐγὼ δὲ Χριστοῦ (1 Cor. 1:12)
                each one of you says, I am **of Paul**, and I [εἰμι, am] **of Apollos**, and I [εἰμι, am] **of Cephas**, and I [εἰμι, am] **of Christ**
         (2) Elliptical form of εἰμι
            (a) Gen. sing. masc.
                ὅτι καθὼς αὐτὸς Χριστοῦ, οὕτως καὶ ἡμεῖς (2 Cor. 10:7)
                that even as he [ἐστιν, **belongs to**] **Christ**, so also [do] we
            (b) Gen. pl. masc. and gen. pl. neut.
                ἢ Ἰουδαίων ὁ θεὸς μόνον; οὐχὶ καὶ ἐθνῶν; ναὶ καὶ ἐθνῶν
                (Rom. 3:29)
                or does God [ἐστιν, **belong to**] **Jews** only? and [ἐστιν, **does he not belong to**] **Gentiles** also? Yes! [ἐστιν, **he belongs to**] **Gentiles** also

(3) Infinitive εἶναι

εἴ τις πέποιθεν ἑαυτῷ Χριστοῦ εἶναι (2 Cor. 10:7)

if anyone is persuaded in himself **to belong to Christ**

(4) Elliptical participle

ἀπαρχὴ Χριστός, ἔπειτα οἱ τοῦ Χριστοῦ ἐν τῇ παρουσίᾳ αὐτοῦ
(1 Cor. 15:23)

Christ the firstfruits, then those [ὄντες, **who belong to**] **Christ** at
his coming

2. Genitive of relationship. This is often considered the same as the genitive
   of possession. However, this function points out a familial, social, or
   spiritual relationship between two or more individuals or groups.

   a. Gen. sing. masc.

   μὴ καὶ σὺ ἐκ τῶν μαθητῶν εἶ τοῦ ἀνθρώπου τούτου; (John 18:17)

   are you also [one] of **this man's disciples?**

   b. Gen. sing. fem.

   μετεκαλέσατο τοὺς πρεσβυτέρους τῆς ἐκκλησίας (Acts 20:17)

   he called for **the elders of the church**

   c. Gen. sing. neut.

   παραλαμβάνει τὸν πατέρα τοῦ παιδίου καὶ τὴν μητέρα (Mark 5:40)

   he took along **the father of the child** and the mother

   d. Gen. pl. masc.

   τότε προσῆλθεν αὐτῷ ἡ μήτηρ τῶν υἱῶν Ζεβεδαίου (Matt. 20:20)

   then **the mother of the sons of Zebedee** came to him

3. Objective genitive. This genitive modifies a noun of action and is the object
   of that action. The context must determine this function.

   a. Gen. sing. masc.

   ἐὰν δὲ παραβάτης νόμου ᾖς (Rom. 2:25)

   but if you are **a transgressor of law**

   b. Gen. sing. fem.

   ὅτι ἐξηράνθη ὁ θερισμὸς τῆς γῆς (Rev. 14:15)

   for **the harvest of the earth** has become ripe

   c. Gen. sing. neut.

   ἐν ἑαυτοῖς στενάζομεν, υἱοθεσίαν ἀπεκδεχόμενοι,

   τὴν ἀπολύτρωσιν τοῦ σώματος ἡμῶν (Rom. 8:23)

   we groan in ourselves, waiting for adoption, **the redemption of our body**

   d. Gen. pl. fem.

   ἀλλ᾽ ἐν αὐταῖς ἀνάμνησις ἁμαρτιῶν κατ᾽ ἐνιαυτόν (Heb. 10:3)

   but in these things [ἐστιν, there is] **remembering of sins** year after year

4. Subjective genitive. This genitive modifies a noun of action and functions as the subject of that action.
   a. Gen. sing. masc.
      ἀφ' ὑμῶν γὰρ ἐξήχηται **ὁ λόγος τοῦ κυρίου** (1 Thess. 1:8)
      for **the word of the Lord** has sounded out from you
   b. Gen. sing. fem.
      τίς ἡμᾶς χωρίσει ἀπὸ **τῆς ἀγάπης τοῦ Χριστοῦ**; (Rom. 8:35)
      who shall separate us from **the love of Christ**?
   c. Gen. sing. neut.
      ἵνα αὐτὴν ἁγιάσῃ καθαρίσας **τῷ λουτρῷ τοῦ ὕδατος** ἐν ῥήματι
      (Eph. 5:26)
      that he might sanctify her having washed [her] **with the washing of water** in the word
   d. Gen. pl. fem.
      καὶ **ἔργα τῶν χειρῶν σού** εἰσιν οἱ οὐρανοί (Heb. 1:10)
      and the heavens are **the works of your hands**
   e. Sometimes both the subjective and objective ideas may be contained in the same genitive. When this occurs the subjective produces the objective.
      ἡ γὰρ **ἀγάπη τοῦ Χριστοῦ** συνέχει ἡμᾶς (2 Cor. 5:14)
      for **the love of Christ** impels us
5. Descriptive genitive. This genitive describes and qualifies the noun to which it is related.
   a. Gen. sing. masc.
      καὶ **ἡ πληγὴ τοῦ θανάτου αὐτοῦ** ἐθεραπεύθη (Rev. 13:3)
      and **the wound of his death** was healed
   b. Gen. sing. fem.
      ὃ ἐθεασάμεθα καὶ αἱ χεῖρες ἡμῶν ἐψηλάφησαν **περὶ τοῦ λόγου τῆς ζωῆς** (1 John 1:1)
      which we beheld and our hands handled concerning **the word of life**
   c. Gen. sing. neut.
      ἐπέστησαν αὐτοῖς οἱ ἱερεῖς καὶ **ὁ στρατηγὸς τοῦ ἱεροῦ** (Acts 4:1)
      the priests and **the captain of the temple** approached them
   d. Gen. pl. fem.
      ἠκολούθει δὲ αὐτῷ **πολὺ πλῆθος** τοῦ λαοῦ καὶ **γυναικῶν**
      (Luke 23:27)
      and **a large number** of the people and **of women** were following him

6. Apposition includes two ideas, simple apposition and the genitive of apposition.
   a. Simple apposition. The two nouns (or a pronoun and a noun) are equal in idea, the latter restating or renaming the former.
      (1) Gen. sing. masc.
          ἵνα πληρωθῇ τὸ ῥηθὲν **διὰ Ἡσαΐου τοῦ προφήτου** (Matt. 4:14)
          that the word spoken **by Isaiah the prophet** should be fulfilled
      (2) Gen. pl. neut.
          ἐγὼ Παῦλος ὁ δέσμιος τοῦ Χριστοῦ Ἰησοῦ **ὑπὲρ ὑμῶν τῶν ἐθνῶν** (Eph. 3:1)
          I Paul, the prisoner of Christ Jesus **for you Gentiles**
   b. Genitive of apposition is always genitive, whereas the noun before it may be any case. This genitive is often called the genitive of definition.
      (1) Gen. pl. masc.
          ἐποικοδομηθέντες ἐπὶ τῷ θεμελίῳ **τῶν ἀποστόλων καὶ προφητῶν** (Eph. 2:20)
          having been built **upon the foundation, [which is] the apostles and prophets**
      (2) Gen. sing. fem.
          καὶ ἐνδυσάμενοι **τὸν θώρακα τῆς δικαιοσύνης** (Eph. 6:14)
          and having put on **the breastplate of righteousness**
      (3) Gen. sing. neut.
          καὶ εἴ τις λαμβάνει **τὸ χάραγμα τοῦ ὀνόματος αὐτοῦ** (Rev. 14:11)
          and if anyone receives **the mark, [which is] his name**
7. Genitive of direct object occurs with certain verbs. ἀκούω and its compounds may take either the accusative or genitive case as its object.[13] Some other verbs that take a genitive object are ἀντέχω, ἀντιλαμβάνω, ἅπτομαι (only in mid./pass. form), ἀμελέω, βασιλεύω, ἐπιθυμέω, θιγγάνω, καθάπτω, κατακυριεύω, κατηγορέω, κοινωνέω, κυριεύω, μεταλαμβάνω, μιμνήσκομαι, ὀμείρομαι, ὀρέγω, προΐστημι, τυγχάνω, ὑπομιμνήσκω, etc. This genitive occurs with finite verbs, infinitives, and participles.

---

[13] Kittel (*TDNT*, 1:216) states: "The classical rule of the genitive for the persons whom we hear and the accusative for the persons or things about whom or which we hear, is applied even more systematically in the NT." Blass-Debrunner (*BDF*, p. 95, # 173) also state: "The classical rule for ἀκούειν is: the person whose words are heard stands in the genitive, the thing about which one hears in the accusative." C. F. D. Moule (*An Idiom-Book of NT Greek*, 36) says that the facts with regard to ἀκούειν are obscure. He restates the classical rule as: "Genitive of person, Accusative of thing, i.e., one listens to a person (Gen.) but hears him say something (Acc.), but the NT usage varies in a way which defies classification."

a. Finite verbs
  (1) Gen. sing. masc.
     οἵτινες οὐ μὴ γεύσωνται θανάτου ἕως ἂν ἴδωσιν τὸν υἱὸν τοῦ
     ἀνθρώπου ἐρχόμενον ἐν τῇ βασιλείᾳ αὐτοῦ (Matt. 16:28)
     who shall not taste death until they shall see the Son of Man
     coming in his kingdom
  (2) Gen. sing. fem.
     καὶ τὰ πρόβατα **τῆς φωνῆς αὐτοῦ ἀκούει** (John 10:3)
     and the sheep **hear his voice**
  (3) Gen. sing. neut.
     καὶ **ὑπεμνήσθη** ὁ Πέτρος **τοῦ ῥήματος** τοῦ κυρίου (Luke 22:61)
     and Peter **remembered the word** of the Lord
  (4) Gen. pl. masc.
     τότε **ἥψατο τῶν ὀφθαλμῶν αὐτῶν** (Matt. 9:29)
     then **he touched their eyes**
b. Infinitives
  (1) Gen. sing. masc.
     Εἰ δίκαιόν ἐστιν ἐνώπιον τοῦ θεοῦ ὑμῶν **ἀκούειν** μᾶλλον ἢ **τοῦ**
     θεοῦ (Acts 4:19)
     whether it is right before God **to listen** to you rather than **God**
  (2) Gen. sing. fem.
     οἱ δὲ καταξιωθέντες τοῦ αἰῶνος ἐκείνου **τυχεῖν** καὶ **τῆς**
     ἀναστάσεως τῆς ἐκ νεκρῶν (Luke 20:35)
     but those who have been counted worthy **to obtain** that age and
     the resurrection that [οὔσης, is] from the dead
  (3) Gen. sing. neut.
     οὐχ ὡς **τοῦ ἔθνους μου** ἔχων τι **κατηγορεῖν** (Acts 28:19)[14]
     not as having anything **to bring charges against my nation**
  (4) Gen. pl. masc.
     τὸν κοπιῶντα γεωργὸν δεῖ πρῶτον **τῶν καρπῶν μεταλαμβάνειν**
     (2 Tim. 2:6)
     the working farmer must first **share in the fruit**
c. Participles
  (1) Gen. sing. masc.
     τοῦ ἰδίου οἴκου καλῶς **προϊστάμενον** (1 Tim. 3:4)
     ruling his own house well

---

[14] Acts 28:19 text is from GNT, NA & WH: TR & MT have κατηγορῆσαι.

(2) Gen. sing. fem.
πολλῆς εἰρήνης τυγχάνοντες διὰ σοῦ (Acts 24:2)
obtaining great peace through you

(3) Gen. pl. neut.
διάκονοι ἔστωσαν μιᾶς γυναικὸς ἄνδρες, **τέκνων** καλῶς
προϊστάμενοι καὶ τῶν ἰδίων οἴκων (1 Tim. 3:12)
let the deacons be husbands of one wife, **ruling their children**
and their own houses well

(4) Gen. pl. masc.
πᾶς ὁ ἐρχόμενος πρός με καὶ **ἀκούων μου τῶν λόγων** καὶ ποιῶν
αὐτούς (Luke 6:47)
everyone who comes to me and **hears my words** and does them

8. Partitive genitives are largely replaced by the preposition ἀπό and ἐκ.
This genitive indicates a whole, a part of which is indicated by the noun it
modifies. Thus, this genitive is misnamed, because it refers to the whole
rather than a part. It is often used with τις, ἕκαστος, εἷς, λοιπός, and
numerals.

a. Gen. pl. masc.
τίς γὰρ οἶδεν **ἀνθρώπων** τὰ τοῦ ἀνθρώπου εἰ μὴ τὸ πνεῦμα τοῦ
ἀνθρώπου τὸ ἐν αὐτῷ; (1 Cor. 2:11)
for **who among men** knows the things [ὄντα, that] belong to a man,
except the spirit of man that [ὄν, is] in him?

b. Gen. pl. fem.
ἐλεύσονται ἡμέραι ὅτε ἐπιθυμήσετε **μίαν τῶν ἡμερῶν** τοῦ υἱοῦ τοῦ
ἀνθρώπου ἰδεῖν καὶ οὐκ ὄψεσθε (Luke 17:22)
the days will come when you will desire to see **one of the days** of the
son of man and will not see [it]

c. Gen. pl. neut.
καὶ παρεκάλουν αὐτὸν ἵνα, κἂν **τοῦ κρασπέδου τοῦ ἱματίου αὐτοῦ**
ἅψωνται (Mark 6:56)
and they implored him that they might touch **the border of his clothing**

d. Gen. sing. fem.
περὶ τετάρτην φυλακὴν τῆς νυκτὸς ἔρχεται πρὸς αὐτούς περιπατῶν
ἐπὶ τῆς θαλάσσης (Mark 6:48)
about the fourth watch of the night he came to them walking on the
sea

9. Adverbial genitive of time. This genitive usually denotes the time within which something occurs. This category is limited to terms specifically indicating time.

   a. Gen. sing. fem.

      καὶ λατρεύουσιν αὐτῷ **ἡμέρας** καὶ **νυκτὸς** ἐν τῷ ναῷ αὐτοῦ
(Rev. 7:15)

      and they serve him **day** and **night** in his temple

   b. Gen. sing. fem.

      καὶ προσμένει ταῖς δεήσεσιν καὶ ταῖς προσευχαῖς **νυκτὸς** καὶ
ἡμέρας (1 Tim. 5:5)

      and she continues in entreaties and prayers **night** and **day**

   c. Gen. pl. fem.

      καὶ ἕξετε θλῖψιν **ἡμερῶν δέκα** (Rev. 2:10)[15]

      and you will have tribulation **ten days**

   d. Gen. pl. masc.

      φανερωθέντος δὲ ἐπ᾽ ἐσχάτου **τῶν χρόνων** δι᾽ ὑμᾶς (1 Peter 1:20)

      but was made known in the last **of the times** because of you

10. Adverbial genitive of place. This genitive indicates a place where something occurs.

   a. Gen. sing. masc.

      ὃς ἐκάθισεν **ἐν δεξιᾷ τοῦ θρόνου** τῆς μεγαλωσύνης ἐν τοῖς οὐρανοῖς
(Heb. 8:1)

      who sat down **at the right hand of the throne** of the majesty in heaven

   b. Gen. sing. fem.

      καὶ τότε κόψονται **πᾶσαι αἱ φυλαὶ τῆς γῆς** (Matt. 24:30)

      and then **all the tribes on earth** shall mourn

   c. Gen. sing. neut.

      καὶ πέμψον Λάζαρον ἵνα βάψῃ τὸ ἄκρον τοῦ δακτύλου αὐτοῦ
ὕδατος (Luke 16:24)

      and send Lazarus, that he may dip the tip of his finger **in water**

   d. Gen. pl. neut.

      ἔκρυψαν ἑαυτοὺς εἰς τὰ σπήλαια καὶ εἰς **τὰς πέτρας τῶν ὀρέων**
(Rev. 6:15)

      they hid themselves in the caves and **in the rocks of the mountains**

---

[15] Rev. 2:10 text is from GNT & NA: WH has ἔχητε; WH, TR & MT have θλῖψιν; MT has ἡμέρας.

11. Genitive absolute. A noun or pronoun and a participle in the genitive case often function as an unrelated or subordinate clause to the main clause. The noun or pronoun functions as the subject of the participle.

a. Gen. sing. masc.

ὁ γὰρ Ἰησοῦς ἐξένευσεν **ὄχλου ὄντος** ἐν τῷ τόπῳ (John 5:13)

for Jesus had withdrawn, **since a crowd was** in this place

b. Gen. sing. fem.

ἐλθούσης δὲ **τῆς πίστεως** οὐκέτι ὑπὸ παιδαγωγόν ἐσμεν (Gal. 3:25)

and **when/because faith came** we are no longer under a tutor

c. Gen. pl. masc.

ἐν δὲ ταῖς ἡμέραις ταύταις **πληθυνόντων τῶν μαθητῶν** ἐγένετο γογγυσμὸς τῶν Ἑλληνιστῶν πρὸς τοὺς Ἑβραίους (Acts 6:1)

but in these days **when the disciples were multiplying**, there was a murmuring of the Hellenists against the Hebrews

d. Gen. pl. fem.

Ἡμερῶν δὲ **διαγενομένων τινῶν** Ἀγρίππας ὁ βασιλεὺς καὶ Βερνίκη κατήντησαν εἰς Καισάρειαν (Acts 25:13)

and **when certain days had passed**, Agrippa the king and Bernice came down to Caesarea

12. Genitive of content. This genitive indicates the content of the word it qualifies. It is usually preceded by μέστος, πλήρης, πλήρωμα, or some word indicating someone or something as a container.

a. Gen. sing. masc.

ἀκούσαντες δὲ καὶ γενόμενοι **πλήρεις θυμοῦ** ἔκραζον λέγοντες, Μεγάλη ἡ Ἄρτεμις Ἐφεσίων (Acts 19:28)

and when they heard and had become **filled with anger**, they cried out saying, Artemis of the Ephesians [ἐστιν, is] great

b. Gen. pl. masc.

οὐ γὰρ ἦσαν μακρὰν ἀπὸ τῆς γῆς ἀλλὰ ὡς ἀπὸ πηχῶν διακοσίων, σύροντες **τὸ δίκτυον τῶν ἰχθύων** (John 21:8)[16]

for they were not far from land, but about two hundred cubits, dragging the **net of fish**

c. Gen. sing. fem.

πεπληρώκατε τὴν Ἰερουσαλὴμ **τῆς διδαχῆς ὑμῶν** (Acts 5:28)[17]

you have filled Jerusalem **with your teaching**

---

[16] John 21:8 text is from GNT, NA & WH: TR & MT have ἀλλ'.

[17] Acts 5:28 text is from GNT, NA, WH & MT: TR has Ἰερουσαλήμ.

d. Gen. sing. neut. and gen. pl. masc.

μεστὴ ἐλέους καὶ καρπῶν ἀγαθῶν (James 3:17)

[ἐστιν, it is] **full of mercy** and **good fruit**

13. Genitive of comparison follows a comparative adjective or adverb, e.g.,
πλείων, πλεῖον, μείζων, μικρότερον.

a. Gen. sing. masc.

μὴ σὺ μείζων εἶ τοῦ πατρὸς ἡμῶν Ἰακώβ, ὃς ἔδωκεν ἡμῖν τὸ φρέαρ;
(John 4:12)

are you greater than our father Jacob, who gave the well to us?

b. Gen. sing. fem. and gen. sing. neut.

οὐχὶ ἡ ψυχὴ πλεῖόν ἐστιν τῆς τροφῆς καὶ τὸ σῶμα τοῦ ἐνδύματος;
(Matt. 6:25)

is not your life **more than food** and your body **[more] than clothing?**

c. Gen. pl. neut.

πόσῳ μᾶλλον ὑμεῖς διαφέρετε τῶν πετεινῶν (Luke 12:24)

by how much **more you are better than the birds**

d. Gen. pl. masc.

κρείττων γενόμενος τῶν ἀγγέλων (Heb. 1:4)

having become **better than the angels**

14. Genitive of quality or attributive genitive. There are two variations of this.

a. The genitive noun names an attribute or quality of the modified noun.
This functions like an adjective.

(1) Gen. sing. masc.

ζηλῶ γὰρ ὑμᾶς θεοῦ ζήλῳ (2 Cor. 11:2)

for I am deeply concerned over you with a **godly zeal**

(2) Gen. sing. fem.

αὐτὴ ἡ κτίσις ἐλευθερωθήσεται ἀπὸ τῆς δουλείας τῆς φθορᾶς
εἰς τὴν ἐλευθερίαν τῆς δόξης τῶν τέκνων τοῦ θεοῦ (Rom. 8:21)

creation itself shall be set free from the bondage of corruption
into the glorious freedom of the children of God

(3) Gen. sing. neut.

καὶ οἱ πόδες αὐτοῦ ὡς στῦλοι πυρός (Rev. 10:1)

and his feet [εἰσιν, were] as **fiery pillars**

b. The genitive noun functions as the qualified noun, and the head noun
functions as an attribute or quality. This is the reverse of the former
function.

(1) Gen. sing. fem.

οὕτως καὶ ἡμεῖς ἐν καινότητι ζωῆς περιπατήσωμεν (Rom. 6:4)

so also let us walk **in new life**

(2) Gen. sing. masc.

οἵτινες μετήλλαξαν **τὴν ἀλήθειαν τοῦ θεοῦ** ἐν τῷ ψεύδει (Rom. 1:25)

who changed **the true God**[18] into the lie

(3) Gen. sing. neut.

εἰ δὲ τὸ ζῆν ἐν σαρκί, τοῦτό μοι **καρπὸς ἔργου** (Phil. 1:22)

but if to live in the flesh, this [ἐστιν, is] my **fruitful labor**

15. Predicate genitive. The genitive noun stands in a predicate relationship to another genitive word joined by εἰμι, γίνομαι, or a passive participle.

   a. Participle form of εἰμι, sometimes in a genitive absolute construction

     (1) Gen. sing. masc.

ἐποικοδομηθέντες ἐπὶ τῷ θεμελίῳ τῶν ἀποστόλων καὶ προφητῶν, **ὄντος ἀκρογωνιαίου αὐτοῦ Χριστοῦ Ἰησοῦ** (Eph. 2:20)

having been built on the foundation of the apostles and prophets, **Jesus Christ himself being the cornerstone**

     (2) Gen. sing. fem.

πῶς σὺ Ἰουδαῖος ὢν παρ' ἐμοῦ πεῖν αἰτεῖς **γυναικὸς Σαμαρίτιδος οὔσης;** (John 4:9)[19]

how do you being a Jew ask a drink from me **being a Samaritan woman**?

   b. Participle form of γίνομαι

     Gen. sing. masc.

περὶ Ἰούδα **τοῦ γενομένου ὁδηγοῦ** τοῖς συλλαβοῦσι(ν) Ἰησοῦν (Acts 1:16)[20]

concerning Judas **who became [the] guide** to those who arrested Jesus

   c. Passive participle

     (1) Gen. sing. masc.

τοῦ ὁρισθέντος υἱοῦ θεοῦ ἐν δυνάμει (Rom. 1:4)

who was designated son of God in power

     (2) Gen. sing. masc.

καὶ οἱ μάρτυρες ἀπέθεντο τὰ ἱμάτια αὐτῶν παρὰ τοὺς πόδας **νεανίου καλουμένου Σαύλου** (Acts 7:58)

and the witnesses laid down their cloaks alongside the feet **of a young man called Saul**

---

[18] This could also be rendered *the divine truth*.

[19] John 4:9 text is from GNT, NA & WH: TR & MT have πιεῖν and οὔσης γυναικὸς Σαμαρείτιδος: WH has Σαμαρείτιδος.

[20] Acts 1:16 text is from GNT, NA & WH: TR & MT have τὸν Ἰησοῦν.

(3) Gen. sing. fem.

οἱ λεγόμενοι ἀκροβυστία ὑπὸ τῆς λεγομένης περιτομῆς
(Eph. 2:11)

who are called uncircumcision **by that which is called circumcision**

B. Less frequent uses of the genitive.
1. Genitive of separation. This is called ablative of separation in the eight case system. The noun in the genitive indicates separation from the person or thing indicated by the other substantive. This use is found most often with the prepositions ἀπό and ἐκ.

a. Gen. pl. masc.

ἐκτινάξατε τὸν κονιορτὸν **τῶν ποδῶν ὑμῶν** (Matt. 10:14)

shake off the dust **from your feet**

b. Gen. sing. fem.

ἀπηλλοτριωμένοι **τῆς πολιτείας** τοῦ Ἰσραήλ (Eph. 2:12)

having been alienated from the citizenship of Israel

c. Gen. sing. neut.

ἀπέχεσθαι εἰδωλοθύτων καὶ **αἵματος** (Acts 15:29)

to abstain from things offered to idols and **from blood**

2. Genitive complement. The head term is completed by the genitive term and may be a noun, adjective, adverb, or verb.

a. With nouns, such as ὁμοίωμα, κληρόνομος, κοινωνία, μεσίτης

(1) Gen. sing. masc.

εἰ γὰρ σύμφυτοι γεγόναμεν **τῷ ὁμοιώματι τοῦ θανάτου αὐτοῦ**
(Rom. 6:5)

for if we became united with [him] **in the likeness of his death**

(2) Gen. sing. fem.

καὶ **τῆς** κατὰ πίστιν **δικαιοσύνης** ἐγένετο **κληρονόμος**
(Heb. 11:7)

and he became **heir of the righteousness** according to faith

(3) Gen. sing. neut.

οὐχὶ **κοινωνία** ἐστὶν **τοῦ αἵματος** τοῦ Χριστοῦ; (1 Cor. 10:16)

is it not **the fellowship of the blood** of Christ?

(4) Gen. pl. masc.

εἷς γὰρ θεός, εἷς καὶ **μεσίτης θεοῦ** καὶ **ἀνθρώπων** (1 Tim. 2:5)

for [ἐστιν, there is] one God, and one **mediator between God and people**

b. With adjectives (ἀκατάπαυστος, ἄνομος, ἄξιος, ἀνάξιος, ἔννομος)

  (1) Gen. sing. fem.

    καὶ οὐκ **ἀξίους** κρίνετε ἑαυτοὺς **τῆς αἰωνίου ζωῆς** (Acts 13:46)

    and you do not consider yourselves **worthy of eternal life**

  (2) Gen. sing. masc.

    οἱ δὲ πάντες κατέκριναν αὐτὸν **ἔνοχον** εἶναι **θανάτου**
    (Mark 14:64)[21]

    and they all condemned him to be **deserving of death**

  (3) Gen. sing. neut.

    ἔνοχος ἔσται **τοῦ σώματος καὶ τοῦ αἵματος** τοῦ κυρίου
    (1 Cor. 11:27)[22]

    he shall be **guilty of the body and the blood** of the Lord

  (4) Gen. pl. masc.

    ὁ δὲ μὴ γνούς, ποιήσας δὲ **ἄξια πληγῶν**, δαρήσεται ὀλίγας
    (Luke 12:48)

    but he who did not know and did [things] **worthy of blows** shall be
    beaten with few [blows]

c. With adverbs, such as ἀναξίως, ἀξίως

  (1) Gen. sing. masc.

    οὓς καλῶς ποιήσεις προπέμψας **ἀξίως τοῦ θεοῦ** (3 John 6)

    whom you will do well by sending [them] forth **worthily of God**

  (2) Gen. sing. fem.

    παρακαλῶ οὖν ὑμᾶς ἐγὼ ὁ δέσμιος, ἐν κυρίῳ **ἀξίως**
    περιπατῆσαι **τῆς κλήσεως** ἧς ἐκλήθητε (Eph. 4:1)

    I the prisoner in the Lord encourage you to walk **worthily of the
    calling** in which you were called

  (3) Gen. sing. neut.

    μόνον **ἀξίως τοῦ εὐαγγελίου** τοῦ Χριστοῦ πολιτεύεσθε
    (Phil. 1:27)

    only conduct yourselves **worthily of the gospel** of Christ

  (4) Gen. pl. masc.

    ἵνα αὐτὴν προσδέξησθε ἐν κυρίῳ **ἀξίως τῶν ἁγίων** (Rom. 16:2)

    that you may receive her in the Lord **worthily of the saints**

d. With verbs, ἀξιόω, καταξιόω, γεμίζω

  (1) Gen. sing. masc.

    καὶ **ἐγεμίσθη** ὁ ναὸς **καπνοῦ** ἐκ τῆς δόξης τοῦ θεοῦ (Rev. 15:8)

    and the temple **was filled with smoke** from the glory of God

---

[21] Mark 14:64 text is from GNT, NA & WH: TR & MT have εἶναι ἔνοχον.

[22] 1 Cor. 11:27 text is from GNT, NA, WH & MT: TR omits τοῦ before αἵματος.

(2) Gen. sing. fem.

εἰς τὸ **καταξιωθῆναι ὑμᾶς τῆς βασιλείας** τοῦ θεοῦ (2 Thess. 1:5)

that **you may be accounted worthy of the kingdom** of God

(3) Gen. sing. neut.

ὅπως ἀναβλέψῃς καὶ **πλησθῇς πνεύματος ἁγίου** (Acts 9:17)

that you may receive [your] sight and **be filled with the Holy Spirit**

(4) Gen. sing. masc. and fem.

καὶ **ἐπλήσθησαν θάμβους καὶ ἐκστάσεως** ἐπὶ τῷ συμβεβηκότι αὐτῷ (Acts 3:10)

and **they were filled with wonder and amazement** at that which had happened to him

3. Genitive of source or origin. The genitive noun denotes the source or origin of the other person or thing indicated in the other noun. This genitive is often found with the prepositions ἀπό and ἐκ.

a. Gen. sing. and pl. masc.

σοφίαν δὲ λαλοῦμεν ἐν τοῖς τελείοις, σοφίαν δὲ **οὐ τοῦ αἰῶνος τούτου οὐδὲ τῶν ἀρχόντων** τοῦ αἰῶνος τούτου (1 Cor. 2:6)

but we speak wisdom among the mature; but wisdom **not derived from this age or derived from the rulers** of this age

b. Gen. sing. fem.

καὶ ὄχλος **τῆς πόλεως** ἱκανὸς ἦν σὺν αὐτῇ (Luke 7:12)[23]

and a considerable crowd **from the city** was with her

c. Gen. sing. neut.

δεξάμενοι τὸν λόγον ἐν θλίψει πολλῇ μετὰ χαρᾶς **πνεύματος ἁγίου** (1 Thess. 1:6)

having received the word in much tribulation with joy **from the Holy Spirit**

4. Genitive of agency indicates the agent by which an action is performed. The action may be found in a verb or verbal adjective.

a. Gen. sing. fem.

καὶ πιάσας αὐτὸν **τῆς δεξιᾶς χειρὸς** ἤγειρε(ν) αὐτόν (Acts 3:7)[24]

and having taken hold of him **by the right hand** he raised him up

b. Gen. pl. fem.

οὐκ ἐγήγερται **ἐν γεννητοῖς γυναικῶν** μείζων Ἰωάννου τοῦ βαπτιστοῦ (Matt. 11:11)[25]

one greater than John the Baptist has not risen **among those born of women**

---

[23] Luke 7:12 text is from GNT, NA, WH & TR*b*: TR*s* & MT omit ἦν.

[24] Acts 3:7 text is from GNT, NA & WH: TR & MT omit the second αὐτόν.

[25] Matt. 11:11 text is from GNT, NA, TR & MT: WH has Ἰωάνου.

c. Gen. sing. masc.

ἐν οἷς ἐστε καὶ ὑμεῖς **κλητοὶ Ἰησοῦ Χριστοῦ** (Rom. 1:6)

among whom you also are **called by Jesus Christ**

d. **Gen. sing. neut.**

ὁ τοῦ πατρὸς ἡμῶν διὰ πνεύματος ἁγίου **στόματος Δαυὶδ** παιδός σου εἰπών (Acts 4:25)[26]

who by the Holy Spirit **through the mouth of David** our father his servant said

5. Genitive of material. The genitive noun denotes the material of which the other noun consists.

a. Gen. pl. masc.

ἡ οὖν Μαριὰμ λαβοῦσα λίτραν μύρου **νάρδου πιστικῆς πολυτίμου** ἤλειψεν τοὺς πόδας τοῦ Ἰησοῦ (John 12:3)[27]

then Mary took a pound of myrrh **of genuine and expensive perfume** and annointed the feet of Jesus

b. Gen. sing. neut.

οὐδεὶς **ἐπίβλημα ῥάκους ἀγνάφου** ἐπιράπτει ἐπὶ ἱμάτιον παλαιόν (Mark 2:21)

no one sews **a patch of unshrunken cloth** on an old garment

6. Genitive of direction or purpose. The genitive noun indicates the way to or the purpose of the head noun.

a. Gen. pl. masc.

μὴ εἰς **τὴν διασπορὰν τῶν Ἑλλήνων** μέλλει πορεύεσθαι; (John 7:35)

is he about to go to **the dispersion among the Greeks**?

b. Gen. sing. fem.

καὶ ὅτι ἤνοιξεν τοῖς ἔθνεσιν **θύραν πίστεως** (Acts 14:27)

and that he opened **a door of faith** for the Gentiles

c. Gen. pl. neut.

ἐγὼ εἰμι ἡ **θύρα τῶν προβάτων** (John 10:7)

I am **the door for the sheep**

7. Genitive of value or price. This genitive indicates the price or value placed on something, often following certain verbs, e.g., ἀγοράζω, κτάομαι.

a. Gen. sing. fem.

ἠγοράσθητε γὰρ **τιμῆς·** δοξάσατε δὴ τὸν θεὸν ἐν τῷ σώματι ὑμῶν (1 Cor. 6:20)

for you were purchased **for a price**; therefore, glorify God in your body

---

[26] Acts 4:25 text is from GNT, NA; TR & MT have Δαβίδ; WH has Δαυείδ.

[27] John 12:3 text is from GNT, NA & WH; TR & MT have Μαρία.

    b. Gen. sing. masc.
       μισθοῦ ἐξεχύτησαν (Jude 11)
       they abandoned themselves **for monetary gain**
    c. Gen. sing. neut.
       Ἐγὼ **πολλοῦ κεφαλαίου** τὴν πολιτείαν ταύτην ἐκτησάμην
       (Acts 22:28)
       I purchased this citizenship **with a great sum**
    d. Gen. sing. neut.
       Ἑταῖρε, οὐκ ἀδικῶ σε· οὐχὶ **δηναρίου** συνεφώνησάς μοι;
       (Matt. 20:13)
       Friend, I am not treating you unjustly; did you not agree with me
       for a denarius?
  8. Genitive of reference limits the application of the word modified to a
     specific thing.
    a. Gen. sing. masc.
       πᾶς γὰρ ὁ μετέχων γάλακτος ἄπειρος **λόγου** δικαιοσύνης
       (Heb. 5:13)
       for everyone who partakes of milk [ἐστιν, is] inexperienced **with**
       reference to the word of righteousness
    b. Gen. sing. fem.
       καρδία πονηρὰ **ἀπιστίας** (Heb. 3:12)
       a heart evil **with reference to unbelief**

C. Genitives with prepositions state more clearly many of the previous functions
   found without the preposition, as well as other functions. The following
   examples are only a few illustrations of the use of the genitive with various
   prepositions. Further examples are given in the section dealing with
   prepositions.
  1. With ἐκ, gen. of source
     καὶ γὰρ ἐν τούτῳ στενάζομεν, τὸ οἰκητήριον ἡμῶν τὸ **ἐξ οὐρανοῦ**
     ἐπενδύσασθαι ἐπιποθοῦντες (2 Cor. 5:2)
     for we also groan in this, longing to be clothed with our dwelling, which
     [ὄν, is] **from heaven**
  2. With ἀπό, gen. of separation
     ἰῶτα ἓν ἢ μία κεραία οὐ μὴ παρέλθῃ **ἀπὸ τοῦ νόμου** ἕως ἂν πάντα
     γένηται (Matt. 5:18)
     one iota or one letter projection shall not pass **from the law** until all things
     take place
  3. With διά, gen. of means
     οἳ **διὰ πίστεως** κατηγωνίσαντο βασιλείας (Heb. 11:33)
     who **by faith** conquered kingdoms

4. With ἐπί, gen. of place

ἵνα εὖ σοι γένηται καὶ ἔσῃ μακροχρόνιος **ἐπὶ τῆς γῆς** (Eph. 6:3)

in order that it may be well with you, and you may live long **on the earth**

5. With περί, gen. of reference or respect

καὶ αὐτὸς ἱλασμός ἐστιν **περὶ τῶν ἁμαρτιῶν ἡμῶν** (1 John 2:2)

and he himself is the propitiation **for our sins**

6. With μετά, gen. of association

ποῦ ἐστιν τὸ κατάλυμα ὅπου τὸ πάσχα **μετὰ τῶν μαθητῶν μου** φάγω;
(Luke 22:11)

where is the guestroom where I shall eat the passover **with my disciples**?

7. With ὑπό, gen. of agency

νῦν δέ, γνόντες θεόν, μᾶλλον δὲ γνωσθέντες **ὑπὸ θεοῦ** (Gal. 4:9)

but now, having known God, but rather, having been known **by God**

8. With ἐνώπιον, gen. of place

διὰ τοῦτό εἰσιν **ἐνώπιον τοῦ θρόνου τοῦ θεοῦ**, καὶ λατρεύουσιν αὐτῷ
ἡμέρας καὶ νυκτὸς ἐν τῷ ναῷ αὐτοῦ (Rev. 7:15)

for this reason they are **before the throne of God**, and they shall serve him
day and night in his temple

9. With παρά, gen. of source

καθὼς ἐντολὴν ἐλάβομεν **παρὰ τοῦ πατρός** (2 John 4)

even as we received a command **from the Father**

10. With ὑπέρ, gen. of advantage

ἐγὼ γὰρ ὑποδείξω αὐτῷ ὅσα δεῖ αὐτὸν **ὑπὲρ τοῦ ὀνόματός μου** παθεῖν
(Acts 9:16)

for I will show him how much he must suffer **for my name**

11. With κατά, gen. of opposition

οἱ δὲ ἀρχιερεῖς καὶ ὅλον τὸ συνέδριον ἐζήτουν **κατὰ τοῦ Ἰησοῦ**
μαρτυρίαν (Mark 14:55)

and the chief priests and all the sanhedrin were seeking testimony
against Jesus

12. With ἀχρί, gen. of time

ἐγὼ πάσῃ συνειδήσει ἀγαθῇ πεπολίτευμαι τῷ θεῷ **ἄχρι ταύτης τῆς
ἡμέρας** (Acts 23:1)

I have conducted myself with a good conscience toward God **until this day**

13. With ἔμπροσθεν, gen. of place

πᾶς ὃς ἂν ὁμολογήσῃ ἐν ἐμοὶ **ἔμπροσθεν τῶν ἀνθρώπων**, καὶ ὁ υἱὸς τοῦ
ἀνθρώπου ὁμολογήσει ἐν αὐτῷ **ἔμπροσθεν τῶν ἀγγέλων** τοῦ θεοῦ
(Luke 12:8)

whoever will confess me **before men**, the son of man will also confess him
before the angels of God

14. With πρό, gen. of time

σπούδασον **πρὸ χειμῶνος** ἐλθεῖν (2 Tim. 4:21)

make every effort to come **before winter**

15. With ἕως, gen. of destination

διέλθωμεν δὴ **ἕως Βηθλέεμ**, καὶ ἴδωμεν τὸ ῥῆμα τοῦτο τὸ γεγονὸς ὃ ὁ κύριος ἐγνώρισεν ἡμῖν (Luke 2:15)[28]

Let us indeed pass through **unto Bethlehem** and let us see this thing that has come to pass that the Lord made known to us

16. With χωρίς, gen. of separation

νυνὶ δὲ **χωρὶς νόμου** δικαιοσύνη θεοῦ πεφανέρωται (Rom. 3:21)

but now **without the law** the righteousness of God has been made known

III. **The dative case** is the case of personal interest or relations, location, or means, along with other specialized functions.

  A. Most frequent uses. The following classifications are given in the descending order of frequency found in the NT.

    1. Dative of indirect object. This is the essence of the dative case. The person or thing in the dative case receives the direct object of a transitive active verb, and when transposed is the subject of a passive verb.

      a. Dat. sing. masc.

        ἑαυτοὺς ἔδωκαν πρῶτον **τῷ κυρίῳ** (2 Cor. 8:5)

        they gave themselves first **to the Lord**

      b. Dat. pl. fem.

        ὁ ἔχων οὖς ἀκουσάτω τί τὸ πνεῦμα λέγει **ταῖς ἐκκλησίαις** (Rev. 2:11)

        let the one who has ears hear what the Spirit says **to the churches**

      c. Dat. pl. neut.

        καὶ ὅτι ἤνοιξεν **τοῖς ἔθνεσιν** θύραν πίστεως (Acts 14:27)

        and that he opened a door of faith **to the Gentiles**

      d. Dat. pl. masc. with a passive verb

        πᾶσα ἁμαρτία καὶ βλασφημία ἀφεθήσεται **τοῖς ἀνθρώποις** (Matt. 12:31)

        every sin and blasphemy **shall be forgiven to people**

      e. Dat. sing. masc. with a participle

        ὁ γὰρ ἄρτος τοῦ θεοῦ ἐστιν ὁ καταβαίνων ἐκ τοῦ οὐρανοῦ καὶ ζωὴν **διδοὺς τῷ κόσμῳ** (John 6:33)

        for the bread of God is he who descends from heaven and **gives** life **to the world**

---

[28] Luke 2:15 text is from GNT, NA & WH: TR & MT have Βηθλεέμ.

f. Dat. pl. masc. with an infinitive

ἀπέστειλεν τὸν ἄγγελον αὐτοῦ **δεῖξαι τοῖς δούλοις αὐτοῦ** ἃ δεῖ γενέσθαι ἐν τάχει (Rev. 22:6)

he sent his angel **to show to his servants** what must take place soon

2. Dative of means or instrument. The dative indicates the impersonal means by which something is performed.

a. Dat. sing. masc.

ἀπεκύησεν ἡμᾶς **λόγῳ** ἀληθείας (James 1:18)

he gave us [new] birth **by the word** of truth

b. Dat. sing. fem.

πίστει προσενήνοχεν Ἀβραὰμ τὸν Ἰσαὰκ πειραζόμενος (Heb. 11:17)

by faith Abraham offered up Isaac when he was tested

c. Dat. pl. masc.

μηδεὶς ὑμᾶς ἀπατάτω **κενοῖς λόγοις** (Eph. 5:6)

let no one deceive you **by empty words**

d. Dat. pl. neut.

δυνάμεσι(ν) καὶ τέρασιν καὶ **σημείοις**, οἷς ἐποίησεν δι᾽ αὐτοῦ ὁ θεὸς ἐν μέσῳ ὑμῶν (Acts 2:22)

by miracles and wonders and **signs**, which God performed through him in your midst

e. Dat. pl. neut. with a passive verb

εἰδότες ὅτι **οὐ φθαρτοῖς**, ἀργυρίῳ ἢ χρυσίῳ ἐλυτρώθητε (1 Peter 1:18)

knowing that **you were not redeemed by corruptible things**, by silver or gold

f. Dat. sing. fem. with a participle

χάριτί ἐστε **σεσωσμένοι** (Eph. 2:5)

you are **saved by grace**

g. Dat. sing. neut. with an infinitive

πίστει νοοῦμεν **κατηρτίσθαι** τοὺς αἰῶνας **ῥήματι** θεοῦ (Heb. 11:3)

by faith we understand the ages were framed **by the word** of God

3. Dative of direct object. A number of verbs take a dative as a direct object, e.g., ἀκολουθέω, ἀπειθέω, λατρεύω, πιστεύω, προσκυνέω, ὑπακούω.[29]

a. Dat. sing. masc.

αἵτινες **ἠκολούθησαν τῷ Ἰησοῦ** ἀπὸ τῆς Γαλιλαίας (Matt. 27:55)

who **followed Jesus** from Galilee

---

[29] See BDF (pp. 103-4, 108-9) and Goetchius (pp. 307-8) for other verbs.

b. Dat. sing. fem.

οὕτως καὶ οὗτοι **ἀνθίστανται τῇ ἀληθείᾳ** (2 Tim. 3:8)

so also these **resist the truth**

c. Dat. sing. neut.

ὑμεῖς ἀεὶ **τῷ πνεύματι τῷ ἁγίῳ ἀντιπίπτετε** (Acts 7:51)

you always **resist the Holy Spirit**

d. Dat. pl. masc.

πιστεύεις, βασιλεῦ Ἀγρίππα, **τοῖς προφήταις;** (Acts 26:27)

do you believe the prophets, King Agrippa?

e. Dat. pl. masc. with a participle

οὕτως λαλοῦμεν, οὐχ ὡς **ἀνθρώποις ἀρέσκοντες** (1 Thess. 2:4)

so we speak, not as **pleasing men**

f. Dat. sing. masc. with an infinitive

οἱ δὲ ἐν σαρκὶ ὄντες **θεῷ ἀρέσαι** οὐ δύνανται (Rom. 8:8)

and those who are in the flesh are not able **to please God**

4. Dative of apposition. The dative noun may further define, explain, or describe another dative substantive.

a. Dat. sing. masc.

καί ἐσμεν ἐν τῷ ἀληθινῷ, **ἐν τῷ υἱῷ αὐτοῦ Ἰησοῦ Χριστῷ** (1 John 5:20)

and we are in the true one, **in his son Jesus Christ**

b. Dat. sing. fem.

τῆς ἐν σοὶ ἀνυποκρίτου πίστεως, ἥτις ἐνῴκησεν πρῶτον **ἐν τῇ μάμμῃ σου Λωΐδι** (2 Tim. 1:5)

of the unfeigned faith in you, that dwelt first **in your grandmother Lois**

c. Dat. sing. neut.

Τίτῳ γνησίῳ τέκνῳ κατὰ κοινὴν πίστιν (Titus 1:4)

to Titus [my] true child according to the common faith

d. Dat. pl. masc.

ἄνδρας πέμψαι πρὸς ὑμᾶς σὺν τοῖς ἀγαπητοῖς ἡμῶν **Βαρναβᾷ καὶ Παύλῳ, ἀνθρώποις** παραδεδωκόσι(ν) τὰς ψυχὰς αὐτῶν ὑπὲρ τοῦ ὀνόματος τοῦ κυρίου ἡμῶν Ἰησοῦ Χριστοῦ (Acts 15:25-26)[30]

to send to you, with our dear friends, **Barnabas and Paul, men** who have given up their lives for the name of our Lord Jesus Christ

5. Adverbial dative of time. The dative noun often refers in some way to time. It generallly expresses a point in time, **when.**

a. Dat. sing. masc.

καιρῷ γὰρ **ἰδίῳ** θερίσομεν μὴ ἐκλυόμενοι (Gal. 6:9)

for we shall reap **in due time**, if we do not faint

---

[30] Acts 15:25-26 text is from GNT, NA & MT: WH & TR have Βαρνάβα.

b. Dat. sing. fem.
τοῦτον ὁ θεὸς ἤγειρε(ν) ἐν **τῇ τρίτῃ ἡμέρᾳ** (Acts 10:40)[31]
God raised this one **on the third day**

c. Dat. sing. neut.
ἕκαστος ὑμῶν **τῷ σαββάτῳ** οὐ λύει τὸν βοῦν αὐτοῦ ἢ τὸν ὄνον ἀπὸ
τῆς φάτνης, καὶ ἀπαγαγὼν ποτίζει; (Luke 13:15)
does not each of you **on the Sabbath** untie his ox or his donkey from
the manger, and when he has led [it] away give [it] a drink?

d. Dat. pl. masc. This reference is an exception to the general rule in that
it expresses duration of time rather than point of time.
τῷ δὲ δυναμένῳ ὑμᾶς στηρίξαι κατὰ τὸ εὐαγγέλιόν μου καὶ τὸ
κήρυγμα Ἰησοῦ Χριστοῦ, κατὰ ἀποκάλυψιν μυστηρίου **χρόνοις
αἰωνίοις** σεσιγημένου (Rom. 16:25)
now to the one who is able to establish you according to my gospel
and the proclamation of Jesus Christ, according to the revelation of the
mystery having been kept secret **during eternal ages**

6. Dative of interest. This is an extension of the dative of indirect object and
includes the ideas of advantage or disadvantage. The three categories may
be distinguished as follows: the indirect object indicates **to whom**
something is performed, the dative of advantage indicates **for whom**
something is performed (to their benefit), and the dative of disadvantage
indicates **against whom** something is done (to their detriment).

a. Dative of advantage is found often with pronouns.
(1) Dat. sing. masc.
ἐγὼ γὰρ διὰ νόμου νόμῳ ἀπέθανον, ἵνα **θεῷ** ζήσω (Gal. 2:19)
for I by the law died to the law, in order that I might live **for God**

(2) Dat. sing. fem.
μὴ μεριμνᾶτε **τῇ ψυχῇ ὑμῶν** τί φάγητε (Matt. 6:25)
do not be overly concerned **for your life**, what you will eat

(3) Dat. sing. neut.
τὸ δὲ σῶμα οὐ τῇ πορνείᾳ ἀλλὰ **τῷ κυρίῳ** καὶ ὁ κύριος **τῷ
σώμα τι** (1 Cor. 6:13)
but the body [ἐστιν, is] not for fornication but for the Lord, and the
Lord **for the body**

---

[31] Acts 10:40 text is from GNT & NA: WH, TR & MT omit ἐν.

   b. Dative of disadvantage is used mostly with pronouns.
      (1) Dat. sing. masc.
         ἢ τίς βασιλεὺς πορευόμενος ἑτέρῳ **βασιλεῖ** συμβαλεῖν εἰς
         πόλεμον (Luke 14:31)[32]
         or what king goes **against another king** to engage in war
      (2) Dat. pl. neut.
         καὶ ἐπὶ ἡγεμόνας δὲ καὶ βασιλεῖς ἀχθήσεσθε ἕνεκεν ἐμοῦ εἰς
         μαρτύριον αὐτοῖς καὶ **τοῖς ἔθνεσιν** (Matt. 10:18)
         and you shall be !ed before governors and kings because of me for
         a testimony against them and **against the Gentiles**
7. Dative of sphere (also called locative of sphere). This indicates an
   abstract, logical, or figurative realm as compared with a temporal or spatial
   location.
   a. Dat. sing. fem.
      μακάριοι οἱ καθαροὶ **τῇ καρδίᾳ** ὅτι αὐτοὶ τὸν θεὸν ὄψονται
      (Matt. 5:8)
      the pure **in heart** [εἰσιν, are] blessed, for they shall see God
   b. Dat. pl. and sing. fem.
      Ἀδελφοί, μὴ παιδία γίνεσθε **ταῖς φρέσιν** ἀλλὰ **τῇ κακίᾳ** νηπιάζετε
      (1 Cor. 14:20)
      Brothers, do not be little children **in [your] minds**, but be babes **in
      malice**
   c. Dat. sing. neut. and masc.
      προσεύξομαι **τῷ πνεύματι**, προσεύξομαι δὲ καὶ **τῷ νοΐ**
      (1 Cor. 14:15)
      I will pray **with [my] spirit**, and I will also pray **with [my] mind**
8. Dative of possession. This idiom often occurs with an equative or elliptical
   verb and a pronoun, most often found in Luke's writings. The dative of
   possession is used when the emphasis is on the object possessed, and the
   genitive of possession is used when the emphasis is on the possessor.
   a. Dat. pl. masc. pron.
      καὶ οὐκ **ἦν αὐτοῖς** τέκνον (Luke 1:7)
      and **they had** no child
   b. Dat. sing. masc.
      ἄρα οὖν ζῶντος τοῦ ἀνδρὸς μοιχαλὶς χρηματίσει ἐὰν γένηται
      ἀνδρὶ ἑτέρῳ (Rom. 7:3)
      so then while her husband is alive she shall be called an adulteress, if
      she belongs to another man

---

[32] Luke 14:31 text is from GNT, NA & WH; TR & MT have συμβαλεῖν ἑτέρῳ βασιλεῖ.

c. Dat. pl. neut. pronoun and noun phrase

ὑμῖν γάρ **ἐστιν** ἡ ἐπαγγελία καὶ **τοῖς τέκνοις ὑμῶν** (Acts 2:39)

for the promise **belongs to you** and **to your children**

d. Dat. sing. neut.

ἀναστὰς δέ τις ἐν τῷ συνεδρίῳ Φαρισαῖος **ὀνόματι** Γαμαλιήλ (Acts 5:34)

and a Pharisee stood up in the Sanhedrin, **whose name [ἦν, was]** Gamaliel

9. Dative of destination or recipient. This is often found in greetings, salutations, or benedictions, where no verb is found.

a. Dat. sing. masc.

μόνῳ σοφῷ θεῷ, διὰ Ἰησοῦ Χριστοῦ, ᾧ ἡ δόξα εἰς τοὺς αἰῶνας (Rom. 16:27)

to the only wise God, through Jesus Christ, to whom [is] the glory forever

b. Dat. sing. fem.

Παῦλος ἀπόστολος ... **τῇ ἐκκλησίᾳ** τοῦ θεοῦ τῇ οὔσῃ ἐν Κορίνθῳ (2 Cor. 1:1)

Paul an apostle ... **to the church** of God that is in Corinth

c. Dat. sing. fem. and pl. neut.

ὁ πρεσβύτερος **ἐκλεκτῇ κυρίᾳ** καὶ **τοῖς τέκνοις αὐτῆς** (2 John 1)

the elder **to the elect lady** and **her children**

d. Dat. pl. masc.

εἰρήνη **τοῖς ἀδελφοῖς** καὶ ἀγάπη μετὰ πίστεως ἀπὸ θεοῦ πατρὸς καὶ κυρίου Ἰησοῦ Χριστοῦ (Eph. 6:23)

peace **to the brethren** and love with faithfulness from God the father and the Lord Jesus Christ

10. Dative of association or accompaniment. A person or thing is associated with or accompanies the subject in the action of the verb. This occurs frequently with compound verbs with prepositions ἐν, πρός, and σύν.

a. Dat. sing. masc.

τί λέγει ἡ γραφή, ὡς ἐντυγχάνει **τῷ θεῷ** κατὰ τοῦ Ἰσραήλ (Rom. 11:2)

what does the Scripture say, how he pleads **with God** against Israel

b. Dat. sing. fem.

μὴ γίνεσθε ἑτεροζυγοῦντες ἀπίστοις· τίς γὰρ μετοχὴ **δικαιοσύνῃ** καὶ **ἀνομίᾳ** ... ; (2 Cor. 6:14)

do not be unevenly yoked with unbelievers, for what is common [between] **righteousness** and **lawlessness** ... ?

   c. Dat. sing. neut.

οὐ προσανεθέμην **σαρκὶ** καὶ **αἵματι** (Gal. 1:16)

I did not consult **with flesh** and **blood**

   d. Dat. sing. and pl. masc.

πολλοὶ τελῶναι καὶ ἁμαρτωλοὶ ἐλθόντες συνανέκειντο **τῷ Ἰησοῦ** καὶ **τοῖς μαθηταῖς** αὐτοῦ (Matt. 9:10)

many tax collectors and sinners came and were eating **with Jesus** and his **disciples**

11. Dative of comparison. This is often the complement of an adjective of comparison.

   a. Dat. sing. masc.

ὁμοία ἐστὶν ἡ βασιλεία τῶν οὐρανῶν **ἀνθρώπῳ ἐμπόρῳ** (Matt. 13:45)

the kingdom of heaven is **like a merchant man**

   b. Dat. sing. fem.

πλὴν λέγω ὑμῖν, ὅτι **γῇ Σοδόμων** ἀνεκτότερον ἔσται ἐν ἡμέρᾳ κρίσεως ἢ **σοί** (Matt. 11:24)

but I tell you that it shall be **more tolerable for the land** of Sodom in the day of judgment than **for you**

   c. Dat. pl. neut.

ὅμοιοί εἰσιν **παιδίοις** τοῖς ἐν ἀγορᾷ καθημένοις (Luke 7:32)

they are **like children** who are sitting in the market place

12. Dative of place or location (also called the locative of place).

   a. Dat. sing. masc.

καὶ περιθεὶς **καλάμῳ** ἐπότιζεν αὐτόν (Matt. 27:48)

and [they] put [it] **on a reed** and gave him a drink

   b. Dat. sing. fem.

ἀλλὰ προσεληλύθατε **Σιὼν ὄρει** καὶ **πόλει** θεοῦ ζῶντος (Heb. 12:22)

but you have come **to mount Zion** and **to the city** of the living God

   c. Dat. sing. neut.

οἱ δὲ ἄλλοι μαθηταὶ **τῷ πλοιαρίῳ** ἦλθον (John 21:8)

and the other disciples came **in a small boat**

B. Datives of less frequent occurrence.

1. Dative of material. The dative noun indicates the material with which something is performed.

   a. Dat. sing. masc.

οἱ θεμέλιοι τοῦ τείχους τῆς πόλεως **παντὶ λίθῳ τιμίῳ** κεκοσμημένοι (Rev. 21:19)

the foundations of the wall of the city [ἦσαν, were] adorned **with every kind of precious stone**

b. Dat. sing. fem.

δόξῃ καὶ τιμῇ ἐστεφάνωσας αὐτόν (Heb. 2:7)

you crowned him **with glory** and **honor**

c. Dat. sing. neut.

ἐγγεγραμμένη οὐ μέλανι ἀλλὰ πνεύματι θεοῦ ζῶντος (2 Cor. 3:3)

having been written not **with ink** but **with the Spirit** of the living God

d. Dat. pl. masc. and neut.

καί τινων λεγόντων περὶ τοῦ ἱεροῦ, ὅτι λίθοις καλοῖς καὶ ἀναθήμασιν κεκόσμηται (Luke 21:5)

and some were speaking about the temple, that it was adorned **with beautiful stones** and **votive offerings**

2. Dative of respect or reference. The action of an intransitive verb refers to the dative person or thing.

a. Dat. sing. masc.

τελεσθήσεται πάντα τὰ γεγραμμένα διὰ τῶν προφητῶν τῷ υἱῷ τοῦ ἀνθρώπου (Luke 18:31)

all things that have been written through the prophets **with respect to the son** of man shall be fulfilled

b. Dat. pl. and sing. masc.

οὐκ ἐψεύσω ἀνθρώποις ἀλλὰ τῷ θεῷ (Acts 5:4)

you did not lie **to men** but **to God**

c. Dat. sing. fem.

οἵτινες ἀπεθάνομεν τῇ ἁμαρτίᾳ, πῶς ἔτι ζήσομεν ἐν αὐτῇ; (Rom. 6:2)

we who died **with reference to sin**, how shall we yet live in it?

d. Dat. pl. fem.

ἐπεὶ νωθροὶ γεγόνατε ταῖς ἀκοαῖς (Heb. 5:11)

since you have become lazy **in respect to hearing**

3. Dative of agency. The dative may indicate the agent performing the action of a passive verb. Means and agency are different in that means is impersonal and agency is personal.

a. Dat. sing. masc.

ὃς καὶ αὐτὸς ἐμαθητεύθη τῷ Ἰησοῦ (Matt. 27:57)[33]

who also himself **was discipled by Jesus**

b. Dat. sing. neut.

εἰ δὲ πνεύματι ἄγεσθε, οὐκ ἐστὲ ὑπὸ νόμον (Gal. 5:18)

but if **you are led by the Spirit**, you are not under law

---

[33] Matt. 27:57 text is from GNT, NA & WH: TR & MT have ἐμαθήτευσε(ν).

    c. Dat. pl. masc.

πάντα δὲ τὰ ἔργα αὐτῶν ποιοῦσιν **πρὸς τὸ θεαθῆναι τοῖς ἀνθρώποις** (Matt. 23:5)

but they perform all their deeds **to be seen by people**

4. Dative of manner. This indicates the manner with which the action of the verb is performed.

    a. Dat. pl. masc.

τὸ δὲ **ἀνίπτιος χερσὶν** φαγεῖν οὐ κοινοῖ τὸν ἄνθρωπον (Matt. 15:20)

but to eat **with unwashed hands** does not defile the person

    b. Dat. sing. fem.

καὶ παρεκάλει πάντας **τῇ προθέσει** τῆς καρδίας προσμένειν τῷ κυρίῳ (Acts 11:23)

and he exhorted all to continue on with the Lord **with purpose** of heart

5. Cognate dative. The dative noun may repeat the idea expressed in the noun with an emphatic effect.

    a. Dat. sing. masc.

ὁ κακολογῶν πατέρα ἢ μητέρα **θανάτῳ τελευτάτω** (Matt. 15:4)

the one who speaks evil of father or mother, **let him die by death**

    b. Dat. sing. fem.

ἐπιθυμίᾳ ἐπεθύμησα τοῦτο τὸ πάσχα φαγεῖν μεθ' ὑμῶν πρὸ τοῦ με παθεῖν (Luke 22:15)

I have greatly desired to eat this passover with you before I suffer

6. Dative absolute. This is similar in function to the genitive absolute. This use is rare and usually found with a dative noun or pronoun as subject of the dative participle.

Dat. sing. masc.

καὶ **παράγοντι** ἐκεῖθεν **τῷ Ἰησοῦ** ἠκολούθησαν αὐτῷ δύο τυφλοί (Matt. 9:27)[34]

and **as Jesus was passing by** there two blind men followed him

7. Dative of cause. This dative indicates the basis or cause of the verbal action rather than the means of the action.

    a. Dat. sing. masc.

ἐγὼ δὲ **λιμῷ** ὧδε ἀπόλλυμαι (Luke 15:17)

but I am perishing here **because of famine**

    b. Dat. sing. fem.

ὑμεῖς ποτε ἠπειθήσατε τῷ θεῷ, νῦν δὲ ἠλεήθητε **τῇ τούτων ἀπειθείᾳ** (Rom. 11:30)

you formerly disobeyed God, but now you have received mercy **because of their unbelief**

---

[34] Matt. 9:27 text is from GNT, NA, TR & MT: WH omits αὐτῷ.

8. Predicate dative. The dative noun may be the complement of a dative
participle of εἰμι, which is related to another dative substantive.
Dat. pl. masc.
καὶ καταγγέλουσιν ἔθη ἃ οὐκ ἔξεστιν ἡμῖν παραδέχεσθει οὐδὲ ποιεῖν,
Ῥωμαίοις οὖσιν (Acts 16:21)
and they preach customs that are not lawful for us to receive nor to
practice, **since we are Romans**

C. Prepositions used with the dative case. The following are only a small
sampling. More extensive illustrations will be found under the section dealing
with prepositions.
1. ἐν with the dative of place
μετὰ ταῦτα εὑρίσκει αὐτὸν ὁ Ἰησοῦς ἐν τῷ ἱερῷ (John 5:14)
after these things Jesus finds him **in the temple**
2. ἐπί with the dative of sphere
καὶ ἡ σάρξ μου κατασκηνώσει ἐπ' ἐλπίδι (Acts 2:26)
and my flesh shall rest **in hope**
3. σύν with the dative of association or accompaniment
ἀπεθάνετε γάρ, καὶ ἡ ζωὴ ὑμῶν κέκρυπται σὺν τῷ Χριστῷ ἐν τῷ θεῷ
(Col. 3:3)
for you died, and your life has been hid **with Christ** in God
4. παρά with the dative of association
παρὰ ἁμαρτωλῷ ἀνδρὶ εἰσῆλθεν καταλῦσαι (Luke 19:7)
he went in to lodge **with a sinful man**
5. πρός with the dative of place
καὶ θεωρεῖ δύο ἀγγέλους ἐν λευκοῖς καθεζομένους, ἕνα πρὸς τῇ κεφαλῇ
καὶ ἕνα πρὸς τοῖς ποσίν, ὅπου ἔκειτο τὸ σῶμα τοῦ Ἰησοῦ (John 20:12)
and she saw two angels in white sitting, one **at the head** and one **at the
feet,** where the body of Jesus had lain

IV. **The accusative case.** "The root meaning of the accusative embraces three ideas:
the end, or direction, or extent of motion or action."[35]

A. Most frequent uses of the accusative in the NT.
1. The accusative of direct object is the main function and occurs more often
than all the other uses combined, with the exception of the accusative
with prepositions. The direct object is found with all the moods of the
finite verb, with participles, and with infinitives.

---

[35] Dana and Mantey, *A Manual Grammar of the Greek New Testament*, 91-92.

  a. With the finite verb

     (1) Acc. sing. masc. and fem.

        ἀντὶ τούτου καταλείψει ἄνθρωπος **τὸν πατέρα** καὶ **τὴν μητέρα** καὶ προσκολληθήσεται πρὸς τὴν γυναῖκα αὐτοῦ (Eph. 5:31)

        because of this a man shall leave **his father** and **his mother** and shall be devoted to his wife

     (2) Acc. sing. fem.

        ὁ δὲ σπείρων εἰς τὸ πνεῦμα ἐκ τοῦ πνεύματος θερίσει **ζωὴν αἰώνιον** (Gal. 6:8)

        but the one who sows to the Spirit shall reap **eternal life** from the Spirit

     (3) Acc. sing. neut.

        ἀπαγγελῶ **τὸ ὄνομά** σου τοῖς ἀδελφοῖς μου (Heb. 2:12)

        I will declare your **name** to my brothers

     (4) Acc. pl. fem.

        χεῖρας ταχέως μηδενὶ ἐπιτίθει (1 Tim. 5:22)

        lay **hands** on no one quickly

     (5) An elliptical verb may be assumed from the context.

        λέγει αὐτῷ Σίμων Πέτρος, κύριε, μὴ **τοὺς πόδας** μου μόνον ἀλλὰ καὶ **τὰς χεῖρας** καὶ **τὴν κεφαλήν** (John 13:9)

        Simon Peter said to him, Lord, [**νίψαι, wash**] not my **feet** only but also **my hands** and **my head**

  b. With the participle

     (1) Acc. sing. masc.

        σπούδασον σεαυτὸν δόκιμον παραστῆσαι τῷ θεῷ, ἐργάτην ἀνεπαίσχυντον, ὀρθοτομοῦντα **τὸν λόγον** τῆς ἀληθείας (2 Tim. 2:15)

        make every effort to present yourself approved to God, an unashamed workman, **cutting correctly the word** of truth

     (2) Acc. sing. fem.

        καὶ ἐδόξασαν τὸν θεόν **τὸν δόντα ἐξουσίαν τοιαύτην** τοῖς ἀνθρώποις (Matt. 9:8)

        and they praised God **who gave such authority** to men

     (3) Acc. sing. neut. and acc. pl. fem.

        ὁ οὖν ἐπιχορηγῶν ὑμῖν τὸ πνεῦμα καὶ ἐνεργῶν δυνάμεις ἐν ὑμῖν ἐξ ἔργων νόμου ἢ ἐξ ἀκοῆς πίστεως; (Gal. 3:5)

        therefore **the one who gives the Spirit** and **works miracles** among you, [ἐστιν, is it] by works of law or by the hearing of faith?

(4) Acc. pl. neut.

Ἰδού ἔρχομαι ὡς κλέπτης. μακάριος ὁ γρηγορῶν καὶ **τηρῶν τὰ ἱμάτια** αὐτοῦ (Rev. 16:15)

notice, I am coming as a thief: blessed [ἐστιν, is] the one who watches and **keeps** his **garments**

(5) An elliptical participle is sometimes assumed from the previous context.

λόγον ὑγιῆ ἀκατάγνωστον, ἵνα ὁ ἐξ ἐναντίας ἐντράπῃ (Titus 2:8)

[**παρέχων, causing**] **healthy speech**, beyond reproach in order that the opponent may be made ashamed

c. With the infinitive

(1) acc. sing. masc.

τὰ δὲ ἔθνη ὑπὲρ ἐλέους **δοξάσαι τὸν θεόν** (Rom. 15:9)

and the nations **might praise God** for [His] mercies

(2) Acc. sing. fem.

ὥσπερ ὁ υἱὸς τοῦ ἀνθρώπου οὐκ ἦλθεν διακονηθῆναι, ἀλλὰ διακονῆσαι καὶ **δοῦναι τὴν ψυχὴν** αὐτοῦ λύτρον ἀντὶ πολλῶν (Matt. 20:28)

even as the son of man did not come to be served, but to serve and **to give his life** a ransom for many

(3) Acc. sing. neut.

περισσοτέρως ἐσπουδάσαμεν **τὸ πρόσωπον ὑμῶν ἰδεῖν** ἐν πολλῇ ἐπιθυμίᾳ (1 Thess. 2:17)

all the more eagerly we made every effort **to see your face** with great longing

(4) Acc. pl. fem.

ἀδύνατον γὰρ αἷμα ταύρων καὶ τράγων **ἀφαιρεῖν ἁμαρτίας** (Heb. 10:4)

for the blood of bulls and of goats [ἐστιν, is] unable **to take away sins**

(5) The elliptical infinitive is sometimes assumed from the preceding context.

τὸ μὲν πρόσωπον τοῦ οὐρανοῦ γινώσκετε διακρίνειν, **τὰ δὲ σημεῖα τῶν καιρῶν** οὐ δύνασθε; (Matt. 16:3)

you know how to discern the face of the sky, but are you unable [**διακρίνειν, to discern**] **the signs** of the times?

2. Accusative of apposition. The appositional accusative explains, defines, or further describes the previous accusative substantive.
   a. Acc. sing. masc.
      οὐκέτι ὡς δοῦλον, ἀλλ' ὑπὲρ δοῦλον ἀδελφὸν ἀγαπητόν, μάλιστα ἐμοί (Philem. 16)
      no longer as a slave but above **a slave, a dear brother**, especially to me
   b. Acc. sing. fem.
      Ἰωσὴφ υἱὸς Δαυίδ, μὴ φοβηθῇς παραλαβεῖν Μαριὰν τὴν γυναῖκά σου (Matt. 1:20)[36]
      Joseph, son of David, do not fear to take home **Mary, your wife**
   c. Acc. sing. neut.
      ἐν ᾧ καὶ ὑμεῖς ἀκούσαντες τὸν λόγον τῆς ἀληθείας, τὸ εὐαγγέλιον τῆς σωτηρίας ὑμῶν (Eph. 1:13)
      in whom you also heard **the word of truth, the gospel** of your salvation
   d. Acc. pl. masc.
      ἔδωκεν αὐτοῖς ὁ θεὸς πνεῦμα κατανύξεως, ὀφθαλμοὺς τοῦ μὴ βλέπειν (Rom. 11:8)
      God gave them **a spirit of slumber, eyes** that did not see
3. Accusative of time. This accusative using words of time denotes the extent of time indicated by the action of the verb.
   a. Acc. sing. masc.
      ἐν φόβῳ τὸν τῆς παροικίας ὑμῶν χρόνον ἀναστράφητε (1 Peter 1:17)
      live **the time** of your sojourn [in a foreign country] with fear
   b. Acc. sing. fem.
      Σίμων, καθεύδεις; οὐκ ἴσχυσας μίαν ὥραν γρηγορῆται; (Mark 14:37)
      Simon, are you sleeping? were you unable to watch **one hour**?
   c. Acc. pl. masc.
      οὐχ ὑμῶν ἐστιν γνῶναι χρόνους ἢ καιροὺς οὓς ὁ πατὴρ ἔθετο ἐν τῇ ἰδίᾳ ἐξουσίᾳ (Acts 1:7)
      to know **the times** or **the seasons** that the Father placed in His own authority does not belong to you
   d. Acc. pl. fem.
      ὥσπερ γὰρ ἦν Ἰωνᾶς ἐν τῇ κοιλίᾳ τοῦ κήτους τρεῖς ἡμέρας καὶ τρεῖς νύκτος, οὕτως ἔσται ὁ υἱὸς τοῦ ἀνθρώπου ἐν τῇ καρδίᾳ τῆς γῆς τρεῖς ἡμέρας καὶ τρεῖς νύκτος (Matt. 12:40)
      for as Jonah was in the belly of the sea monster **for three days** and **three nights** so shall the son of man be in the heart of the earth **for three days** and **three nights**

---

[36] Matt. 1:20 text is from GNT & NA: WH has Δαυείδ; TR & MT have Δαβίδ and Μαριάμ.

4. Accusative as subject of infinitive. The accusative often functions as the subject of the infinitive. This use is also called the accusative of reference. This accusative may serve a double function, as direct object and subject of infinitive.

   a. Acc. sing. masc.
   κατοικῆσαι τὸν Χριστὸν διὰ τῆς πίστεως ἐν ταῖς καρδίαις ὑμῶν (Eph. 3:17)
   that **Christ may live** in your hearts through faith

   b. Acc. sing. fem.
   πρὸ τοῦ δὲ **ἐλθεῖν τὴν πίστιν** ὑπὸ νόμον ἐφρουρούμεθα (Gal. 3:23)
   but before **faith came** we were confined under the law

   c. Acc. pl. neut.
   ἄφες πρῶτον **χορτασθῆναι τὰ τέκνα** (Mark 7:27)
   allow the children to be fed first

   d. Acc. pl. masc.
   ὃς **πάντας ἀνθρώπους θέλει σωθῆναι** καὶ εἰς ἐπίγνωσιν ἀληθείας **ἐλθεῖν** (1 Tim. 2:4)
   who **wants all people to be saved** and **to come** to the knowledge of the truth

5. Accusative object complement. This is a subset of the double accusative. The object complement is always anarthrous and predicates or asserts something about the direct object.

   a. Acc. sing. masc. (the direct object is a proper name here)
   ὅτι ἐὰν **ὁμολογήσῃς** ἐν τῷ στόματί σου **κύριον Ἰησοῦν** (Rom. 10:9)
   that if **you confess** with your mouth **Jesus as Lord**

   b. Acc. sing. fem. (the direct object here is a pronoun)
   οἱ γὰρ ἑπτὰ **ἔσχον αὐτὴν γυναῖκα** (Luke 20:33)
   for the seven **had her as wife**

   c. Acc. pl. neut. and acc. sing. fem. (the direct object is articular)
   ὁ ποιῶν **τοὺς ἀγγέλους** αὐτοῦ **πνεύματα** καὶ **τοὺς λειτουργοὺς** αὐτοῦ πυρὸς **φλόγα** (Heb. 1:7)
   the one who makes his angels spirits and **his ministers a flame** of fire

   d. Acc. pl. masc. (the direct object is a pronoun)
   δι' ἣν αἰτίαν οὐκ **ἐπαισχύνεται ἀδελφοὺς αὐτοὺς καλεῖν** (Heb. 2:11)
   on account of which cause he is not ashamed **to call them brothers**

6. Accusative supplementary participle. The direct object sometimes functions as the one performing the action of an accusative participle.

   a. Acc. sing. masc.
   εἶδεν δόξαν θεοῦ καὶ **Ἰησοῦν ἑστῶτα** ἐκ δεξιῶν τοῦ θεοῦ (Acts 7:55)
   he saw the glory of God, and **Jesus standing** at the right hand of God

b. Acc. sing. fem.

ὁ Ἰησοῦς ἐπιγνοὺς ἐν ἑαυτῷ τὴν ἐξ αὐτοῦ δύναμιν ἐξελθοῦσαν
(Mark 5:30)

when Jesus **knew** in himself **that power went out** of him

c. Acc. sing. neut.

ἀλλ' ὁ πέμψας με βαπτίζειν ἐν ὕδατι ἐκεῖνός μοι εἶπεν, ἐφ' ὃν ἂν
ἴδῃς τὸ πνεῦμα καταβαῖνον καὶ μένον ἐπ' αὐτόν, οὗτός ἐστιν ὁ
βαπτίζων ἐν πνεύματι ἁγίῳ (John 1:33)

but the one who sent me to baptize with water, that one said to me,
upon whom **you see the Spirit coming down** and **remaining** on him, this
is the one who baptizes with the Holy Spirit

d. Acc. pl. masc.

εἶδεν σχιζομένους τοὺς οὐρανούς (Mark 1:10)

he saw the heavens divided

7. Predicate accusative. An accusative noun or pronoun functions as a
complement of a passive participle in the accusative case after the
infinitives εἶναι or γενέσθαι when the subject of the infinitive is
accusative.

a. Acc. sing. masc. with εἶναι

πέποιθάς τε σεαυτὸν ὁδηγὸν εἶναι τυφλῶν (Rom. 2:19)

and you have persuaded **yourself to be a guide** of the blind

b. Acc. sing. fem. with εἶναι

δι' ὀλίγων ἔγραψα, παρακαλῶν καὶ ἐπιμαρτυρῶν ταύτην εἶναι
ἀληθῆ χάριν τοῦ θεου (1 Peter 5:12)

I wrote briefly, exhorting and testifying **this to be the true grace** of God

c. Acc. sing. masc. with a passive participle

τί οὖν ποιήσω Ἰησοῦν τὸν λεγόμενον Χριστόν; (Matt. 27:22)

what then shall I do with respect to **Jesus who is called Christ**?

d. Acc. sing. masc. with γενέσθαι

καὶ εἶπεν αὐτοῖς ὁ Ἰησοῦς, Δεῦτε ὀπίσω μου, καὶ ποιήσω ὑμᾶς
γενέσθαι ἁλιεῖς ἀνθρώπων (Mark 1:17)[37]

and Jesus said to them, "come after me and I will make **you to become
fishers** of men"

e. Acc. sing. fem. with a passive participle

ὃν ἐτίθουν καθ' ἡμέραν πρὸς τὴν θύραν τοῦ ἱεροῦ τὴν λεγομένην
Ὡραίαν (Acts 3:2)

whom they laid daily at **the door** of the temple, **which is called Beautiful**

---

[37] Compare Matt. 4:19, where the construction is an object complement, ποιήσω ὑμᾶς ἁλιεῖς ἀνθρώπων. This illustrates
the relationship between the predicate accusative and the object complement.

B. Less frequent uses of the accusative noun.
  1. Accusative of reference
    a. Acc. sing. masc.
      τί οὖν ποιήσω Ἰησοῦν τὸν λεγόμενον Χριστόν; (Matt. 27:22)
      what then shall I do **with respect to Jesus** who is called Christ?
    b. Acc. sing. neut.
      πεπίστευμαι τὸ εὐαγγέλιον τῆς ἀκροβυστίας (Gal. 2:7)
      I have been entrusted **with the gospel** of the uncircumcised
    c. Acc. pl. masc.
      ὃς γὰρ ἂν ἐπαισχυνθῇ με καὶ τοὺς ἐμοὺς λόγους (Luke 9:26)
      for whoever has been ashamed **with respect to** me and **my words**
  2. Accusative with oaths, a special function of the accusative of reference.
    a. Acc. sing. masc. and fem.
      μὴ ὀμνύετε μήτε τὸν οὐρανόν μήτε τὴν γῆν μήτε ἄλλον τινὰ ὅρκον
      (James 5:12)
      do not swear, neither **by heaven**, neither **by the earth**, neither **by any other oath**
    b. Acc. sing. masc.
      ὁρκίζω σε τὸν θεόν, μή με βασανίσῃς (Mark 5:7)
      I adjure you **by God**, do not torment me
    c. Acc. sing. masc.
      ὁρκίζω ὑμᾶς τὸν Ἰησοῦν ὃν Παῦλος κηρύσσει (Acts 19:13)[38]
      I adjure you **by Jesus**, whom Paul preaches
    d. Acc. sing. masc.
      Ἐνορκίζω ὑμᾶς τὸν κύριον ἀναγνωσθῆναι τὴν ἐπιστολὴν πᾶσι(ν) τοῖς ἀδελφοῖς (1 Thess. 5:27)[39]
      I adjure you **by the Lord** [that] this epistle be read to all the brothers
  3. Cognate accusative. The direct object contains the same idea and/or the same root as the verb and denotes emphasis.
    a. Acc. sing. masc.
      ἀγωνίζου τὸν καλὸν ἀγῶνα τῆς πίστεως (1 Tim. 6:12)
      fight the good fight of faith
    b. Acc. sing. fem.
      ἐάν τις ἴδῃ τὸν ἀδελφὸν αὐτοῦ **ἁμαρτάνοντα ἁμαρτίαν** μὴ πρὸς θάνατον (1 John 5:16)
      if anyone should see his brother **sin a sin** not unto death

---

[38] Acts 19:13 text is from GNT, NA & WH: TR & MT have ὁρκίζομεν and the article ὁ before Παῦλος.
[39] 1 Thess. 5:27 text is from GNT, NA & WH: TR & MT have ὁρκίζω and τοῖς ἁγίοις ἀδελφοῖς.

c. Acc. sing. neut.

ὅτι δωρεὰν τὸ τοῦ θεοῦ **εὐαγγέλιον εὐηγγελισάμην** ὑμῖν
(2 Cor. 11:7)

that freely **I announced the gospel** of God to you

d. Acc. pl. masc.

μὴ **θησαυρίζετε** ὑμῖν **θησαυροὺς** ἐπὶ τῆς γῆς (Matt. 6:19)

do not treasure up for yourselves **treasures** on the earth

4. Double accusative. Certain verbs require two accusatives as objects.

a. Acc. sing. masc.

ἕτοιμοι ἀεὶ πρὸς ἀπολογίαν **παντὶ τῷ αἰτοῦντι ὑμᾶς λόγον**
περὶ τῆς ἐν ὑμῖν ἐλπίδος (1 Peter 3:15)[40]

[ἔστε, be] ready always for a defence **to everyone who asks you an
account** concerning the hope in you

b. Acc. sing. fem.

καὶ ὅτε ἐνέπαιξαν αὐτῷ ἐξέδυσαν αὐτὸν τὴν χλαμύδα
(Matt. 27:31)

and when they mocked him, **they stripped him of his cloak**

c. Acc. sing. neut.

διὰ τοῦτο **ἔχρισέν σε** ὁ θεὸς ὁ θεός σου **ἔλαιον** ἀγαλλιάσεως παρὰ
τοὺς μετόχους σου (Heb. 1:9)

because of this God, your God, **anointed you with the oil** of rejoicing
above your companions

d. Acc. pl. fem.

ὃς **ὑμᾶς ἀναμνήσει τὰς ὁδούς μου** τὰς ἐν Χριστῷ (1 Cor. 4:17)

who **will remind you of my ways** that [οὔσας, are] in Christ

5. Accusative of manner or adverbial accusative. This is especially true of
adjectives. However, there are some nouns that function as adverbs.

a. Acc. sing. masc.

ποσάκις ἠθέλησα ἐπισυνάξαι τὰ τέκνα σου, **ὃν τρόπον** ὄρνις τὴν
ἑαυτῆς νοσσιὰν ὑπὸ τὰς πτέρυγας, καὶ οὐκ ἠθελήσατε (Luke 13:34)

I often wanted to gather your children **in the same way** a hen [gathers]
her brood under her wings, but you did not want [that]

b. Acc. sing. fem.

δωρεὰν ἐλάβετε, **δωρεὰν** δότε (Matt. 10:8)

you received **freely**, give **freely**

---

[40] 1 Peter 3:15 text is from GNT, NA & WH: TR & MT have δέ after ἕτοιμοι.

   c. Acc. sing. neut.
   ἀκούω σχίσματα ἐν ὑμῖν ὑπάρχειν, καὶ **μέρος** τι πιστεύω
   (1 Cor. 11:18)
   I hear divisions exist among you, and I **partly** believe [it]
   d. Acc. pl. fem.
   κατακλίνατε αὐτοὺς **κλισίας** ὡσεὶ ἄνα πεντήκοντα (Luke 9:14)[41]
   make them sit down **in rows** of about fifty
6. Accusative of measure indicates quantity (how much, extent) or distance
   in space (how far).
   a. Acc. sing. masc.
   ἀνέπεσαν οὖν οἱ ἄνδρες **τὸν ἀριθμὸν** ὡς πεντακισχίλιοι
   (John 6:10)[42]
   then the men reclined, **the number** about five thousand
   b. Acc. sing. fem.
   καὶ αὐτὸς ἀπεσπάσθη ἀπ᾽ αὐτῶν ὡσεὶ λίθου **βολήν** (Luke 22:41)
   and he was withdrawn from them about **a throw** of a stone (a stone's
   throw)
   c. Acc. pl. neut.
   καὶ ἰδοὺ δύο ἐξ αὐτῶν ἐν αὐτῇ τῇ ἡμέρᾳ ἦσαν πορευόμενοι εἰς
   κώμην **ἀπέχουσαν σταδίους ἐξήκοντα** ἀπὸ Ἰερουσαλήμ
   (Luke 24:13)[43]
   and, behold, two of them on the same day were going into a village
   [that was] **sixty stades distance** from Jerusalem

C. Accusatives with prepositions. The prepositions both enhance and enlarge the
   categories of the accusative without the prepositions.
   1. With εἰς, accusative of goal or end
      οὕτως γὰρ πλουσίως ἐπιχορηγηθήσεται ὑμῖν ἡ εἴσοδος **εἰς τὴν αἰώνιον
      βασιλείαν** τοῦ κυρίου ἡμῶν καὶ σωτῆρος Ἰησοῦ Χριστοῦ (2 Peter 1:11)
      for in this way the entrance **into the eternal kingdom** of our Lord and Savior
      Jesus Christ shall be abundantly granted
   2. With κατά, accusative of reference
      καὶ σχεδὸν ἐν αἵματι πάντα καθαρίζεται **κατὰ τὸν νόμον** (Heb. 9:22)
      and almost all things are purified with blood **according to the law**

---

[41] Luke 9:14 text is from GNT, NA & WH: TR & MT omit ὡσεὶ.
[42] John 6:10 text is from GNT, NA & WH: TR & MT have ἀνέπεσον and ὡσεί for ὡς.
[43] Luke 24:13 text is from GNT, NA & WH: TR & MT have ἦσαν πορευόμενοι ἐν αὐτῇ τῇ ἡμέρᾳ.

3. With πρός, accusative of place
   ὅτι δι᾽ αὐτοῦ ἔχομεν τὴν προσαγωγὴν οἱ ἀμφότεροι ἐν ἑνὶ πνεύματι
   πρὸς τὸν πατέρα (Eph. 2:18)
   for through him we both have an approach **to the father** in one spirit
4. With διά, causal accusative
   καὶ πολλῷ πλείους ἐπίστευσαν **διὰ τὸν λόγον αὐτοῦ** (John 4:41)
   and many more believed **because of his word**
5. With ἐπί, accusative of place
   καὶ πεσὼν **ἐπὶ τὴν γῆν** ἤκουσεν φωνὴν λέγουσαν αὐτῷ, Σαούλ, Σαούλ,
   τί με διώκεις; (Acts 9:4)
   and after he fell **on the ground** he heard a voice saying to him, Saul, Saul,
   why are you persecuting me?
6. With μετά, accusative of time
   αὕτη ἡ διαθήκη ἣν διαθήσομαι πρὸς αὐτοὺς **μετὰ τὰς ἡμέρας ἐκείνας**,
   λέγει κύριος (Heb. 10:16)
   this [ἐστιν, is] the covenant that I will covenant with them **after these
   days**, the Lord says
7. With παρά, accusative of place
   καὶ οἱ μάρτυρες ἀπέθεντο τὰ ἱμάτια αὐτῶν **παρὰ τοὺς πόδας** νεανίου
   καλουμένου Σαύλου (Acts 7:58)
   and the witnesses laid their garments **at the feet** of a young man named
   Saul
8. With ὑπό, accusative of authority
   εἰ δὲ πνεύματι ἄγεσθε, οὐκ ἐστὲ **ὑπὸ νόμον** (Gal. 5:18)
   but if you are being led by the Spirit, you are not **under law**
9. With περί, accusative of time
   ἀνέβη Πέτρος ἐπὶ τὸ δῶμα προσεύξασθαι **περὶ ὥραν ἕκτην** (Acts 10:9)
   Peter went up on the housetop to pray **about the sixth hour**
10. With ὑπέρ, accusative of comparison
    οὐκ ἔστιν μαθητὴς **ὑπὲρ τὸν διδάσκαλον**, οὐδὲ δοῦλος **ὑπὲρ τὸν κύριον
    αὐτοῦ** (Matt. 10:24)
    a disciple is not **superior to his teacher**, nor a **slave superior to his owner**

V. **The vocative case**. The vocative case involves direct address to one or more
persons. The vocative plural form is always like the nominative plural form and/or
like the nominative neuter singular and plural forms, but most often the nominative
singular form is distinct from the vocative case. Most vocatives are nouns, but
some adjectives have vocative forms when they modify vocative nouns or are
used as substantives. There is only one distinct vocative participle form in the
Greek New Testament (i.e., κεκονιαμένε, perfect passive, Acts 23:3), although
some participles function as attributives or substantives as vocatives. The
nominative case is often used in direct address like the vocative. However, the
nominative case normally (with few exceptions) uses the article in such functions,
whereas the vocative never has the article.

A. Introduced by ὦ.
   1. ὦ indicates emphasis or deep emotion (except in Acts).
      a. With single term
         Ὦ γύναι, μεγάλη σου ἡ πίστις (Matt. 15:28)
         O woman, your faith [ἐστιν, is] great
      b. With attributive adjectival and attributive participial phrase
         Ὦ γενεὰ ἄπιστος καὶ διεστραμμένη, ἕως πότε ἔσομαι πρὸς ὑμᾶς καὶ
         ἀνέξομαι ὑμῶν; (Luke 9:41)
         O unbelieving and perverted generation, how long shall I be with you
         and bear with you?
      c. With substantive adjectival phrase
         Ὦ ἀνόητοι καὶ βραδεῖς τῇ καρδίᾳ τοῦ πιστεύειν ἐπὶ πᾶσιν οἷς
         ἐλάλησεν οἱ προφῆται (Luke 24:25)
         O fools and slow in heart to believe all things that the prophets spoke
      d. With participial phrase in apposition to vocative
         λογίζῃ δὲ τοῦτο, **ὦ ἄνθρωπε ὁ κρίνων** τοὺς τὰ τοιαῦτα πράσσοντας
         καὶ **ποιῶν** αὐτά (Rom. 2:3)
         but you consider this, **O man, who judges** those who practise such
         things and **do** the same things [yourself]
      e. With noun and attributive adjectival phrase
         Ὦ ἀνόητοι Γαλάται, τίς ὑμᾶς ἐβάσκανεν (Gal. 3:1)
         O foolish Galatians, who bewitched you
   2. In Acts, ὦ has no special emphasis.
      a. Masc. sing.
         τὸν μὲν πρῶτον λόγον ἐποιησάμην περὶ πάντων, **ὦ Θεόφιλε** (Acts 1:1)
         I made the first account of all things, **O Theophilus**

b. Masc. pl.

ἔδει μέν, **ὦ ἄνδρες**, πειθαρχήσαντάς μοι μὴ ἀνάγεσθαι ἀπὸ τῆς
Κρήτης κερδῆσαί τε τὴν ὕβριν ταύτην καὶ τὴν ζημίαν (Acts 27:21)
you should, **O men**, have obeyed me and not set sail from Crete and as
a result obtained this disaster and loss

B. Most vocatives are used without ὦ. The vocative term is usually a personal
name, a title, or a descriptive term or phrase. Occasionally a common noun is
personalized and functions in a vocative role.

1. A personal name

a. Masc. sing.

εἶπεν πρὸς αὐτόν, **Ζακχαῖε**, σπεύσας κατάβηθι (Luke 19:5)
he said to him, **Zacchaeus**, come down quickly

b. Masc. sing.

φωνῇ μεγάλῃ ἐκραύγασεν, **Λάζαρε**, δεῦρο ἔξω (John 11:43)
he cried with a loud voice, **Lazarus**, come outside

c. Masc. sing.

καί φησιν, **Κορνήλιε**, εἰσηκούσθη σου ἡ προσευχή (Acts 10:31)
and he said, **Cornelius**, your prayer has been heard

d. Masc. pl.

οἴδατε δὲ καὶ ὑμεῖς, **Φιλιππήσιοι** (Phil. 4:15)
and you yourselves also know, **Philippians**

2. A title

a. Masc. sing.

κύριε, βοήθει μοι (Matt. 15:25)
Lord, help me

b. Masc. sing.

Διδάσκαλε, οὐ μέλει σοι ὅτι ἀπολλύμεθα; (Mark 4:38)
Teacher, is it not a concern to you that we are perishing?

c. Masc. sing.

νῦν ἀπολύεις τὸν δοῦλόν σου, **δέσποτα**, κατὰ τὸ ῥῆμά σου,
ἐν εἰρήνῃ (Luke 2:29)
let your servant depart now in peace, **master**, according to your word

d. Masc. sing.

πάτερ, δόξασόν σου τὸ ὄνομα (John 12:28)
Father, glorify your name

3. A descriptive adjective as a substantive

a. Masc. sing.

φίλε, χρῆσόν μοι τρεῖς ἄρτους (Luke 11:5)
friend, lend me three loaves of bread

b. Masc. pl.
 Ἀγαπητοί, ἀγαπῶμεν ἀλλήλους (1 John 4:7)
 dear friends, let us love one another
c. Masc. pl.
 καθαρίσατε χεῖρας, **ἁμαρτωλοί**, καὶ ἁγνίσατε καρδίας, **δίψυχοι**
 (James 4:8)
 wash [your] hands, **sinners**, and purify [your] hearts, **double minded**
d. Masc. pl.
 ἄφρονες, οὐχ ὁ ποιήσας τὸ ἔξωθεν καὶ τὸ ἔσωθεν ἐποίησεν;
 (Luke 11:40)
 fools, did not he who made the outside make the inside also?

4. A descriptive phrase, attributive adjective with noun
a. Masc. sing.
 Εὖ, **δοῦλε ἀγαθὲ καὶ πιστέ**, ἐπὶ ὀλίγα ἧς πιστός (Matt. 25:23)
 Well done, **good and faithful servant**, you were faithful over a few things
b. Masc. sing.
 Διδάσκαλε ἀγαθέ, τί ποιήσας ζωὴν αἰώνιον κληρονομήσω;
 (Luke 18:18)
 good teacher, after I have done what thing shall I inherit eternal life?
c. Masc. sing.
 πάτερ ἅγιε, τήρησον αὐτοὺς ἐν τῷ ὀνόματί σου (John 17:11)
 holy Father, keep them in your name
d. Masc. pl.
 ὅθεν, ἀδελφοὶ ἅγιοι, κλήσεως ἐπουρανίου μέτοχοι (Heb. 3:1)
 wherefore, **holy brothers, partakers** of the heavenly calling

5. A personalized common noun functioning as a vocative
a. Fem. sing.
 καὶ ἐρῶ τῇ ψυχῇ μου, **ψυχή**, ἔχεις πολλὰ ἀγαθὰ κείμενα εἰς ἔτη
 πολλά· ἀναπαύου, φάγε, πίε, εὐφραίνου (Luke 12:19)
 and I will say to my soul, **soul**, you have many goods laid up for many
 years, rest! eat! drink! be merry!
c. Masc. sing.
 ποῦ σου, **θάνατε**, τὸ νῖκος; (1 Cor. 15:55)[44]
 where is your victory, **death**
d. Masc. sing.
 Εὐφραίνου ἐπ᾽ αὐτῇ, **οὐρανέ** (Rev. 18:20)
 rejoice over her, **O heaven**

---

[44] 1 Cor. 15:55 text is from GNT, NA & WH: TR & MT have κέντρον for νῖκος.

C. The vocative may be repeated for emphasis.
1. Masc. sing.
ὕστερον δὲ ἔρχονται καὶ αἱ λοιπαὶ παρθένοι λέγουσαι, **κύριε κύριε,**
ἄνοιξον ἡμῖν (Matt. 25:11)
but afterward the other virgins also came and said, **"Lord, Lord**, open to us"
2. Masc. sing.
προσελθόντες δὲ διήγειραν αὐτόν λέγοντες, **Ἐπιστάτα ἐπιστάτα,**
ἀπολλύμεθα (Luke 8:24)
and they came to [him] and awoke him saying,**"Master, master**, we are
perishing"
3. Fem. sing.
Ἰερουσαλήμ Ἰερουσαλήμ, ἡ ἀποκτείνουσα τοὺς προφήτας (Luke 13:34)
Jerusalem, Jerusalem, who killed the prophets
4. Masc. sing.
Σίμων, Σίμων, ἰδού, ὁ σατανᾶς ἐξητήσατο ὑμᾶς τοῦ σινιάσαι ὡς τὸν
σῖτον (Luke 22:31)
Simon, Simon, behold, Satan has demanded to sift you as wheat

D. A second vocative may function in apposition to the first vocative.
1. Masc. sing.
Ἐξομολογοῦμαί σοι, **πάτερ, κύριε** τοῦ οὐρανοῦ καὶ τῆς γῆς
(Matt. 11:25)
I praise you **Father, Lord** of heaven and earth
2. Masc. sing.
τί ἐμοὶ καὶ σοί, **Ἰησοῦ υἱὲ** τοῦ θεοῦ τοῦ ὑψίστου; (Mark 5:7)
what is it to me and you, **Jesus, son** of the most high God?
3. Neut. and masc. sing.
ταύτην τὴν παραγγελίαν παρατίθεμαί σοι, **τέκνον Τιμόθεε** (1 Tim. 1:18)
I commit this charge to you, **son Timothy**
4. Masc. pl.
γνωστὸν οὖν ἔστω ὑμῖν, **ἄνδρες ἀδελφοί,** ὅτι διὰ τούτου ὑμῖν ἄφεσις
ἁμαρτιῶν καταγγέλλεται (Acts 13:38)
therefore, let it be known to you, **men, brothers**, that through this man
forgiveness of sins is announced to you

E. The word in apposition to the vocative may be a nominative case.
1. Masc. sing. articular noun
καὶ ἔλεγεν, **Αββα ὁ πατήρ,**πάντα δυνατά σοι (Mark 14:36)
and he said, **"Abba, Father**, all things [ἐστιν, are] possible to you"

2. Masc. sing. article
πάτερ ἡμῶν ὁ ἐν τοῖς οὐρανοῖς (Matt. 6:9)
our Father who [ὤν, is] in heaven

3. Masc. pl. noun and participle
Ἄνδρες Ἰσραηλῖται καὶ οἱ φοβούμενοι τὸν θεόν, ἀκούσατε (Acts 13:16)
Men, Israelites, and those who fear God, listen

4. Masc. attributive adjectival participle
Διὸ ἀναπολόγητος εἶ, ὦ ἄνθρωπε πᾶς ὁ κρίνων (Rom. 2:1)
wherefore you are inexcusable, **O man, everyone who judges**

5. Masc. sing. anarthrous noun
Ἐλέησόν με, κύριε υἱὸς Δαυίδ (Matt. 15:22)[45]
have mercy on me, **Lord, son** of David

F. The vocative is often followed by a genitive pronoun or noun indicating relationship.
1. Neut. pl.
τεκνία μου, ταῦτα γράφω ὑμῖν ἵνα μὴ ἁμάρτητε (1 John 2:1)
my little children, I write these things to you that you may not sin

2. Masc. pl.
τότε Πέτρος πλησθεὶς πνεύματος ἁγίου εἶπεν πρὸς αὐατούς Ἄρχοντες τοῦ λαοῦ καὶ πρεσβύτεροι (Acts 4:8)
then Peter, filled with the Holy Spirit, said to them, **rulers of the people** and elders

3. Masc. pl.
τὸ λοιπόν, ἀδελφοί μου, χαίρετε ἐν κυρίῳ (Phil. 3:1)
finally, **my brothers**, rejoice in the Lord

4. Masc. sing.
Υἱέ μου, μὴ ὀλιγώρει παιδείας κυρίου (Heb. 12:5)
my son, do not despise the Lord's discipline

G. The vocative may function as a predicate after a passive verb.
Masc. sing.
Ῥαββουνι ὃ λέγεται διδάσκαλε (John 20:16)[46]
Rabboni, **which means teacher**

---

[45] Matt. 15:22 text is from GNT & NA: TR & MT have υἱὲ Δαβίδ; WH has Δαυείδ.
[46] John 20:16 text is from GNT & NA: WH has Ῥαββουνεί: TR & MT have Ῥαββουνί.

H. The vocative may be modified by an attributive participle.
Masc. pl.
ἡμεῖς δὲ ὀφείλομεν εὐχαριστεῖν τῷ θεῷ πάντοτε περὶ ὑμῶν, ἀδελφοὶ
ἠγαπημένοι ὑπὸ κυρίου (2 Thess. 2:13)
but we ought to thank God always for you, **brothers beloved** by the Lord

I. The vocative noun may function as an attributive.
Masc. sing.
Σαοὺλ ἀδελφέ, ὁ κύριος ἀπεσταλκέ(ν) με (Acts 9:17)
brother Saul, the Lord has sent me

VI. **Occasionally, a noun may function as an attributive adjective.**

A. Dat. sing. masc.
καὶ ἐβαπτίζοντο ἐν τῷ Ἰορδάνῃ ποταμῷ ὑπ᾽ αὐτοῦ (Matt. 3:6)[47]
and they were baptized **in the Jordan River** by him

B. Acc. sing. fem.
καὶ πρὸς οὐδεμίαν αὐτῶν ἐπέμφθη Ἠλίας εἰ μὴ εἰς Σάρεπτα τῆς Σιδωνίας
πρὸς γυναῖκα χήραν (Luke 4:26)[48]
and to none of them was Elijah sent except to Sarepta of Sidon, **to a widow
woman**

Select Bibliography for Nouns

Barnwell, Katharine. "Vocative Phrase." *Notes on Translation* 53: 9-17.
Best, John E. "A Supplement to 'Grammar Notes' by Phillip R. Williams." Dallas Theological Seminary, 1981.
Chapman, Benjamin. *New Testament-Greek Notebook*. Grand Rapids: Baker, 1983.
Crenshaw, Curtis I. "Grammatical Studies on the Greek Noun." Master's thesis, Dallas Theological Seminary, 1975.
Countess, Robert H. "Thank God for the Genitive!" *Journal of the Evangelical Theological Society* 12 (1969): 117-22.
Geytenbeek, Helen. "A Classification of the Adnominal Genitives of I Peter." *Notes on Translation* 61: 21-32.

[47] Matt. 3:6 text is from GNT, NA & WH: TR & MT omit ποταμῷ.
[48] Luke 4:26 text is from GNT & NA: WH has Ἠλείας; TR & MT have Σιδῶνος.

Greenlee, J. Harold. "The Genitive Case in the New Testament." *Bible Translator* 1 (April 1950): 68-70.

Harner, Philip B. "Qualitative Anarthrous Predicate Nouns." *Journal of Biblical Literature* 92 (March 1973): 75-78.

Harrison, Gessner. *A Treatise on the Greek Prepositions, and on the Cases of Nouns With Which These Are Used*. Philadelphia: Lippincott, 1958.

Kilpatrick, G. D. "The Order of Some Noun and Adjective Phrases in the New Testament." *Novum Testamentum* 5 (July 1962): 111-14.

Marshall, Alfred. "The Genitive of Quality in the New Testament." *Bible Translator* 3 (1952): 14-16.

McGhee, H. William. "The Greek Article and the Abstract Noun." Master's thesis, Tennessee Temple Univ., 1985.

Moeller, Henry R. and Arnold Kramer. "An Overlooked Structural Pattern in New Testament Greek." *Novum Testamentum* 5 (July 1962): 25-35.

Moulton, Harold K. "Of." *Bible Translator* 19 (1968): 18-25.

Nelson, Dotson M., Jr. "The Articular and Anarthrous Predicate Nominative in the Greek New Testament." Th.D. diss., Southern Baptist Theological Seminary, 1944.

Nida, Eugene A. "Equivalents of the Genitive in Other Languages." *Bible Translator* 1 (April 1950): 70-72.

Nole, John A. "The Exegetical Significance of the Case of the Object of ΑΚΟΥΩ." Master's thesis, Grace Theological Seminary, 1977.

Porter, Stanley E. "The Adjectival Attributive Genitive in the New Testament: A Grammatical Study." *Trinity Journal* 4, n.s. 1 (1983): 3-17.

Roberts, J. W. "The Genitive with Nouns of Action." *Restoration Quarterly* 1 (1957): 35-40.

_____. "Exegetical Helps: the Greek Noun with and without the Article." *Restoration Quarterly* 14, no. 1 (1971): 28-47.

Scomp, Henry A. "The Case Absolute in the New Testament." *Bibliotheca Sacra* (January 1902): 76-84; (April 1902): 325-40.

Slaten, Arthur W. *Qualitative Nouns in the Pauline Epistles and Their Translation in the Revised Version*. Chicago: Univ. of Chicago, 1918.

Wallace, Daniel B. "The Semantics and Exegetical Significance of the Object-Complement Construction in the New Testament." *Grace Theological Journal* 3, no. 2 (1982): 163-75.

_____. "The Relation of Adjective to Noun in Anarthrous Constructions in the New Testament." *Novum Testamentum* 26 (April 1984): 128-67.

_____. "The Semantic Range of the Article-Noun-Καί-Noun Plural Construction in the New Testament." *Grace Theological Journal* 6, no. 1 (1985): 91-112.

Waterman, G. Henry. "The Greek Verbal Genitive" In *Current Issues in Biblical and Patristic Interpretation*, edited by Gerald F. Hawthorne. Grand Rapids: Eerdmans, (1975): 289-93.

Williams, Philip R. *Grammar Notes on the Noun and the Verb and Certain Other Items.* Tacoma, Wash.: Northwest Baptist Seminary, 1976.

PARTICLES

Forms. The term *particle* has reference to a *small part* of something. In grammar it basically has reference to a short and indeclinable part of speech. Some grammarians classify conjunctions and particles together. Others include all indeclinable forms, e.g., adverbs, conjunctions, prepositions, and interjections. In this manual, the term will refer to all indeclinable words that are not included among the adverbs, conjunctions, negatives, and prepositions. Dana and Mantey refer to particles as the "odds and ends" of Greek grammar.[1]

Functions. An alphabetic consideration of the most frequently used particles follows.

A. ἀμήν, an emphatic particle, meaning **so let it be, truly, amen**.
   1. Used with a doxology
      a. At the end of a doxology
         ᾧ ἐστιν ἡ δόξα καὶ τὸ κράτος εἰς τοὺς αἰῶνας τῶν αἰώνων, **ἀμήν**
         (1 Peter 4:11)
         to whom belongs the glory and the power forever and ever, **amen**
      b. At the beginning and end of a doxology
         Ἀμήν, ἡ εὐλογία καὶ ἡ δόξα καὶ ἡ σοφία καὶ ἡ εὐχαριστία καὶ ἡ τιμὴ καὶ ἡ δύναμις καὶ ἡ ἰσχὺς τῷ θεῷ ἡμῶν εἰς τοὺς αἰῶνας τῶν αἰώνων· **ἀμήν** (Rev. 7:12)
         Amen, blessing and glory and wisdom and gratitude and honor and power and might [belongs] to our God forever and ever, **amen**
   2. As a particle of affirmation, used with λέγω, introducing a solemn statement
      a. Used only by Jesus, as found in the synoptic gospels
         Ἀμὴν λέγω ὑμῖν, ἐὰν μὴ στραφῆτε καὶ γένησθε ὡς τὰ παιδία, οὐ μὴ εἰσέλθητε εἰς τὴν βασιλείαν τῶν οὐρανῶν (Matt. 18:3)
         truly I tell you, unless you convert and become as little children, you shall not enter the kingdom of heaven
      b. Used only by Jesus, but doubled for emphasis in John's gospel
         Ἀμὴν ἀμὴν λέγω ὑμῖν ὅτι ὁ τὸν λόγον μου ἀκούων καὶ πιστεύων τῷ πέμψαντί με ἔχει ζωὴν αἰώνιον (John 5:24)
         truly truly I tell you that the one who hears my word and believes the one who sent me has eternal life
   3. Used with an article as a substantive
      a. Nom. sing. masc.
         τάδε λέγει ὁ Ἀμήν, ὁ μάρτυς ὁ πιστὸς καὶ ἀληθινός (Rev. 3:14)
         the Amen, the faithful and true witness, says these things

---

[1] Dana and Mantey, *A Manual Grammar of the Greek New Testament*, 258.

b. Acc. sing. neut.

ἐπεὶ ἐὰν εὐλογῇς ἐν πνεύματι ὁ ἀναπληρῶν τὸν τόπον τοῦ ἰδιώτου πῶς ἐρεῖ **τὸ Ἀμὴν** ἐπὶ τῇ σῇ εὐχαριστίᾳ; ἐπειδὴ τί λέγεις οὐκ οἶδε(ν) (1 Cor. 14:16)[2]

otherwise if you bless with the spirit, how will the one who occupies the place of the uninstructed say **Amen** at your giving of thanks since he does not know what you are saying?

B. ἄν, unable to be translated by a single English word, is used with the various moods.
  1. With the indicative mood
    a. With the imperfect tense
      (1) Indicating repeated action in past time
        καὶ τὰ κτήματα καὶ τὰς ὑπάρξεις ἐπίπρασκον καὶ διεμέριζον αὐτὰ πᾶσι(ν) **καθότι ἄν τις χρείαν εἶχε(ν)** (Acts 2:45)
        and they were selling their properties and possessions and were distributing them to all **according as anyone had need**
      (2) In the apodosis of a contrary to fact condition
        εἰ ὁ θεὸς πατὴρ ὑμῶν ἦν **ἠγαπᾶτε ἄν** ἐμέ (John 8:42)
        if God were your Father, **you would have loved** me
    b. With the aorist tense
      (1) In the apodosis of a contrary to fact condition
        εἰ γὰρ ἔγνωσαν, **οὐκ ἄν** τὸν κύριον τῆς δόξης **ἐσταύρωσαν** (1 Cor. 2:8)
        for if they had known, **they would not have crucified the Lord** of glory
      (2) With οὐκ as an interrogative expecting an affirmative answer
        οὐκ ἄν ἐπαύσαντο προσφερόμεναι . . . ; (Heb. 10:2)
        since **would they not have ceased** to be offered . . . ?
    c. With the future tense and relative pronoun
      ὃς δ' **ἄν ἀπολέσει** τὴν ψυχὴν αὐτοῦ ἕνεκεν ἐμοῦ καὶ τοῦ εὐαγγελίου σώσει αὐτήν (Mark 8:35)[3]
      but whoever will lose his life on account of me and the gospel shall save it
    d. With the pluperfect tense in the apodosis of a contrary to fact condition
      εἰ ἐμὲ ᾔδειτε, καὶ τὸν πατέρα μου **ἄν ᾔδειτε** (John 8:19)
      if you had known me, **you would have known** my Father also

---

[2] 1 Cor. 14:16 text is from GNT, NA & WH: TR & MT have τῷ πνεύματι: MT has εὐλογήσῃς.

[3] Mark 8:35 text is from GNT, NA & WH: TR & MT have ἀπολέσῃ: MT has τὴν ἑαυτοῦ ψυχήν and οὗτος σώσει. This is parallel to Luke 9:24, which also has the aorist subjunctive, ἀπολέσῃ. The equivalency of the future indicative and the aorist subjunctive is found in other verbal functions.

2. With the subjunctive mood and the aorist tense
   a. After relative pronouns (ὅς, ἥ, ὅ, and ὅστις)
      (1) Nom. sing. masc.
         πᾶς γὰρ ὃς ἂν ἐπικαλέσηται τὸ ὄνομα κυρίου σωθήσεται
         (Rom. 10:13)
         for **everyone who shall call on** the name of the Lord shall be saved
      (2) Gen. sing. neut.
         ἀφ᾽ οὗ ἂν ἐγερθῇ ὁ οἰκοδεσπότης καὶ ἀποκλείσῃ τὴν θύραν
         (Luke 13:25)
         from the time the master of the house **has arisen** and shut the door
      (3) Dat. sing. neut.
         ἐν ᾧ δ᾽ ἄν τις τολμᾷ, ἐν ἀφροσύνῃ λέγω, τολμῶ κἀγώ (2 Cor. 11:21)
         but wherein anyone is daring, I am speaking foolishly, I also am daring
      (4) Acc. sing. masc.
         Ἐλεήσω **ὃν ἂν ἐλεῶ**, καὶ οἰκτειρήσω **ὃν ἂν οἰκτίρω** (Rom. 9:15)[4]
         I will have mercy **on whomever I have mercy**, and I will have
         compassion **on whomever I have compassion**
   b. With the temporal particle ἕως
      πρὸς τίνα δὲ τῶν ἀγγέλων εἴρηκέν ποτε, κάθου ἐκ δεξιῶν μου, **ἕως ἂν
      θῶ** τοὺς ἐχθρούς σου ὑποπόδιον τῶν ποδῶν σου; (Heb. 1:13)
      but to which of the angels did he ever say, sit here at my right hand,
      until I put your enemies under your feet?
   c. With adjective ὅσος
      καὶ νῦν οἶδα ὅτι **ὅσα ἂν αἰτήσῃ** τὸν θεόν δώσει σοι ὁ θεός (John 11:22)
      and now I know that **whatever you ask** God, God will give [it] to you
   d. With ὅπως, a purpose conjunction
      (1) Introducing a purpose clause
         καὶ σοῦ δὲ αὐτῆς τὴν ψυχὴν διελεύσεται ῥομφαία, **ὅπως ἂν
         ἀποκαλυφθῶσιν** ἐκ πολλῶν καρδιῶν **διαλογισμοί** (Luke 2:35)
         and for you also a sword shall pass through your soul, **in order that
         the thoughts** of many hearts **may be revealed**
      (2) Introducing a substantive object clause
         καθὼς γέγραπται, Ὅπως **ἂν δικαιωθῇς** ἐν τοῖς λόγοις σου (Rom. 3:4)
         even as it is written, **that you might be justified** in your words
   e. With ὡς
      (1) Introducing a temporal clause
         τὰ δὲ λοιπὰ **ὡς ἂν ἔλθω** διατάξομαι (1 Cor. 11:34)
         and the other things, **whenever I come**, I will set in order

---

[4] Rom. 9:15 text is from GNT & NA: WH, TR & MT have οἰκτείρω.

(2) Meaning, **as if**

ἵνα μὴ δόξω **ὡς ἂν** ἐκφοβεῖν ὑμᾶς διὰ τῶν ἐπιστολῶν (2 Cor. 10:9)

that I may not seem **as if** I were intimidating you through my epistles

f. With ὅπου, introducing a local clause

οὗτοι οἱ ἀκολουθοῦντες τῷ ἀρνίῳ **ὅπου ἂν ὑπάγῃ** (Rev. 14:4)[5]

these [εἰσιν, are] those who follow the lamb **wherever he goes**

g. With ἄχρις οὗ, introducing a temporal clause

πλὴν ὃ ἔχετε κρατήσατε **ἄχρι(ς) οὗ ἂν ἥξω** (Rev. 2:25)

but hold fast what you have **until I come**

C. ἄρα, inferential particle.
1. At the beginning of a sentence

ἄρα εἰ καὶ ἔγραψα ὑμῖν, οὐχ ἕνεκεν τοῦ ἀδικήσαντος (2 Cor. 7:12)[6]

therefore even though I wrote to you, [I wrote] not for the sake of the one who did wrong

2. In questions

γενομένης δὲ ἡμέρας ἦν τάραχος οὐκ ὀλίγος ἐν τοῖς στρατιώταις, τί **ἄρα** ὁ Πέτρος ἐγένετο (Acts 12:18)

and when day arrived there was no small stir among the soldiers, what **then** had become of Peter

3. In the apodosis of conditional sentences, translated **then, as a result**

εἰ δὲ ἐν δακτύλῳ θεοῦ ἐγὼ ἐκβάλλω τὰ δαιμόνια, **ἄρα** ἔφθασεν ἐφ᾽ ὑμᾶς ἡ βασιλεία τοῦ θεοῦ (Luke 11:20)[7]

but if I cast out demons by the finger of God, **then** the kingdom of God has come upon you

4. Meaning **so then, consequently, for**

ἐπεὶ **ἄρα** τὰ τέκνα ὑμῶν ἀκάθαρτά ἐστιν, νῦν δὲ ἅγιά ἐστιν (1 Cor. 7:14)

for otherwise your children are unclean, but now they are holy

D. γε, a postpositive, emphatic, enclitic particle that emphasizes the word(s) appended to it.
1. εἰ δὲ μή γε, meaning **otherwise**
   a. After an affirmative clause

   κἂν μὲν ποιήσῃ καρπὸν εἰς τὸ μέλλον· **εἰ δὲ μή γε**, ἐκκόψεις αὐτήν (Luke 13:9)[8]

   if then it should bear fruit in the next year, **otherwise** you shall cut it dow

---

[5] Rev. 14:4 text is from GNT & NA: WH has ὑπάγει: TR & MT have οὗτοί εἰσιν: MT has ὅπου ἐάν.

[6] 2 Cor. 7:12 text is from GNT, NA & WH: TR & MT have εἵνεκεν.

[7] Luke 11:20 text is from GNT, NA & WH: TR & MT omit ἐγώ.

[8] Luke 13:9 text is from GNT & NA: WH has εἰ δὲ μήγε: TR & MT have καρπόν· εἰ δὲ μή γε, εἰς τὸ μέλλον.

b. After a negative clause

καὶ οὐδεὶς βάλλει οἶνον νέον εἰς ἀσκοὺς παλαιούς· εἰ δὲ μή γε, ῥήξει ὁ οἶνος ὁ νέος τοὺς ἀσκούς, καὶ αὐτὸς ἐκχυθήσεται καὶ οἱ ἀσκοὶ ἀπολοῦνται (Luke 5:37)[9]

and no one puts new wine into old skins, **otherwise** the new wine will burst the skins and it will be poured out and the skins will be destroyed

2. εἴ γε, meaning **if indeed, inasmuch as**

εἴ γε ἠκούσατε τὴν οἰκονομίαν τῆς χάριτος τοῦ θεοῦ τῆς δοθείσης μοι εἰς ὑμᾶς (Eph. 3:2)

if indeed you heard of the administration of the grace of God, which was given to me for you

3. ἄρα γε, meaning **indeed then**, and καί γε, meaning **even though indeed**

ζητεῖν τὸν θεόν, εἰ **ἄρα γε** ψηλαφήσειαν αὐτὸν καὶ εὕροιεν, **καί γε** οὐ μακρὰν ἀπὸ ἑνὸς ἑκάστου ἡμῶν ὑπάρχοντα (Acts 17:27)[10]

to seek God **if indeed then** they might feel after him and find [him] **even though indeed** he is not far from each one of us

4. διά γε, meaning **yet because of**

διά γε τὴν ἀναίδειαν αὐτοῦ ἐγερθεὶς δώσει αὐτῷ ὅσων χρῄζει (Luke 11:8)

yet because of his persistance he will rise and give him as much as he needs

5. ἀλλά γε, meaning **at least**

εἰ ἄλλοις οὐκ εἰμὶ ἀπόστολος, **ἀλλά γε** ὑμῖν εἰμι (1 Cor. 9:2)

if I am not an apostle to others, **at least** I am to you

6. ὅς γε, meaning **who indeed**

ὅς γε τοῦ ἰδίου υἱοῦ οὐκ ἐφείσατο ἀλλὰ ὑπὲρ ἡμῶν πάντων παρέδωκεν αὐτόν (Rom. 8:32)

who indeed spared not his own son, but delivered him for us all

7. ὄφελόν γε, meaning **would that indeed**

χωρὶς ἡμῶν ἐβασιλεύσατε· καὶ **ὄφελόν γε** ἐβασιλεύσατε (1 Cor. 4:8)

you reigned without us, and **would that indeed** you did reign

E. ἴδε is properly the 2d person singular imperative of εἶδον, translated **you see**, but it became stereotyped as a particle.

1. Functioning verbally as an equative verb with predicate nominative

a. Nom. sing. masc.

ἠγέρθη, οὐκ ἔστιν ὧδε· **ἴδε ὁ τόπος** ὅπου ἔθηκαν αὐτόν (Mark 16:6)

he has risen, he is not here; **here is the place** where they laid him

---

[9] Luke 5:37 text is from GNT & NA: WH has εἰ δὲ μήγε: TR & MT have ὁ νέος οἶνος.

[10] Acts 17:27 text is from GNT, NA & WH: TR & MT have ζητεῖν τὸν κύριον and TR has καίτοιγε for καί γε.

b. Nom. sing. masc.

καὶ λέγει, Ἴδε ὁ ἀμνὸς τοῦ θεοῦ ὁ αἴρων τὴν ἁμαρτίαν τοῦ κόσμου (John 1:29)

and he said, **here is the lamb** of God, who takes away the sin of the world

c. Nom. sing. fem. and nom. pl. masc.

λέγει, Ἴδε ἡ μήτηρ μου καὶ οἱ ἀδελφοί μου (Mark 3:34)

he said **here is my mother** and **my brothers**

2. Functioning as an imperative four times in the NT with a direct object

a. Acc. sing. fem.

Ἴδε οὖν χρηστότητα καὶ ἀποτομίαν θεοῦ (Rom. 11:22)

notice then **the kindness** and **severity** of God

b. Acc. pl. fem.

εἶτα λέγει τῷ Θωμᾷ, φέρε τὸν δάκτυλόν σου ὧδε καὶ ἴδε τὰς χεῖράς μου (John 20:27)

then he said to Thomas, bring your finger here, and **see my hands**

c. With an object clause introduced by ὅτι

ἐραύνησον καὶ ἴδε ὅτι ἐκ τῆς Γαλιλαίας προφήτης οὐκ ἐγείρεται (John 7:52)[11]

search and **see that** no prophet arises out of Galilee

d. With an elliptical object clause

καὶ εἶπεν, ποῦ τεθείκατε αὐτόν; λέγουσιν αὐτῷ, κύριε, ἔρχου καὶ ἴδε (John 11:34)

and he said, where have you laid him? they said to him, Lord, come and **see**

[ποῦ τεθείκαμεν αὐτόν, **where we have laid him**]

3. Introducing something contrary to expectation

ἴδε οὗτος βαπτίζει καὶ πάντες ἔρχονται πρὸς αὐτόν (John 3:26)

notice, this one baptizes, and all are coming to him

4. Drawing special attention

Διδάσκαλε, ἴδε ποταποὶ λίθοι καὶ ποταπαὶ οἰκοδομαί (Mark 13:1)

Teacher, **notice** what great stones and what great buildings

F. ἰδού, demonstrative particle.

1. Without a finite verb, functioning verbally with a predicate nominative

a. Nom. sing. fem. and nom. pl. masc.

εἶπεν, Ἰδοὺ ἡ μήτηρ μου καὶ οἱ ἀδελφοί μου (Matt. 12:49)[12]

he said, **this is** my **mother** and my **brothers**

[11] John 7:52 text is from GNT, NA & WH: TR & MT have προφήτης ἐκ τῆς Γαλιλαίας οὐκ ἐγήγερται: MT has ἐρεύνησον.
[12] ἰδού is synonymous with ἴδε. See Mark 3:34.

b. Nom. sing. fem.

εἶπεν δὲ Μαριάμ, Ἰδοὺ ἡ δούλη κυρίου (Luke 1:38)

and Mary said, **here is the servant girl** of the Lord

c. Nom. sing. pronoun

ὁ δὲ εἶπεν, Ἰδοὺ ἐγώ, κύριε (Acts 9:10)

and he said, **here I am**, Lord

2. Drawing the attention of one's audience

ὁ δὲ εἶπεν αὐτοῖς, Ἰδοὺ εἰσελθόντων ὑμῶν εἰς τὴν πόλιν συναντήσει ὑμῖν ἄνθρωπος κεράμιον ὕδατος βαστάζων (Luke 22:10)

and he said to them, "**pay attention**, after you enter the city a person will meet you carrying a pitcher of water"

3. Introducing something new

a. After a genitive absolute

πορευομένων δὲ αὐτῶν ἰδού τινες τῆς κουστωδίας ἐλθόντες εἰς τὴν πόλιν ἀπήγγειλαν τοῖς ἀρχιερεῦσιν ἅπαντα τὰ γενόμενα (Matt. 28:11)[13]

and while they were going, **notice**, some of the guard went into the city and reported all things that happened to the chief priests

b. With καί

ὡς ἀγνοούμενοι, καὶ ἐπιγινωσκόμενοι, ὡς ἀποθνῄσκοντες καὶ ἰδοὺ ζῶμεν (2 Cor. 6:9)

as being unknown and yet well known, as dying **and yet take note** we are alive

G. μέν, postpositive affirmative, adversative, or emphatic particle.

1. Introduces a concessive clause

σὺ μὲν γὰρ καλῶς εὐχαριστεῖς, ἀλλ᾽ ὁ ἕτερος οὐκ οἰκοδομεῖται (1 Cor. 14:17)

for you **indeed** give thanks well, but the other person is not edified

2. Adversative with δέ, left untranslated

τὰ αὐτὰ γράφειν ὑμῖν ἐμοὶ μὲν οὐκ ὀκνηρόν, ὑμῖν δὲ ἀσφαλές (Phil. 3:1)

to write the same things to you [ἐστιν, is] not irksome to me **but** [ἐστιν, is] safe for you

3. With the adjective ἄλλος

ᾧ μὲν γὰρ διὰ τοῦ πνεύματος δίδοται λόγος σοφίας, ἄλλῳ δὲ λόγος γνώσεως κατὰ τὸ αὐτὸ πνεῦμα (1 Cor. 12:8)

for the word of wisdom is given by the Spirit **to one, and to another** the word of knowledge according to the same Spirit

---

[13] Matt. 28:11 text is from GNT, NA & WH: TR & MT have τινές.

3. As an alternative pronoun
   a. With the article
   ἐσχίσθη δὲ τὸ πλῆθος τῆς πόλεως, καὶ οἱ μὲν ἦσαν σὺν τοῖς Ἰουδαίοις
   οἱ δὲ σὺν τοῖς ἀποστόλοις (Acts 14:4)
   and the multitude of the city was divided; and **some** were with the Jews,
   and some [ἦσαν, were] with the apostles
   b. With the relative pronoun
   (1) Nom. sing. masc.
   ὃς μὲν γὰρ κρίνει ἡμέραν παρ' ἡμέραν, ὃς δὲ κρίνει πᾶσαν
   ἡμέραν (Rom. 14:5)[14]
   for **one** considers one day above another day, **and one** considers every
   day alike
   (2) Dat. sing. masc.
   καὶ ᾧ μὲν ἔδωκεν πέντε τάλαντα, ᾧ δὲ δύο, ᾧ δὲ ἕν, ἑκάστῳ
   κατὰ τὴν ἰδίαν δύναμιν (Matt. 25:15)
   and he gave five talents **to one, and to another** [ἔδωκεν, he gave] two,
   and to another [ἔδωκεν, he gave] one
   (3) Acc. sing. masc.
   ἐκεῖ ἐσταύρωσαν αὐτόν καὶ τοὺς κακούργους, ὃν μὲν ἐκ δεξιῶν
   ὃν δὲ ἐξ ἀριστερῶν (Luke 23:33)
   they crucified him and the criminals there, **one** on the right side
   and one on the left
   (4) Acc. sing. neut.
   ἢ οὐκ ἔχει ἐξουσίαν ὁ κεραμεὺς τοῦ πηλοῦ ἐκ τοῦ αὐτοῦ
   φυράματος ποιῆσαι ὃ μὲν εἰς τιμὴν σκεῦος ὃ δὲ εἰς ἀτιμίαν;
   (Rom. 9:21)
   or does not the potter have power over the clay, from the same lump
   to make **one** vessel unto honor **and one** unto dishonor?
   (5) Nom. pl. neut.
   ἐν μεγάλῃ δὲ οἰκίᾳ οὐκ ἔστιν μόνον σκεύη χρυσᾶ καὶ ἀργυρᾶ,
   ἀλλὰ καὶ ξύλινα καὶ ὀστράκινα, καὶ ἃ μὲν εἰς τιμήν ἃ δὲ εἰς
   ἀτιμίαν (2 Tim. 2:20)
   but in a spacious house there are not only vessels of gold and silver,
   but also of wood and stone, and **some** to honor **and some** to dishonor

---

[14] Rom. 14:5 text is from GNT, NA & WH; TR & MT omit γάρ.

H. ναί, affirmative or emphatic particle, meaning **yes, indeed.**
   1. Affirmative answer to a question
      σὺ Ῥωμαῖος εἶ; ὁ δὲ ἔφη, **Ναί** (Acts 22:27)
      are you a Roman? and he said, **"Yes!"**
   2. Introducing a statement of emphatic agreement
      Ναί, κύριε ὁ θεὸς ὁ παντοκράτωρ, ἀληθιναὶ καὶ δίκαιαι αἱ κρίσεις σου
      (Rev. 16:7)
      Certainly, Lord God Almighty, your judgments [εἰσιν, are] true and just
   3. With the article as substantive and without the article as predicate
      ἤτω δὲ **ὑμῶν τὸ ναὶ ναὶ** καὶ τὸ οὒ οὔ (James 5:12)
      but let **your yes** be **yes** and [ἤτω ὑμῶν, let your] no be no
   4. Affirmative and emphatic
      ναί λέγω ὑμῖν, ἐκζητηθήσεται ἀπὸ τῆς γενεᾶς ταύτης (Luke 11:51)
      indeed, I tell you, it shall be required of this generation
   5. As a solemn exclamation of assurance
      Ἰδού, ἔρχεται μετὰ τῶν νεφελῶν, καὶ ὄψεται αὐτὸν πᾶς ὀφθαλμὸς καὶ
      οἵτινες αὐτὸν ἐξεκέντησαν, καὶ κόψονται ἐπ᾽ αὐτὸν πᾶσαι αἱ φυλαὶ τῆς
      γῆς **ναί,** ἀμήν (Rev. 1:7)
      behold, he is coming with the clouds, and every eye shall see him, even those
      who pierced him, and all the tribes of the earth shall mourn because of him.
      yes indeed, amen!

I. ὅπου, particle of place.
   1. Literal sense
      a. With indicative mood
         (1) With present tense
             ὅπου γάρ **ἐστιν** ὁ θησαυρὸς ὑμῶν, ἐκεῖ καὶ ἡ καρδία ὑμῶν ἔσται
             (Luke 12:34)
             for **where** your treasure **is,** your heart will be there also
         (2) With imperfect tense
             ὅπου ἦν κῆπος, εἰς ὃν εἰσῆλθεν αὐτὸς καὶ οἱ μαθηταὶ αὐτοῦ
             (John 18:1)
             where there was a garden, into which he and his disciples entered
         (3) With aorist tense
             οὕτως δὲ φιλοτιμούμενον εὐαγγελίζεσθαι, οὐχ **ὅπου ὠνομάσθη**
             Χριστός (Rom. 15:20)
             and so being ambitious to preach the gospel **where** Christ **was** not
             named

    (4) With implicit (elliptical) verb

    οἶδα ποῦ κατοικεῖς, **ὅπου** ὁ θρόνος τοῦ Σατανᾶ (Rev. 2:13*a*)[15]

    I know where you dwell, **where** the throne of Satan [ἐστιν, **is**]

  b. With subjunctive mood

    ποῦ ἐστιν τὸ κατάλυμα **ὅπου** τὸ πάσχα μετὰ τῶν μαθητῶν μου **φάγω;**
    (Luke 22:11)

    where is the guest room **where I shall eat** the passover with my disciples?

  c. With ἐάν or ἄν and the subjunctive

    (1) With aorist tense

    καὶ **ὅπου ἐὰν εἰσέλθῃ**, εἴπατε τῷ οἰκοδεσπότῃ (Mark 14:14)

    and **wherever he enters**, say to the house owner

    (2) With present tense

    ὅπου ἐὰν ᾖ τὸ πτῶμα, ἐκεῖ συναχθήσονται οἱ ἀετοί (Matt. 24:28)[16]

    wherever the carcass **is**, the vultures will be gathered there

2. Figurative sense

  a. With implicit (elliptical) verb

    ὅπου γὰρ ζῆλος καὶ ἐριθεία, ἐκεῖ ἀκαταστασία καὶ πᾶν φαῦλον
    πρᾶγμα (James 3:16)

    for **where** jealousy and selfish ambition [ἐστιν, **exist**], disorder and every
    evil thing [ἐστιν, **exists**] there

  b. With present indicative

    ὅπου οὐκ ἔνι Ἕλλην καὶ Ἰουδαῖος, περιτομὴ καὶ ἀκροβυστία,
    Βάρβαρος, Σκύθης, δοῦλος, ἐλεύθερος, ἀλλὰ τὰ πάντα καὶ ἐν πᾶσιν
    Χριστός (Col. 3:11)

    where there is no Greek nor Jew, circumcision nor uncircumcision,
    Barbarian, Scythian, slave, freeman; but Christ [ἐστιν, is] all and
    in all

J. ὅταν, temporal particle.

  1. With the subjunctive mood

    a. With present tense, indicating action contemporaneous with the main
      clause

      διὸ εὐδοκῶ ἐν ἀσθενείαις . . . **ὅταν** γὰρ **ἀσθενῶ**, τότε δυνατός εἰμι
      (2 Cor. 12:10)

      wherefore I delight in weaknesses . . . for **when I am weak**, then I am
      strong

---

[15] Rev. 2:13 text is from GNT, NA & WH: TR & MT have οἶδα τὰ ἔργα σου καί.

[16] Matt. 24:28 text is from GNT, NA & WH: TR & MT have ὅπου γὰρ ἐάν.

b. With aorist tense, indicating action prior to that of the τότε clause

ἐλεύσονται δὲ ἡμέραι, καὶ **ὅταν ἀπαρθῇ** ἀπ᾽ αὐτῶν ὁ νυμφίος, τότε
νηστεύσουσιν ἐν ἐκείναις ταῖς ἡμέραις (Luke 5:35)

but the days will come **when** the bridegroom **will be taken away**
from them, then they will fast in those days

2. With the indicative mood

a. With present tense, translated **whenever**

εἶπε(ν) δὲ αὐτοῖς, ὅταν προσεύχησθε λέγετε, πάτερ, ἁγιασθήτω
τὸ ὄνομά σου (Luke 11:2)[17]

and he said to them, **whenever you pray**, say, "Father, let your name be
sanctified"

b. With future tense

καὶ **ὅταν δώσουσιν** τὰ ζῷα δόξαν καὶ τιμὴν καὶ εὐχαριστίαν τῷ
καθημένῳ ἐπὶ τῷ θρόνῳ (Rev. 4:9)

and **whenever** the living creatures **shall give** glory and honor and gratitude
to the one who sits on the throne

c. With imperfect tense

καὶ τὰ πνεύματα τὰ ἀκάθαρτα, **ὅταν** αὐτὸν **ἐθεώρουν, προσέπιπτον**
αὐτῷ καὶ **ἔκραζον** λέγοντες ὅτι Σὺ εἶ ὁ υἱὸς τοῦ θεοῦ (Mark 3:11)[18]

and the unclean spirits, **whenever they saw** him, **fell down before** him, and
cried out, "You are the son of God"

d. With aorist tense

καὶ **ὅταν** ὀψὲ **ἐγένετο**, ἐξεπορεύοντο ἔξω τῆς πόλεως (Mark 11:19)[19]

and **when** evening **arrived**, they went out of the city

K. ὅτε, temporal particle with indicative mood.

1. Often functioning as a conjunction

a. With present tense

διαθήκη γὰρ ἐπὶ νεκροῖς βεβαία, ἐπεὶ μήποτε ἰσχύει **ὅτε ζῇ**
ὁ διαθέμενος (Heb. 9:17)

for a will [ἐστιν, is] valid at the time of the death, since it is never in
force **while** the one who made the will **is alive**

b. With imperfect tense

ὅτε ἦς νεώτερος, ἐζώννυες σεαυτόν καὶ περιεπάτεις ὅπου ἤθελες
(John 21:18)

when you were young you dressed yourself and walked wherever you
wanted

---

[17] Luke 11:2 text is from GNT, NA & WH: TR & MT have πάτερ ἡμῶν ὁ ἐν τοῖς οὐρανοῖς.

[18] Mark 3:11 text is from GNT & NA: WH has λέγοντα: TR & MT have ἐθεώρει, προσέπιπτεν, and ἔκραζε(ν) λέγοντα.

[19] Mark 11:19 text is from GNT, NA & WH: TR & MT have ὅτε and ἐξεπορεύετο.

   c. With aorist tense
     ἔτι γὰρ ἐν τῇ ὀσφύϊ τοῦ πατρὸς ἦν, **ὅτε συνήντησεν** αὐτῷ **Μελχισεδέκ**
     (Heb. 7:10)[20]
     for he was yet in his father's loins **when Melchisedek met** him
   d. With perfect tense
     ὅτε δὲ γέγονα ἀνήρ, κατήργηκα τὰ τοῦ νηπίου (1 Cor. 13:11)[21]
     but **when I became** a man I set aside infantile things
  2. In place of the relative pronoun after a noun indicating time
   a. With present tense
     ἔρχεται νύξ **ὅτε οὐδεὶς δύναται** ἐργάζεσθαι (John 9:4)
     night is coming **when no one is able** to work
   b. With future tense
     ἐλεύσονται ἡμέραι **ὅτε ἐπιθυμήσετε** μίαν τῶν ἡμερῶν τοῦ υἱοῦ τοῦ
     ἀνθρώπου ἰδεῖν καὶ οὐκ ὄψεσθε (Luke 17:22)
     the days will come **when you will desire** to see one of the days of the son
     of man and you will not see

L. **ποτε**, an enclitic temporal particle.
  1. Of time
   a. With affirmative statement
     ἐχάρην δὲ ἐν κυρίῳ μεγάλως ὅτι **ἤδη ποτὲ** ἀνεθάλετε τὸ ὑπὲρ ἐμοῦ
     φρονεῖν (Phil. 4:10)
     but I rejoiced greatly in the Lord, that **now at last** [your] thinking of me
     bloomed again
   b. After negative statement
     οὐ γὰρ θελήματι ἀνθρώπου ἠνέχθη προφητεία **ποτέ** (2 Peter 1:21)
     for prophecy was not brought **at any time** by the will of man
  2. With present tense
     τίς **στρατεύεται** ἰδίοις ὀψωνίοις **ποτέ**; (1 Cor. 9:7)
     who **at any time serves as a soldier** at his own expense?
  3. With imperfect tense
     ἦτε γάρ **ποτε** σκότος, νῦν δὲ φῶς ἐν κυρίῳ (Eph. 5:8)
     for **you were once** darkness, but now [ἐστε, you are] light in the Lord
  4. With elliptical verb
     οἵ ποτε οὐ λαός, νῦν δὲ λαὸς θεοῦ (1 Peter 2:10)[22]
     who at one time [ὄντες, were] not a people but now [ὄντες/εἰσιν, are] the
     people of God

[20] Heb. 7:10 text is from GNT, NA & WH: TR & MT have ὁ Μελχισεδέκ.
[21] 1 Cor. 13:11 text is from GNT, NA & WH: TR & MT have ὅτε δέ.
[22] 1 Peter 2:10 text is from GNT, NA & WH: TR & MT have οἱ ποτέ.

M. πότε, interrogative particle of time, meaning **when?**
 1. With direct questions
 Διδάσκαλε, **πότε** οὖν ταῦτα ἔσται; (Luke 21:7)
 Teacher, **when** then shall these things be?
 2. With indirect questions
 γρηγορεῖτε οὖν· οὐκ οἴδατε γὰρ **πότε** ὁ κύριος τῆς οἰκίας ἔρχεται
 (Mark 13:35)
 watch therefore; for you do not know **when** the owner of the house will come
 3. With ἕως, meaning **how long?**
 Ὦ γενεὰ ἄπιστος καὶ διεστραμμένη, **ἕως πότε** ἔσομαι πρὸς ὑμᾶς καὶ
 ἀνέξομαι ὑμῶν; (Luke 9:41)
 O unbelieving and perverted generation, **how long** shall I be with you and put
 up with you?

N. πῶς, interrogative particle, translated **how? in what way?**
 1. With indicative mood
 a. With direct questions
 (1) With present tense
 καὶ **πῶς** ἡμεῖς **ἀκούομεν** ἕκαστος τῇ ἰδίᾳ διαλέκτῳ ἡμῶν ἐν ᾗ
 ἐγεννήθημεν (Acts 2:8)
 and **how does** each one of us **hear** in our own mother tongue in which
 we were born
 (2) With aorist tense
 πῶς οὖν **ἐλογίσθη**; ἐν περιτομῇ ὄντι ἢ ἐν ἀκροβυστίᾳ; οὐκ ἐν
 περιτομῇ ἀλλ᾽ ἐν ἀκροβυστίᾳ (Rom. 4:10)
 how then was it **accounted**? while he lived in circumcision, or in
 uncircumcision? not in circumcision, but in uncircumcision
 (3) With future tense
 πῶς οὐχὶ μᾶλλον ἡ διακονία τοῦ πνεύματος **ἔσται** ἐν δόξῃ;
 (2 Cor. 3:8)
 how shall the ministry of the Spirit not **be** with glory?
 b. With indirect questions
 (1) With present tense
 αὐτοὶ γὰρ οἴδατε **πῶς** δεῖ μιμεῖσθαι ἡμᾶς (2 Thess. 3:7)
 for you yourselves know **how one ought** to imitate us
 (2) With imperfect tense
 ἔλεγον οὖν οἱ Ἰουδαῖοι, Ἴδε **πως ἐφίλει** αὐτόν (John 11:36)
 the Jews then were saying, notice **how he loved** him
 (3) With aorist tense
 καὶ διηγήσατο αὐτοῖς **πῶς** ἐν τῇ ὁδῷ **εἶδεν** τὸν κύριον (Acts 9:27)
 and he related to them **how he saw** the Lord along the way

    (4) With perfect tense
       μνημόνευε οὖν **πῶς εἴληφας** καὶ ἤκουσας (Rev. 3:3)
       remember then **how you have received** and heard
  2. With the aorist subjunctive in deliberative questions
    ὄφεις, γεννήματα ἐχιδνῶν, **πῶς φύγητε** ἀπὸ τῆς κρίσεως τῆς γεέννης;
    (Matt. 23:33)
    serpents, offspring of vipers, **how shall you escape** from the judgment of
    Gehenna?
  3. With the present optative in deliberative questions
    ὁ δὲ εἶπεν, **πῶς γὰρ ἂν δυναίμην** ἐὰν μή τις ὁδηγήσει με; (Acts 8:31)
    and he said, for **how shall I be able** unless someone guide me?

O. πώς, enclitic particle, meaning **perhaps**.
  1. With εἴ
    a. With future indicative
       εἴ πως ἤδη ποτὲ **εὐοδωθήσομαι** ἐν τῷ θελήματι τοῦ θεοῦ ἐλθεῖν πρὸς
       ὑμᾶς (Rom. 1:10)
       if perhaps already **I shall succeed** by the will of God to come to you
    b. With aorist subjunctive
       εἴ πως καταντήσω εἰς τὴν ἐξανάστασιν τὴν ἐκ νεκρῶν (Phil. 3:11)
       if perhaps I may arrive at the resurrection that [οὖσαν, is] from the dead
    c. With present optative
       εἴ πως δύναιντο καταντήσαντες εἰς Φοίνικα παραχειμάσαι
       (Acts 27:12)[23]
       if perhaps they might be able to spend the winter after having arrived at
       Phoenix
  2. With μή and the aorist subjunctive
    ὥστε τοὐναντίον μᾶλλον ὑμᾶς χαρίσασθαι καὶ παρακαλέσαι, **μή πως** τῇ
    περισσοτέρᾳ λύπῃ **καταποθῇ ὁ τοιοῦτος** (2 Cor. 2:7)
    so that on the other hand you should forgive and encourage [him], **lest such
    a one should be overwhelmed** with greater grief

Select Bibliography for Particles

Denniston, J. D. *The Greek Particles.* Oxford, 1954.
Thrall, Margaret E. *Greek Particles in the New Testament.* Leiden: E. J. Brill, 1962.

---

[23] Acts 27:12 text is from GNT, NA, WH & MT; TR has εἴπως.

PREPOSITIONS

Forms. A preposition is a word used primarily as an aid in expressing relations between substantives (adjectives, nouns, participles, and infinitives). Prepositions generally do not change their form, although there are special rules for accents, vowels, and compounds. Prepositions fall into two basic categories called proper and improper prepositions.

I. **The proper prepositions** have several distinctive characteristics as follows.

    A. The accents.

        1. The accent (except for εἰς, ἐκ, and ἐν) is always on the ultima, the last syllable of the word, e.g., ἀνά, ἀντί, διά, ἀπό, κατά, μετά, παρά, περί, πρό, πρός, σύν, ὑπέρ, and ὑπό.

        2. Occasionally the enclitic prepositions εἰς and ἐν are also accented.

           a. εἰς before another enclitic

           καὶ εἰσερχομένου αὐτοῦ **εἴς τινα κώμην** ἀπήντησαν αὐτῷ δέκα λεπροὶ ἄνδρες (Luke 17:12)

           and while he was entering **into a certain village**, ten leprous men met him

           b. ἐν before another enclitic

           βλέπετε, ἀδελφοί, μήποτε ἔσται **ἔν τινι** ὑμῶν καρδία πονηρὰ ἀπιστίας (Heb. 3:12)

           beware, brothers, lest there shall be **in any** of you an evil heart of unbelief

    B. The proper prepositions are often used to form compound words, which add a new idea to the basic word or intensify the meaning. The following are samples of some of the most frequent words found in the NT.

        1. Adjectives: διάβολος, ἐκλεκτός.

        2. Nouns: ἀπόστολος, διαθήκη, διακονία, ἐκκλησία, ἐντολή, ἐπιθυμία, καταβολή, μετάνοια, παραβολή, παράκλησις, ὑπομονή.

        3. Verbs: ἀποθνῄσκω, ἀποκρίνομαι, ἀποκτείνω, ἀπόλλυμι, ἀπολύω, ἀποστέλλω, εἰσέρχομαι, ἐκβάλλω, ἐπιγινώσκω, καταβαίνω, παραδίδωμι, παρακαλέω, παραλαμβάνω.

    C. The proper prepositions that end in a vowel (except for περί and πρό) often delete the final vowel (ellision) when followed by another word beginning with a vowel.

        1. When the word following the preposition has a smooth breathing, the final vowel of the preposition is generally replaced with an apostrophe.

a. Illustrations of this rule

　　(1) ἀπό

　　　　πάντα οὕτως διαμένει **ἀπ' ἀρχῆς** κτίσεως (2 Peter 3:4)

　　　　all things thus continue **from the beginning** of creation

　　(2) ἐπί

　　　　καὶ οὕτως εἶδον τοὺς ἵππους ... καὶ τοὺς καθημένους

　　　　ἐπ' αὐτῶν (Rev. 9:17)

　　　　and thus I saw the horses ... and those who were sitting **on th**

　　(3) κατά

　　　　καὶ ἀπολύσας τοὺς ὄχλους ἀνέβη εἰς τὸ ὄρος **κατ' ἰδίαν**

　　　　προσεύξασθαι (Matt. 14:23)

　　　　and when he had dismissed the crowds he went up into the

　　　　mountain **privately** to pray

　　(4) μετά

　　　　καὶ περιπατήσουσιν **μετ' ἐμοῦ** ἐν λευκοῖς (Rev. 3:4)

　　　　and they shall walk **with me** in white

　　(5) ὑπό

　　　　ἔλεγεν οὖν τοῖς ἐκπορευομένοις ὄχλοις βαπτισθῆναι **ὑπ' αὐτ**

　　　　(Luke 3:7)

　　　　he spoke then to the crowds coming out to be baptized **by him**

b. Exceptions to this rule; e.g., when the final vowel is not deleted befo

　　a smooth breathing

　　(1) ἀντί

　　　　ἐκεῖνον λαβὼν δὸς αὐτοῖς **ἀντὶ ἐμοῦ** καὶ σοῦ (Matt. 17:27)

　　　　take it and give to them **for me** and you

　　(2) ἀπό

　　　　Ἰωσὴφ ὁ **ἀπὸ Ἀριμαθαίας**, εὐσχήμων βουλευτής (Mark 15:43)

　　　　Joseph who [ὤν, was] **from Arimathea**, an honorable counselor

　　(3) ἐπί

　　　　εἰσῆλθεν εἰς τὸν οἶκον τοῦ θεοῦ **ἐπὶ Ἀβιάθαρ** (Mark 2:26)

　　　　he entered the house of God **in [the days] of Abiathar**

　　(4) μετά

　　　　εὗρόν με ἡγνισμένον ἐν τῷ ἱερῷ, οὐ **μετὰ ὄχλου** οὐδὲ μετὰ

　　　　θορύβου (Acts 24:18)

　　　　they found me purified in the temple, not **with a crowd** nor with

　　　　disturbance

　　(5) παρά

　　　　ὁ Ἰησοῦς εἶπεν αὐτοῖς, **παρὰ ἀνθρώποις** τοῦτο ἀδύνατόν ἐστι

　　　　(Matt. 19:26)

　　　　Jesus said to them, this is impossible **with men**

(6) ὑπό

Κορνήλιος ἑκατοντάρχης, ἀνὴρ δίκαιος καὶ φοβούμενος τὸν
θεόν, μαρτυρούμενός τε **ὑπὸ ὅλου τοῦ ἔθνους** τῶν Ἰουδαίων,
ἐχρηματίσθη **ὑπὸ ἀγγέλου ἁγίου** (Acts 10:22)

Cornelius, a centurion, a just man who feared God and was
witnessed to **by the entire nation** of Jews, was divinely instructed
by a holy angel

2. When the initial vowel of the word following the preposition has the rough
breathing, the preposition's final vowel is deleted and the final consonant
is changed to a double consonant.

a. Illustrations of this rule

(1) ἀντί, always before ὧν

ἀνθ᾽ ὧν τὴν ἀγάπην τῆς ἀληθείας οὐκ ἐδέξαντο εἰς τὸ σωθῆναι
αὐτούς (2 Thess. 2:10)

because they did not receive the love of the truth in order that they
might be saved

(2) ἀπό

οὐ γὰρ λαλήσει **ἀφ᾽ ἑαυτοῦ** (John 16:13)

for he will not speak **from himself**

(3) ἐπί

ἐπιποθούντων ὑμᾶς διὰ τὴν ὑπερβάλλουσαν χάριν τοῦ θεοῦ
ἐφ᾽ ὑμῖν (2 Cor. 9:14)

longing for you because of the surpassing grace of God **upon you**

(4) κατά

καὶ ἀσπασάμενος αὐτοὺς ἐξηγεῖτο **καθ᾽ ἓν ἕκαστον** ὧν
ἐποίησεν ὁ θεὸς ἐν τοῖς ἔθνεσιν διὰ τῆς διακονίας αὐτοῦ
(Acts 21:19)

and when he had saluted them he related **one by one** the things
God did among the Gentiles through his ministry

(5) μετά

μεθ᾽ ἧς ἐπόρνευσαν οἱ βασιλεῖς τῆς γῆς (Rev. 17:2)

with whom the kings of the earth committed fornication

(6) ὑπό

φανερούμενοι ὅτι ἐστὲ ἐπιστολὴ Χριστοῦ διακονηθεῖσα
ὑφ᾽ ἡμῶν (2 Cor. 3:3)

being manifested that you are Christ's epistle ministered **by us**

b. Exceptions to this rule; e.g., when the final vowel is not deleted or the
final consonant doubled before a rough breathing

(1) κατά

οὐχὶ σαρκικοί ἐστε καὶ **κατὰ ἄνθρωπον** περιπατεῖτε; (1 Cor. 3:3)

are you not fleshly and walk **according to man**?

(2) ἀπό

καὶ οἱ γραμματεῖς οἱ **ἀπὸ Ἱεροσολύμων** καταβάντες ἔλεγον (Mark 3:22)[1]

and the scribes who came down **from Jerusalem** said

(3) μετά

ἵνα **μετὰ ἡσυχίας** ἐργαζόμενοι τὸν ἑαυτῶν ἄρτον ἐσθίωσιν (2 Thess. 3:12)

that, working **with quietness**, they may eat their own bread

(4) ἐπί

ὃς ὤφθη **ἐπὶ ἡμέρας πλείους** τοῖς συναναβᾶσιν αὐτῷ ἀπὸ τῆς Γαλιλαίας εἰς Ἰερουσαλήμ (Acts 13:31)

who appeared **for many days** to those who came up with him from Galilee to Jerusalem

(5) παρά

διεγόγγυζον, λέγοντες, ὅτι **παρὰ ἁμαρτωλῷ ἀνδρί**, εἰσῆλθεν καταλῦσαι (Luke 19:7)

they murmured, saying, "he has entered to lodge **with a sinful man**"

3. With two prepositions, διά and παρά, the final vowel is sometimes replaced with an apostrophe, whether before a smooth or rough breathing mark.

a. διά

(1) Before smooth breathing

δι᾽ ὀλίγων ἔγραψα, παρακαλῶν καὶ ἐπιμαρτυρῶν ταύτην εἶναι ἀληθῆ χάριν τοῦ θεοῦ (1 Peter 5:12)

I wrote **briefly**, exhorting and testifying [that] this is the true grace of God

(2) Before rough breathing

τῷ δὲ θεῷ χάρις τῷ πάντοτε θριαμβεύοντι ἡμᾶς ἐν τῷ Χριστῷ καὶ τὴν ὀσμὴν τῆς γνώσεως αὐτοῦ φανεροῦντι **δι᾽ ἡμῶν** ἐν παντὶ τόπῳ (2 Cor. 2:14)

but thanks to God who always leads us triumphant in Christ and makes manifest the fragrance of knowing him **through us** in every place

(3) Exceptions to δι᾽ before an initial vowel. Proper nouns beginning with a vowel; i.e., Ἰερεμίου, Ἡσαΐου, Ἰησοῦ, are preceded by διά, and once εἴδους is preceded by διά.

οὗ ἐξέχεεν ἐφ᾽ ἡμᾶς πλουσίως **διὰ Ἰησοῦ** Χριστοῦ τοῦ σωτῆρος ἡμῶν (Titus 3:6)

which he poured out on us richly **through Jesus** Christ our savior

---

[1] Mark 3:22 text is from GNT, NA, TR & MT; WH has Ἱεροσολύμων.

Prepositions

189

  (1) Before smooth breathing
  καὶ διὰ τὸ ὁμότεχνον εἶναι ἔμενεν **παρ᾽ αὐτοῖς** (Acts 18:3)
  and because [he] was of the same trade, he remained **with them**
  (2) Before rough breathing
  τί ἄπιστον κρίνεται **παρ᾽ ὑμῖν** εἰ ὁ θεὸς νεκροὺς ἐγείρει;
  (Acts 26:8)
  why is it considered incredible **with you** if God raises the dead?
  (3) Exceptions to παρ᾽ before an initial vowel. The following are
  preceded by παρά: proper names beginning with a vowel (e.g.,
  Ἰωάννου, Ἰησοῦ, Ἐπαφροδίτου); one pronoun, ἀλλήλων; one noun,
  ἀνθρώπου, ἀνθρώπων; and one adjective, ἁμαρτωλῷ.
  δεξάμενος **παρὰ Ἐπαφροδίτου** τὰ παρ᾽ ὑμῶν (Phil. 4:18)
  having received **from Epaphroditus** the things from you
4. One preposition, ἐκ, changes the final consonant before both a smooth and
   a rough breathing mark.
   a. With smooth breathing
   καὶ φωνὴν **ἐξ οὐρανοῦ** γενέσθαι (Luke 3:22)
   and a voice came **from heaven**
   b. With rough breathing
   νῦν δὲ ὑπάγω πρὸς τὸν πέμψαντά με, καὶ οὐδεὶς **ἐξ ὑμῶν** ἐρωτᾷ με,
   ποῦ ὑπάγεις; (John 16:5)
   but now I am going to the one who sent me, and none **of you** asks me,
   "where are you going?"

II. **Forty-two improper prepositions occur in the NT.** Only a few of these are given
consideration in this book, e.g., ἄχρι(ς), ἔμπροσθεν, ἐνώπιον, ἔξω, ἕως, χωρίς.
A few improper prepositions are postpositive, following the substantive rather
than preceding it.
διδάσκοντες ἃ μὴ δεῖ, **αἰσχροῦ κέρδους χάριν** (Titus 1:11)
teaching what they ought not, **for the purpose of base gain**

Functions. Prepositions are used to help in expressing relationships between
substantives and verbs. "They mark the direction and relative position of the action,
motion, or state expressed by the verb."[2] The substantives may be adjectives,
adverbs, nouns, pronouns, infinitives, or participles. "In the Koine all the prepositions
become increasingly elastic and their sense has to be determined more often by the

---

[2] Dana and Mantey, *A Manual Grammar of the Greek Testament*, 97.

context than was earlier the case. . . . Such elasticity makes it dangerous to press doctrinal distinctions as though our authors were writing classical Greek."[3]

I. **Proper prepositions.**

 A. ἀντί with the genitive indicates, among others, substitution, equivalence, reason, exchange, and contrast.

  1. Meaning **in the place of, replaced by**
   ὃς ἀντὶ τῆς προκειμένης αὐτῷ χαρᾶς ὑπέμεινεν σταυρόν (Heb. 12:2)
   who **in place of the joy set before** him endured the cross

  2. Meaning **for, equivalent to**
   a. With adjectives
    μὴ ἀποδιδόντες κακὸν ἀντὶ κακοῦ . . . τοὐναντίον δὲ εὐλογοῦντες
    (1 Peter 3:9)
    not rendering evil **equivalent to evil** . . . but rather blessing
   b. With nouns
    ἠκούσατε ὅτι ἐρρέθη, ὀφθαλμὸν ἀντὶ ὀφθαλμοῦ καὶ ὀδόντα ἀντὶ
    ὀδόντος (Matt. 5:38)
    you heard that it was said, an eye **for an eye** and a tooth **for a tooth**

  3. Meaning **on behalf of**, equivalent to ὑπέρ
   a. With adjective
    καὶ γὰρ ὁ υἱὸς τοῦ ἀνθρώπου οὐκ ἦλθεν διακονηθῆναι ἀλλὰ
    διακονῆσαι καὶ δοῦναι τὴν ψυχὴν αὐτοῦ λύτρον ἀντὶ πολλῶν
    (Mark 10:45)
    for even the son of man did not come to be ministered to but to minister and to give his life a ransom **on behalf of many**
   b. With pronoun
    καὶ τὸν ἀναβάντα πρῶτον ἰχθὺν ἆρον, καὶ ἀνοίξας τὸ στόμα αὐτοῦ
    εὑρήσεις στατῆρα· ἐκεῖνον λαβὼν δὸς αὐτοῖς ἀντὶ ἐμοῦ καὶ σοῦ
    (Matt. 17:27)
    and take the first fish that comes up, and when you have opened its mouth you will find a coin; take it and give to them **on behalf of me** and **you**

  4. Gen. of cause, meaning **because**
   ἀνθ᾽ ὧν τὴν ἀγάπην τῆς ἀληθείας οὐκ ἐδέξαντο εἰς τὸ σωθῆναι αὐτούς
   (2 Thess. 2:10)
   because they did not receive the love of the truth in order that they might be saved

---

[3] Moulton and Turner, *A Grammer of New Testament Greek: Syntax*, 261.

5. Meaning **in exchange for**

ὡς Ἠσαῦ, ὃ **ἀντὶ βρώσεως μιᾶς** ἀπέδετο τὰ πρωτοτόκια ἑαυτοῦ
(Heb. 12:16)

as Esau, who **in exchange for one meal** sold his own birthright

6. With infinitive, meaning **instead of**

ἀντὶ τοῦ λέγειν ὑμᾶς, ἐὰν ὁ κύριος θελήσῃ καὶ ζήσομεν καὶ
ποιήσομεν τοῦτο ἢ ἐκεῖνο (James 4:15)[4]

instead you should say, if the Lord wills, we shall live and do this or that

B. ἀπό, with genitive, primarily indicates separation or source. However, there are several other meanings associated with this preposition. We find some overlap of meaning with ἐκ, παρά, and ὑπό.

1. Genitive of separation

a. With adjectives

πιστὸς δέ ἐστιν ὁ κύριος, ὃς στηρίξει ὑμᾶς καὶ φυλάξει **ἀπὸ τοῦ
πονηροῦ** (2 Thess. 3:3)

but the Lord is faithful, who will establish and keep you **from the evil one**

b. With adverbs

καὶ τὸ καταπέτασμα τοῦ ναοῦ ἐσχίσθη εἰς δύο **ἀπ᾽ ἄνωθεν** ἕως
κάτω (Mark 15:38)[5]

and the veil of the temple was torn in two **from the top** to the bottom

c. With nouns

κρύψατε ἡμᾶς **ἀπὸ προσώπου** τοῦ καθημένου ἐπὶ τοῦ θρόνου καὶ
ἀπὸ τῆς ὀργῆς τοῦ ἀρνίου (Rev. 6:16)

hide us **from the face** of the one who sits upon the throne and **from the wrath** of the lamb

d. With pronouns

ὑπὲρ τούτου τρὶς τὸν κύριον παρεκάλεσα, ἵνα ἀποστῇ **ἀπ᾽ ἐμοῦ**
(2 Cor. 12:8)

for this I requested the Lord three times that it might depart **from me**

e. With participles

ἵνα ῥυσθῶ **ἀπὸ τῶν ἀπειθούντων** ἐν τῇ Ἰουδαίᾳ (Rom. 15:31)

that I may be delivered **from those who are disobedient** in Judea

2. Genitive of source

a. With pronouns

καίπερ ὢν υἱός, ἔμαθεν **ἀφ᾽ ὧν** ἔπαθεν τὴν ὑπακόην (Heb. 5:8)

though he was a son, he learned obedience **from the things** he suffered

---

[4] James 4:15 text is from GNT, NA & TR*b*: WH has θέλῃ; TR*s* & MT have ζήσωμεν and ποιήσωμεν.

[5] Mark 15:38 text is from GNT, NA & WH: TR & MT have ἀπὸ ἄνωθεν.

b. With nouns

τὴν ἁγίαν Ἰερουσαλήμ, καταβαίνουσαν ἐκ τοῦ οὐρανοῦ **ἀπὸ τοῦ θεοῦ** (Rev. 21:10)[6]

the holy Jerusalem, coming down out of heaven **from God**

c. With participles

ἀπὸ δὲ τῶν δοκούντων εἶναί τι, ὁποῖοί ποτε ἦσαν οὐδέν μοι διαφέρει (Gal. 2:6)

but **from those who had the reputation** of being something, whatever they were, it makes no difference to me

3. Genitive of time

a. With adverbs

ἀπὸ τοῦ νῦν ἀνθρώπους ἔσῃ ζωγρῶν (Luke 5:10)

from now on you shall be catching men

b. With nouns

ἐπεὶ ἔδει αὐτὸν πολλάκις παθεῖν **ἀπὸ καταβολῆς** κόσμου (Heb. 9:26)

since, then, it was necessary for him to suffer often **from the foundation** of the world

c. With pronouns

ὑμεῖς ἐπίστασθε, ἀπὸ πρώτης ἡμέρας **ἀφ᾽ ἧς** ἐπέβην εἰς τὴν Ἀσίαν (Acts 20:18)

you know, from the first day **since** I arrived in Asia

4. Genitive of origin

a. The city of origin

Ἰησοῦν τὸν **ἀπὸ Ναζαρέθ** (Acts 10:38)

Jesus the one **from Nazareth**

b. The country of origin

τινὲς δὲ **ἀπὸ τῆς Ἀσίας** Ἰουδαῖοι (Acts 24:19)

but some Jews [ἦσαν, were] **from Asia**

5. Genitive of the originator of the action

a. With adjectives

καὶ ὑμεῖς χρῖσμα ἔχετε **ἀπὸ τοῦ ἁγίου** (1 John 2:20)

and you yourselves have an anointing **from the holy one**

b. With nouns

καὶ τότε ὁ ἔπαινος γενήσεται ἑκάστῳ **ἀπὸ τοῦ θεοῦ** (1 Cor. 4:5)

and then praise shall belong to each one **from God**

c. With adverbs

δεῖ δὲ καὶ μαρτυρίαν καλὴν ἔχειν **ἀπὸ τῶν ἔξωθεν** (1 Tim. 3:7)[7]

but he must also have a good testimony **from those outside**

---

[6] Rev. 21:10 text is from GNT, NA, WH & MT: TR has Ἱερουσαλήμ.

[7] 1 Tim. 3:7 text is from GNT, NA & WH: TR & MT have δεῖ δὲ αὐτὸν καί.

d. With participles

ἀπὸ ὁ ὢν καὶ ὁ ἦν καὶ ὁ ἐρχόμενος (Rev. 1:4)[8]

from the one who is and who was and **who is coming**

6. Partisan genitive, indicating members of a group

a. With adjectives

ᾧ καὶ δεκάτην **ἀπὸ πάντων** ἐμέρισεν Ἀβραάμ (Heb. 7:2)

to whom also Abraham divided a tenth **of all**

b. With nouns

ἐπέβαλεν Ἡρῴδης ὁ βασιλεὺς τὰς χεῖρας κακῶσαί τινας τῶν **ἀπὸ τῆς ἐκκλησίας** (Acts 12:1)

Herod the king put his hands on some of those who [ὄντων, were members] **of the church**

c. With pronouns

προσεφώνησεν τοὺς μαθητὰς αὐτοῦ, καὶ ἐκλεξάμενος **ἀπ᾽ αὐτῶν** δώδεκα, οὓς καὶ ἀποστόλους ὠνόμασεν (Luke 6:13)

he summoned his disciples and chose out twelve **from among them**, whom he also named apostles

7. Genitive of agency or instrumental with passive verb

a. With finite verbs

(1) With nouns

καὶ **ἐδικαιώθη** ἡ σοφία **ἀπὸ τῶν ἔργων αὐτῆς** (Matt. 11:19)

and wisdom **is justified by its deeds**

(2) With pronouns

ὅτι **ἀναπέπαυται** τὸ πνεῦμα αὐτοῦ **ἀπὸ πάντων ὑμῶν** (2 Cor. 7:13)

because his spirit **was refreshed by you all**

b. With infinitives

πρῶτον δὲ δεῖ αὐτὸν πολλὰ παθεῖν καὶ **ἀποδοκιμασθῆναι ἀπὸ τῆς γενεᾶς ταύτης** (Luke 17:25)

but first he must suffer many things and **be rejected by this generation**

c. With participles

κατενεχθεὶς ἀπὸ τοῦ ὕπνου ἔπεσεν ἀπὸ τοῦ τριστέγου κάτω καὶ ἤρθη νεκρός (Acts 20:9)

having been overcome by sleep, he fell down from the third floor and was taken up dead

---

[8] In Rev. 1:4 (GNT, NA & WH: TR has ἀπὸ τοῦ ὁ ὤν; MT has ἀπὸ θεοῦ ὁ ὤν), ἀπό is used with the nominative participle as an indeclinable phrase and may have been a set phrase among Christians indicating the eternity and unchangeableness of God (A. T. Robertson, *A Grammar of the Greek New Testament in the Light of Historical Research*, 734-35). ὁ ὤν, in reference to the divine name is found in Ex. 3:14 and may have been regarded as indeclinable in Greek (Moulton and Turner, *A Grammar of New Testament Greek: Syntax*, 230).

8. To indicate distance from some point
   a. With adjectives
      οὐ μακρὰν ἀπὸ ἑνὸς ἑκάστου ἡμῶν ὑπάρχοντα (Acts 17:27)
      he is **not far from each one of us**
   b. With adverbs
      καὶ ὅσοι τὴν θάλασσαν ἐργάζονται, ἀπὸ μακρόθεν ἔστησαν
      (Rev. 18:17)
      and as many as trade by sea **stood at a distance**
   c. With nouns
      οὐ μακρὰν εἶ ἀπὸ τῆς βασιλείας τοῦ θεοῦ (Mark 12:34)
      you are **not far from the kingdom** of God
9. Indicating caution, fear, shame
   a. With nouns
      προσέχετε δὲ ἀπὸ τῶν ἀνθρώπων· παραδώσουσιν γὰρ ὑμᾶς εἰς
      συνέδρια (Matt. 10:17)
      but **beware of men**, for they will deliver you to the sanhedrin
   b. With participles
      μὴ φοβηθῆτε ἀπὸ τῶν ἀποκτεινόντων τὸ σῶμα καὶ μετὰ ταῦτα μὴ
      ἐχόντων περισσοτερόν τι ποιῆσαι (Luke 12:4)
      do not be afraid of those who kill the body, and after these things do
      not have anything more to do
10. Genitive of cause
   a. With adjectives
      ἔβαλον οὖν, καὶ οὐκέτι αὐτὸ ἑλκύσαι ἴσχυον ἀπὸ τοῦ πλήθους τῶν
      ἰχθύων (John 21:6)
      they cast [τὸ δίκτυον, the net] therefore, and **they were unable**
      to draw it **because of the large number of fish**
   b. With nouns
      καὶ ἐζήτει ἰδεῖν τὸν Ἰησοῦν τίς ἐστιν καὶ οὐκ ἠδύνατο ἀπὸ
      τοῦ ὄχλου, ὅτι τῇ ἡλικίᾳ μικρὸς ἦν (Luke 19:3)
      and he was seeking to see Jesus, who he was, and **he was unable**
      because of the crowd, because he was small in stature
11. Adverbial genitive
   a. With μέρος
      ὅτι πώρωσις ἀπὸ μέρους τῷ Ἰσραὴλ γέγονεν (Rom. 11:25)
      that hardness **in part** has happened to Israel
   b. With nouns
      ἐὰν μὴ ἀφῆτε ἕκαστος τῷ ἀδελφῷ αὐτοῦ ἀπὸ τῶν καρδιῶν ὑμῶν
      (Matt. 18:35)
      unless each of you will forgive his brother **sincerely**

C. διά, with genitive and accusative, among others, indicates agency, space, time, and cause.
  1. With genitive
    a. Genitive of means, instrumentality, intermediate agent
      (1) Genitive of person
        (a) With nouns
            τὸ πνεῦμα τὸ ἅγιον ἐλάλησεν **διὰ Ἡσαΐου** τοῦ προφήτου
            πρὸς τοὺς πατέρας (Acts 28:25)
            the Holy Spirit spoke **through Isaiah** the prophet to the fathers
        (b) With pronouns
            καὶ ἡ πίστις ἡ **δι᾽ αὐτοῦ** ἔδωκεν αὐτῷ τὴν ὁλοκληρίαν
            ταύτην ἀπέναντι πάντων ὑμῶν (Acts 3:16)
            and the faith that [οὖσα, is] **by him** gave to him this
            complete soundness before you all
      (2) Genitive of thing
          ἵνα μὴ δόξω ὡς ἂν ἐκφοβεῖν ὑμᾶς **διὰ τῶν ἐπιστολῶν**
          (2 Cor. 10:9)
          so that I may not seem to intimidate you **by means of [my] epistles**
    b. Genitive of place
      (1) With adjectives
          αὐτὸς δὲ διελθὼν **διὰ μέσου αὐτῶν** ἐπορεύετο (Luke 4:30)
          but when he passed **through their midst** he went on his way
      (2) With nouns
          καὶ οὐκ ἤφιεν ἵνα τις διενέγκῃ σκεῦος **διὰ τοῦ ἱεροῦ**
          (Mark 11:16)
          and he did not permit that anyone should carry a vessel **through the
          temple**
    c. Genitive of time (extent), meaning **during, in, through**
      (1) With adjectives
          αὐτὸς δὲ ὁ κύριος τῆς εἰρήνης δῴη ὑμῖν τὴν εἰρήνην **διὰ παντός**
          (2 Thess. 3:16)
          but may the Lord of peace himself give you peace **continually**
      (2) Rarely to indicate an interval of time, **after**
          ἔπειτα **διὰ δεκατεσσάρων ἐτῶν** πάλιν ἀνέβην εἰς Ἱεροσόλυμα
          (Gal. 2:1)
          then **after fourteen years** I went up again into Jerusalem
      (3) With nouns
          ἐγὼ καταλύσω τὸν ναὸν τοῦτον τὸν χειροποίητον καὶ **διὰ
          τριῶν ἡμερῶν** ἄλλον ἀχειροποίητον οἰκοδομήσω (Mark 14:58)
          I will destroy this temple that was made with hands, and **in three
          days** I will build another made without hands

2. With accusative
   a. Causal
      (1) With nouns
          καὶ τὰς ψυχὰς τῶν πεπλεκισμένων διὰ τὴν μαρτυρίαν
          Ἰησοῦ καὶ διὰ τὸν λόγον τοῦ θεοῦ (Rev. 20:4)
          and the souls of those who were beheaded **because of the
          testimony** of Jesus and **because of the word** of God
      (2) With pronouns
          διὰ τοῦτο εὐφραίνεσθε, οἱ οὐρανοὶ καὶ οἱ ἐν αὐτοῖς
          σκηνοῦντες (Rev. 12:12)
          because of this rejoice you heavens and you who inhabit them
      (3) With infinitives
          ὁ δέ, διὰ τὸ μένειν αὐτὸν εἰς τὸν αἰῶνα ἀπαράβατον ἔχει τὴν
          ἱερωσύνην (Heb. 7:24)
          but **because he remains** forever, he has the priesthood
          unchangeable
   b. Combined with interrogative pronoun
      διὰ τί ὑμεῖς οὐ πιστεύετέ μοι; (John 8:46)[9]
      why do you not believe me?

D. εἰς, with accusative, among others indicates motion, direction, purpose, time,
   result, reference, and opposition.
   1. Accusative of place after verbs of motion toward a place, translated **into,
      unto, to**
      a. With adjectives
         εἰς τὰ ἴδια ἦλθεν, καὶ οἱ ἴδιοι αὐτὸν οὐ παρέλαβον (John 1:11)
         he came **to his own,** and his own people did not receive him
      b. With adverbs
         καὶ ἦλθον εἰς τὸ πέραν τῆς θαλάσσης (Mark 5:1)
         and they went **to the other side** of the lake
      c. With nouns
         ἀλλὰ ἀποταξάμενος αὐτοῖς ἐξῆλθον εἰς Μακεδονίαν (2 Cor. 2:13)
         but when I had said farewell to them, I went out **into Macedonia**
      d. With pronouns
         οὐδέν ἐστιν ἔξωθεν τοῦ ἀνθρώπου εἰσπορευόμενον εἰς αὐτόν ὃ
         δύναται κοινῶσαι αὐτόν (Mark 7:15)[10]
         there is nothing outside of the person entering **into him** that is
         able to make him impure

---

[9] John 8:46 text is from GNT, NA, WH & MT: TR has διατί.
[10] Mark 7:15 text is from GNT & NA: WH has οὐδὲν ἔστιν; TR & MT have αὐτὸν κοινῶσαι.

2. Accusative of direction after verbs of looking, pointing, sending, speaking, translated **unto, to**
   a. With nouns
      ἀναβλέψας εἰς τὸν οὐρανὸν εὐλόγησεν καὶ κατέκλασεν τοὺς ἄρτους καὶ ἐδίδου τοῖς μαθηταῖς (Mark 6:41)
      when he looked up **to heaven** he blessed and broke the loaves and gave to his disciples
   b. With pronouns
      ἐκηρύξαμεν εἰς ὑμᾶς τὸ εὐαγγέλιον τοῦ θεοῦ (1 Thess. 2:9)
      we proclaimed the gospel of God **to you**
3. Accusative of goal, purpose, end
   a. Object of πιστεύω
      (1) With nouns
          καὶ ἡμεῖς εἰς Χριστὸν Ἰησοῦν ἐπιστεύσαμεν (Gal. 2:16)
          and we believed **in Christ Jesus**
      (2) With pronouns
          περὶ ἁμαρτίας μέν, ὅτι οὐ πιστεύουσιν εἰς ἐμέ (John 16:9)
          concerning sin, because they do not believe **in me**
   b. Purpose, end, goal
      (1) With nouns
          κηρύσσων βάπτισμα μετανοίας εἰς ἄφεσιν ἁμαρτιῶν (Luke 3:3)
          proclaiming the baptism of repentance **for the forgiveness** of sins
      (2) With pronouns
          εἰς ὃ ἐτέθην ἐγὼ κῆρυξ καὶ ἀπόστολος (1 Tim. 2:7)
          for which I was appointed a preacher and an apostle
   c. To change something into something else
      ὁ ἥλιος μεταστραφήσεται εἰς σκότος καὶ ἡ σελήνη εἰς αἷμα (Acts 2:20)
      the sun shall be turned **into darkness** and the moon **into blood**
4. Accusative of time
   a. With adjectives
      ἀφωμοιωμένος δὲ τῷ υἱῷ τοῦ θεοῦ, μένει ἱερεὺς εἰς τὸ διηνεκές (Heb. 7:3)
      and being made like the son of God, he remains a priest **for all time**
   b. With nouns
      εἰ βρῶμα σκανδαλίζει τὸν ἀδελφόν μου, οὐ μὴ φάγω κρέα εἰς τὸν αἰῶνα (1 Cor. 8:13)
      if meat causes my brother to stumble, I will never eat flesh **forever**

   c. With participles
     ἀποθησαυρίζοντας ἑαυτοῖς θεμέλιον καλὸν εἰς τὸ μέλλον
     (1 Tim. 6:19)
     laying up for themselves a good foundation **for the future**

5. Predicate εἰς with εἰμί, γίνομαι, passive verb and elliptical verb
   a. With εἰμί
     καὶ **ἔσομαι** αὐτοῖς **εἰς θεόν** καὶ αὐτοὶ **ἔσονταί** μου **εἰς λαόν**
     (Heb. 8:10)
     and **I will be** their **God**, and **they shall be** my **people**
   b. With γίνομαι
     ἡ λύπη ὑμῶν **εἰς χαρὰν** γενήσεται (John 16:20)
     your grief **shall become joy**
   c. With passive verb
     ἐπίστευσεν δὲ Ἀβραὰμ τῷ θεῷ, καὶ **ἐλογίσθη** αὐτῷ **εἰς δικαιοσύνην**
     (Rom. 4:3)
     and Abraham believed God, and **it was counted** to him for **righteousness**
   d. With elliptical verb
     ἐν τῷ νῦν καιρῷ τὸ ὑμῶν περίσσευμα **εἰς τὸ** ἐκεινων ὑστέρημα
     (2 Cor. 8:14)
     in the present time your abundance [**γένηται, should be**] **for their deficiency**

6. εἰς sometimes functions for ἐν
   a. With adjectives
     ἦλθεν ὁ Ἰησοῦς καὶ ἔστη **εἰς τὸ μέσον** καὶ λέγει αὐτοῖς, Εἰρήνη ὑμῖν
     (John 20:19)
     Jesus came and stood **in the midst** and said to them, Peace to you
   b. With adverbs
     ὑμῖν γάρ ἐστιν ἡ ἐπαγγελία καὶ τοῖς τέκνοις ὑμῶν καὶ πᾶσιν τοῖς
     εἰς μακράν (Acts 2:39)
     for the promise belongs to you and to your children, and to all who
     [οὖσιν, are] **at a distance**
   c. With nouns
     ἐγὼ γὰρ οὐ μόνον δεθῆναι ἀλλὰ καὶ ἀποθανεῖν **εἰς Ἰερουσαλὴμ**
     ἑτοίμως ἔχω ὑπὲρ τοῦ ὀνόματος τοῦ κυρίου Ἰησοῦ (Acts 21:13)[11]
     for I am ready not only to be bound but also to die **in Jerusalem**
     for the name of the Lord Jesus

---

[11] Acts 21:13 text is from GNT, NA, WH & MT: TR has Ἰερουσαλήμ.

d. With pronouns

τοῦ λαβεῖν αὐτοὺς ἄφεσιν ἁμαρτιῶν καὶ κλῆρον ἐν τοῖς
ἡγιασμένοις πίστει τῇ εἰς ἐμέ (Acts 26:18)

that they may receive forgiveness of sins and an inheritance among
those who are sanctified by faith that [οὔσῃ, is] **in me**

7. Accusative of result of an action or stated condition

a. With adjectives

θεοῦ γὰρ διάκονός ἐστίν σοι εἰς τὸ ἀγαθόν (Rom. 13:4)

for he is a servant of God to you, **resulting in good**

b. With nouns

νῦν χαίρω, οὐχ ὅτι ἐλυπήθητε, ἀλλ᾽ ὅτι ἐλυπήθητε εἰς μετάνοιαν
(2 Cor. 7:9)

now I rejoice, not because you were grieved, but because you were
grieved **resulting in repentance**

8. Accusative of purpose or result with infinitive

a. Purpose

εἰς τὸ στηρίξαι ὑμῶν τὰς καρδίας ἀμέμπτους ἐν ἁγιωσύνῃ
ἔμπροσθεν τοῦ θεοῦ καὶ πατρὸς ἡμῶν (1 Thess. 3:13)

in order that your hearts may be established blameless in sanctification
before our God and Father

b. Result

εἰς τὸ εἶναι αὐτὸν δίκαιον καὶ δικαιοῦντα τὸν ἐκ πίστεως Ἰησοῦ
(Rom. 3:26)

so that he is just and justifies the one [ὄντα, who is] of faith in Jesus

9. Accusative of respect or reference

a. With adjectives

οἴδαμεν δὲ ὅτι τοῖς ἀγαπῶσιν τὸν θεὸν πάντα συνεργεῖ εἰς ἀγαθόν
(Rom. 8:28)

but we know that for those who love God he works all things **for good**

b. With nouns

Μάρκον ἀναλαβὼν ἄγε μετὰ σεαυτοῦ· ἔστιν γάρ μοι εὔχρηστος
εἰς διακονίαν (2 Tim. 4:11)

take Mark and bring [him] with you, for he is useful to me **with respect
to ministry**

c. With pronouns

ἐπεὶ δοκιμὴν ζητεῖτε τοῦ ἐν ἐμοὶ λαλοῦντος Χριστοῦ, ὃς εἰς ὑμᾶς
οὐκ ἀσθενεῖ ἀλλὰ δυνατεῖ ἐν ὑμῖν (2 Cor. 13:3)

since you seek a proof of Christ speaking in me, who is not weak **with
any reference to you** but is strong in you

10. Accusative of opposition or hostility, translated **against**
    a. With nouns
        οὕτως δὲ ἁμαρτάνοντες εἰς τοὺς ἀδελφούς, καὶ τύπτοντες αὐτῶν τὴν
        συνείδησιν ἀσθενοῦσαν εἰς Χριστὸν ἁμαρτάνετε (1 Cor. 8:12)
        now in this way when you sin **against the brothers** and wound their
        weak conscience, you sin **against Christ**
    b. With pronouns
        κύριε, ποσάκις ἁμαρτήσει εἰς ἐμὲ ὁ ἀδελφός μου καὶ ἀφήσω αὐτῷ;
        (Matt. 18:21)
        Lord, how often shall my brother sin **against me** and shall I forgive him?
11. Adverbially
    a. With adjectives
        ὅθεν καὶ σῴζειν εἰς τὸ παντελὲς δύναται τοὺς προσερχομένους δι
        αὐτοῦ τῷ θεῷ (Heb. 7:25)
        wherefore also he is able to save **completely** those who approach
        God through him
    b. With nouns
        ἀγαπήσας τοὺς ἰδίους τοὺς ἐν τῷ κόσμῳ εἰς τέλος ἠγάπησεν αὐτούς
        (John 13:1)
        having loved his own who [ὄντας, were] in the world, he loved them
        absolutely
12. Interrogative with τί
    καὶ λέγει αὐτῷ, Ὀλιγόπιστε, εἰς τί ἐδίστασας; (Matt. 14:31)
    and he said to him, "Little faith one, **why** did you doubt?"

E. ἐκ, with genitive, among others, indicates source, separation, partitive,
    partison, direction, cause, place, and time.
    1. Genitive of origin, source, or family
        a. With adverbs
            ὑμεῖς ἐκ τῶν κάτω ἐστέ, ἐγὼ ἐκ τῶν ἄνω εἰμί (John 8:23
            you are **from below**, I am **from above**
        b. With adjectives
            λόγον ὑγιῆ ἀκατάγνωστον, ἵνα ὁ ἐξ ἐναντίας ἐντραπῇ (Titus 2:8)
            sound speech, beyond reproach, in order that the one [ὤν, who is]
            of the opposition may be ashamed
        c. With nouns
            καὶ ἐγεμίσθη ὁ ναὸς καπνοῦ ἐκ τῆς δόξης τοῦ θεοῦ καὶ ἐκ τῆς
            δυνάμεως αὐτοῦ (Rev. 15:8)
            and the temple was filled with smoke **from the glory** of God and
            from his power

d. With pronouns
ἔχομεν δὲ τὸν θησαυρὸν τοῦτον ἐν ὀστρακίνοις σκεύεσιν, ἵνα ἡ
ὑπερβολὴ τῆς δυνάμεως ᾖ τοῦ θεοῦ καὶ μὴ **ἐξ ἡμῶν** (2 Cor. 4:7)
but we have this treasure in earthen vessels, in order that the
extraordinary quality of power may be of God and not **from us**

e. With participles
ἡ πεισμονὴ οὐκ **ἐκ τοῦ καλοῦντος** ὑμᾶς (Gal. 5:8)
this persuasion [ἐστιν, is] not **from the one who called** you

2. Genitive of separation
a. With adjectives
καὶ ὑμεῖς πεφυσιωμένοι ἐστέ, καὶ οὐχὶ μᾶλλον ἐπενθήσατε, ἵνα
ἀρθῇ **ἐκ μέσου ὑμῶν** ὁ τὸ ἔργον τοῦτο πράξας (1 Cor. 5:2)[12]
and you are puffed up and did not rather mourn, that the one who did
this deed might be taken **out of your midst**

b. With nouns
οἶδεν κύριος εὐσεβεῖς **ἐκ πειρασμοῦ** ῥύεσθαι (2 Peter 2:9)
the Lord knows how to deliver the godly **from temptation**

c. With pronouns
ὁ Ἰησοῦς ἐπιγνοὺς ἐν ἑαυτῷ τὴν **ἐξ αὐτοῦ** δύναμιν ἐξελθοῦσαν
(Mark 5:30)
Jesus knew in himself that power had departed **from him**

3. Partitive genitive
a. With nouns
ἦσαν ὁμοῦ Σίμων Πέτρος καὶ Θωμᾶς ὁ λεγόμενος Δίδυμος καὶ
Ναθαναὴλ ὁ ἀπὸ Κανᾶ τῆς Γαλιλαίας καὶ οἱ τοῦ Ζεβεδαίου καὶ
ἄλλοι **ἐκ τῶν μαθητῶν αὐτοῦ** δύο (John 21:2)
there were together Simon Peter and Thomas, who was called Didymus,
and Nathanael, who [ὤν, was] from Cana of Galilee, and the [sons]
of Zebedee and two others **of his disciples**

b. With adjectives
τίς **ἐκ τῶν δύο** ἐποίησεν τὸ θέλημα τοῦ πατρός; (Matt. 21:31)
who **of the two** performed the will of his father?

c. With pronouns
ἐξ αὐτῶν ἀποκτενεῖτε καὶ σταυρώσετε, καὶ **ἐξ αὐτῶν** μαστιγώσετε
ἐν ταῖς συναγωγαῖς ὑμῶν (Matt. 23:34)
you will kill and crucify [some] **of them**, and you will scourge
[some] **of them** in your synagogues

---

[12] 1 Cor. 5:2 text is from GNT, NA & WH; TR & MT have ἐξαρθῇ and τὸ ἔργον τοῦτο ποιήσας.

   d. With participles

     πάντες γὰρ ἐκ τοῦ περισσεύοντος αὐτοῖς ἔβαλον, αὕτη δὲ
     ἐκ τῆς ὑστερήσεως αὐτῆς πάντα ὅσα εἶχεν ἔβαλεν (Mark 12:44)
     for they all cast [in] **from their abundance**, but she from her poverty
     cast in all that she had

4. Partisan genitive, belonging to a group or unified entity

   a. With adjectives

     Θωμᾶς δέ εἷς ἐκ τῶν δώδεκα ὁ λεγόμενος Δίδυμος (John 20:24)
     but Thomas, one **of the twelve**, who is called Didymus

   b. With nouns

     ἐὰν εἴπῃ ὁ πούς, ὅτι οὐκ εἰμὶ χείρ, οὐκ εἰμὶ ἐκ τοῦ σώματος
     (1 Cor. 12:15)
     if the foot should say, because I am not a hand, I am not [a member]
     of the body

   c. With pronouns

     σὺν Ὀνησίμῳ τῷ πιστῷ καὶ ἀγαπητῷ ἀδελφῷ, ὅς ἐστιν ἐξ ὑμῶν
     (Col. 4:9)
     with Onesimus, the faithful and beloved brother, who is [one] **of you**

5. Genitive of direction, from which something comes

    καὶ ὁ τρίτος ἄγγελος ἐσάλπισεν, καὶ ἔπεσεν ἐκ τοῦ οὐρανοῦ
    ἀστὴρ μέγας (Rev. 8:10)
    and the third angel blew a trumpet, and a great star fell **out of heaven**

6. Genitive of cause, translated **because of, as a result of**

   a. With adjectives

     τὸ μὲν γὰρ κρίμα ἐξ ἑνὸς εἰς κατάκριμα (Rom. 5:16)
     for indeed the judgment [ἦν, was] to condemnation **because of one**

   b. With nouns

     μὴ ἐκ λύπης ἢ ἐξ ἀνάγκης· ἱλαρὸν γὰρ δότην ἀγαπᾷ ὁ θεός
     (2 Cor. 9:7)
     not of grief or **of necessity**; for God loves a cheerful giver

7. Genitive of place, meaning **where**

    καὶ σὺν αὐτῷ σταυροῦσιν δύο λῃστάς, ἕνα ἐκ δεξιῶν καὶ ἕνα
    ἐξ εὐωνύμων αὐτοῦ (Mark 15:27)
    and they crucified two robbers with him, one **on the right side** and
    one **on his left side**

8. Genitive of time, meaning **beginning from, for**

    εἰσὶν γὰρ εὐνοῦχοι οἵτινες ἐκ κοιλίας μητρὸς ἐγεννήθησαν οὕτως
    (Matt. 19:12)
    for there are eunuchs, which were so born **from [their] mother's womb**

9. Genitive of descent from
   καὶ ἦν Ἄννα προφῆτις, θυγάτηρ Φανουήλ, ἐκ φυλῆς Ἀσήρ
   (Luke 2:36)[13]
   and Anna was a prophetess, a daughter of Phanuel, **from the tribe of Asher**
10. Adverbial genitive
    a. With adjectives
       ἐκ δευτέρου χωρὶς ἁμαρτίας ὀφθήσεται τοῖς αὐτὸν
       ἀπεκδεχομένοις εἰς σωτηρίαν (Heb. 9:28)
       he shall appear **a second time** apart from sin to those who eagerly
       wait for him for salvation
    b. With nouns
       ὑμεῖς δέ ἐστε σῶμα Χριστοῦ καὶ μέλη ἐκ μέρους (1 Cor. 12:27)
       now you are the body of Christ, and members **individually**
11. Genitive of material, of which something is made
    καὶ οἱ δώδεκα πυλῶνες δώδεκα μαργαρῖται, ἀνὰ εἷς ἕκαστος τῶν
    πυλώνων ἦν ἐξ ἑνὸς μαργαρίτου (Rev. 21:21)
    and the twelve gates [εἰσιν, were] twelve pearls; each one of the gates
    was **of one pearl**

F. ἐν with the dative case. "The uses of this preposition are so many-sided, and
   often so easily confused, that a strictly systematic treatment is impossible.
   It must suffice to list the main categories, which will help in establishing
   the usage in individual cases."[14]
   1. Dative of place, spatial, meaning **in** (within which an action takes place or
      a state of being exists)
      a. Meaning **in**
         (1) With adjectives
             φωνὴ βοῶντος ἐν τῇ ἐρήμῳ, ἑτοιμάσατε τὴν ὁδὸν κυρίου
             (Luke 3:4)
             the voice of one crying **in the desert place**, prepare the way of the
             Lord
         (2) With pronouns
             μὴ θορυβεῖσθε· ἡ γὰρ ψυχὴ αὐτοῦ ἐν αὐτῷ ἐστιν (Acts 20:10)
             do not be distressed; for his life is **in him**

---

[13] Luke 2:36 text is from GNT, NA, WH & MT: TR has Ἄννα.
[14] BDF, p. 258

(3) With nouns

καὶ ἀφέντες τὸν ὄχλον παραλαμβάνουσιν αὐτὸν ὡς ἦν
ἐν τῷ πλοίῳ (Mark 4:36)

and when they dismissed the crowd, they took him along as he was
in the boat

b. Meaning **among**

(1) With adjectives

ἐγὼ δὲ **ἐν μέσῳ ὑμῶν** εἰμι ὡς ὁ διακονῶν (Luke 22:27)

but I am **among you** as one who serves

(2) With nouns

γενομένης δὲ ἡμέρας ἦν τάραχος οὐκ ὀλίγος **ἐν τοῖς
στρατιώταις**, τί ἄρα ὁ Πέτρος ἐγένετο (Acts 12:18)

and when daylight came there was no small consternation
among the soldiers [as to] where Peter had gone

(3) With pronouns

τὰ μὲν σημεῖα τοῦ ἀποστόλου κατειργάσθη **ἐν ὑμῖν** ἐν πάσῃ
ὑπομονῇ (2 Cor. 12:12)

indeed, the signs of an apostle were performed **among you** with
all patience

(4) With participles

ὅτι Χριστοῦ εὐωδία ἐσμὲν τῷ θεῷ **ἐν τοῖς σῳζομένοις** καὶ
ἐν τοῖς ἀπολλυμένοις (2 Cor. 2:15)

for we are a fragrance of Christ to God **among those who are being
saved** and **among those who are perishing**

c. Meaning **to be clothed with**

(1) With adjectives

καὶ θεωρεῖ δύο ἀγγέλους **ἐν λευκοῖς** καθεζομένους (John 20:12)

and she saw two angels sitting **in white [clothes]**

(2) With nouns

οὐδὲ Σολομὼν **ἐν πάσῃ τῇ δόξῃ αὐτοῦ** περιεβάλετο ὡς ἐν
τούτων (Matt. 6:29)

neither Solomon **in all his splendor** was clothed as one of these

2. Dative of sphere, influence, control, or domain

a. Meaning **influence, control, or domain**

(1) With nouns

ἄχρι γὰρ καὶ ὑμῶν ἐφθάσαμεν **ἐν τῷ εὐαγγελίῳ** τοῦ Χριστοῦ
(2 Cor. 10:14)

for unto you also we came **in the gospel** of Christ

(2) With adjectives

ἐν παντὶ καὶ ἐν πᾶσιν μεμύημαι καὶ χορτάζεσθαι καὶ πεινᾶν
(Phil. 4:12)[15]

in everything and **in all respects** I have learned both to be filled
and to hunger

(3) With pronouns

ἐγὼ γὰρ ἔμαθον ἐν οἷς εἰμι αὐτάρκης εἶναι (Phil. 4:11)

for I have learned to be content (self-sufficient) **in whatever
circumstances** I am

b. Spiritual relationships

(1) With κυρίῳ

οὐ τὸ ἔργον μου ὑμεῖς ἐστε ἐν κυρίῳ; (1 Cor. 9:1)

are you not my work **in the Lord**?

(2) With Χριστῷ

τῷ δὲ θεῷ χάρις τῷ πάντοτε θριαμβεύοντι ἡμᾶς ἐν τῷ Χριστῷ
(2 Cor. 2:14)

but thanks to God who always causes us to triumph **in Christ**

(3) With Χριστῷ Ἰησοῦ

καὶ ἡ εἰρήνη τοῦ θεοῦ ἡ ὑπερέχουσα πάντα νοῦν
φρουρήσει τὰς καρδίας ὑμῶν καὶ τὰ νοήματα ὑμῶν ἐν Χριστῷ
Ἰησοῦ (Phil. 4:7)

and the peace of God that surpasses all understanding will guard
your hearts and your minds **in Christ Jesus**

(4) With pronouns

ὁ μένων ἐν ἐμοί κἀγὼ ἐν αὐτῷ, οὗτος φέρει καρπὸν πολύν
(John 15:5)

the one who abides **in me**, and I **in him**, this one bears much fruit

(5) With participles

ἐχαρίτωσεν ἡμᾶς ἐν τῷ ἠγαπημένῳ (Eph. 1:6)

he highly favored us **in the beloved one**

(6) With ὄνομα

ὅτι ἐν τῷ ὀνόματι Ἰησοῦ Χριστοῦ τοῦ Ναζωραίου ὃν ὑμεῖς
ἐσταυρώσατε, ὃν ὁ θεὸς ἤγειρεν ἐκ νεκρῶν, ἐν τούτῳ οὗτος
παρέστηκεν ἐνώπιον ὑμῶν ὑγιής (Acts 4:10)

that **in the name** of Jesus Christ the Nazarene, whom you crucified,
whom God raised from the dead, in this [name] this one stands
before you whole

---

[15] Phil. 4:12 text is from GNT, NA & MT: WH & TR have πεινᾶν.

c. Indicating mental or thought processes
   (1) With nouns
   τί ταῦτα διαλογίζεσθε **ἐν ταῖς καρδίαις ὑμῶν**; (Mark 2:8)
   why do you ponder these things **in your hearts**
   (2) With pronouns
   ὡς δὲ **ἐν ἑαυτῷ** διηπόρει ὁ Πέτρος τί ἂν εἴη τὸ ὅραμα ὃ εἶδεν
   (Acts 10:17)
   and as Peter was greatly perplexed **in himself** what the vision
   that he saw might signify
3. Dative of time
   a. Meaning **within which, during**
      (1) With nouns
      ἐν δὲ ταῖς ἡμέραις ταύταις πληθυνόντων τῶν μαθητῶν ἐγένετο
      γογγυσμὸς τῶν Ἑλληνιστῶν πρὸς τοὺς Ἑβραίους (Acts 6:1)
      now **in these days** when the disciples multiplied there arose
      a complaint from the Hellenists against the Hebrews
      (2) With nouns and participles
      οὐ μόνον **ἐν τῷ αἰῶνι τούτῳ** ἀλλὰ καὶ **ἐν τῷ μέλλοντι** (Eph. 1:21)
      not only **in this age** but also **in the coming** [αἰῶνι, age]
      (3) With infinitives
      καὶ ἦν ὁ λαὸς προσδοκῶν τὸν Ζαχαρίαν καὶ ἐθαύμαζον **ἐν τῷ**
      χρονίζειν ἐν τῷ ναῷ αὐτόν (Luke 1:21)[16]
      and the people were looking for Zacharias; and they were
      wondering because **he delayed** in the temple
   b. Point of time, at the time of an event
      (1) With adjectives
      καὶ ἐγένετο **ἐν μιᾷ** τῶν ἡμερῶν καὶ αὐτὸς ἦν διδάσκων
      (Luke 5:17)
      and it took place [that] **on one** of those days he was teaching
      (2) With adverbs
      ἐν τῷ μεταξὺ ἠρώτων αὐτὸν οἱ μαθηταί (John 4:31)
      in the meantime his disciples were asking him
      (3) With nouns
      ἀνταποδοθήσεται γάρ σοι **ἐν τῇ ἀναστάσει** τῶν δικαίων
      (Luke 14:14)
      for it shall be repaid to you **at the resurrection** of the righteous

---

[16] Luke 1:21 text is from GNT, NA & WH: TR & MT have αὐτὸν ἐν τῷ ναῷ.

(4) With pronouns
ἦλθεν δὲ ἡ ἡμέρα τῶν ἀζύμων, ἐν ᾗ ἔδει θύεσθαι τὸ πάσχα
(Luke 22:7)
and the day of unleavened bread came **in which** the passover
[lamb] must be killed

(5) With infinitives
καὶ ἐγένετο ἐν τῷ **ἐλθεῖν αὐτὸν** εἰς οἶκόν τινος τῶν ἀρχόντων
τῶν Φαρισαίων σαββάτῳ φαγεῖν ἄρτον (Luke 14:1)
and it took place **when he entered** the house of one of the rulers
of the Pharisees on a sabbath to eat bread

c. Introducing an activity whose time is given, meaning **when, while,
during**
ἀσπάζεται ὑμᾶς Ἐπαφρᾶς ὁ ἐξ ὑμῶν, δοῦλος Χριστοῦ Ἰησοῦ,
πάντοτε ἀγωνιζόμενος ὑπὲρ ὑμῶν **ἐν ταῖς προσευχαῖς** (Col. 4:12)
Epaphras greets you, who [ὢν εἷς, is one] of you, a servant of Christ
Jesus, always striving on your behalf **in his prayers**

4. Dative of means, translated **by**
a. With things
δουλεύων τῷ κυρίῳ μετὰ πάσης ταπεινοφροσύνης καὶ δακρύων καὶ
πειρασμῶν τῶν συμβάντων μοι **ἐν ταῖς ἐπιβουλαῖς** τῶν Ἰουδαίων
(Acts 20:19)
serving the Lord with all humility and tears and trials, which happened
to me **by the plots** of the Jews

b. With persons
εἴ γε αὐτὸν ἠκούσατε καὶ **ἐν αὐτῷ** ἐδιδάχθητε (Eph. 4:21)[17]
if indeed you heard him and were taught **by him**

5. Dative of accompaniment or association, translated **with**
a. With nouns
ὥστε ἑορτάζωμεν, μὴ **ἐν ζύμῃ παλαιᾷ**, μηδὲ **ἐν ζύμῃ κακίας** καὶ
πονηρίας ἀλλ᾽ **ἐν ἀζύμοις** εἰλικρινείας καὶ ἀληθείας (1 Cor. 5:8)[18]
therefore, let us celebrate a festival, not **with old leaven**, nor
with leaven of wickedness and malice, but **with unleavened [bread]**
of sincerity and truth

b. With pronouns
καὶ πῶς ἡμεῖς ἀκούομεν ἕκαστος τῇ ἰδίᾳ διαλέκτῳ ἡμῶν **ἐν ᾗ**
ἐγεννήθημεν (Acts 2:8)
and how do we each one hear in our own dialect **with which** we were
born

---

[17] Eph. 4:21 text is from GNT, NA, WH & MT: TR has εἴγε.
[18] 1 Cor. 5:8 text is from GNT, NA, TR & MT: WH has εἰλικρινίας.

6. Dative with certain verbs
    a. With πιστεύω
       μετανοεῖτε καὶ **πιστεύετε** ἐν τῷ εὐαγγελίῳ (Mark 1:15)
       repent and **believe the gospel**
    b. With ὁμολογέω
       λέγω δὲ ὑμῖν, πᾶς ὃς ἂν ὁμολογήσῃ ἐν ἐμοὶ ἔμπροσθεν τῶν
       ἀνθρώπων, καὶ ὁ υἱὸς τοῦ ἀνθρώπου ὁμολογήσει ἐν αὐτῷ ἔμπροσθεν
       τῶν ἀγγέλων τοῦ θεοῦ (Luke 12:8)
       but I tell you, whoever **will confess me** before men, the son of man
       also **will confess him** before the angels of God
7. Adverbial dative
    a. With adjectives
       καὶ ἐν κρυπτῷ ἐλάλησα οὐδέν (John 18:20)
       and I spoke nothing **secretly**
    b. With nouns
       σπεῦσον καὶ ἔξελθε ἐν τάχει ἐξ Ἰερουσαλήμ (Acts 22:18)[19]
       make haste and go out of Jerusalem **quickly**
8. Dative of cause
    a. With nouns
       παρέδωκεν αὐτοὺς ὁ θεὸς ἐν ταῖς ἐπιθυμίαις τῶν καρδιῶν αὐτῶν εἰς
       ἀκαθαρσίαν (Rom. 1:24)
       God delivered them over to uncleanness **because of the desires** of their
       hearts
    b. With pronouns
       ἐν αὐτῷ γὰρ ζῶμεν καὶ κινούμεθα καὶ ἐσμέν (Acts 17:28)[20]
       for **because of him** we live and move about and exist

G. ἐπί (with genitive, dative, and accusative) has a basic idea of **on** or **upon**
someone or something. Although the preposition is used with all three oblique
cases, the difference in meaning between the cases are not necessarily or
apparently distinctive. There is frequently a confusion of the cases in the
various manuscripts as well as two different cases being used in the same
sentence with little or no change of meaning. For example:
Gen. and acc. ὅταν καθίσῃ ὁ υἱὸς τοῦ ἀνθρώπου ἐπὶ φρόνου δόξης αὐτοῦ,
                καθήσεσθε καὶ ὑμεῖς ἐπὶ δώδεκα θρόνους (Matt. 19:28)[21]
                when the son of man shall sit **on the throne** of his glory,
                you also shall sit **on twelve thrones**

---

[19] Acts 22:18 text is from GNT, NA, WH & MT: TR has Ἰερουσαλήμ.
[20] Acts 17:28 text is from GNT, NA & WH: TR & MT have καί ἐσμεν.
[21] Matt. 19:28 text is from GNT, NA & WH: TR & MT have καθίσεσθε.

Dat. and acc. διαμερισθήσονται πατὴρ ἐπὶ υἱῷ καὶ υἱὸς ἐπὶ πατρί . . .
πενθερὰ ἐπὶ τὴν νύμφην αὐτῆς καὶ νύμφη ἐπὶ τὴν πενθεράν
(Luke 12:53)

they will be divided father **against son** and son **against father** . . .
mother-in-law **against** her **daughter-in-law** and daughter-in-law
against the mother-in-law

Dat. and gen. οὓς μὲν ἐπὶ σανίσιν, οὓς δὲ ἐπί τινων τῶν ἀπὸ τοῦ πλοίου
(Acts 27:44)

some **on planks** and others **on some of the things** from the boat

Thus, the following analysis, in descending frequency, will present the
functions in the case most often used, with footnotes to similar uses in other
case(s).

1. With accusative
   a. Accusative of place
      (1) Meaning **on, upon**
          (a) With adjectives
              καὶ ἔπεσεν ἐκ τοῦ οὐρανοῦ ἀστὴρ μέγας καιόμενος ὡς
              λαμπάς καὶ ἔπεσεν ἐπὶ τὸ τρίτον τῶν ποταμῶν (Rev. 8:10)
              and a great star fell from heaven burning as a lamp, and it fell
              on the third of the rivers
          (b) With nouns[22]
              ἰδού ὁ βασιλεύς σου ἔρχεται καθήμενος ἐπὶ πῶλον ὄνου
              (John 12:15)
              behold, your king is coming, sitting **on a colt** of an ass
          (c) With pronouns
              καὶ εἶδον θρόνους, καὶ ἐκάθισαν ἐπ᾽ αὐτούς (Rev. 20:4)
              and I saw thrones, and they sat **on them**
      (2) Meaning **near, at, to, before**
          (a) With pronouns
              καὶ ἐλθὼν ἐπ᾽ αὐτήν οὐδὲν εὖρεν εἰ μὴ φύλλα (Mark 11:13)
              and when he came **to it**, he found nothing except leaves

---

[22] ἐπί with the dative of place is found in Eph. 2:20. ἐποικοδομηθέντες **ἐπὶ τῷ θεμελίῳ** τῶν ἀποστόλων καὶ προφητῶν, being built **upon the foundation** of the apostles and prophets. ἐπί with the genitive of place is found in Rev. 19:21: καὶ οἱ λοιποὶ ἀπεκτάνθησαν ἐν τῇ ῥομφαίᾳ τοῦ καθημένου **ἐπὶ τοῦ ἵππου**, and the rest were killed by the sword belonging to the one sitting **on the horse**.

(b) With nouns[23]

κατεπέστησαν ὁμοθυμαδὸν οἱ Ἰουδαῖοι τῷ Παύλῳ, καὶ ἤγαγον αὐτὸν **ἐπὶ τὸ βῆμα** (Acts 18:12)

the Jews with one mind rose up against Paul and led him **to the judgment seat**

b. Accusative of authority, power, influence, rule, translated **over, upon**[24]

(1) With nouns

καὶ βασιλεύσει **ἐπὶ τὸν οἶκον** Ἰακὼβ εἰς τοὺς αἰῶνας (Luke 1:33)

and he shall reign **over the house** of Jacob forever

(2) With pronouns

καὶ κατέστησεν αὐτὸν ἡγούμενην **ἐπ᾽ Αἴγυπτον** καὶ **ἐφ᾽ ὅλον τὸν οἶκον αὐτοῦ** (Acts 7:10)[25]

and he appointed him ruler **over Egypt** and **his entire household**

c. Accusative of direction

καὶ ἀπὸ μὲν τῆς ἀληθείας τὴν ἀκοὴν ἀποστρέψουσιν, **ἐπὶ** δὲ τοὺς **μύθους** ἐκτραπήσονται (2 Tim. 4:4)

and they shall turn away their ear from the truth, and they shall be turned **to fables**

d. Accusative of hostility, opposition

(1) With nouns[26]

ἐγένετο δὲ ἐν ἐκείνῃ τῇ ἡμέρᾳ διωγμὸς μέγας **ἐπὶ τὴν ἐκκλησίαν** τὴν ἐν Ἱεροσολύμοις (Acts 8:1)[27]

and a great persecution took place on that day **against the church** that [οὖσην, was] in Jerusalem

(2) With pronouns

εἰ δὲ καὶ ὁ σατανᾶς **ἐφ᾽ ἑαυτὸν** διεμερίσθη, πῶς σταθήσεται ἡ βασιλεία αὐτοῦ; (Luke 11:18)

and if Satan also is divided **against himself**, how shall his kingdom stand?

---

[23] ἐπί, with the genitive of place, is found in Luke 22:40: γενόμενος δὲ **ἐπὶ τοῦ τόπου** εἶπεν αὐτοῖς, προσεύχεσθε μὴ εἰσελθεῖν εἰς πειρασμόν, and when he came **to the place** he said to them, "pray that you do not enter into temptation." ἐπί, with the dative of place, is found in John 5:2: ἐστιν δὲ ἐν τοῖς Ἱεροσολύμοις **ἐπὶ τῇ προβατικῇ** κολυμβήθρα, now there is in Jerusalem a pool **at the sheepgate.**

[24] ἐπί, with the genitive of authority, is found in Rev. 17:18: καὶ ἡ γυνὴ ἣν εἶδες, ἔστιν ἡ πόλις ἡ μεγάλη, ἡ ἔχουσα βασιλείαν **ἐπὶ τῶν βασιλέων** τῆς γῆς, and the woman that you saw is the great city, who has authority **over the king** of the earth. ἐπί, with the dative of authority, occurs in Matt. 24:47 with a participle: ἀμὴν λέγω ὑμῖν ὅτι **ἐπὶ πᾶσιν τοῖς ὑπάρχουσιν** αὐτοῦ καταστήσει αὐτόν, truly I tell you that he will set him **over all his property.**

[25] Acts 7:10 text is from GNT, NA & WH: TR & MT omit ἐφ᾽.

[26] ἐπί, with a dative of hostility, is found in Acts 11:19: οἱ μὲν οὖν διασπαρέντες ἀπὸ τῆς θλίψεως τῆς γενομένης **ἐπὶ Στεφάνῳ**, those indeed then who were scattered by the trouble that took place **against Stephen.**

[27] Acts 8:1 text is from GNT, NA, TR & MT: WH has Ἱεροσολύμοις.

e. Accusative of time, over a period of time

(1) With nouns[28]

πίστει τὰ τείχη Ἰεριχὼ ἔπεσαν, κυκλωθέντα **ἐπὶ ἑπτὰ ἡμέρας** (Heb. 11:30)[29]

by faith the walls of Jericho fell, having been encircled **for seven days**

(2) With adjectives

ἐφ᾽ ἱκανόν τε ὁμιλήσας ἄχρι(ς) αὐγῆς, οὕτως ἐξῆλθεν (Acts 20:11)

and having conversed **for a long time** until daybreak, he thus departed

(3) With adverbs (indicating point of time)

ἐγένετο δὲ **ἐπὶ τὴν αὔριον** συναχθῆναι αὐτῶν τοὺς ἄρχοντας (Acts 4:5)

and it took place **on the next day** [that] their rulers were gathered together

f. Accusative of purpose[30]

(1) With nouns

ἡ δὲ περιοχὴ τῆς γραφῆς ἣν ἀνεγίνωσκεν ἦν αὕτη· Ὡς πρόβατον **ἐπὶ σφαγὴν** ἤχθη (Acts 8:32)

and the passage of scripture that he was reading was this, as a sheep he was led **to slaughter**

(2) With participles

οἱ μὲν γὰρ . . . κατὰ τὸ δοκοῦν αὐτοῖς ἐπαίδευον, ὁ δὲ **ἐπὶ τὸ συμφέρον** εἰς τὸ μεταλαβεῖν τῆς ἁγιότητος αὐτοῦ (Heb. 12:10)

for they indeed . . . disciplined according to what seemed good to them; but he **for our profit**, that we should partake of his holiness

(3) With pronouns

ὁ δὲ Ἰησοῦς εἶπεν αὐτῷ, Ἑταῖρε, **ἐφ᾽ ὃ** πάρει; (Matt. 26:50)

and Jesus said to him, "Friend, **for what purpose** have you come?"

2. With dative

a. With verbs expressing feelings, opinions, meaning **over, on, at**

(1) With nouns

καὶ ὠργίσθη ὁ δράκων **ἐπὶ τῇ γυναικί** (Rev. 12:17)

and the dragon was angry **with the woman**

---

[28] ἐπί, with a genitive of time, occurs in Mark 2:26: πῶς εἰσῆλθεν εἰς τὸν οἶκον τοῦ θεοῦ **ἐπὶ Ἀβιάθαρ**, how he entered the house of God **during the time of Abiathar**. ἐπί, with a dative of time, occurs in 2 Cor. 1:4: ὁ παρακαλῶν ἡμᾶς **ἐπὶ πάσῃ τῇ θλίψει ἡμῶν**, who encourages us **during all our tribulation**.

[29] Heb. 11:30 text is from GNT & NA: WH & TR*b* have Ἰεριχώ; TR & MT have ἔπεσε(ν).

[30] Eph. 2:10 has the dative of purpose with ἐπί: αὐτοῦ γάρ ἐσμεν ποίημα, κτισθέντες ἐν Χριστῷ Ἰησοῦ **ἐπὶ ἔργοις ἀγαθοῖς**, for we are his creation, created in Christ Jesus **for good works**.

(2) With adjectives
λέγω ὑμῖν, γίνεται χαρὰ ἐνώπιον τῶν ἀγγέλων τοῦ θεοῦ **ἐπὶ ἑνὶ ἁμαρτωλῷ** μετανοοῦντι (Luke 15:10)[31]
I tell you there is joy in the presence of the angels of God **over one sinner** repenting

(3) With pronouns[32]
καὶ ἰδὼν αὐτὴν ὁ κύριος ἐσπλαγχνίσθη **ἐπ᾽ αὐτῇ** καὶ εἶπεν αὐτῇ, μὴ κλαῖε (Luke 7:13)
and when the Lord saw her he had compassion **on her** and said to her, "stop crying"

(4) With participles
καὶ ἐπλήσθησαν θάμβους καὶ ἐκστάσεως **ἐπὶ τῷ συμβεβηκότι αὐτῷ** (Acts 3:10)
and they were filled with wonder and amazement **at that which happened** to him

b. With dative, indicating that on which a state of being, action, or result is based, translated **by, on the basis of**

(1) With adjectives
διαθήκη γὰρ **ἐπὶ νεκροῖς** βεβαία, ἐπεὶ μήποτε ἰσχύει ὅτε ζῇ ὁ διαθέμενος (Heb. 9:17)
for a will [ἐστιν, is] confirmed **on the basis of the dead**, since [a will] is not in force while the testator lives

(2) With pronouns
καὶ οὕτως εἰς πάντες ἀνθρώπους ὁ θάνατος διῆλθεν, **ἐφ᾽ ᾧ** πάντες ἥμαρτον (Rom. 5:12)
and so death passed upon all people, **on the basis that** all sinned

(3) With nouns[33]
γέγραπται ὅτι οὐκ **ἐπ᾽ ἄρτῳ μόνῳ** ζήσεται ὁ ἄνθρωπος (Luke 4:4)
it is written, "a person shall not live **on the basis of bread only**"

c. With dative of cause, translated **for, because of**

(1) With participles
ὅτι πάντες ἐδόξαζον τὸν θεὸν **ἐπὶ τῷ γεγονότι** (Acts 4:21)
for all were praising God **because of that which had happened**

[31] Luke 15:10 text is from GNT, NA & WH: TR & MT have χαρὰ γίνεται.
[32] 2 Cor. 1:23 has ἐπί with the accusative with verbs expressing feelings, opinions, etc.: ἐγὼ δὲ μάρτυρα τὸν θεὸν ἐπικαλοῦμαι **ἐπὶ τὴν ἐμὴν ψυχήν**, but I call God as witness **upon my soul**.
[33] ἐπί, with the genitive, is found in 2 Cor. 13:1: **ἐπὶ στόματος** δύο μαρτύρων καὶ τριῶν σταθήσεται πᾶν ῥῆμα, **by the testimony** of two and three witnesses every matter shall be established.

(2) With nouns[34]

καὶ μὴ μετανοησάντων **ἐπὶ τῇ ἀκαθαρσίᾳ** καὶ **πορνείᾳ** καὶ **ἀσελγείᾳ** ᾗ ἔπραξαν (2 Cor. 12:21)

and have not repented **for the uncleanness** and **fornication** and **debauchery** that they practised

d. With dative ὀνόματι, **in connection with, by the use of, naming**

οὐδεὶς γάρ ἐστιν ὃς ποιήσει δύναμιν **ἐπὶ τῷ ὀνόματί** μου καὶ δυνήσεται ταχὺ κακολογῆσαί με (Mark 9:39)

for there is no one who shall perform a miracle **in my name** and shall be able quickly to speak evil of me

e. With dative as object of πιστεύω, ἐλπίζε, and πείθω[35]

(1) With pronouns and nouns

ἵνα μὴ **πεποιθότες ὦμεν ἐφ᾽ ἑαυτοῖς** ἀλλ᾽ **ἐπὶ τῷ θεῷ** τῷ **ἐγείροντι** τοὺς νεκρούς (2 Cor. 1:9)

that **we should** not **trust in ourselves**, but **in the God who raises** the dead

(2) With nouns

ὅτι **ἠλπίκαμεν ἐπὶ θεῷ ζῶντι** (1 Tim. 4:10)

for **we have hoped in the living God**

3. With genitive. Almost every kind of genitive with ἐπί was footnoted above, except for one of note, the genitive of place, **before**, of lawsuits.

a. With adjectives

τολμᾷ τις ὑμῶν πρᾶγμα ἔχων πρὸς τὸν ἕτερον κρίνεσθαι **ἐπὶ τῶν ἀδίκων** καὶ οὐχὶ **ἐπὶ τῶν ἁγίων**; (1 Cor. 6:1)

dare any of you, having a matter against the other, to go to law **before the unjust** and not **before the saints**?

b. With nouns

καὶ ἐὰν ἀκουσθῇ τοῦτο **ἐπὶ τοῦ ἡγεμόνος**, ἡμεῖς πείσομεν (Matt. 28:14)

and if this should be heard **before the governor**, we will persuade [him]

---

[34] Rev. 1:7 has the accusative of cause with ἐπί: καὶ κόψονται **ἐπ᾽ αὐτὸν** πᾶσαι αἱ φυλαὶ τῆς γῆς, and all the tribes of the earth shall wail **because of him.**

[35] ἐπί, with the accusative after these verbs, is found in Acts 22:19: κύριε, αὐτοὶ ἐπίστανται, ὅτι ἐγὼ ἤμην φυλακίζων καὶ δέρων κατὰ τὰς συναγωγὰς **τοὺς πιστεύοντας ἐπί σε**, Lord, they themselves know that I was imprisoning and beating in every synagogue **those who were believing in you.**

c. With pronouns

διὸ προήγαγον αὐτὸν ἐφ᾽ ὑμῶν καὶ μάλιστα ἐπὶ σοῦ, βασιλεῦ
Ἀγρίππα (Acts 25:26)

therefore I brought him **before you**, and especially **before you** King
Agrippa

H. κατά, with the genitive and accusative, indicates among others, opposition,
   space, standard, reason, respect, and place.
   1. With the genitive. Contrary to many grammars and lexicons, the primary
      meaning of κατά with the genitive in the NT is not **down from** nor **down
      upon** but **against**, indicating opposition or hostility.
      a. With genitive of opposition
         (1) With adjectives
             κατὰ πρεσβυτέρου κατηγορίαν μὴ παραδέχου, ἐκτὸς εἰ μὴ
             ἐπὶ δύο ἢ τριῶν μαρτύρων (1 Tim. 5:19)

             do not receive an accusation **against an elder**, except before two
             or three witnesses
         (2) With nouns
             καὶ ῥήτορος Τερτύλλου τινός, οἵτινες ἐνεφάνισαν τῷ ἡγεμόνι
             κατὰ τοῦ Παύλου (Acts 24:1)

             and an orator, Tertullus, who informed the governor **against Paul**
         (3) With pronouns
             πολλοὶ γὰρ ἐψευδομαρτύρουν **κατ᾽ αὐτοῦ**, καὶ ἴσαι αἱ
             μαρτυρίαι οὐκ ἦσαν (Mark 14:56)

             for many were bringing false testimony **against him**, but their
             testimonies were not in agreement
      b. With genitive of place, meaning **throughout**
         καὶ φήμη ἐξῆλθεν **καθ᾽ ὅλης τῆς περιχώρου** περὶ αὐτοῦ (Luke 4:14)
         and news went out **throughout all the surrounding country** concerning
         him
      c. With genitive of oaths, what one swears by
         τῷ γὰρ Ἀβραὰμ ἐπαγγειλάμενος ὁ θεός, ἐπεὶ **κατ᾽ οὐδενὸς** εἶχεν
         μείζονος ὀμόσαι, ὤμοσεν **καθ᾽ ἑαυτοῦ** (Heb. 6:13)
         for when God made promise to Abraham, since **by no one greater**
         did he have to swear, he swore **by himself**
      d. With genitive of place, meaning **down (from)**
         καὶ ὥρμησεν ἡ ἀγέλη **κατὰ τοῦ κρημνοῦ** εἰς τὴν θάλασσαν
         (Mark 5:13)
         and the herd rushed **down the steep slope** into the sea

2. With accusative
   a. With the accusative of norm, meaning **in accordance with**
      (1) With nouns
         καινοὺς δὲ οὐρανοὺς καὶ γῆν καινὴν **κατὰ τὸ ἐπάγγελμα αὐτοῦ** προσδοκῶμεν (2 Peter 3:13)
         but we are looking for new heavens and a new earth **according to his promise**
      (2) With participles
         κατὰ τὸ εἰρημένον, οὕτως ἔσται τὸ σπέρμα σου (Rom. 4:18)
         according to that which was spoken, so shall be your seed
   b. With causal accusative, **because of, as a result of, on the basis of**
      (1) With adverbial accusative
         ποτε ἐν τῷ Ἰουδαϊσμῷ, ὅτι **καθ' ὑπερβολὴν** ἐδίωκον τὴν ἐκκλησίαν τοῦ θεοῦ (Gal. 1:13)
         for you heard of my former conduct in Judea, that I **beyond comparison** persecuted the church of God
      (2) With nouns
         κατὰ δὲ **τὴν σκληρότητά** σου καὶ **ἀμετανόητον καρδίαν** θησαυρίζεις σεαυτῷ ὀργὴν ἐν ἡμέρᾳ ὀργῆς (Rom. 2:5)
         but **because of your stubbornness** and **unrepentant heart** you store up for yourself wrath in the day of wrath
   c. With accusative of time
      (1) Meaning **during, in**
         ἄγγελος κυρίου **κατ' ὄναρ** ἐφάνη αὐτῷ (Matt. 1:20)
         an angel of the Lord appeared to him **during a dream**
      (2) Distributively
         ὥσπερ ὁ ἀρχιερεὺς εἰσέρχεται εἰς τὰ ἅγια **κατ' ἐνιαυτὸν** ἐν αἵματι ἀλλοτρίῳ (Heb. 9:25)
         even as the high priest enters into the holy places **year after year** with another's blood
   d. With accusative of respect
      (1) With adjectives
         τὰ τέκνα, ὑπακούετε τοῖς γονεῦσιν **κατὰ πάντα** (Col. 3:20)
         children, obey your parents **in all respects**
      (2) With pronouns
         ὅταν Λυσίας ὁ χιλίαρχος καταβῇ, διαγνώσομαι τὰ **καθ' ὑμᾶς** (Acts 24:22)
         when Lysias the chiliarch comes down, I will determine the things **in regard to you**

(3) With nouns
Ἑβραῖος ἐξ Ἑβραίων, **κατὰ νόμον** Φαρισαῖος (Phil. 3:5)
a Hebrew of Hebrews, **with respect to the law** a Pharisee

e. With accusative of place
(1) Meaning **throughout**
καὶ ἀπῆλθεν **καθ᾽ ὅλην τὴν πόλιν** κηρύσσων ὅσα ἐποίησεν
αὐτῷ ὁ Ἰησοῦς (Luke 8:39)
and he departed proclaiming **throughout the entire city** what
Jesus did for him

(2) Distributively
καὶ καταστήσῃς **κατὰ πόλιν** πρεσβυτέρους, ὡς ἐγώ σοι
διεταξάμην (Titus 1:5)
and you should appoint elders **in every city** as I directed you

f. With accusative of direction, **toward, before**
ὑπεπλεύσαμεν τὴν Κρήτην **κατὰ Σαλμώνην** (Acts 27:7)
we sailed under the lee of Crete **toward Salmone**

g. With numerals, distributively
δύνασθε γὰρ **καθ᾽ ἕνα** πάντες προφητεύειν (1 Cor. 14:31)
for you all are able to prophecy **one by one**

I. μετά, with genitives and accusatives, indicates among others, association,
attendant circumstances, space, opposition, and time.
1. With genitives
a. With genitive of association, accompaniment
(1) With nouns
μέλλει γὰρ ὁ υἱὸς τοῦ ἀνθρώπου ἔρχεσθαι ἐν τῇ δόξῃ τοῦ
πατρὸς αὐτοῦ **μετὰ τῶν ἀγγέλων αὐτοῦ** (Matt. 16:27)
for the son of man is about to come in the glory of his father
with his angels

(2) With pronouns
καὶ ἡ φωνὴ ἡ πρώτη ἣν ἤκουσα ὡς σάλπιγγος λαλούσης **μετ᾽**
ἐμοῦ (Rev. 4:1)
and the first voice that I heard [ἦν, was] like a trumpet speaking
with me

(3) With participles
δίωκε δὲ δικαιοσύνην πίστιν ἀγάπην εἰρήνην **μετὰ τῶν**
ἐπικαλουμένων τὸν κύριον ἐκ καθαρᾶς καρδίας (2 Tim. 2:22)
but pursue righteousness, faith, love, peace **with those who call**
upon the Lord from a pure heart

(4) With adjectives

ἢ τίς μερὶς πιστῷ **μετὰ ἀπίστου**; (2 Cor. 6:15)

or what share [has a] believer **with an unbeliever**?

b. With genitive of attendant circumstances, with something that takes place

ὅθεν **μεθ᾽ ὅρκου** ὡμολόγησεν αὐτῇ δοῦναι ὃ ἐὰν αἰτήσηται (Matt. 14:7)

wherefore he promised **with an oath** to give her whatever she asks

c. With genitive of place, meaning **among**

(1) With adjectives

τί ζητεῖτε τὸν ζῶντα **μετὰ τῶν νεκρῶν** . . . ; (Luke 24:5)

why are you looking for the living **among the dead** . . . ?

(2) With nouns

καὶ ἦν **μετὰ τῶν θηρίων** (Mark 1:13)

and he was **among the wild animals**

(3) With pronouns

ἰδοὺ ἡ σκηνὴ τοῦ θεοῦ μετὰ τῶν ἀνθρώπων, καὶ σκηνώσει **μετ᾽ αὐτῶν** (Rev. 21:3)

behold, the tabernacle of God is among men, and he will dwell **among them**

d. With genitive of hostility

(1) With adjectives

καὶ ἐδόθη αὐτῷ ποιῆσαι πόλεμον **μετὰ τῶν ἁγίων** (Rev. 13:7)[36]

and it was given him to wage war **against the saints**

(2) With nouns

ἀλλὰ ἀδελφὸς **μετὰ ἀδελφοῦ** κρίνεται καὶ τοῦτο ἐπὶ ἀπίστων . . . ; (1 Cor. 6:6)

but does a brother go to law **against a brother**, and this before unbelievers . . . ?

(3) With pronouns

καὶ πολεμήσω **μετ᾽ αὐτῶν** ἐν τῇ ῥομφαίᾳ τοῦ στόματός μου (Rev. 2:16)

and I will war **against them** with the sword of my mouth

(4) With participles

καὶ τὰ στρατεύματα αὐτῶν συνηγμένα ποιῆσαι τὸν πόλεμον **μετὰ τοῦ καθημένου** ἐπὶ τοῦ ἵππου (Rev. 19:19)[37]

and their armies were gathered to wage war **against the one sitting** on the horse

---

[36] Rev. 13:7 text is from GNT, NA, WH & MT: TR has πόλεμον ποιῆσαι.

[37] Rev. 19:19 text is from GNT, NA, MT & WH: TR has ποιῆσαι πόλεμον.

2. With accusatives
   a. With accusative of time, translated **after**
      (1) With adjectives
          καὶ **μετὰ μικρὸν** πάλιν οἱ παρεστῶτες ἔλεγον τῷ Πέτρῳ
          (Mark 14:70)
          and **after a little while** again those standing by spoke to Peter
      (2) With nouns
          ἡμεῖς δὲ ἐξεπλεύσαμεν **μετὰ τὰς ἡμέρας** τῶν ἀζύμων ἀπὸ
          Φιλίππων (Acts 20:6)
          but we sailed away from Philippi **after the days** of unleavened
          bread
      (3) With pronouns
          ἀνάβα ὧδε, καὶ δείξω σοι ἃ δεῖ γενέσθαι **μετὰ ταῦτα** (Rev. 4:1)
          come up here, and I will show you what must take place **after these
          things**
      (4) With infinitives
          ἀλλὰ **μετὰ τὸ ἐγερθῆναί** με προάξω ὑμᾶς εἰς τὴν Γαλιλαίαν
          (Mark 14:28)
          but **after I have risen**, I will go before you into Galilee
   b. With accusative of place, translated **behind**
      μετὰ δὲ τὸ δεύτερον **καταπέτασμα** σκηνὴ ἡ λεγομένη Ἅγια Ἁγίων
      (Heb. 9:3)
      and **behind the second veil** the tent that is called the Holy of Holies

J. παρά, with genitives, datives, and accusatives, indicates, among others,
   source, association, space, comparison, and opposition.
   1. With genitive of source or origin, **from**
      a. With nouns
         οὐ φέρουσιν κατ᾽ αὐτῶν **παρὰ κυρίῳ** βλάσφημον κρίσιν
         (2 Peter 2:11)
         they do not bring a slanderous accusation against them **from the
         Lord**
      b. With pronouns
         συμβουλεύω σοι ἀγοράσαι **παρ᾽ ἐμοῦ** χρυσίον πεπυρωμένον
         ἐκ πυρός, ἵνα πλουτήσῃς (Rev. 3:18)
         I advise you to purchase **from me** gold refined by fire so that you may
         be rich

2. With datives
   a. With dative of company, association, meaning **with, among**
     (1) With pronouns
       καὶ ὅταν ἀναγνωσθῇ **παρ' ὑμῖν** ἡ ἐπιστολή (Col. 4:16)
       and when the epistle is read **among you**
     (2) With nouns
       διεγόγγυζον λέγοντες ὅτι **παρὰ ἁμαρτωλῷ ἀνδρὶ** εἰσῆλθεν
       καταλῦσαι (Luke 19:7)
       they were murmuring, saying, "he has entered to lodge **with a sinful man**"
   b. With dative of sphere, before someone's judgment, translated **with, in**
     (1) With nouns
       μία ἡμέρα **παρὰ κυρίῳ** ὡς χίλια ἔτη (2 Peter 3:8)
       one day **with the Lord** [ἐστιν, is] as a thousand years
     (2) With pronouns
       τί ἄπιστον κρίνεται **παρ' ὑμῖν** εἰ ὁ θεὸς νεκροὺς ἐγείρει;
       (Acts 26:8)
       why is it considered incredible **with you** if God raises the dead?
   c. With dative of place, **near, beside**
     εἰστήκεισαν δὲ **παρὰ τῷ σταυρῷ** τοῦ Ἰησοῦ ἡ μήτηρ αὐτοῦ, καὶ ἡ
     ἀδελφὴ τῆς μητρὸς αὐτοῦ (John 19:25)
     and his mother and his mother's sister stood **near the cross** of Jesus
3. With accusatives
   a. With accusative of comparison, often with comparative adjective
     (1) With pronouns
       αὐτὰ δὲ τὰ ἐπουράνια **κρείττοσιν θυσίας παρὰ ταύτας**
       (Heb. 9:23)
       but the heavenly things themselves **with better sacrifices than these**
     (2) With nouns
       πίστει **πλείονα θυσίαν** Ἄβελ **παρὰ Κάϊν** προσήνεγκεν τῷ θεῷ
       (Heb. 11:4)[38]
       by faith Abel offered to God **a better sacrifice than Cain**
     (3) With participles
       μηδὲν **πλέον παρὰ τὸ διατεταγμένον** ὑμῖν πράσσετε (Luke 3:13)
       collect **nothing more than what is commanded** to you

---

[38] Heb. 11:4 text is from GNT, NA & MT: WH has **Κάϊν**: TR has **Ἄβελ**.

    b. With accusative of place, meaning **by the side of, near, at, on, alongside**

        (1) Meaning **at the edge of, by the side of**

            καὶ αὐτὸς ἦν ἑστὼς **παρὰ τὴν λίμνην** Γεννησαρέτ (Luke 5:1)

            and he was standing **at the edge of the lake** Gennesaret

        (2) Meaning **near, at**

            καὶ οἱ μάρτυρες ἀπέθεντο τὰ ἱμάτια αὐτῶν **παρὰ τοὺς πόδας**
            νεανίου καλουμένου Σαύλου (Acts 7:58)

            and the witnesses laid their garments **at the feet** of a young
            man named Saul

        (3) Meaning **on**

            καὶ ἐγένετο ἐν τῷ σπείρειν ὃ μὲν ἔπεσεν **παρὰ τὴν ὁδόν**
            (Mark 4:4)

            and it happened while he was sowing, some fell **on the roadway**

    c. With accusative of adversity, meaning **against, contrary to**

        ὃς **παρ' ἐλπίδα** ἐπ' ἐλπίδι ἐπίστευσεν (Rom. 4:18)

        who **against hope** believed in hope

K. περί, with genitives and accusatives, indicates, among others, advantage,
reference, purpose, place, time, and respect.

    1. With genitives

        a. With genitive of advantage

            (1) With adjectives

                τὸ **περὶ πολλῶν** ἐκχυννόμενον εἰς ἄφεσιν ἁμαρτιῶν
                (Matt. 26:28)[39]

                which is poured out **for many** for the purpose of forgiving sins

            (2) With pronouns

                προσευχόμενοι ἅμα καὶ **περὶ ἡμῶν** (Col. 4:3)

                praying at the same time also **for us**

            (3) With nouns

                ὀφείλει καθὼς **περὶ τοῦ λαοῦ**, οὕτω(ς) καὶ περὶ αὐτοῦ
                προσφέρειν περὶ ἁμαρτιῶν (Heb. 5:3)[40]

                he must offer **for sins** even as **for the people**, so also
                for himself

        b. With genitive of reference, meaning **concerning, about, with reference
        to**

            (1) With adjectives

                εἰ κακῶς ἐλάλησα, μαρτύρησον **περὶ τοῦ κακοῦ** (John 18:2)

                if I spoke evily, testify **concerning the evil**

---

[39] Matt. 26:28 text is from GNT, NA & WH: TR & MT have ἐκχυνόμενον.
[40] Heb. 5:3 text is from GNT, NA & WH: TR & MT have ἑαυτοῦ for αὐτοῦ; TR has ὑπὲρ ἁμαρτιῶν.

(2) With the article preceding περί

κηρύσσων τὴν βασιλείαν τοῦ θεοῦ καὶ διδάσκων τὰ περὶ τοῦ
κυρίου Ἰησοῦ (Acts 28:31)

preaching the kingdom of God and teaching **the things
concerning the Lord Jesus**

(3) With nouns

τότε συνῆκαν οἱ μαθηταὶ ὅτι περὶ Ἰωάννου τοῦ βαπτιστοῦ
εἶπεν αὐτοῖς (Matt. 17:13)

then the disciples understood that he spoke to them **about
John the Baptist**

(4) With pronouns

πᾶσαν τὴν μέριμναν ὑμῶν ἐπιρίψαντες ἐπ᾽ αὐτόν, ὅτι αὐτῷ
μέλει περὶ ὑμῶν (1 Peter 5:7)[41]

casting all your care upon him, for he cares **for you**

c. With genitive of purpose, with ἁμαρτία, meaning **to take away**

ὅτι καὶ Χριστὸς ἅπαξ περὶ ἁμαρτιῶν ἔπαθεν, δίκαιος ὑπὲρ ἀδίκων
(1 Peter 3:18)

for Christ also suffered once **to take away sins**, the just for the unjust

2. With accusatives

a. With accusative of place, translated **around, about, near**

(1) With nouns

λυσιτελεῖ αὐτῷ εἰ λίθος μυλικὸς περίκειται
περὶ τὸν τράχηλον αὐτοῦ καὶ ἔρριπται εἰς τὴν θάλασσαν
(Luke 17:2)

it is profitable for him if a millstone is placed **around his neck**
and he is thrown into the sea

(2) With pronouns

ἰδὼν δὲ ὁ Ἰησοῦς ὄχλον περὶ αὐτόν, ἐκέλευσεν
ἀπελθεῖν εἰς τὸ πέραν (Matt. 8:18)[42]

and when Jesus saw many people **around him**, he commanded to
depart to the other side

---

[41] 1 Peter 5:7 text is from GNT, NA & WH: TR & MT have ἐπιρρίψαντες.
[42] Matt. 8:18 text is from GNT, NA & WH: TR & MT haave πολλοὺς ὄχλους.

b. Accusative of time, translated **about, near**

ἐγένετο δέ μοι πορευομένῳ καὶ ἐγγίζοντι τῇ Δαμασκῷ **περὶ**
μεσημβρίαν ἐξαίφνης ἐκ τοῦ οὐρανοῦ περιαστράψαι φῶς ἱκανὸν
περὶ ἐμέ (Acts 22:6)

and it happened, while I was journeying and drawing near to Damascus
a bright light **about midday** suddenly shone out of heaven around me

c. Accusative of respect, translated **with regard** or **respect to**

   (1) With adjectives

   περὶ πάντα, σεαυτὸν παρεχόμενος τύπον καλῶν ἔργων
   (Titus 2:7)

   showing yourself a pattern of good works **with respect to all things**

   (2) With nouns

   ἄνθρωποι κατεφθαρμένοι τὸν νοῦν, ἀδόκιμοι **περὶ τὴν πίστιν**
   (2 Tim. 3:8)

   men depraved in mind, worthless **with respect to the faith**

L. **πρό,** with genitive, indicating space and time.

1. With genitive of place, translated **before, in front of, at**

   ἀπήγγειλεν ἑστάναι τὸν Πέτρον **πρὸ τοῦ πυλῶνος** (Acts 12:14)
   she reported [that] Peter was standing **in front of the porch**

2. With genitive of time, **before** an even

   a. With nouns

   οὐκ ἄρα σὺ εἶ ὁ Αἰγύπτιος ὁ **πρὸ τούτων τῶν ἡμερῶν** ἀναστατώσας;
   (Acts 21:38)

   are you not then the Egyptian who **before these days** caused a
   disturbance?

   b. With infinitives

   καὶ νῦν δόξασόν με σύ, πάτερ παρὰ σεαυτῷ τῇ δόξῃ ᾗ εἶχον
   πρὸ τοῦ τὸν κόσμον εἶναι παρὰ σοί (John 17:5)

   and now, father, you glorify me, with yourself, with the glory I had with
   you **before the world existed**

   c. With pronouns

   ἐν ᾧ δὲ ἔρχομαι ἐγὼ ἄλλος **πρὸ ἐμοῦ** καταβαίνει (John 5:7)
   but while I am coming another steps down **before me**

M. **πρός,** with genitive, datives, and accusatives, indicating, among others,
   advantage, space, purpose, indirect object, reference, opposition, and time

1. With genitive of advantage (only once)

   τοῦτο γὰρ **πρὸς τῆς ὑμετέρας σωτηρίας** ὑπάρχει (Acts 27:34)
   for this is necessary **for your safety**

2. With dative of place, translated **near, at, around, close to**

καὶ θεωρεῖ δύο ἀγγέλους ἐν λευκοῖς καθεζομένους, ἕνα **πρὸς τῇ κεφαλῇ** καὶ ἕνα **πρὸς τοῖς ποσίν**, ὅπου ἔκειτο τὸ σῶμα τοῦ Ἰησοῦ (John 20:12)

and she saw two angels in white sitting, one **at the head** and one **at the feet** where the body of Jesus had lain

3. With accusatives

a. With accusative of place or person

(1) Meaning **toward, to**

(a) With nouns

καὶ ἡρπάσθη τὸ τέκνον αὐτῆς **πρὸς τὸν θεόν** (Rev. 12:5)

and her child was carried away **to God**

(b) With adjectives

πρὸς οὐδεμίαν αὐτῶν ἐπέμφθη Ἠλίας (Luke 4:26)[43]

Elijah was sent **to none** of them

(c) With pronouns

ἑτοίμως ἔχω ἐλθεῖν **πρὸς ὑμᾶς** (2 Cor. 12:14)

I am ready to come **to you**

(d) With participles

νῦν δὲ ὑπάγω **πρὸς τὸν πέμψαντά** με (John 16:5)

but now I am going **for the one who sent** me

(2) Meaning **at, near, be in company with**

(a) With pronouns

ἀλλ’ ἐν χάριτι θεοῦ, ἀνεστράφημεν ἐν τῷ κόσμῳ, περισσοτέρως δὲ **πρὸς ὑμᾶς** (2 Cor. 1:12)

but by the grace of God we conducted ourselves in the world, but even much more **with you**

(b) With nouns

καὶ ὅτε εἶδον αὐτόν, ἔπεσα **πρὸς τοὺς πόδας** αὐτοῦ ὡς νεκρός (Rev. 1:17)

and when I saw him, I fell **at** his **feet** as dead

b. With accusative of speaking to or with someone, like the dative of indirect object

(1) With nouns

παρακαλῶ δὲ ὑμᾶς ... συναγωνίσασθαί μοι ἐν ταῖς προσευχαῖς ὑπὲρ ἐμοῦ **πρὸς τὸν θεόν** (Rom. 15:30)

but I encourage you ... to assist me by your prayers for me **to God**

---

[43] Luke 4:26 text is from GNT, NA, TR*b* & MT: WH has Ἠλείας; TR*s* has Ἠλίας.

(2) With pronouns

ἀλλ᾽ ὁ λαλήσης **πρὸς αὐτόν**, Υἱός μου εἶ σύ (Heb. 5:5)

but the one who said **to him**, you are my son

(3) With participles

ἔλεγεν δὲ **πρὸς τοὺς κεκλημένους** παραβολήν (Luke 14:7)

but he spoke a parable **to those who had been invited**

c. With accusative of purpose

(1) With nouns

τὰ γὰρ ὅπλα τῆς στρατείας ἡμῶν οὐ σαρκικὰ ἀλλὰ δυνατὰ τῷ θεῷ **πρὸς καθαίρεσιν** ὀχυρωμάτων (2 Cor. 10:4)

for the weapons of our warfare are not carnal but powerful with God **for the destruction** of fortresses

(2) With adjectives

ἡ δὲ εὐσέβεια **πρὸς πάντα** ὠφέλιμός ἐστιν (1 Tim. 4:8)

but godliness is profitable **for everything**

(3) With infinitives

πάντα δὲ τὰ ἔργα αὐτῶν ποιοῦσιν **πρὸς τὸ θεαθῆναι** τοῖς ἀνθρώποις (Matt. 23:5)

but they perform all their works **in order to be seen** by people

d. With accusative of reference, meaning **with respect to, for**

(1) With nouns

πρεσβείαν ἀποστείλας ἐρωτᾷ τὰ **πρὸς εἰρήνην** (Luke 14:32)

when he sends an ambassador he asks the [terms] **with regard to peace**

(2) With pronouns

τοῦτο δὲ οὐδεὶς ἔγνω τῶν ἀνακειμένων **πρὸς τί** εἶπεν αὐτῷ (John 13:28)

but no one of those who were dining understood **why** he said [this] to him

e. With accusative of opposition, hostility, meaning **against**

(1) With adjectives

τολμᾷ τις ὑμῶν, πρᾶγμα ἔχων **πρὸς τὸν ἕτερον** κρίνεσθαι ἐπὶ τῶν ἀδίκων καὶ οὐχὶ ἐπὶ τῶν ἁγίων; (1 Cor. 6:1)

does anyone of you, when he has a matter **against another**, dare to go to law before the unrighteous and not before the saints?

(2) With nouns

οὔπω μέχρις αἵματος ἀντικατέστητε **πρὸς τὴν ἁμαρτίαν** ἀνταγωνιζόμενοι (Heb. 12:4)

you have not yet resisted unto blood while struggling **against sin**

(3) With pronouns

ζητήματα δέ τινα περὶ τῆς ἰδίας δεισιδαιμονίας εἶχον **πρὸς αὐτόν** (Acts 25:19)

but they had **against him** certain questions concerning their own superstition

f. With accusative of time

(1) With adjectives

ἡ γὰρ σωματικὴ γυμνασία **πρὸς ὀλίγον** ἐστὶν ὠφέλιμος (1 Tim. 4:8)

for bodily exercise is profitable **for a little time**

(2) With nouns

οἷς οὐδὲ **πρὸς ὥραν** εἴξαμεν τῇ ὑποταγῇ, ἵνα ἡ ἀλήθεια τοῦ εὐαγγελίου διαμείνῃ πρὸς ὑμᾶς (Gal. 2:5)

to whom we did not yield in subjection, not even **for an hour**, in order that the truth of the gospel might remain with you

(3) With participles

πᾶσα δὲ παιδεία **πρὸς μὲν τὸ παρὸν** οὐ δοκεῖ χαρᾶς εἶναι ἀλλὰ λύπης (Heb. 12:11)

but no discipline **for the present time** seems to be pleasant but painful

N. σύν, with the dative of association and accompaniment

1. To be with someone

a. Preceded by article with elliptical participle

ἀλλ' οὐδὲ Τίτος **ὁ σὺν ἐμοί**, Ἕλλην ὤν (Gal. 2:3)

but neither Titus **who [ὤν, was] with me**, being a Greek

b. With nouns

ἀσπάζονται ὑμᾶς **οἱ σὺν ἐμοὶ ἀδελφοί** (Phil. 4:21)

the brothers with me greet you

c. With participles

οἱ δὲ σὺν ἐμοὶ ὄντες τὸ μὲν φῶς ἐθεάσαντο (Acts 22:9)

and **those who were with me** saw the light

2. To remain with someone

καὶ εἰσῆλθεν **τοῦ μεῖναι σὺν αὐτοῖς** (Luke 24:29)

and he entered in **to remain with them**

3. To go or travel with someone

εἰσῄει ὁ Παῦλος **σὺν ἡμῖν** πρὸς Ἰάκωβον (Acts 21:18)

Paul **went in with us** to James

4. To experience something with someone

θεὶς τὰ γόνατα αὐτοῦ **σὺν πᾶσιν αὐτοῖς** προσηύξατο (Acts 20:36)

when he had bowed his knees **he prayed with them all**

O. ὑπέρ, with the genitive and accusative, indicating substitution, advantage, cause, reference, and comparison
  1. With genitives
    a. With genitive of substitution, meaning **for, in behalf of**
      (1) With adjectives
        ἕως οὗ προσηνέχθη **ὑπὲρ ἑνὸς ἑκάστου** αὐτῶν ἡ προσφορά
        (Acts 21:26)
        until the offering was offered **for each one** of them
      (2) With pronouns
        τοῦτό ἐστιν τὸ σῶμά μου, τὸ **ὑπὲρ ὑμῶν** διδόμενον (Luke 22:19)
        this is my body, which is given **for you**
      (3) With nouns
        ὁ ποιμὴν ὁ καλὸς τὴν ψυχὴν αὐτοῦ τίθησιν **ὑπὲρ τῶν προβάτων**
        (John 10:11)
        the good shepherd lays down his life **for the sheep**
    b. With genitive of advantage, meaning **for, in behalf of, for the benefit of**
      (1) With adjectives
        ὅτι κατὰ θεὸν ἐντυγχάνει **ὑπὲρ ἁγίων** (Rom. 8:27)
        for he intercedes **for the saints** according to [the will of] God
      (2) With nouns
        ἐγὼ δὲ ἥδιστα δαπανήσω καὶ ἐκδαπανηθήσομαι **ὑπὲρ τῶν ψυχῶν**
        ὑμῶν (2 Cor. 12:15)
        but I will most gladly spend freely and be exhausted **for your lives**
      (3) With pronouns
        καὶ **ὑπὲρ αὐτῶν** ἐγὼ ἁγιάζω ἐμαυτόν (John 17:19)
        and I sanctify myself **for them**
      (4) With participles
        καὶ προσεύχεσθε **ὑπὲρ τῶν διωκόντων** ὑμᾶς (Matt. 5:44)[44]
        and pray **for those who persecute** you
    c. With genitive of cause
      (1) With pronouns
        εἰς τὸ καταξιωθῆναι ὑμᾶς τῆς βασιλείας τοῦ θεοῦ, **ὑπὲρ ἧς καὶ**
        πάσχετε (2 Thess. 1:5)
        that you may be considered worthy of the kingdom of God,
        because of which you also suffer

---

[44] Matt. 5:44 text is from GNT, NA & WH: TR & MT add ἐπηρεαζόντων ὑμᾶς καί after ὑπὲρ τῶν.

(2) With nouns

ἐγὼ γὰρ ὑποδείξω αὐτῷ ὅσα δεῖ αὐτὸν **ὑπὲρ τοῦ ὀνόματός μου** παθεῖν (Acts 9:16)

for I will show him how much he must suffer **because of my name**

d. With genitive of reference

(1) With pronouns

ὑπὲρ τούτου τρὶς τὸν κύριον παρεκάλεσα, ἵνα ἀποστῇ ἀπ᾽ ἐμοῦ (2 Cor. 12:8)

with reference to this, I implored the Lord three times that it might leave me

(2) With nouns

εἴτε **ὑπὲρ Τίτου**, κοινωνὸς ἐμός (2 Cor. 8:23)

whether **in regard to Titus**, [ἐστιν, he is] my partner

2. With accusative of comparison or excelling, meaning **surpassing, beyond, more than, superior to**

a. With adjectives

καὶ αὐτὸν ἔδωκεν κεφαλὴν **ὑπὲρ πάντα** τῇ ἐκκλησίᾳ (Eph. 1:22)

and he gave him [to be] head **over and above all things** to the church

b. With nouns

εἶδον, Βασιλεῦ, οὐρανόθεν **ὑπὲρ τὴν λαμπρότητα** τοῦ ἡλίου περιλάμψαν με φῶς (Acts 26:13)

I saw, O king, from heaven a light shining around me **surpassing the brilliance** of the sun

c. With pronouns

ὁ φιλῶν πατέρα ἢ μητέρα **ὑπὲρ ἐμὲ** οὐκ ἔστιν μου ἄξιος (Matt. 10:37)

the one who loves father or mother **more than me** is not worthy of me

P. ὑπό, with the genitive and accusative, indicating agency and place

1. With the genitive, indicating agency with a passive verb. The preposition is found more often with the participle than with the finite verb and infinitive combined. The agent is usually a person or persons, but occasionally a thing is the agent.

a. With the participle

(1) The agent as a noun

ἡμεῖς δὲ ὀφείλομεν εὐχαριστεῖν τῷ θεῷ πάντοτε περὶ ὑμῶν, ἀδελφοὶ **ἠγαπημένοι ὑπὸ κυρίου** (2 Thess. 2:13)

and we ought always to thank God for you, brothers, **beloved by the Lord**

(2) The agent as a pronoun

οἱ δὲ Φαρισαῖοι καὶ οἱ νομικοὶ τὴν βουλὴν τοῦ θεοῦ ἠθέτησαν εἰς ἑαυτοὺς **μὴ βαπτισθέντες ὑπ᾽ αὐτοῦ** (Luke 7:30)

but the Pharisees and the lawyers rejected the counsel of God for themselves, **not having been baptized by him**

(3) The agent as a noun with an attributive adjective

ἡ ἐπιστολὴ ἡμῶν ὑμεῖς ἐστε, ἐγγεγραμμένη ἐν ταῖς καρδίαις ἡμῶν, **γινωσκομένη καὶ ἀναγινωσκομένη ὑπὸ πάντων ἀνθρώπων** (2 Cor. 3:2)

you are our epistle, written in our hearts, **known** and **read by all people**

(4) The agent as an adjective

καὶ ἔσεσθε **μισούμενοι ὑπὸ πάντων** διὰ τὸ ὄνομά μου (Mark 13:13)

and you shall be **hated by all** because of my name

(5) The agent as a participle

χειραγωγούμενος ὑπὸ τῶν συνόντων μοι ἦλθον εἰς Δαμασκόν (Acts 22:11)

being led by the hand of those who were with me I went into Damascus

(6) The agent personified

καὶ οἱ ἀστέρες τοῦ οὐρανοῦ ἔπεσαν εἰς τὴν γῆν, ὡς συκῆ βάλλει τοὺς ὀλύνθους αὐτῆς, **ὑπὸ ἀνέμου μεγάλου σειομένη** (Rev. 6:13)

and the stars of heaven fell to the earth, as a fig tree drops its unripe figs **while being shaken by a mighty wind**

b. With the finite verb

(1) The agent as a noun

ἵνα μὴ **πλεονεκτηθῶμεν ὑπὸ τοῦ Σατανᾶ** (2 Cor. 2:11)

lest **we should be taken advantage of by Satan**

(2) The agent as a pronoun

ὅταν **κληθῇς ὑπό τινος** εἰς γάμους, μὴ κατακλιθῇς εἰς τὴν πρωτοκλισίαν (Luke 14:8)

when **you are invited by anyone** to a wedding, do not recline at the table in the place of honor

(3) The agent as an adjective

χωρὶς δὲ πάσης ἀντιλογίας τὸ ἔλαττον **ὑπὸ τοῦ κρείττονος εὐλογεῖται** (Heb. 7:7)

and without any contradiction the inferior **is blessed by the better**

(4) The agent as a noun with an attributive adjective
ἱναντί γὰρ ἡ ἐλευθερία μου **κρίνεται ὑπὸ ἄλλης συνειδήσεως;**
(1 Cor. 10:29)
for why is my freedom **being judged by another's conscience?**
(5) The agent as a substantive participle
ὑπὸ τῶν ἀκουσάντων εἰς ἡμᾶς **ἐβεβαιώθη** (Heb. 2:3)
it was confirmed to us **by those who heard**

c. With the infinitive
(1) The agent as a noun
συνέβη **βαστάζεσθαι** αὐτὸν **ὑπὸ τῶν στρατιωτῶν** διὰ τὴν βίαν
τοῦ ὄχλου (Acts 21:35)
it came about [that] he **was carried by the soldiers** because of the
violence of the crowd
(2) The agent as a pronoun
ἐγὼ γὰρ ὤφειλον **ὑφ' ὑμῶν συνίστασθαι** (2 Cor. 12:11)
for I myself ought **to be recommended by you**

2. With the accusative, **under**
a. With the accusative of place
ποσάκις ἠθέλησα ἐπισυνάξαι τὰ τέκνα σου ὃν τρόπον ὄρνις τὴν
ἑαυτῆς νοσσιὰν **ὑπὸ τὰς πτέρυγας,** καὶ οὐκ ἠθελήσατε (Luke 13:34)
how often I wanted to gather your children as a bird [ἐπισυνάγει,
gathers] her brood **under her wings** and you wouldn't [let me]
b. With the accusative indicating authority, power, command
ἁμαρτία γὰρ ὑμῶν οὐ κυριεύσει· οὐ γάρ ἐστε **ὑπὸ νόμον** ἀλλὰ
ὑπὸ χάριν (Rom. 6:14)[45]
for sin shall not reign over you; for you are not **under law**, but **under
grace**

II. **Improper prepositions**. Adverbs used frequently as prepositions.

A. ἄχρι(ς) with genitive
1. With adverb of time, translated **until**
πολλάκις προεθέμην ἐλθεῖν πρὸς ὑμᾶς, καὶ ἐκωλύθην **ἄχρι τοῦ δεῦρο**
(Rom. 1:13)
often I made plans to come to you, but I was prevented **until now**

<hr>

[45] Rom. 6:14 text is from GNT, NA & WH: TR & MT have ἀλλ'.

2. With nouns
   a. With genitive of place, **as far as**
      καὶ ἐξῆλθεν αἷμα ἐκ τῆς ληνοῦ **ἄχρι τῶν χαλινῶν** τῶν ἵππων
      (Rev. 14:20)
      and blood came out of the winepress **as far as the bridles** of the horses
   b. With genitive of time, **until**
      καὶ ἔσῃ τυφλός, μὴ βλέπων τὸν ἥλιον **ἄχρι καιροῦ** (Acts 13:11)
      and you shall be blind, not seeing the sun, **until the time** [appointed
      by God]
3. With pronouns
   a. With genitive of place, **as far as**
      ἀλλὰ κατὰ τὸ μέτρον τοῦ κανόνος οὗ ἐμέρισεν ἡμῖν ὁ θεὸς μετροῦ,
      ἐφικέσθαι **ἄχρι καὶ ὑμῶν** (2 Cor. 10:13)
      but according to the measure of the rule that God assigned to us,
      a measure to reach even **to you**
   b. With genitive of time, **as long as**
      ἀλλὰ παρακαλεῖτε ἑαυτοὺς καθ᾽ ἑκάστην ἡμέραν, **ἄχρις οὗ** τὸ
      σήμερον καλεῖται (Heb. 3:13)
      but exhort one another each day, **as long as** it is called today

B. ἔμπροσθεν, with genitive, indicating place and rank
   1. With genitive of place, translated **before, in front of, in the sight of, in the
      presence of**
      a. With adjectives
         ὁ δὲ ἠρνήσατο **ἔμπροσθεν πάντων** λέγων, οὐκ οἶδα τί λέγεις
         (Matt. 26:70)
         and he denied **before all**, saying, I do not know what you are saying
      b. With nouns
         εἰς τὸ στηρίξαι ὑμῶν τὰς καρδίας ἀμέμπτους ἐν ἁγιωσύνῃ
         ἔμπροσθεν τοῦ θεοῦ (1 Thess. 3:13)
         in order to establish your hearts blameless in holiness **before God**
      c. With pronouns
         τοσαῦτα δὲ αὐτοῦ σημεῖα πεποιηκότος **ἔμπροσθεν αὐτῶν** οὐκ
         ἐπίστευον εἰς αὐτόν (John 12:37)
         but, even though he had done so many miracles **in their sight**, they did
         not believe in him
   2. With genitive of rank
      ὁ ὀπίσω μου ἐρχόμενος **ἔμπροσθέν μου** γέγονεν (John 1:15)
      the one who is coming after me has **rank higher than I**

C. ἐνώπιον with genitive of place, meaning **before, in the sight of, in the presence of**
   1. With adjectives
      ἱκανοὶ δὲ . . . συνενέγκαντες τὰς βίβλους κατέκαιον **ἐνώπιον πάντων**
      (Acts 19:19)
      and many . . . brought their books and burned [them] **before all**
   2. With nouns
      καὶ ἀνέβη ὁ καπνὸς τῶν θυμιαμάτων ταῖς προσευχαῖς τῶν ἁγίων ἐκ
      χειρὸς τοῦ ἀγγέλου **ἐνώπιον τοῦ θεοῦ** (Rev. 8:4)
      and the smoke of the incense ascended with the prayers of the saints
      from the hand of the angel **before God**
   3. With pronouns
      ἀναστὰς πορεύσομαι πρὸς τὸν πατέρα μου καὶ ἐρῶ αὐτῷ, πάτερ,
      ἥμαρτον εἰς τὸν οὐρανὸν καὶ **ἐνώπιόν σου** (Luke 15:18)
      I will arise and go to my father, and I will say to him, "Father, I have
      sinned against heaven and **before you**"

D. ἔξω with genitive of place
   διὸ καὶ Ἰησοῦς, ἵνα ἁγιάσῃ διὰ τοῦ ἰδίου αἵματος τὸν λαόν, **ἔξω τῆς πύλης**
   ἔπαθεν (Heb. 13:12)
   wherefore Jesus also, in order that he might sanctify the people by his own
   blood, suffered **outside the gate**

E. ἕως with genitive
   1. With genitive of time
      a. With adverbs
         ἔσται γὰρ τότε θλῖψις μεγάλη οἵα οὐ γέγονεν ἀπ᾽ ἀρχῆς κόσμου
         ἕως τοῦ νῦν (Matt. 24:21)
         for then shall be great tribulation, which has not been from the
         beginning of the world **until the present time**
      b. With nouns
         ἐγὼ μεθ᾽ ὑμῶν εἰμι πάσας τὰς ἡμέρας **ἕως τῆς συντελείας** τοῦ αἰῶνος
         (Matt. 28:20)
         I am with you always **until the close** of the age
      c. With pronouns
         οἵτινες ἀνεθεμάτισαν ἑαυτοὺς μήτε φαγεῖν μήτε πιεῖν **ἕως οὗ**
         ἀνέλωσιν αὐτόν (Acts 23:21)
         who bound themselves with an oath neither to eat nor drink **until**
         they should kill him

   d. With infinitives
      καὶ διερχόμενος εὐηγγελίζετο τὰς πόλεις πάσας **ἕως τοῦ ἐλθεῖν**
      αὐτὸν εἰς Καισάρειαν (Acts 8:40)
      and as he was passing through he preached the gospel in all cities,
      until he came to Caesarea
2. With genitive of place
   a. With nouns
      ἁρπαγέντα τὸν τοιοῦτον **ἕως τρίτου οὐρανοῦ** (2 Cor. 12:2)
      such a person [was] snatched away **to the third heaven**
   b. With pronouns
      καὶ ἦλθον **ἕως αὐτοῦ** καὶ κατεῖχον αὐτὸν τοῦ μὴ πορεύεσθαι ἀπ᾽
      αὐτῶν (Luke 4:42)
      and they came **up to him** and were detaining him so that he might not
      depart from them
3. Genitive of sequence or series
   κάλεσον τοὺς ἐργάτας καὶ ἀπόδος αὐτοῖς τὸν μισθὸν ἀρξάμενος ἀπὸ
   τῶν ἐσχάτων **ἕως τῶν πρώτων** (Matt. 20:8)
   call the workers, and pay them their wages, from the last **to the first**

F. χωρίς with genitive of separation
   1. With nouns
      οἱ δὲ ἐσθίοντες ἦσαν ἄνδρες ὡσεὶ πεντακισχίλιοι **χωρὶς γυναικῶν καὶ**
      παιδίων (Matt. 14:21)
      and those who ate were about five thousand men, **apart from women and**
      children
   2. With pronouns
      a. Prepositive
         ὅτι **χωρὶς ἐμοῦ** οὐ δύνασθε ποιεῖν οὐδέν (John 15:5)
         for **without me** you are unable to do anything
      b. Postpositive only once in the NT
         εἰρήνην διώκετε μετὰ πάντων, καὶ τὸν ἁγιασμόν, **οὗ χωρὶς** οὐδεὶς
         ὄψεται τὸν κύριον (Heb. 12:14)
         pursue peace with all [people], and sanctification, **without which**
         no one will see the Lord
   3. With participles
      πῶς οὖν ἐπικαλέσωνται εἰς ὃν οὐκ ἐπίστευσαν; πῶς δὲ πιστεύσωσιν οὗ
      οὐκ ἤκουσαν; πῶς δὲ ἀκούσωσιν **χωρὶς κηρύσσοντος**; (Rom. 10:14)
      how then shall they call on whom they did not believe? and how shall they
      believe whom they did not hear? and how shall they hear **without someone**
      preaching?

Select Bibliography for Prepositions

Allen, J. P. "The Force of Prepositions in Compound Verbs in the Perfect Tense in John's Gospel and Epistles." Doctoral diss., Southern Baptist Theological Seminary, 1940.

Argyle, W. "An Alleged Semitism." *Expository Times* 66 (1954-1955): 177; 67 (1955-1956): 247.

Atkinson, Basil F. C. *The Theology of Prepositions.* London: Tyndale, 1943.

Beckwith, I. T. "The Articular Infinitve with εἰς." *Journal of Biblical Literature* 15 (1896): 155-67.

Beverage, John M. "The Preposition ἐκ in Johannine Literature." Master's thesis, Dallas Theological Seminary, 1953.

Blackwelder, Boice, W. "The Causal Use of Prepositions in the Greek New Testament." Th.D. diss., Northern Baptist Theological Seminary, 1951.

Blakeney, E. H. "ὑπέρ with Genitive in N.T." *Expository Times* 55 (1944): 306.

Bratcher, Robert G. "'The Name' in Prepositional Phrases in the New Testament. "*Bible Translator* 14: 72-80.

Davies, R. E. "Christ in Our Place—the Contribution of the Prepositions." *Tyndale Bulletin* 21 (1970): 71-91.

Ferguson, Everett. "'When You Come Together': ἐπὶ τὸ αὐτό in Early Christian Literature." *Restoration Quarterly* 16, no. 3-4 (1973): 202-8.

Greenlee, J. Harold. "The Preposition ΕΙΣ in the New Testament." *Bible Translator* 3 (1952): 12-14.

Griffin, B. Glenn. "A Fresh Approach to Acts 2:38." Master's thesis, Dallas Theological Seminary, 1983.

Harris, Murray J. "Appendix: Prepositions and Theology in the Greek New Testament," pp. 1171–1215. *New International Dictionary of New Testament Theology.* Edited by Colin Brown. 3 vols. Grand Rapids: Zondervan, 1978.

Harrison, Gessner. *A Treatise on the Greek Prepositions, and on the Cases of Nouns with which These Are Used.* Philadelphia: Lippincott, 1958.

Hartman, L. "'Into the Name of Jesus.' A Suggestion Concerning the Earliest Meaning of the Phrase." *New Testament Studies* 20 (1973-74): 432-40.

Hendrickson, William. "The Meaning of the Greek Preposition 'ANTI' in the New Testament." Th.D. diss., Princeton Theological Seminary, 1948.

Hutton, W. R. "Considerations for the Translation of Greek EN." *Bible Translator* 9 (1958): 163-70.

Kendall, Wm. Frederick. "Paul's Use of Ἀντί and Ὑπέρ." Th.D. diss., Southern Baptist Theological Seminary, 1935.

Kennedy, A. A. "Two Exegetical Notes on St. Paul. I. A Special use of ἐν." *Expository Times* 28 (1916-17): 322f.

Lipscomb, Davis. "The Use of EN and EIS in the New Testament and the Contemporaneous Nonliterary Papyri." Doctoral diss., Southern Baptist Theological Seminary, 1930.

Mantey, Julius R. "The Causal Use of EIS in the New Testament." *Journal of Biblical Literature* 70, part 1 (1951): 45–48.

_____. "On Causal ΕΙΣ Again." *Journal of Biblical Literature* 70 (December 1951): 309–11.

_____. "Unusual Meanings for Prepositions in the Greek N.T." *Expositor* 25 (1923): 453–60.

Marcus, Ralph. "The Elusive Causal ΕΙΣ." *Journal of Biblical Literature* 70 (March 1951): 43–44.

_____. "On Causal ΕΙΣ." *Journal of Biblical Literature* 70 (September 1951): 129–30.

Mitchell, M. M. "Concerning περὶ δέ in 1 Corinthians." *Novum Testamentum* 31 (1989): 229–56.

O'Rourke, John. "ΕΙΣ and EN in John." *Bible Translator* 25, no. 1 (January 1974): 139–42.

Ricketson, Robert Fleming. "The Ablative After ΔΙΑ." Th.D. diss., Southwestern Baptist Theological Seminary, 1944.

Southern, Paul. "The New Testament Use of the Preposition KATA with Special Reference to its Distributive Aspects." Doctoral diss., Southern Baptist Theological Seminary, 1948.

Turner, Nigel. "An Alleged Semitism." *Expository Times* 66 (1954–55): 252–54.

_____. "The Preposition EN in the New Testament." *Bible Translator* 10, no. 3 (1959): 113–20.

Waltke, Bruce Kenneth. "The Theological Significance of ANTI and ΥΠΕΡ in the New Testa ment." Th.D. diss., Dallas Theological Seminary, 1958.

Wedderburn, A. J. M. "Some Observations on Paul's Use of the Phrases 'in Christ' and 'with Christ.'" *Journal for the Study of the New Testament* 25 (1985): 83–97.

Wuest, Kenneth S. "Prepositions and Synonyms in Greek Exposition." *Bibliotheca Sacra* 117, no. 467 (July 1960): 234–41.

PRONOUNS

Pronouns are words that take the place of nouns to eliminate repetition. We will look at the various pronouns found in the Greek NT: personal, relative, indefinite, interrogative, demonstrative, possessive, reciprocal, and reflexive.

I. Personal pronouns.
Forms.

1 pers. sing. nom. ἐγώ (I) is usually emphatic.

        gen. ἐμοῦ, μου
        dat. ἐμοί, μοι
        acc. ἐμέ, με

ἐμοῦ, ἐμοί, and ἐμέ are always accented and are emphatic except when related to a preposition. μου, μοι, and με do not have their own accent and are always unemphatic.

2 pers. sing. nom. σύ (you) is usually emphatic.

        gen. σοῦ
        dat. σοί
        acc. σέ

σοῦ, σοί, and σέ when accented are considered emphatic except when related to a preposition.

1 pers. pl. nom. ἡμεῖς (we) is usually emphatic.

        gen. ἡμῶν
        dat. ἡμῖν
        acc. ἡμᾶς

2 pers. pl. nom. ὑμεῖς (you) is usually emphatic.

        gen. ὑμῶν
        dat. ὑμῖν
        acc. ὑμᾶς

3 pers. sing. (he, she, they)			3 pers. pl. (they)		
masc.	fem.	neut.	masc.	fem.	neut.
αὐτός	αὐτή	αὐτό	αὐτοί	αὐταί	αὐτά
αὐτοῦ	αὐτῆς	αὐτοῦ	αὐτῶν	αὐτῶν	αὐτῶν
αὐτῷ	αὐτῇ	αὐτῷ	αὐτοῖς	αὐταῖς	αὐτοῖς
αὐτόν	αὐτήν	αὐτό	αὐτούς	αὐτάς	αὐτά

Functions.
A. As personal pronoun.
   1. Nominative as subject of verb. These are the only substantives (nouns or pronouns) that can be an explicit subject of a first or second singular or plural verb.

235

a. 1 pers. sing. ἐγώ

οὐδὲ ἐγὼ λέγω ὑμῖν ἐν ποίᾳ ἐξουσίᾳ ταῦτα ποιῶ (Mark 11:33)

neither **do I tell** you by what authority I am doing these things

b. 1 pers. pl. ἡμεῖς

λέγει αὐτοῖς Σίμων Πέτρος, ὑπάγω ἁλιεύειν. λέγουσιν αὐτῷ, ἐρχόμεθα καὶ ἡμεῖς σὺν σοί (John 21:3)

Simon Peter said to them, "I am going fishing." they said to him, **"we also are coming** with you"

c. 2 pers. sing. σύ

σὺ εἶ ὁ Χριστός ὁ υἱὸς τοῦ θεοῦ τοῦ ζῶντος (Matt. 16:16)

you are the Christ, the son of the living God

d. 2 pers. pl. ὑμεῖς

καὶ ὑμεῖς πεφυσιωμένοι ἐστέ, καὶ οὐχὶ μᾶλλον ἐπενθήσατε (1 Cor. 5:2)

and **you yourselves are conceited** and have not rather mourned

e. 3 pers. sing. αὐτός

αὐτὸς δὲ σωθήσεται, οὕτως δὲ ὡς διὰ πυρός (1 Cor. 3:15)

but **he himself shall be saved**, yet so as through fire

f. 3 pers. pl. αὐτοί

ἀλλὰ ἐλθόντες αὐτοὶ ἡμᾶς ἐξαγαγέτωσαν (Acts 16:37)

but **let they themselves come and bring** us **out**

2. Genitive—the substantive modified by the genitive is usually articular.

a. Genitive of possession or relationship

(1) Gen. sing. 1 pers.

πέμψω τὸν υἱόν μου τὸν ἀγαπητόν (Luke 20:13)

I will send **my beloved son**

(2) Gen. sing. 2 pers.

ἀγαπήσεις τὸν πλησίον σου ὡς σεαυτόν (James 2:8)

you shall love **your neighbor** as yourself

(3) Gen. sing. 3 pers.

οὐ γὰρ αὐτοῦ τὰ νοήματα ἀγνοοῦμεν (2 Cor. 2:11)

for we are not ignorant of **his designs**

(4) Gen. pl. 1 pers.

νῦν γὰρ ἐγγύτερον ἡμῶν ἡ σωτηρία ἢ ὅτε ἐπιστεύσαμεν (Rom. 13:11)

for now **our salvation** [ἐστιν, is] nearer than when we believed

(5) Gen. pl. 2 pers.

πείθεσθε τοῖς ἡγουμένοις ὑμῶν καὶ ὑπείκετε, αὐτοὶ γὰρ ἀγρυπνοῦσιν ὑπὲρ τῶν ψυχῶν ὑμῶν (Heb. 13:17)

obey your leaders and submit; for they care **for your souls**

(6) Gen. pl. 3 pers.

καὶ πᾶν ὄρος καὶ νῆσος **ἐκ τῶν τόπων αὐτῶν** ἐκινήθησαν
(Rev. 6:14)

and every mountain and island were moved **out of their places**

b. Objective genitive

παρακαλῶ οὖν ὑμᾶς, **μιμηταί μου** γίνεσθε (1 Cor. 4:16)

I exhort you therefore, be **imitators of me**

c. Subjective genitive

μεγάλα καὶ θαυμαστὰ **τὰ ἔργα σου**, κύριε ὁ θεὸς ὁ παντοκράτωρ
(Rev. 15:3)

great and wonderful [εἰσιν/ἐστιν, are] **your works**, Lord God Almighty

d. Object of certain verbs, such as ἀκούω, ἅπτω (mid. or pass.),
βασιλεύω, γεύομαι, μνψμονεύω

παρακαλῶ **ἀκούσαί σε ἡμῶν** συντόμως τῇ σῇ ἐπιεικείᾳ (Acts 24:4)

I request you **to hear us** briefly, based on your graciousness

e. Object of preposition

ἡ χάρις **μετὰ πάντων ὑμῶν** (Titus 3:15)

grace [be] **with you all**

f. Genitive of comparison

ὁ δὲ ὀπίσω μου ἐρχόμενος **ἰσχυρότερός μού** ἐστιν (Matt. 3:11)

but the one who comes after me is **greater than I**

g. Genitive pronoun as subject of genitive absolute construction

συνυπουργούντων καὶ **ὑμῶν** ὑπὲρ ἡμῶν τῇ δεήσει (2 Cor. 1:11)

you also **are helping** in prayer for us

h. Predicate genitive after forms of εἰμι as possessive

οὗτός ἐστιν ὁ κληρονόμος· δεῦτε ἀποκτείνωμεν αὐτόν, καὶ **ἡμῶν
ἔσται** ἡ κληρονομία (Mark 12:7)

this is the heir; come, let us kill him, and the inheritance **shall belong to
us**

i. Genitive complement with adjectives

ὁ φιλῶν πατέρα ἢ μητέρα ὑπὲρ ἐμὲ οὐκ ἔστιν **μου ἄξιος**
(Matt. 10:37)

the one who loves father or mother more than me is not **worthy of me**

j. Genitives with prepositions

(1) With ἀπό

οὗτος ὁ λαὸς τοῖς χείλεσίν με τιμᾷ, ἡ δὲ καρδία αὐτῶν πόρρω
ἀπέχει **ἀπ᾽ ἐμοῦ** (Mark 7:6)

this people honors me with their lips, but their heart is far away
from me

(2) With διά

ἥτις κατεργάζεται δι' ἡμῶν εὐχαριστίαν τῷ θεῷ (2 Cor. 9:11)
which works **through us** gratitude to God

(3) With ἐκ

εἶπέν τις ἐξ αὐτῶν ἴδιος αὐατῶν προφήτης, Κρῆτες ἀεὶ ψεῦσται
(Titus 1:12)
one **of them** said, their own prophet, "Cretans [εἰσιν, are]
always liars"

(4) With ἐπί

ἔχουσιν ἐπ' αὐτῶν βασιλέα (Rev. 9:11)[1]
they have a king **over them**

(5) With μετά

μετ' οὐ πολὺ δὲ ἔβαλεν κατ' αὐτῆς ἄνεμος τυφωνικός
(Acts 27:14)
and after a short time a whirlwind came **against it**

(6) With παρά

καὶ ἀκούσαντες οἱ παρ' αὐτοῦ ἐξῆλθον κρατῆσαι αὐτόν
(Mark 3:21)
and when **those who belonged to him** heard, they went out to lay
hold of him

(7) With περί

καὶ ἠρώτησαν αὐτὸν περὶ αὐτῆς (Luke 4:38)
and they asked him **about her**

(8) With πρό

ἐν ᾧ δὲ ἔρχομαι ἐγώ, ἄλλος πρὸ ἐμοῦ καταβαίνει (John 5:7)
but while I am going, another person steps down **before me**

(9) With ὑπέρ

καθὼς καὶ ὁ Χριστὸς ἠγάπησεν τὸν ἐκκλησίαν, καὶ ἑαυτὸν
παρέδωκεν ὑπὲρ αὐτῆς (Eph. 5:25)

(10) With ὑπό

κἀκεῖνοι ἀκούσαντες ὅτι ζῇ καὶ ἐθεάθη ὑπ' αὐτῆς ἠπίστησαν
(Mark 16:11)
and when they heard that he is alive and was seen **by her** they did
not believe

3. With the dative

a. With dative of indirect object

καὶ εἶπεν, νεανίσκε, σοὶ λέγω, ἐγέρθητι (Luke 7:14)
and he said, "young man, **I tell you**, arise"

---

[1] Rev. 9:11 text is from GNT, NA, WH, TR*b* & MT; TR*s* has ἐφ' αὐτῶν.

b. With dative of direct object with certain verbs
   καὶ **ἠπίστουν αὐταῖς** (Luke 24:11)
   and **they did not believe them**

c. With dative of disadvantage
   οὐαὶ ὑμῖν, γραμματεῖς καὶ Φαρισαῖοι, ὑποκριταί (Matt. 23:29)
   woe to you, scribes and Pharisees, hypocrites

d. With dative of advantage
   κάλεσον τοὺς ἐργάτας καὶ **ἀπόδος αὐτοῖς** τὸν μισθόν (Matt. 20:8)
   call the workers and **give to them** their wages

e. With dative of possession with an equative verb
   ἡμεῖς ἀφήκαμεν πάντα καὶ ἠκολουθήσαμέν σοι· τί ἄρα **ἔσται ἡμῖν**;
   (Matt. 19:27)
   we have left everything and followed you; what then **shall be ours**?

f. Dative subject of dative absolute participle construction
   καὶ **ἐμβάντι αὐτῷ** εἰς τὸ πλοῖον, ἠκολούθησαν αὐτῷ οἱ μαθηταὶ
   αὐτοῦ (Matt. 8:23)
   and **when he embarked** into the ship, his disciples followed him

g. Dative object of prepositions
   (1) With ἐν
       τὸ γὰρ **ἐν αὐτῇ** γεννηθὲν ἐκ πνεύματός ἐστιν ἁγίου (Matt. 1:20)
       for that conceived **in her** is from the Holy Spirit
   (2) With ἐπί
       ἦν δὲ σπήλαιον, καὶ λίθος ἐπέκειτο **ἐπ᾽ αὐτῷ** (John 11:38)
       now it was a cave, and a stone was lying **on it**
   (3) With σύν
       ἀσπάζονται ὑμᾶς οἱ **σὺν ἐμοὶ** ἀδελφοί (Phil. 4:21)
       the brothers **with me** greet you

4. With the accusative
   a. Accusative of direct object
      οὕτως **ἡμᾶς λογιζέσθω** ἄνθρωπος ὡς ὑπηρέτας Χριστοῦ (1 Cor. 4:1)
      so let a person **consider us** servants of Christ
   b. Accusative subject of infinitive
      καὶ ὅτι διὰ πολλῶν θλίψεων δεῖ **ἡμᾶς εἰσελθεῖν** εἰς τὴν βασιλείαν
      τοῦ θεοῦ (Acts 14:22)
      and that through many trials **we must enter** the kingdom of God
   c. Accusative subject of a supplementary participle
      κύριε, πότε **σὲ εἴδομεν πεινῶντα**, ἢ **διψῶντα** (Matt. 25:44)
      Lord, when did we see **you hungry** or **thirsty**

d. With prepositions
  (1) With διά
      καὶ χαίρω δι᾽ ὑμᾶς, ἵνα πιστεύσητε, ὅτι οὐκ ἤμην ἐκεῖ
      (John 11:15)
      and I rejoice **on your account**, so that you may believe that I wɛ
      not there
  (2) With εἰς
      περὶ ἁμαρτίας μέν, ὅτι οὐ πιστεύουσιν εἰς ἐμέ (John 16:9)
      concerning sin, because they do not believe **in me**
  (3) With ἐπί
      εὑρὼν δὲ ὁ Ἰησοῦς ὀνάριον ἐκάθισεν ἐπ᾽ αὐτό (John 12:14)
      and when Jesus found a young donkey he sat **upon it**
  (4) With περί
      ὡς Σόδομα καὶ Γόμορρα καὶ αἱ περὶ αὐτὰς πόλεις (Jude 7)
      as Sodom and Gomorrah, and the cities **around them**
  (5) With πρός
      Ἰερουσαλήμ, Ἰερουσαλήμ, ἡ ἀποκτείνουσα τοὺς προφήτας κα
      λιθοβολοῦσα τοὺς ἀπεσταλμένους πρὸς αὐτήν (Matt. 23:37)[2]
      Jerusalem, Jerusalem, who kills the prophets and stones those
      who have been sent **to her**

B. Intensive pronouns. Although αὐτός functions as a personal pronoun,
   especially in the oblique cases (genitive, dative, and accusative), the intensivɛ
   use involves the nominative as well as the other cases.
   1. Nominative
      a. Nominative double pronouns for emphasis
         (1) 1 pers. sing.
             ἀνάστηθι· καὶ ἐγὼ αὐτὸς ἄνθρωπός εἰμι (Acts 10:26)
             rise up, **I also myself** am a man
         (2) 1 pers. pl.
             ἡμεῖς καὶ αὐτοὶ ἐν ἑαυτοῖς στενάζομεν (Rom. 8:23)
             even **we ourselves** groan within ourselves
         (3) 2 pers. pl.
             Δεῦτε ὑμεῖς αὐτοὶ κατ᾽ ἰδίαν εἰς ἔρημον τόπον (Mark 6:31)
             come **you yourselves** privately into a deserted place
      b. First attributive position, meaning **the same**
         οὐ πᾶσα σὰρξ ἡ αὐτὴ σάρξ (1 Cor. 15:39)
         not all flesh [ἐστιν, is] **the same flesh**

---

[2] Matt. 23:37 text is from GNT, NA, WH & MT: TR has Ἰερουσαλήμ, Ἰερουσαλήμ.

c. Articular substantive

σὺ δὲ ὁ αὐτὸς εἶ καὶ τὰ ἔτη σου οὐκ ἐκλείψουσιν (Heb. 1:12)

but you are **the same**, and your years will not end

d. Predicate position

αὐτο τὸ πνεῦμα συμμαρτυρεῖ τῷ πνεύματι ἡμῶν (Rom. 8:16)

the Spirit Himself bears witness with our spirit

e. With personal names αὐτός is used without the article and means **himself**

αὐτὸς Δαυὶδ λέγει αὐτὸν κύριον (Mark 12:37)[3]

David himself calls him Lord

2. With the genitive

a. Double pronouns are emphatic.

(1) Singular

καὶ σοῦ δὲ αὐτῆς τὴν ψυχὴν διελεύσεται ῥομφαία (Luke 2:35)

and a sword shall pass through **your own soul** also

(2) Plural

καὶ ἐξ ὑμῶν αὐτῶν ἀναστήσονται ἄνδρες λαλοῦντες διεστραμμένα (Acts 20:30)

and **from among you yourselves** men shall rise up speaking perverted things

b. First attributive position

ἢ οὐκ ἔχει ἐξουσίαν ὁ κεραμεὺς τοῦ πηλοῦ, ἐκ τοῦ αὐτου φυράματος ποιῆσαι ὃ μὲν εἰς τιμὴν σκεῦος ὃ δὲ εἰς ἀτιμίαν; (Rom. 9:21)

or does not the potter have authority over the clay, to make **out of the same lump** one vessel unto honor and another unto dishonor?

c. Second attributive position

ἐν σκηναῖς κατοικήσας μετὰ Ἰσαὰκ καὶ Ἰακὼβ τῶν συγκληρονόμων τῆς ἐπαγγελίας τῆς αὐτῆς (Heb. 11:9)

dwelling in tents with Isaac and Jacob the joint heirs **of the same promise**

d. Articular substantive, meaning **the same**

καὶ αὐτὸς παραπλησίως μετέσχεν τῶν αὐτῶν (Heb. 2:14)

he also in like manner partook **of the same**

3. With the dative

a. Second attributive position

καὶ ποιμένες ἦσαν ἐν τῇ χώρᾳ τῇ αὐτῇ (Luke 2:8)

and there were shepherds **in the same country**

---

[3] Mark 12:37 text is from GNT & NA: TR & MT have αὐτὸς οὖν Δαβίδ; WH has Δαυείδ.

b. First attributive position

κατ᾿ ἐνιαυτὸν **ταῖς αὐταῖς θυσίαις** ἃς προσφέρουσιν εἰς τὸ διηνεκὲς
οὐδέποτε δύναται τοὺς προσερχομένους τελειῶσαι (Heb. 10:1)
year by year **with the same sacrifices**, which they offer perpetually
are never able to perfect those who approach

c. Double pronoun, emphatic

ἐν **ὑμῖν αὐτοῖς** κρίνατε (1 Cor. 11:13)
decide **among yourselves**

4. With the accusative

a. First attributive position

καὶ πᾶς μὲν ἱερεὺς ἕστηκεν καθ᾿ ἡμέραν λειτουργῶν, καὶ **τὰς αὐτὰς**
πολλάκις προσφέρων **θυσίας** (Heb. 10:11)
and every priest stands daily ministering and often offering **the same
sacrifices**

b. Articular substantive

(1) Direct object

ἀπεστάλκαμεν οὖν Ἰούδαν καὶ Σίλαν, καὶ αὐτοὺς διὰ λόγου
ἀπαγγέλλοντας **τὰ αὐτά** (Acts 15:27)
we have sent then Judas and Silas, they also by report will
tell [you] **the same things**

(2) Object of preposition

συνερχομένων οὖν ὑμῶν **ἐπὶ τὸ αὐτό**, οὐκ ἔστιν κυριακὸν
δεῖπνον φαγεῖν (1 Cor. 11:20)
when then you gather together **in the same place**, it is not to
eat the Lord's supper

II. **Relative pronouns** are used to connect substantives that are related to each other.
Although classified as definite and indefinite (ὅς and ὅστις respectively), little if
any distinction is found between the two in the NT.

Forms.   sing.   pl.
                  masc.   fem.   neut.   masc.   fem.   neut.
Definite nom.   ὅς   ἥ   ὅ   οἵ   αἵ   ἅ
Indefinite   ὅστις   ἥτις   ὅ τι   οἵτινες αἵτινες ἅτινα

A. The relative pronoun agrees with its antecedent in gender and number but not
necessarily in case. The case is determined by its function in the specific
clause.

ἀπαγγέλλομεν ὑμῖν **τὴν ζωὴν τὴν αἰώνιον ἥτις** ἦν πρὸς τὸν πατέρα
(1 John 1:2)
we report to you **the eternal life that** was with the father

B. The indefinite relative pronoun is always in the nominative form except for ἕως ὅτου, a genitive singular neuter, translated **until, while**.

Functions.

A. Nominative case subject of finite verb.
    1. Nom. sing. masc.
        τὸν φωτισμὸν τοῦ εὐαγγελίου τῆς δόξης τοῦ Χριστοῦ, **ὅς ἐστιν** εἰκὼν τοῦ θεοῦ (2 Cor. 4:4)
        the light of the gospel of the glory of Christ, **who is** the image of God
    2. Nom. pl. neut.
        a. With singular verb
            ἅ ἐστιν σκιὰ τῶν μελλόντων (Col. 2:17)
            which are a shadow of things to come
        b. With plural verb
            ἔχεις ὀλίγα ὀνόματα ἐν Σάρδεσιν **ἃ οὐκ ἐμόλυναν** τὰ ἱμάτια αὐτῶν (Rev. 3:4)
            you have a few names in Sardis, **who have not defiled** their garments

B. With the genitive case.
    1. Genitive of relationship
        γυνή . . . **ἧς** εἶχεν **τὸ θυγάτριον αὐτῆς** πνεῦμα ἀκάθαρτον (Mark 7:25)
        a woman . . . **whose daughter** had an unclean spirit
    2. With preposition διά
        καὶ εἷς κύριος Ἰησοῦς Χριστός, **δι' οὗ** τὰ πάντα καὶ ἡμεῖς δι' αὐτοῦ (1 Cor. 8:6)
        and one Lord Jesus Christ, **by whom** all things [ἐστιν/εἰσιν, exist] and we [ἐσμεν, live] through him

C. With the dative case.
    1. Dative of apposition
        ἕκαστος **ἐν τῇ κλήσει ᾗ** ἐκλήθη, ἐν ταύτῃ μενέτω (1 Cor. 7:20)
        each one **in the calling in which** he was called, let him remain in it
    2. With preposition ἐν
        καινοὺς δὲ οὐρανοὺς καὶ γῆν καινὴν κατὰ τὸ ἐπάγγελμα αὐτοῦ προσδοκῶμεν, **ἐν οἷς** δικαιοσύνη κατοικεῖ (2 Peter 3:13)
        but we await new heavens and a new earth, **in which** righteousness dwells

D. With the accusative case.
  1. As direct object
     καὶ ἤνοιξεν ἡ γῆ τὸ στόμα αὐτῆς καὶ κατέπιεν τὸν ποταμὸν **ὃν ἔβαλεν**
     ὁ δράκων ἐκ τοῦ στόματος αὐτοῦ (Rev. 12:16)
     and the earth opened its mouth and swallowed the river **that the**
     dragon cast out of his mouth
  2. With the preposition εἰς
     μετῴκισεν αὐτὸν εἰς τὴν γῆν ταύτην εἰς ἣν ὑμεῖς νῦν κατοικεῖτε
     (Acts 7:4)
     he removed himself into this land **in which** you now dwell

III. **Indefinite pronouns.**

Forms are enclitic, or without an accent, except when followed by another
enclitic; when it has an accent, it is always on the second syllable.

	sing.		pl.	
	Masc. and fem.	neut.	masc. and fem.	neut.
Nom.	τις	τι	τινες	τινα

Functions.

A. Substantival use.
  1. Nominative case as subject of finite verb
     a. Singular
        οὐδὲ τὸν πατέρα **τις ἐπιγινώσκει** εἰ μὴ ὁ υἱός (Matt. 11:27)
        neither does **anyone know** the father except the son
     b. Plural
        ἔχων πίστιν καὶ ἀγαθὴν συνείδησιν, ἥν **τινες** ἀπωσάμενοι
        περὶ τὴν πίστιν ἐναυάγησαν (1 Tim. 1:19)
        having faith and a good conscience, which **some** having rejected
        have suffered shipwreck concerning the faith
  2. Genitive case
     a. Subjective genitive
        εἴ **τινος** τὸ ἔργον κατακαήσεται, ζημιωθήσεται (1 Cor. 3:15)
        if **anyone's work** shall be burned up, he shall forfeit [it]
     b. With preposition ὑπό
        πάντα μοι ἔξεστιν, ἀλλ᾽ οὐκ ἐγὼ ἐξουσιασθήσομαι **ὑπό τινος**
        (1 Cor. 6:12)
        all things are permissible for me, but I will not be mastered **by anything**

3. Dative case
   a. Dative of direct object
      ἵνα ἐρχομένου Πέτρου κἂν ἡ σκιὰ **ἐπισκιάσῃ τινὶ** αὐτῶν
      (Acts 5:15)
      that while Peter is coming even his shadow **might overshadow one**
      of them
   b. With preposition ἐν
      βλέπετε, ἀδελφοί, μήποτε ἔσται **ἔν τινι** ὑμῶν καρδία πονηρὰ
      ἀπιστίας (Heb. 3:12)
      beware, brothers, lest there shall be **in any one** of you an evil heart of
      unbelief
4. Accusative case
   a. Direct object of finite verb
      καὶ **ἀποστέλλουσιν** πρὸς αὐτόν **τινας** τῶν Φαρισαίων καὶ τῶν
      Ἡρωδιανῶν ἵνα αὐτὸν ἀγρεύσωσιν λόγῳ (Mark 12:13)
      and **they sent** to him **some** of the Pharisees and of the Herodians, in
      order that they might catch him in discourse
   b. Subject of infinitive
      ὥστε **μὴ ἰσχύειν τινὰ** παρελθεῖν διὰ τῆς ὁδοῦ ἐκείνης (Matt. 8:28)
      so that **no one was able** to pass by that road

B. Attributive use.
   1. Nominative case
      a. Singular functioning as an indefinite article
         κριτής τις ἦν ἔν τινι πόλει (Luke 18:2)
         a judge was in a city
      b. Plural
         παρεισέδυσαν γάρ **τινες ἄνθρωπος**, οἱ πάλαι προγεγραμμένοι εἰς
         τοῦτο τὸ κρίμα (Jude 4)
         for **some men** slipped in stealthily, who long ago were written before
         unto this judgment
   2. Genitive case
      a. Singular
         καὶ **περί τινος** Ἰησοῦ τεθνηκότος, ὃν ἔφασκεν ὁ Παῦλος ζῆν
         (Acts 25:19)[4]
         and **concerning one Jesus** who had died, whom Paul affirmed to be
         alive

---

[4] Acts 25:19 text is from GNT & NA: WH, TR & MT have ζῆν.

b. Plural

ἡμερῶν δὲ διαγενομένων **τινῶν** Ἀγρίππας ὁ βασιλεὺς καὶ Βερνίκη κατήντησαν εἰς Καισάρειαν (Acts 25:13)

and after **certain days** had passed Agrippa the king and Bernice came down to Caesarea

3. Dative case

ἄγοντες παρ' ᾧ ξενισθῶμεν **Μνάσωνί** τινι Κυπρίῳ (Acts 21:16)

bring [one] with whom we might lodge, **a certain Mnason**, a Cypriote

4. Accusative case

   a. Singular

   καὶ εὑρών **τινα** Ἰουδαῖον ὀνόματι Ἀκύλαν (Acts 18:2)

   and having found **a certain Jew** whose name [was] Aquila

   b. Plural

   ἦμεν δὲ ἐν ταύτῃ τῇ πόλει διατρίβοντες **ἡμέρας τινάς** (Acts 16:12)

   and we were staying in this city **certain days**

IV. **Interrogative pronouns.**

Forms. The forms are exactly the same spelling as the indefinite pronouns, except that the acute accent is always on the first syllable and never changes to a grave.

Functions. It is the regular pronoun for introducing questions.

A. The nominative form is generally the subject of a third person finite verb.

1. Indirect questions

   a. With indicatives

   αὐτὸς γὰρ ἐγίνωσκεν **τί ἦν** ἐν τῷ ἀνθρώπῳ (John 2:25)

   for he himself knew **what was** in man

   b. With subjunctives

   βάλλοντες κλῆρον ἐπ' αὐτὰ **τίς τί ἄρῃ** (Mark 15:24)

   casting lots on them [to decide] **who should take** what

   c. With optative

   καὶ ἐπυνθάνετο **τίς εἴη** καὶ τί ἐστιν πεποιηκώς (Acts 21:33)

   and he inquired **who he might be** and what he had been doing

2. Direct questions

   a. With future indicative

   τίς με **ῥύσεται** ἐκ τοῦ σώματος τοῦ θανάτου τούτου; (Rom. 7:24)

   who shall deliver me from the body of this death?

    b. With present indicative
       τίς στρατεύεται ἰδίοις ὀψωνίοις ποτέ; (1 Cor. 9:7)
       who serves as a soldier at his own expense at anytime?
    c. With aorist indicative
       τίς σε **κατέστησεν** ἄρχοντα καὶ δικαστήν; (Acts 7:35)
       who appointed you ruler and judge?
  3. When used with a first or second person equative singular verb, τίς is the predicate nominative.
    a. 1 pers. sing.
       ἐγὼ τίς **ἤμην** δυνατὸς κωλῦσαι τὸν θεόν; (Acts 11:17)[5]
       I was who [to be] able to hinder God?
    b. 2 pers. sing.
       ἔλεγον οὖν αὐτῷ, Σὺ τίς εἶ; (John 8:25)
       they said then to him, "**you are who?**"

B. The genitive case.
  1. Genitive of possession
     καὶ λέγει αὐτοῖς, τίνος ἡ εἰκὼν αὕτη καὶ ἡ ἐπιγραφή; (Matt. 22:20)
     and he said to them, "**whose image** and **inscription** [ἐστιν, is] this?"
  2. Genitive of relationship
     τί ὑμῖν δοκεῖ περὶ τοῦ Χριστοῦ; τίνος υἱός ἐστιν; (Matt. 22:42)
     what does it seem to you concerning Christ? **whose son** is he?
  3. Genitive with preposition
     περὶ τίνος ὁ προφήτης λέγει τοῦτο; (Acts 8:34)
     concerning whom does the prophet say this?

C. The dative case.
  1. Dative complement with verb ὁμοιόω or adjective ὅμοιος
     τίνι οὖν ὁμοιώσω τοὺς ἀνθρώπους τῆς γενεᾶς ταύτης καὶ τίνι εἰσὶν ὅμοιοι (Luke 7:31)
     to what, then, **shall I compare** the men of this generation and **they are like what**?
  2. As an attributive adjective
     δι᾽ οὗ καὶ σῴζεσθε, τίνι λόγῳ εὐηγγελισάμην ὑμῖν εἰ κατέχετε (1 Cor. 15:2)
     by which you also are saved, if you retain **what word** I preached to you

---

[5] Acts 11:17 text is from GNT, NA & WH: TR & MT have ἐγὼ δὲ τίς.

  3. Indirect object
     τίνι γὰρ εἶπέν ποτε **τῶν ἀγγέλων**, υἱός μου εἶ σύ; (Heb. 1:5)
     for **to whom of the angels** did he ever say, "you are my son?"

D. The accusative case.
  1. When used adverbially, τί means **why?**
     τί με ζητεῖτε ἀποκτεῖναι; (John 7:19)
     why are you seeking to kill me?
  2. Accusative with preposition
     a. διὰ τί (TR and MT have Διατί)
        διὰ τί οὖν οὐκ ἐπιστεύσατε αὐτῷ; (Matt. 21:25)
        why, then, did you not believe him?
     b. εἰς τί
        εἰς τί ἡ ἀπώλεια αὕτη τοῦ μύρου γέγονεν; (Mark 14:4)
        for what reason has this waste of the ointment been made?
  3. Accusative of direct object
     τίνα με λέγουσιν οἱ ἄνθρωποι εἶναι; (Mark 8:27)
     whom do men claim me to be?

V. **Demonstrative pronouns.**

Forms.

	sing.			pl.		
	Masc.	fem.	neut.	masc.	fem.	neut.
A.	οὗτος	αὕτη	τοῦτο	οὗτοι	αὗται	ταῦτα

That which is relatively near, translated **this, this (one), these**

| B. | | ἐκεῖνος | ἐκείνη | ἐκεῖνο | ἐκεῖνοι | ἐκεῖναι | ἐκεῖνα |

That which is relatively distant, translated **that, that (person), those**

Functions.

A. The demonstrative οὗτος is used as a substantive, or it modifies another
   substantive. Approximately 71 percent of the pronouns are substantive and 29
   percent of the pronouns modify a substantive.
   1. The substantival use is found in both numbers, three genders, and all four
      cases. Sixty-four percent of the substantives are found in the neuter gender
      and 29 percent in the masculine. Thirty-nine percent are found in the
      nominative case and 46 percent in the accusative case.

a. Nominative case
  (1) The pronoun may be used as the subject of a finite verb.
      καὶ **οὗτοι ἔγνωσαν** ὅτι σύ με ἀπέστειλας (John 17:25)
      and **these knew** that you sent me
  (2) The pronoun may be used as the subject of an equative verb.
      οὗτός ἐστιν ὁ υἱός μου ὁ ἀγαπητός (Matt. 3:17)
      this is my beloved son
  (3) The pronoun may be used as the subject of an elliptical or implied
      equative verb.
      εἴ τις ἐν λόγῳ οὐ πταίει, **οὗτος** τέλειος ἀνήρ (James 3:2)
      if anyone does not stumble in speech, **this one [ἐστιν, is]** a perfect
      man
b. Genitive case
  (1) The pronoun may be found with a comparative adjective.
      καὶ **μείζονα τούτων** ποιήσει (John 14:12)
      and he will do **greater things than these**
  (2) Certain verbs take their object in the genitive case.
      ὑμῶν δὲ ὁ πατὴρ οἶδεν ὅτι **χρῄζετε τούτων** (Luke 12:30)
      and your father knows that **you need these things**
  (3) The pronoun may be used as an object of a preposition.
      ἕνεκεν τούτου καταλείψει ἄνθρωπος τὸν πατέρα αὐτοῦ καὶ
      τὴν μητέρα (Mark 10:7)
      for this reason a man shall leave his father and his mother
c. Dative case
  (1) The pronoun may be used as an indirect object of a verb.
      τούτῳ πάντες οἱ προφῆται μαρτυροῦσιν (Acts 10:43)
      all the prophets bear witness **to this one**
  (2) The pronoun may be used as an object of a preposition.
      ταῦτα μελέτα, **ἐν τούτοις** ἴσθι (1 Tim. 4:15)
      practice these things, live **in them**
  (3) The pronoun may be used as a dative of association.
      τούτοις ἀρκεσθησόμεθα (1 Tim. 6:8)
      we will be content **with these things**
d. Accusative case
  (1) The pronoun may be used as the direct object of a verb.
      τοῦτον ὁ θεὸς ἀρχηγὸν καὶ σωτῆρα ὕψωσεν τῇ δεξιᾷ
      αὐτοῦ (Acts 5:31)
      God exalted this one a prince and savior at his right hand
  (2) The pronoun may be used as the object of a preposition.
      διὰ τοῦτο ἔχρισέν σε ὁ θεός (Heb. 1:9)
      because of this God anointed you

(3) The pronoun may function as the subject of an infinitive, also called an accusative of respect.

ὅθεν ἀναγκαῖον ἔχειν τι καὶ **τοῦτον** ὃ προσενέγκῃ (Heb. 8:3)
wherefore it [ἦν, was] necessary for **this one** also **to have** something to offer

2. When the pronoun modifies a substantive, the article precedes the substantive, whereas the pronoun may precede the article or follow the substantive. It is always in the predicate position.

   a. The pronoun follows the substantive (postposition) 77 percent of the time.

      (1) Nominative case

      καὶ ὁ ἄνθρωπος **οὗτος** δίκαιος καὶ εὐλαβής (Luke 2:25)
      and **this man** [ἦν, was] just and reverent

      (2) Genitive case

      ἀλλὰ πρόβατα ἔχω ἃ οὐκ ἔστιν ἐκ τῆς αὐλῆς **ταύτης** (John 10:16)
      but I have other sheep that are not **of this fold**

      (3) Dative case

      ὥστε παρακαλεῖτε ἀλλήλους ἐν τοῖς λόγοις **τούτοις** (1 Thess. 4:18)
      wherefore encourage one another **with these words**

      (4) Accusative case

      ἀπήγγειλεν δὲ ὁ δεσμοφύλαξ **τοὺς λόγους τούτους** πρὸς τὸν Παῦλον (Acts 16:36)
      and the jailor reported **these words** to Paul

   b. The pronoun precedes the article (pre-position) 23 percent of the time.

      (1) Nominative case

      οὗτοι οἱ ἄνθρωποι δοῦλοι τοῦ θεοῦ τοῦ ὑψίστου εἰσίν (Acts 16:17)
      these men are servants of the most high God

      (2) Genitive case

      ἐγὼ πάσῃ συνειδήσει ἀγαθῇ πεπολίτευμαι τῷ θεῷ ἄχρι **ταύτης** τῆς ἡμέρας (Acts 23:1)
      I in all good conscience have lived for God to **this day**

      (3) Dative case

      ἐφ' ὅσον εἰμὶ ἐν **τούτῳ** τῷ σκηνώματι (2 Peter 1:13)
      as long as I am **in this tent**

      (4) Accusative case

      καὶ **ταύτην** τὴν ἐντολὴν ἔχομεν ἀπ' αὐτοῦ (1 John 4:21)
      and we have **this command** from Him

B. The demonstrative ἐκεῖνος is used both substantivally and adjectivally, modifying a substantive. It is found 60 percent of the time modifying a substantive and 40 percent of the time as a substantive.
1. When modifying a substantive, 72.5 percent of the time the pronoun is postpositional and 27.5 percent of the time pre-positional.
   a. Postpositional
      (1) Nominative case
         μακάριοι **οἱ δοῦλοι ἐκεῖνοι** (Luke 12:37)
         those servants [εἰσιν, are] blessed
      (2) Genitive case
         καὶ ἐσώθη ἡ γυνὴ **ἀπὸ τῆς ὥρας ἐκείνης** (Matt. 9:22)
         and the woman was healed **from that hour**
      (3) Dative case
         τί ποιήσει **τοῖς γεωργοῖς ἐκείνοις**; (Matt. 21:40)
         what will he do **to those farmers**?
      (4) Accusative case
         πᾶσαν **τὴν ὀφειλὴν ἐκείνην** ἀφῆκά σοι (Matt. 18:32)
         I forgave you all **that debt**
   b. Pre-positional
      (1) Nominative case
         ἐμνήσθημεν ὅτι **ἐκεῖνος ὁ πλάνος** εἶπεν ἔτι ζῶν (Matt. 27:63)
         we remember that **that deceiver** said while he was yet alive
      (2) Genitive case
         ἦν γὰρ μεγάλη ἡ ἡμέρα **ἐκείνου τοῦ σαββάτου** (John 19:31)
         for the day of **that sabbath** was great
      (3) Dative case
         τότε νηστεύσουσιν **ἐν ἐκείναις ταῖς ἡμέραις** (Luke 5:35)
         then they will fast **in those days**
      (4) Accusative case
         σπουδάσωμεν οὖν εἰσελθεῖν **εἰς ἐκείνην τὴν κατάπαυσιν** (Heb. 4:11)
         be diligent therefore to enter **into that rest**
2. Substantival use of ἐκεῖνος
   a. Nominative case
      (1) Subject of finite verb
         περὶ γὰρ ἐμοῦ **ἐκεῖνος ἔγραψεν** (John 5:46)
         for **that one wrote** about me
      (2) Subject of equative verb
         καθὼς **ἐκεῖνος δίκαιός ἐστιν** (1 John 3:7)
         even as **that one is** righteous

b. Genitive case
  (1) Genitive of possession
      ἵνα ὑμεῖς τῇ ἐκείνου πτωχείᾳ πλουτήσητε (2 Cor. 8:9)
      that you may be enriched by the poverty **of that one**
  (2) Genitive of relationship
      σὺ μαθητὴς εἶ ἐκείνου (John 9:28)
      you are a disciple **of that one**
  (3) Subjective genitive
      εἰ δὲ τοῖς ἐκείνου γράμμασιν οὐ πιστεύετε (John 5:47)
      but if you do not believe **the writings of that one**
c. Dative case
  (1) Dative of indirect object
      καὶ ἐκείνοις εἶπεν (Matt. 20:4)
      and **he said to those [people]**
  (2) Dative of direct object with certain verbs
      οὐδὲ ἐκείνοις ἐπίστευσαν (Mark 16:13)
      neither **did they believe them**
d. Accusative case
  (1) Accusative of direct object
      μὴ τῷ βρώματί σου ἐκεῖνον ἀπόλλυε ὑπὲρ οὗ Χριστὸς
      ἀπέθανεν (Rom. 14:15)
      do not with your food destroy **that one** for whom Christ died
  (2) Object of preposition
      καὶ μετὰ τὸ ψωμίον τότε εἰσῆλθεν εἰς ἐκεῖνον ὁ σατανᾶς
      (John 13:27)
      and after the morsel, then Satan entered **into that one**
  (3) Accusative subject of infinitive
      ἐκεῖνον δεῖ αὐξάνειν, ἐμὲ δὲ ἐλαττοῦσθαι (John 3:30)
      that one must increase, but I must decrease

VI. **Possessive pronouns.**

Forms.

	masc.	fem.	neut.	translation
1 pers. sing.	ἐμός	ἐμή	ἐμόν	**my, mine**
2 pers. sing.	σός	σή	σόν	**your, yours**
1 pers. pl.	ἡμέτερος	ἡμετέρα	ἡμέτερον	**our, ours**
2 pers. pl.	ὑμέτερος	ὑμετέρα	ὑμέτερον	**your, yours**

Functions. The possessive pronoun indicates possession.

A. It is used as an attributive.
  1. First attributive position
    a. Nom. sing. 1 pers. sing.
      πεποιθὼς ἐπὶ πάντας ὑμᾶς ὅτι **ἡ ἐμὴ χαρὰ** πάντων ὑμῶν ἐστιν
      (2 Cor. 2:3)
      having confidence in you all, that **my joy** belongs to you all
    b. Gen. sing. 2 pers. pl.
      τοῦτο γὰρ **πρὸς τῆς ὑμετέρας σωτηρίας** ὑπάρχει (Acts 27:34)
      for this is **for your safety**
    c. Dat. sing. 2 pers. sing.
      πῶς ἐρεῖ τὸ ἀμὴν **ἐπὶ τῇ σῇ εὐχαριστίᾳ**; (1 Cor. 14:16)
      how will he say "Amen" **at your giving of thanks**?
    d. Acc. sing. 1 pers. pl.
      ὅσα γὰρ προεγράφη, εἰς **τὴν ἡμετέραν διδασκαλίαν** ἐγράφη
      (Rom. 15:4)
      for whatever was written before was written **for our instruction**
  2. Second attributive position
    a. Nom. sing. 2 pers. sing.
      ὁ λόγος ὁ σὸς ἀλήθειά ἐστιν (John 17:17)
      your word is truth
    b. Gen. pl. 1 pers. sing.
      ἀλλὰ ὑμεῖς οὐ πιστεύετε, ὅτι οὐκ ἐστὲ ἐκ **τῶν προβάτων τῶν ἐμῶν**
      (John 10:26)[6]
      but you do not believe because you are not **of my sheep**
    c. Dat. pl. 2 pers. pl
      καὶ **ἐν τῷ νόμῳ** δὲ **τῷ ὑμετέρῳ** γέγραπται (John 8:17)
      but **in your law** also it is written
    d. Acc. sing. 1 pers. sing.
      καὶ ἡ κρίσις ἡ ἐμὴ δικαία ἐστιν, ὅτι οὐ ζητῶ **τὸ θέλημα τὸ ἐμόν**
      (John 5:30)
      and my judgment is just because I do not seek **my own will**
  3. Anarthrous attributive use
    a. Nom. pl. 1 pers. sing.
      ἐν τούτῳ γνώσονται πάντες ὅτι **ἐμοὶ μαθηταί** ἐστε, ἐὰν ἀγάπην
      ἔχητε ἐν ἀλλήλοις (John 13:35)
      by this all shall know that you are **my disciples**, if you have love
      toward one another

---

[6] John 10:26 text is from GNT, NA & WH: TR & MT have ἀλλ' and οὐ γάρ ἐστε.

    b. Acc. sing. 1 pers. sing.

       καὶ εὑρεθῶ ἐν αὐτῷ, μὴ ἔχων **ἐμὴν δικαιοσύνην** τὴν ἐκ νόμου
       (Phil. 3:9)

       and [ἵνα, that] I may be found in him, not having **my own
       righteousness** that [οὖσαν, is] of the law

B. It is used as a substantive.

   1. Nom. pl. 2 pers. sing.

      καὶ τὰ ἐμὰ πάντα σά ἐστιν καὶ **τὰ σὰ** ἐμά (John 17:10)

      and all my things are yours, and **your things** [ἐστιν, are] mine

   2. Gen. pl. 1 pers. pl.

      καὶ αὐτὸς ἱλασμός ἐστιν περὶ τῶν ἁμαρτιῶν ὑμῶν, οὐ **περὶ τῶν
      ἡμετέρων** δὲ μόνον (1 John 2:2)

      and he himself is the satisfaction for our sins, but not **for ours** only

   3. Dat. sing. 1 pers. pl.

      ἢ οὐκ ἔξεστί(ν) μοι ὃ θέλω ποιῆσαι **ἐν τοῖς ἐμοῖς**; (Matt. 20:15)[7]

      or is it unlawful for me to do what I wish **with my own [money]**? [No!]

   4. Acc. sing. 2 pers. pl.

      εἰ τὸν λόγον μου ἐτήρησαν, καὶ **τὸν ὑμέτερον** τηρήσουσιν (John 15:20)

      if they kept my word, they will also keep **yours**

C. It is used as a predicate with an equative verb.

   1. Nom. pl. 2 pers. sing.

      ὁ δὲ εἶπεν αὐτῷ, τέκνον, σὺ πάντοτε μετ᾽ ἐμοῦ εἶ, καὶ πάντα τὰ
      ἐμὰ **σά ἐστιν** (Luke 15:31)

      but he said to him, "son, you are always with me and all my possessions
      are yours"

   2. Nom. sing. 1 pers. sing.

      καὶ ὁ λόγος ὃν ἀκούετε **οὐκ ἔστιν ἐμός** ἀλλὰ τοῦ πέμψαντός με
      πατρός (John 14:24)

      and the word that you hear **is not mine** but from the father who sent
      me

VII. **Reciprocal pronouns** refer to mutual relations.

    Forms. ἀλλήλων, ἀλλήλοις, ἀλλήλους, only in the oblique plural cases.

---

[7] Matt. 20:15 text is from GNT & NA: WH omits ἤ; TR & MT have ποιῆσαι ὃ θέλω.

Functions.

A. Genitive case.
1. Genitive of possession
   ἀλλήλων τὰ βάρη βαστάζετε (Gal. 6:2)
   carry **the burdens of one another**
2. Genitive of relationship
   λαλεῖτε ἀλήθειαν ἕκαστος μετὰ τοῦ πλησίον αὐτοῦ, ὅτι ἐσμὲν
   ἀλλήλων μέλη (Eph. 4:25)
   let each one speak truth with his neighbor, for we are **members of one
   another**
3. Genitive object of preposition
   καὶ ἔλεγον μετ᾽ ἀλλήλων ἐν τῷ ἱερῷ ἑστηκότες (John 11:56)
   and they were speaking **with one another** while standing in the temple

B. Dative case.
1. Dative of indirect object
   ὅμοιοί εἰσιν παιδίοις τοῖς ἐν ἀγορᾷ καθημένοις καὶ προσφωνοῦσιν
   ἀλλήλοις (Luke 7:32)
   they are like children who are sitting in the market place and **calling to one
   another**
2. Dative object of preposition
   ὁ δὲ θεὸς τῆς ὑπομονῆς καὶ τῆς παρακλήσεως δῴη ὑμῖν τὸ αὐτὸ
   φρονεῖν ἐν ἀλλήλοις (Rom. 15:5)
   now the God of patience and encouragement give you the same mind
   among one another
3. Dative of direct object with certain verbs
   ἀλλὰ διὰ τῆς ἀγάπης δουλεύετε ἀλλήλοις (Gal. 5:13)
   but through love **serve one another**

C. Accusative case.
1. Accusative of direct object
   ἦμεν γάρ ποτε καὶ ἡμεῖς ἀνόητοι . . . μισοῦντες ἀλλήλους (Titus 3:3)
   for we ourselves also were once foolish . . . **hating one another**
2. Accusative object of preposition
   a. With πρός
      καὶ συνελάλουν πρὸς ἀλλήλους (Luke 4:36)
      and they were discussing **with one another**

b. With εἰς

καὶ πλεονάζει ἡ ἀγάπη ἑνὸς ἑκάστου πάντων ὑμῶν εἰς ἀλλήλους
(2 Thess. 1:3)

and the love of each one of you all increases **toward one another**

VIII. **Reflexive pronouns.**

Forms.

	gen.	dat.	acc.	translation
1 pers. sing.	ἐμαυτοῦ	ἐμαυτῷ	ἐμαυτόν	**myself**
2 pers. sing.	σεαυτοῦ	σεαυτῷ	σεαυτόν	**yourself**
3 pers. sing.	ἑαυτοῦ	ἑαυτῷ	ἑαυτόν	**himself, itself**
3 pers. pl.	ἑαυτῶν	ἑαυτοῖς	ἑαυτούς	**ourselves, yourselves, themselves**

The plural forms are in agreement in person with the subject of the verb and are thus variously translated as above

Functions.

A. Singular.
   1. Genitive case
     a. Genitive of possession

       καὶ νῦν τὸ κατέχον οἴδατε, εἰς τὸ ἀποκαλυφθῆναι αὐτὸν ἐν τῷ
       ἑαυτοῦ καίρῳ (2 Thess. 2:6)

       and now you know what restrains, in order that he might be revealed
       in his own time

     b. Genitive of relationship

       ὡς ἐὰν τροφὸς θάλπῃ τὰ **ἑαυτῆς** τέκνα (1 Thess. 2:7)[8]

       as a nurse cherishes **her own children**

     c. Genitive object of preposition

       (1) With ἀπό

          οὐδεὶς αἴρει αὐτὴν ἀπ᾽ ἐμοῦ, ἀλλ᾽ ἐγὼ τίθημι αὐτὴν
          ἀπ᾽ ἐμαυτοῦ (John 10:18)

          no one takes it from me, but I lay it down **of myself**

       (2) With περί

          σὺ **περὶ σεαυτοῦ** μαρτυρεῖς· ἡ μαρτυρία σου οὐκ ἔστιν
          ἀληθής (John 8:13)

          you testify **concerning yourself**; your testimony is not true

---

[8] 1 Thess. 2:7 text is from GNT, NA & WH; TR & MT have ὡς ἄν.

2. Dative case
   a. Dative of advantage
      (1) 1 pers. sing.
          κατέλιπον ἐμαυτῷ ἑπτακισχιλίους ἄνδρας, οἵτινες οὐκ
          ἔκαμψαν γόνυ τῇ Βάαλ (Rom. 11:4)
          I have kept for myself seven thousand men who did not bow the
          knee to Baal
      (2) 2 pers. sing.
          ἔπεχε σεαυτῷ καὶ τῇ διδασκαλίᾳ, ἐπίμενε αὐτοῖς
          (1 Tim. 4:16)
          take heed to yourself and to the teaching; continue in them
      (3) 3 pers. sing.
          ἀνείλατο αὐτὸν ἡ θυγάτηρ Φαραώ, καὶ ἀνεθρέψατο αὐτὸν
          ἑαυτῇ εἰς υἱόν (Acts 7:21)[9]
          the daughter of Pharaoh adopted him and reared him **for herself**
          a son
   b. Dative object of preposition
      Ἰησοῦς οὖν πάλιν ἐμβριμώμενος **ἐν ἑαυτῷ** ἔρχεται εἰς τὸ μνημεῖον
      (John 11:38)
      Jesus, then again deeply moved **within himself**, came to the tomb
3. Accusative case
   a. Accusative of direct object
      περὶ πάντα, **σεαυτὸν παρεχόμενος** τύπον καλῶν ἔργων (Titus 2:7)
      concerning all things **showing yourself** an example of good works
   b. Accusative of direct object and subject of infinitive
      πρὸ γὰρ τούτων τῶν ἡμερῶν ἀνέστη Θευδᾶς, **λέγων εἶναί** τινα
      ἑαυτόν (Acts 5:36)
      for before these days Theudas arose, **claiming himself to be**
      somebody
   c. Accusative object of preposition
      (1) With **ἐπί**
          καὶ ἐὰν βασιλεία **ἐφ᾽ ἑαυτὴν** μερισθῇ, οὐ δύναται
          σταθῆναι ἡ βασιλεία ἐκείνη (Mark 3:24)
          and if a kingdom is divided **against itself**, that kingdom is unable
          to stand

---

[9] Acts 7:21 text is from GNT, NA & WH: TR has ἀνείλετο; MT has ἀνείλετο ἡ θυγάτηρ.

(2) With πρός

κἀγὼ ἐὰν ὑψωθῶ ἐκ τῆς γῆς, πάντας ἑλκύσω **πρὸς ἐμαυτόν**
(John 12:32)

and if I am lifted up from the earth, I will draw all people **to myself**

B. Plural.
1. Genitive case
   a. Genitive of possession, 2 pers. pl.

   ἢ οὐκ οἴδατε ὅτι τὸ σῶμα ὑμῶν ναὸς τοῦ ἐν ὑμῖν ἁγίου
   πνεύματός ἐστιν οὗ ἔχετε ἀπὸ θεοῦ, καὶ **οὐκ ἐστὲ ἑαυτῶν**;
   (1 Cor. 6:19)

   or do you not know that your body is the temple of the Holy Spirit, which [ὄντος, is] in you, which you have from God, and **you do not belong to yourselves**

   b. Genitive of relationship, 3 pers. pl.

   οὕτως ὀφείλουσιν καὶ οἱ ἄνδρες ἀγαπᾶν **τὰς ἑαυτῶν** γυναῖκας ὡς
   τὰ ἑαυτῶν σώματα (Eph. 5:28)[10]

   so husbands ought to love **their own wives** as their own bodies

   c. Genitive object of preposition, 1 pers. pl.

   οὐχ ὅτι **ἀφ᾽ ἑαυτῶν** ἱκανοί ἐσμεν λογίσασθαί τι ὡς **ἐξ ἑαυτῶν**
   (2 Cor. 3:5)

   not that we are sufficient **of ourselves** to consider anything as **from ourselves**

2. Dative case
   a. Dative of advantage, 3 pers. pl.

   ἀποθησαυρίζοντας **ἑαυτοῖς** θεμέλιον καλὸν εἰς τὸ μέλλον
   (1 Tim. 6:19)

   treasuring up **for themselves** a good foundation for the future

   b. Dative object of preposition
   (1) With ἐν, 1 pers. pl.

   ἀλλὰ αὐτοὶ **ἐν ἑαυτοῖς** τὸ ἀπόκριμα τοῦ θανάτου ἐσχήκαμεν
   (2 Cor. 1:9)

   but we ourselves have the decision of death **within ourselves**

   (2) With παρ᾽, 2 pers. pl.

   μὴ γίνεσθε φρόνιμοι **παρ᾽ ἑαυτοῖς** (Rom. 12:16)

   do not be wise **in yourselves**

---

[10] Eph. 5:28 text is from GNT, NA & WH: TR & MT omit καί; MT has ἀγαπᾶν.

3. Accusative case
   a. Accusative of direct object
      (1) 1 pers. pl.
      καθαρίσωμεν ἑαυτοὺς ἀπὸ παντὸς μολυσμοῦ σαρκὸς καὶ
      πνεύματος (2 Cor. 7:1)
      let us cleanse ourselves from every defilement of flesh and spirit
      (2) 2 pers. pl.
      ἑαυτοὺς πειράζετε εἰ ἐστὲ ἐν τῇ πίστει, ἑαυτοὺς
      δοκιμάζετε (2 Cor. 13:5)
      examine yourselves if you are in the faith; **prove yourselves**
      (3) 3 pers. pl.
      καί εἰσιν εὐνοῦχοι οἵτινες εὐνούχισαν ἑαυτοὺς διὰ τὴν
      βασιλείαν τῶν οὐρανῶν (Matt. 19:12)
      and there are eunuchs who **have made themselves eunuchs**
      because of the kingdom of heaven
   b. Accusative object of preposition
      (1) With εἰς, 2 pers. pl.
      ἕκαστος καθὼς ἔλαβεν χάρισμα, εἰς ἑαυτοὺς αὐτὸ
      διακονοῦντες (1 Peter 4:10)
      each one as he has received a gift, ministering it **to one another**
      (2) With πρός, 3 pers. pl.
      καὶ ἔλεγον **πρὸς ἑαυτάς** τίς ἀποκυλίσει ἡμῖν τὸν
      λίθον ἐκ τῆς θύρας τοῦ μνημείου; (Mark 16:3)
      and they said **to one another**, who will roll away the stone from
      the door of the tomb for us?

Select Bibliography for Pronouns

Argyle, A.W. "The Causal Use of the Relative Pronouns in the Greek New Testament."
    Bible Translator 6 (1955): 165-69.
Cadbury, H. J. "The Relative Pronouns in Acts and Elsewhere." *Journal of Biblical
    Literature* (1923): 150-57.
Hatch, W. H. P. "The Possessive Pronoun in the New Testament." *Anglical Theological
    Review* 26 (1941): 250-53.
Kilpatrick, G. D. "The Possessive Pronoun in the New Testament." *Journal of
    Theological Studies* 42 (1941): 184-86.
Lofthouse, W. F. "'I' and 'We' in the Pauline Letters." *Bible Translator* 6: 72-80.

Matthew, John P. "When does 'We' include 'You'?" *Bible Translator* 27, no. 2 (April 1976): 237-40.

Moulton, Harold K. "Pronouns in the New Testament." *Bible Translator* 21: 36-44.

O'Rourke, John J. "The Article as Pronoun in the Synoptic Gospels." *Catholic Biblical Quarterly* 37, no. 4 (1975): 492-99.

_____. "Paul's Use of the Article as a Pronoun." *Catholic Biblical Quarterly* 34 (1972): 59-65.

Pickett, Velma A. "Those Problem Pronouns, We, Us and Our in the New Testament." *Bible Translator* 15, no. 2 (1964): 88-92.

Spottorno, Mme. V. "The Relative Pronoun in the New Testament." *New Testament Studies* 28 (1982): 132-41.

Sturz, Harry A. "Analysis of Word Order and Emphasis in the Greek New Testament: With Special Treatment of the Pronouns ME and EME." Master's thesis, Grace Theological Seminary, 1962.

Wifstrand, Albert. "A Problem Concerning the Word Order in the New Testament." *Studia Theologica* 3: 172-84.

Wilson, Ambrose J. "Emphasis in the New Testament." *Journal of Theological Studies* 10 (1909): 255-66.

FINITE VERBS

Indicative Mood

Verbs are divided into three groups: finite, infinitive, and participle. Finite verbs have five elements: person (first, second, third), number (singular and plural), mood (indicative, subjunctive, imperative, and optative), tense (present, future, imperfect, aorist, perfect, and pluperfect), and voice (active, middle, and passive). Each of these elements will be treated separately along the way. Person and number will be a part of each classification in all four moods as well as tense and voice.

I. **The Indicative Mood** is generally considered the mood of fact, reality, or certainty. However, this is only one aspect of the indicative mood, as it also includes other features: the future tense indicates the expected and anticipated, which may or may not become true; and the interrogative, which includes questions of fact and questions of possibility or impossibility and everything in between. This is the only mood that includes all six tenses. Thus, the classification of the indicative will be considered only with such concepts that include all six tenses.

The declarative indicative expresses an assertion or negation of a simple fact, past, present, or future. The interrogative indicative asks a question of a simple fact, past, present, or future. The potential indicative includes several concepts: wish, command, obligation, and condition. As command is primarily a feature of the indicative future, it will be treated under that tense. Since obligation and wish are primarily characteristics of the aorist, imperfect, and present tenses, they will be considered under those tenses. Only the conditional sentence will be considered under the potential concept.

The kinds of statements, voice, and tense will be discussed and illustrated as found in the indicative mood. Each classification will include all three persons in both numbers except where that person and number is not found in the NT.

A. Major kinds of indicatives.
  1. The declarative indicative states a simple fact in the past, present, or future.
    a. 1 pers. sing. aor. act. indic.
       ὅτι πάντα ἃ **ἤκουσα** παρὰ τοῦ πατρός μου **ἐγνώρισα** ὑμῖν
       (John 15:15)
       for everything that **I heard** from my father **I made known** to you
    b. 2 pers. sing. impf. act. indic.
       ὅτε **ἦς** νεώτερος **ἐζώννυες** σεαυτόν καὶ **περιεπάτεις** ὅπου **ἤθελες**
       (John 21:18)
       when **you were** young **you dressed** yourself and **walked** wherever **you wanted**

c. 3 pers. sing. fut. act. indic.

καὶ ὁ πατήρ μου ἀγαπήσει αὐτόν (John 14:23)

and **my father will love** him

d. 1 pers. pl. pres. act. indic.

καὶ γὰρ οἱ ὄντες ἐν τῷ σκήνει **στενάζομεν** βαρούμενοι (2 Cor. 5:4)

for, indeed, **we who are** in this tent **groan**, being burdened

e. 2 pers. pl. perf. act. indic.

αὐτὸς γὰρ ὁ πατὴρ φιλεῖ ὑμᾶς, ὅτι ὑμεῖς ἐμὲ **πεφιλήκατε** (John 16:27)

for the father himself loves you, because **you have loved** me

f. 3 pers. pl. plupf. act. indic.

οἱ δὲ **διάκονοι ᾔδεισαν** οἱ ἠντληκότες τὸ ὕδωρ (John 2:9)

but **the servants** who had drawn the water **knew**

2. The interrogative indicative states a question.

   a. With or without an interrogative adverb or pronoun

     (1) 1 pers. sing. impf. indic.

ἐγὼ τίς **ἤμην** δυνατὸς κωλῦσαι τὸν θεόν; (Acts 11:17)

I was who (or who **was** I) [to be] able to hinder God?

     (2) 2 pers. sing. perf. act. indic.

πεντήκοντα ἔτη οὔπω ἔχεις, καὶ Ἀβραὰμ **ἑώρακας;** (John 8:57)

you are not yet fifty years [old], and **have you seen** Abraham?

     (3) 3 pers. sing. pres. act. indic.

τίς γάρ σε **διακρίνει;** τί δὲ ἔχεις ὃ οὐκ ἔλαβες; (1 Cor. 4:7)

for **who makes** you **different?** and what do you have that you did not receive?

     (4) 1 pers. pl. fut. act. indic.

τί οὖν **ἐροῦμεν;** ὁ νόμος ἁμαρτία; (Rom. 7:7)

what, then, **shall we say?** [ἐστιν, is] the law sin?

     (5) 3 pers. pl. aor. act. indic.

τίνες εἰσίν καὶ **πόθεν ἦλθον;** (Rev. 7:13)

who are they, and **from where did they come?**

   b. With οὐ, οὐκ, or οὐχί, expecting an affirmative answer

     (1) 2 pers. sing. pres. act. indic.

οὐ πιστεύεις ὅτι ἐγὼ ἐν τῷ πατρὶ καὶ ὁ πατὴρ ἐν ἐμοί ἐστι(ν); (John 14:10)

do you not believe that I [εἰμι, am] in the father and the father is in me? [Yes]

     (2) 3 pers. sing. impf. act. indic.

οὐχὶ ταῦτα **ἔδει** παθεῖν τὸν Χριστόν . . . ; (Luke 24:26)

was it not necessary for Christ to suffer these things . . . ? [Yes]

    (3) 3 pers. sing. perf. pass. indic.

        οὐ γέγραπται ὅτι ὁ οἶκός μου οἶκος προσευχῆς κληθήσεται...;
        (Mark 11:17)

        is it not written, "my house shall be called a house of prayer?"
        [Yes]

    (4) 2 pers. pl. aor. act. indic.

        οὐκ ἀνέγνωτε τὸ ῥηθὲν ὑμῖν ὑπὸ τοῦ θεοῦ . . . ; (Matt. 22:31)

        did you not read what was spoken to you by God . . .? [Yes]

    (5) 2 pers. pl. plupf. act. indic.

        οὐκ ᾔδειτε ὅτι ἐν τοῖς τοῦ πατρός μου δεῖ εἶναί με (Luke 2:49)

        did you not know that I must be about the [affairs] of my father?
        [Yes]

    (6) 3 pers. pl. fut. act. indic.

        οὐκ ἐροῦσιν ὅτι μαίνεσθε; (1 Cor. 14:23)

        will they not say that you are mad? [Yes]

  c. With μή, expecting a negative answer

    (1) 1 pers. sing. pres. act. indic.

        μὴ κατὰ ἄνθρωπον ταῦτα λαλῶ; (1 Cor. 9:8)

        do I speak these things according to man? [No]

    (2) 3 pers. sing. fut. act. indic.

        μὴ ἐρεῖ τὸ πλάσμα τῷ πλάσαντι, τί με ἐποίησας οὕτως;
        (Rom. 9:20)

        will the thing formed say to the one who formed [it], why did you
        make me so? [No]

    (3) 3 pers. sing. aor. act. indic.

        μή τις ἐκ τῶν ἀρχόντων ἐπίστευσεν εἰς αὐτόν . . . ; (John 7:48)

        has anyone of the rulers **believed** in him . . .? [No]

    (4) 2 pers. pl. perf. pass. indic.

        μὴ καὶ ὑμεῖς πεπλάνησθε; (John 7:47)

        have you also **been deceived**? [No]

3. Conditional statements in the indicative are found with the particle εἰ.

  a. First class conditional or simple condition. The meaning of "since" for εἰ
      must be obtained from other information in the context, not from εἰ.
      The truth of either condition or conclusion is not implied in this
      construction. This condition is found about 300 times in the NT.

    (1) 1 pers. sing. aor. act. indic.

        εἰ κακῶς ἐλάλησα, μαρτύρησον περὶ τοῦ κακοῦ (John 18:23)

        if I spoke wrongly, testify concerning the wrong

    (2) 1 pers. sing. impf. mid./pass. dep. indic.

        εἰ καὶ μετεμελόμην . . . νῦν χαίρω (2 Cor. 7:8-9)

        even if I was sorry . . . I now rejoice

(3) 3 pers. sing. perf. act. indic.

κύριε, εἰ κεκοίμηται σωθήσεται (John 11:12)

Lord, **if he sleeps** he will get well

(4) 2 pers. pl. pres. act. indic.

ἀφίετε εἴ τι ἔχετε κατά τινος (Mark 11:25)

forgive **if you have** anything against someone

(5) 2 pers. pl. fut. act. indic.

ἀλλ᾽ εἰ ἀγαθοποιοῦντες καὶ πάσχοντες ὑπομενεῖτε, τοῦτο χάρις παρὰ θεῷ (1 Peter 2:20*b*)

but **if you endure** while doing good and yet suffer, this [ἐστιν, is] grace with God

b. Second class conditional or contrary to fact. The statement by the speaker or writer is believed to be contrary to fact, and in the NT most often is in reality. Only a past time indicative is used in the protasis and often with ἄν in the apodosis. The apodosis makes a nonfact statement It is found about 47 times in the NT.

(1) 2 pers. sing. impf. act. indic. indicates a present-time condition

εἰ ἐκ τοῦ κόσμου ἦτε, ὁ κόσμος ἂν τὸ ἴδιον ἐφίλει (John 15:19)

if you were of the world, **the world would love** its own

(2) 3 pers. sing. aor. pass. indic. indicates a past-time condition

καλὸν ἦν αὐτῷ εἰ οὐκ ἐγεννήθη ὁ ἄνθρωπος ἐκεῖνος (Matt. 26:24)

it was good for him **if that man had not been born**

(3) 3 pers. sing. plupf. act. indic. indicates a past-time condition

εἰ ᾔδει ὁ οἰκοδεσπότης ποίᾳ φυλακῇ ὁ κλέπτης ἔρχεται, ἐγρηγόρησεν ἄν (Matt. 24:43)

if the master of the house had known in what watch the thief would come, **he would have watched**

B. Voice. The subject is related to the action of the verb in a variety of ways. The name of the quality that indicates that relationship is called "voice." The Greek language includes three voices: active, middle, and passive. All Greek verbs have voice except εἰμι with its compounds and φημι. Thus, voice is part of neither the form nor the function of these verbs.

1. Active voice. The subject is described as directly performing the action of the verb or causing the action.

a. Simple active, the subject performs the action.

(1) 1 pers. sing. perf. act. indic.

τὸν δρόμον τετέλεκα, τὴν πίστιν τετήρηκα (2 Tim. 4:7)

I have finished the course, **I have kept** the faith

(2) 2 pers. sing. aor. act. indic.

καὶ ἐτήρησάς μου τὸν λόγον (Rev. 3:8)

and **you kept** my word

(3) 3 pers. sing. plupf. act. indic.

ὁ δὲ Πέτρος εἱστήκει πρὸς τῇ θύρᾳ ἔξω (John 18:16)

but **Peter had been standing** at the door outside

(4) 1 pers. pl. impf. act. indic.

καὶ καθίσαντες ἐλαλοῦμεν ταῖς συνελθούσαις γυναιξίν
(Acts 16:13)

and after we sat down **we began speaking** to the women who had
gathered together

(5) 2 pers. pl. pres. act. indic.

τοὺς πτωχοὺς γὰρ πάντοτε ἔχετε μεθ᾽ ἑαυτῶν (John 12:8)

for **you have** the poor with you always

(6) 3 pers. pl. fut. act. indic.

καὶ οἱ δοῦλοι αὐτοῦ λατρεύσουσιν αὐτῷ (Rev. 22:3)

and his **servants shall serve** him

b. Causative active. The subject causes the action.

(1) 1 pers. sing. fut. act. indic.

καὶ ποιήσω ὑμᾶς γενέσθαι ἁλιεῖς ἀνθρώπων (Mark 1:17)[1]

and **I will cause** you to become fishers of men

(2) 3 pers. sing. pres. act. indic.

ὅτι τὸν ἥλιον αὐτοῦ ἀνατέλλει ἐπὶ πονηροὺς καὶ ἀγαθούς
(Matt. 5:45)

for **he causes** his sun **to shine** upon the evil and the good

(3) 3 pers. sing. impf. act. indic.

ἐγὼ ἐφύτευσα, Ἀπολλῶς ἐπότισεν, ἀλλὰ ὁ θεὸς ηὔξανεν
(1 Cor. 3:6)[2]

I planted, Apollos watered, but **God caused the increase**

(4) 3 pers. pl. impf. act. indic.

καὶ ἐποίουν χαρὰν μεγάλην πᾶσιν τοῖς ἀδελφοῖς (Acts 15:3)

and **they caused** great joy among all the brothers

c. Stative active. This is a function primarily of the present tense, but it
is often found in the other tenses as well. Certain verbs have a stative
sense: e.g., ἀσθενέω, γέμω, γίνομαι, διψάω, εἰρηεύω, ἔχω, ζάω,
ἰσχύω, κάμνω, μεθύω, μένω, πεινάω, πλουτίζω (1 Cor. 1:5), πτωχεύω,
σιγάω, σιωπάω, ὑγιαίνω, ὑστερέω, χωρέω.

---

[1] Mark 1:17 text is from GNT, NA, TR & MT: WH has ἁλεεῖς.

[2] 1 Cor. 3:6 text is from GNT & NA: WH, TR & MT have Ἀπολλώς; TR & MT have ἀλλ᾽.

(1) 1 pers. sing. plupf. act. indic.

κἀγὼ οὐκ ᾔδειν αὐτόν, ἀλλ᾽ ἵνα φανερωθῇ τῇ Ἰσραήλ
(John 1:31)

and I did not know him, except that he should be made manifest
to Israel

(2) 2 pers. sing. fut. act. indic.

τήν τε γὰρ ἐπιθυμίαν οὐκ ᾔδειν εἰ μὴ ὁ νόμος ἔλεγεν, **οὐκ
ἐπιθυμήσεις** (Rom. 7:7)

for I had not known lustful craving except the law said,
"you shall not covet"

(3) 3 pers. sing. pres. act. indic.

ἡ δικαιοσύνη αὐτοῦ μένει εἰς τὸν αἰῶνα (2 Cor. 9:9)

his righteousness remains forever

(4) 1 pers. pl. perf. act. indic.

οἴδαμεν γὰρ τὸν εἰπόντα, ἐμοὶ ἐκδίκησις, ἐγὼ ἀνταποδώσω
(Heb. 10:30)

for **we know** him who said, "vengeance [ἐστιν, is] mine, I will
repay"

(5) 2 pers. pl. aor. act. indic.

ποσάκις ἠθέλησα ἐπισυνάξαι τὰ τέκνα σου . . . καὶ **οὐκ
ἠθελήσατε** (Luke 13:34)

how often I wanted to gather your children . . . and
you would not

(6) 3 pers. pl. impf. act. indic.

πολλοὺς γὰρ ἐθεράπευσεν, ὥστε ἐπιπίπτειν αὐτῷ ἵνα
αὐτοῦ ἅψωνται ὅσοι εἶχον μάστιγας (Mark 3:10)

for he healed many, so that they approached him in order that
they might touch him **as many as had** illness

2. The middle voice, except for deponents, describes the subject as
participating in the results of the action in some way.

a. Deponent verbs have middle (mid./pass. in the present, imperfect and
perfect tenses) forms, but active meanings. The large majority of middle
verbs are deponent, e.g., ἀποκρίνομαι, ἀσπάζομαι, γίνομαι, δέχομαι,
δύναμαι, ἔρχομαι (and compound verbs), κάθημαι, πορεύομαι (and
compounds), προσεύχομαι, φοβέομαι.

(1) 1 pers. sing. aor. mid. dep. indic.

ἐγενόμην ἐν πνεύματι ἐν τῇ κυριακῇ ἡμέρᾳ (Rev. 1:10)

I was in the Spirit on the Lord's day

(2) 2 pers. sing. pres. mid./pass. dep. indic.

κύριε, ἐὰν θέλῃς **δύνασαί** με καθαρίσαι (Matt. 8:2)

Lord, if you will, **you are able** to cleanse me

(3) 3 pers. sing. perf. mid./pass. dep. indic.

καὶ πληροφορηθεὶς ὅτι ὃ **ἐπήγγελται**, δυνατός ἐστιν καὶ ποιῆσαι (Rom. 4:21)

and being fully assured that what **he had promised** he is able also to perform

(4) 2 pers. pl. fut. mid. dep. indic.

καθήσεσθε καὶ ὑμεῖς ἐπὶ δώδεκα θρόνους (Matt. 19:28)[3]

you yourselves also shall sit on twelve thrones

(5) 3 pers. pl. impf. mid./pass. dep. indic.

οἱ μὲν οὖν **ἐπορεύοντο** χαίροντες ἀπὸ προσώπου τοῦ συνεδρίου (Acts 5:41)

and they therefore **went on their way** rejoicing from the presence of the sanhedrin

(6) 3 pers. pl. fut. mid. dep. indic.

καὶ **ὄψονται** τὸ πρόσωπον αὐτοῦ (Rev. 22:4)

and **they shall see** his face

b. Middle with active sense, but not truly a deponent verb

(1) 1 pers. sing. pres. mid./pass. indic.

ταύτην τὴν παραγγελίαν **παρατίθεμαί** σοι, τέκνον Τιμόθεε (1 Tim. 1:18)

I entrust this charge to you son Timothy

(2) 3 pers. sing. fut. mid. indic.

καὶ πᾶσα γλῶσσα **ἐξομολογήσεται** τῷ θεῷ (Rom. 14:11)

and every tongue **shall confess** to God

(3) 3 pers. sing. plupf. mid. indic.

ἀπολελύσθαι ἐδύνατο ὁ ἄνθρωπος οὗτος εἰ μὴ **ἐπεκέκλητο** Καίσαρα (Acts 26:32)

this man could have been set free except **he had appealed to** Caesar

(4) 1 pers. pl. aor. mid. indic.

ἀπειπάμεθα τὰ κρυπτὰ τῆς αἰσχύνης (2 Cor. 4:2)

we renounced the hidden things of shame

(5) 3 pers. pl. impf. mid. indic.

διεκρίνοντο πρὸς αὐτὸν οἱ ἐκ περιτομῆς (Acts 11:2)

those [ὄντες, who were] of the circumcision **contended** with him

---

[3] Matt. 19:28 text is from GNT, NA & WH; TR & MT have **καθίσεσθε**.

c. Reflexive middle. The subject of the verb acts upon itself with a reflexive force.

    (1) 3 pers. sing. fut. mid. indic.

    ὁ νικῶν οὕτως **περιβαλεῖται** ἐν ἱματίοις λευκοῖς (Rev. 3:5)[4]

    the one who overcomes **shall** thus **clothe himself** in white garments

    (2) 2 pers. pl. pres. mid. indic.

    πλανᾶσθε μὴ εἰδότες τὰς γραφὰς μηδὲ τὴν δύναμιν τοῦ θεοῦ (Matt. 22:29)

    you deceive yourselves because you do not know the Scriptures nor the power of God

    (3) 2 pers. pl. aor. mid. indic.

    ὅσοι γὰρ εἰς Χριστὸν ἐβαπτίσθητε, Χριστὸν **ἐνεδύσασθε** (Gal. 3:27)

    for as many of you as were baptized into Christ, **you clothed yourselves** [with] Christ

d. Middle with a different meaning than the active: e.g., ἅπτω, to kindle; ἅπτομαι, to touch; ἄρχω, to rule; ἄρχομαι, to begin

    (1) 3 pers. sing. aor. mid. indic.

    καὶ πάλιν **ἤρξατο** διδάσκειν παρὰ τὴν θάλασσαν (Mark 4:1)

    and again **he began** to teach by the sea

    (2) 3 pers. sing. pres. mid./pass. indic.

    καὶ ὁ πονηρὸς οὐχ **ἅπτεται** αὐτοῦ (1 John 5:18)

    and **the wicked one does not touch** him

    (3) 3 pers. pl. fut. mid. indic.

    τότε **ἄρξονται** λέγειν τοῖς ὄρεσιν (Luke 23:30)

    then **they will begin** to say to the mountains

e. Middle intensive, with emphasis on the subject

    (1) 1 pers. sing. pres. mid./pass. indic.

    ἐγὼ δὲ μάρτυρα τὸν θεὸν **ἐπικαλοῦμαι** ἐπὶ τὴν ἐμὴν ψυχήν (2 Cor. 1:23)

    but **I myself call on** God as witness upon my soul

    (2) 3 pers. sing. aor. mid. indic.

    καθὼς **ἐξελέξατο** ἡμᾶς ἐν αὐτῷ πρὸ καταβολῆς κόσμου (Eph. 1:4)

    even as **he himself chose** us in him before the foundation of the world

---

[4] Rev. 3:5 text is from GNT, NA & WH: TR & MT have οὗτος for οὕτως.

f. Reciprocal middle, only in the plural
   (1) 3 pers. pl. plupf. mid. indic.
   ἤδη γὰρ **συνετέθειντο** οἱ Ἰουδαῖοι, ἵνα ἐάν τις αὐτὸν
   ὁμολογήσῃ Χριστόν, ἀποσυνάγωγος γένηται (John 9:22)
   for already **the Jews had agreed among themselves** that if anyone
   confessed him as Christ, he should be put out of the synagogue
   (2) 3 pers. pl. pres. mid./pass. indic.
   καὶ σταυροῦσιν αὐτὸν καὶ **διαμερίζονται** τὰ ἱμάτια αὐτοῦ
   (Mark 15:24)[5]
   and they crucified him and **divided** his garments **among themselves**

3. The passive voice describes the subject as receiving the action of the verb.
   Because the passive and middle voices have the same forms in the present,
   imperfect, and perfect tenses, it is sometimes difficult to distinguish them.
   Context and the specific meaning of the verb are the determining criteria.
   a. Theological passive is used to avoid naming God directly as the agent
      or God is implied as the agent.
      (1) 1 pers. sing. perf. pass. indic.
      οὐχ ὅτι ἤδη ἔλαβον, ἢ ἤδη **τετελείωμαι** (Phil. 3:12)
      not that I already received, or already **have been perfected [by God]**
      (2) 3 pers. sing. fut. pass. indic.
      αἰτεῖτε καὶ **δοθήσεται** ὑμῖν (Matt. 7:7)
      ask and **it shall be given** to you [by God]
      (3) 1 pers. pl. pres. pass. indic.
      αὐτοὶ γὰρ οἴδατε ὅτι εἰς τοῦτο **κείμεθα** (1 Thess. 3:3)
      for you yourselves know that **we are appointed [by God]** for this
      purpose
      (4) 2 pers. pl. aor. pass. indic.
      εἰ οὖν **συνηγέρθητε** τῷ Χριστῷ, τὰ ἄνω ζητεῖτε (Col. 3:1)
      if then **you were raised together** with Christ, seek the things above
      (5) 3 pers. pl. impf. pass. indic.
      μᾶλλον δὲ **προσετίθεντο** πιστεύοντες τῷ κυρίῳ (Acts 5:14)
      but rather **believers were being added** to the Lord
   b. Passive with agent indicated by a preposition
      (1) 3 pers. sing. pres. pass. indic.
      ἁγιάζεται γὰρ διὰ λόγου θεοῦ καὶ ἐντεύξεως (1 Tim. 4:5)
      for **it is sanctified by the word of God** and **prayer**

---

[5] Mark 15:24 text is from GNT, NA & WH: TR has σταυρώσαντες αὐτὸν διεμέριζον; MT has σταυρώσαντες αὐτὸν διαμερίζονται.

(2) 1 pers. sing. perf. pass. indic.

οὐδὲν γὰρ ἐμαυτῷ σύνοιδα, ἀλλ᾽ οὐκ ἐν τούτῳ δεδικαίωμαι
(1 Cor. 4:4)

for I am conscious of nothing against myself; but **I am not justified by this**

(3) 1 pers. pl. fut. pass. indic.

κατηλλαγέντες **σωθησόμεθα** ἐν τῇ ζωῇ αὐτοῦ (Rom. 5:10)

having been reconciled, **we shall be saved by his life**

(4) 2 pers. pl. aor. pass. indic.

καὶ μὴ λυπεῖτε τὸ πνεῦμα τὸ ἅγιον τοῦ θεοῦ, ἐν ᾧ
ἐσφραγίσθητε εἰς ἡμέραν ἀπολυτρώσεως (Eph. 4:30)

and do not grieve the Holy Spirit of God **by whom you were sealed** unto the day of redemption

(5) 3 pers. pl. impf. pass. indic.

καὶ **ἐσκανδαλίζοντο** ἐν αὐτῷ (Mark 6:3)

and **they were offended by him**

c. The agent of the passive is sometimes indicated by the dative case

(1) 3 pers. sing. perf. pass. indic.

ἡ γὰρ ὕπανδρος γυνὴ τῷ ζῶντι ἀνδρὶ **δέδεται νόμῳ**
(Rom. 7:2)

for the married woman **is bound by law** to the living husband

(2) 3 pers. sing. impf. pass. indic.

ὁ δὲ ἑκατοντάρχης τῷ κυβερνήτῃ καὶ τῷ ναυκλήρῳ μᾶλλον
ἐπείθετο ἢ τοῖς ὑπὸ Παύλου (Acts 27:11)

and **the centurion was being persuaded by the steersman** and **the shipmaster** rather than by the things spoken by Paul

3) 2 pers. pl. aor. pass. indic.

ἐν ᾧ καὶ πιστεύσαντες ἐσφραγίσθητε τῷ πνεύματι . . .
τῷ ἁγίῳ (Eph. 1:13)

having believed in him **you** also **were sealed by the Holy Spirit**

(4) 3 pers. pl. pres. pass. indic.

ὅσοι γὰρ πνεύματι θεοῦ **ἄγονται**, οὗτοι υἱοὶ θεοῦ εἰσιν
(Rom. 8:14)[6]

for as many as **are led by the Spirit** of God, these are the sons of God

---

[6] Rom. 8:14 text is from GNT & NA: WH has εἰσίν; TR & MT have εἰσιν υἱοὶ θεοῦ.

d. The agent of the passive may be unexpressed, unspecified, insignificant, or defined from the context.

   (1) 1 pers. sing. pres. pass. indic.

περὶ ἐλπίδος καὶ ἀναστάσεως νεκρῶν ἐγὼ **κρίνομαι** (Acts 23:6)

I am being judged concerning the hope and resurrection of the dead

   (2) 3 pers. sing. plupf. pass. indic.

τεθεμελίωτο γὰρ ἐπὶ τὴν πέτραν (Matt. 7:25)

for **it had been founded** upon the rock

   (3) 3 pers. sing. impf. pass. indic.

ὁ μὲν οὖν Πέτρος **ἐτηρεῖτο** ἐν τῇ φυλακῇ (Acts 12:5)

Peter then **was being kept** in the prison

   (4) 3 pers. sing. perf. pass. indic.

κύριε, ὁ παῖς μου **βέβληται** ἐν τῇ οἰκίᾳ παραλυτικός (Matt. 8:6)

Lord, **my servant lies** in the house a paralytic

   (5) 3 pers. pl. aor. pass. indic.

ὅτι τὰ δικαιώματά σου **ἐφανερώθησαν** (Rev. 15:4)

for your **righteous deeds were made known**

e. Deponent passive, only in future and aorist tenses

   (1) 1 pers. sing. aor. pass. dep. indic.

ἀδελφοί, **οὐκ ἠδυνήθην** λαλῆσαι ὑμῖν ὡς πνευματικοῖς (1 Cor. 3:1)

brothers, **I was unable** to speak to you as to spiritual ones

   (2) 3 pers. sing. fut. pass. dep. indic.

ὤμοσεν κύριος καὶ **οὐ μεταμεληθήσεται** (Heb. 7:21)

the Lord swore and **will not repent**

4. Voiceless verb, εἰμι, equative copula, **I am**

a. The first person singular of all tenses has only two possible subjects, explicit ἐγώ or the implicit pronoun. This principle is true of all verbs as well as εἰμι.

   (1) Explicit ἐγώ

     (a) Pres. indic.

ἐγώ εἰμι ὁ πρῶτος καὶ ὁ ἔσχατος (Rev. 1:17)

I am the first and the last

     (b) Impf. indic.

ἐγὼ ἤμην ἐν πόλει Ἰόππῃ προσευχόμενος (Acts 11:5)

I was in the city of Joppa praying

     (c) Fut. indic.

ἐγὼ ἔσομαι αὐτῷ εἰς πατέρα (Heb. 1:5)

I shall be a father to him

(2) Implicit pronoun
   (a) Pres. indic.
     οὐκ **εἰμί** ἱκανὸς λῦσαι τὸν ἱμάντα τῶν ὑποδημάτων
     αὐτοῦ (Luke 3:16)
     I am not worthy to untie the thong of his sandals
   (b) Impf. indic.
     καὶ χαίρω δι᾽ ὑμᾶς, ἵνα πιστεύσητε, ὅτι οὐκ **ἤμην** ἐκεῖ
     (John 11:15)
     and I rejoice on your account, that you may believe, because
     I was not there
   (c) Fut. indic.
     ὅτι ἵλεως **ἔσομαι** ταῖς ἀδικίαις αὐτῶν (Heb. 8:12)
     because **I will be** merciful to their unrighteousnesses
 b. The second person singular of all tenses has only two possible subjects,
   explicit σύ or the implicit pronoun.
  (1) Explicit σύ
   (a) Pres. indic.
     υἱός μου **εἶ** σύ, ἐγὼ σήμερον γεγέννηκά σε (Heb. 5:5)
     you are my son, today I have begotten you
   (b) Impf. indic.
     καὶ σὺ **ἦσθα** μετὰ Ἰησοῦ τοῦ Γαλιλαίου (Matt. 26:69)
     and **you were** with Jesus the Galilean
  (2) Implicit pronoun
   (a) Pres. indic.
     οἶδά σου τὰ ἔργα, ὅτι οὔτε ψυχρὸς **εἶ** οὔτε
     ζεστός (Rev. 3:15)
     I know your works, that **you are** neither cold nor hot
   (b) Impf. indic.
     ὅτε **ἦς** νεώτερος, ἐζώννυες σεαυτόν (John 21:18)
     when **you were** young you dressed yourself
   (c) Fut. indic.
     ἵνα εὖ σοι γένηται καὶ **ἔσῃ** μακροχρόνιος ἐπὶ τῆς
     γῆς (Eph. 6:3)
     that it may be well with you, and **you shall have** long life on the
     earth

c. The first person plural of all tenses has only two possible subjects, explicit ἡμεῖς or the implicit pronoun.
  (1) Explicit ἡμεῖς
    (a) Pres. indic.
       καὶ **ἡμεῖς** ὁμοιοπαθεῖς **ἐσμεν** ὑμῖν ἄνθρωποι
       (Acts 14:15)
       we also **are** men of like feelings with you
    (b) Impf. indic.
       ἦμεν γάρ ποτε καὶ **ἡμεῖς** ἀνόητοι (Titus 3:3)
       for **we** also **ourselves were** once without intelligence
  (2) Implicit pronoun
    (a) Pres. indic.
       οὐκ **ἐσμὲν** παιδίσκης τέκνα ἀλλὰ τῆς ἐλευθέρας
       (Gal. 4:31)
       we are not children of the slave girl but of the free [woman]
    (b) Impf. indic.
       ἦμεν δὲ ἐν ταύτῃ τῇ πόλει διατρίβοντες ἡμέρας
       τινάς (Acts 16:12)
       but **we were** staying in this city some days
    (c) Fut. indic.
       ἀλλὰ καὶ τῆς ἀναστάσεως **ἐσόμεθα** (Rom. 6:5)
       but **we shall be** also [τῷ ὁμοιώματι, in the likeness] of his resurrection
d. The second person plural of all tenses has only two possible subjects, explicit ὑμεῖς or the implicit pronoun.
  (1) Explicit ὑμεῖς
    (a) Pres. indic.
       ὑμεῖς καθαροί **ἐστε** διὰ τὸν λόγον ὃν λελάληκα ὑμῖν
       (John 15:3)
       you are clean because of the word that I have spoken to you
    (b) Fut. indic.
       καὶ **ὑμεῖς** **ἔσεσθέ** μοι εἰς υἱοὺς καὶ θυγατέρας
       (2 Cor. 6:18)
       and **you shall be** my sons and daughters
  (2) Implicit pronoun
    (a) Pres. indic.
       εἰ ταῦτα οἴδατε, μακάριοί **ἐστε** ἐὰν ποιῆτε αὐτά
       (John 13:17)
       if you know these things, **you are** blessed if you do these things

(b) Impf. indic.

εἰ ἐκ τοῦ κόσμου ἦτε, ὁ κόσμος ἂν τὸ ἴδιον ἐφίλει
(John 15:19)

if **you were** of the world, the world would love its own

(c) Fut. indic.

καὶ ἔσεσθε μισούμενοι ὑπὸ πάντων διὰ τὸ ὄνομά μου
(Luke 21:17)

and **you shall be** hated by all because of my name

e. The third person singular and plural has the possibility of a variety of subjects: adjectives, nouns, pronouns and participles. The identification of the subject sometimes requires extra discernment in that both the subject and the predicate may be in the nominative case. The following rules will help guide in identifying the subject as opposed to the predicate nominative.

(1) A proper noun is normally the subject.

(a) 3 pers. sing. pres. indic.

Λουκᾶς ἐστιν μόνος μετ᾽ ἐμοῦ (2 Tim. 4:11)
Luke is alone with me

(b) 3 pers. sing. impf. indic.

καὶ ἦν Ἄννα προφῆτις (Luke 2:36)[7]
and **Hanna was a prophetess**

(2) When two proper names are joined by an equative verb the first is the subject and the second is a metaphor.

3 pers. sing. pres. indic.

τὸ γὰρ Ἀγὰρ Σινᾶ ὄρος ἐστιν ἐν τῇ Ἀραβίᾳ (Gal. 4:25)[8]
for **Hagar represents Mount Sinai** in Arabia

(3) When two articular substantives are joined by εἰμι, the two substantives are interchangeable, but the first one is to be considered the subject.

(a) 3 pers. sing. pres. indic.

καὶ ἡ γυνὴ ἣν εἶδες ἐστιν ἡ πόλις ἡ μεγάλη
(Rev. 17:18)

and **the woman** that you say **represents the great city**

(b) 3 pers. pl. impf. indic.

ὅτι οἱ ἔμποροί σου ἦσαν οἱ μεγιστᾶνες τῆς γῆς
(Rev. 18:23)

for **your merchants were the great ones** of the earth

---

[7] Luke 2:36 text is from GNT, NA, WH & MT: TR has Ἄννα.

[8] Gal. 4:25 text is from GNT, NA & MT: WH has Ἄγαρ; TR has Ἄγαρ.

(4) The articular substantive joined by εἰμι to an anarthrous adjective or noun is always the subject regardless of the position in the sentence.

   (a) 3 pers. sing. pres. indic.
   ῥίζα γὰρ πάντων τῶν κακῶν ἐστιν ἡ φιλαργυρία
   (1 Tim. 6:10)
   for **the love of money is a root** of all kinds of evils

   (b) 3 pers. sing. impf. indic.
   εἰ ὁ θεὸς πατὴρ ὑμῶν ἦν, ἠγαπᾶτε ἂν ἐμέ (John 8:42)
   if **God were your father**, you would have loved me

   (c) 3 pers. sing. fut. indic.
   καὶ ἔσται ὁ μισθὸς ὑμῶν πολύς (Luke 6:35)
   and **your reward shall be great**

(5) A pronoun is normally the subject.

   (a) Impf. indic.
   ἀληθῶς θεοῦ υἱὸς ἦν οὗτος (Matt. 27:54)
   truly **this man was [the] son** of God

   (b) Pres. indic.
   ἥτις ἐστὶν ἐντολὴ πρώτη ἐν ἐπαγγελίᾳ (Eph. 6:2)
   which is the first command with a promise

   (c) Fut. indic.
   καὶ αὐτοὶ λαοὶ αὐτοῦ ἔσονται (Rev. 21:3)
   and **they shall be his people**

(6) When two pronouns are joined by an equative verb, the first one is the subject.
   3 pers. sing. pres. indic.
   τί οὖν ἐστιν τὸ γεγραμμένον τοῦτο . . . ; (Luke 20:17)
   what then **is this** that has been written . . . ?

f. The predicate of εἰμι consists of substantives, adjectives, adverbs, and prepositions. This is true of all three persons and both numbers.

(1) The substantives indicate identity, real or metaphoric.

   (a) 3 pers. sing. pres. indic.
   οὗτός ἐστιν Ἰωάννης ὁ βαπτιστής (Matt. 14:2)[9]
   this one **is John** the Baptist

   (b) 3 pers. sing. impf. indic.
   ἀλλ᾽ ὅτι κλέπτης ἦν (John 12:6)
   but because **he was a thief**

---

[9] Matt. 14:2 text is from GNT, NA, TR & MT: WH has Ἰωάνης.

(c) 3 pers. sing. fut. indic.
    καὶ αὐτὸς ἔσται μοι υἱός (Rev. 21:7)
    and **he shall be my son**

(2) The adjectives indicate an attribute assigned to the subject.
  (a) 3 pers. sing. pres. indic.
    οἴδαμεν γὰρ ὅτι ὁ νόμος **πνευματικός ἐστιν** (Rom. 7:14)
    for we know that the law **is spiritual**
  (b) 3 pers. sing. impf. indic.
    ἦν γὰρ **ἐναντίος** ὁ ἄνεμος (Matt. 14:24)
    for the wind **was contrary**
  (c) 3 pers. sing. fut. indic.
    καὶ **ἔσται** ὁ μισθὸς ὑμῶν **πόλυς** (Luke 6:35)
    and your reward **shall be great**

(3) The predicate adverbs indicate location or manner.
  (a) 3 pers. sing. pres. indic.
    οὐκ ἔστιν ὧδε· ἠγέρθη γάρ (Matt. 28:6)
    he is not here; for he has risen
  (b) 3 pers. sing. impf. indic.
    καὶ **ἦν** ἡ μήτηρ τοῦ Ἰησοῦ **ἐκεῖ** (John 2:1)
    and the mother of Jesus **was there**
  (c) 3 pers. sing. fut. indic.
    οὕτως ἔσται τὸ σπέρμα σου (Rom. 4:18)
    your seed **shall be so**

(4) The predicate prepositional phrases indicate source, association,
    or a predicate accusative with εἰς.
  (a) 3 pers. sing. pres. indic.
    ἀναμιμνήσκω σε ἀναζωπυρεῖν τὸ χάρισμα τοῦ θεοῦ,
    ὅ **ἐστιν ἐν σοί** (2 Tim. 1:6)
    I remind you to rekindle the gift of God, which **is in you**
  (b) 3 pers. sing. impf. indic.
    καὶ χάρις θεοῦ **ἦν ἐπ' αὐτό** (Luke 2:40)
    and the grace of God **was upon him**
  (c) 3 pers. sing. fut. indic.
    ὧν τὸ τέλος **ἔσται κατὰ τὰ ἔργα αὐτῶν** (2 Cor. 11:15)
    whose end **shall be according to their works**
  (d) 3 pers. pl. fut. indic.
    καὶ **ἔσονται** οἱ δύο **εἰς σάρκα μίαν** (Matt. 19:5)
    and **the two shall be one flesh**

(5) The predicate genitive indicates possession.
  (a) 3 pers. sing. pres. indic.
      τῶν γὰρ τοιούτων ἐστὶν ἡ βασιλεία τοῦ θεοῦ
      (Luke 18:16)
      for the kingdom of God **belongs to such**
  (b) 3 pers. pl. impf. indic.
      καὶ οἱ ὀδόντες αὐτῶν ὡς λεόντων ἦσαν (Rev. 9:8)
      and their teeth **were** as **lion's [teeth]**
  (c) 3 pers. sing. fut. indic.
      καὶ ἡμῶν ἔσται ἡ κληρονομία (Mark 12:7)
      and the inheritance **shall be ours**
(6) The predicate dative often indicates possession as well. The
    classical distinction focuses on the genitive of possession
    emphasizing the possessor and the dative of possession
    emphasizing the object of possession.
  (a) 3 pers. sing. pres. indic.
      ἐὰν γὰρ εὐαγγελίζωμαι, οὐκ ἔστιν μοι καύχημα
      (1 Cor. 9:16)
      for if I preach the gospel, **boasting does not belong to me**
  (b) 3 pers. sing. impf. indic.
      ὅτι θυγάτηρ μονογενὴς ἦν αὐτῷ ὡς ἐτῶν δώδεκα
      (Luke 8:42)
      for **an only daughter was his**, about twelve years [old]
  (c) 3 pers. sing. fut. indic.
      ἡμεῖς ἀφήκαμεν πάντα καὶ ἠκολουθήσαμέν σοι· τί
      ἄρα ἔσται ἡμῖν; (Matt. 19:27)
      we have left everything and followed you; **what then shall
      belong to us**?
(7) The predicate may be a periphrastic participle. When an anarthrous
    participle is joined with any tense of εἰμι, a periphrastic construction
    occurs. The tense of the verb and the participle join in an emphatic
    expression.
  (a) 3 pers. sing. pres. indic., with perf. ptc., intensive perf.
      οὐδὲν γὰρ ἐστιν κεκαλυμμένον ὃ οὐκ ἀποκαλυφθήσεται
      (Matt. 10:26)
      for **nothing is concealed** that shall not be disclosed
  (b) 3 pers. sing. impf. indic., with pres. ptc., iterative imperf.
      ἦν δὲ τὰς ἡμέρας ἐν τῷ ἱερῷ διδάσκων (Luke 21:37)
      and **he was teaching** daily in the temple

(c) 3 pers. sing. fut. indic., with pres. ptc., progressive fut.

καὶ Ἰερουσαλὴμ ἔσται πατουμένη ὑπὸ ἐθνῶν
(Luke 21:24)[10]

and **Jerusalem shall be trampled on** by Gentiles

(8) The subject and the predicate may have an elliptical or implied verb.

(a) 3 pers. sing. pres. indic.

πλήρωμα οὖν νόμου ἡ ἀγάπη (Rom. 13:10)

love therefore [**ἐστιν, is**] **the fulfillment** of the law

(b) 3 pers. sing. impf. indic.

οὐ γὰρ διὰ νόμου ἡ ἐπαγγελία τῷ ᾿Αβραὰμ ἢ τῷ
σπέρματι αὐτοῦ . . . ἀλλὰ διὰ δικαιοσύνης πίστεως
(Rom. 4:13)

for the promise to Abraham or to his son [**ἦν, was**] not through
the law . . . but [**ἦν, was**] through the righteousness of faith

(c) 3 pers. sing. fut. indic.

οὐκ ἐπίστασθε τὸ τῆς αὔριον ποία ἡ ζωὴ ὑμῶν (James 4:14)

you do not know what **your life** [**ἔσται, shall be**] **tomorrow**

(9) The verb εἰμι occurs without a predicate in the sense of existence.

(a) 3 pers. sing. pres. indic.

καθὼς γέγραπται ὅτι οὐκ ἔστιν δίκαιος οὐδὲ εἷς
(Rom. 3:10)

even as it is written, "**a righteous man does not exist**, not even
one"

(b) 3 pers. sing. impf. indic.

ἅγιος ἅγιος ἅγιος κύριος ὁ θεὸς ὁ παντοκράτωρ,
ὁ ἦν καὶ ὁ ὢν καὶ ὁ ἐρχόμενος (Rev. 4:8)

holy, holy, holy, Lord God Almighty **who lived** and who is and
who is coming

(c) 3 pers. sing. fut. indic.

καὶ ὁ θάνατος οὐκ ἔσται ἔτι (Rev. 21:4)

and **death shall exist no longer**

C. Tense usually has reference to the temporal aspect of a verb: past, present, or
future. Only in the indicative mood is this time factor of any importance. The
kind of action is always predominant over the time of action.

---

[10] Luke 21:24 text is from GNT, NA, WH & MT: TR has Ἰερουσαλήμ.

1. The present tense is inclusive of linear, punctiliar and perfective action and thus some have designated it a zero tense. However, aspect or kind of action is the main emphasis. The present tense is classified according to the following categories: descriptive, aoristic, iterative, customary, gnomic, historical, futuristic, perfective, past action continuing into the present, stative, tendential, impersonal, explanatory, elliptical, and present of indirect discourse. These classifications are based on three contributing factors: the basic idea of the tense, the meaning of the verb, and the significance of the context. All three factors enter into the determination of the specific function of a given verb in speech or in writing.

   a. Descriptive or progressive present, action in progress at the present time

      (1) 1 pers. sing. pres. mid./pass. dep. indic.

      ἀλήθειαν λέγω ἐν Χριστῷ, **οὐ ψεύδομαι** (Rom. 9:1)

      I speak truth in Christ, **I am not lying**

      (2) 2 pers. sing. pres. act. indic.

      ἀξιοῦμεν δὲ παρὰ σοῦ ἀκοῦσαι ἃ **φρονεῖς** (Acts 28:22)

      but we consider [it] fitting to hear from you what **you are thinking**

      (3) 3 pers. sing. pres. pass. indic.

      εὐχαριστῶ τῷ θεῷ μου . . . ὅτι **ἡ πίστις ὑμῶν
      καταγγέλλεται** ἐν ὅλῳ τῷ κόσμῳ (Rom. 1:8)

      I thank my God . . . that **your faith is being announced** in the whole world

      (4) 1 pers. pl. pres. act. indic.

      ἀλλὰ τὴν μέλλουσαν **ἐπιζητοῦμεν** (Heb. 13:14)

      but **we are looking for** the coming [city]

      (5) 2 pers. pl. pres. act. indic.

      Ἰησοῦν **ζητεῖτε** τὸν Ναζαρηνὸν τὸν ἐσταυρωμένον· ἠγέρθη (Mark 16:6)

      you are seeking Jesus the Nazarene who was crucified: he is risen

      (6) 3 pers. pl. pres. mid./pass. dep. indic.

      ἐλπίδα ἔχων εἰς τὸν θεόν, ἣν καὶ **αὐτοὶ οὗτοι προσδέχονται** (Acts 24:15)

      having hope in God, which [hope] **they themselves** also **wait for**

   b. Aoristic present, expressing undefined action performed in the very act of speaking. Actually there are two types of this usage: action that is identical and simultaneous in time with the act of speaking, and action that is characteristic of a pronouncement, often illustrated by the verb λέγω.

(1) Identical and simultaneous action with the act of speaking
  (a) 1 pers. sing. pres. mid./pass. dep. indic.
      ἀσπάζομαι ὑμᾶς ἐγὼ Τέρτιος ὁ γράψας τὴν ἐπιστολὴν
      ἐν κυρίῳ (Rom. 16:22)
      I Tertius who wrote this epistle **greet** you in the Lord
  (b) 1 pers. pl. pres. act. indic.
      ὁρκίζομεν ὑμᾶς τὸν Ἰησοῦν ὃν ὁ Παῦλος κηρύσσει
      (Acts 19:13)[11]
      we adjure you by Jesus, whom Paul preaches
  (c) 3 pers. pl. pres. mid./pass. dep. indic.
      ἀσπάζονται ὑμᾶς αἱ ἐκκλησίαι τῆς Ἀσίας
      (1 Cor. 16:19)
      the churches of Asia **greet** you
(2) Action as a pronouncement
  (a) 1 pers. sing. pres. act. indic.
      ἀλήθειαν λέγω ἐν Χριστῷ, οὐ ψεύδομαι (Rom. 9:1)
      I speak truth in Christ, I am not lying
  (b) 3 pers. sing. pres. act. indic.
      ζῶ ἐγώ, λέγει κύριος (Rom. 14:11)
      I live, **the Lord says**
  (c) 1 pers. pl. pres. mid./pass. dep. indic.
      δεόμεθα ὑπὲρ Χριστοῦ, καταλλάγητε τῷ θεῷ
      (2 Cor. 5:20)
      we beg on behalf of Christ, be reconciled to God
c. Iterative present, repeated action intermittently
  (1) 1 pers. sing. pres. act. indic.
      ἰδοὺ ἕστηκα ἐπὶ τὴν θύραν καὶ κρούω (Rev. 3:20)
      behold I stand at the door and **repeatedly knock**
  (2) 2 pers. sing. pres. act. indic.
      οἴδαμεν ὅτι ὀρθῶς λέγεις καὶ διδάσκεις (Luke 20:21)
      we know that **you speak** and **teach** correctly
  (3) 3 pers. sing. pres. act. indic.
      ἐν ᾧ δὲ ἔρχομαι, ἐγὼ ἄλλος πρὸ ἐμοῦ καταβαίνει
      (John 5:7)
      but while I am coming **another steps down** before me

---

[11] Acts 19:13 text is from TR & MT: GNT, NA & WH have ὁρκίζω and omit ὁ.

(4) 1 pers. pl. pres. act. indic.

εὐχαριστοῦμεν τῷ θεῷ πάντοτε περὶ πάντων ὑμῶν
(1 Thess. 1:2)

we thank God always for you all

(5) 2 pers. pl. pres. act. indic.

πολλοὶ προφῆται καὶ δίκαιοι ἐπεθύμησαν ἰδεῖν ἃ **βλέπετε**
καὶ οὐκ εἶδαν, καὶ ἀκοῦσαι ἃ **ἀκούετε** καὶ οὐκ ἤκουσαν
(Matt. 13:17)

many prophets and righteous men have desired to see what **you
see** and did not see, and to hear what **you hear** and did not hear

(6) 3 pers. pl. pres. mid./pass. dep. indic.

ἴδε οὗτος βαπτίζει καὶ **πάντες ἔρχονται** πρὸς αὐτόν
(John 3:26)

behold this one baptizes and **all are coming** to him

d. Customary or habitual present, repeated activity on a regular or habitual
basis

(1) 1 pers. sing. pres. act. indic.

νηστεύω δὶς τοῦ σαββάτου (Luke 18:12)

I fast twice a week

(2) 2 pers. sing. pres. act. indic.

σὺ ὃ **σπείρεις** οὐ ζῳοποιεῖται ἐὰν μὴ ἀποθάνῃ
(1 Cor. 15:36)

what **you sow** does not come to life except it dies

(3) 3 pers. sing. pres. act. indic.

καὶ τὸ στόμα αὐτῶν **λαλεῖ** ὑπέρογκα (Jude 16)

and **their mouth habitually speaks** haughty things

(4) 1 pers. pl. pres. act. indic.

ἡμεῖς **προσκυνοῦμεν** ὃ οἴδαμεν (John 4:22)

we customarily worship what we know

(5) 2 pers. pl. pres. act. indic.

καὶ ὅταν γένηται **ποιεῖτε** αὐτὸν υἱὸν γεέννης
διπλότερον ὑμῶν (Matt. 23:15)

and when it happens **you customarily make** him a son of Gehenna
twice as much as you

(6) 3 pers. pl. pres. act. indic.

οὐδὲ γὰρ οἱ περιτεμνόμενοι αὐτοὶ νόμον **φυλάσσουσιν**
(Gal. 6:13)

for **neither those who are circumcised keep** the law

e. Gnomic present, expressing timeless, universal or proverbial statements
  (1) 2 pers. sing. pres. mid./pass. dep. indic.
      ὅτι **οὐ δύνασαι** μίαν τρίχα λευκὴν ποιῆσαι ἢ μέλαιναν
      (Matt. 5:36)[12]
      because **you are unable** to make one hair white or black
  (2) 3 pers. sing. pres. act. indic.
      ἱλαρὸν γὰρ δότην **ἀγαπᾷ ὁ θεός** (2 Cor. 9:7)
      for **God loves** a cheerful giver
  (3) 2 pers. pl. pres. mid./pass. dep. indic.
      οὐ δύνασθε θεῷ δουλεύειν καὶ μαμωνᾷ (Luke 16:13)
      you are unable to serve God and mammon
  (4) 3 pers. pl. pres. act. indic.
      οὐ χρείαν **ἔχουσιν** οἱ **ἰσχύοντες** ἰατροῦ (Mark 2:17)
      those who are well have no need of a physician
f. The historical present is restricted to the third person singular or plural verbs. It is limited to narrative literature and is preceded by a temporal statement which gives the temporal framework. There are several uses of the historical present as set forth below.
  (1) The vivid description transfers a past event into the present in Matthew, Luke, and Acts.
      (a) 3 pers. pl. pres. act. indic.
          τότε **προσέρχονται** αὐτῷ οἱ **μαθηταὶ** Ἰωάννου
          (Matt. 9:14)[13]
          then **the disciples** of John **came** to him
      (b) 3 pers. sing. pres. act. indic.
          καὶ μεθ᾽ ἡμέρας ἓξ **παραλαμβάνει ὁ Ἰησοῦς** τὸν
          Πέτρον καὶ Ἰάκωβον καὶ Ἰωάννην τὸν ἀδελφὸν αὐτοῦ, καὶ
          ἀναφέρει αὐτοὺς εἰς ὄρος ὑψηλὸν κατ᾽ ἰδίαν
          (Matt. 17:1)[14]
          and after six days **Jesus took** Peter and James and John his brother, and **led** them into a high mountain privately
  (2) With verbs of speaking it may be an idiom without any sense of vividness
      (a) 3 pers. sing. pres. act. indic.
          ὁ Παῦλος **λέγει** τῷ χιλιάρχῳ (Acts 21:37)
          Paul said to the chiliarch

---

[12] Matt. 5:36 text is from GNT, NA & WH: TR & MT have ἢ μέλαιναν ποιῆσαι.
[13] Matt. 9:14 text is from GNT, NA, TR & MT: WH has Ἰωάνου.
[14] Matt. 17:1 text is from GNT, NA, TR & MT: WH has Ἰωάνου.

(b) 3 pers. pl. pres. act. indic.

λέγουσιν αὐτῷ οἱ μαθηταὶ αὐτοῦ (Mark 14:12)

his disciples said to him

(3) In Mark, the historical present is used as a discourse function.

(a) 3 pers. sing. pres. act. indic. (to begin a paragraph)

καὶ ἀναβαίνει εἰς τὸ ὄρος (Mark 3:13)

and **he went up** into the mountain

(b) 3 pers. pl. pres. act. indic. (to begin a new event)

καὶ ἀφέντες τὸν ὄχλον παραλαμβάνουσιν αὐτὸν ὡς
ἦν ἐν τῷ πλοίῳ (Mark 4:36)

and having left the crowd **they took** him **along** since he was
in the ship

(4) Chains of historical presents are found in John
3 pers. sing. pres. act. indic. (John 2:3–10)

λέγει ἡ μήτηρ τοῦ Ἰησοῦ πρὸς αὐτόν . . . (John 2:3)

the mother of Jesus **said** to him . . .

λέγει αὐτῇ ὁ Ἰησοῦς . . . (John 2:4)

Jesus said to her . . .

λέγει ἡ μήτηρ αὐτοῦ τοῖς διακόνοις . . . (John 2:5)

his mother said to the servants . . .

λέγει αὐτοῖς ὁ Ἰησοῦς . . . (John 2:7)

Jesus said to them . . .

καὶ λέγει αὐτοῖς . . . (John 2:8)

and **he said** to them . . .

φωνεῖ τὸν νυμφίον ὁ ἀρχιτρίκλινος καὶ λέγει αὐτῷ
(John 2:9-10)

the head waiter called the bridegroom and **he said** to him

g. Futuristic present, indicating future time with a present verb.

(1) 1 pers. sing. pres. mid./pass. dep. indic.

Μακεδονίαν γὰρ διέρχομαι (1 Cor. 16:5)

for **I am going through** Macedonia

(2) 3 pers. sing. pres. act. indic.

καὶ ἰδοὺ προάγει ὑμᾶς εἰς τὴν Γαλιλαίαν (Matt. 28:7)

and behold **he is going before** you into Galilee

(3) 2 pers. sing. pres. act. indic.

νῦν ἀπολύεις τὸν δοῦλόν σου, δέσποτα (Luke 2:29)[15]

now **let** your servant **depart**, Lord

---

[15] ἀπολύεις in Luke 2:29 is called a futuristic imperative (Blass, Debrunner, Funk, *A Greek Grammar of the New Testament*, 323);
see also *Problems of NT Translation* by Goodspeed, pp. 77-79.

(4) 1 pers. pl. pres. act. indic.

οἰκοδομὴν ἐκ θεοῦ ἔχομεν, οἰκίαν ἀχειροποίητον
(2 Cor. 5:1)

we will have a building of God, a house not made with hands

(5) 2 pers. pl. pres. act. indic.

μικρὸν καὶ **οὐ θεωρεῖτέ** με (John 16:17)

a little while and **you will not see** me

(6) 3 pers. pl. pres. act. indic.

καὶ **οὐχ ἔχουσιν** ἀνάπαυσιν ἡμέρας καὶ νυκτός (Rev. 14:11)

and **they will not have** rest day and night

(7) Present tense μέλλω with the infinitive has a future sense

μέλλει γὰρ ὁ υἱὸς τοῦ ἀνθρώπου **ἔρχεσθαι** ἐν τῇ δόξῃ τοῦ
πατρὸς αὐτοῦ μετὰ τῶν ἀγγέλων αὐτοῦ (Matt. 16:27)

for the son of man **is about to come (will come)** in the glory of his
father with his angels

h. Perfective present, a present state based upon a past action, often a
citation of Scripture

(1) 1 pers. sing. pres. act. indic.

τί τοῦτο **ἀκούω** περὶ σοῦ; (Luke 16:2)

what [ἐστιν, is] this **I have heard** about you?

(2) 3 pers. sing. pres. act. indic.

λέγει γὰρ **ἡ γραφή** (1 Tim. 5:18)

for **the scripture says**

(3) 1 pers. pl. pres. act. indic.

ἀκούομεν γάρ τινας περιπατοῦντας ἐν ὑμῖν ἀτάκτως
(2 Thess. 3:11)

for **we have heard** some are walking disorderly among you

(4) 2 pers. pl. pres. indic.

τίς ἡ αἰτία δι᾽ ἣν **πάρεστε**; (Acts 10:21)

what [ἐστιν, is] the reason for which **you have come**?

(5) 3 pers. pl. pres. act. indic.

ἀμὴν λέγω ὑμῖν, **ἀπέχουσι(ν)** τὸν μισθὸν αὐτῶν (Matt. 6:2)

truly I tell you, **they have received** their reward

i. Durative present of past action continuing into the present, often with
an adverb or temporal word or phrase

(1) 1 pers. sing. pres. act. indic.

ἰδοὺ τοσαῦτα ἔτη **δουλεύω** σοι (Luke 15:29)

behold, **I have been serving** you these many years

(2) 3 pers. sing. pres. act. indic.

πάντα οὕτω(ς) **διαμένει** ἀπ᾽ ἀρχῆς κτίσεως (2 Peter 3:4)

all things thus **have continued** from the beginning of creation

(3) 2 pers. sing. pres. indic.

τέκνον, **σὺ πάντοτε** μετ᾽ ἐμοῦ **εἶ**, καὶ πάντα τὰ ἐμὰ σά
ἐστιν (Luke 15:31)

son, **you have always been** with me, and all my things are yours

(4) 2 pers. pl. pres. indic.

ἀπ᾽ ἀρχῆς μετ᾽ ἐμοῦ **ἐστε** (John 15:27)

you have been with me from the beginning

j. Tendential or conative present describes an action attempted or
intended but not performed.

(1) 1 pers. sing. pres. mid./pass. dep. indic.

θλῖψιν δὲ τῇ σαρκὶ ἕξουσιν οἱ τοιοῦτοι· ἐγὼ δὲ ὑμῶν
φείδομαι (1 Cor. 7:28)[16]

and such shall have trouble in the flesh; but **I intend to spare** you

(2) 2 pers. sing. pres. act. indic.

ἐν ὀλίγῳ με **πείθεις** Χριστιανὸν ποιῆσαι (Acts 26:28)[17]

in a little time **you are trying to persuade** to make me a Christian

(3) 3 pers. sing. pres. act. indic.

ἀγνοῶν ὅτι **τὸ χρηστὸν** τοῦ θεοῦ εἰς μετάνοιάν σε **ἄγει**
(Rom. 2:4)

not knowing that **the goodness** of God **leads** you to repentance

(4) 1 pers. pl. pres. act. indic.

περὶ καλοῦ ἔργου **οὐ λιθάζομέν** σε ἀλλὰ περὶ βλασφημίας
(John 10:33)

we are not about to stone you for a good work, but for blasphemy

(5) 2 pers. pl. pres. act. indic.

κατηργήθητε ἀπὸ Χριστοῦ, **οἵτινες** ἐν νόμῳ **δικαιοῦσθε**
(Gal. 5:4)

you have been released from Christ, **you who attempt to be
justified** by the law

(6) 3 pers. pl. pres. act. indic.

οὗτοι **ἀναγκάζουσιν** ὑμᾶς περιτέμνεσθαι (Gal. 6:12)

these attempt to force you to be circumcised

k. Impersonal verbs are found in the 3 pers. sg. only, e.g., συμφέρει, δεῖ,
ἔξεστιν, λυσιτελεῖ, πρέπει, μέλει and sometimes ἐστιν.

(1) δεῖ

δεῖ γὰρ **ταῦτα** γενέσθαι πρῶτον (Luke 21:9)

for **these things must** happen first

---

[16] 1 Cor. 7:28 text is from GNT, NA & MT: WH & TR have θλίψιν.
[17] Acts 26:28 text is from GNT, NA & WH: TR & MT have γένεσθαι for ποιῆσαι.

(2) πρέπει

ἀλλ' ὃ **πρέπει** γυναιξὶν ἐπαγγελλομέναις θεοσέβειαν
(1 Tim. 2:10)

but **what is fitting** for women professing godliness

(3) συμφέρει

συμφέρει ὑμῖν ἵνα ἐγὼ ἀπέλθω (John 16:7)

it is better for you that I go away

(4) μέλει

ὅτι αὐτῷ **μέλει** περὶ ὑμῶν (1 Peter 5:7)

for **it is a care** to him concerning you

(5) ἔξεστιν

πάντα μοι **ἔξεστιν**, ἀλλ' οὐ πάντα συμφέρει (1 Cor. 6:12)

all things are lawful for me, but not all things are beneficial

(6) ἐστιν

οὐκ **ἀρεστόν ἐστιν** ἡμᾶς καταλείψαντας τὸν λόγον τοῦ θεοῦ
διακονεῖν τραπέζαις (Acts 6:2)

for us to neglect the word of God to serve tables **is not desirable**

I. Stative present is indicated by such verbs as have a lexical meaning
indicating a state, such as εἰμι, ἔχω, μένω, γινώσκω, θέλω, ζάω, etc.

(1) 1 pers. sing. pres. act. indic.

ἐγὼ χρείαν **ἔχω** ὑπὸ σοῦ βαπτισθῆναι (Matt. 3:14)

I have need to be baptized by you

(2) 2 pers. sing. pres. indic.

ἄξιος **εἶ** λαβεῖν τὸ βιβλίον (Rev. 5:9)

you are worthy to take the book

(3) 3 pers. sing. pres. act. indic.

πῶς ἡ ἀγάπη τοῦ θεοῦ **μένει** ἐν αὐτῷ; (1 John 3:17)

how **does the love** of God **abide** in him?

(4) 1 pers. pl. pres. act. indic.

εἰ **ὑπομένομεν**, καὶ συμβασιλεύσομεν (2 Tim. 2:12)

if **we endure**, we will also reign

(5) 2 pers. pl. pres. act. indic.

μετῴκισεν αὐτὸν εἰς τὴν γῆν ταύτην εἰς ἣν ὑμεῖς νῦν
κατοικεῖτε (Acts 7:4)

he resettled him in this land in which **you** now **live**

(6) 3 pers. pl. pres. act. indic.

οἵτινες ἔξωθεν μὲν **φαίνονται** ὡραῖοι ἔσωθεν δὲ **γέμουσιν**
ὀστέων νεκρῶν (Matt. 23:27)

which outside **appear** beautiful but inside **are full** of dead men's
bones

m. Explanatory present, including interpretive, linguistic, metaphoric, and representative statements
  (1) 1 pers. sing. pres. indic. (metaphorical)
     φῶς εἰμι τοῦ κόσμου (John 9:5)
     I am the light of the world
  (2) 3 pers. sing. pres. pass. indic. (translation, linguistic)
     ἐν Ἰόππῃ δέ τις ἦν μαθήτρια ὀνόματι Ταβιθά, ἡ διερμηνευομένη **λέγεται Δορκάς** (Acts 9:36)
     and a disciple was living in Joppa whose name [ἦν, was] Tabitha, which translated **means Dorcas**
  (3) 1 pers. pl. pres. indic. (metaphorical)
     ὅτι Χριστοῦ εὐωδία ἐσμὲν τῷ θεῷ (2 Cor. 2:15)
     for **we are a sweet perfume** of Christ to God
  (4) 2 pers. pl. pres. indic. (simile)
     ὅτι ἐστὲ ὡς τὰ μνημεῖα τὰ ἄδηλα (Luke 11:44)
     for **you are like the unseen tombs**
  (5) 3 pers. pl. pres. indic. (representative)
     καὶ τὰ δέκα κέρατα ἃ εἶδες δέκα βασιλεῖς εἰσιν (Rev. 17:12)
     and **the ten horns** that you saw **represent** ten kings
n. Elliptical present—the verb is implied from the context
  (1) 1 pers. sing. pres. act. indic.
     πόσον ὀφείλεις τῷ κυρίῳ μου; ὁ δὲ εἶπεν, ἑκατὸν βάτους ἐλαίου (Luke 16:5-6)
     how much do you owe my lord? and he said, [ὀφείλω, **I owe**] a hundred baths of oil
  (2) 2 pers. sing. pres. act. indic.
     ὅτι οὐ φρονεῖς τὰ τοῦ θεοῦ ἀλλὰ τὰ τῶν ἀνθρώπων (Matt. 16:23)
     for you are not thinking the things of God, but [φρονεῖς, **you are thinking**] the things of men
  (3) 3 pers. sing. pres. act. indic.
     πρεσβύτας νηφαλίους εἶναι, σεμνούς (Titus 2:2)
     older men [δεῖ, **ought**] to be sober, worthy of respect
  (4) 1 pers. pl. pres. act. indic.
     τίνα ζητεῖτε; ... Ἰησοῦν τὸν Ναζωραῖον (John 18:4-5)
     whom are you looking for? . . . [ζητοῦμεν, **we are looking for**] Jesus the Nazarene

(5) 2 pers. pl. pres. act. indic.

ὑμεῖς ἀεὶ τῷ πνεύματι τῷ ἁγίῳ ἀντιπίπτετε ὡς οἱ
πατέρες ὑμῶν καὶ ὑμεῖς (Acts 7:51)

you always resist the Holy Spirit, as **your fathers**
[ἀντιπίπτουσιν, resisted], **you** also [ἀντιπίπτετε, resist]

(6) 3 pers. pl. pres. act. indic.

οἷς οὐκ ἐγὼ μόνος εὐχαριστῶ ἀλλὰ καὶ πᾶσαι αἱ ἐκκλησίαι
τῶν ἐθνῶν (Rom. 16:4)

to whom not only I give thanks but also all the churches of the
Gentiles [εὐχαριστοῦσιν, **give thanks**]

o. Present of indirect discourse, including mental thoughts and perception
as well as speech. The English tense translation will be determined by
the context.

(1) 1 pers. sing. pres. indic.

ὅταν ὑψώσητε τὸν υἱὸν τοῦ ἀνθρώπου, τότε γνώσεσθε ὅτι
ἐγὼ εἰμι (John 8:28)

when you lift up the son of man, then **you shall know that I am**

(2) 3 pers. sing. pres. act. indic.

εἰδὼς ὅτι ὀλίγον καιρὸν ἔχει (Rev. 12:12)

knowing that he has a little time

(3) 3 pers. sing. pres. indic.

ἔγνω οὖν ὄχλος πολὺς ἐκ τῶν Ἰουδαίων ὅτι ἐκεῖ ἐστιν
(John 12:9)

then a large crowd of Jews **knew that he was there**

(4) 3 pers. pl. pres. act. indic.

ἀλλ' ὅτε εἶδον ὅτι οὐκ ὀρθοποδοῦσιν πρὸς τὴν ἀλήθειαν
(Gal 2:14)

but when **I saw that they were not walking** according to the truth

(5) 3 pers. pl. pres. indic.

ὁ Παῦλος οὗτος πείσας μετέστησεν ἱκανὸν ὄχλον, **λέγων ὅτι**
οὐκ εἰσὶν θεοὶ οἱ διὰ χειρῶν γινόμενοι (Acts 19:26)

this Paul persuaded and turned away a great crowd, **saying, "gods**
do not exist that are made by hands"

p. Present periphrastic participle: present εἰμι and present participle; the
linear, stative, or iterative sense is highlighted. The verb can be any
person or number and the participle will always be nominative
anarthrous, but may be any gender and voice.

(1) 1 pers. sing. pres. indic. and nom. sing. masc. pres. act. ptc.

καὶ ἰδοὺ ζῶν εἰμι εἰς τοὺς αἰῶνας τῶν αἰώνων (Rev. 1:18)

and, behold, **I am alive** forevermore

(2) 3 pers. sing. pres. indic. and nom. sing. neut. pres. mid./pass. dep.ptc.

οὐδέν ἐστιν ἔξωθεν τοῦ ἀνθρώπου **εἰσπορευόμενον** εἰς αὐτὸν ὃ δύναται κοινῶσαι αὐτόν (Mark 7:15)

nothing from outside of the person **is entering** into him which is able to defile him

(3) 1 pers. pl. pres. indic. and nom. pl. masc. pres. act. ptc.

οὐ γάρ ἐσμεν ὡς οἱ πολλοὶ **καπηλεύοντες** τὸν λόγον τοῦ θεοῦ (2 Cor. 2:17)

for **we are not corrupting** the word of God as many [are]

(4) 3 pers. pl. pres. indic. and nom. pl. masc. pres. pass. ptc.

καὶ γὰρ εἴπερ **εἰσὶν λεγόμενοι** θεοί . . . (1 Cor. 8:5)

for even if **they are called** gods . . .

(5) 3 pers. pl. pres. indic. and two ptcs., nom. pl. masc. perf. act. ptc. and nom. pl. masc. pres. act. ptc.

ἰδοὺ **οἱ ἄνδρες**, οὓς ἔθεσθε ἐν τῇ φυλακῇ, **εἰσὶν** ἐν τῷ ἱερῷ **ἑστῶτες** καὶ **διδάσκοντες** τὸν λαόν (Acts 5:25)

behold **these men**, whom you put in prison, **are standing** in the temple and **teaching** the people

q. Perfect periphrastic participle, pres. εἰμι and perf. ptc., emphasizing the present result of the past completed action

(1) 1 pers. sing. pres. indic. and nom. sing. masc. perf. act. ptc.

εἶπεν δὲ ὁ Παῦλος, ἐπὶ τοῦ βήματος Καίσαρος **ἑστώς εἰμι** (Acts 25:10)

but Paul said, "**I stand** before the judgment seat of Ceasar"

(2) 3 pers. sing. pres. indic. and nom. sing. neut. perf. pass. ptc.

εἰ δὲ καὶ **ἔστιν κεκαλυμμένον** τὸ εὐαγγέλιον ἡμῶν ἐν τοῖς ἀπολλυμένοις **ἐστὶν κεκαλυμμένον** (2 Cor. 4:3)

but even if **our gospel is hidden, it is hidden** among those who are perishing

(3) 1 pers. pl. pres. indic. and nom. pl. masc. perf. pass. ptc.

καὶ γάρ **ἐσμεν εὐηγγελισμένοι** καθάπερ κἀκεῖνοι (Heb. 4:2)

for **we** also **have the gospel preached** even as they

(4) 2 pers. pl. pres. indic. and nom. pl. masc. perf. pass. ptc.

καὶ ὑμεῖς **πεφυσιωμένοι ἐστέ** (1 Cor. 5:2)

and **you yourselves are puffed up**

(5) 3 pers. pl. pres. indic. and. nom. pl. masc. perf. pass. ptc.

οἱ δὲ νῦν οὐρανοὶ καὶ ἡ γῆ τῷ αὐτῷ λόγῳ **τεθησαυρισμένοι εἰσίν** (2 Peter 3:7)

but **the** present **heavens** and **the earth are preserved** by the same word

2. **Future Tense.** Two ideas are expressed in this tense, the futuristic idea and the volitive, an expression of the will.
   a. Futuristic
      (1) Predictive future, usually aoristic or punctilliar in action
         (a) 1 pers. sing. fut. act. indic.
            εἶπεν αὐτοῖς, λύσατε τὸν ναὸν τοῦτον καὶ ἐν
            τρισὶν ἡμέραις ἐγερῶ αὐτόν (John 2:19)
            he said to them, you destroy this temple, and within three days
            I will raise it
         (b) 2 pers. sing. fut. act. indic.
            καὶ ὡσεὶ περιβόλαιον ἑλίξεις αὐτούς, ὡς ἱμάτιον
            καὶ ἀλλαγήσονται (Heb. 1:12)[18]
            and as a cloak **you shall roll** them **up**, and as a garment they
            shall be changed
         (c) 3 pers. sing. fut. act. indic.
            οὗτοι μετὰ τοῦ ἀρνίου πολεμήσουσιν, καὶ τὸ ἀρνίον
            νικήσει αὐτούς (Rev. 17:14)
            these shall make war against the lamb, and **the lamb will
            overcome** them
         (d) 1 pers. pl. fut. act. indic.
            οὐκ οἴδατε ὅτι ἀγγέλους κρινοῦμεν . . . ;
            (1 Cor. 6:3)
            do you not know that **we shall judge** angels . . . ?
         (e) 2 pers. pl. fut. act. and mid. dep. indic.
            ἐλεύσονται ἡμέραι ὅτε ἐπιθυμήσετε μίαν τῶν ἡμέρων
            τοῦ υἱοῦ τοῦ ἀνθρώπου ἰδεῖν καὶ οὐκ ὄψεσθε (Luke 17:22)
            the days will come, when **you will desire** to see one of the days
            of the son of man, and **you shall not see**
         (f) 3 pers. pl. fut. mid. dep. indic.
            ὁ οὐρανὸς καὶ ἡ γῆ παρελεύσονται (Mark 13:31)
            heaven and **earth shall pass away**
      (2) Progressive, iterative, or stative future action. The future tense is
         by nature aoristic in action, but certain contexts indicate continuous
         action.
         (a) 1 pers. sing. fut. act. indic.
            ὃ δὲ ποιῶ, καὶ ποιήσω (2 Cor. 11:12)
            and what I do **I will** also **continue doing**

---

[18] Heb. 1:12 text is from GNT, NA & WH: TR & MT omit ὡς ἱμάτιον.

(b) 2 pers. sing. fut. act. indic.

καὶ ἔσῃ τυφλὸς μὴ βλέπων τὸν ἥλιον ἄχρι καιροῦ
(Acts 13:11)

and **you shall be** blind, unable to see the sun for a time

(c) 3 pers. sing. fut. act. indic.

ἐκεῖ ἔσται ὁ κλαυθμὸς καὶ ὁ βρυγμὸς τῶν ὀδόντων
(Matt. 22:13)

weeping and **gnashing** of teeth **shall be there**

(d) 1 pers. pl. fut. act. indic.

καὶ οὕτως **πάντοτε** σὺν κυρίῳ **ἐσόμεθα** (1 Thess. 4:17)

and so **we shall always be** with the Lord

(e) 2 pers. pl. fut. act. indic.

μελλήσετε δὲ ἀκούειν πολέμους καὶ ἀκοὰς πολέμων
(Matt. 24:6)

but **you will repeatedly** hear of wars and rumors of wars

(f) 3 pers. pl. fut. act. indic.

ἀλλ᾽ **ἔσονται** ἱερεῖς τοῦ θεοῦ καὶ τοῦ Χριστοῦ
(Rev. 20:6)

but **they shall be** priests of God and of Christ

(3) Simple future, what will soon occur, likely in the immediate future.

(a) 1 pers. sing. fut. act. indic.

ἐρωτήσω ὑμᾶς **κἀγὼ** λόγον ἕνα (Matt. 21:24)

I also will ask you one thing

(b) 2 pers. sing. fut. mid. dep. indic.

παρ᾽ οὗ **δυνήσῃ** αὐτὸς ἀνακρίνας περὶ πάντων τούτων
ἐπιγνῶναι ὧν ἡμεῖς κατηγοροῦμεν αὐτοῦ (Acts 24:8)

from whom **you yourself shall be able** to know after examining
concerning all these things of which we accuse him

(c) 1 pers. pl. fut. act. indic.

καταβάτω νῦν ἀπὸ τοῦ σταυροῦ καὶ **πιστεύσομεν** ἐπ᾽
αὐτόν (Matt. 27:42)[19]

let him now come down from the cross and **we will believe** on
him

(d) 3 pers. sing. fut. act. indic.

ἀλλ᾽ **ἐρεῖ** τις, σὺ πίστιν ἔχεις, κἀγὼ ἔργα ἔχω
(James 2:18)

but **someone will say**, "you have faith and I have works"

---

[19] Matt. 27:42 text is from GNT, NA and WH: TRs and MT have ἐπ᾽ αὐτῷ: TRb has αὐτῷ.

(e) 2 pers. pl. fut. act. indic.

καὶ εἶπεν πρὸς αὐτούς, πάντως **ἐρεῖτέ** μοι τὴν
παραβολὴν ταύτην (Luke 4:23)

and he said to them, perhaps **you will tell** me this parable

(f) 3 pers. pl. fut. pass. indic.

καὶ ἐὰν ἀπολύσω αὐτοὺς νήστεις εἰς οἶκον αὐτῶν,
ἐκλυθήσονται ἐν τῇ ὁδῷ (Mark 8:3)

and if I send them home hungry, **they will become faint** along
the way

(4) Future promise or personal commitment to one or more persons.

(a) 1 pers. sing. fut. mid. dep. indic.

ὅτι ἐὰν ἔλθω εἰς τὸ πάλιν **οὐ φείσομαι** (2 Cor. 13:2)

for if I come again **I will not spare**

(b) 2 pers. sing. fut. indic.

σήμερον μετ᾽ ἐμοῦ **ἔσῃ** ἐν τῷ παραδείσῳ (Luke 23:43)

today **you will be** with me in paradise

(c) 3 pers. sing. fut. act. indic.

αὐτὸς γὰρ **σώσει** τὸν λαὸν αὐτοῦ ἀπὸ τῶν ἁμαρτιῶν
αὐτῶν (Matt. 1:21)

for **he himself shall save** his people from their sins

(d) 1 pers. pl. fut. act. indic.

καὶ ἐὰν ἀκουσθῇ τοῦτο ἐπὶ τοῦ ἡγεμόνος, ἡμεῖς
πείσομεν αὐτὸν καὶ ὑμᾶς ἀμερίμνους **ποιήσομεν**
(Matt. 28:14)

and if this should be heard by the governor, **we will persuade**
him and **we will make** you free from worry

(e) 2 pers. pl. fut. indic.

καὶ ἔσομαι ὑμῖν εἰς πατέρα, καὶ ὑμεῖς **ἔσεσθέ** μοι εἰς υἱοὺς
καὶ θυγατέρας (2 Cor. 6:18)

and I will be your father and **you shall be** my sons and daughters

(f) 3 pers. pl. fut. indic.

καὶ ἔσομαι αὐτοῖς εἰς θεόν, καὶ **αὐτοὶ ἔσονταί** μοι εἰς λαόν
(Heb. 8:10)

and I will be their God, and **they shall be** my people

(5) Future assurance or guarantee of what will be true.

(a) 1 pers. sing. fut. mid. dep. indic.

τότε δὲ **ἐπιγνώσομαι** καθὼς καὶ ἐπεγνώσθην
(1 Cor. 13:12)

but then **I shall know** even as also I have been known

(b) 2 pers. sing. fut. pass. indic.

ἐὰν ὁμολογήσῃς ἐν τῷ στόματί σου κύριον Ἰησοῦν καὶ
πιστεύσῃς ἐν τῇ καρδίᾳ σου ὅτι ὁ θεὸς αὐτὸν ἤγειρεν
ἐκ νεκρῶν, **σωθήσῃ** (Rom. 10:9)
if you confess with your mouth Jesus as Lord and shall believe
in your heart that God raised him from the dead, **you shall be
saved**

(c) 3 pers. sing. fut. indic.

καὶ **ἔσται** ὁ **μισθὸς ὑμῶν** πολύς (Luke 6:35)
and **your reward shall be** great

(d) 1 pers. pl. fut. indic.

οἴδαμεν ὅτι ἐὰν φανερωθῇ, ὅμοιοι αὐτῷ **ἐσόμεθα**
(1 John 3:2)
we know that if he appears **we shall be** like him

(e) 2 pers. pl. fut. mid. dep. indic.

οἶδα ὅτι **οὐκέτι ὄψεσθε** τὸ πρόσωπόν μου (Acts 20:25)
I know that **you will no longer see** my face

(f) 3 pers. pl. fut. mid. dep. indic.

μακάριοι οἱ καθαροὶ τῇ καρδίᾳ, ὅτι **αὐτοὶ** τὸν θεὸν
ὄψονται (Matt. 5:8)
the pure in heart [εἰσιν, are] blessed, for **they shall see** God

(6) Gnomic future refers to a general or universal, theological or
aphoristic truth, or axiom.

(a) 2 pers. sing. fut. pass. indic.

ἐκ γὰρ τῶν λόγων σου **δικαιωθήσῃ** καὶ ἐκ τῶν λόγων σου
καταδικασθήσῃ (Matt. 12:37)
for by your words **you shall be justified** and by your words
you shall be condemned

(b) 3 pers. sing. fut. indic.

ὅπου γάρ ἐστιν ὁ θησαυρὸς ὑμῶν, ἐκεῖ καὶ **ἡ καρδία
ὑμῶν ἔσται** (Luke 12:34)
for where your treasure is, **your heart will be** there also

(c) 2 pers. pl. fut. mid. dep. indic.

ἀπὸ τῶν καρπῶν αὐτῶν **ἐπιγνώσεσθε** αὐτούς (Matt. 7:16)
by their fruits **you shall know** them

(d) 3 pers. pl. fut. mid. dep. indic.

τυφλὸς δὲ τυφλὸν ἐὰν ὁδηγῇ **ἀμφότεροι** εἰς βόθυνον
πεσοῦνται (Matt. 15:14)
but if the blind leads the blind, **both will fall** into a ditch

(7) Future with οὐ μή, indicates emphatic negation. The aorist subjunctive also often functions the same way.

  (a) 1 pers. sing. fut. act. indic.

  καὶ **οὐ μὴ ἐξαλείψω** τὸ ὄνομα αὐτοῦ ἐκ τῆς βίβλου τῆς ζωῆς (Rev. 3:5)

  and **I will in no wise blot** his name out of the book of life

  (b) 3 pers. sing. fut. indic.

  κύριε, **οὐ μὴ ἔσται** σοι τοῦτο (Matt. 16:22)

  Lord, **this shall never happen** to you

(8) Future with εἰ is occasionally used to indicate strong negation. It translates oaths from the Hebrew language.

  (a) 3 pers. sing. fut. pass. indic.

  ἀμὴν λέγω ὑμῖν, **εἰ δοθήσεται** τῇ γενεᾷ ταύτῃ σημεῖον (Mark 8:12)

  truly I tell you, **a sign shall not be given** to this generation

  (b) 3 pers. pl. fut. mid. dep. indic.

  ὡς ὤμοσα ἐν τῇ ὀργῇ μου, **εἰ εἰσελεύσονται** εἰς τὴν κατάπαυσίν μου (Heb. 4:3)

  as I swore in my anger, **they shall not enter** into my rest

(9) Elliptical future verb is implied rather than explicit.

  (a) 3 pers. sing. fut. indic.

  ἔσομαι τῷ λαλοῦτι βάρβαρος, καὶ **ὁ λαλῶν** ἐν ἐμοὶ βάρβαρος (1 Cor. 14:11)

  I shall be a barbarian to the one who speaks, and **the one who speaks [ἔσται, shall be]** a barbarian to me

  (b) 1 pers. pl. fut. act. indic.

  βλέπομεν γὰρ ἄρτι δι᾽ ἐσόπτρου ἐν αἰνίγματι, τότε δὲ πρόσωπον πρὸς πρόσωπον (1 Cor. 13:12)

  for now we see through a mirror dimly, but then **[βλέψομεν, we shall see]** face to face

  (c) 3 pers. pl. fut. indic.

  πολλοὶ δὲ ἔσονται πρῶτοι ἔσχατοι καὶ **ἔσχατοι** πρῶτοι (Matt. 19:30)

  but many first shall be last, and **the last [ἔσονται, shall be]** first

(d) 2 pers. pl. fut. indic.

εἰδότες ὅτι ὡς κοινωνοί ἐστε τῶν παθημάτων, οὕτω(ς)
καὶ τῆς παρακλήσεως (2 Cor. 1:7)[20]
knowing that as you are sharers of the sufferings, so also
[**ἔσεσθε κοινωνοί, you shall be sharers**] of the encouragement

(10) Periphrastic future. The future forms of εἰμι join with an
anarthrous participle, either present or perfect, and give emphasis
to the present progressive action, or to the perfect complete action.

(a) Future with present participle

[1] 3 pers. sing. fut. indic. and nom. sing. fem. pres. pass. ptc.

καὶ Ἰερουσαλὴμ ἔσται πατουμένη ὑπὸ ἐθνῶν
(Luke 21:24)[21]
and **Jerusalem will be trampled** by Gentiles

[2] 2 pers. sing. fut. indic. and nom. sing. masc. pres. act. and
mid./pass. dep. participles

καὶ ἰδοὺ ἔσῃ σιωπῶν καὶ μὴ δυνάμενος λαλῆσαι
ἄχρι ἧς ἡμέρας γένηται ταῦτα (Luke 1:20)
and behold **you shall be silent** and **unable** to speak
until the day in which these things take place

[3] 2 pers. pl. fut. indic. and nom. pl. masc. pres. pass. ptc.

καὶ ἔσεσθε μισούμενοι ὑπὸ πάντων διὰ τὸ ὄνομα
μου (Mark 13:13)
and **you will be hated** by all because of my name

[4] 3 pers. pl. fut. indic. and nom. pl. masc. pres. act. ptc.

καὶ οἱ ἀστέρες ἔσονται ἐκ τοῦ οὐρανοῦ πίπτοντες
(Mark 13:25)[22]
and **the stars shall be falling** out of the sky

(b) Future with perfect participle

[1] 1 pers. sing. fut. indic. and nom. sing. masc. perf. act. ptc.
(perfect with present sense)

ἐγὼ ἔσομαι πεποιθὼς ἐπ᾽ αὐτῷ (Heb. 2:13)
I will trust in him

---

[20] 2 Cor. 1:7 text is from GNT, NA & WH: TR & MT have ὥσπερ for ὡς.

[21] Luke 21:24 text is from GNT, NA, WH & MT: TR has Ἰερουσαλήμ.

[22] Mark 13:25 text is from GNT, NA & WH: TR & Mt have τοῦ οὐρανοῦ ἔσονται ἐκπίπτοντες.

[2] 3 pers. sing. fut. indic. and nom. sing. neut. perf. pass. ptc.
(perfect with completed action)
καὶ ὃ ἐὰν δήσῃς ἐπὶ τῆς γῆς ἔσται δεδεμένον ἐν
τοῖς οὐρανοῖς, καὶ ὃ ἐὰν λύσῃς ἐπὶ τῆς γῆς ἔσται
λελυμένον ἐν τοῖς οὐρανοῖς (Matt. 16:19)
and whatever you bind on earth **shall have been bound** in
heaven, and whatever you release on earth **shall have been
released** in heaven

[3] 3 pers. pl. fut. indic. and nom. pl. masc. perf. pass. ptc.
(perfect with present sense)
ἔσονται γὰρ ἀπὸ τοῦ νῦν **πέντε** ἐν ἑνὶ οἴκῳ
διαμεμερισμένοι (Luke 12:52)[23]
for from now on **five will be divided** in one house

b. Volitive Future, an expression of the will.
(1) Future purpose. The first person (singular and plural), the relative
pronoun, and ἵνα, and μήποτε may express purpose or intention.
(a) 1 pers. sing. fut. mid. dep. and act. indic.
ἀναστὰς **πορεύσομαι** πρὸς τὸν πατέρα μου καὶ **ἐρῶ** αὐτῷ . . .
(Luke 15:18)
I will arise and **go** to my father, and **I will say** to him . . .
(b) 1 pers. pl. fut. act. indic.
καὶ τοῦτο **ποιήσομεν**, ἐάνπερ ἐπιτρέπῃ ὁ θεός (Heb. 6:3)
and **we will do** this if God permits
(c) 1 pers. sing. fut. pass. indic. with οὐκ expresses a negative
purpose or a refusal to do something.
πάντα μοι ἔξεστιν, ἀλλ' **οὐκ ἐγὼ ἐξουσιασθήσομαι** ὑπό
τινος (1 Cor. 6:12)
all things are lawful for me, but **I myself will not be mastered** by
anything
(d) The future may express purpose or intention when introduced by
the relative pronoun.
[1] 3 pers. sing. fut. act. indic.
πιστὸς δὲ ὁ θεός, ὃς οὐκ **ἐάσει** ὑμᾶς
πειρασθῆναι ὑπὲρ ὃ δύνασθε (1 Cor. 10:13)
but God is faithful, **who will not allow** you to be tempted
beyond what you are able

---

[23] Luke 12:52 text is from GNT, NA & WH: TR & MT have ἐν οἴκῳ ἑνί.

[2] 3 pers. pl. fut. indic.

ταῦτα παράθου πιστοῖς ἀνθρώποις, **οἵτινες ἱκανοὶ ἔσονται** καὶ ἑτέρους διδάξαι (2 Tim. 2:2)

commit these things to faithful men, **who shall be qualified** to teach others also

(e) ἵνα may introduce a purpose clause or μήποτε a negative purpose clause.

[1] 3 pers. sing. fut. indic.

ἵνα ἔσται ἡ ἐξουσία αὐτῶν ἐπὶ τὸ ξύλον τῆς ζωῆς (Rev. 22:14)

in order that their authority shall be over the tree of life

[2] 3 pers. pl. fut. act. indic.

ἵνα ἀπὸ τοῦ καρποῦ τοῦ ἀμπελῶνος **δώσουσιν** αὐτῷ (Luke 20:10)

in order that they shall give him of the fruit of the vineyard

[3] 3 pers. pl. fut. act. indic.

μήποτε καταπατήσουσιν αὐτοὺς ἐν τοῖς ποσὶν αὐτῶν (Matt. 7:6)

lest they shall trample them under their feet

(2) The future is often used in an imperatival or command sense in the second person.

(a) 2 pers. pl. fut. indic.

ἅγιοι **ἔσεσθε**, ὅτι ἐγὼ ἅγιος εἰμί (1 Peter 1:16)

you shall be holy, for I am holy

(b) 2 pers. sing. fut. act. indic.

κύριον τὸν θεόν σου **προσκυνήσεις** καὶ αὐτῷ μόνῳ **λατρεύσεις** (Matt. 4:10)

you shall worship the Lord your God, and **you shall serve** only him

(c) 2 pers. sing. fut. act. indic. with οὐ indicates prohibition.

οὐ **μοιχεύσεις**, οὐ **φονεύσεις**, οὐ **κλέψεις** (Rom. 13:9)

you shall not commit adultery, you shall not murder, you shall not steal

(3) Prescriptive future. The future third person often functions as an indirect command or prescription of what ought to be, or with οὐ, what ought not to be.

(a) 3 pers. pl. fut. indic.

καὶ **ἔσονται** οἱ δύο εἰς σάρκα (Matt. 19:5)

and **the two shall be** one flesh

(b) 3 pers. sing. fut. act. and pass. indic.

ἕνεκεν τούτου **καταλείψει ἄνθρωπος** τὸν πατέρα αὐτου
καὶ τὴν μητέρα καὶ **προσκολληθήσεται** πρὸς τὴν γυναῖκα
αὐτοῦ (Mark 10:7)[24]

because of this **a man shall leave** his father and mother and
shall be joined to his wife

(c) 3 pers. sing. fut. act. indic. with οὐ

ἁμαρτία γὰρ ὑμῶν **οὐ κυριεύσει** (Rom. 6:14)

for **sin shall not rule over** you

3. Imperfect tense expresses action going on in past time. That action may be
descriptive, iterative, customary, inceptive, potential, aoristic, stative,
tendential, with pluperfect sense, elliptical, impersonal, and periphrastic.

a. Descriptive imperfect indicates linear or progressive action that was going
on in past time.

(1) 1 pers. sing. impf. act. indic.

εἶπεν δὲ αὐτοῖς, **ἐθεώρουν** τὸν Σατανᾶν ὡς ἀστραπὴν ἐκ τοῦ
οὐρανοῦ πεσόντα (Luke 10:18)

and he said to them, "**I was observing** Satan falling from heaven as
lightning

(2) 2 pers. sing. impf. mid./pass. dep. indic.

Σαοὺλ ἀδελφέ, ὁ κύριος ἀπέσταλκέν με, Ἰησοῦς ὁ ὀφθείς σοι
ἐν τῇ ὁδῷ ᾗ **ἤρχου** (Acts 9:18)

brother Saul, the Lord has sent me, Jesus, who appeared to you on
the road which **you were traveling**

(3) 3 pers. sing. impf. act. indic.

καὶ ὁ **λόγος** τοῦ θεοῦ **ηὔξανεν** (Acts 6:7)

and **the word** of God **was increasing**

(4) 3 pers. pl. impf. act. indic.

ἤκουον δὲ αὐτοῦ ἄχρι τούτου τοῦ λόγου (Acts 22:22)

and **they were listening** to him until this word

(5) 1 pers. pl. impf. pass. indic.

συναρπασθέντος δὲ τοῦ πλοίου καὶ μὴ δυναμένου ἀντοφθαλμεῖν
τῷ ἀνέμῳ ἐπιδόντες **ἐφερόμεθα** (Acts 27:15)

now because the ship was caught and unable to face the wind we
gave up and **let ourselves be driven**

---

[24] Mark 10:7 text is from GNT, NA, TR & MT: WH omits προσκολληθήσεται πρὸς τὴν γυναῖκα αὐτοῦ.

(6) 2 pers. pl. impf. mid./pass. dep. indic.

τί ἐν τῇ ὁδῷ πρὸς ἑαυτοὺς **διελογίζεσθε**; (Mark 9:33)[25]

what **were you discussing** among yourselves along the way?

b. Stative imperfect

(1) 1 pers. sing. impf. indic.

ταῦτα δὲ ὑμῖν ἐξ ἀρχῆς οὐκ εἶπον ὅτι μεθ᾽ ὑμῶν **ἤμην** (John 16:4)

I did not tell you these things from the beginning because **I was** with you

(2) 2 pers. sing. impf. indic.

καὶ σὺ **ἦσθα** μετὰ Ἰησοῦ τοῦ Γαλιλαίου (Matt. 26:69)

you also **were** with Jesus the Galilean

(3) 3 pers. sing. impf. act. indic.

ἐπεὶ κατ᾽ οὐδενὸς **εἶχεν** μείζονος ὀμόσαι, ὤμοσεν καθ᾽ ἑαυτοῦ (Heb. 6:13)

since **he had** no one greater by whom to swear, he swore by himself

(4) 1 pers. pl. impf. act. indic.

εἶτα τοὺς μὲν τῆς σαρκὸς ἡμῶν πατέρας **εἴχομεν** παιδευτὰς καὶ ἐνετρεπόμεθα (Heb. 12:9)

furthermore **we had** fathers of our flesh as disciplinarians and we respected [αὐτούς, them]

(5) 2 pers. pl. impf. indic.

καὶ ταῦτά τινες **ἦτε** (1 Cor. 6:11)

and **some of you were** these things

(6) 3 pers. pl. impf. indic.

συνῆσαν αὐτῷ οἱ **μαθηταί** (Luke 9:18)

his disciples were with him

c. Potential imperfect with ἄν, obligation, wish

(1) 1 pers. sing. impf. indic.

εἰ γὰρ ἔτι ἀνθρώποις ἤρεσκον, Χριστοῦ δοῦλος οὐκ ἄν **ἤμην** (Gal. 1:10)[26]

for if I yet were pleasing men, **I would not be** a servant of Christ

(2) 2 pers. sing. impf. act. indic.

οὐκ **εἶχες** ἐξουσίαν κατ᾽ ἐμοῦ οὐδεμίαν εἰ μὴ ἦν δεδομένον σοι ἄνωθεν (John 19:11)[27]

you would not have power against me at all unless it had been given to you from above

---

[25] Mark 9:33 text is from TR & MT: GNT, NA & WH omit πρὸς ἑαυτούς.
[26] Gal. 1:10 text is from TR & MT: GNT, NA & WH omit γάρ.
[27] John 19:11 text is from GNT, NA & WH: TR & MT have οὐδεμίαν κατ᾽ ἐμοῦ and σοι δεδομένον.

    (3) 3 pers. sing. impf. act. indic.

εἰ γὰρ αὐτοὺς Ἰησοῦς κατέπαυσεν, **οὐκ ἂν** περί ἄλλης **ἐλάλει**
μετὰ ταῦτα ἡμέρας (Heb. 4:8)

for if Joshua had given them rest, **he would not have spoken** about
another day after these things

    (4) 1 pers. pl. impf. act. indic.

λέγετε ὅτι δοῦλοι ἀρχεῖοί ἐσμεν, ὃ **ὠφείλομεν** ποιῆσαι
πεποιήκαμεν (Luke 17:10)[28]

say that we are unprofitable servants, what **we ought** to do, we have
done

    (5) 2 pers. pl. impf. act. indic.

εἰ ὁ θεὸς πατὴρ ὑμῶν ἦν, **ἠγαπᾶτε ἂν** ἐμέ (John 8:42)

if God were your father, **you would love** me

    (6) 3 pers. pl. impf. act. indic.

τινὲς δὲ **ἤθελον** ἐξ αὐτῶν πιάσαι αὐτόν (John 7:44)

and **some** of them **wanted** to seize him

  d. Iterative imperfect, repeated action in past time

    (1) 1 pers. sing. impf. act. indic.

πολλοὶ γὰρ περιπατοῦσιν οὓς πολλάκις **ἔλεγον** ὑμῖν (Phil. 3:18)

for many walk of whom **I spoke** to you often

    (2) 3 pers. sing. impf. act. indic.

καὶ **ἐδίδασκεν** αὐτοὺς ἐν παραβολαῖς πολλά (Mark 4:2)

and **he repeatedly taught** them with many parables

    (3) 1 pers. pl. impf. act. indic.

καὶ γὰρ ὅτε πρὸς ὑμᾶς ἦμεν, **προελέγομεν** ὑμῖν ὅτι μέλλομεν
θλίβεσθαι (1 Thess. 3:4)

for also when we were with you, **we told you before**, that we are
going to suffer trials

    (4) 3 pers. pl. impf. act. indic.

καὶ **πολλοὶ** τῶν Κορινθίων ἀκούοντες **ἐπίστευον** καὶ
ἐβαπτίζοντο (Acts 18:8)

and **many** of the Corinthians hearing **believed** and **were baptized**

  e. Customary imperfect—what is usually, customarily, or habitually
performed.

    (1) 2 pers. sing. impf. act. indic.

ὅτε ἦς νεώτερος, **ἐζώννυες** σεαυτὸν καὶ **περιεπάτεις** ὅπου **ἤθελες**
(John 21:18)

when you were young **you used to clothe** yourself and **walk**
wherever **you wanted**

---

[28] Luke 17:10 text is from GNT, NA & WH: TR & MT have ὅτι before ὅ.

    (2) 1 pers. sing. impf. act. indic.

ὅτε ἤμην νήπιος, **ἐλάλουν** ὡς νήπιος, **ἐφρόνουν** ὡς νήπιος
(1 Cor. 13:11)[29]

when I was a child, **I used to speak** as a child, **I used to think** as a child

    (3) 3 pers. sing. impf. act. indic.

καὶ **πᾶς ὁ λαὸς ὤρθριζεν** πρὸς αὐτὸν ἐν τῷ ἱερῷ ἀκούειν αὐτοῦ (Luke 21:38)

and **all the people regularly got up early in the morning** to hear him in the temple

    (4) 3 pers. pl. impf. act. indic.

ὃν **ἐτίθουν** καθ᾽ ἡμέραν πρὸς τὴν θύραν τοῦ ἱεροῦ (Acts 3:2)

whom **they placed** daily at the door of the temple

f. Inceptive imperfect, indicating the beginning of an action

    (1) 3 pers. sing. impf. act. indic.

καὶ παραχρῆμα ἀνέβλεψεν, καὶ **ἠκολούθει** αὐτῷ δοξάζων τὸν θεόν (Luke 18:43)

and immediately he received sight, and **he began following** him, praising God

    (2) 1 pers. pl. impf. act. indic.

καὶ καθίσαντες **ἐλαλοῦμεν** ταῖς συνελθούσαις γυναιξίν (Acts 16:13)

and when we sat down **we began speaking** to the women who were gathered together

    (3) 3 pers. pl. impf. act. indic.

καὶ ἔκστασις ἔλαβεν ἅπαντας καὶ **ἐδόξαζον** τὸν θεόν (Luke 5:26)

and astonishment came upon all, and **they began praising** God

g. Aoristic imperfect, idiom of λέγω and other words of speaking

    (1) 1 pers. sing. impf. act. indic.

ἔλεγον εἰ βούλοιτο πορεύεσθαι εἰς Ἱεροσόλυμα (Acts 25:20)
I asked if he would be willing to go to Jerusalem

    (2) 3 pers. sing. impf. act. indic.

συνελθόντων δὲ αὐτῶν **ἔλεγεν** πρὸς αὐτούς (Acts 28:17)
and when they gathered together **he spoke** to them

    (3) 3 pers. pl. impf. act. indic.

καί τινες τῶν ἐκεῖ ἑστηκότων **ἔλεγον** αὐτοῖς (Mark 11:5)
and **some** of those standing there **spoke** to them

---

[29] 1 Cor. 13:11 text is from GNT, NA & WH: TR & MT have ὡς νήπιος ἐλάλουν, ὡς νήπιος ἐφρόνουν.

h. Tendential imperfect, an attempt or intention, but without accomplishment.
   (1) 1 pers. sing. impf. act. indic.
      καὶ κατὰ πάσας τὰς συναγωγὰς πολλάκις τιμωρῶν αὐτοὺς ἠνάγκαζον βλασφημεῖν (Acts 26:11)
      and often in all the synagogues **I attempted to force** [αὐτούς, them] to blaspheme by punishing them
   (2) 3 pers. sing. impf. act. indic.
      ὁ δὲ Ἰωάννης διεκώλυεν αὐτόν (Matt. 3:14)[30]
      and **John tried to forbid** him
   (3) 3 pers. pl. impf. act. indic.
      καὶ ἐκάλουν αὐτὸ ἐπὶ τῷ ὀνόματι τοῦ πατρὸς αὐτοῦ Ζαχαρίαν (Luke 1:59)
      and **they tried to name** him after the name of his father Zacharias
i. Elliptical imperfect, the verb is implied rather than explicit.
   (1) 1 pers. sing. impf. indic.
      ξένος ἤμην καὶ συνηγάγετέ με, γυμνός καὶ περιεβάλετέ με (Matt. 25:35-36)
      I was a stranger and you took me in, [**ἤμην, I was**] **naked** and you clothed me
   (2) 3 pers. sing. impf. indic.
      ἄνθρωποι δύο ἀνέβησαν εἰς τὸ ἱερὸν προσεύξασθαι, ὁ εἷς Φαρισαῖος καὶ ὁ ἕτερος τελώνης (Luke 18:10)
      two men went up into the temple to pray; **the one [ἦν, was]** a Pharisee and **the other [ἦν, was]** a tax collector
   (3) 3 pers. pl. impf. indic.
      καὶ ἤμεθα τέκνα φύσει ὀργῆς ὡς καὶ οἱ λοιποί (Eph. 2:3)
      and we were children of wrath by nature as also **the rest** [**ἦσαν** τέκνα φύσει ὀργῆς, **were** children of wrath by nature]
j. Imperfect with a pluperfect sense
   (1) 3 pers. sing. impf. mid./pass. dep. indic.
      δεῦτε ἴδετε τὸν τόπον ὅπου ἔκειτο (Matt. 28:6)
      come see the place where **he had been lying**
   (2) 3 pers. pl. impf. act. indic.
      ὡς δὲ πλείους ἡμέρας διέτριβον ἐκεῖ (Acts 25:14)
      and when **they had stayed** there many days

---

[30] Matt. 3:14 text is from GNT, NA, TR & MT: WH has Ἰωάνης.

k. Impersonal imperfect, only in the third person

ταῦτα δὲ ἔδει ποιῆσαι κἀκεῖνα μὴ ἀφίεναι (Matt. 23:23)

but **it was necessary** to do these things and not to leave those things

l. Periphrastic imperfect. The imperfect of εἰμί is joined with a present participle and emphasizes the progressive, iterative, or stative sense of the imperfect tense.

(1) 1 pers. sing. impf. indic. and nom. sing. masc. pres. act. ptc.

καὶ **αὐτὸς ἤμην ἐφεστὼς** καὶ **συνευδοκῶν** καὶ **φυλάσσων**
τὰ ἱμάτια τῶν ἀναιφούντων αὐτόν (Acts 22:20)

and **I myself was standing** and **approving** and **guarding** the garments of those who were killing him

(2) 3 pers. sing. impf. indic. and nom. sing. masc. pres. act. ptc.

ἐπείδη **ἐπιποθῶν ἦν** πάντας ὑμᾶς (Phil. 2:26)

since **he was longing for** you all

(3) 2 pers. pl. impf. indic. and nom. pl. masc. pres. pass. ptc.

ἦτε γὰρ ὡς πρόβατα **πλανώμενοι** (1 Peter 2:25)

for **you were being led astray** as sheep

(4) 3 pers. pl. impf. indic. and nom. pl. masc. pres. mid./pass. dep. ptc.

ἦσαν δέ τινες τῶν γραμματέων ἐκεῖ **καθήμενοι** καὶ
διαλογιζόμενοι ἐν ταῖς καρδίαις αὐτῶν (Mark 2:6)

now **some** of the scribes **were sitting** there and **reasoning** in their hearts

4. Aorist tense expresses undefined action as to its progress. It usually refers to past-time action as an event regardless of how long the event was in progress. The aorist does not describe a once for all event but an undefined event (undefined as to the progress or the completion of the action), and indicates the perspective of the author or speaker. An event that is described by Matthew in the aorist tense (4:23, ἐθεράπευσεν) is described in Luke in the imperfect tense (6:18, ἐθεραπεύοντο). The following classifications are found within the aorist tense rather than specifically expressed by the aorist tense. They are determined by the meaning of the verb and the context.

a. Historical or constative aorist is most often used in narrative and may be viewed from three aspects: instantaneous or momentary action; comprehensive or an extended act or state; and collective, pointing out a series or an aggregate of repeated acts.

(1) Momentary action, referring to a specific instance of action

(a) 2 pers. sing. aor. act. indic.

ἐλαίῳ τὴν κεφαλήν μου **οὐκ ἤλειψας** (Luke 7:46)

you did not anoint my head with oil

(b) 1 pers. sing. aor. act. indic.

ἔπειτα διὰ δεκατεσσάρων ἐτῶν πάλιν **ἀνέβην** εἰς Ἱεροσόλυμα
μετὰ Βαρναβᾶ (Gal. 2:1)[30]

then after fourteen years again **I went up** to Jerusalem with
Barnabas

(c) 3 pers. sing. aor. act. indic.

ἡ δὲ **ἤνοιξεν** τοὺς ὀφθαλμοὺς αὐτῆς, καὶ ἰδοῦσα τὸν Πέτρον
ἀνεκάθισεν (Acts 9:40)

and **she opened** her eyes; and when she saw Peter **she sat up**

(d) 1 pers. pl. aor. act. indic.

οἷς **οὐδὲ** πρὸς ὥραν **εἴξαμεν** τῇ ὑποταγῇ (Gal. 2:5)

to whom **we did not yield** even for a moment

(e) 2 pers. pl. aor. pass. indic.

ὅσοι γὰρ εἰς Χριστὸν **ἐβαπτίσθητε**, Χριστὸν ἐνεδύσασθε
(Gal. 3:27)

for **as many of you who were baptized** into Christ have put on
Christ

(f) 3 pers. pl. aor. act. indic.

καὶ αἱ ἕτοιμοι **εἰσῆλθον** μετ᾽ αὐτοῦ εἰς τοὺς γάμους
(Matt. 25:10)

and **those who were ready went in** with him to the wedding

(2) Comprehensive, expressing an extended act or state, often with
stative verbs

(a) 1 pers. sing. aor. act. indic.

ὅτι κατὰ τὴν ἀκριβεστάτην αἵρεσιν τῆς ἡμετέρας
θρησκείας **ἔζησα** Φαρισαῖος (Acts 26:5)

that according to the strictest sect of our religion **I lived** a Pharisee

(b) 2 pers. sing. aor. act. indic.

τέκνον, τί **ἐποίησας** ἡμῖν οὕτως; (Luke 2:48)

child, why **did you do** this to us?

(c) 3 pers. sing. aor. act. indic. and 1 pers. pl. aor. mid. dep. indic.

καὶ ὁ λόγος σὰρξ ἐγένετο καὶ **ἐσκήνωσεν** ἐν ἡμῖν, καὶ
ἐθεασάμεθα τὴν δόξαν αὐτοῦ (John 1:14)

and the Word became flesh and **lived** among us, and **we beheld**
his glory

(d) 2 pers. pl. aor. act. indic.

καὶ νῦν, ἀδελφοί, οἶδα ὅτι κατὰ ἄγνοιαν **ἐπράξατε** (Acts 3:17)

and now, brothers, I know that in ignorance **you acted**

---

[30] Gal. 2:1 text is from GNT, NA & WH: TR & MT have Βαρνάβα.

(e) 3 pers. pl. aor. act. indic.

οὗτοι οἱ ἔσχατοι μίαν ὥραν ἐποίησαν (Matt. 20:12)

these last men worked one hour

(3) Collective action indicating a series or an aggregate of repeated acts

(a) 1 pers. sing. aor. act. indic.

ἅπαξ ἐλιθάσθην τρὶς ἐναυάγησα (2 Cor. 11:25)

once I was stoned, three times **I was shipwrecked**

(b) 2 pers. sing. aor. act. indic.

μακαρία ἡ κοιλία ἡ βαστάσασά σε καὶ μαστοὶ οὓς ἐθήλασας
(Luke 11:27)

blessed [ἐστιν, is] the womb that carried you and the breasts
that **you did suck**

(c) 3 pers. sing. aor. mid. dep. indic.

οἷά μοι ἐγένετο ἐν Ἀντιοχείᾳ, ἐν Ἰκονίῳ, ἐν Λύστροις
(2 Tim. 3:11)

which things happened to me in Antioch, in Iconium, in Lystra

(d) 1 pers. pl. aor. act. indic.

συνεπέμψαμεν δὲ αὐτοῖς τὸν ἀδελφὸν ἡμῶν ὃν ἐδοκιμάσαμεν
ἐν πολλοῖς πολλάκις σπουδαῖον ὄντα (2 Cor. 8:22)

and we sent our brother to them, whom **we proved** often to be
diligent in many things

(e) 3 pers. pl. aor. act. indic.

οἱ γὰρ ἑπτὰ ἔσχον αὐτὴν γυναῖκα (Mark 12:23)

for **the seven had** her as wife

(f) 2 pers. pl. aor. act. indic.

ὅτι καὶ ἐν Θεσσαλονίκῃ καὶ ἅπαξ καὶ δίς εἰς τὴν
χρείαν μοι ἐπέμψατε (Phil. 4:16)

because also in Thessalonica both once and again **you sent**
to my need

b. Ingressive or inceptive aorist, placing focus on the beginning of the
action or entrance into a state or condition

(1) 1 pers. sing. aor. mid. dep. indic.

ὅ ἐστιν ἡ ἐκκλησία, ἧς ἐγενόμην ἐγὼ διάκονος (Col. 1:24-5)

which is the church, of which **I became** a servant

(2) 2 pers. sing. aor. act. indic.

ὅτι εἴληφας τὴν δύναμίν σου τὴν μεγάλην, καὶ ἐβασίλευσας
(Rev. 11:17)

because you have taken your great power and **you have begun to
reign**

(3) 3 pers. sing. aor. act. indic.

γινώσκετε γὰρ τὴν χάριν τοῦ κυρίου ἡμῶν Ἰησοῦ Χριστοῦ, ὅτι δι' ὑμᾶς **ἐπτώχευσεν** πλούσιος ὤν (2 Cor. 8:9)

for you know the grace of our Lord Jesus Christ, that though he was rich **he became poor** for you

(4) 1 pers. pl. aor. pass. indic.

μετὰ δὲ τρεῖς μῆνας **ἀνήχθημεν** ἐν πλοίῳ (Acts 28:11)

and after three months **we set sail** in a ship

(5) 2 pers. pl. aor. act. indic.

καὶ ὑμεῖς πεφυσιωμένοι ἐστέ, καὶ **οὐχὶ** μᾶλλον **ἐπενθήσατε** (1 Cor. 5:2)

and you are puffed up and **did not** rather **begin to mourn**

(6) 3 pers. pl. aor. act. indic.

καὶ θαυμάσαντες ἐπὶ τῇ ἀποκρίσει αὐτοῦ **ἐσίγησαν** (Luke 20:26)

and wondering at his answer **they became silent**

c. Effective or culminative aorist, placing some emphasis on the conclusion, end, or result of the action

(1) 1 pers. sing. aor. pass. indic.

τότε δὲ ἐπιγνώσομαι καθὼς καὶ **ἐπεγνώσθην** (1 Cor. 13:12)

but then I shall know even as also **I have been known**

(2) 2 pers. sing. aor. act. and pass. indic.

σὺ δὲ μένε ἐν οἷς **ἔμαθες** καὶ **ἐπιστώθης** (2 Tim. 3:14)

but you remain in those things that **you learned** and **have been convinced**

(3) 2 pers. pl. aor. act. indic.

ἤδη **ἐπλουτήσατε**, χωρὶς ἡμῶν ἐβασιλεύσατε (1 Cor. 4:8)

already **you have been enriched**; without us you have begun to reign

(4) 3 pers. sing. aor. act. indic.

ὅτε **ἐτέλεσεν** ὁ **Ἰησοῦς** διατάσσων τοῖς δώδεκα μαθηταῖς αὐτοῦ, μετέβη ἐκεῖθεν (Matt. 11:1)

when **Jesus finished** commanding his twelve disciples, he departed from there

(5) 3 pers. pl. aor. act. indic.

οἱ δὲ **ἀρχιερεῖς** καὶ οἱ **πρεσβύτεροι ἔπεισαν** τοὺς ὄχλους ἵνα αἰτήσωνται τὸν Βαραββᾶν, τὸν δὲ Ἰησοῦν ἀπολέσωσιν (Matt. 27:20)

but **the chief priests** and **the elders persuaded** the people that they should ask for Barabbas and should destroy Jesus

(6)	1 pers. pl. aor. pass. indic.

διὰ τοῦτο ἔχοντες τὴν διακονίαν ταύτην καθὼς **ἠλεήθημεν**
(2 Cor. 4:1)

therefore, having this ministry, even as **we received mercy**

d.	Potential aorist, something should, could, or would have been done if a certain condition had been met, often with ἄν.

(1)	1 pers. sing. 2 aor. mid. dep. indic.

εἰ μὲν ἦν ἀδίκημά τι ἢ ῥαδιούργημα πονηρόν, ὦ Ἰουδαῖοι,
κατὰ λόγον **ἂν ἀνεσχόμην** ὑμῶν (Acts 18:14)[31]

if indeed it was some crime or wicked prank, O Jews, **I would have
listened** to you according to reason

(2)	2 pers. sing. aor. act. indic.

σὺ ἂν ᾔτησας αὐτόν καὶ ἔδωκεν ἄν σοι ὕδωρ ζῶν (John 4:10)

you would have asked him, and he would have given you living water

(3)	3 pers. sing. aor. pass. indic.

καὶ εἰ μὴ ἐκολόβωσεν κύριος τὰς ἡμέρας, οὐκ **ἂν ἐσώθη πᾶσα
σάρξ** (Mark 13:20)

and unless the Lord shortened the days, **no flesh would be saved**

(4)	1 pers. pl. aor. pass. indic.

εἰ μὴ κύριος Σαβαὼθ ἐγκατέλιπεν ἡμῖν σπέρμα, ὡς Σόδομα ἂν
ἐγενήθημεν καὶ ὡς Γόμορρα **ἂν ὡμοιώθημεν** (Rom. 9:29)

unless the Lord of Sabaoth had left us a seed, **we would have been**
as Sodom and **we would have been** like Gomorrah

(5)	2 pers. pl. aor. act. indic.

εἰ ἠγαπᾶτέ με, **ἐχάρητε ἄν** (John 14:28)

if you loved me, **you would have rejoiced**

e.	Dramatic aorist indicates present action or state, often with the adverb νῦν or verbs of emotion.

(1)	1 pers. sing. aor. act. indic.

οὗτός ἐστιν ὁ υἱός μου ὁ ἀγαπητός, ἐν ᾧ **εὐδόκησα** (Matt. 17:5)

this is my beloved son in whom **I am well pleased**

(2)	3 pers. sing. aor. pass. indic.

Ἰησοῦν ζητεῖτε τὸν Ναζαρηνὸν τὸν ἐσταυρωμένον· **ἠγέρθη**,
οὐκ ἔστιν ὧδε (Mark 16:6)

you are looking for Jesus the Nazarene who was crucified; **he is risen**,
he is not here

---

[31]	Acts 18:14 text is from GNT, NA & WH: TR & MT have εἰ μὲν οὖν ἦν and ἠνεσχόμην.

(3) 1 pers. pl. aor. pass. indic.

κύριε, **ἐμνήσθημεν** ὅτι ἐκεῖνος ὁ πλάνος εἶπεν ἔτι ζῶν, μετὰ τρεῖς ἡμέρας ἐγείρομαι (Matt. 27:63)

sir, **we remember** that that deceiver said while he was yet alive, "after three days I will rise"

(4) 2 pers. pl. aor. act. indic.

ἐνέγκατε ἀπὸ τῶν ὀψαρίων ὧν **ἐπιάσατε** νῦν (John 21:10)

bring of the fish that **you** just now **caught**

(5) 3 pers. pl. aor. act. indic.

ἐπὶ τῆς Μωϋσέως καθέδρας **ἐκάθισαν** οἱ γραμματεῖς καὶ οἱ Φαρισαῖοι (Matt. 23:2)[32]

the scribes and **the Pharisees sit** on Moses' seat

f. Futuristic or proleptic aorist, a future event with the certainty of a past action.

(1) 1 pers. sing. aor. act. indic.

καθὼς ἐμὲ **ἀπέστειλας** εἰς τὸν κόσμον, **κἀγὼ ἀπέστειλα** αὐτοὺς εἰς τὸν κόσμον (John 17:18)

even as you sent me into the world, **I also will send** them into the world

(2) 2 pers. sing. aor. act. indic.

ἐάν σου ἀκούσῃ, **ἐκέρδησας** τὸν ἀδελφόν σου (Matt. 18:15)

if he hears you, **you will gain** your brother

(3) 2 pers. pl. aor. pass. and act. indic.

κατηργήθητε ἀπὸ Χριστοῦ, οἵτινες ἐν νόμῳ δικαιοῦσθε, τῆς χάριτος **ἐξεπέσατε** (Gal. 5:4)[33]

you have been released from Christ, you who are being justified by law; **you have fallen** from grace

(4) 3 pers. sing. aor. pass. indic.

ὅτι ἐν αὐταῖς **ἐτελέσθη** ὁ θυμὸς τοῦ θεοῦ (Rev. 15:1)

because **the wrath** of God **will be completed** in them

(5) 3 pers. pl. aor. act. indic.

καὶ **ἔζησαν**, καὶ **ἐβασίλευσαν** μετὰ τοῦ Χριστοῦ χίλια ἔτη (Rev. 20:4)[34]

and **they will live** and **reign** with Christ a thousand years

---

[32] Matt. 23:2 text is from GNT & NA: WH has Μωϋσέως; TR & MT have Μωσέως.

[33] Gal. 5:4 text is from GNT, NA & WH: TR & MT have τοῦ Χριστοῦ.

[34] Rev. 20:4 text is from GNT, NA, WH & MT: TR omits τοῦ before Χριστοῦ; TRs and MT have τὰ χίλια ἔτη.

g. Aorist with perfect sense in the English
   (1) 1 pers. sing. aor. pass. indic.
   εἰς ὃ **ἐτέθην ἐγὼ** κῆρυξ καὶ ἀπόστολος καὶ διδάσκαλος
   (2 Tim. 1:11)
   to which **I have been appointed** a herald and apostle and teacher
   (2) 2 pers. sing. aor. act. indic.
   καὶ εἴπατε ᾿Αρχίππῳ, βλέπε τὴν διακονίαν ἣν **παρέλαβες**
   ἐν κυρίῳ, ἵνα αὐτὴν πληροῖς (Col. 4:17)
   and tell Archippus, "take heed to the ministry that **you have received**
   in the Lord, that you fulfill it"
   (3) 1 pers. pl. aor. act. indic.
   εἴτε γὰρ **ἐξέστημεν** θεῷ· εἴτε σωφρονοῦμεν, ὑμῖν (2 Cor. 5:13)
   for whether **we are out of our minds**, [ἐστιν, it is] to God;
   whether we are of a sound mind, [ἐστιν, it is] for you
   (4) 2 pers. pl. aor. act. indic.
   παρακαλῶ δὲ ὑμᾶς, ἀδελφοί, σκοπεῖν τοὺς τὰς διχοστασίας καὶ
   τὰ σκάνδαλα παρὰ τὴν διδαχὴν ἣν ὑμεῖς **ἐμάθετε** ποιοῦντας
   (Rom. 16:17)
   but I exhort you, brothers, to consider those who cause divisions
   and offences contrary to the teaching that **you have learned**
h. Epistolary aorist—the author writes from the perspective of the reader
   (1) 1 pers. sing. aor. act. indic.
   δι᾿ ὀλίγων **ἔγραψα**, παρακαλῶν καὶ ἐπιμαρτυρῶν ταύτην εἶναι
   ἀληθῆ χάριν τοῦ θεοῦ (1 Peter 5:12)
   I wrote briefly, exhorting and testifying this to be the true grace of
   God
   (2) 3 pers. sing. aor. act. indic.
   ὅτι τὴν μὲν παράκλησιν ἐδέξατο, σπουδαιότερος δὲ ὑπάρχων
   αὐθαίρετος **ἐξῆλθεν** πρὸς ὑμᾶς (2 Cor. 8:17)
   for, indeed, he received the exhortation, but, being more eager,
   of his own accord **he went out** to you
   (3) 1 pers. pl. aor. act. indic.
   συνεπέμψαμεν δὲ αὐτοῖς τὸν ἀδελφὸν ἡμῶν (2 Cor. 8:22)
   and **we sent with** them our brother
i. Aorist for English pluperfect, an event antecedent to another event
   mentioned in a past tense
   (1) 3 pers. sing. aor. act. indic.
   ὅτε οὖν **ἔνιψεν** τοὺς πόδας αὐτῶν . . . εἶπεν αὐτοῖς (John 13:12)
   then when **he had washed** their feet . . . he said to them

(2) 3 pers. pl. aor. mid. dep. indic.

καὶ ἐπελάθοντο λαβεῖν ἄρτους, καὶ εἰ μὴ ἕνα ἄρτον οὐκ εἶχον μεθ᾽ ἑαυτῶν ἐν τῷ πλοίῳ (Mark 8:14)

and **they had forgotten** to take loaves of bread and except for one loaf they did not have [τι, any] with them in the boat

j. Gnomic aorist, a nontemporal, general, universal, proverbial, or theological truth.

(1) 3 pers. sing. aor. act. indic.

οὐδεὶς γάρ ποτε τὴν ἑαυτοῦ σάρκα ἐμίσησεν (Eph. 5:29)

for **no one** ever **hated** his own flesh

(2) 3 pers. pl. aor. act. indic.

οἱ δὲ τοῦ Χριστοῦ Ἰησοῦ τὴν σάρκα ἐσταύρωσαν σὺν τοῖς παθήμασι(ν) καὶ ταῖς ἐπιθυμίαις (Gal. 5:24)[35]

but **they who** belong to Christ Jesus **have crucified** the flesh with its passions and lusts

k. Elliptical aorist—the aorist is implied from the context.

(1) 3 pers. sing. aor. mid. dep. indic.

τὸ σάββατον διὰ τὸν ἄνθρωπον ἐγένετο καὶ οὐχ ὁ ἄνθρωπος διὰ τὸ σάββατον (Mark 2:27)

the sabbath came into existence because of man, but **man [did] not** [**ἐγένετο, come into existence**] because of the sabbath

(2) 2 pers. pl. aor. pass. dep. indic.

ὁ δὲ λέγει αὐτοῖς, διὰ τὴν ὀλιγοπιστίαν ὑμῶν (Matt. 17:20)[36]

and he said to them [**οὐκ ἠδυνήθητε** ἐκβαλεῖν αὐτό, **you were unable** to cast it out] because of your little faith

(3) 1 pers. pl. aor. act. indic.

καὶ λέγουσιν αὐτῷ, ἑπτά (Mark 8:20)

and they said to him, "[**ἤραμεν, we took up**] seven [κοφίνους, baskets]"

(4) 3 pers. pl. aor. pass. indic.

ὁ νόμος καὶ οἱ προφῆται μέχρι Ἰωάννου (Luke 16:16)

the law and the prophets [**εὐηγγελίσθησαντο, were proclaimed**] until John

5. Perfect tense is the tense of completed action focusing on the existence of the finished results. It implies a process that has reached its completion and now exists in a finished state. The following categories are determined by the meaning of the verb and the context.

---

[35] Gal. 5:24 text is from GNT, NA & WH: TR & MT omit Ἰησοῦ.
[36] Matt. 17:20 text is from GNT, NA & WH: TR & MT have ὁ δὲ Ἰησοῦς εἶπεν and διὰ τὴν ἀπιστίαν.

a. Intensive perfect, past action with emphasis placed on the results of the action.

   (1) 1 pers. sing. perf. act. indic.

      ἤδη **κέκρικα** ὡς παρὼν τὸν οὕτως τοῦτο κατεργασάμενον (1 Cor. 5:3)

      I have judged already, as being present, the one who thus has performed this deed

   (2) 2 pers. sing. perf. pass. indic.

      δέδεσαι γυναικί; μὴ ζήτει λύσιν. **λέλυσαι** ἀπὸ γυναικός; μὴ ζήτει γυναῖκα (1 Cor. 7:27)

      have you been bound to a wife? do not seek separation. **have you been set free** from a wife? do not seek a wife

   (3) 3 pers. sing. perf. act. indic.

      θύρα γάρ μοι **ἀνέῳγεν** μεγάλη καὶ ἐνεργής, καὶ ἀντικείμενοι πολλοί (1 Cor. 16:9)

      for **a** great and effective **door has been opened** to me, and those who oppose [εἰσιν, are] many

   (4) 1 pers. pl. perf. act. indic.

      δι᾽ οὗ καὶ τὴν προσαγωγὴν **ἐσχήκαμεν** τῇ πίστει εἰς τὴν χάριν ταύτην ἐν ᾗ **ἐστήκαμεν** (Rom. 5:2)

      through whom also **we have obtained** access by faith into this grace in which **we stand**

   (5) 2 pers. pl. perf. act. indic.

      αὐτὸς γὰρ ὁ πατὴρ φιλεῖ ὑμᾶς, ὅτι ὑμεῖς ἐμὲ **πεφιλήκατε** καὶ **πεπιστεύκατε** ὅτι ἐγὼ παρὰ τοῦ θεοῦ ἐξῆλθον (John 16:27)

      for the father himself loves you, for **you have loved** me and **have believed** that I came from God

   (6) 3 pers. pl. perf. act. indic.

      καὶ **αἱ βοαὶ** τῶν θερισάντων εἰς τὰ ὦτα κυρίου Σαβαὼθ **εἰσεληλύθασιν** (James 5:4)

      and **the cries** of those who have reaped **have entered** into the ears of the Lord of Sabaoth

b. Consummative perfect, action completed in the past with no specific focus on the results.

   (1) 1 pers. sing. perf. act. indic.

      τὸν δρόμον **τετέλεκα**, τὴν πίστιν τετήρηκα (2 Tim. 4:7)

      I have finished the course, I have kept the faith

(2) 2 pers. sing. perf. act. indic.

πέντε γὰρ ἄνδρας ἔσχες, καὶ νῦν ὃν ἔχεις οὐκ ἔστίν σου ἀνήρ·
τοῦτο ἀληθὲς **εἴρηκας** (John 4:18)

for you have had four husbands, and the one you now have is not
your husband; **you said** this correctly

(3) 3 pers. sing. perf. act. indic.

καὶ εἶπεν ὁ δοῦλος, κύριε, **γέγονεν** ὃ ἐπέταξας (Luke 14:22)

and the servant said, "master, what you commanded **has been done**"

(4) 1 pers. pl. perf. act. indic.

εἰ καὶ **ἐγνώκαμεν** κατὰ σάρκα Χριστόν, ἀλλὰ νῦν οὐκέτει
γινώσκομεν (2 Cor. 5:16)[37]

even if **we have known** Christ according to the flesh, yet now we no
longer know [αὐτόν, him]

(5) 2 pers. pl. perf. act. indic.

ἐγὼ ἀπέστειλα ὑμᾶς θερίζειν ὃ **οὐχ ὑμεῖς κεκοπιάκατε** (John 4:38)

I sent you to reap that on which **you have not labored**

(6) 3 pers. pl. perf. act. indic.

δοκεῖτε ὅτι οἱ Γαλιλαῖοι οὗτοι ἁμαρτωλοὶ παρὰ πάντας
Γαλιλαίους ἐγένοντο, ὅτι ταῦτα **πεπόνθασιν**; (Luke 13:2)[38]

do you think that these Galileans were sinful more than all
Galileans, because **they suffered** these things?

c. Iterative perfect, indicating repetitive but completed action.

(1) 1 pers. sing. perf. act. indic.

μή τινα ὧν **ἀπέσταλκα** πρὸς ὑμᾶς, δι᾽ αὐτοῦ ἐπλεονέκτησα ὑμᾶς;
(2 Cor. 12:17)

any of whom **I sent** to you, did I take advantage of you by him?

(2) 2 pers. sing. perf. act. indic.

ὃς ἦν μετὰ σοῦ πέραν τοῦ Ἰορδάνου, ᾧ **σὺ μεμαρτύρηκας**, ἴδε
οὗτος βαπτίζει, καὶ πάντες ἔρχονται πρὸς αὐτόν (John 3:26)

he who was with you across the Jordan, to whom **you repeatedly
bore witness**, behold, this one baptizes, and all are coming to him

(3) 3 pers. sing. perf. act. indic.

ἐν παντὶ τόπῳ **ἡ πίστις ὑμῶν** ἡ πρὸς τὸν θεὸν **ἐξελήλυθεν**
(1 Thess. 1:8)

in every place **your faith**, which [οὖσα, is] toward God, **has gone forth**

---

[37] 2 Cor. 5:16 text is from GNT, NA & WH: TR & MT have εἰ δὲ καί.
[38] Luke 13:2 text is from GNT, NA & WH: TR & MT have τοιαῦτα.

(4) 1 pers. pl. perf. act. indic.
ὃ ἦν ἀπ' ἀρχῆς, ὃ **ἀκηκόαμεν**, ὃ **ἑωράκαμεν** τοῖς ὀφθαλμοῖς
(1 John 1:1)
what was from the beginning, which **we have heard**, which **we have
seen** with our eyes

(5) 2 pers. pl. perf. act. indic.
ἀλλ' εἶπον ὑμῖν ὅτι καὶ **ἑωράκατέ** με καὶ οὐ πιστεύετε (John 6:36)
but I told you that **you** also **have seen** me and yet do not believe

(6) 3 pers. pl. perf. act. indic.
νῦν δὲ καὶ **ἑωράκασιν** καὶ μεμισήκασιν καὶ ἐμὲ καὶ τὸν
πατέρα μου (John 15:24)
but now **they have** both **seen** and hated both me and my Father

d. Perfect as present. Certain verbs lend themselves to this, e.g., οἶδα (old
2d perfect form), and ἕστηκα.

(1) 1 pers. sing. 2d perf. act. indic.
οἶδα γὰρ ᾧ πεπίστευκα (2 Tim. 1:12)
for **I know** whom I have believed

(2) 2 pers. sing. perf. act. indic.
λῦσον τὸ ὑπόδημα τῶν ποδῶν σου, ὁ γὰρ τόπος ἐφ' ᾧ **ἕστηκας** γῆ
ἁγία ἐστίν (Acts 7:33)
loose the sandal from your feet, for the place on which **you stand** is
holy ground

(3) 3 pers. sing. perf. act. indic.
ἰδού, ὁ κριτὴς πρὸ τῶν θυρῶν **ἕστηκεν** (James 5:9)
behold, **the judge is standing** before the doors

(4) 1 pers. pl. 2d perf. act. indic.
οἴδαμεν ὅτι οὐδὲν εἴδωλον ἐν κόσμῳ (1 Cor. 8:4)
we know that an idol [ἐστιν, is] nothing in the world

(5) 2 pers. pl. 2d perf. act. indic.
αὐτοὶ γὰρ ἀκριβῶς **οἴδατε** ὅτι ἡμέρα κυρίου ὡς κλέπτης ἐν
νυκτὶ οὕτως ἔρχεται (1 Thess. 5:2)[39]
for **you yourselves know** well that the day of the Lord shall so
come as a thief in the night

(6) 3 pers. pl. 2d perf. act. indic.
οὗτοι δὲ ὅσα μὲν **οὐκ οἴδασιν** βλασφημοῦσιν (Jude 10)
but these speak evil of whatever **they do not understand**

---

[39] 1 Thess. 5:2 text is from GNT, NA & WH: TR & MT have ἡ ἡμέρα.

e. Aoristic perfect, functioning as a simple aorist, often when words of speaking are used.
  (1) 1 pers. sing. perf. act. indic.
    κἀιείρηκα αὐτῷ, κύριέ μου, σὺ οἶδας (Rev. 7:14)
    and **I said** to him, "my Lord, you know"
  (2) 2 pers. sing. perf. mid. indic.
    Καίσαρα ἐπικέκλησαι, ἐπὶ Καίσαρα πορεύσῃ (Acts 25:12)
    you have appealed to Caesar, to Caesar you will go
  (3) 3 pers. sing. perf. act. indic.
    καὶ εἴληφεν ἐκ τῆς δεξιᾶς τοῦ καθημένου ἐπὶ τοῦ θρόνου
    (Rev. 5:7)
    and **he took** [it] out of the hand of the one sitting on the throne
  (4) 2 pers. pl. perf. act. indic.
    ἀποκριθεὶς δὲ ὁ Σίμων εἶπεν, δεήθητε ὑμεῖς ὑπέρ ἐμοῦ πρὸς τὸν
    κύριον, ὅπως μηδὲν ἐπέλθῃ ἐπ᾽ ἐμὲ ὧν εἰρήκατε (Acts 8:24)
    and Simon said, "pray to the Lord for me, that nothing of which
    you spoke shall come upon me"

f. Gnomic perfect, expressing general, universal, theological, or proverbial truth.
  (1) 3 pers. sing. perf. act. indic.
    ὁ γὰρ ἀγαπῶν τὸν ἕτερον νόμον πεπλήρωκεν (Rom. 13:8)
    for **the one who loves** the other person **has fulfilled** the law
  (2) 3 pers. sing. perf. pass. indic.
    ὁ δὲ διακρινόμενος ἐὰν φάγῃ κατακέκριται, ὅτι οὐκ ἐκ
    πίστεως (Rom. 14:23)
    but **he who wavers is condemned**, if he eats, because [ἐστιν, it is]
    not of faith

6. Pluperfect tense, representing an action as complete, with the results existing at some point in past time. It is found only in the indicative mood.
  a. Pluperfect as imperfect. Sometimes the imperfect best translates the pluperfect.
    (1) 1 pers. sing. plupf. act. indic.
      ἔφη τε ὁ Παῦλος, οὐκ ᾔδειν, ἀδελφοί, ὅτι ἐστὶν ἀρχιερεύς
      (Acts 23:5)
      and Paul said, "**I did not know**, brothers, that he is high priest"
    (2) 2 pers. sing. plupf. act. indic.
      ᾔδεις ὅτι ἐγὼ ἄθρωπος αὐστηρός εἰμι (Luke 19:22)
      you knew that I am an austere man
    (3) 3 pers. sing. plupf. act. indic.
      καὶ πᾶς ὁ ὄχλος ἐπὶ τὸν αἰγιαλὸν εἱστήκει (Matt. 13:2)
      and **all the people were standing** on the shore

(4) 2 pers. pl. plupf. act. indic.

τί ὅτι ἐζητεῖτέ με; **οὐκ ᾔδειτε** ὅτι ἐν τοῖς τοῦ πατρός μου δεῖ εἶναί με; (Luke 2:49)

why [ἐστιν, is it] that you were looking for me? **did you not know** that I must be involved in the things of my Father?

(5) 3 pers. pl. plupf. act. indic.

εἱστήκεισαν δὲ **οἱ δοῦλοι** καὶ **οἱ ὑπηρέται** ἀνθρακιὰν πεποιηκότες, ὅτι ψῦχος ἦν (John 18:18)

but **the servants** and **officers were standing**, having made a fire of coals, for it was cold

b. Intensive pluperfect, emphasizing the results.

(1) 3 pers. sing. plupf. act. indic.

καὶ ὧδε εἰς τοῦτο **ἐληλύθει** ἵνα δεδεμένους αὐτοὺς ἀγάγῃ ἐπὶ τοὺς ἀρχιερεῖς (Acts 9:21)

for **he had come** here for this purpose, that he might lead them bound to the chief priests

(2) 3 pers. pl. plupf. act. indic.

παρέθεντο αὐτοὺς τῷ κυρίῳ εἰς ὃν **πεπιστεύκεισαν** (Acts 14:23)

they committed them to the Lord, in whom **they had believed**

c. Consummative pluperfect—indicating completed action in past time.

(1) 3 pers. sing. plupf. act. indic.

πολλοῖς γὰρ χρόνοις **συνηρπάκει** αὐτόν (Luke 8:29)[40]

for **it had seized** him many times

(2) 3 pers. pl. plupf. act. indic.

ἐγίνωσκεν γὰρ ὅτι διὰ φθόνον **παραδεδώκεισαν** αὐτὸν οἱ ἀρχειρεῖς (Mark 15:10)

for he knew that because of envy **the chief priests had delivered** him

d. Periphrastic pluperfect. The imperfect of εἰμι and a perfect anarthrous participle emphasize past completed action.

(1) 1 pers. sing. impf. indic. and nom. sing. masc. perf. act. ptc. plus two pres. act. ptc. emphasize past linear action.

καὶ αὐτὸς **ἤμην ἐφεστὼς** καὶ **συνευδοκῶν** καὶ **φυλάσσων** τὰ ἱμάτια τῶν ἀναιρούντων αὐτόν (Acts 22:20)

and **I myself was standing** and **consenting** and **guarding** the garments of those who were killing him

(2) 3 pers. sing. impf. indic. and nom. sing. fem. perf. pass. ptc.

ἦν γὰρ **ἡ ἐκκλησία συγκεχυμένη** (Acts 19:32)

for **the church was confused**

---

[40] Dana and Mantey (*A Manual Grammar of the Greek New Testament*, 206) call this an iterative pluperfect, and their point is well taken because of πολλοῖς χρόνοις.

(3) 3 pers. pl. impf. indic. and nom. pl. masc. perf. pass. ptc.

καὶ ἐπίστευσαν ὅσοι ἦσαν τεταγμένοι εἰς ζωὴν αἰώνιον
(Acts 13:48)

and **as many as belonged** to eternal life believed

(4) 1 pers. pl. impf. indic. and nom. pl. masc. perf. pass. ptc.

οὕτω(ς) καὶ ἡμεῖς, ὅτε ἦμεν νήπιοι, ὑπὸ τὰ στοιχεῖα τοῦ κόσμου ἤμεθα δεδουλωμένοι (Gal. 4:3)[41]

so also we, when we were minors, **we were enslaved** under the elements of the world

(5) 3 pers. sing. impf. indic. and nom. sing. masc. aor. pass. ptc.
One example of an aorist participle with the imperfect indicative of εἰμι equals a pluperfect periphrastic.

ὅστις ἦν διὰ στάσιν τινὰ γενομένην ἐν τῇ πόλει καὶ φόνον βληθεὶς ἐν τῇ φυλακῇ (Luke 23:19)

who for a certain insurrection, which occurred in the city, and for murder **had been cast** into prison

Select Bibliography for the Indicative Mood

Allen, J. P. "The Force of Prepositions in Compound Verbs in the Perfect Tense in John's Gospel and Epistles." Doctoral diss., Southern Baptist Theological Seminary, 1940.

Baima, John K. "Making Valid Conclusions from Greek Conditional Sentences." Master's thesis, Grace Theological Seminary, 1986.

Battle, John A., Jr. "The Present Indicative in New Testament Exegesis." Th.D. diss., Grace Theological Seminary, 1975.

Beekman, John. "Analyzing and Translating the Questions of the New Testament." *Notes on Translation* 44: 3-21.

Boyer, James L. "First Class Conditions: What Do They Mean?" *Grace Theological Journal* 2, no. 1 (Spring 1981): 75-113.

_____. "Second Class Conditions in the New Testament Greek." *Grace Theological Journal* 3, no. 1 (Spring 1982): 81-88.

Burton, Ernest DeWitt. *Syntax of the Moods and Tenses in the New Testament Greek.* 3d ed. Edinburgh: T & T Clark, 1965.

Buth, Randy. "Mark's Use of the Historical Present." *Notes on Translation* 65: 7-13.

---

[41] Gal. 4:3 text is from GNT, NA & WH: TR & MT have ἦμεν for ἤμεθα δεδουλωμένοι.

Christopher, Gregory T. "Determining the Voice of New Testament Verbs Whose Middle and Passive Forms are Identical: A Consideration of the Perfect Middle/Passive." Master's thesis, Grace Theological Seminary, 1985.

Cline, George J. "The Middle Voice in the New Testament." Master's thesis, Grace Theological Seminary, 1983.

Clock, A. V. "The Aorist and Its English Equivalents." Master's thesis, Dallas Theological Seminary, 1954.

Davis, William H. "The Place of the Greek Tenses in the Province of New Testament Interpretation." *Review and Expositor* 18, no. 4 (October 1921): 375-86.

Deer, Donald S. "The Implied Agent in Greek Passive Verb Forms in the Gospel of Matthew." *Bible Translator* 18: 164-67.

_____. "The Implied Agent in Passive Forms in the Gospel of Matthew." Master's thesis, The Hartford Seminary Foundation, 1966.

_____. "The Interpretation and Translation of Constructions with a Passive Meaning in the Greek of the Synoptic Gospels." *Bible Translator* 26, no. 3 (July 1975): 338-46.

Denio, F. B. "Translation of the Aorist Tense in the Indicative Mood." *Bibliotheca Sacra* (April 1884): 386-89.

Elliott, William E. "Conditional Sentences in the New Testament." Th.D. diss., Grace Theological Seminary, 1981.

Emden, Cecil S. "St. Mark's Use of the Imperfect Tense." *Expository Times* 65 (October 1953-September 1954): 146-49.

France, R. T. "The Exegesis of Greek Tenses in the New Testament." *Notes on Translation* 46 (December 1972): 3–12.

Gallagher, R. E. "The Present Periphrastic in the New Testament." Th.D. diss., Dallas Theological Seminary, 1965.

Gault, Jo Ann Marie. "The Discourse Function of ΚΑΙ ΕΓΕΝΕΤΟ in Luke and Acts." Master's thesis, Multnomah School of the Bible, 1984.

Goodwin, William Watson. *Syntax of the Moods and Tenses of the Greek Verb.* New York: St. Martin's, 1965.

Greenlee, J. Harold. "'If' in the New Testament." *Bible Translator* 13, no. 1 (1962): 39-43.

_____. "Verbs in the New Testament." *Bible Translator* (April 1952): 71-75.

Hawkins, John C. "The Historic Present in Mark." In *Horae Synopticae.* Reprint. Grand Rapids: Baker, 1968.

Kuehne, C. "Topics on the Tenses . . . Keeping the Aorist in its Place." *Journal of Theology* 16, no. 3 (1976): 2-10.

_____. "Topics on the Tenses . . . The Viewpoints of the Aorist." *Journal of Theology* 18, no. 3 (1978): 2-10.

_____. "Topics on the Tenses . . . Translating the Aorist Indicative." *Journal of Theology* 18, no. 2 (1978): 19-26.

Kujne, John H. "Greek Conditional Sentences." *Bible Translator* 13 (October 1962): 223-24.

Levinsohn, Stephen H. "Preliminary Observations on the Use of the Historical Present in Mark." *Notes on Translation* 65: 13-28.

McGaughy, Lance C. *Towards a Descriptive Analysis of EINAI as a Linking Verb in New Testament Greek.* Published by the Society of Biblical Literature for the Linguistics Seminar. Dissertation series, no. 6, 1972.

McKay, K. L. "On the Perfect and Other Aspects in New Testament Greek." *Novum Testamentum* 23, no. 4 (1981): 289-329.

Marshall, Alfred. "οὐ and μή in Questions." *Bible Translator* 4, (1953): 41-42.

Orth, L. S., Jr. "The Rendering of the Greek Perfect Tense into English." Master's thesis, Dallas Theological Seminary, 1956.

Osborn, Carroll D. "The Present Indicative in Matthew 19:9." *Restoration Quarterly* (1981): 193-203.

Pritchett, W. Kendrick. "The Conditional Sentence in Attic Greek." *American Journal of Philology* 76, no. 1 (1965): 1-17.

Reilin, J. "The Use and Translation of Kai Egeneto, 'and it happened,' in the New Testament." *Bible Translator* 16, no. 4 (October 1965): 153-63.

Reynolds, Stephen M. "The Zero Tense in Greek, A Critical Note." *Westminster Theological Journal* 32 (1969): 68-72.

Roberts, J. W. "Some Aspects of Conditional Sentences in the Greek New Testament." *Bible Translator* 15, no. 2 (1964): 70-76.

Ryl, G. L. "The Significance of the Middle Voice in the Greek New Testament." Master's thesis, Dallas Theological Seminary, 1962.

Sears, Vaudrey Washington. "The Use of the Future Tense in the New Testament." Th.D. diss., Southern Baptist Theological Seminary, 1950.

Smith, Charles R. "Errant Aorist Interpreters." *Grace Theological Journal* 2, no. 2 (Fall 1982): 205-26.

Stagg, Frank. "The Abused Aorist." *Journal of Biblical Literature* 91 (June 1972): 222-31.

Tune, Cecil L. "The Use of Conditional Sentences in Hebrews." Master's thesis, Dallas Theological Seminary, 1973.

Turner, C. H. "Notes and Studies: Auxiliary and Quasi-Auxiliary Verbs." *Journal of Theological Studies* 28, no. 2 (1927): 349-62.

Waters, Dan Riley. "Conditional Sentences in Romans." Master's thesis, Dallas Theological Seminary, 1976.

Weymouth, Richard F. *On the Rendering into English of the Greek Aorist and Perfect.* London: James Clarke, 1890.

Wootton, R. W. F. "The Implied Agent in Greek Passive Verbs in Mark, Luke, and John." *Bible Translator* 19: 159-64.

Wuest, Kenneth S. "The Eloquence of Greek Tenses and Moods." *Bibliotheca Sacra* 117, no. 466 (April 1960): 134-43.

FINITE VERBS

Subjunctive Mood

II. **Subjunctive mood**. This is generally called the mood of probability, expressing a measure of uncertainty. This mood is found in the present, aorist, and perfect tenses. The following treatment looks at the kinds of subjunctives, voice, and tense.

   A. Kinds of subjunctives. These are basically divided into two groups: independent and dependent clauses.

      1. Independent subjunctives are independent clauses as compared with subordinate or dependent clauses. They fall into five categories: hortatory, deliberative, imperatival, emphatic negative, and prohibitive.

         a. Hortatory subjunctives indicate an exhortation, challenge, or invitation in the first person plural, encouraging others to participate in the action. This takes the place of the first person imperative form, which is not found in Greek or English. It is generally translated as "let us do . . ."

            (1) Positive exhortation

               (a) 1 pers. sing. aor. act. subj. (rarely found in the singular)

ἀδελφέ, **ἄφες ἐκβάλω** τὸ κάρφος τὸ ἐν τῷ ὀφθαλμῷ σου (Luke 6:42)

brother, **you let me pull out** the speck that [ὄν, is] in your eye

               (b) 1 pers. pl. aor. act. subj.

καθαρίσωμεν ἑαυτοὺς ἀπὸ παντὸς μολυσμοῦ σαρκὸς καὶ πνεύματος (2 Cor. 7:1)

let us cleanse ourselves from every defilement of flesh and spirit

            (2) Negative exhortation with μή, μηδέ, or μηκέτι

              1 pers. pl. pres. act. subj.

μηκέτι οὖν ἀλλήλους **κρίνωμεν** (Rom. 14:13)

let us, then, **no longer repeatedly criticize** one another

         b. Deliberative subjunctive, asking a question that contemplates or asks the advisability of doing or not doing a certain thing. The question may be real (expecting an answer) or rhetorical, direct or indirect.

            (1) 2 pers. sing. aor. act. subj. (with interrogative pronoun)

εἶπε(ν) δὲ ὁ κύριος τοῦ ἀμπελῶνος, **τί ποιήσω**; (Luke 20:13)

and the owner of the vineyard said, "**what shall I do**?"

            (2) 3 pers. sing. aor. mid. dep. subj. (with interrogative pronoun)

ὅτι εἰ ἐν τῷ ὑγρῷ ξύλῳ ταῦτα ποιοῦσιν, ἐν τῷ ξηρῷ **τί γένηται**; (Luke 23:31)

for if they do these things during the green tree, **what will happen** during the dry [tree]?

(3) 1 pers. pl. pres. act. subj. (with interrogative pronoun)

τί ποιῶμεν ἵνα ἐργαζώμεθα τὰ ἔργα τοῦ θεοῦ; (John 6:28)

what shall be do that we might produce the works of God?

(4) 1 pers. pl. aor. act. subj. (with θέλω)

θέλεις οὖν ἀπελθόντες συλλέξωμεν αὐτά; (Matt. 13:28)

do you wish, then, that we go **and gather** them?

(5) 2 pers. pl. aor. act. subj. (with interrogative adverb)

πῶς φύγητε ἀπὸ τῆς κρίσεως τῆς γεέννης; (Matt. 23:33)

how shall you flee from the judgment of Gehenna?

(6) 3 pers. pl. aor. act. subj. (indirect question with interrogative pronoun)

καὶ οὐχ εὕρισκον τὸ τί ποιήσωσιν (Luke 19:48)

and they did not find **what they should do**

c. Imperatival ἵνα or ἵνα μή. ἵνα sometimes introduces an imperatival clause. This is a controversial classification, as Greek grammarians are not in agreement in their discussion of this use of ἵνα. The major grammars give some attention to this matter, and several articles in theological journals give even more extensive coverage (see bibliography). The ranges of agreement or disagreement include such terms as unacceptable, doubtful, not certain, possible, conceivable, probable, unmistakable, and certain.

(1) 1 pers. sing. pres. act. subj.

ἵνα μὴ λέγω σοι ὅτι καὶ σεαυτόν μοι προσοφείλεις (Philem. 19)

I do not want to remind you that you owe me yourself also

(2) 2 pers. sing. perf. act. subj. (perf. with pres. meaning)

ἐὰν δὲ βραδύνω, ἵνα εἰδῇς πῶς δεῖ ἐν οἴκῳ θεοῦ ἀναστρέφεσθαι (1 Tim. 3:15)

but if I delay, **you must know** how to conduct yourself in the house of God

(3) 3 pers. sing. pres. act. subj.

ἵνα μηδὲν αὐτοῖς λείπῃ (Titus 3:13)

let nothing be lacking to them

(4) 1 pers. pl. pres. act. subj.

μόνον τῶν πτωχῶν ἵνα μνημονεύωμεν (Gal. 2:10)

only **let us remember** the poor

(5) 2 pers. pl. pres. pass. subj.

ἵνα καὶ ὑμεῖς ὑποτάσσησθε τοῖς τοιούτοις (1 Cor. 16:16)

you must also **be subject** to such

(6) 3 pers. pl. pres. act. subj.

ἵνα σωφρονίζωσιν τὰς νέας φιλάνδρους εἶναι (Titus 2:4)

let them encourage the young women to love their husbands

d. Emphatic negative with οὐ μή (only in the aorist tense). This is similar to οὐ μή with the future indicative.

(1) 1 pers. sing. aor. act. subj.

κάθημαι βασίλισσα καὶ χήρα οὐκ εἰμί καὶ πένθος οὐ μὴ ἴδω (Rev. 18:7)

I sit a queen, and I am not a widow, and **I will never see** mourning

(2) 2 pers. sing. aor. act. subj.

ἀμὴν λέγω σοι, οὐ μὴ ἐξέλθῃς ἐκεῖθεν ἕως ἂν ἀποδῷς τὸν ἔσχατον κοδράντην (Matt. 5:26)

truly I tell you, **you will not come out** from there until you repay the last penny

(3) 3 pers. sing. aor. act. subj.

καὶ **φωνὴ** νυμφίου καὶ νύμφης οὐ μὴ ἀκουσθῇ ἐν σοὶ ἔτι (Rev. 18:23)

and **the voice** of the bridegroom and the bride **shall no longer be heard** by you

(4) 1 pers. pl. aor. act. subj.

ἡμεῖς οἱ ζῶντες οἱ περιλειπόμενοι εἰς τὴν παρουσίαν τοῦ κυρίου οὐ μὴ φθάσωμεν τοὺς κοιμηθέντας (1 Thess. 4:15)

we who are alive who remain unto the coming of the Lord **shall not at all precede** those who sleep

(5) 2 pers. pl. aor. act. subj.

ἀκοῇ ἀκούσετε καὶ οὐ μὴ συνῆτε, καὶ βλέποντες βλέψετε καὶ οὐ μὴ ἴδητε (Acts 28:26)

by hearing **you** will hear and **will not at all understand**, and by seeing **you** will see and **will not at all perceive**

(6) 3 pers. pl. aor. act. subj.

καὶ οἱ πυλῶνες αὐτῆς οὐ μὴ κλεισθῶσιν ἡμέρας, νὺξ γὰρ οὐκ ἔσται ἐκεῖ (Rev. 21:25)

and **her gates shall never be closed** by day, for night shall not exist there

e. Prohibitive subjunctive with μή, μηδείς, μηδέ, μήποτε (only in aorist)

(1) 2 pers. sing. aor. act. subj.

σφράγισον ἃ ἐλάλησαν αἱ ἑπτὰ βρονταί, καὶ μὴ αὐτὰ γράψῃς (Rev. 10:4)

seal what the seven thunders said and **do not write** them

(2)   3 pers. sing. aor. act. subj.

μή τις οὖν αὐτὸν ἐξουθενήσῃ (1 Cor. 16:11)

let no one therefore **despise** him

(3)   2 pers. pl. aor. act. subj.

μὴ ἀδικήσητε τὴν γῆν (Rev. 7:3)

do not harm the earth

2. Dependent subjunctives are subordinate clauses introduced by some conjunction, adverb, particle, or relative pronoun. These indicators point out various functions: purpose, substantive, condition, concessive, temporal, relative, local, result, comparative, warning, or periphrastic clauses.

    a. Purpose clauses, introduced by ἵνα or ὅπως (with two exceptions, Matt. 6:4 and Luke 16:28, found only in the aorist tense)

       (1)   1 pers. sing. aor. act. subj. with ἵνα

τί ποιήσω ἵνα ζωὴν αἰώνιον **κληρονομήσω**; (Mark 10:17)

what shall I do **in order that I may inherit** eternal life?

       (2)   2 pers. sing. pres. act subj. with ἵνα

τάχα γὰρ διὰ τοῦτο ἐχωρίσθη πρὸς ὥραν, ἵνα αἰώνιον αὐτὸν **ἀπέχῃς** (Philem. 15)

for perhaps he departed for an hour **in order that you might receive** him forever

       (3)   3 pers. sing. pres. mid./pass. dep. subj. with ὅπως

ἵνα πέμψῃς αὐτὸν εἰς τὸν οἶκον τοῦ πατρός μου, ἔχω γὰρ πέντε ἀδελφούς, ὅπως **διαμαρτύρηται** αὐτοῖς (Luke 16:27-28)

that you will send him to my father's home, for I have five brothers, **in order that he may witness** to them

       (4)   1 pers. pl. perf. act. subj. with ἵνα (perf. with pres. meaning)

ἡμεῖς δὲ οὐ τὸ πνεῦμα τοῦ κόσμου ἐλάβομεν ἀλλὰ τὸ πνεῦμα τὸ ἐκ τοῦ θεοῦ, ἵνα **εἰδῶμεν** τὰ ὑπὸ τοῦ θεοῦ χαρισθέντα ἡμῖν (1 Cor. 2:12)

but we did not receive the spirit of the world but the spirit that [ὄν, is] of God **in order that we might know** the things that have been freely given to us by God

       (5)   2 pers. pl. pres. mid./pass. dep. subj. with ἵνα, negative purpose

ἐν οἴκῳ ἐσθιέτω, ἵνα μὴ εἰς κρίμα **συνέρχησθε**
(1 Cor. 11:34)

let him eat at home, **lest you come together** for judgment

(6) 3 pers. pl. aor. act. subj. with ἵνα

πάντα ὑπομένω διὰ τοὺς ἐκλεκτούς, ἵνα καὶ αὐτοὶ
σωτηρίας τύχωσιν (2 Tim. 2:10)

I endure all things for the sake of the elect, **in order that they** also
might obtain salvation

b. Substantive subjunctive clauses function as nouns or complementary
to adjectives. They function as subjects of impersonal verbs, indirect
objects, or appositional (epexegetical) to other nouns, pronouns, or
verbs. These clauses are introduced by ἵνα, ἵνα μή, or ὅπως.

(1) 2 pers. sing. aor. act. subj. (complementary of adj. with ἵνα)

κύριε, οὐκ εἰμὶ **ἱκανὸς ἵνα** μου ὑπὸ τὴν στέγην **εἰσέλθῃς**
(Matt. 8:8)

Lord, I am not **worthy that you should come in** under my roof

(2) 1 pers. sing. aor. mid. dep. subj. (appositional/epexegetical with
ὅπως and pronoun)

εἰς αὐτὸ τοῦτο ἐξήγειρά σε **ὅπως ἐνδείξωμαι** ἐν σοὶ τὴν
δύναμιν μου (Rom. 9:17)

for this very purpose I raised you up, **that I might show** my power
in you

(3) 3 pers. sing. aor. act. subj. with ἵνα and object clause

εἰς ὃ καὶ **προσευχόμεθα** πάντοτε περὶ ὑμῶν, **ἵνα** ὑμᾶς
ἀξιώσῃ τῆς κλήσεως ὁ **θεὸς ἡμῶν** (2 Thess. 1:11)

for which also **we pray** always for you **that our God would count**
you **worthy** of His calling

(4) 1 pers. pl. pres. act. subj. with ἵνα and pronoun

καὶ **αὕτη** ἐστὶν ἡ ἀγάπη, **ἵνα περιπατῶμεν** κατὰ τὰς
ἐντολὰς αὐτοῦ (2 John 6)

and **this** is love, **that we walk** according to his commands

(5) 2 pers. pl. aor. act. subj. with ἵνα and noun

συνίστημι δὲ ὑμῖν **Φοίβην** . . . **ἵνα** . . . **παραστῆτε**
αὐτῇ ἐν ᾧ ἂν ὑμῶν χρήζῃ πράγματι (Rom. 16:1-2)

I recommend to you **Phoebe** . . . **that** . . . **you may assist** her in
whatever matter she may need from you

(6) 3 pers. pl. aor. act. subj. (ἵνα μή may introduce a substantive that
functions as the subject of an impersonal verb)

καὶ ἐδόθη αὐτοῖς ἵνα μὴ ἀποκτείνωσιν αὐτούς (Rev. 9:5)[1]

and **it was granted** them **that they should not kill** them

---

[1] ἀποκτείνωσιν is parsed as pres. subj. by Guillemette, Stegenga, Wigram, and Yeagor; as aor. subj. by Frieberg; but as
pres. or aor. subj. by Zerwick, and Reinicker and Rodgers.

c. Conditional subjunctive, with ἐάν or ἐὰν μή in the protasis of a third class probable future condition.

(1) 1 pers. sing. pres. act. subj.

ἐὰν δὲ **βραδύνω**, ἵνα εἰδῇς πῶς δεῖ ἐν οἴκῳ θεοῦ ἀναστρέφεσθαι (1 Tim. 3:15)

but **if I delay**, that you may know how to conduct yourself in the house of God

(2) 2 pers. sing. aor. act. subj.

ἐὰν τοῦτον **ἀπολύσῃς**, οὐκ εἶ φίλος τοῦ Καίσαρος (John 19:12)

if you release this one, you are not a friend of Caesar

(3) 3 pers. sing. aor. act. subj.

ἐὰν ὁ **κύριος θελήσῃ** καὶ ζήσομεν καὶ ποιήσομεν τοῦτο ἢ ἐκεῖνο (James 4:15)

if the Lord wills, we shall both live and do this or that

(4) 1 pers. pl. pres. act. subj.

ἐὰν **διψᾷ**, πότιζε αὐτόν (Rom. 12:20)

if [ὁ ἐχθρός σου, your enemy] thirsts, give him drink

(5) 2 pers. pl. aor. act. subj.

ἐὰν . . . μὴ **δῶτε** δὲ αὐτοῖς τὰ ἐπιτήδεια τοῦ σώματος (James 2:15-16)

but **if you do not give** them the things needful for the body

(6) 3 pers. pl. aor. act. subj.

μή πως ἐὰν **ἔλθωσι(ν)** σὺν ἐμοὶ **Μακεδόνες** καὶ **εὕρωσιν** ὑμᾶς ἀπαρασκευάστους (2 Cor. 9:4)

lest **if Macedonians come** with me and **find** you unprepared

d. Concessive subjunctives are introduced by ἐάν, καὶ ἐάν, ἐὰν καί, or κἄν.

(1) 1 pers. sing. aor. mid. dep. subj.

ἐάν τε γὰρ περισσότερόν τι **καυχήσωμαι** περὶ τῆς ἐξουσίας ἡμῶν (2 Cor. 10:8)

for **even if I should boast** more abundantly concerning our authority

(2) 3 pers. sing. pres. act. subj.

ἐὰν δὲ καὶ **ἀθλῇ** τις (2 Tim. 2:5)

but **although someone competes in a contest**

(3) 2 pers. pl. aor. act. subj.

ἀλλὰ **κἄν** τῷ ὄρει τούτῳ **εἴπητε** (Matt. 21:21)

but **even if you will say** to this mountain

(4) 3 pers. pl. aor. act. subj.

κἂν θανάσιμόν τι πίωσιν καὶ οὐ μὴ αὐτοὺς βλάψῃ
(Mark 16:18)[2]

even if they drink anything poisonous it shall not hurt them

e. Temporal subjunctive with ὅταν, **when, whenever,** or μέχρις οὗ, **until.**
Other adverbs, conjunctions, or particles that introduce temporal
clauses are: ἐπάν, **whenever;** ὡς ἐάν, **whenever;** and ἡνίκα ἄν,
whenever; ὁσάκις ἐάν, **as often as;** ὡς ἄν, **whenever;** ἄχρις οὗ, **until.**
See also letter (*g*) below.

   (1) 1 pers. sing. aor. act. subj.

   ἐλεύσομαι δὲ πρὸς ὑμᾶς ὅταν Μακεδονίαν διέλθω
   (1 Cor. 16:5)

   but I will come to you **when I shall pass through** Macedonia

   (2) 2 pers. sing. pres. act. subj.

   ἀλλ' ὅταν δοχὴν ποιῇς, κάλει πτωχούς (Luke 14:13)[3]

   but **whenever you prepare** a feast, invite the poor

   (3) 3 pers. sing. pres. act. subj.

   ἐν ταῖς ἡμέραις τῆς φωνῆς τοῦ ἑβδόμου ἀγγέλου, ὅταν
   μέλλῃ σαλπίζειν (Rev. 10:7)

   in the days of the voice of the seventh angel, **when he is about**
   to blow the trumpet

   (4) 1 pers. pl. pres. act. subj.

   χαίρομεν γὰρ ὅταν ἡμεῖς ἀσθενῶμεν, ὑμεῖς δὲ δυνατοὶ ἦτε
   (2 Cor. 13:9)

   for we rejoice **whenever we are weak**, and you are strong

   (5) 2 pers. pl. aor. act. subj.

   ὅταν ἴδητε ταῦτα γινόμενα (Luke 21:31)

   when you shall see these things happening

   (6) 3 pers. pl. aor. act. subj.

   καὶ ὅταν τελέσωσι(ν) τὴν μαρτυρίαν αὐτῶν (Rev. 11:7)

   and **when they shall complete** their testimony

f. Relative subjunctive clauses are introduced by a relative pronoun and
ἐάν, ἄν, or ἂν μή. The relative pronoun may be in any case, gender,
or number.

   (1) 1 pers. sing. aor. act. subj.

   καὶ δεῦρο εἰς τὴν γῆν ἣν ἄν σοι δείξω (Acts 7:3)

   and come into the land **that I will show** you

---

[2] Mark 16:18 text is from GNT, NA, WH & MT: TR βλάψει.
[3] Luke 14:13 text is from GNT, NA & WH: TR & MT have ποιῇς δοχήν.

(2) 2 pers. sing. aor. act. subj.

καὶ ὅ τι ἂν προσδαπανήσῃς ἐγὼ ἐν τῷ ἐπανέρχεσθαί με
ἀποδώσω σοι (Luke 10:35)

and **whatever you spend more** I will repay you when I return

(3) 3 pers. sing. pres. act. subj.

καὶ παραστῆτε αὐτῇ ἐν ᾧ ἂν ὑμῶν χρῄζῃ πράγματι
(Rom. 16:2)

and help her **with whatever** things **she may need** from you

(4) 1 pers. pl. pres. act. subj.

καὶ ὃ ἐὰν αἰτῶμεν λαμβάνομεν ἀπ᾽ αὐτοῦ (1 John 3:22)

and **whatever we ask** we receive from him

(5) 2 pers. pl. aor. act. subj.

οὓς ἐὰν δοκιμάσητε δι᾽ ἐπιστολῶν τούτους πέμψω
(1 Cor. 16:3)

whomever you approve by epistles I will send them

(6) 3 pers. pl. pres. mid. pass. dep. subj.

καὶ εἰς ἣν ἂν πόλιν εἰσέρχησθε καὶ δέχωνται ὑμᾶς,
ἐσθίετε τὰ παρατιθέμενα ὑμῖν (Luke 10:8)

and **into whatever city** you enter, and **they receive** you, eat the
things set before you

g. Temporal subjunctive clauses with ἕως, ἕως ἄν or ἕως οὗ (or ὅτου)

(1) 1 pers. sing. aor. act. subj.

καὶ περιζωσάμενος διακόνει μοι ἕως φάγω καὶ πίω
(Luke 17:8)

and when you have girded yourself, serve me **while I eat** and **drink**

(2) 2 pers. sing. aor. act. subj.

οὐ μὴ ἐξέλθῃς ἐκεῖθεν, ἕως ἂν ἀποδῷς τὸν ἔσχατον
κοδράντην (Matt. 5:26)

you will never depart from there, **until you repay** the last penny

(3) 3 pers. sing. aor. act. subj.

καὶ πορεύεται ἐπὶ τὸ ἀπολωλὸς ἕως εὕρῃ αὐτό; (Luke 15:4)

and will he go after the lost **until he finds** it?

(4) 2 pers. pl. aor. act. subj.

οὐ μή με ἴδητε ἀπ᾽ ἄρτι ἕως ἂν εἴπητε, εὐλογημένος ὁ
ἐρχόμενος ἐν ὀνόματι κυρίου (Matt. 23:39)

you will not see me from now on **until you shall say**, blessed
[ἐστιν, is] the one coming in the name of the Lord

(5) 3 pers. pl. aor. act. subj.

οἵτινες οὐ μὴ γεύσωνται θανάτου **ἕως ἂν ἴδωσι(ν)** τὴν βασιλείαν τοῦ θεοῦ ἐληλυθυῖαν ἐν δυνάμει (Mark 9:1)

who shall not at all taste death **until they shall see** the kingdom of God come in power

h. Local subjunctive clauses indicate a place where something happens or exists and are introduced by ὅπου ἐάν, ὅπου ἄν, and οὗ ἐάν, which mean **wherever**.

(1) 1 pers. sing. pres. mid./pass. dep. subj.

ἵνα ὑμεῖς με προπέμψητε **οὗ ἐὰν πορεύωμαι** (1 Cor. 16:6)

in order that you may send me on my journey **wherever I go**

(2) 2 pers. sing. pres. mid./pass. dep. subj.

ἀκολουθήσω σοι **ὅπου ἐὰν ἀπέρχῃ** (Luke 9:57)

I will follow you **wherever you go**

(3) 3 pers. sing. aor. act. subj.

καὶ **ὅπου ἐὰν εἰσέλθῃ** εἴπατε τῷ οἰκοδεσπότῃ . . . (Mark 14:14)

and **wherever he enters**, say to the householder . . .

(4) 2 pers. pl. aor. act. subj.

ὅπου ἐὰν εἰσέλθητε εἰς οἰκίαν, ἐκεῖ μένετε (Mark 6:10)

wherever you enter a house, remain there

i. Negative result clauses may be introduced by ἵνα μή, ὅπως μή, or μηδέ.

(1) 3 pers. sing. pres. act. subj.

ἵνα μὴ ὑετὸς βρέχῃ τὰς ἡμέρας τῆς προφητείας αὐτῶν (Rev. 11:6)[4]

so that rain should not fall during the days of their prophecy

(2) 2 pers. pl. pres. act. subj.

ταῦτα γὰρ ἀλλήλοις ἀντίκειται, **ἵνα μὴ** ἃ ἐὰν θέλητε ταῦτα **ποιῆτε** (Gal. 5:17)[5]

for these things oppose one another **so that you may not do** these things that you want [to do]

---

[4] Rev. 11:6 text is from GNT, NA, WH & MT: TR has βρέχῃ ὑετὸς ἐν ἡμέραις αὐτῶν τῆς προφητείας.

[5] Gal. 5:17 text is from GNT, NA & WH: TR & MT have ταῦτα δὲ ἀντίκειται ἀλλήλοις. Burton classifies this as purpose in *Syntax of the Moods and Tenses in New Testament Greek*, 94, par. 222.

(3) 3 pers. pl. pres. mid./pass. dep. subj. and pres. act. subj. combined in one verse.

ὅπως οἱ θέλοντες διαβῆναι ἔνθεν πρὸς ὑμᾶς μὴ δύνωνται, μηδὲ ἐκεῖθεν πρὸς ἡμᾶς διαπερῶσιν (Luke 16:26)[6]

so that those who want to cross over from here to you **are unable, neither do they cross over** from there to us

j. Comparative subjunctive clauses with ὡς, all 3 pers. sing.

3 pers. sing. pres. mid./pass. subj.

ὡς . . . καὶ καθεύδῃ καὶ ἐγείρηται νύκτα καὶ ἡμέραν (Mark 4:26-27)

as . . . also he sleeps and **gets up** night and day

k. Warning or caution clauses with βλέπω μή.

3 pers. sing. aor. act. subj.

ὥστε ὁ δοκῶν ἑστάναι βλεπέτω μὴ πέσῃ (1 Cor. 10:12)

therefore, let the one who thinks he stands **beware lest he fall**

l. Elliptical subjunctive verbs

(1) 1 pers. sing. pres. subj.

ἵνα ἡ ἀγάπη ἣν ἠγάπησάς με ἐν αὐτοῖς ᾖ, κἀγὼ ἐν αὐτοῖς (John 17:26)

in order that the love with which you love me may be in them, and I [ᾦ, **may be**] in them

(2) 2 pers. sing. aor. act. subj.

ἐγὼ δὲ λέγω ὑμῖν μὴ ὀμόσαι ὅλως, μήτε ἐν τῷ οὐρανῷ (Matt. 5:34)

but I tell you not to swear at all, **neither [ὀμόσῃς, swear]** by heaven

(3) 3 pers. sing. aor. act. subj.

μήποτέ σε παραδῷ ὁ ἀντίδικος τῷ κριτῇ, καὶ ὁ κρίτης τῷ ὑπηρέτῃ (Matt. 5:25)[7]

lest the opponent deliver you to the judge, and **the judge [παραδῷ σε, deliver you]** to the officer

(4) 1 pers. pl. aor. act. subj.

ἔλεγον δέ, μὴ ἐν τῇ ἑορτῇ (Matt. 26:5)

and they said, [κρατήσωμεν αὐτόν, "**let us** not **take him**] at the feast"

---

[6] Luke 16:26 text is from GNT, NA & WH: TR & MT have οἱ ἐκεῖθεν; TR has ἐντεῦθεν.

[7] Matt. 5:25 text is from GNT, NA & WH: TR & MT have ὁ κρίτης σε παραδῷ τῷ ὑπηρέτῃ.

(5) 2 pers. pl. aor. act. subj.

ὅταν ἴδητε τὴν νεφέλην ἀνατέλλουσαν ἐπὶ δυσμῶν εὐθέως
λέγετε ὅτι ὄμβρος ἔρχεται καὶ γίνεται οὕτως καὶ ὅταν
νότου πνέοντα, λέγετε ὅτι καύσων ἔσται (Luke 12:54-55)
when you see the cloud rising in the west, immediately you
say that there will come a rainstorm, and it so happens,
and when [**ἴδητε, you see**] the wind blowing you say that
there will be heat

(6) 3 pers. pl. aor. act. subj.

ὅταν δὲ ἔλθῃ ὁ υἱὸς τοῦ ἀνθρώπον ἐν τῇ δόξῃ αὐτοῦ καὶ
πάντες οἱ ἄγγελοι μετ᾽ αὐτοῦ (Matt. 25:31)
but when the son of man will come in his splendor and **all
his angels [ἔλθωσιν, will come]** with him

m. Periphrastic clause with pres. subjunctive of εἰμι and perf. ptc.

(1) 3 pers. sing. pres. subj. ᾖ and nom. sing. masc. perf. pass. ptc.

μὴ κατακλιθῇς εἰς τὴν πρωτοκλισίαν, μήποτε
ἐντιμότερός σου ᾖ κεκλημένος ὑπ᾽ αὐτοῦ (Luke 14:8)
do not sit in the first place, **lest one more honorable** than you
may have been invited by him

(2) 2 pers. pl. pres. subj. ἦτε and nom. pl. masc. perf. pass. ptc.

ἵνα ... ἦτε δὲ κατηρτισμένοι ἐν τῷ αὐτῷ νοΐ
(1 Cor. 1:10)
but that **you may be knit together** with the same mind

(3) 3 pers. sing. pres. subj. ᾖ and nom. sing. neut. perf. pass. ptc.

οὐδεὶς δύναται ἐλθεῖν πρός με ἐὰν μὴ ᾖ δεδομένον αὐτῷ
ἐκ τοῦ πατρός (John 6:65)
no one is able to come to me except **it had been given** to him by
my Father

(4) 3 pers. sing. pres. subj. ᾖ and nom. sing. fem. perf. pass. ptc.

αἰτεῖτε καὶ λήμψεσθε, ἵνα ἡ χαρὰ ὑμῶν ᾖ πεπληρωμένη
(John 16:24)[8]
ask and you shall receive, in order that **your joy may be full**

(5) 3 pers. pl. pres. subj. ᾖ and nom. pl. masc. perf. pass. ptc.

ἐγὼ ἐν αὐτοῖς καὶ σὺ ἐν ἐμοί, ἵνα ὦσιν τετελειωμένοι
εἰς ἕν (John 17:23)
I in them, and you in me, that **they may be perfect** in one

---

[8] John 16:24 text is from GNT, NA & WH: TR & MT have λήψεσθε.

B. Voice in the subjunctive mood.
  1. Active voice
     a. Simple active
        (1) 1 pers. sing. pres. act. subj. (negative purpose with ἵνα μή)
             ἵνα μὴ ἐπ' ἀλλότριον θεμέλιον οἰκοδομῶ (Rom. 15:20)
             lest I build on another's foundation
        (2) 2 pers. sing. aor. act. subj. (prohibitive subj. with μή)
             καὶ τὸ ἔλαιον καὶ τὸν οἶκον μὴ ἀδικήσῃς (Rev. 6:6)
             and **do not damage** the oil and the wine
        (3) 3 pers. sing. pres. act. subj. (epexegetical or appositional ἵνα)
             δότε κἀμοὶ τὴν ἐξουσίαν ταύτην ἵνα ᾧ ἐὰν ἐπιθῶ τὰς
             χεῖρας λαμβάνῃ πνεῦμα ἅγιον (Acts 8:19)
             give this power to me also, **that** on whomever I place my hands
             he shall receive the Holy Spirit
        (4) 1 pers. pl. pres. act. subj. (epexegetical ἵνα)
             καὶ αὕτη ἐστὶν ἡ ἀγάπη, ἵνα περιπατῶμεν κατὰ τὰς
             ἐντολὰς αὐτοῦ (2 John 6)
             and this is love, **that we walk** according to his commands
        (5) 2 pers. pl. pres. act. subj. (temporal subj. with ὁσάκις ἐάν)
             τοῦτο ποιεῖτε, ὁσάκις ἐὰν πίνητε, εἰς τὴν ἐμὴν
             ἀνάμνησιν (1 Cor. 11:25)[9]
             do this, **as often as you drink [it]**, in remembering me
        (6) 3 pers. pl. pres. act. subj. (imperatival ἵνα)
             ἵνα σωφρονίζωσιν τὰς νέας φιλάνδρους εἶναι (Titus 2:4)
             let them encourage the young women to love their husbands
     b. Stative active, normally in the present tense
        (1) 1 pers. sing. pres. act. subj. (negative conditional with ἐὰν μή)
             ἐὰν ταῖς γλώσσαις τῶν ἀνθρώπων λαλῶ καὶ τῶν ἀγγέλων,
             ἀγάπην δὲ μὴ ἔχω (1 Cor. 13:1)
             if I speak in the languages of men and of angels, but **I do not have**
             love
        (2) 2 pers. sing. aor. act. subj. (emphatic negative with οὐ μή)
             καὶ οὐ μὴ γνῷς ποίαν ὥραν ἥξω ἐπὶ σέ (Rev. 3:3)
             and **you will not know** what hour I will come to you
        (3) 3 pers. sing. pres. act. subj. (caution or warning with βλέπω μή)
             βλέπετε μή τις ὑμᾶς πλανήσῃ (Matt. 24:4)
             beware lest anyone deceives you

---

[9] 1 Cor. 11:25 text is from GNT, NA & WH; TR & MT have ὁσάκις ἂν πίνητε.

(4) 1 pers. pl. pres. act. subj. (deliberative subj.)

ἐπιμένωμεν τῇ ἁμαρτίᾳ, ἵνα ἡ χάρις πλεονάσῃ; (Rom. 6:1)[10]

shall we continue in sin in order that grace may abound?

(5) 2 pers. pl. pres. act. subj. (purpose ἵνα)

ταῦτα λελάληκα ὑμῖν **ἵνα** ἐν ἐμοὶ εἰρήνην **ἔχητε**
(John 16:33)

I have spoken these things to you, **in order that you may have** peace in me

(6) 3 pers. pl. aor. act. subj. (conditional with ἐάν)

σωθήσεται δὲ διὰ τῆς τεκνογονίας, **ἐὰν μείνωσιν** ἐν πίστει καὶ ἀγάπῃ καὶ ἁγιασμῷ μετὰ σωφροσύνης (1 Tim. 2:15)

but she shall be saved through childbearing, **if they remain** in faith and love and holiness with good judgment

2. Middle voice

   a. Deponent middle, with middle form but active meaning

     (1) 1 pers. sing. pres. mid./pass. dep. (conditional with ἐάν)

ἐὰν γὰρ εὐαγγελίζωμαι, οὐκ ἔστι(ν) μοι καύχημα
(1 Cor. 9:16)

for **if I preach the gospel,** I have no boasting

     (2) 2 pers. sing. aor. mid. dep. subj. (prohibitive subj. with μηδέ)

μὴ ἅψῃ **μηδὲ γεύσῃ** μηδὲ θίγῃς (Col. 2:21)

do not touch, **neither taste**, neither handle

     (3) 3 pers. sing. pres. mid./pass. dep. subj. (imperatival ἵνα)

ἡ δὲ γυνὴ **ἵνα φοβῆται** τὸν ἄνδρα (Eph. 5:33)[11]

and **let the wife respect** her husband

     (4) 1 pers. pl. pres. mid./pass. dep. subj. (hortatory subj.)

προσερχώμεθα οὖν μετὰ παρρησίας τῷ θρόνῳ τῆς χάριτος
(Heb. 4:16)

therefore, **let us approach** the throne of grace with boldness

     (5) 2 pers. pl. aor. mid. dep. subj. (prohibitive with μηδείς)

καὶ **μηδένα** κατὰ τὴν ὁδὸν **ἀσπάσησθε** (Luke 10:4)

and **greet no one** along the way

---

[10] Since there is no interrogative indicator, ἐπιμένωμεν could function as a hortatory subjunctive with no change in the theological thrust of Paul's argument. Paul is anticipating his advocate's thinking when he says, **let us continue in sin that grace may abound.** A.T. Robertson (*Grammar of the Greek New Testament in the Light of Historical Research*, 934) states, "There is no great amount of difference between the hortatory (volitive) subjunctive and the deliberative."

[11] ἵνα φοβῆται functions in the same way as the preceding ἀγαπάτω in Eph. 5:33.

(6) 3 pers. pl. aor. mid. dep. subj. (emphatic negative with οὐ μή)

 ἀμὴν λέγω ὑμῖν ὅτι εἰσί(ν) τινες . . . οἵτινες οὐ μὴ
 γεύσωνται θανάτου ἕως ἂν ἴδωσι(ν) τὴν βασιλείαν τοῦ
 θεοῦ ἐληλυθυῖαν ἐν δυνάμει (Mark 9:1)

 truly I tell you that there are some . . . **who shall not taste** death
 until they see the kingdom of God come in power

b. Middle voice with active sense but not a true deponent

(1) 1 pers. sing. aor. mid. subj. (deliberative with τί)

 εἶπε(ν) τῇ μητρὶ αὐτῆς, **τί αἰτήσωμαι**; (Mark 6:24)[12]

 she said to her mother, **"what shall I ask?"**

(2) 2 pers. sing. aor. mid. subj. (appositional or epexegetical ἵνα)

 τούτου χάριν ἀπέλιπόν σε ἐν Κρήτῃ, **ἵνα** τὰ λείποντα
 ἐπιδιορθώσῃ (Titus 1:5)[13]

 I left you in Crete for this purpose, **that you might set right**
 the remaining things

(3) 3 pers. sing. pres. mid./pass. subj. (conditional with ἐάν)

 οἴδαμεν δὲ ὅτι καλὸς ὁ νόμος **ἐάν** τις αὐτῷ νομίμως
 χρῆται (1 Tim. 1:8)

 but we know that the law [ἐστιν, is] good, **if anyone uses** it
 lawfully

(4) 1 pers. pl. pres. mid./pass. subj. (conditional with ἐάν)

 ὅτι **ἐάν** τι **αἰτώμεθα** κατὰ τὸ θέλημα αὐτοῦ ἀκούει ἡμῶν
 (1 John 5:14)

 that **if we ask** anything according to his will he hears us

(5) 2 pers. pl. aor. mid. subj. (purpose with ἵνα)

 ὑπομονῆς γὰρ ἔχετε χρείαν **ἵνα** τὸ θέλημα τοῦ θεοῦ
 ποιήσαντες **κομίσησθε** τὴν ἐπαγγελίαν (Heb. 10:36)

 for you have need of patience, **in order that** after you have
 performed the will of God **you may receive** the promise

(6) 3 pers. pl. aor. mid. subj. (emphatic negative with οὐ μή)

 κἀγὼ δίδωμι αὐτοῖς ζωὴν αἰώνιον, καὶ **οὐ μὴ ἀπόλωνται**
 εἰς τὸν αἰῶνα (John 10:28)[14]

 and I give to them eternal life, and **they shall never perish**
 forever

---

[12] Mark 6:24 text is from GNT, NA, WH & TR; MT has αἰτήσομαι.

[13] Titus 1:5 text is from GNT & NA; WH has ἀπέλειπον; TR & MT have κατέλιπον.

[14] John 10:28 text is from GNT, NA & WH; TR & MT have ζωὴν αἰώνιον δίδωμι αὐτοῖς.

c. Middle voice with active meaning different from the active voice,
    e.g., ἅπτω, ἄρχω
    (1) 1 pers. sing. aor. mid. subj. (conditional with ἐάν)
         ἐὰν μόνον **ἅψωμαι** τοῦ ἱματίου αὐτοῦ σωθήσομαι
         (Matt. 9:21)
         if only **I may touch** his clothing I shall be healed
    (2) 2 pers. sing. aor. mid. subj. (temporal clause with ὅταν)
         ὅταν . . . καὶ τότε **ἄρξῃ** μετὰ αἰσχύνης τὸν ἔσχατον
         τόπον κατέχειν (Luke 14:8-9)[15]
         when . . . and then **you will begin** with shame to take the last place
    (3) 3 pers. sing. aor. mid. subj. (conditional with ἐάν)
         ἐὰν . . . χρονίζει ὁ **κύριός** μου ἔρχεσθαι καὶ **ἄρξηται**
         τύπτειν τοὺς παῖδας καὶ τὰς παιδίσκας (Luke 12:45)
         if . . . **my lord** delays in coming and **he [the servant] begins** to
         strike his servants and maidservants
    (4) 3 pers. pl. aor. mid. subj. (purpose ἵνα)
         πολλοὺς γὰρ ἐθεράπευσεν, ὥστε ἐπιπίπτειν αὐτῷ **ἵνα**
         αὐτοῦ **ἅψωνται** (Mark 3:10)
         for he healed many so that they pressed upon him, **in order that
         they might touch** him
    (5) 2 pers. pl. aor. mid. subj. (temporal clause with οὗ ἄν)
         ἀφ' οὗ ἂν ἐγερθῇ ὁ οἰκοδεσπότης καὶ ἀποκλείσῃ τὴν
         θύραν καὶ **ἄρξησθε** ἔξω ἑστάναι καὶ κρούειν τὴν θύραν
         (Luke 13:25)
         after the householder has risen and locked the door and **you begin**
         to stand outside and knock on the door
    (6) 3 pers. pl. aor. mid. subj. (negative purpose with ἵνα μήποτε)
         ἵνα μήποτε θέντος αὐτοῦ θεμέλιον καὶ μὴ ἰσχύοντος
         ἐκτελέσαι **πάντες** οἱ **θεωροῦντες ἄρξωνται** αὐτῷ ἐμπαίζειν
         (Luke 14:29)[16]
         lest after he laid a foundation and was not able to finish [it], **all
         those who see [it] will begin** to mock him

---

[15] Luke 14:8-9 text is from GNT, NA & WH: TR & MT have μετ'.
[16] Luke 14:29 text is from GNT & NA: WH has μή ποτε; TR & MT have ἐμπαίζειν αὐτῷ.

d. Middle reflexive

  (1) 2 pers. sing. aor. mid. subj. (purpose with ἵνα)

συμβουλεύω σοι ἀγοράσαι παρ' ἐμοῦ χρυσίον πεπυρωμένον
ἐκ πυρός ἵνα πλουτήσῃς, καὶ ἱμάτια λευκά, ἵνα
περιβάλῃ καὶ μὴ φανερωθῇ ἡ αἰσχύνη τῆς γυμνότητός σου
(Rev. 3:18)

I counsel you to purchase from me gold purified by fire in order that
you may be rich, and white clothings **in order that you may clothe
yourself** and the shame of your nakedness should not be made
known

  (2) 3 pers. sing. pres. mid./pass. subj. (comparative with ὡς)

ὡς . . . καὶ **καθεύδῃ** καὶ **ἐγείρηται** νύκτα καὶ ἡμέραν
(Mark 4:26-27)

as . . . also he **sleeps** and **gets up** night and day

  (3) 1 pers. pl. aor. mid. subj. (hortatory subj.)

ἀποθώμεθα οὖν τὰ ἔργα τοῦ σκότους, **ἐνδυσώμεθα** δὲ τὰ
ὅπλα τοῦ φωτός (Rom. 13:12)[17]

let us cast off the works of darkness, and **let us clothe ourselves**
with the armor of light

  (4) 2 pers. pl. aor. mid. subj. (prohibitve subj. with μή)

ἀλλὰ ὑποδεδεμένους σανδάλια, καὶ **μὴ ἐνδύσησθε** δύο
χιτῶνας (Mark 6:9)[18]

but after you have put on sandals, **do not put on** two tunics

  (5) 3 pers. pl. aor. mid. subj. (exceptive clause with ἐὰν μή)

καὶ ἀπ' ἀγορᾶς **ἐὰν μὴ βαπτίσωνται** οὐκ ἐσθίουσι(ν)
(Mark 7:4)[19]

and [coming] from the market they do not eat **unless they have
washed themselves**

e. Middle voice with passive meaning. "The middle sense is not always
right; the passive is sometimes better."[20]

  (1) 1 pers. sing. aor. mid. subj. (purpose ἵνα)

ἵνα ἐν χαρᾷ ἐλθὼν πρὸς ὑμᾶς διὰ θελήματος θεοῦ
συναναπαύσωμαι ὑμῖν (Rom. 15:32)[21]

in order that when I come to you in joy by the will of God **I may be
refreshed by you**

---

[17] Rom. 13:12 text is from GNT, NA & WH: TR & MT have καὶ ἐνδυσώμεθα.

[18] Mark 6:9 text is from GNT, NA & TR*s*: WH, TR & MT have ἀλλ'; WH & TR*b* have ἐδύσασθαι.

[19] Mark 7:4 text is from GNT & NA: WH has ἐὰν μὴ ῥαντίσωνται; TR & MT have ἀπό.

[20] Andt and Gingrich, *A Greek-English Lexicon of the New Testament,* 263.

[21] Rom. 15:32 text is from GNT, NA, WH & MT: TR has ἔλθω for ἐλθών.

(2) 3 pers. sing. aor. mid. subj. (ἵνα substantive clause as subject
of impersonal verb)

καὶ ἐδόθη αὐτῇ ἵνα περιβάληται βύσσινον λαμπρὸν καθαρόν
(Rev. 19:8)

and **it was given** to her **that she should be clothed** with fine bright
clean linen[22]

(3) 2 pers. pl. aor. mid. subj. (temporal clause with ἕως οὗ)

ὑμεῖς δὲ καθίσατε ἐν τῇ πόλει ἕως οὗ ἐνδύσησθε ἐξ ὕψους
δύναμιν (Luke 24:49)[23]

but you remain in the city **until you shall be clothed** with power
from heaven

f. Middle intensive, with emphasis on the subject of the verb

(1) 3 pers. sing. aor. mid. subj. (ἵνα substantive clause as subject
of impersonal verb)

οὕτως οὐκ ἔστιν θέλημε ἔμπροσθεν τοῦ πατρὸς ὑμῶν τοῦ ἐν
οὐρανοῖς ἵνα ἀπόληται ἓν τῶν μικρῶν τούτων (Matt. 18:14)

so it is not the will before your Father who [ὄντος, is] in
heaven **that one** of these little ones **should perish**

(2) 1 pers. pl. aor. mid. subj. (hortatory subj.)

ἀπειλησώμεθα αὐτοῖς μηκέτι λαλεῖν ἐπὶ τῷ ὀνόματι τούτῳ
μηδενὶ ἀνθρώπων (Acts 4:17)

let us threaten them to speak no longer to no one in this name

3. Passive voice

a. Theological passive, where the implied agent is God

(1) 1 pers. sing. aor. pass. subj. (purpose ἵνα)

τί με δεῖ ποιεῖν ἵνα σωθῶ; (Acts 16:30)

what must I do **in order that I might be saved**?

(2) 2 pers. sing. aor. pass. subj. (purpose ὅπως)

Σαοὺλ ἀδελφέ, ὁ κύριος ἀπεσταλκέ(ν) με . . . ὅπως
ἀναβλέψῃς καὶ πλησθῇς πνεύματος ἁγίου (Acts 9:17)

brother Saul, the Lord sent me . . . **in order that you may** receive
sight and **be filled** with the Holy Spirit

(3) 3 pers. sing. aor. pass. subj. (epexegetical ἵνα)

ἐλήλυθεν ἡ ὥρα ἵνα δοξασθῇ ὁ υἱὸς τοῦ ἀνθρώπου
(John 12:23)

the hour has come **that the son** of man **should be glorified**

---

[22] περιβάληται in Rev. 19:8 could be middle reflexive, **"that she should clothe herself."**

[23] Luke 24:49 text is from GNT, NA & WH: TR & MT have πόλει Ἰερουσαλήμ (MT has Ἰερουσαλήμ) and δύναμιν ἐξ
ὕψους.

(4) 1 pers. pl. aor. pass. subj. (purpose ἵνα)
εἴπερ συμπάσχομεν ἵνα καὶ **συνδοξασθῶμεν** (Rom. 8:17)
if we suffer with [him] **in order that we may** also **be glorified witl [him]**

(5) 2 pers. pl. aor. pass. subj. (emphatic negation with οὐ μή)
καὶ μὴ καταδικάζετε, καὶ **οὐ μὴ καταδικασθῆτε**
(Luke 6:37)[24]
and do not condemn, and **you shall not be condemned**

(6) 3 pers. pl. aor. pass. subj. (emphatic negation with οὐ μή)
καὶ οἱ πυλῶνες αὐτῆς **οὐ μὴ κλεισθῶσιν** ἡμέρας, νὺξ γὰρ
οὐκ ἔσται ἐκεῖ (Rev. 21:25)
and **its gates shall never be closed** during the day, for night
shall not exist there

b. Passive deponent subjunctive, passive form with active meaning

(1) 1 pers. sing. aor. pass. dep. subj. (emphatic negation with οὐ μή
καὶ τῶν ἁμαρτιῶν αὐτῶν **οὐ μὴ μνησθῶ** ἔτι (Heb. 8:12)[25]
and **I will not remember** their sins anymore

(2) 2 pers. sing. aor. pass. dep. subj. (prohibitive with μή)
μὴ οὖν **ἐπαισχυνθῇς** τὸ μαρτύριον τοῦ κυρίου ἡμῶν
(2 Tim. 1:8)
do not then **be ashamed of** the witness of our Lord

(3) 3 pers. sing. aor. pass. dep. subj. (conditional with ἐάν)
ἀλλ᾽ ἐάν τις ἀπὸ νεκρῶν **πορευθῇ** πρὸς αὐτοὺς
μετανοήσουσιν (Luke 16:30)
but **if anyone goes** to them from the dead they will repent

(4) 1 pers. pl. aor. pass. dep. subj. (hortatory)
φοβηθῶμεν οὖν μήποτε καταλειπομένης ἐπαγγελίας
εἰσελθεῖν εἰς τὴν κατάπαυσιν αὐτοῦ (Heb. 4:1)
let us fear then lest a promise being left to enter into his rest

(5) 2 pers. pl. aor. pass. dep. subj. (prohibitive with μή)
τὸν δὲ φόβον αὐτῶν **μὴ φοβηθῆτε** (1 Peter 3:14)
but **do not fear** their intimidation

(6) 3 pers. pl. aor. pass. dep. subj. (deliberative with τί)
καὶ οὐκ ᾔδεισαν **τί ἀποκριθῶσι(ν)** αὐτῷ (Mark 14:40)[26]
and they did not know **what they should answer** him

---

[24] Luke 6:37 text is from GNT, NA & WH: TR & MT omit καί before μή.
[25] Heb. 8:12 text is from GNT, NA & WH: TR & MT have τῶν ἁμαρτιῶν αὐτῶν καὶ τῶν ἀνομιῶν αὐτῶν.
[26] Mark 14:40 text is from GNT, NA & WH: TR & MT have αὐτῷ ἀποκριθῶσι(ν).

c. Passive subjunctive with agent expressed by preposition

(1) 1 pers. sing. aor. pass. subj.

ἐμοὶ δὲ εἰς ἐλάχιστόν ἐστιν **ἵνα ὑφ' ὑμῶν ἀνακριθῶ**
(1 Cor. 4:3)

but **that I should be judged by you** is an insignificant matter to me

(2) 2 pers. sing. aor. pass. subj. (temporal subj. with ὅταν)

ὅταν κληθῇς ὑπό τινος εἰς γάμους, μὴ κατακλιθῇς εἰς τὴν
πρωτοκλισίαν (Luke 14:8)

when you are invited by anyone to a wedding, do not sit in the
place of honor

(3) 3 pers. sing. aor. pass. subj. (emphatic negation with οὐ μή)

ὁ νικῶν **οὐ μὴ ἀδικηθῇ** ἐκ τοῦ θανάτου τοῦ δευτέρου
(Rev. 2:11)

the one who overcomes will not be hurt by the second death

(4) 1 pers. pl. aor. pass. subj. (purpose ἵνα)

καὶ ἡμεῖς εἰς Χριστὸν Ἰησοῦν ἐπιστεύσαμεν, **ἵνα**
δικαιωθῶμεν ἐκ πίστεως Χριστοῦ (Gal. 2:16)

and we ourselves believed in Christ Jesus **in order that we might**
be justified by faith in [or by the faithfulness of] Christ

(5) 3 pers. pl. aor. pass. subj. (purpose ὅπως)

μὴ σαλπίσῃς ἔμπροσθέν σου ὥσπερ οἱ ὑποκριταὶ ποιοῦσιν . . .
ὅπως δοξασθῶσιν ὑπὸ τῶν ἀνθρώπων (Matt. 6:2)

do not blow a trumpet before you as the hypocrites do . . . **in order**
that they might be praised by the people

d. Passive subjunctive with agent unexpressed, unimportant, or found in
the context

(1) 1 pers. sing. aor. pass. subj. (negative purpose with ἵνα μή)

εἰ ἐκ τοῦ κόσμου τούτου ἦν ἡ βασιλεία ἡ ἐμή, οἱ
ὑπηρέται οἱ ἐμοὶ ἠγωνίζοντο ἄν, **ἵνα μὴ παραδοθῶ** τοῖς
Ἰουδαίοις (John 18:36)

if my kingdom were of this world, my servants would have fought,
in order that I should not be delivered to the Jews

(2) 2 pers. sing. aor. pass. subj. (negative purpose with μή)

σκοπῶν σεαυτόν, μὴ καὶ **σὺ πειρασθῇς** (Gal. 6:1)

considering yourself, **lest you** also **should be tempted**

(3) 3 pers. sing. pres. pass. subj. (negative purpose with ἵνα μή)

ἵνα μὴ ὁ λόγος τοῦ θεοῦ **βλασφημῆται** (Titus 2:5)

lest the word of God **should be defamed**

  (4) 2 pers. pl. pres. pass. subj. (imperatival ἵνα)

ἵνα καὶ ὑμεῖς ὑποτάσσησθε τοῖς τοιούτοις (1 Cor. 16:16)

you must also **be subject** to such

  (5) 3 pers. pl. aor. pass. subj. (purpose with ἵνα)

οὓς παρέδωκα τῷ Σατανᾷ, ἵνα παιδευθῶσι(ν) μὴ βλασφημεῖν (1 Tim. 1:20)

whom I delivered up to Satan **in order that they might be taught** not to blaspheme

e. Passive subjunctive with agent in dative case

  (1) 1 pers. sing. aor. pass. subj. (negative purpose with μή πως)

φοβοῦμαι γὰρ μή πως ἐλθὼν οὐχ οἵους θέλω εὕρω ὑμᾶς κἀγὼ εὑρεθῶ ὑμῖν οἷον οὐ θέλετε (2 Cor. 12:20)

for I fear **lest** when I come I will find you such as I do not want and **I shall be found by you** such as you do not want

  (2) 2 pers. sing. aor. pass. subj. (prohibitive subj. with μή πως)

σὺ οὖν μὴ πεισθῇς αὐτοῖς (Acts 23:21)

do not then **be persuaded by them**

  (3) 3 pers. sing. aor. pass. subj. (negative purpose with ἵνα μή)

ἵνα μὴ σκληρυνθῇ τις ἐξ ὑμῶν ἀπάτῃ τῆς ἁμαρτίας (Heb. 3:13)

lest anyone of you **should be hardened by the deceitfulness** of sin

  (4) 1 pers. pl. aor. pass. subj. (negative purpose with ἵνα μή)

κρινόμενοι δὲ ὑπὸ τοῦ κυρίου παιδευόμεθα, ἵνα μη σὺν τῷ κόσμῳ κατακριθῶμεν (1 Cor. 11:32)

but if we are judged we are disciplined by the Lord, **so that we should not be condemned** with **the world**

f. Passive subjunctive with an active meaning

  (1) 3 pers. sing. aor. pass. subj. (temporal clause with ἀφ’ οὗ ἄν)

ἀφ’ οὗ ἂν ἐγερθῇ ὁ οἰκοδεσπότης καὶ ἀποκλείσῃ τὴν θύραν (Luke 13:25)

after the householder gets up and locks the door

  (2) 2 pers. pl. aor. pass. subj. (substantive object clause with ἵνα)

πάντοτε ἀγωνιζόμενος ὑπὲρ ὑμῶν ἐν ταῖς προσευχαῖς, ἵνα σταθῆτε τέλειοι καὶ πεπληροφορημένοι ἐν παντὶ θελήματι τοῦ θεοῦ (Col. 4:12)

always agonizing for you in our prayers, **that you will stand** complete and assured in all the will of God

    g. Passive subjunctive with a middle reflexive sense

       (1) 1 pers. sing. aor. pass. subj. (purpose with ἵνα)

         καὶ ἐμοὶ οὐδέποτε ἔδωκας ἔριφον ἵνα μετὰ τῶν φίλων μου
         εὐφρανθῶ (Luke 15:29)

         and you never gave me a kid **in order that I might enjoy myself**
         with my friends

       (2) 2 pers. sing. aor. pass. subj. (prohibitive with νή)

         καὶ τὸν θέλοντα ἀπὸ σοῦ δανίσασθαι **μὴ ἀποστραφῇς**
         (Matt. 5:42)[27]

         and **do not turn yourself away from** from the one who wants to
         borrow from you

  4. Voiceless subjunctive, εἰμι, only in the present tense

    a. 1 pers. sing. pres. subj. (purpose ἵνα)

      ἔπεμψα αὐτὸν, ἵνα . . . χαρῆτε **κἀγὼ** ἀλυπότερος **ὦ** (Phil. 2:28)

      I sent him **in order that** . . . you might rejoice **and [that] I may be** less
      sorrowful

    b. 2 pers. sing. pres. subj. (conditional with ἐάν)

      ἐὰν δὲ παραβάτης νόμου **ᾖς** (Rom. 2:25)

      but **if you are** a transgressor of the law

    c. 3 pers. sing. pres. subj. (negative purpose with ἵνα μή)

      ἵνα ἡ πίστις ὑμῶν **μὴ ᾖ** ἐν σοφίᾳ ἀνθρώπων (1 Cor. 2:5)

      so that your faith should not be in the wisdom of men

    d. 1 pers. pl. pres. subj. (epexegetical ἵνα)

      οὐχ ἵνα ἡμεῖς δόκιμοι φανῶμεν, ἀλλ᾽ **ἵνα** ὑμεῖς τὸ καλὸν ποιῆτε,
      ἡμεῖς δὲ ὡς ἀδόκιμοι **ὦμεν** (2 Cor. 13:7)

      not that we should appear approved, but **that** you may do what is right
      and **we may be** as disapproved

    e. 2 pers. pl. pres. subj. (epexegetical or appositional ἵνα)

      καὶ τοῦτο προσεύχομαι . . . **ἵνα ἦτε** εἰλικρινεῖς καὶ
      ἀπρόσκοποι εἰς ἡμέραν Χριστοῦ (Phil. 1:9-10)

      and I pray this . . . **that you may be** pure and blameless in the day of
      Christ

    f. 3 pers. pl. pres. subj. (imperatival ἵνα)

      ἵνα καὶ οἱ ἔχοντες γυναῖκας ὡς μὴ ἔχοντες **ὦσι(ν)** (1 Cor. 7:29)

      let those who have wives **be** as those who have none

---

[27] Matt. 5:42 text is from GNT, NA & WH: TR & MT have δανείσασθαι.

C. Tense. Subjunctives are found only in the aorist, present, and perfect tenses. However, the perfect subjunctives are all forms of οἶδα, a second perfect form with a present sense. Thus, in essense only aorist and present forms of the subjunctive exist. The tense does not indicate the time of the action, past or present, but the kind of action. The aorist tense refers to punctiliar or undefined action, whereas the present tense refers to stative, durative, or repeated (iterative) action.

1. Present tense.
    a. Certain verbs have a basic meaning which is stative or linear and thus are found in the present tense when a subjunctive is required (with only a few exceptions); e.g., εἰμι, βλέπω, ἔχω, θέλω, βούλομαι, ἀγαπάω, περισσεύω, μέλλω, τηρέω, γρηγορεύω, φρονέω.
        (1) 1 pers. sing. pres. act. subj. (temporal with ὅταν)
             ὅταν γὰρ ἀσθενῶ τότε δυνατός εἰμι (2 Cor. 12:10)
             for **when I am weak** then I am strong
        (2) 2 pers. sing. pres. act. subj. (purpose with ἵνα)
             συμβουλεύω σοι . . . κολλούριον ἐγχρῖσαι τοὺς ὀφθαλμούς σου ἵνα βλέπῃς (Rev. 3:18)
             I counsel you to put eyesalve on your eyes **in order that you may see**
        (3) 3 pers. sing. pres. act. subj. (appositional with ἵνα)
             καὶ τοῦτο προσεύχομαι, ἵνα ἡ ἀγάπη ὑμῶν ἔτι μᾶλλον καὶ μᾶλλον περισσεύῃ (Phil. 1:9)
             and I pray this, **that your love may abound** yet more and more
        (4) 1 pers. pl. pres. act. subj. (purpose with ἵνα)
             ἵνα ἤρεμον καὶ ἡσύχιον βίον διάγωμεν (1 Tim. 2:2)
             in order that we may live a tranquil and quiet life
        (5) 2 pers. pl. pres. act. subj. (epexegetical or appositional with ἵνα)
             πληρώσατέ μου τὴν χαρὰν ἵνα τὸ αὐτὸ φρονῆτε (Phil. 2:2)
             fulfill my joy, **that you may continually think** the same thing
        (6) 3 pers. pl. pres. act. subj. (negative purpose with ἵνα μή)
             οἱ πατέρες, μὴ ἐρεθίζετε τὰ τέκνα ὑμῶν, ἵνα μὴ ἀθυμῶσιν (Col. 3:21)
             parents, do not repeatedly irritate your children, **lest they should be repeatedly discouraged**
    b. ἄγωμεν is an idiomatic form in the present subjunctive.
       1 pers. pl. pres. act. subj. (hortatory)
       ἐγείρεσθε ἄγωμεν· ἰδού ὁ παραδιδούς με ἤγγικεν (Mark 14:42)
       arise, **let us be going**, notice, the one who betrays me has arrived

c. Present tense may indicate a progressive or iterative sense.
   (1) 1 pers. sing. pres. act. subj. (purpose with ἵνα)

   ἀποκαλύψαι τὸν υἱὸν αὐτοῦ ἐν ἐμοί, **ἵνα εὐαγγελίζωμαι**
   αὐτὸν ἐν τοῖς ἔθνεσιν (Gal. 1:16)

   to reveal his son in me **in order that I might repeatedly preach** him
   among the Gentiles

   (2) 2 pers. sing. pres. mid./pass. dep. subj. (epexegetical or
   appositional ἵνα)

   ταύτην τὴν παραγγελίαν παρατίθεμαί σοι, τέκνον, Τιμόθεε
   ... **ἵνα στρατεύῃ** ἐν αὐταῖς τὴν καλὴν στρατείαν (1 Tim. 1:18)

   I entrust this command to you, son Timothy ... **that you continually
   fight** with them the good fight

   (3) 3 pers. sing. pres. act. subj. (indirect deliberative)

   ὁ δὲ υἱὸς τοῦ ἀνθρώπου οὐκ ἔχει **ποῦ** τὴν κεφαλὴν **κλίνῃ**
   (Matt. 8:20)

   but the son of man does not have [a place] **where he may lay** his
   head

   (4) 1 pers. pl. pres. act. subj. (hortatory)

   εἰ ζῶμεν πνεύματι, πνεύματι καὶ **στοιχῶμεν** (Gal. 5:25)

   if we are living with the Spirit, **let us** also **be walking** with the Spirit

   (5) 2 pers. pl. pres. act. subj. (purpose with ἵνα)

   ἵνα ὁμοθυμαδὸν ἐν ἑνὶ στόματι **δοξάζητε** τὸν θεόν (Rom. 15:6)

   that unanimously with one mouth **you may constantly glorify** God

   (6) 3 pers. pl. pres. act. subj. (ἵνα object clause)

   καὶ καθὼς θέλετε **ἵνα ποιῶσιν** ὑμῖν οἱ **ἄνθρωποι**, ποιεῖτε
   αὐτοῖς ὁμοίως (Luke 6:31)[28]

   and even as you wish **that people should do** for you, do for them
   in the same manner

2. Aorist tense indicates action in summary, without reference to its
   progress, state, repetition, or results.
   a. All subjunctive prohibitions (μή with subjunctive) are found in the
   aorist tense. μή with the present imperative forbids the continuation
   of some activity, whereas the aorist subjunctive forbids the beginning
   of an activity.
   (1) 2 pers. sing. aor. act. subj.

   μὴ φοβοῦ, ἀλλὰ **λάλει** καὶ **μὴ σιωπήσῃς** (Acts 18:9)

   do not be afraid, but **continue speaking**, and **do not become silent**

---

[28] Luke 6:31 text is from GNT, NA & WH: TR & MT have καὶ ὑμεῖς ποιεῖτε.

(2) 2 pers. pl. aor. mid. dep. subj.

καὶμηδένα κατὰ τὴν ὁδὸν ἀσπάσησθε (Luke 10:4)

and **greet no one** along the way

b. All emphatic negations in the subjunctive mood are found in the aorist tense. In fact the use of οὐ μή is found both with the aorist subjunctive and the future indicative. Thus, the similarity between the two are are seen in their aoristic, undefined statements.

(1) 3 pers. pl. fut. mid. dep. indic. and aor. act. subj.

ὁ οὐρανὸς καὶ ἡ γῆ παρελεύσεται, οἱ δὲ λόγοι μου οὐ μὴ παρέλθωσι(ν) (Matt. 24:35)[29]

heaven and **earth will pass away,** but **my words shall never pass away**

(2) 3 pers. sing. aor. act. subj.

πάλιν λέγω, μή τίς με δόξῃ ἄφρονα εἶναι (2 Cor. 11:16)

again I say, **let no one consider** me to be a fool

Select Bibliography for the Subjunctive Mood

Baima, John K. "Making Valid Conclusions from Greek Conditional Sentences." Master's thesis, Grace Theological Seminary, 1986.

Beekman, John. "Analyzing and Translating the Questions of the New Testament." *Notes on Translation* 44: 3-21.

Boyer, James L. "Third (and Fourth) Class Conditions." *Grace Theological Journal* 3, no. 2 (1982): 163-75.

_____. "Other Conditional Elements in New Testament Greek." *Grace Theological Journal* 4, no. 2 (Fall 1983): 173-88.

_____. *Supplemental Manual of Information: Subjunctive Verbs.* Winona Lake, Ind.: Morgan Library, Grace Theological Seminary, 1985.

_____. "The Classification of Subjunctives: A Statistical Study." *Grace Theological Journal* 7, no. 1 (1986): 3-19.

Buse, S. Ivor. "Substitutes for the Imperative in the New Testament." *Expository Times* 57 (1946): 250.

Cadoux, D. J. "The Imperatival Use of ἵνα in the New Testament." *Journal of Theological Studies* 42 (1941): 165-73.

---

[29] Matt. 24:35 text is from GNT, NA & WH: TR & MT have παρελεύσονται.

Curry, W. B. "The Nature and Use of the ἵνα Clause in the New Testament." Doctoral diss., Southwestern Baptist Seminary, 1949.

Deer, D. S.   "More about the Imperatival ἵνα." *Bible   Translator* 24, no. 3   (1972): 328-29.

Elliott, William E. "Conditional Sentences in the New Testament." Th.D diss., Grace Theological Seminary, 1981.

Fernando, Andrew P. "Translation of Questions and Prohibitions in Greek." *Bible Translator* 27, no. 1 (January 1976): 138-42.

George, A. R. "The Imperatival Use of ἵνα in the New Testament." *Journal of Theological Studies* 45 (1944): 56-60.

Greenlee, J. Harold. "ἵνα Substantive Clauses in the New Testament." *Asbury Seminarian* 2 (1947): 154-63.

_____. "ἵνα Clauses and Related Expressions." *Bible Translator* 6 (1955): 12-16.

_____. "'If' in the New Testament." *Bible Translator* 13, no. 1 (1962): 39-43.

Kujne, John H. "Greek Conditional Sentences." *Bible Translator* 13 (October 1962): 223-24.

Marshall, Alfred. "οὐ and μή in Questions." *Bible Translator* 4 (1953): 41-42.

Meecham, H. G. "The Imperatival Use of ἵνα in the New Testament." *Journal of Theological Studies* 43 (1942): 179-80.

Morrice, W. G. "The Imperatival ἵνα." *Bible Translator* 23, no. 3 (1972): 326-30.

Muraoka, Takamitsy. "The Use of ΩΣ in the Greek Bible." *Novum Testamentum* 7 (1964): 51-72.

_____. "Purpose of Result? ΩΣΤΕ in Biblical Greek." *Novum Testamentum* 15 (July 1973): 205-19.

Pritchett, W. Kendrick. "The Conditional Sentence in Attic Greek." *American Journal of Philology* 76, no. 1 (1955): 1-17.

Roberts, J. W. "Some Aspects of Conditional Sentences in the Greek New Testament." *Bible Translator* 15, no. 2 (1964): 70-76.

Robertson, A. T. "The Causal Use of ἵνα." In *Studies in Early Christianity,* edited by Shirley Jackson Case. New York: Century, 1928.

Tune, Cecil L. "The Use of Conditional Sentences in Hebrews." Master's thesis, Dallas Theological Seminary, 1973.

Waters, Dan Rile. "Conditional Sentences in Romans." Master's thesis, Dallas Theological Seminary, 1976.

Verbs: Imperative Mood

III. **Imperative mood.** The mode of command that expresses volitional possibility.
The term *imperative* includes a variety of concepts: command, direction, charge,
injoin, order, require, impose, decree, dictate, prescribe, demand, forbid, prohibit,
warn, threaten, counsel, exhort, advise, recommend, suggest, request, invite,
dare, challenge, permit. The response to an imperative depends upon the
authority of the person speaking or writing and the relationship of the person(s)
addressed.
   A. Kinds of Imperatives.
      1. Imperative of direct command, only in the second person. A command can
         be addressed to a group in two different ways: distributively, to each and
         every member—**πληροῦσθε** ἐν πνεύματι (Eph. 5:18), **be filled** by the
         Spirit; collectively or corporately, all members participate in the process
         in some way—καὶ εἶπεν αὐτοῖς, πορευθέντες εἰς τὸν κόσμον ἅπαντα
         κηρύξατε τὸ εὐαγγέλιον πάσῃ τῇ κτίσει (Mark 16:15), and he said to
         them, "go into all the world and **preach** the gospel to every creature."
         a. 2 pers. sing. pres. act. imper.
            τίμα τὸν πατέρα σου καὶ τὴν μητέρα σου (Mark 7:10)
            honor your father and your mother
         b. 2 pers. sing. pres. act. and perf. pass. imper.
            καὶ διεγερθεὶς ἐπετίμησεν τῷ ἀνέμῳ καὶ εἶπεν τῇ θαλάσσῃ,
            Σιώπα, πεφίμωσο (Mark 4:39)
            and when he was aroused he rebuked the wind and said to the sea,
            "be silent, be muzzled"
         c. 2 pers. pl. pres. act. and aor. mid. dep. imper.
            ὑπάγετε ἀσφαλίσασθε ὡς οἴδατε (Matt. 27:65)
            go make [it] secure as you know [how]
      2. Prohibitive imperative with μή, μηδείς, μηδέ, μηκέτι, only in the present
         tense. The prohibitive subjunctive is found with μή in the aorist tense and
         in the future indicative with οὐ.
         a. 2 pers. sing. pres. mid./pass. dep. imper.
            μὴ φοβοῦ, τὸ μικρὸν ποίμνιον· ὅτι εὐδόκησεν ὁ πατὴρ ὑμῶν
            δοῦναι ὑμῖν τὴν βασιλείαν (Luke 12:32)
            do not fear, little flock; for your father is delighted to give you the
            kingdom
         b. 3 pers. sing. pres. act. imper.
            μηδείς σου **περιφρονείτω** (Titus 2:15)
            let no one despise you

345

    c. 2 pers. pl. pres. act. imper.

    μὴ καταλαλεῖτε ἀλλήλων, ἀδελφοί (James 4:11)

    do not speak against one another, brothers

    d. 3 pers. pl. pres. mid./pass. dep. imper.

    καὶ οἱ ἐν ταῖς χώραις μὴ εἰσερχέσθωσαν εἰς αὐτήν (Luke 21:21)

    and **let not those [ὄντες, who are]** in the districts **enter** into her

3. Imperative of exhortation, not so much a command as an encouragement to do or be something

    a. 2 pers. sing. pres. act. imper.

    καὶ ὅστις σε ἀγγαρεύσει μίλιον ἕν, **ὕπαγε** μετ' αὐτοῦ δύο
    (Matt. 5:41)

    and whoever will force you [ὑπάγειν, to go] one mile, **go** with him two [miles]

    b. 3 pers. sing. pres. act. imper.

    τὸ δὲ ἔργον ἑαυτοῦ **δοκιμαζέτω** ἕκαστος (Gal. 6:4)

    but **let each one prove** his own work

    c. 2 pers. pl. aor. act. imper.

    ἄρατε τὸν ζυγόν μου ἐφ' ὑμᾶς, καὶ **μάθετε** ἀπ' ἐμοῦ (Matt. 11:29)

    take my yoke upon you and **learn** from me

    d. 3 pers. pl. pres. act. imper.

    τότε οἱ ἐν τῇ Ἰουδαίᾳ **φευγέτωσαν** εἰς τὰ ὄρη (Luke 21:21)

    then **let those [ὄντες, who are]** in Judea **flee** into the mountains

4. Imperative of invitation

    a. 2 pers. sing. pres. act. imper.

    καὶ λέγει αὐτῷ, Ἀκολούθει μοι (Mark 2:14)

    and he said to him, "**Follow** me"

    b. 3 pers. sing. pres. mid./pass. dep. and act. imper.

    ἐάν τις διψᾷ, **ἐρχέσθω** πρός με καὶ **πινέτω** (John 7:37)

    if anyone thirsts, **let him come** to me and **drink**

    c. 2 pers. pl. aor. act. imper.

    οὐκ ἔστιν ὧδε, ἠγέρθη γὰρ καθὼς εἶπεν, δεῦτε **ἴδετε** τὸν τόπον ὅπου ἔκειτο (Matt. 28:6)

    he is not here; for he has risen, even as he said; "come, **see** the place where he was lying"

    d. 3 pers. pl. aor. act. imper.

    αἰνεῖτε, πάντα τὰ ἔθνη, τὸν κύριον καὶ **ἐπαινεσάτωσαν** αὐτὸν **πάντες οἱ λαοί** (Rom. 15:11)[1]

    praise the Lord, all nations, and **let all peoples laud** him

---

[1] Rom. 15:11 text is from GNT, NA & WH: TR & MT have τὸν κύριον πάντα τὰ ἔθνη καὶ ἐπαινέσατε.

5. Imperative of request, petition, supplication, or prayer, normally used in the aorist tense.
    a. 2 pers. sing. aor. act. imper.
        λέγει πρὸς αὐτὸν ἡ γυνή, κύριε, **δός** μοι τοῦτο τὸ ὕδωρ (John 4:15)
        the woman said to him, "Sir, **give** me this water"
    b. 3 pers. pl. aor. pass. imper.
        σκοτισθήτωσαν οἱ ὀφθαλμοὶ αὐτῶν τοῦ μὴ βλέπειν (Rom. 11:10)
        let their eyes be darkened so that they will not see
    c. 3 pers. sing. aor. act. imper.
        πάτερ μου, εἰ δυνατόν ἐστι(ν), **παρελθάτω** ἀπ᾽ ἐμοῦ τὸ
        ποτήριον τοῦτο (Matt. 26:39) [2]
        my Father, if it is possible, **let this cup pass** from me
    d. 2 pers. pl. aor. pass. dep. imper.
        ἀποκριθεὶς δὲ ὁ Σίμων εἶπεν, **δεήθητε** ὑμεῖς ὑπὲρ ἐμοῦ πρὸς
        τὸν κύριον (Acts 8:24)
        and Simon said, "**you pray** to the Lord for me"
6. Imperative of demand, much stronger than a request
    a. 2 pers. sing. pres. act. imper.
        καὶ ἐπῆραν τὴν φωνὴν αὐτῶν λέγοντες, **αἶρε** ἀπὸ τῆς γῆς τὸν
        τοιοῦτον (Acts 22:22)
        and they lifted up their voice and said, ""**away** from the earth with
        such a person"
    b. 3 pers. sing. aor. pass. imper.
        οἱ δὲ περισσῶς ἔκραζον λέγοντες, **σταυρωθήτω** (Matt. 27:23)
        and they continued crying out even more, saying, "**let him be crucified**"
7. Imperative of permission, giving permission to another person or persons to do something
    a. 3 pers. sing. and 3 pers. pl. pres. act. imper.
        ὃ θέλει **ποιείτω**, οὐχ ἁμαρτάνει· **γαμείτωσαν** (1 Cor. 7:36)
        let him do what he wants, he does not sin; **let them marry**
    b. 2 pers. pl. pres. act. and mid. imper.
        καὶ ἔρχεται τὸ τρίτον καὶ λέγει αὐτοῖς, **καθεύδετε** τὸ λοιπὸν
        καὶ **ἀναπαύεσθε** (Mark 14:41)
        and he came the third time and said to them, "**you may sleep on** now
        and **take your rest**"
    c. 2 pers. pl. aor. act. imper.
        λύσατε τὸν ναὸν τοῦτον, καὶ ἐν τρισὶν ἡμέραις ἐγερῶ αὐτόν
        (John 2:19)
        you may destroy this temple, and I will raise it up in three days

---

[2] Matt. 26:39 text is from GNT, NA & WH: TR & MT have παρελθέτω.

    d. 3 pers. pl. aor. act. imper.

      εἰ δὲ οὐκ ἐγκρατεύονται, γαμησάτωσαν (1 Cor. 7:9)

      but if they do not abstain, **let them marry**

8. Imperative of a challenge or dare by one person to another

    a. 2 pers. sing. aor. act. imper.

      εἰ υἱὸς εἶ τοῦ θεοῦ, βάλε σεαυτὸν κάτω (Matt. 4:6)

      if you are the son of God, **throw** yourself down

    b. 2 pers. pl. aor. act. imper.

      λάβετε αὐτὸν ὑμεῖς, καὶ κατὰ τὸν νόμον ὑμῶν **κρίνατε** αὐτόν
      (John 18:31)

      you take him and **judge** him according to your law

9. Imperative of greeting, an idiom with the verbs χαίρω and ῥώννυμι

    a. 2 pers. sing. pres. act. imper.

      καὶ ἤρξαντο ἀσπάζεσθαι αὐτόν, Χαῖρε, βασιλεῦ τῶν Ἰουδαίων
      (Mark 15:18)

      and they began to greet him, **"Good day,** king of the Jews"

    b. 2 pers. pl. pres. act. imper.

      καὶ ἰδοὺ Ἰησοῦς ὑπήντησεν αὐταῖς λέγων, Χαίρετε
      (Matt. 28:9)[3]

      and, behold, Jesus met them saying, **"Good morning"**

    c. 2 pers. pl. perf. pass. imper.

      ἐξ ὧν διατηροῦντες ἑαυτοὺς εὖ πράξετε. ἔρρωσθε (Acts 15:29)

      from which if you keep yourselves, you will do well. **Farewell**

10. Exclamatory imperative, drawing the attention of a person or persons

    a. 2 pers. sing. pres. act. imper.

      καὶ λέγει αὐτῷ ὁ Ἰησοῦς, ὅρα μηδενὶ εἴπῃς (Matt. 8:4)

      and Jesus said to him, **"See** [that] you speak to no one"

    b. 2 pers. pl. pres. act. imper.

      ὁρᾶτε ὅτι ἐξ ἔργων δικαιοῦται ἄνθρωπος καὶ οὐκ ἐκ πίστεως
      μόνον (James 2:24)[4]

      you see that a person is justified by works and not by faith only

11. Imperative of warning or caution with βλέπω μή or προσέχω

    a. 3 pers. sing. pres. act. imper.

      ὥστε ὁ δοκῶν ἑστάναι βλεπέτω μὴ πέσῃ (1 Cor. 10:12)

      so that the one who thinks he stands, **let him beware lest** he falls

---

[3] Matt. 28:9 text is from GNT, NA & WH: TR has ὁ Ἰησοῦς ἀπήντησεν; MT has Ἰησοῦς ἀπήντησεν.

[4] James 2:24 text is from GNT, NA & WH: TR & MT have ὁρᾶτε τοίνυν.

b. 2 pers. pl. pres. act. imper.

προσέχετε ἀπὸ τῶν γραμματέων τῶν θελόντων περιπατεῖν ἐν στολαῖς (Luke 20:46)

beware of the scribes, who desire to walk about in long flowing robes

12. Periphrastic imperative, indicating descriptive or stative action

a. 2 pers. sing. pres. indic. and nom. sing. masc. pres. act. ptc.

ὅτι ἐν ἐλαχίστῳ πιστὸς ἐγένου, **ἴσθι** ἐξουσίαν **ἔχων** ἐπάνω δέκα πόλεων (Luke 19:17)

because you were faithful with a very little, **be having** (or **you shall have**) authority over ten cities

b. 3 pers. pl. pres. indic. and. nom. pl. fem. perf. pass. ptc. with present sense

ἔστωσαν ὑμῶν αἱ ὀσφύες περιεζωσμέναι καὶ οἱ λύχνοι καιόμενοι (Luke 12:35)

let your loins be fastened with a belt and [ἔστωσαν, let your] lamps be burning

13. Elliptical imperative verbs are often taken from the context.

a. 3 pers. sing. pres. mid./pass. dep. imper.

γινέσθω δὲ ὁ θεὸς ἀληθής, **πᾶς** δὲ **ἄνθρωπος** ψεύστης (Rom. 3:4)

but let God be true, but [**γινέσθω, let**] **every man** [be] a liar

b. 3 pers. pl. pres. imper.

ἔστωσαν ὑμῶν αἱ ὀσφύες περιεζωσμέναι καὶ **οἱ λύχνοι** καιόμενοι (Luke 12:35)

let your loins be fastened with a belt and [**ἔστωσαν ὑμῶν, let your**] **lamps** [be] burning

14. Third person imperatives are frequent in NT Greek but are not found in English. Thus, they are a problem for English understanding and translation.

The third person imperatives may be classified as follows.

a. An indirect imperative is directed to a member of a specific class identified in the immediate context.

(1) 3 pers. sing. pres. act. imper.

εἴ τις ἔχει ὦτα ἀκούειν ἀκουέτω (Mark 4:23)

if anyone has ears to hear, let him listen

(2) 3 pers. sing. aor. mid. dep. and act. imper.

τότε ὁ Ἰησοῦς εἶπεν τοῖς μαθηταῖς αὐτοῦ, **εἴ τις θέλει** ὀπίσω μου ἐλθεῖν, **ἀπαρνησάσθω** ἑαυτόν καὶ **ἀράτω** τὸν σταυρὸν αὐτοῦ καὶ **ἀκολουθείτω** μοι (Matt. 16:24)

then Jesus said to his disciples, "**if anyone wants to come after me, let him deny** himself, and **let him take up** his cross, and let him follow me"

(3) 3 pers. pl. pres. act. imper.

τότε οἱ ἐν τῇ Ἰουδαίᾳ φευγέτωσαν εἰς τὰ ὄρη (Luke 21:21)

then **let those [ὄντες, who are] in Judea flee** to the mountains

b. An indirect imperative is given to a second person by referring to something belonging to that person: "your hand," "your will," "your name," etc. The use of the personal pronoun points out the indirect reference.

(1) 3 pers. sing. pres. act. imper.

μηδεὶς ὑμᾶς ἀπατάτω κενοῖς λόγοις (Eph. 5:6)

do not permit anyone to deceive you with empty words

(2) 3 pers. sing. aor. pass. imper.

τὸ ἐπιεικὲς ὑμῶν γνωσθήτω πᾶσιν ἀνθρώποις (Phil. 4:5)

let your forbearing spirit be made known to all people

c. An indirect imperative is presented to a third party, who is to respond.

(1) 3 pers. sing. aor. act. imper.

καταβάτω νῦν ἀπὸ τοῦ σταυροῦ, ἵνα ἴδωμεν καὶ πιστεύσωμεν (Mark 15:32)

let him now **come down** from the cross in order that we may see and believe

(2) 3 pers. pl. aor. act. imper.

ὁ δὲ Παῦλος ἔφη πρὸς αὐτούς, δείραντες ἡμᾶς δημοσίᾳ ἀκατακρίτους, ἀνθρώπους Ῥωμαίους ὑπάρχοντας, ἔβαλαν εἰς φυλακήν, καὶ νῦν λάθρα ἡμᾶς ἐκβάλλουσιν; οὐ γάρ, ἀλλὰ ἐλθόντες αὐτοὶ ἡμᾶς ἐξαγαγέτωσαν (Acts 16:37)[5]

but Paul said to them, "they have beaten us publicly uncondemned, even though we were Romans, and threw [ἡμᾶς, us] into prison, and now will they put us out secretly? No indeed! but **let they themselves** come **and bring** us **out**"

d. An indirect imperative is given to everyone in the defined audience with a distributive sense indicated by ἕκαστος.

(1) 3 pers. sing. pres. act. imper.

ἕκαστος δὲ βλεπέτω πῶς ἐποικοδομεῖ (1 Cor. 3:10)

but **let each one take heed** how he builds

(2) 3 pers. sing. aor. pass. imper.

καὶ βαπτισθήτω ἕκαστος ὑμῶν ἐπὶ τῷ ὀνόματι Ἰησοῦ Χριστοῦ (Acts 2:38)

and **let each one of you be baptized** in the name of Jesus Christ

---

[5] Acts 16:37 text is from GNT, NA & WH: TR & MT have ἔβαλον; TR has λάθρα; MT omits ἡμᾶς after αὐτοί.

e. An indirect imperative may be given for instructional purposes.

    (1) 3 pers. sing. pres. act. imper.

      ὃ οὖν ὁ θεὸς συνέζευξεν **ἄνθρωπος μὴ χωριζέτω** (Mark 10:9)

      what, then, God has joined together, **let no person separate**

    (2) 3 pers. pl. pres. act. imper.

      προφῆται δὲ **δύο ἢ τρεῖς λαλείτωσαν**, καὶ οἱ ἄλλοι

      διακρινέτωσαν (1 Cor. 14:29)

      but **let two or three prophets speak**, and **let the others judge**

f. An indirect imperative is used in a curse or imprecatory prayer.

    (1) 3 pers. sing. aor. pass. dep. imper. and 3 pers. sing. pres. imper.

      γέγραπται γὰρ ἐν βίβλῳ ψαλμῶν, **γενηθήτω ἡ ἔπαυλις αὐτοῦ**

      ἔρημος καὶ **μὴ ἔστω ὁ κατοικῶν** ἐν αὐτῇ (Acts 1:20)

      for it is written in the book of Psalms, **"let his residence be** empty

      and **let no one live** in it"

    (2) 3 pers. pl. aor. pass. imper.

      σκοτισθήτωσαν οἱ ὀφθαλμοὶ αὐτῶν τοῦ μὴ βλέπειν

      (Rom. 11:10)

      let their eyes be darkened so that they will not see

g. An indirect imperative is used in legal decrees.

    (1) 3 pers. sing. pres. act. imper.

      τίμα τὸν πατέρα σου καὶ τὴν μητέρα σου, καὶ, ὁ κακολογῶν

      πατέρα ἢ μητέρα **θανάτῳ τελευτάτω** (Mark 7:10)

      honor your father and your mother; and the one who speaks evil

      of father or mother, **let him die by death**

    (2) 3 pers. sing. aor. act. imper.

      ὃς ἂν ἀπολύσῃ τὴν γυναῖκα αὐτοῦ, **δότω** αὐτῇ ἀποστάσιον

      (Matt. 5:31)

      whoever shall put away his wife, **let him give** her a certificate

      of divorce

B. Voice in the imperative mood.

  1. Active voice

    a. Simple active

      (1) 2 pers. sing. pres. act. imper.

        καὶ εἷς ἐκ τῶν πρεσβυτέρων λέγει μοι, **μὴ κλαῖε** (Rev. 5:5)

        and one of the elders said to me, **"stop weeping"**

      (2) 2 pers. pl. pres. and aor. act. imper.

        ὑπάγετε ἀπαγγείλατε τοῖς ἀδελφοῖς μου ἵνα ἀπέλθωσιν

        εἰς τὴν Γαλιλαίαν (Matt. 28:10)

        go tell my brothers that they should go into Galilee

        (3) 3 pers. sing. pres. act. imper.

            ἂν δὲ τοῦτο μὴ λανθανέτω ὑμᾶς, ἀγαπητοί, ὅτι μία ἡμέρα παρὰ κυρίῳ ὡς χίλια ἔτη καὶ χίλια ἔτη ὡς ἡμέρα μία (2 Peter 3:8)

            but **let not this one thing escape** your **notice**, beloved, that one day [ἐστιν, is] as a thousand years to the Lord and a thousand years [ἐστιν, is] as one day

        (4) 3 pers. pl. aor. act. imper.

            καὶ **προσκυνησάτωσαν** αὐτῷ **πάντες ἄγγελοι** θεοῦ (Heb. 1:6)

            and **let all the angels** of God **worship** him

   b. Causal active

        (1) 2 pers. sing. aor. act. imper.

            σκοτισθήτωσαν οἱ ὀφθαλμοὶ αὐτῶν τοῦ μὴ βλέπειν, καὶ τὸν νῶτον αὐτῶν διὰ παντὸς **σύγκαμψον** (Rom. 11:10)[6]

            let their eyes be darkened so that they will not see and **cause** their backs **to bend** continually

        (2) 3 pers. sing. pres. act. imper.

            τοῦ λοιποῦ κόπους μοι **μηδεὶς παρεχέτω** (Gal. 6:17)

            from now on, **let no one cause** me trouble

   c. Stative active, primarily in the present tense

        (1) 2 pers. sing. pres. act. imper.

            σὺ δὲ **μένε** ἐν οἷς ἔμαθες καὶ ἐπιστώθης (2 Tim. 3:14)

            but **you remain** in the things that you learned and were assured of

        (2) 3 pers. sing. pres. act. imper.

            ἐὰν δὲ μὴ ᾖ διερμηνευτής, **σιγάτω** ἐν ἐκκλησίᾳ (1 Cor. 14:28)

            but if there is no translator, **let him remain silent** in the church

        (3) 2 pers. pl. pres. act. imper.

            ἀλλήλων τὰ βάρη **βαστάζετε** (Gal. 6:2)

            carry the burdens of one another

        (4) 3 pers. pl. pres. act. imper.

            ἀλλὰ μᾶλλον **δουλευέτωσαν**, ὅτι πιστοί εἰσιν (1 Tim. 6:2)

            but rather **let them serve** [αὐτούς, them] because they are believers

 2. Middle voice in the imperative mood

   a. Deponent middle (mid./pass. in pres. tense)

        (1) 3 pers. sing. pres. mid./pass. dep. imper. (exhortation)

            ὁ δὲ καυχώμενος ἐν κυρίῳ **καυχάσθω** (2 Cor. 10:17)

            but he who boasts, **let him boast** in the Lord

---

[6] Rom. 11:10 text is from GNT, NA, TR*b* & MT: WH has σύνκαμψον; TR*s* has διαπαντός.

    (2) 2 pers. sing. pres. mid./pass. dep. imper. (prohibitive with μή)

κατὰ πρεσβυτέρου κατηγορίαν **μὴ παραδέχου** ἐκτὸς εἰ μὴ ἐπὶ δύο ἢ τριῶν μαρτύρων (1 Tim. 5:19)

do not receive an accusation against an elder except before two or three witnesses

    (3) 2 pers. pl. pres. mid./pass. dep. imper. (exhortation)

καὶ τὴν τοῦ κυρίου ἡμῶν μακροθυμίαν σωτηρίαν **ἡγεῖσθε** (2 Peter 3:15)

and **regard** the patience of our Lord [to be] salvation

    (4) 3 pers. pl. aor. mid. dep. imper.

προσκαλεσάσθω τοὺς πρεσβυτέρους τῆς ἐκκλησίας, καὶ **προσευξάσθωσαν** ἐπ᾽ αὐτόν (James 5:14)

let him call for the elders of the church, and **let them pray** over him

  b. Reflexive middle

    (1) 2 pers. sing. pres. mid./pass. imper.

ἔχοντες μόρφωσιν εὐσεβείας τὴν δὲ δύναμιν αὐτῆς ἠρνημένοι, καὶ τούτους **ἀποτρέπου** (2 Tim. 3:5)

being religious in appearance, but denying its power, **turn yourself away from** these things also

    (2) 3 pers. sing. pres. mid./pass. imper.

εἰ δὲ αἰσχρὸν γυναικὶ τὸ κείρασθαι ἢ ξυρᾶσθαι, **κατακαλυπτέσθω** (1 Cor. 11:6)

but if to be shorn or shaven [ἐστιν, is] a shame; **let her cover herself**

    (3) 2 pers. pl. aor. mid. imper.

ἐνδύσασθε τὴν πανοπλίαν τοῦ θεοῦ (Eph. 6:11)

clothe yourselves with the full armor of God

    (4) 3 pers. pl. pres. mid./pass. imper.

οὐ γὰρ ἐπιτρέπεται αὐταῖς λαλεῖν, ἀλλὰ **ὑποτασσέσθωσαν**, καθὼς καὶ ὁ νόμος λέγει (1 Cor. 14:34)

for it is not permitted for them to speak; but **let them submit themselves**, even as the law says

  c. Middle with active meaning different from the active meaning

    (1) 2 pers. sing. pres. mid./pass. imper. (prohibitive with μή)

μή μου **ἅπτου**, οὔπω γὰρ ἀναβέβηκα πρὸς τὸν πατέρα (John 20:17)

do not hold me, for I have not yet ascended to my father

    (2)   2 pers. pl. pres. mid./pass. imper. (prohibitive with μή)

         καὶ ἀκαθάρτου μὴ ἅπτεσθε· κἀγὼ εἰσδέξομαι ὑμᾶς
         (2 Cor. 6:17)

         and **do not touch** the unclean thing, and I will receive you

3.   Passive voice

     a.   Deponent passive

         (1)   2 pers. sing. aor. pass. dep. imper. (command)

             καὶ λέγω τούτῳ, **πορεύθητι**, καὶ πορεύεται (Matt. 8:9)

             and I tell this one, **"go,"** and he goes

         (2)   3 pers. sing. aor. pass. dep. imper. (request, prayer)

             γενηθήτω τὸ θέλημά σου (Matt. 6:10)

             let your will be done

         (3)   2 pers. pl. aor. pass. dep. imper. (exhortation)

             φοβήθητε τὸν θεόν καὶ δότε αὐτῷ δόξαν (Rev. 14:7)

             fear God, and give glory to Him

     b.   Theological passive

         (1)   2 pers. sing. aor. pass. imper. (command)

             καὶ ἀναβλέψας εἰς τὸν οὐρανὸν ἐστέναξεν, καὶ λέγει αὐτῷ,
             Εφφαθα, ὅ ἐστιν, **Διανοίχθητι** (Mark 7:34)[7]

             and when he lifted up his eyes to heaven he sighed and said
             to him, "ephata," which means, **"be opened"**

         (2)   3 pers. sing. aor. pass. imper. (exhortation)

             ὁ γέλως ὑμῶν εἰς πένθος **μετατραπήτω** καὶ ἡ χαρὰ εἰς
             κατήφειαν (James 4:9)[8]

             let your laughter be turned to mourning, and [**ὑμῶν μετατραπήτω,**
             let your] joy [be turned] to gloominess

         (3)   2 pers. pl. aor. pass. imper. (invitation)

             σώθητε ἀπὸ τῆς γενεᾶς τῆς σκολιᾶς ταύτης (Acts 2:40)

             be saved from this crooked generation

     c.   Agent or instrument of passive verb indicated by a preposition

         (1)   3 pers. sing. aor. pass. imper. (exhortation)

             ἕκαστος ἐν τῷ ἰδίῳ νοῒ **πληροφορείσθω** (Rom. 14:5)

             let each one be fully assured by his own mind

         (2)   2 pers. sing. pres. pass. imper. (prohibitive with μή)

             μὴ νικῶ ὑπὸ τοῦ κακοῦ ἀλλὰ νίκα ἐν τῷ ἀγαθῷ τὸ κακόν
             (Rom. 12:21)

             do not be conquered by evil, but conquer evil by good

---

[7]   Mark 7:34 text is from GNT & NA: WH, TR & MT have Ἐφφαθά.

[8]   James 4:9 text is from GNT, NA & WH: TR & MT have μεταστραφήτω.

(3) 2 pers. pl. pres. pass. imper. (exhortation)
καὶμὴ μεθύσκεσθε οἴνῳ, ἐν ᾧ ἐστιν ἀσωτία, ἀλλὰ
πληροῦσθε ἐν πνεύματι (Eph. 5:18)
and do not be drunk with wine, in which is debauchery, but
be filled with [or, **by**] **the spirit**

(4) 3 pers. pl. pres. pass. imper. (exhortation)
ὥστε καὶ οἱ πάσχοντες κατὰ τὸ θέλημα τοῦ θεοῦ πιστῷ
κτίστῃ παρατιθέσθωσαν τὰς ψυχὰς αὐτῶν ἐν ἀγαθοποιΐᾳ
(1 Peter 4:19)[9]
wherefore also **let those who suffer** according to the will of God
entrust their lives to a faithful creator **by doing good**

d. Passive with agent unexpressed, whether unimportant or implied
within context

(1) 2 pers. sing. aor. pass. imper. (command)
τούτους παραλαβὼν ἁγνίσθητι σὺν αὐτοῖς (Acts 21:24)
take them and **be purified** with them

(2) 3 pers. sing. pres. pass. imper. (prohibitive with μή)
καὶ μὴ βαρείσθω ἡ ἐκκλησία, ἵνα ταῖς ὄντως χήραις
ἐπαρέσκῃ (1 Tim. 5:16)
and **do not let the church be burdened**, in order that it [the
church] may help those who are really widows

(3) 2 pers. pl. pres. pass. imper. (prohibitive with μή)
ὅταν δὲ ἀκούσητε πολέμους καὶ ἀκοὰς πολέμων, μὴ
θροεῖσθε (Mark 13:7)
but when you hear of wars and reports of wars, **do not be troubled**

(4) 3 pers. pl. pres. pass. imper. (exhortation)
οἱ καλῶς προεστῶτες πρεσβύτεροι διπλῆς τιμῆς
ἀξιούσθωσαν (1 Tim. 5:17)
let the elders who manage well be counted worthy of double honor

e. Passive with active meaning

(1) 2 pers. sing. pres. mid./pass. imper. (permission)
καὶ ἐρῶ τῇ ψυχῇ μου, Ψυχή, ἔχεις πολλὰ ἀγαθὰ κείμενα
εἰς ἔτη πολλά, ἀναπαύου, φάγε, πίε, εὐφραίνου
(Luke 12:19)
and I will say to my soul, "soul, you have many goods laid
up for many years; rest, eat, drink, **rejoice**"

---

[9] 1 Peter 4:19 text is from GNT & NA: WH omits αὐτῶν; TR & MT have ὡς after θεοῦ; TR has ἑαυτῶν for αὐτῶν.

(2) 2 pers. pl. aor. pass. imper. (invitation)

καὶ πάλιν λέγει, **Εὐφράνθητε**, ἔθνη, μετὰ τοῦ λαοῦ αὐτοῦ (Rom. 15:10)

and again he says, "**rejoice**, nations, with his people"

f. Passive with dative as agent

(1) 2 pers. sing. pres. pass. imper. (prohibitive with μή)

ἀγαπητοί, **μὴ ξενίζεσθε** τῇ ἐν ὑμῖν **πυρώσει** πρὸς πειρασμον ὑμῖν γινομένῃ (1 Peter 4:12)

beloved friends, **do not be surprised by the burning** among you, for the trial taking place against you

(2) 3 pers. sing. aor. pass. imper. (exhortation)

τὸ ἐπιεικὲς ὑμῶν **γνωσθήτω** πᾶσιν ἀνθρώποις (Phil. 4:5)

let your forbearing spirit be known by all people

(3) 2 pers. pl. pres. pass. imper. (exhortation)

καὶ **μὴ συσχηματίζεσθε** τῷ αἰῶνι τούτῳ, ἀλλὰ **μεταμορφοῦσθε** τῇ ἀνακαινώσει τοῦ νοός (Rom. 12:2)

and **do not be guided by this age**, but **be transformed by the renewal** of [your] mind

g. Passive with reflexive sense

(1) 2 pers. sing. aor. pass. imper. (command)

εἶπεν δὲ τὸ πνεῦμα τῷ Φιλίππῳ, πρόσελθε καὶ **κολλήθητι** τῷ ἄρματι τούτῳ (Acts 8:29)

and the Spirit said to Philip, "**join yourself** to the chariot"

(2) 2 pers. pl. aor. pass. imper. (exhortation)

ταπεινώθητε οὖν ὑπὸ τὴν κραταιὰν χεῖρα τοῦ θεοῦ (1 Peter 5:6)

humble yourselves, then, under the mighty hand of God

4. Voiceless verb, εἰμι

a. 2 pers. sing. pres. imper. (command)

καὶ φεῦγε εἰς Αἴγυπτον, καὶ **ἴσθι** ἐκεῖ ἕως ἂν εἴπω σοι (Matt. 2:13)

and flee into Egypt, and **live** there until I speak to you

b. 3 pers. sing. pres. imper. (exhoration)

γνωστὸν οὖν **ἔστω** ὑμῖν ὅτι τοῖς ἔθνεσιν ἀπεστάλη τοῦτο τὸ σωτήριον τοῦ θεοῦ (Acts 28:28)[10]

let it be known, then, to you, that this salvation of God has been sent to the nations

c. 3 pers. pl. pres. imper.

διάκονοι **ἔστωσαν** μιᾶς γυναικὸς ἄνδρες (1 Tim. 3:12)

let those who serve be husbands of one wife

---

[10] Acts 28:28 text is from GNT, NA & WH: TR & MT omit τοῦτο.

C. Tense. The imperative is found in three tenses: present, aorist, and perfect. The perfect occurs only five times in the NT and with a present sense; thus, in reality the imperative occurs only in the present and aorist tenses. The present tense denotes progressive, iterative, or stative action, rather than temporal action. Tense in the sense of past, present, or future is not found in the imperative mood. The present tense prohibitive rather calls for the cessation of an action already going on (as made clear from the context) or to avoid such an action as a general precept. The aorist denotes undefined action as to progress or state. Buist Fanning makes a distinction between *general precepts* and *specific commands*.

> *General precept*: A moral regulation which is broadly applicable; a rule for conduct to be applied in multiple situations; a comman or prohibition to be followed by an individual or a group not only in the immediate situation in which it is given, but also in subsequent (repeated or continuing) circumstances in which the precept is appropriate. *Specific command*: An order or request for action to be done in a particular instance. The speaker commands or prohibits some attitude or action, but does so only in reference to the immediate circumstances and hearers involved: he does not intend to regulate conduct in broader terms.[11]

As a general (not universal) rule or guideline, the present tense is the normal tense for a general precept, and the aorist is the normal tense for a specific command.

1. Present tense
   a. The prohibitive imperative with μή, μηδείς, μηδέ, and μηκέτι is always in the present tense. The prohibitive aorist with μή is used only in the subjunctive mood, and the prohibitive future is found with οὐ in the indicative.
      (1) 2 pers. sing. pres. act. imper. (prohibitive pres. imper. with μή)
         μὴ ἕνεκεν βρώματος **κατάλυε** τὸ ἔργον τοῦ θεοῦ (Rom. 14:20)
         do not destroy the work of God for the sake of meat
      (2) 2 pers. sing. aor. act. subj. (prohibitive aor. subj. with μή)
         καὶ τὸ ἔλαιον καὶ τὸν οἶνον **μὴ ἀδικήσῃς** (Rev. 6:6)
         and **do not damage** the oil and the wine
      (3) 2 pers. sing. fut. act. indic. (prohibitive fut. indic. with οὐ)
         ἠκούσατε ὅτι ἐρρέθη τοῖς ἀρχαίοις, **οὐ φονεύσεις** (Matt. 5:21)
         you have heard that it was said to the men of ancient times,
         "you shall not commit murder"

---

[11] Buist Fanning, *Verbal Aspect in New Testament Greek* (Oxford: Clarendon, 1990), 327-28.

b. The progressive, iterative, customary, or habitual sense is prominent in the present tense.
   (1) 2 pers. pl. pres. act. imper. (exhortation)
       κἀγὼ ὑμῖν λέγω, **αἰτεῖτε**, καὶ δοθήσεται ὑμῖν· **ζητεῖτε**, καὶ εὑρήσετε· **κρούετε**, καὶ ἀνοιγήσεται ὑμῖν (Luke 11:9)
       and I say to you, **repeatedly ask**, and it shall be give to you; **constantly seek**, and you shall find; **continually knock**, and it shall be opened to you
   (2) 2 pers. sing. pres. act. imper. (exhortation)
       σὺ δὲ ἀπελθὼν **διάγγελλε** τὴν βασιλείαν τοῦ θεοῦ (Luke 9:60)
       but **you** go and **proclaim** the kingdom of God
c. The general precept is usually in the present tense.
   (1) 2 pers. sing. pres. act. imper. (command)
       ὁ γὰρ θεὸς εἶπεν, **τίμα** τὸν πατέρα καὶ τὴν μητέρα (Matt. 15:4)
       for God said, "**Honor** your father and your mother"
   (2) 2 pers. pl. pres. act. imper. (exhortation)
       καὶ καθὼς θέλετε ἵνα ποιῶσιν ὑμῖν οἱ ἄνθρωποι **ποιεῖτε** αὐτοῖς ὁμοίως (Luke 6:31)[12]
       even as you want people to treat you, **you treat** them in the same way
d. Idiomatic use of present imperatives in specific commands (e.g., ἀκολουθέω, ἐγείρω, ἔρχομαι, περιπατέω, πορεύομαι, ὑπάγω, φέρω)
   (1) 2 pers. sing. pres. mid./pass. dep. imper. (command)
       ἐγερθεὶς παράλαβε τὸ παιδίον καὶ τὴν ματέρα αὐτοῦ, καὶ **πορεύου** εἰς γῆν Ἰσραήλ (Matt. 2:20)
       arise and take the child and his mother and **go** into the land of Israel
   (2) 2 pers. pl. pres. act. imper. (command)
       ὑπάγετε εἴπατε τοῖς μαθηταῖς αὐτοῦ καὶ τῷ Πέτρῳ, ὅτι προάγει ὑμᾶς εἰς τὴν Γαλιλαίαν (Mark 16:7)
       Go tell his disciples and Peter, that he is going before you into Galilee

---

[12] Luke 6:31 text is from GNT, NA & WH: TR & MT have καὶ ὑμεῖς ποιεῖτε.

2. Aorist tense in the imperative mood
   a. The aorist tense is normally used in prayers. However, in Luke the present tense is used for one of the petitions of the Lord's prayer.
      (1) 3 pers. sing. aor. act. and pass. imper. (request)
      πάτερ ἡμῶν ὁ ἐν τοῖς οὐρανοῖς, **ἁγιασθήτω τὸ ὄνομά σου**· **ἐλθέτω ἡ βασιλεία σου. γενηθήτω τὸ θέλημά σου** . . . τὸν ἄρτον ἡμῶν τὸν ἐπιούσιον **δὸς** ἡμῖν σήμερον· καὶ **ἄφες** ἡμῖν τὰ ὀφειλήματα ἡμῶν . . . καὶ **μὴ εἰσενέγκῃς** ἡμᾶς εἰς πειρασμόν, ἀλλὰ **ῥῦσαι** ἡμᾶς ἀπὸ τοῦ πονηροῦ (Matt. 6:9-13)
      our Father who [ὤν, is] in heaven, **let your name be sanctified**; **let your kingdom come**; let your will be done . . . **give** us today our needed bread; and **forgive** us our debts . . . and **do not bring** us into temptation, but **deliver** us from the evil one
      (2) 3 pers. sing. pres. act. imper. (request)
      τὸν ἄρτον ἡμῶν τὸν ἐπιούσιον **δίδου** ἡμῖν τὸ καθ' ἡμέραν (Luke 11:3)
      give us our needed bread daily
   b. The specific command is usually in the aorist tense.
      (1) 2 pers. sing. aor. mid. imper. (command)
      καὶ εἶπεν αὐτῷ, ὕπαγε, **νίψαι** εἰς τὴν κολυμβήθραν τοῦ Σιλωάμ (John 9:7)
      and he said to him, "go, **wash yourself** in the pool of Siloam"
      (2) 2 pers. pl. aor. act. imper. (command)
      πορευθέντες **ἀπαγγείλατε** Ἰωάννῃ ἃ εἴδετε καὶ ἠκούσατε (Luke 7:22)[13]
      go and **report** to John what you have seen and heard
   c. The aorist tense is sometimes used idiomatically in a general precept with some verbs.
      (1) 3 pers. sing. aor. pass. imper. (exhortation)
      πᾶσα πικρία καὶ **θυμὸς** καὶ **ὀργὴ** καὶ **κραυγὴ** καὶ **βλασφημία ἀρθήτω** ἀφ' ὑμῶν (Eph. 4:31)
      let every king of bitterness and **rage** and **anger** and **quarreling** and **abusive speech be removed** from you
      (2) 2 pers. pl. aor. mid. imper. (exhortation)
      ἐνδύσασθε τὸν κύριον Ἰησοῦν Χριστόν, καὶ τῆς σαρκὸς πρόνοιαν μὴ ποιεῖσθε εἰς ἐπιθυμίας (Rom. 13:14)
      clothe yourselves with the Lord Jesus Christ and do not make provision for the flesh to lust

---

[13] Luke 7:22 text is from GNT, NA, TR & MT: WH has Ἰωάνῃ.

Select Bibliography for the Imperative Mood

Bakker, W. F. *The Greek Imperative*. Amsterdam: Adolf M. Hakkert, 1966.

Bammel, E. "The Command in 1 Peter 2:17." *New Testament Studies* 11 (1964-65): 279-81.

Barrett, Walter C. "The Use of Tense in the Imperative Mood in First Corinthians." M.Th. thesis, Dallas Theological Seminary, 1973.

Boyer, James L. "A Classification of Imperatives: A Statistical Study." *Grace Theological Journal* 8, no. 1 (1987): 35-54.

_____. *Supplemental Manual of Information: Imperative Verbs*. Winona Lake, Ind.: Morgan Library, Grace Theological Seminary, 1987.

Burton, Ernest De Witt. *Syntax of the Moods and Tenses in New Testament Greek*. 3d ed. Edinburgh: T & T Clark, 1955.

Daube, David. "The Participle and Imperative in 1 Peter." 2d ed. Edited by E.G.Selwyn. *The First Epistle of Peter*. Grand Rapids: Baker, 1981, 467-88.

Elliott, Ray. "Functions of the Third Person Imperative Verb Forms in the Greek New Testament." *Notes on Translation* 69: 30-31.

Fanning, Buist M. *Verbal Aspect in the Greek of the New Testament*. Oxford: Clarendon, 1990.

Fernando, Andrew P. "Translation of Questions and Prohibitions in Greek." *Bible Translator* 27, no. 1 (January 1976): 138-42.

Glaze, Judy. "The Septuagintal Use of the Third Person Imperative." Master's thesis, Harding Graduate School of Religion, 1979.

Heidt, William. "Translating New Testament Imperatives." Catholic Biblical Quarterly 13 (1951): 253-56.

McKay, K. L. "Aspect in Imperatival Construction in New Testament Greek." *Novum Testamentum* 27, no. 3 (1985): 201-26.

Morrice, William G. "Translating the Greek Imperative." Bible Translator 24, no. 2 (January 1973): 129-34.

Mozley, F. W. "Notes on the Biblical Use of the Present and Aorist Imperative." *Journal of Theological Studies* 4 (1903): 279-82.

Osborn, Carroll D. "The Third Person Imperative in Acts 2:38." *Restoration Quarterly* (1979-80): 81-84.

Porter, Stanley E. *Verbal Aspect in the Greek of the New Testament with Reference to Tense and Mood*. New York: Peter Lang, 1989.

Thorley, John. "Aktionsart in New Testament Greek: Infinitive and Imperative." *Novum Testamentum* 31, no. 4 (1989): 290-315.

Wallace, Daniel B. "ὀργίζεσθε in Ephesians 4:26; command or condition?" *Criswell Theological Review* 3, no. 2 (1984): 353-72.

FINITE VERBS

Optative Mood

IV. **Optative mood**. The term *optative* means "to wish." It is the mood of possibility. However, it is impossible to state one concept or definition that will fit all of the uses of this mood.

  A. Kinds of optatives. There are two basic functions of the optative: volitive and potential.
    1. Volitive, expression of the will
      a. Expression of a wish or a prayer
        (1) 1 pers. sing. aor. mid. dep. opt. (optative of request)
          ναὶ ἀδελφέ, ἐγώ σου ὀναίμην ἐν κυρίῳ (Philem. 20)[1]
          yes, brother, **may I benefit** from you in the Lord
        (2) 3 pers. sing. aor. act. opt. (optative of a prayer for blessing)
          ὁ δὲ θεὸς τῆς εἰρήνης . . . **καταρτίσαι** ὑμᾶς . . . εἰς τὸ
          ποιῆσαι τὸ θέλημα αὐτοῦ (Heb. 13:20-21)
          may the God of peace . . . **perfect** you . . . to do His will
        (3) 3 pers. sing. aor. pass. opt. (optative of benediction)
          καὶ ὁλόκληρον ὑμῶν τὸ πνεῦμα καὶ ἡ ψυχὴ καὶ τὸ σῶμα
          ἀμέμπτως ἐν τῇ παρουσίᾳ τοῦ κυρίου ἡμῶν Ἰησοῦ Χριστοῦ
          τηρηθείη (1 Thess. 5:23*b*)
          and **may your whole spirit** and **soul** and **body be kept** blamelessly at the coming of our Lord Jesus Christ
      b. Expression of a strong emphatic wish or prayer
        (1) 3 pers. sing. aor. mid. dep. opt (μὴ γένοιτο)[2]
          τί οὖν ἐροῦμεν; ὁ νόμος ἁμαρτία; **μὴ γένοιτο** (Rom. 7:7)
          what, then, shall we say? [ἐστιν, is] the law sin? **Absolutely not!**
        (2) 3 pers. sing. aor. mid. dep. opt. (γένοιτο, optative of willing permission)
          εἶπεν δὲ Μαριάμ, ἰδού ἡ δούλη κυρίου· γένοιτό μοι κατὰ
          τὸ ῥῆμά σου (Luke 1:38)
          and Mary said, "here [ἐστιν, is] the handmaid of the Lord; **let it happen** to me according to your word"

---

[1] Philem. 20 is "the only NT example of the first person optative to express a wish" (C. F. D. Moule, *An Idiom-Book of New Testament Greek*, 23). This verse is "the only proper optative without ἄν which is not 3d person" (J. H. Moulton, *Grammar of New Testament Greek*, 1:194-95).

[2] NASB translates μὴ γένοιτο, "may it never be." NRJB translates it, "Certainly not!" KJV, "God forbid." NIV uses various phrases, "Not at all!" "By no means!" "Absolutely not!" "May it never be." "Certainly not!" "Far from it." "Never." "It is used as an exclamation of revulsion, indignant and strong rejection" (James Boyer, "The Classification of Optatives: A Statistical Study." *Grace Theological Journal* 9, no. 1 [1988]: 130).

361

   (3) 3 pers. sing. aor. act. opt. (adverse wish, curse, imprecation)

        καὶ ἀποκριθεὶς εἶπεν αὐτῇ, μηκέτι εἰς τὸν αἰῶνα ἐκ σοῦ **μηδεὶς καρπὸν φάγοι** (Mark 11:14)[3]

        and he said to it, "**let no one eat** fruit anymore from you forever"

2. Potential optatives. The term *potential* limits the action: that is, it is dependent upon certain circumstances or conditions. The NT uses of the potential optative are limited to questions and conditional statements.

   a. Direct questions

      (1) 1 pers. sing. pres. mid./pass. dep. opt.

          ὁ δὲ εἶπε(ν), **πῶς γὰρ ἂν δυναίμην** ἐὰν μή τις ὁδηγήσει με; (Acts 8:31)[4]

          but he said, "**how can I** unless someone guides me?"

      (2) 3 pers. sing. pres. act. opt.

          καί τινες ἔλεγον· **τί ἂν θέλοι** ὁ σπερμολόγος οὗτος λέγειν; (Acts 17:18)

          and some were saying, "**what could this babbler wish** to say?"

   b. Indirect questions

      (1) 3 pers. sing. pres. act. opt. (with τί ἄν)

          ἐνένευον δὲ τῷ πατρὶ αὐτοῦ τὸ **τί ἂν θέλοι** καλεῖσθαι αὐτό (Luke 1:62)[5]

          and they were making signs to his father **what he wanted** him to be named

      (2) 3 pers. pl. aor. act. opt. (with εἰ)

          ζητεῖν τὸν θεόν, εἰ ἄρα γε **ψηλαφήσειαν** αὐτὸν καὶ **εὕροιεν** (Acts 17:27)[6]

          to seek God, **whether** perhaps **they might grope after** him and **might find** [him]

   c. The potential optative is found in the protasis of a conditional statement, but the apodosis is left incomplete or absent. Thus, it is not a true fourth class condition.

      (1) 3 pers. sing. aor. act. opt.

          τοσαῦτα εἰ **τύχοι** γένη φωνῶν εἰσιν ἐν κόσμῳ (1 Cor. 14:10)[7]

          if it so happens [that] many kinds of voices exist

---

[3] Mark 11:14 text is from GNT, NA & WH: TR & MT have ὁ Ἰησοῦς εἶπεν αὐτῇ μηκέτι ἐκ σου ἐν τὸν αἰῶνα.

[4] Acts 8:31 text is from GNT, NA & WH: TR & MT have ὁδηγήσῃ.

[5] Luke 1:62 text is from GNT, NA & WH: TR & MT have αὐτόν for αὐτό.

[6] Acts 17:27 text is from GNT, NA & WH: TR & MT have τὸν κύριον for τὸν θεόν; TR*b* has εἰ ἄραγε.

[7] 1 Cor. 14:10 text is from GNT & NA: WH has εἰσίν; TR & MT have ἐστιν for εἰσιν.

(2) 3 pers. pl. aor. act. opt.

οὓς ἔδει ἐπὶ σοῦ παρεῖναι καὶ κατηγορεῖν **εἴ τι ἔχοιεν** πρὸς ἐμέ
(Acts 24:19)[8]

who ought to appear before you and accuse **whether they might
have anything** against me

B. Voices with optatives.
   1. Active voice
      a. Simple active
         (1) 3 pers. sing. aor. act. opt. (strong wish or prayer/benediction)
            ὁ δὲ **θεὸς** τῆς εἰρήνης . . . **καταρτίσαι** ὑμᾶς ἐν παντὶ ἀγαθῷ
            (Heb. 13:20–21)[9]

            now **may the God** of peace . . . **perfect** you in every good [thing]
         (2) 2 pers. pl. pres. act. opt. (potential indirect question with εἰ)
            ἀλλ᾽ **εἰ** καὶ **πάσχοιτε** διὰ δικαιοσύνην, μακάριοι
            (1 Peter 3:14)

            but **if you** also **suffer** on account of righteousness, [ἐστε, you are]
            blessed
         (3) 3 pers. pl. aor. act. opt. (potential indirect question with εἰ)
            ζητεῖν τὸν θεόν, **εἰ** ἄρα γε **ψηλαφήσειαν** αὐτὸν καὶ εὕροιεν
            (Acts 17:27)[10]

            to seek God, **whether** perhaps **they might grope after** him and
            might find [him]
      b. Stative active
         (1) 3 pers. sing. pres. act. opt. (indirect question with εἰ)
            καὶ ὃ σπείρεις, οὐ τὸ σῶμα τὸ γενησόμενον σπείρεις ἀλλὰ
            γυμνὸν κόκκον **εἰ τύχοι** σίτου ἤ τινος τῶν λοιπῶν (1 Cor. 15:37)
            and whatever you sow, you do not sow the body, which shall be
            but bare seed, **whether it happens to be** wheat or one of the
            other [seeds]
         (2) 3 pers. pl. pres. act. opt. (potential indirect question with εἰ)
            οὓς ἔδει ἐπὶ σοῦ παρεῖναι καὶ κατηγορεῖν **εἴ τι ἔχοιεν**
            πρὸς ἐμέ (Acts 24:19)[11]
            who ought to appear before you and accuse, **whether they might
            have anything** against me

---

[8] Acts 24:19 text is from GNT, NA & WH: TR*s* & MT have δεῖ; TR & MT have πρός με.

[9] Heb. 13:20-21 text is from GNT, NA & WH: TR & MT have ἔργῳ ἀγαθῷ.

[10] Acts 17:27 text is from GNT, NA & WH: TR & MT have τὸν κύριον for τὸν θεόν; TR*b* has εἰ ἄραγε.

[11] Acts 24:19 text is from GNT, NA & WH: TR*s* & MT have δεῖ; TR & MT have πρός με.

2. Middle voice, all middle optative forms are deponent.
   a. 1 pers. sing. pres. mid./pass. dep. opt. (potential indirect question with πῶς ἄν)
      ὁ δὲ εἶπεν, πῶς γὰρ ἂν δυναίμην ἐὰν μή τις ὁδηγήσει με; (Acts 8:31)[12]
      but he said, **"how can I** unless someone guides me?"
   b. 3 pers. sing. aor. mid. dep. opt. (strong wish or prayer)
      ἐμοὶ δὲ μὴ γένοιτο καυχᾶσθαι εἰ μὴ ἐν τῷ σταυρῷ τοῦ κυρίου ἡμῶν Ἰησοῦ Χριστοῦ (Gal. 6:14)
      but **may I not boast** except in the cross of our Lord Jesus Christ
   c. 3 pers. pl. pres. mid./pass. dep. opt. (indirect question with εἰ)
      κόλπον δέ τινα κατενόουν ἔχοντα αἰγιαλὸν εἰς ὃν ἐβουλεύοντο εἰ δύναιντο ἐξῶσαι τὸ πλοῖον (Acts 27:39)[13]
      but they were looking at a bay having a beach, into which they were deciding **whether they were able** to run the ship ashore
3. Passive voice, theological passive
   3 pers. sing. aor. pass. opt. (strong wish or prayer/benediction)
   ἔλεος ὑμῖν καὶ εἰρήνη καὶ ἀγάπη πληθυνθείη (Jude 2)
   may mercy and **peace** and **love be multiplied** to you
4. Voiceless εἰμι
   3 pers. sing. pres. opt. (indirect question)
   προσδοκῶντος δὲ τοῦ λαοῦ, καὶ διαλογιζομένων πάντων ἐν ταῖς καρδίαις αὐτῶν περὶ τοῦ Ἰωάννου, μήποτε αὐτὸς εἴη ὁ Χριστός (Luke 3:15)[14]
   but while the people were expecting and all were considering in their hearts concerning John, **whether or not he might be** the Christ

C. Tense. Of the sixty-eight times the optative is found in the NT, twenty-three verbs are in the present tense and forty-five verbs are in the aorist tense.
   1. Present tense
      a. Most present tense optatives are stative.
         3 pers. sing. pres. opt.
         ἐπυνθάνετο τί εἴη τοῦτο (Luke 18:36)
         he inquired **what this might mean**

---

[12] Acts 8:31 text is from GNT, NA & WH: TR & MT have ὁδηγήσῃ.

[13] Acts 27:39 text is from GNT, NA & WH: TR & MT have ἐβουλεύσαντο.

[14] Luke 3:15 text is from GNT, NA, TR & MT: WH has Ἰωάνου.

b. Iterative or progressive present
2 pers. pl. pres. act. opt.

ἀλλ᾽ εἰ καὶ **πάσχοιτε** διὰ δικαιοσύνην, μακάριοι (1 Peter 3:14)
but **if you** also **suffer** on account of righteousness, [ἐστε, you are]
blessed

2. Aorist tense indicates undefined action as to progress, state, or results.

a. 3 pers. sing. aor. pass. opt. (negative prayer)
ἐν τῇ πρώτῃ μου ἀπολογίᾳ οὐδείς μοι παρεγένετο, ἀλλὰ πάντες με
ἐγκατέλιπον· **μὴ** αὐτοῖς **λογισθείη** (2 Tim. 4:16)
at my first defense no one stood with me, but all deserted me; **may it
not be counted** against them

b. 3 pers. pl. aor. act. opt. (future aoristic action)
καὶ διελάλουν πρὸς ἀλλήλους **τί ἂν ποιήσαιεν** τῷ Ἰησοῦ
(Luke 6:11)[15]
and they were discussing with one another **what they might do** to
Jesus

Select Bibliography for the Optative Mood

Baima, John K. "Making Valid Conclusions from Greek Conditional Sentences."
Master's thesis, Grace Theological Seminary, 1986.

Boyer, James L. "Third (and Fourth) Class Conditions." *Grace Theological Journal* 2
(1982): 163-75.

_____. "Other Conditional Elements in New Testament Greek." *Grace
Theological Journal* 4, no. 2 (Fall 1983): 173-88.

_____. "The Classification of Optatives: A Statistical Study." *Grace Theological
Journal* 9, no. 1 (1988): 129-40.

_____. *Supplemental Manual of Information: Optative Verbs.* Winona Lake, Ind.:
Morgan Library, Grace Theological Seminary, 1985.

Burton, Ernest De Witt. *Syntax of the Moods and Tenses in the New Testament Greek.* 3d ed.
Edinburgh: T & T Clark, 1965.

de Plooy, Gerhard P. V. "The Use of the Optative in Luke-Acts: Grammatical
Classifications and Implications for Translation." *Scriptura* 19 (1986): 25-43.

Elliott, William E. "Conditional Sentences in the New Testament." Th.D. diss., Grace
Theological Seminary, 1981.

Fanning, Buist M. *Verbal Aspect in New Testament Greek.* Oxford: Clarendon, 1990.

---

[15] Luke 6:11 text is from GNT, NA & WH: TR & MT have ποιήσειαν.

Greenlee, J. Harold. "'If' in the New Testament." *Bible Translator* 13, no. 1 (1962): 39-43.

Heinz, Vincent A. "The Optative Mood in the Greek New Testament." Master's thesis, Dallas Theological Seminary, 1962.

Kujne, John H. "Greek Conditional Sentences." *Bible Translator* 13 (October 1962): 223-24.

Porter, Stanley E. *Verbal Aspect in the Greek of the New Testament with Reference to Tense and Mood.* New York: Peter Lang, 1989.

Roberts, J. W. "Some Aspects of Conditional Sentences in the Greek New Testament." *Bible Translator* 15, no. 2 (1964): 70-76.

Wuest, Kenneth S. "The Eloquence of Greek Tenses and Moods." *Bibliotheca Sacra* 117, no. 466 (April 1960): 134-43.

INFINITIVES

Infinitives differ from finite verbs in that infinitives have no person or plural number. The infinitive is always singular in number (though used with plural substantives) and always neuter in gender, thus differing from the participle that has both number and all three genders. Infinitives function as both verbs and nouns and thus are called verbal nouns. Infinitives are found in four tenses: present, aorist, perfect, and future.

I. **Kinds of infinitives**. Infinitives may function as substantives and adverbs, but without losing the function of a verb.

    A. Substantive infinitives.
        1. Subject infinitive of impersonal verbs (e.g., δεῖ, ἔξεστιν, γίνομαι)
            a. Aor. act. infin.
            δεῖ σε πάλιν **προφητεῦσαι** ἐπὶ λαοῖς καὶ ἔθνεσιν καὶ γλώσσαις καὶ βασιλεῦσιν πολλοῖς (Rev. 10:11)
            you must prophesy again as to many peoples and nations and languages and kings
            b. Pres. act. infin.
            εἰ ἄνθρωπον Ῥωμαῖον καὶ ἀκατάκριτον **ἔξεστιν ὑμῖν μαστίζειν**; (Acts 22:25)
            is it lawful for you to scourge a man [who is] a Roman and uncondemned?
        2. Subject of linking verb, εἰμι
            a. Aor. act. infin.
            εὐκοπώτερον δέ **ἐστιν τὸν οὐρανὸν καὶ τὴν γῆν παρελθεῖν** ἢ τοῦ νόμου **μίαν κεραίαν πεσεῖν** (Luke 16:17)
            but **for heaven and earth to pass away is** easier than for **one tittle** of the law **to fall**
            b. Pres. act. infin.
            οὐκ ἀρεστόν **ἐστιν ἡμᾶς** καταλείψαντας τὸν λόγον τοῦ θεοῦ **διακονεῖν** τραπέζαις (Acts 6:2)
            for us to leave the word of God **to attend** tables is not appropriate
            c. Perf. act. infin.
            κρεῖττον γὰρ **ἦν αὐτοῖς μὴ ἐπεγνωκέναι** τὴν ὁδὸν τῆς δικαιοσύνης ἢ ἐπιγνοῦσιν ὑποστρέψαι ἐκ τῆς παραδοθείσης αὐτοῖς ἁγίας ἐντολῆς (2 Peter 2:21)
            for **it is** better **for them not to have known** the way of righteousness than after having known [it] to turn from the holy commandment delivered to them

3. Subject of passive verb
   a. Aor. act. infin.

   καὶ ἔκραξεν φωνῇ μεγάλῃ τοῖς τέσσαρσιν ἀγγέλοις οἷς **ἐδόθη**
   αὐτοῖς **ἀδικῆσαι** τὴν γῆν καὶ τὴν θάλασσαν (Rev. 7:2)

   and he cried out with a loud voice to the four angels to whom **it was**
   given to injure the earth and the sea

   b. Pres. act. infin.

   ὅτι **ὑμῖν ἐχαρίσθη** τὸ ὑπὲρ Χριστοῦ, οὐ μόνον **τὸ εἰς αὐτὸν**
   πιστεύειν ἀλλὰ καὶ τὸ ὑπὲρ αὐτοῦ **πάσχειν** (Phil. 1:29)

   because **it was granted to you** on behalf of Christ, not only **to believe**
   on him but also **to suffer** on his behalf

4. Subject of other verbs
   a. Aor. act. infin.

   τὸ δὲ ἀνίπτοις χερσὶν **φαγεῖν οὐ κοινοῖ** τὸν ἄνθρωπον (Matt. 15:20)

   but **to eat** with unwashed hands **does not defile** the person

   b. Pres. act. infin.

   τὸ γὰρ **θέλειν παράκειταί** μοι (Rom. 7:18)

   for **to will is present with** me

5. Subject of elliptical verb
   a. Pres. act. infin.

   Σαούλ, Σαούλ, τί με διώκεις; σκληρόν **σοι** πρὸς κέντρα **λακτίζειν**
   (Acts 26:14)

   Saul, Saul, why are you persecuting me? **for you to kick** against
   goads [**ἐστιν, is**] hard

   b. Aor. act. infin.

   χωρὶς δὲ πίστεως ἀδύνατον **εὐαρεστῆσαι** (Heb. 11:6)

   but apart from faith [**ἐστιν, it is**] impossible **to please** [him]

B. Infinitives may function as objects or complements of another verb.
   1. Verbs that entirely or primarily take an infinitive complement, e.g.,
      δύναμαι, θέλω, ἄρχομαι, ὀφείλω, βούλομαι, ἰσχύω, ἐπιτρέπω, μέλλω,
      τολμάω
      a. Aor. act. infin.

      καὶ **οὐκ ἴσχυον ἀντιστῆναι** τῇ σοφίᾳ καὶ τῷ πνεύματι ᾧ ἐλάλει
      (Acts 6:10)

      and **they were unable to resist** the wisdom and the spirit with
      which he was speaking

      b. Pres. act. infin.

      οὗτος ὁ ἄνθρωπος **ἤρξατο οἰκοδομεῖν** καὶ οὐκ ἴσχυσεν ἐκτελέσαι
      (Luke 14:30)

      this man began to build, and he was unable to finish

    c. Perf. act. infin. with θέλω

       θέλω δὲ **ὑμᾶς εἰδέναι** ὅτι παντὸς ἀνδρὸς ἡ κεφαλὴ ὁ Χριστός ἐστιν
       (1 Cor. 11:3)

       but **I want you to know** that Christ is the head of every man

    d. Fut. infin. with μέλλω

       ἐσήμανεν διὰ τοῦ πνεύματος λιμὸν μεγάλην **μέλλειν ἔσεσθαι** ἐφ᾽
       ὅλην τὴν οἰκουμένην (Acts 11:28)

       he signified by the Spirit [that] a great famine **is about to take place**
       over the whole world

  2. Verbs that usually take a direct object but often have an infinitive
    as complement, e.g., ζητέω, ἔχω, ἀφίημι, ποιέω, δίδωμι

    a. Aor. act. infin. with ζητέω

       καὶ ἦν διδάσκων τὸ καθ᾽ ἡμέραν ἐν τῷ ἱερῷ, **οἱ δὲ ἀρχιερεῖς καὶ**
       οἱ γραμματεῖς ἐζήτουν αὐτὸν **ἀπολέσαι** (Luke 19:47)

       and he was teaching daily in the temple; and **the chief priests** and **the**
       scribes were seeking to destroy him

    b. Pres. act. infin. with ποιέω

       καλῶς πάντα πεποίηκεν, καὶ τοὺς κωφοὺς **ποιεῖ ἀκούειν**, καὶ τοὺς
       ἀλάλους **λαλεῖν** (Mark 7:37)

       he has done all things well; **he caused** both the deaf **to hear** and the
       mute **to speak**

C. Infinitive of indirect discourse. The infinitive may function as an object of a
   verb expressing thought or verbal communication in a statement, question,
   command, or prohibition, usually after such verbs as follows: λέγω, δοκέω,
   παραγγέλλω, νομίζω, κρίνω, κελεύω, ὑπομιμνήσκω, διατάσσω, πείθω,
   ἐλπίζω, ἐρωτάω, αἰτέω.

  1. Pres. act. infin. with μή, prohibitive

    λέγω γὰρ διὰ τῆς χάριτος τῆς δοθείσης μοι, παντὶ τῷ ὄντι ἐν ὑμῖν,
    μὴ ὑπερφρονεῖν παρ᾽ ὃ δεῖ φρονεῖν (Rom. 12:3)

    for **I say** through the grace that has been given to me, to everyone
    who is among you, **do not think more highly** than one ought to think

  2. Aor. pass. infin.

    σταθεὶς δὲ ὁ Ἰησοῦς **ἐκέλευσεν αὐτὸν ἀχθῆναι** πρὸς αὐτόν (Luke 18:40)

    and when Jesus stood still, **he commanded him to be brought** to him

  3. Fut. mid. dep. infin.

    τίσιν δὲ **ὤμοσεν μὴ εἰσελεύσεσθαι** εἰς τὴν κατάπαυσεν αὐτοῦ, εἰ μὴ
    τοῖς ἀπειθήσασιν; (Heb. 3:18)

    and to whom **did he swear [that they] will not enter** into his rest
    except to those who disobeyed?

4. Perf. act. infin.

ὥστε ὁ δοκῶν ἑστάναι βλεπέτω μὴ πέσῃ (1 Cor. 10:12)

so that **the one who thinks he stands**, let him beware lest he fall

II. **Adverbial infinitives** may express purpose or result with verbs of motion and sending, e.g, ἀποστέλλω, πέμπω, ἔρχομαι (and its compounds), πορεύομαι (and compounds), βαίνω (and compounds).

A. Infinitive of purpose.

1. Aor. act. infin.

ὅτε δὲ ἤγγισεν ὁ καιρὸς τῶν καρπῶν, ἀπέστειλεν τοὺς δούλους αὐτοῦ πρὸς τοὺς γεωργοὺς **λαβεῖν** τοὺς καρποὺς αὐτοῦ (Matt. 21:34)

and when the time of fruit drew near, **he sent his servants** to the farmers **to receive** the fruit

2. Pres. act. infin.

μετέβη ἐκεῖθεν τοῦ **διδάσκειν** καὶ **κηρύσσειν** ἐν ταῖς πόλεσιν αὐτῶν (Matt. 11:1)

he departed from there **to teach** and **to preach** in their cities

B. Infinitive of result introduced by ὥστε or ὡς.

1. Pres. act. infin.

καὶ ἐγένετο ὡσεὶ νεκρός, **ὥστε τοὺς πολλοὺς λέγειν** ὅτι ἀπέθανεν (Mark 9:26)[1]

and he became as dead, **so that many [people] said**, "he is dead"

2. Aor. act. infin.

τοῦτο δὲ ἐγένετο ἐπὶ ἔτη δύο, **ὥστε πάντας τοὺς κατοικοῦντας** τὴν Ἀσίαν **ἀκοῦσαι** τὸν λόγον τοῦ κυρίου (Acts 19:10)

and this took place for two years, **so that all those who lived** in Asia **heard** the word of the Lord

C. Articular (always a neuter article) infinitives with prepositions. Not all articular infinitives are found in prepositional phrases, but all infinitives with prepositions are articular. In descending order of frequency, the infinitive is found with the following prepositions: εἰς, ἐν, διά, μετά, πρός, πρίν or πρὶν ἤ, πρό, ἀντί, ἕνεκεν, ἕως. The following classifications are based on the adverbial meanings.

---

[1] Mark 9:26 text is from GNT, NA & WH: TR & MT omit τούς.

1. Purpose infinitive with εἰς or πρός
   a. Aor. pass. infin.
      πάντα δὲ τὰ ἔργα αὐτῶν ποιοῦσιν **πρὸς τὸ θεαθῆναι** τοῖς ἀνθρώποις
      (Matt. 23:5)
      and they perform all their works **in order to be seen** by people
   b. Pres. act. infin.
      ὁ δὲ θεὸς τῆς ἐλπίδος πληρῶσαι ὑμᾶς πάσης χαρᾶς καὶ εἰρήνης
      ἐν τῷ πιστεύειν, **εἰς τὸ περισσεύειν** ὑμᾶς ἐν τῇ ἐλπίδι (Rom. 15:13)
      now the God of hope fill you with every kind of joy and peace in
      believing, **in order that you may abound** in hope
2. Temporal infinitive clauses
   a. With ἐν, **while, as, when**
      (1) Pres. act. infin.
          καὶ **ἐν τῷ σπείρειν** αὐτὸν ἃ μὲν ἔπεσεν παρὰ τὴν ὁδόν
          (Matt. 13:4 and Luke 8:5)
          and **while he sowed** some [seed] fell alongside the road
      (2) Aor. mid. dep. infin.
          ἐν δὲ τῷ ἄρξασθαί με λαλεῖν ἐπέπεσεν τὸ πνεῦμα τὸ ἅγιον
          ἐπ᾽ αὐτούς (Acts 11:15)
          and **when I began to speak** the Holy Spirit fell on them
   b. With μετά, **after**
      οἷς καὶ παρέστησεν ἑαυτὸν ζῶντα **μετὰ τὸ παθεῖν** αὐτόν (Acts 1:3)
      to whom also he presented himself alive **after he had suffered**
   c. With πρό, **before**
      (1) Aor. act. infin.
          ἡμεῖς δέ, **πρὸ τοῦ ἐγγίσαι** αὐτόν, ἕτοιμοί ἐσμεν τοῦ ἀνελεῖν
          αὐτόν (Acts 23:15)
          and we ourselves, **before he draws near**, are ready to put him to
          death
      (2) Pres. act. infin.
          καὶ νῦν δόξασόν με σύ, πάτερ, παρὰ σεαυτῷ, τῇ δόξῃ ᾗ εἶχον
          πρὸ τοῦ τὸν κόσμον εἶναι παρὰ σοί (John 17:5)
          and now, Father, you glorify me with yourself, with the glory that
          I had with you **before the world existed**
   d. With πρίν or πρὶν ἤ, **before**
      Aor. act. infin.
      ἔφη αὐτῷ ὁ Ἰησοῦς, ἀμὴν λέγω σοι ὅτι ἐν ταύτῃ τῇ νυκτί
      πρὶν ἀλέκτορα φωνῆσαι τρὶς ἀπαρνήσῃ με (Matt. 26:34)
      Jesus said to him, "I tell you truly, that during this night, **before a
      rooster crows**, you will deny me three times"

   e. With ἕως, **until**
      Aor. act. infin.
      καὶ διερχόμενος εὐηγγελίζετο τὰς πόλεις πάσας ἕως τοῦ ἐλθεῖν
      αὐτὸν εἰς Καισάρειαν (Acts 8:40)
      and while passing through he evangelized all the cities, **until he came
      to Caesarea**
3. Causal infinitives with διά, **because**
   a. Pres. act. infin.
      οἵτινες ἀνακρίναντές με ἐβούλοντο ἀπολῦσαι διὰ τὸ μηδεμίαν
      αἰτίαν θανάτου ὑπάρχειν ἐν ἐμοί (Acts 28:18)
      who after examining me wanted to release me, **because there existed
      no cause** of death in me
   b. Perf. pass. infin.
      προσέρηξεν ὁ ποταμὸς τῇ οἰκίᾳ ἐκείνῃ, καὶ οὐκ ἴσχυσεν
      σαλεῦσαι αὐτὴν διὰ τὸ καλῶς οἰκοδομῆσθαι αὐτήν (Luke 6:48)[2]
      the river burst on that house, and it was not able to shake it
      because it was well built

D. Imperatival infinitives stand alone as the main verb of a sentence, often
   in a context of other imperatives.
   1. Pres. act. infin.
      εὐλογεῖτε τοὺς διώκοντας ὑμᾶς, εὐλογεῖτε καὶ μὴ καταρᾶσθε. χαίρειν
      μετὰ χαιρόντων, καὶ κλαίειν μετὰ κλαιόντων (Rom. 12:14-15)
      bless those who persecute you; bless and do not curse. **Rejoice** with
      those who rejoice, and **weep** with those who weep
   2. Aor. mid. infin.
      ἀποθέσθαι ὑμᾶς κατὰ τὴν προτέραν ἀναστροφὴν τὸν παλαιὸν
      ἄνθρωπον (Eph. 4:22)
      you put off from yourselves the old person according to your former
      conduct

E. Infinitives may complement modifying nouns, adjectives, and pronouns.
   1. Infinitive complement of nouns, e.g., ἐξουσία, χρεία, ἀνάγκη, καιρός
      a. Aor. act. infin.
         ὁ δὲ Ἰησοῦς εἶπεν αὐτοῖς, οὐ χρείαν ἔχουσιν ἀπελθεῖν, δότε αὐτοῖς
         ὑμεῖς φαγεῖν (Matt. 14:16)
         but Jesus said to them, "they have **no need to depart**; you yourselves
         give them [something] to eat"

---

[2] Luke 6:48 text is from GNT, NA & WH: TR & MT have προσέρρηξεν and τεθεμελίωτο γὰρ ἐπὶ τὴν πέτραν for the causal
infinitive clause.

b. Pres. act. infin.

ἵνα δὲ εἰδῆτε ὅτι **ἐξουσίαν** ἔχει ὁ υἱὸς τοῦ ἀνθρώπου ἐπὶ τῆς γῆς **ἀφιέναι** ἁμαρτίας (Matt. 9:6)

but that you may know that the son of man has **authority** on earth **to forgive** sins

c. Fut. infin.

μηνυθείσης δέ μοι **ἐπιβουλῆς** εἰς τὸν ἄνδρα **ἔσεσθαι** (Acts 23:30)[3]

but when **a plot** was revealed to me **to be** against the man

d. Perf. pass. infin.

ὡς γὰρ ὑπάγεις μετὰ τοῦ ἀντιδίκου σου ἐπ᾽ ἄρχοντα, ἐν τῇ ὁδῷ δὸς **ἐργασίαν ἀπαλλάχθαι** ἀπ᾽ αὐτοῦ (Luke 12:58)

for while you are going with your opponent to the magistrate, on the way make **an effort to be released** from him

2. Infinitive complement of adjectives; e.g., ἄξιος, δύνατος, ἕτοιμος, ἵκανος

a. Aor. act. infin.

ἔρχεται δὲ ὁ ἰσχυρότερός μου, οὗ οὐκ εἰμὶ **ἱκανὸς λῦσαι** τὸν ἱμάντα τῶν ὑποδημάτων αὐτοῦ (Luke 3:16)

but the one who is greater than I is coming, of whom I am not **worthy to loose** the thongs of his sandals

b. Pres. act. infin.

οὐδεὶς **ἄξιος** εὑρέθη ἀνοῖξαι καὶ ἀναγνῶναι τὸ βιβλίον, οὔτε **βλέπειν** αὐτό (Rev. 5:4)[4]

no one was found **worthy** to open and to read the book, or **to see** it

3. Infinitive complement or appositional of pronouns; e.g., οὗτος, τί, ὅς

a. Aor. act. infin.

τί ἐστιν εὐκοπώτερον, **εἰπεῖν**, ἀφέωνταί σοι αἱ ἁμαρτίαι σου, ἢ **εἰπεῖν**, ἔγειρε καὶ περιπάτει; (Luke 5:23)[5]

what is easier **to say**, "your sins are forgiven you," or **to say**, "rise up and walk"

b. Pres. mid. and act. infin.

θρησκεία καθαρὰ καὶ ἀμίαντος παρὰ τῷ θεῷ καὶ πατρὶ **αὕτη** ἐστίν, **ἐπισκέπτεσθαι** ὀρφανοὺς καὶ χήρας ἐν τῇ θλίψει αὐτῶν, ἄσπιλον ἑαυτὸν **τηρεῖν** ἀπὸ τοῦ κόσμου (James 1:27)

pure religion and undefiled before God and Father is **this**, **to visit** orphans and widows in their trouble and **to keep** oneself spotless from the world

---

[3] Acts 23:30 text is from GNT, NA & WH: TR & MT have μέλλειν ἔσεσθαι.

[4] Rev. 5:4 text is from TR & MT: GNT, NA & WH omit καὶ ἀναγνῶναι.

[5] Luke 5:23 text is from GNT, NA & WH: TR & MT have ἔγειραι.

   c. Perf. pass. infin.

τοῦτο δηλοῦντος τοῦ πνεύματος τοῦ ἁγίου, **μήπω πεφανερῶσθαι τὴν** τῶν ἁγίων **ὁδὸν** ἔτι τῆς πρώτης σκηνῆς ἐχούσης στάσιν (Heb. 9:8)

the Holy Spirit signifying **this**, not yet **had the way** into the holy place **been made known** while the first tabernacle had a standing

F. Periphrastic infinitive, εἶναι with an acc. sing. masc. pres. pass. ptc.

καὶ ἐγένετο ἐν τῷ εἶναι αὐτὸν ἐν τόπῳ τινὶ **προσευχόμενον** (Luke 11:1)

and it happened **while he was praying** in a certain place

II. **Voice** with the infinitive is essentially the same as with finite verbs.

   A. Active voice.
      1. Simple active
         a. Aor. act. infin.

καὶ οὐκ ἴσχυον **ἀντιστῆναι** τῇ σοφίᾳ καὶ τῷ πενύματι ᾧ ἐλάλει (Acts 6:10)

and they were unable **to resist** the wisdom and the spirit by which he was speaking

         b. Pres. act. infin.

διδάσκοντες αὐτοὺς **τηρεῖν** πάντα ὅσα ἐνετειλάμην ὑμῖν (Matt. 28:20)

teaching them **to keep** all things that I commanded you

      2. Stative active, normally in the present tense, with verbs having a lexical meaning indicating a state or condition, e.g., ζάω, ἔχω, μένω, ἀκούω
         Pres. act. infin.

καὶ μὴ εὑροῦσαι τὸ σῶμα αὐτοῦ ἦλθον, λέγουσαι καὶ ὀπτασίαν ἀγγέλων ἑωρακέναι, οἳ λέγουσιν **αὐτὸν ζῆν** (Luke 24:23)[6]

and not having found his body, they came, claiming to have seen a vision of angels, who claim **he is alive**

   B. Middle voice.
      1. Deponent middle, a middle form with an active meaning
         a. Aor. mid. dep. infin.

προτρεψάμενοι οἱ ἀδελφοὶ ἔγραψαν τοῖς μαθηταῖς **ἀποδέξασθαι** αὐτόν (Acts 18:27)

the brothers wrote to the disciples exhorting [them] **to receive** him

---

[6] Luke 24:23 text is from GNT, NA & MT: WH & TR has ζῆν.

b. Pres. mid./pass. dep. infin.

καὶἐγένετο ἐν τῷ **προσεύχεσθαι αὐτὸν** τὸ εἶδος τοῦ προσώπου
αὐτοῦ ἕτερον, καὶ ὁ ἱματισμὸς αὐτοῦ λευκὸς ἐξαστράπτων
(Luke 9:29)

and it happened **while he was praying** [that] the appearance of his face
[was] changed and his clothing [was] white like lightning

c. Fut. mid. dep. infin.

τίσιν δὲ ὤμοσεν **μὴ εἰσελεύσεσθαι** εἰς τὴν κατάπαυσιν αὐτοῦ, εἰ μὴ
τοῖς ἀπειθήσασιν; (Heb. 3:18)

but to whom did he swear **they shall not enter** into his rest, except
to those who disobeyed

2. Middle with an active sense but not deponent
   a. Aor. mid. infin.

ἀντιλεγόντων δὲ τῶν Ἰουδαίων ἠναγκάσθην **ἐπικαλέσασθαι**
Καίσαρα (Acts 28:19)

but when the Jews spoke against [it] I was compelled **to appeal** to
Caesar

   b. Pres. mid./pass. infin.

ἡμεῖς δὲ ἠλπίζομεν ὅτι αὐτός ἐστιν ὁ μέλλων **λυτροῦσθαι** τὸν
Ἰσραήλ (Luke 24:21)

but we were hoping that he is the one who is about **to redeem** Israel

3. Middle reflexive
   a. Aor. mid. infin.

καὶ **ἐνδύσασθαι** τὸν καινὸν ἄνθρωπον τὸν κατὰ θεὸν κτισθέντα ἐν
δικαιοσύνη καὶ ὁσιότητι τῆς ἀληθείας (Eph. 4:24)

and **clothe yourself** with the new person, who according to God
was created in righteousness and holiness of the truth

   b. Pres. mid./pass. infin.

ὑμεῖς ἐπίστασθε ὡς ἀθέμιτόν ἐστιν ἀνδρὶ Ἰουδαίῳ **κολλᾶσθαι** ἢ
προσέρχεσθαι ἀλλοφύλῳ (Acts 10:28)

you know that it is unlawful for a Jewish man **to unite himself** or come
near to one of another race

4. Middle intensive
   a. Pres. mid./pass. infin.

τίς ἔτι χρεία κατὰ τὴν τάξιν Μελχισέδεκ ἕτερον **ἀνίστασθαι** ἱερέα
(Heb. 7:11)[7]

what need yet [existed] according to the order of Melchisedek **for
another priest to arise**

---

[7] Heb. 7:11 text is from GNT, NA & MT: WH & TR has Μελχισεδέκ.

    b. Aor. mid. infin.

    μὴ βουλόμενός τινας ἀπολέσθαι ἀλλὰ πάντες εἰς μετάνοιαν χωρῆσαι (2 Peter 3:9)

    not willing for **any to perish** but for all to come to repentance

5. Middle with an active meaning different from the active form

    a. Aor. mid. infin.

    ὅτι ὁ καιρὸς **τοῦ ἄρξασθαι** τὸ κρίμα ἀπὸ τοῦ οἴκου τοῦ θεοῦ (1 Peter 4:17)

    for [it is] the time **to begin** the judgment from the house of God

    b. Pres. mid./pass. infin.

    καλὸν ἀνθρώπῳ γυναικὸς **μὴ ἅπτεσθαι** (1 Cor. 7:1)

    [ἐστιν, it is] good for a man **not to touch** a woman

C. Passive voice.

   1. Most passives have no agent expressed, because it is either unimportant or it is implied in the context.

    a. Aor. pass. infin.

    ἐγένετο δὲ ἐν τῷ **βαπτισθῆναι** ἅπαντα τὸν λαόν (Luke 3:21)

    now it happened **when all the people were baptized**

    b. Pres. pass. infin.

    καὶ γὰρ κινδυνεύομεν **ἐγκαλεῖσθαι** στάσεως περὶ τῆς σήμερον (Acts 19:40)

    for we also are in danger **of being accused** of discord concerning this day

    c. Perf. pass. infin.

    Ἀγρίππας δὲ τῷ Φήστῳ ἔφη, **ἀπολελύσθαι** ἐδύνατο ὁ ἄνθρωπος οὗτος εἰ μὴ ἐπεκέκλητο Καίσαρα (Acts 26:32)

    and Agrippa said to Festus, "this man could **have been released** if he had not appealed to Caesar"

   2. Theological passive, where the agent is assumed to be God

    a. Aor. pass. infin.

    καὶ ἦλθεν ἡ ὀργή σου καὶ ὁ καιρὸς τῶν νεκρῶν **κριθῆναι** (Rev. 11:18)

    and your wrath has come, and the time for the dead **to be judged**

    b. Pres. pass. infin.

    ὁ καὶ τῆς μελλούσης **ἀποκαλύπτεσθαι** δόξης κοινωνός (1 Peter 5:1)

    who also [am] a partner of the glory about **to be revealed**

3. Deponent passive, with an active meaning
   a. Aor. pass. infin.
      μνησθῆναι τῶν προειρημένων ῥημάτων ὑπὸ τῶν ἁγίων προφητῶν
      (2 Peter 3:2)
      to remember the words spoken before by the holy prophets
   b. Perf. pass. infin.
      Χριστὸν διάκονον **γεγενῆσθαι** περιτομῆς ὑπὲρ ἀληθείας θεοῦ
      (Rom. 15:8)
      Christ has become a servant of the circumcision for the truth of God
4. Passive with an active meaning
   Aor. pass. infin.
   ὅτι ἦλθεν ἡ ἡμέρα ἡ μεγάλη τῆς ὀργῆς αὐτῶν, καὶ τίς δύναται
   σταθῆναι; (Rev. 6:17)[8]
   for the great day of his wrath has come, and who is able **to stand?**
5. Passive agent with the preposition ὑπό
   a. Aor. pass. infin.
      ἔλεγεν οὖν τοῖς ἐκπορευομένοις ὄχλοις **βαπτισθῆναι ὑπ᾽ αὐτοῦ**
      (Luke 3:7)
      he said, then, to the crowds who were coming out **to be baptized
      by him**
   b. Pres. pass. infin.
      ὃν ὁ θεὸς ἀνέστησεν λύσας τὰς ὠδῖνας τοῦ θανάτου, καθότι οὐκ
      ἦν δυνατὸν **κρατεῖσθαι αὐτὸν ὑπ᾽ αὐτοῦ** (Acts 2:24)
      whom God raised up, when he set free the birth pains of death, in view
      of the fact that it was not possible **for him to be held by it**
6. Passive agent with the preposition ἐν
   a. Aor. pass. infin.
      καὶ ἀπὸ πάντων ὧν οὐκ ἠδυνήθητε ἐν νόμῳ Μωϋσέως δικαιωθῆναι
      (Acts 13:38)[9]
      and from all things which you were unable **to be justified by the law
      of Moses**
   b. Pres. pass. infin.
      τὸ μηδένα **σαίνεσθαι** ἐν ταῖς θλίψεσιν ταύταις (1 Thess. 3:3)[10]
      that no one should be disturbed by these trials

---

[8] Rev. 6:17 text is from GNT, NA & WH: TR & MT have αὐτοῦ for αὐτῶν.

[9] Acts 13:38 text is from GNT, NA & WH: TR & MT have ἐν τῷ νόμῳ Μωσέως in verse 38.

[10] 1 Thess. 3:3 text is from GNT, NA & WH: TR & MT have τῷ μηδένα.

7. Passive agent with the dative case
   a. Aor. pass. infin.
      σπουδάσατε ἄσπιλοι καὶ ἀμώμητοι **αὐτῷ εὑρεθῆναι** ἐν εἰρήνῃ
      (2 Peter 3:14)
      put forth effort **to be found by him** spotless and blameless in peace
   b. Pres. pass. infin.
      καλὸν γὰρ χάριτι **βεβαιοῦσθαι** τὴν **καρδίαν** (Heb. 13:9)
      for [ἐστιν, it is] good **for the heart to be established by grace**
   c. Perf. pass. infin.
      πίστει νοοῦμεν **κατηρτίσθαι** τοὺς **αἰῶνας ῥήματι** θεοῦ (Heb. 11:3)
      by faith we perceive [that] **the worlds were created by the word** of
      God
8. Passive agent with the preposition διά
   a. Aor. pass. infin.
      δυνάμει **κραταιωθῆναι διὰ** τοῦ **πνεύματος αὐτοῦ** εἰς τὸν ἔσω
      ἄνθρωπον (Eph. 3:16)
      to be strengthened by his Spirit with power in the inner person
   b. Pres. pass. infin.
      οὕτως λαλεῖτε καὶ οὕτως ποιεῖτε ὡς **διὰ νόμου** ἐλευθερίας
      μέλλοντες **κρίνεσθαι** (James 2:12)
      so speak and so do as [those who are] about **to be judged by the law**
      of liberty

D. Voiceless εἶναι.
   1. Pres. infin.
      πεπεισμένος γάρ ἐστιν **Ἰωάννην προφήτην εἶναι** (Luke 20:6)[11]
      for they were persuaded **[that] John was a prophet**
   2. Fut. infin.
      ἐλπίδα ἔχων εἰς τὸν θεόν ἣν καὶ αὐτοὶ οὗτοι προσδέχονται, **ἀνάστασιν**
      μέλλειν ἔσεσθαι δικαίων τε καὶ ἀδίκων (Acts 24:15)
      having hope in God, which they themselves also expect, **there is going**
      to be a resurrection both of the just and the unjust

III. **Tense in the infinitives.** Infinitives are found in four tenses: present, aorist,
perfect, and future. The following are only representative of the possibilities.

A. The present tense is used when progressive, iterative, or stative action
   is described.

---

[11] Luke 20:6 text is from GNT, NA, TR & MT; WH has Ἰωάνην.

1. Progressive or descriptive infinitives
   a. Pres. mid./pass. dep. and act. infin.
      ὥστε ἐξίστησθαι πάντας καὶ δοξάζειν τὸν θεόν (Mark 2:12)
      so that **all were amazed** and **glorified** God
   b. Pres. act. infin.
      διαπονούμενοι διὰ τὸ διδάσκειν αὐτοὺς τὸν λαόν, καὶ
      καταγγέλειν ἐν τῷ Ἰησοῦ τὴν ἀνάστασιν τὴν ἐκ νεκρῶν
      (Acts 4:2)
      being annoyed **because they were teaching** the people and **proclaiming**
      in Jesus the resurrection, which [οὖσην, is] from the dead
2. Stative present infinitive
   Pres. act. infin.
   καὶ οὐκ ἀπεκρίθη αὐτῷ πρὸς οὐδὲ ἓν ῥῆμα, ὥστε θαυμάζειν τὸν
   ἡγεμόνα λίαν (Matt. 27:14)
   and he did not answer him not even one word, so that **the governor
   marveled** exceedingly
3. Gnomic present infinitive
   Pres. mid./pass. dep. infin.
   ἓξ ἡμέραι εἰσίν ἐν αἷς δεῖ ἐργάζεσθαι (Luke 13:14)
   there are six days during which **it is necessary to work**

B. The aorist tense considers the action as undefined as far as progress,
   state, or repetition. However, the context indicates the ingressive,
   consummative, or constative sense.
   1. Ingressive aorist infinitives emphasizing the beginning of the action
      Aor. act. infin.
      μετὰ δὲ τὸ σιγῆσαι αὐτοὺς ἀπεκρίθη Ἰάκωβος (Acts 15:13)
      but **after they became silent** James answered
   2. Consummative aorist looking at the effect or conclusion of the action
      Aor. act. infin.
      καὶ πέπεισμαι ὅτι δυνατός ἐστιν τὴν παραθήκην μου **φυλάξαι** εἰς
      ἐκείνην τὴν ἡμέραν (2 Tim. 1:12)
      and I am persuaded that he is able **to guard** my deposit until that day

C. The perfect tense indicates a state based on previous action, stative action,
   and completed action.
   1. Intensive action, emphasizing the result of previous action
      Perf. pass. infin.
      πίστει νοοῦμεν **κατηρτίσθαι τοὺς αἰῶνας** ῥήματι θεοῦ (Heb. 11:3)
      by faith we understand **the worlds to have been created** by the word of
      God

    2. Completed action
       Perf. act. infin.
       ὥστε με . . . πεπληρωκέναι τὸ εὐαγγέλιον τοῦ Χριστοῦ (Rom. 15:19)
       so that I . . . **have fully preached** the gospel of Christ
    3. Stative action with οἶδα and ἵστημι
       Perf. act. infin.
       καὶ ἄρξησθε ἔξω ἐστάναι καὶ κρούειν τὴν θύραν (Luke 13:25)
       and you begin **to stand** outside and to knock on the door

  D. The future infinitive is limited to the future of εἰμι and one future
     middle deponent verb.
     1. Fut. infin.
        ἐτήμανεν διὰ τοῦ πνεύματος λιμὸν μεγάλην μέλλειν **ἔσεσθαι** ἐφ'
        ὅλην τὴν οἰκουμένην (Acts 11:28)[12]
        he signified by the Spirit [that] a great famine was about **to occur** over
        all the inhabited world
     2. Fut. mid. dep. infin. of indirect discourse
        τίσιν δὲ ὤμοσεν **μὴ εἰσελεύσεσθαι** εἰς τὴν κατάπαυσιν αὐτοῦ,
        εἰ μὴ τοῖς ἀπειθήσασιν; (Heb. 3:18)
        but to whom did he swear **[that they] shall not enter** into his rest, except
        to those who disobeyed?

IV. **The infinitive is often found with two substantival accusatives.** The distinction
    between the subject and the object or complement is determined by word order.
    The first accusative functions as the subject, and the second functions as the
    object or complement.[13] The following examples are only representative of this
    principle.

  A. When the infinitive precedes both accusatives.
     1. Noncopulative infin.
        a. Pres. act. infin.
           καθώς ἐστιν δίκαιον ἐμοὶ τοῦτο φρονεῖν ὑπὲρ πάντων ὑμῶν,
           διὰ τὸ ἔχειν με ἐν τῇ καρδίᾳ ὑμᾶς (Phil. 1:7)
           even as it is right for me to think this concerning all of you,
           because I have you in [my] heart

---

[12] Acts 11:28 text is from GNT & NA: WH has ἐσήμαινεν; TR & MT have μέγαν.

[13] This is based upon the article by Jeffrey T. Reed, "The Infinitive with Two Substantival Accusatives," *Novum Testamentum* 33, no. 1 (1991): 1-27. Out of 95 examples in the NT, 87 support this principle. The seven "exceptions" indicate some emphasis or theme distinctive.

  b. Aor. act. infin.

  τηρῆσαί σε τὴν ἐντολὴν ἄσπιλον (1 Tim. 6:14)

  [that] you keep the commandment spotless

2. Copulative infin.

  εὐτόνως γὰρ τοῖς Ἰουδαίοις διακατηλέγχετο δημοσίᾳ ἐπιδεικνὺς
  διὰ τῶν γραφῶν **εἶναι τὸν Χριστὸν Ἰησοῦν** (Acts 18:28)[14]

  for he was refuting completely [both] vigorously and publicly,
  demonstrating through the scriptures **[that] the Christ is Jesus**

B. When the infinitive comes between the two accusatives.
  1. Noncopulative infin.
    a. Pres. act. infin.

      ἐπιθυμοῦμεν δὲ **ἕκαστον** ὑμῶν **τὴν αὐτὴν ἐνδείκνυσθαι σπουδὴν**
      πρὸς τὴν πληροφορίαν τῆς ἐλπίδος ἄχρι τέλους (Heb. 6:11)

      but we desire **[that] each one** of you **show the same zeal** with regard
      to the certainty of the hope unto the end

    b. Aor. act. infin.

      τοῦτο δὲ ἐγένετο ἐπὶ ἔτη δύο, **ὥστε πάντας τοὺς κατοικοῦντας**
      τὴν Ἀσίαν **ἀκοῦσαι τὸν λόγον** τοῦ κυρίου (Acts 19:10)

      and this took place for two years, **so that all those who lived** in Asia
      heard the word of the Lord

    c. Perf. act. infin.

      ὥστε με ἀπὸ Ἰερουσαλὴμ καὶ κύκλῳ μέχρι τοῦ Ἰλλυρικοῦ
      πεπληρωκέναι τὸ εὐαγγέλιον τοῦ Χριστοῦ (Rom. 15:19)[15]

      so that from Jerusalem and all around Illyricum **I have full proclaimed
      the gospel** of Christ

  2. Copulative infin.

    δἰ ὀλίγων ἔγραψα, παρακαλῶν καὶ ἐπιμαρτυρῶν **ταύτην εἶναι ἀληθῆ**
    χάριν τοῦ θεοῦ (1 Peter 5:12)

    I wrote briefly, exhorting and witnessing **[that] this is the true grace** of God

C. When the infinitive follows the two accusatives.
  1. Copulative infin.

    πάλιν λέγω, μή τίς με δόξῃ **ἄφρονα εἶναι** (2 Cor. 11:16)

    I say [it] again, let no one consider **me to be a fool**

---

[14] The KJV, NKJV, NIV, NASB, J. B. Phillips, and Charles Williams all state that "Jesus is the Christ" or the equivalent. However, the *Revised Standard Version* has "the Christ was Jesus."

[15] Rom. 15:19 text is from GNT, NW, WH & MT: TR has Ἰερουσαλήμ.

2. Noncopulative infin.
   a. Pres. act. infin.
      ἐὰν δὲ καὶ χωρισθῇ, μενέτω ἄγαμος ἢ τῷ ἀνδρὶ καταλλαγήτω,
      καὶ ἄνδρα γυναῖκα μὴ ἀφιέναι (1 Cor. 7:11)
      but if she also is separated, let her remain unmarried or let her be
      reconciled to her husband; and **do not let the husband leave his wife**
   b. Aor. act. infin.
      καὶ ἤρξατο διδάσκειν αὐτοὺς ὅτι δεῖ τὸν υἱὸν τοῦ ἀνθρώπου
      (Mark 8:31)
      and he began to teach them that **the son** of man **must suffer many
      things**

Select Bibliography for Infinitives

Allen, Hamilton Ford. "The Use of the Infinitive in Polybius compared with the Use of
the Infinitive in Biblical Greek." Ph.D. diss., Univ. of Chicago, 1907.

Boyer, James L. *Supplemental Manual of Information: Infinitive Verbs.* Winona Lake, Ind.:
Morgan Library, Grace Theological Seminary, 1985.

_____. "The Classification of Infinitives: A Statistical Study." *Grace Theological
Journal* 6, no. 1 (1985): 3-27.

Higgins, Martin J. "New Testament Result Clauses With Infinitive." *Catholic Biblical
Quarterly* 12 (1961): 233-41.

Kilpatrick, G. D. "The Articular Infinitive in the New Testament." *Journal of Theological
Studies* 4, no. 1 (April 1990): 95-97.

Lovelady, Edgar J. "Infinitive Clause Syntax in the Gospels." Master's thesis, Grace
Theological Seminary, 1976.

Lovik, Gordon H. "The Future Infinitive in the Greek New Testament." *Calvary Baptist
Theological Journal* (Fall 1985): 13-15.

McGaughy, Lance C. *Toward a Descriptive Analysis of* EINAI *as a Linking Verb.* Published
by the Society of Biblical Literature for the Linguistics Seminar. Dissertation
series, no. 6, 1972.

Moeller, Henry R., and Arnold Kramer. "An Overlooked Structural Pattern in New
Testament Greek." *Novum Testamentum* 5 (1963): 25-35.

Reed, Jeffrey T. "The Infinitive with two Substantival Accusatives: An Ambiguous
Construction?" *Novum Testamentum* 33, no. 1 (1991): 1-27.

Thorley, John. "Aktionsart in New Testament Greek: Infinitive and Imperative." *Novum
Testamentum* 31, no. 4 (1989): 290-315.

Votaw, Clyde Weber. "The Use of the Infinitive in Biblical Greek." Doctoral diss.,
Univ. of Chicago, 1896.

PARTICIPLES

The participle is a verbal adjective having tense and voice like a verb, and case, gender, and number like an adjective. Participles function as adjectives, adverbs, substantives, and verbs. All articular participles are either adjectival or substantival, and all adverbial and verbal participles are anarthrous. However, not all anarthrous participles are adverbial, but may be adjectival, adverbial, substantival, and verbal. The following classifications are based on the articular and anarthrous uses of the participle.

I. **Adjectival participles** modify nouns and pronouns. Usually both the participle and the noun have the article.

   A. Attributive participle.
      1. First attributive position participles function both as a true attributive and in an appositional sense.
         a. Attributive participles are found in the present, aorist, and perfect tenses and in all four cases (not the vocative).
            (1) Nom. sing. masc. pres. act. ptc.

               καθὼς ἀπέστειλέν με ὁ **ζῶν πατήρ** (John 6:57)
               even as **the living father** sent me

            (2) Gen. sing. fem. pres. act. ptc.

               ἔσται γὰρ καιρὸς ὅτε **τῆς ὑγιαινούσης διδασκαλίας** οὐκ ἀνέξονται (2 Tim. 4:3)
               for there will be a time when they will not bear **the sound teaching**

            (3) Dat. sing. fem. perf. pass. ptc.

               τοῦτον **τῇ ὡρισμένῃ βουλῇ** καὶ προγνώσει τοῦ θεοῦ ἔκδοτον (Acts 2:23)
               this one [was] delivered up **by the determinate counsel** and foreknowledge of God

            (4) Acc. pl. fem. pres. mid./pass. dep. ptc.

               οἱ δὲ Ἰουδαῖοι παρώτρυναν **τὰς σεβομένας γυναῖκας** (Acts 13:50)
               but the Jews incited **the worshiping women**

         b. Appositional sense is translated like a relative pronoun phrase or clause.
            (1) Nom. pl. masc. aor. act. ptc.

               καὶ ὁ **πέμψας** με **πατήρ**, ἐκεῖνος μεμαρτύρηκε(ν) περὶ ἐμοῦ (John 5:37)[1]
               and **the father who sent** me, he has witnessed concerning me

---

[1] John 5:37 text is from GNT, NA & WH: TR & MT have αὐτός.

(2) Gen. pl. neut. perf. pass. ptc.

μνησθῆναι τῶν προειρημένων ῥημάτων ὑπὸ τῶν ἁγίων προφητῶν (2 Peter 3:2)

to be mindful **of the words that were spoken before** by the holy prophets

(3) Dat. sing. fem. aor. pass. ptc.

ἀνάγκην ἔσχον γράψαι ὑμῖν, παρακαλῶν ἐπαγωνίζεσθαι τῇ ἅπαξ **παραδοθείσῃ** τοῖς ἁγίοις **πίστει** (Jude 3)

I had to write to you, exhorting [you] to contend **for the faith that was** once **handed down** to the saints

(4) Acc. pl. neut. pres. pass. ptc.

οὐδ᾽ αὐτὸν οἶμαι τὸν κόσμον χωρῆσαι τὰ γραφόμενα βιβλία (John 21:25)[2]

I suppose not even the world itself could contain **the books that would be written**

2. Second attributive position participles function as a true attributive and in an appositional sense.

  a. Second attributives

    (1) Nom. sing. masc. pres. mid./pass. ptc.

    ἐκεῖνος ἦν ὁ λύχνος ὁ καιόμενος καὶ φαίνων (John 5:35)

    he was **the burning** and shining **lamp**

    (2) Gen. sing. masc. pres. act. ptc.

    σὺ εἶ ὁ Χριστός ὁ υἱὸς τοῦ θεοῦ τοῦ ζῶντος (Matt. 16:16)

    you are the Christ, the son **of the living God**

    (3) Dat. sing. masc. pres. mid./pass. dep. ptc.

    ὃς οὐχὶ μὴ ἀπολάβῃ πολλαπλασίονα ἐν τῷ καιρῷ τούτῳ καὶ ἐν τῷ αἰῶνι τῷ ἐρχομένῳ ζωὴν αἰώνιον (Luke 18:30)[3]

    who shall not receive much more in this time and in the **coming age** eternal life?

    (4) Acc. pl. neut. perf. pass. ptc.

    ἐν ᾧ δυνήσεσθε πάντα τὰ βέλη τοῦ πονηροῦ (Eph. 6:16)

    with which you shall be able to quench **all the fiery darts** of the wicked one

  b. Appositional sense

    (1) Nom. sing. masc. pres. act. ptc.

    καὶ ὁ διάβολος ὁ πλανῶν αὐτοὺς ἐβλήθη εἰς τὴν λίμνην τοῦ πυρός (Rev. 20:10)

    and **the devil who deceived** them was thrown into the lake of fire

---

[2] John 21:25 text is from GNT, NA & WH: TR & MT have οὐδέ.

[3] Luke 18:30 text is from GNT & NA: WH has λάβῃ; TR & MT have ὃς οὐ μή.

(2) Gen. sing. neut. aor. pass. ptc.

ἐγνώρισαν **περὶ τοῦ ῥήματος τοῦ λαληθέντος** αὐτοῖς περὶ τοῦ παιδίου τούτου (Luke 2:17)[4]

they made known **concerning the word that was spoken** to them about this child

(3) Dat. sing. masc. pres. act. ptc.

ἱκανὸν μὲν οὖν χρόνον διέτριψαν παρρησιαζόμενοι **ἐπὶ τῷ κυρίῳ τῷ μαρτυροῦντι** ἐπὶ τῷ λόγῳ τῆς χάριτος (Acts 14:3)[5]

they stayed then a long time speaking boldly **in the Lord who witnessed** to the word of his grace

(4) Acc. pl. masc. perf. pass. ptc.

λῦσον **τοὺς τέσσαρας ἀγγέλους τοὺς δεδεμένους** ἐπὶ τῷ ποταμῷ τῷ μεγάλῳ Εὐφράτῃ (Rev. 9:14)

release **the four angels who are bound** at the great river Euphrates

(5) Acc. sing. neut. fut. mid. dep. ptc.

καὶ ὃ σπείρεις, οὐ **τὸ σῶμα τὸ γενησόμενον** σπείρεις ἀλλὰ γυμνὸν κόκκον (1 Cor. 15:37)

and what you sow, you do not sow **the body that shall come into existence**, but a bare grain

3. Anarthrous attributive participle

   a. Nom. pl. fem. pres. mid./pass. ptc.

   καὶ ὤφθησαν αὐτοῖς **διαμεριζόμεναι γλῶσσαι** ὡσεὶ πυρός (Acts 2:3)

   and **divided tongues** as of fire appeared to them

   b. Gen. sing. masc. pres. act. ptc.

   φοβερὸν τὸ ἐμπεσεῖν εἰς χεῖρας **θεοῦ ζῶντος** (Heb. 10:31)

   [ἐστιν, it is] frightful to fall into the hands **of the living God**

   c. Dat. sing. masc. pres. act. ptc.

   ᾧ καλῶς ποιεῖτε προσέχοντες, ὡς **λύχνῳ φαίνοντι** ἐν αὐχμηρῷ τόπῳ (2 Peter 1:19)

   to which you do well by taking heed, as **to a shining lamp** in a dark place

   d. Voc. sing. masc. perf. pass. ptc. (the only vocative ptc. in the NT)

   τότε ὁ Παῦλος πρὸς αὐτὸν εἶπεν, τύπτειν σε μέλλει ὁ θεός, **τοῖχε κεκονιαμένε** (Acts 23:3)

   then Paul said to him, "God is about to strike you, **you whitewashed wall**"

---

[4] Luke 2:17 text is from GNT, NA & WH: TR & MT have διεγνώρισαν.

[5] Acts 14:3 text is from GNT & NA: WH, TR & MT omit ἐπί before τῷ λόγῳ.

e. Acc. pl. masc. aor. mid. dep. ptc.

τότε ἔδοξεν τοῖς ἀποστόλοις καὶ τοῖς πρεσβυτέροις σὺν ὅλῃ
τῇ ἐκκλησίᾳ, **ἐκλεξαμένους ἄνδρας** ἐξ αὐτῶν πέμψαι εἰς
Ἀντιόχειαν σὺν τῷ Παύλῳ καὶ Βαρνάβᾳ (Acts 15:22)[6]
then it seemed good to the apostles and the elders with all the
church to send **chosen men** from [among] them into Antioch with
Paul and Barnabas

B. Predicate participle.
 1. Articular participle as predicate nominative of linking or equative verb
  a. Nom. sing. masc. pres. act. ptc.

  θεὸς γάρ **ἐστιν ὁ ἐνεργῶν** ἐν ὑμῖν καὶ τὸ θέλειν καὶ τὸ ἐνεργεῖν
  ὑπὲρ τῆς εὐδοκίας (Phil. 2:13)
  for **God is the one who is working** in you both to will and to perform
  according to his good pleasure

  b. Nom. pl. masc. pres. mid./pass. dep. ptc.

  καὶ εἶπέν μοι, **οὗτοί εἰσιν οἱ ἐρχόμενοι** ἐκ τῆς θλίψεως τῆς
  μεγάλης (Rev. 7:14)
  and he said to me, "**these are the ones who came** out of the great
  tribulation"

  c. Nom. pl. masc. aor. act. ptc.

  οὐχ **οὗτός ἐστιν ὁ πορθήσας** εἰς Ἰερουσαλὴμ τοὺς ἐπικαλουμένους
  τὸ ὄνομα τοῦτο; (Acts 9:21)[7]
  is this one not **he who made havoc** of those who called on this name
  in Jerusalem?

  d. Nom. sing. masc. fut. act. ptc.

  ᾔδει γὰρ ἐξ ἀρχῆς ὁ Ἰησοῦς τίνες εἰσὶν οἱ μὴ πιστεύοντες, καὶ **τίς
  ἐστιν ὁ παραδώσων** αὐτόν (John 6:64)
  for Jesus knew from the beginning who they are who do not believe
  and **who is the one who will betray** him

  e. Nom. pl. masc. perf. act. ptc.

  ὑμεῖς δέ **ἐστε οἱ διαμεμενηκότες** μετ᾽ ἐμοῦ ἐν τοῖς πειρασμοῖς
  μου (Luke 22:28)
  but **you are the ones who have remained** with me in my temptations

 2. Anarthrous/articular participle as predicate nominative with elliptical verbs
  a. Nom. sing. masc. pres. act. ptc.

  ζῶν γὰρ **ὁ λόγος** τοῦ θεοῦ καὶ ἐνεργής (Heb. 4:12)
  for **the word** of God [ἐστιν, is] **living** and energetic

---

[6] Acts 15:22 text is from GNT, NA, WH & TR: MT has Βαρναβᾷ.
[7] Acts 9:21 text is from GNT, NA & WH: TR & MT have ἐν for εἰς; TR has Ἱερουσαλήμ.

b. Nom. sing. masc. pres. act. ptc.

ὅτι ἄλλος ἐστὶν ὁ σπείρων καὶ ἄλλος ὁ θερίζων (John 4:37)

for one is the one who sows, and **another [ἐστιν, is] the one who reaps**

c. Nom. sing. masc. aor. act. ptc.

ὅτι ὁ **θεὸς** ὁ εἰπών, ἐκ σκότους φῶς λάμψει (2 Cor. 4:6)

for **God [ἐστιν, is] the one who commanded** the light to shine out of darkness

d. Nom. pl. masc. perf. pass. ptc.

οἱ **θεμέλιοι** τοῦ τείχους τῆς πόλεως παντὶ λίθῳ τιμίῳ **κεκοσμημένοι** (Rev. 21:19)

the foundations of the wall of the city **[ἦσαν, were] adorned** with every kind of precious stone

C. Predicate accusative participle with the infinitive and participle of εἰμι.

1. Acc. sing. masc. pres. mid./pass. dep. ptc.

καὶ ἐγένετο ἐν τῷ εἶναι αὐτὸν **προσευχόμενον** (Luke 9:18)

and it happened **while he was praying**

2. Acc. pl. masc. perf. pass. ptc.

καὶ **ὑμᾶς** ποτε **ὄντας ἀπηλλοτριωμένους** καὶ ἐχθροὺς τῇ διανοίᾳ ἐν τοῖς ἔργοις τοῖς πονηροῖς (Col. 1:21)

and **you who** once **were alienated** and enemies in your mind by wicked works

D. Accusative object complement participle.

1. Acc. sing. neut. pres. act. ptc.

οἷς καὶ **παρέστησεν ἑαυτὸν ζῶντα** μετὰ τὸ παθεῖν αὐτόν (Acts 1:3)

to whom also **he presented himself alive** after he suffered

2. Acc. sing. masc. perf. pass. ptc.

ὁ **Φῆλιξ κατέλιπεν τὸν Παῦλον δεδεμένον** (Acts 24:27)

Felix left Paul bound

II. **Substantival participles** are found in all four cases (not vocative) and both numbers, and are both articular and anarthrous.

A. Nominative case participle.

1. Nominative subject of finite verb

a. Nom. sing. masc. pres. act. ptc.

λέγει ὁ **μαρτυρῶν** ταῦτα, Ναί, ἔρχομαι ταχύ (Rev. 22:20)

the one who testifies these things **says,** "yes I am coming quickly"

    b. Nom. sing. masc. perf. act. ptc.

       ὁ ἑωρακὼς ἐμέ ἑώρακεν τὸν πατέρα (John 14:9)

       the one who has seen me **has seen** the father

    c. Nom. sing. neut. pres. mid./pass. dep. ptc.

       καὶ οὐκ ᾔδει ὅτι ἀληθές ἐστιν τὸ γινόμενον διὰ τοῦ ἀγγέλου
       (Acts 12:9)

       and he was unaware that **the thing that was happening** by the angel
       was real

    d. Nom. pl. masc. aor. act. ptc.

       καὶ διηγήσαντο αὐτοῖς οἱ ἰδόντες πῶς ἐγένετο τῷ δαιμονιζομένῳ
       (Mark 5:16)

       and **those who saw [it] related** to them how it happened to the one who
       was demonized

  2. Nominative subject of an elliptical verb

    a. Nom. sing. masc. pres. act. ptc.

       ἰδού, ἔρχομαι ὡς κλέπτης. μακάριος ὁ γρηγορῶν καὶ τηρῶν τὰ
       ἱμάτια αὐτοῦ (Rev. 16:15)

       behold, I am coming as a thief. **the one who watches** and **keeps**
       his garments [ἐστιν, **is**] **blessed**

    b. Nom. sing. masc. aor. mid. ptc.

       τίς ὁ ἁψάμενός μου; (Luke 8:45)

       the one who touched me [ἐστιν, **is who**]?

    c. Nom. pl. masc. perf. pass. ptc.

       μακάριοι οἱ εἰς τὸ δεῖπνον τοῦ γάμου τοῦ ἀρνίου κεκλημένοι
       (Rev. 19:9)

       those who have been invited to the wedding supper of the lamb
       [εἰσιν, **are**] **blessed**

    d. Nom. sing. masc. fut. act. ptc.

       καὶ τίς ὁ κακώσων ὑμᾶς . . . ; (1 Peter 3:13)

       and **the one who will injure** you [ἐστιν, **is**] **who** . . . ?

  3. Articular participle as appositional

    a. Appositional to common noun

      (1) nom. sing. masc. pres. ptc. and pres. mid./pass. dep. ptc.

         ἅγιος ἅγιος ἅγιος κύριος ὁ θεὸς ὁ παντοκράτωρ, ὁ ἦν καὶ
         ὁ ὢν καὶ ὁ ἐρχόμενος (Rev. 4:8)

         holy, holy, holy, Lord **God** almighty, who was and **who is** and
         who is coming

      (2) Nom. sing. masc. aor. act. ptc.

         ἐγώ εἰμι ὁ ἄρτος ὁ ζῶν ὁ ἐκ τοῦ οὐρανοῦ καταβάς (John 6:51)
         I am the living **bread that came down** from heaven

(3) Nom. sing. neut. perf. pass. ptc.

οὐδὲ γὰρ **ὄνομά** ἐστιν ἕτερον ὑπὸ τὸν οὐρανὸν **τὸ δεδομένον** ἐν ἀνθρώποις ἐν ᾧ δεῖ σωθῆναι ἡμᾶς (Acts 4:12)

for there is no other **name that has been given** under heaven among people, by which we must be saved

b. Appositional to proper noun

(1) Nom. sing. masc. pres. act. ptc.

ᾔδει δὲ καὶ **Ἰούδας ὁ παραδιδοὺς** αὐτὸν τὸν τόπον (John 18:2)

but **Judas who** also **betrayed** him knew the place

(2) Nom. sing. masc. aor. act. ptc.

ἀσπάζομαι ὑμᾶς ἐγὼ **Τέρτιος ὁ γράψας** τὴν ἐπιστολὴν ἐν κυρίῳ (Rom. 16:22)

I, **Tertius, who wrote** this epistle, greet you in the Lord

c. Appositional to pronoun

(1) Nom. sing. masc. pres. act. ptc.

τίς γὰρ μείζων, ὁ ἀνακείμενος ἢ **ὁ διακονῶν**; (Luke 22:27)

for **who** [ἐστιν, is] greater, the one who reclines [at the table] or **the one who serves**?

(2) Nom. sing. masc. aor. act. ptc.

αὐτὸς γὰρ ἐστιν ἡ εἰρήνη ἡμῶν, **ὁ ποιήσας** τὰ ἀμφότερα ἕν (Eph. 2:14)

for **he** is our peace **who made** both one

d. Appositional to adjective

(1) Nom. sing. masc. pres. act. ptc.

τάδε λέγει ὁ ἅγιος, ὁ ἀληθινός, **ὁ ἔχων** τὴν κλεῖν Δαυίδ (Rev. 3:7)[8]

the holy one, the true one, the one who has the key of David says these things

(2) Nom. sing. masc. aor. act. ptc.

αἳ ὅτε ἦν ἐν τῇ Γαλιλαίᾳ ἠκολούθουν αὐτῷ καὶ διηκόνουν αὐτῷ, καὶ **ἄλλαι πολλαὶ αἱ συναναβᾶσαι** αὐτῷ εἰς Ἱεροσόλυμα (Mark 15:41)[9]

who when he was in Galilee followed him and ministered to him, and **many others who came with** him to Jerusalem

4. Articular participle as a hanging nominative

a. Nom. sing. masc. aor. act. ptc.

ὁ δὲ **ὑπομείνας** εἰς τέλος, **οὗτος** σωθήσεται (Matt. 24:13)

but **the one who remains** to the end, **this one** shall be saved

---

[8] Rev. 3:7 text is from GNT & NA: WH has Δαυείδ; TR has κλεῖδα τοῦ Δαβίδ; MT has τὴν κλεῖν τοῦ Δαβίδ.

[9] Mark 15:41 text is from GNT & NA: WH has Ἱεροσόλυμα; TR & MT have αἲ καὶ ἦν.

   b. Nom. sing. masc. pres. act. ptc.

      καὶ ὁ νικῶν καὶ ὁ τηρῶν ἄχρι τέλους τὰ ἔργα μου, δώσω αὐτῷ ἐξουσίαν ἐπὶ τῶν ἐθνῶν (Rev. 2:26)

      and **the one who overcomes** and **the one who keeps** my works unto the end, I will give **to him** authority over the nations

5. Articular participle as nominative of address

   a. Nom. pl. masc. pres. act. ptc.

      διὰ τοῦτο εὐφραίνεσθε, οἱ οὐρανοὶ καὶ οἱ ἐν αὐτοῖς σκηνοῦντες (Rev. 12:12)

      because of this, rejoice you heavens and **you who live** in them

   b. Nom. pl. masc. perf. pass. ptc.

      τότε ἐρεῖ ὁ βασιλεὺς τοῖς ἐκ δεξιῶν αὐτοῦ, Δεῦτε οἱ εὐλογημένοι τοῦ πατρός μου (Matt. 25:34)

      then the king will say to those [οὖσιν, who are] at his right hand, "Come, **you who are blessed** of my father"

B. Genitive case participles are similar in possibilities to genitive nouns. The following examples, in a declining order of frequency, are representative of about 80 percent of the genitive substantives in the NT. Most are present tense.

  1. Articular appositional gen. sing. neut. pres. act. ptc.

    φύλαξον διὰ πνεύματος ἁγίου τοῦ ἐνοικοῦντος ἐν ἡμῖν (2 Tim. 1:14)

    keep **by the Holy Spirit who dwells** in us

  2. Partitive gen. pl. masc. pres. mid./pass. ptc.

    τοῦτο δὲ οὐδεὶς ἔγνω τῶν ἀνακειμένων πτὸς τί εἶπεν αὐτῷ (John 13:28)

    but **no one of those reclining** [at the table] knew why he said this to him

  3. Possessive gen. sing. masc. pres. mid./pass. dep. ptc.

    καὶ εἶδον ἐπὶ τὴν δεξιὰν τοῦ καθημένου ἐπὶ τοῦ θρόνου βιβλίον (Rev. 5:1)

    and I saw a book at the right hand **of the one who was sitting** on the throne

  4. Gen. sing. masc. pres. act. ptc. object of prep. ἐκ

    πάντες γὰρ ἐκ τοῦ περισσεύοντος αὐτοῖς ἔβαλον (Mark 12:44)

    for all cast [in] **out of** their **abundance**

  5. Gen. sing. masc. pres. act. ptc. object of prep. ἀπό

    ἵνα ῥυσθῶ ἀπὸ τῶν ἀπειθούντων ἐν τῇ Ἰουδαίᾳ (Rom. 15:31)

    that I may be delivered **from those who disobey** in Judea

  6. Descriptive gen. pl. neut. pres. act. ptc.

    ἅ ἐστιν σκιὰ τῶν μελλόντων, τὸ δὲ σῶμα τοῦ Χριστοῦ (Col. 2:17)

    which are **a shadow of coming things,** but the body [ἐστιν, is] of Christ

7. Gen. pl. masc. pres. act. ptc. object of prep. περί

ταῦτα ἔγραψα ὑμῖν **περὶ τῶν πλανώντων** ὑμᾶς (1 John 2:26)

I wrote these things to you **concerning those who are attempting to deceive** you

8. Objective gen. pl. neut. pres. mid./pass. dep. ptc.

ἀποψυχόντων ἀνθρώπων ἀπὸ φόβου καὶ **προσδοκίας τῶν ἐπερχομένων** τῇ οἰκουμένῃ (Luke 21:26)

people fainting because of fear and **expectation of those things that are coming upon** the world

9. Subjective gen. sing. masc. aor. act. ptc.

ἡμᾶς δεῖ ἐργάζεσθαι τὰ ἔργα **τοῦ πέμψαντός** με ἕως ἡμέρα ἐστίν (John 9:4)[10]

we must work **the works of the one who sent** me while it is day

10. Gen. pl. masc. aor. act. ptc. of relationship

ὥστε μαρτυρεῖτε ἑαυτοῖς, ὅτι **υἱοί** ἐστε **τῶν φονευσάντων** τοὺς προφήτας (Matt. 23:31)

so that you testify against yourselves, that you are **sons of those who murdered** the prophets

C. Dative case participles.

1. Indirect object participles

a. Dat. sing. masc. pres. mid./pass. dep. ptc.

καὶ ὅταν δώσουσιν τὰ ζῷα δόξαν καὶ τιμὴν καὶ εὐχαριστίαν **τῷ καθημένῳ** ἐπὶ τῷ θρόνῳ (Rev. 4:9)[11]

and when the living creatures shall give glory and honor and thanksgiving **to the one who sits** on the throne

b. Dat. pl. masc. aor. act. ptc.

τίς εἶ; ἵνα ἀπόκρισιν δῶμεν **τοῖς πέμψασιν** ἡμᾶς (John 1:22)

you are who? (who are you?) that we may give an answer **to those who sent** us

c. Dat. pl. masc. perf. pass. ptc.

εἴπατε **τοῖς κεκλημένοις**, ἰδού τὸ ἄριστόν μου ἡτοίμακα (Matt. 22:4)[12]

say **to those who have been invited**, "behold, I have prepared my dinner"

---

[10] John 9:4 text is from GNT, NA & WH: TR & MT have ἐμὲ δεῖ.

[11] Rev. 4:9 text is from GNT & NA: WH has ἐπὶ τοῦ θρόνου; TR has ζῷα and ἐπὶ τοῦ θρόνου; MT has δῶσι τὰ ζῷα and ἐπὶ τοῦ θρόνου.

[12] Matt. 22:4 text is from GNT, NA & WH: TR & MT have ἡτοίμασα.

  2. Articular appositional participles

    a. Dat. sing. masc. pres. act. ptc.

      τῷ **νικῶντι** δώσω **αὐτῷ** φαγεῖν ἐκ τοῦ ξύλου τῆς ζωῆς (Rev. 2:7)

      I will give **to him who overcomes** to eat of the tree of life

    b. Dat. pl. masc. aor. act. ptc.

      οὗτοι οἱ ἔσχατοι μίαν ὥραν ἐποίησαν, καὶ ἴσους ἡμῖν αὐτοὺς
      ἐποίησας **τοῖς βαστάσασι(ν)** τὸ βάρος τῆς ἡμέρας (Matt. 20:12)

      these last worked one hour, and you made them equal **to us who have
      borne** the burden of the day

    c. Dat. pl. masc. perf. pass. ptc.

      οὐ παντὶ τῷ λαῷ, ἀλλὰ **μάρτυσιν τοῖς προκεχειροτονημένοις**
      ὑπὸ τοῦ θεοῦ (Acts 10:41)

      not to all the people, but **to witnesses who had been chosen before
      by God**

  3. Dative of direct object with certain verbs

    a. Dat. pl. neut. pres. pass. ptc.

      ἧς ὁ κύριος διήνοιξεν τὴν καρδίαν προσέχειν **τοῖς λαλουμένοις**
      ὑπὸ τοῦ Παύλου (Acts 16:14)

      whose heart the Lord opened to follow **the words spoken** by Paul

    b. Dat. sing. masc. aor. act. ptc.

      καὶ προσκυνήσατε **τῷ ποιήσαντι** τὸν οὐρανὸν καὶ τὴν γῆν
      (Rev. 14:7)

      and worship **the one who made** heaven and earth

  4. Dative object of prep. ἐν

    a. Dat. sing. masc. pres. act. ptc.

      καὶ ὤμοσεν **ἐν τῷ ζῶντι** εἰς τοὺς αἰῶνας τῶν αἰώνων (Rev. 10:6)

      and he swore **by the one who lives** forever and ever

    b. Dat. pl. masc. perf. pass. ptc.

      τοῦ λαβεῖν αὐτοὺς ἄφεσιν ἁμαρτιῶν καὶ κλῆρον **ἐν τοῖς
      ἡγιασμένοις** πίστει τῇ εἰς ἐμέ (Acts 26:18)

      that they may receive forgiveness of sins and an inheritance **among
      those who have been sanctified** by faith that [οὔσῃ, is] in me

  5. Dative participle of advantage

    a. Dat. sing. masc. aor. act. and pass. ptc.

      ἵνα οἱ ζῶντες μηκέτι ἑαυτοῖς ζῶσιν ἀλλὰ **τῷ ὑπὲρ αὐτῶν
      ἀποθανόντι** καὶ **ἐγερθέντι** (2 Cor. 5:15)

      in order that those who live should no longer live for themselves
      but **for the one who died** for them and **was raised**

b. Dat. sing. masc. pres. act. ptc.
πάντα δυνατὰ τῷ πιστεύοντι (Mark 9:23)
all things [ἐστιν/εἰσιν, are] possible **to the one who believes**
c. Dat. pl. masc. perf. pass. ptc.
ὕστερον δὲ καρπὸν εἰρηνικὸν τοῖς δι᾽ αὐτῆς γεγυμνασμένοις
ἀποδίδωσιν δικαιοσύνης (Heb. 12:11)
but afterward it produces peaceful fruit of righteousness **for those who
have been trained** by it
6. Dative participle of disadvantage
a. Dat. pl. fem. pres. act. ptc.
οὐαὶ δὲ ταῖς ἐν γαστρὶ ἐχούσαις καὶ ταῖς θηλαζούσαις ἐν
ἐκείναις ταῖς ἡμέραις (Mark 13:17)
but **woe to those who are pregnant** and to those who nurse in
those days
b. Dat. sing. masc. aor. act. ptc.
ἡ γὰρ κρίσις ἀνέλεος τῷ μὴ ποιήσαντι ἔλεος (James 2:13)[13]
for judgment [ἔσται, will be] without mercy **to the one who did
not perform** mercy
c. Dat. pl. masc. perf. pass. ptc.
τοῖς δὲ μεμιαμμένοις καὶ ἀπίστοις οὐδὲν καθαρόν (Titus 1:15)[14]
but nothing [ἐστιν, is] pure **to those who are defiled** and unbelieving

D. Accusative participles.
1. Accusative participle as direct object
a. Direct object of finite verb
(1) Articular acc. pl. masc. pres. act. ptc.
καὶ πλανᾷ τοὺς κατοικοῦντας ἐπὶ τῆς γῆς (Rev. 13:14)
and **he deceives those who live** on the earth
(2) Anarthrous acc. pl. masc. pres. act. ptc.
πεινῶντας ἐνέπλησεν ἀγαθῶν καὶ πλουτοῦντας
ἐξαπέστειλεν κενούς (Luke 1:53)
he filled the hungry with good things, and **he sent the rich away**
empty
(3) Articular acc. sing. masc. aor. act. ptc.
ὁ δεχόμενος ὑμᾶς ἐμὲ δέχεται, καὶ ὁ ἐμὲ δεχόμενος δέχεται
τὸν ἀποστείλαντά με (Matt. 10:40)
the one who receives you receives me, and the one who receives
me **receives the one who sent** me

---

[13] James 2:13 text is from GNT, NA, WH & MT: TR has ἀνίλεως.
[14] Titus 1:15 text is from GNT, NA & WH: TR & MT have μεμιασμένοις.

(4) Articular acc. sing. masc. perf. pass. ptc.

ἔρχεται ὁ πονηρὸς καὶ **ἁρπάζει τὸ ἐσπαρμένον** ἐν τῇ καρδίᾳ αὐτοῦ (Matt. 13:19)

the evil one comes and **snatches the seed sown** in his heart

b. Direct object of infinitive

(1) Articular acc. pl. neut. pres. act. ptc.

ἤρξατο αὐτοῖς **λέγειν τὰ μέλλοντα** αὐτῷ συμβαίνειν (Mark 10:32)

he began **to tell** them **the things that were about** to happen to him

(2) Articular acc. pl. masc. aor. act. ptc.

καὶ περιεβλέπετο **ἰδεῖν τὴν** τοῦτο **ποιήσασαν** (Mark 5:32)

and he looked around **to see the woman who had done** this

(3) Articular acc. sing. neut. 2 perf. act. ptc.

ἦλθεν γὰρ ὁ υἱὸς τοῦ ἀνθρώπου **ζητῆσαι** καὶ **σῶσαι τὸ ἀπολωλός** (Luke 19:10)

for the son of man came **to seek** and **to save that which is lost**

c. Direct object of participle

(1) Articular acc. pl. neut. pres. act. ptc.

ἀνθρωπός τις ἦν πλούσιος ὃς εἶχεν οἰκονόμον, καὶ οὗτος διεβλήθη αὐτῷ ὡς **διασκορπίζων τὰ ὑπάρχοντα** (Luke 16:1)

a certain man was rich, who had a manager, and this one was accused by him as **squandering his property**

(2) Articular acc. sing. masc. aor. act. ptc.

καὶ πᾶς ὁ ἀγαπῶν **τὸν γεννήσαντα** ἀγαπᾷ καὶ τὸν γεγεννημένον ἐξ αὐτοῦ (1 John 5:1)

and everyone who loves **the one who begets** also loves the one who has been begotten of him

(3) Articular acc. pl. neut. perf. pass. ptc.

μακάριος ὁ ἀναγινώσκων καὶ οἱ ἀκούοντες τοὺς λόγους τῆς προφητείας καὶ **τηροῦντες τὰ** ἐν αὐτῇ **γεγραμμένα** (Rev. 1:3)

blessed [ἐστιν, is] the one who reads and **those** who hear the words of the prophecy and **who keep the things that are written** in it

2. Articular appositional participles

a. Acc. pl. masc. pres. act. ptc.

καὶ τί τὸ ὑπερβάλλον μέγεθος τῆς δυνάμεως αὐτοῦ εἰς ἡμᾶς **τοὺς πιστεύοντας** (Eph. 1:19)

and what [ἐστιν, is] the surpassing greatness of his power **toward us who believe**

b. Acc. sing. masc. aor. act. ptc.

οἵτινες παρεισάξουσιν αἱρέσιες ἀπωλείας καὶ τὸν ἀγοράσαντα αὐτοὺς δεσπότην ἀνούμενοι (2 Peter 2:1)

who shall bring in destructive heresies, and denying **the Lord who purchased** them

c. Acc. pl. masc. perf. act. ptc.

εἶπεν δὲ καὶ πρός τινας τοὺς πεποιθότας ἐφ᾽ ἑαυτοῖς ὅτι εἰσὶν δίκαιοι (Luke 18:9)

and he spoke also **to some who trusted** in themselves that they are righteous

3. Accusative participle as subject of infinitive

Acc. sing. masc. pres. mid./pass. dep. ptc.

πιστεῦσαι γὰρ δεῖ τὸν προσερχόμενον τῷ θεῷ (Heb. 11:6)

for **the one who approaches must believe** in God

4. Accusative participle as an object of a preposition

a. Accusative object of πρός

(1) Acc. sing. masc. aor. act. ptc.

νῦν δὲ ὑπάγω πρὸς τὸν πέμψαντά με (John 16:5)

but now I am going **to the one who sent** me

(2) Acc. pl. masc. perf. pass. ptc.

ἔλεγεν δὲ πρὸς τοὺς κεκλημένους παραβολήν (Luke 14:7)

but he was speaking a parable **to those who had been invited**

b. Accusative object of ἐπί

(1) Acc. sing. masc. aor. act. ptc.

τοῖς πιστεύουσιν ἐπὶ τὸν ἐγείραντα Ἰησοῦν τὸν κύριον ἡμῶν ἐκ νεκρῶν (Rom. 4:24)

to those who believe **on him who raised** Jesus our Lord from the dead

(2) Acc. sing. neut. perf. act. ptc.

καὶ πορεύεται ἐπὶ τὸ ἀπολωλός ἕως εὕρῃ αὐτό (Luke 15:4)

and he goes **after that which is lost** until he finds it

c. Accusative object of κατά

(1) Acc. sing. neut. perf. pass. ptc.

καὶ ἐν τῷ εἰσαγαγεῖν τοὺς γονεῖς τὸ παιδίον Ἰησοῦν τοῦ ποιῆσαι αὐτοὺς κατὰ τὸ εἰθισμένον τοῦ νόμου περὶ αὐτοῦ (Luke 2:27)

and when the parents brought in the child Jesus that they might perform for him **according to the custom** of the law

   (2) Acc. sing. masc. aor. act. ptc.

ἀλλὰ **κατὰ τὸν καλέσαντα** ὑμᾶς ἅγιον καὶ αὐτοὶ ἅγιοι
ἐν πάσῃ ἀναστροφῇ γενήθητε (1 Peter 1:15)

but **according as the one who called** you [is] holy, you also
yourselves be holy in all [your] conduct

  d. Accusative object of διά

    (1) Acc. pl. masc. pres. act. ptc.

οὐχὶ πάντες εἰσὶν λειτουργικὰ πνεύματα εἰς διακονίαν
ἀποστελλόμενα **διὰ τοὺς μέλλοντας** κληρονομεῖν σωτηρίαν;
(Heb. 1:14)

are they all not ministering spirits sent forth for service **on account
of those who are about** to inherit salvation?

    (2) Acc. sing. masc. aor. act. ptc.

ἐὰν δέ τις ὑμῖν εἴπῃ, τοῦτο ἱερόθυτόν ἐστι(ν), μὴ
ἐσθίετε **δί ἐκεῖνον τὸν μηνύσαντα** καὶ τὴν συνείδησιν
(1 Cor. 10:28)[15]

but if anyone says to you, "this is offered to idols," do not eat
because of the one who informed [you]

5. Granville Sharp's rule applied to participles. Two singular personal
substantives joined by **καί** with the first one articular and the second
anarthrous refer to the same person.

  a. Nom. sing. masc. pres. act. ptc.

καὶ **πᾶς ὁ ἀκούων** μου τοὺς λόγους τούτους **καὶ μὴ ποιῶν**
αὐτούς ὁμοιωθήσεται ἀνδρὶ μωρῷ (Matt. 7:26)

and **everyone who hears** these words of mine **and does not do** them
shall be likened to a foolish man

  b. Gen. sing. masc. pres. act. ptc.

κατέναντι οὗ ἐπίστευσεν θεοῦ **τοῦ ζωοποιοῦντος** τοὺς νεκρούς
καὶ λαλοῦντος τὰ μὴ ὄντα ὡς ὄντα (Rom. 4:17)[16]

before God whom he believed, **who makes** the dead **live and calls**
the things that do not live as living

  c. Dat. sing. masc. pres. and aor. act. ptc.

τῷ ἀγαπῶντι ἡμᾶς **καὶ λύσαντι** ἡμᾶς ἐκ τῶν ἁμαρτιῶν ἡμῶν
ἐν τῷ αἵματι αὐτοῦ (Rev. 1:5)[17]

to the one who loves us **and set** us free from our sins by his blood

---

[15] 1 Cor. 10:28 text is from GNT, NA & WH: TR & MT have εἰδωλόθυτόν.

[16] Rom. 4:17 text is from GNT & NA: WH, TR & MT have ζωοποιοῦντος.

[17] Rev. 1:5 text is from GNT, NA & WH: TR & MT have λούσαντι; TR has ἀγαπήσαντι.

d. Acc. sing. masc. aor. act. ptc.

θεὸν τὸν ἐγείραντα αὐτὸν ἐκ νεκρῶν καὶ δόξαν αὐτῷ δόντα, ὥστε τὴν πίστιν ὑμῶν καὶ ἐλπίδα εἶναι εἰς θεόν (1 Peter 1:21)
God, **who raised** him from the dead **and gave** glory to him so that your faith and hope might be in God

III. **Adverbial or circumstantial participles** are always anarthrous. They indicate various subordinate clauses, e.g., temporal, causal, manner, instrumental, concessive, purpose, conditional, and complementary. Most are found in the aorist tense, followed by the present and perfect tenses, and once in the future. About 83 percent are found in the nominative case, about 14 percent in the genitive case, about 2 percent in the accusative, and 0.5 percent in the dative case.

A. Temporal participles indicate a time relationship with the main verb. The present tense indicates simultaneous action with the main verb, the aorist tense indicates antecedent action, the perfect tense indicates simultaneous or antecedent action depending on the context, and the future tense indicates subsequent action.

1. Nominative case
   a. Nom. pl. masc. pres. act. ptc.

   καὶ ταῦτα λέτοντες μόλις **κατέπαυσαν** τοὺς ὄχλους τοῦ μὴ θύειν αὐτοῖς (Acts 14:18)
   and **while they were speaking,** with difficulty **they stopped** the crowds from sacrificing to them

   b. Nom. sing. masc. aor. act. ptc.

   καὶ **ποιήσας** φραγέλλιον ἐκ σχοινίων πάντας **ἐξέβαλεν** ἐκ τοῦ ἱεροῦ (John 2:15)
   and **when he made** a whip of cords, **he drove** them all out of the temple

2. Genitive absolute involves a genitive substantive (pronoun, noun, adjective, or participle) as subject of a genitive participle in a subordinate relationship (often detached) to the rest of the sentence.

   a. Gen. pl. masc. pres. pass. ptc.

   εἴπατε ὅτι οἱ μαθηταὶ αὐτοῦ νυκτὸς ἐλθόντες **ἔκλεψαν** αὐτὸν **ἡμῶν κοιμωμένων** (Matt. 28:13)
   say that "his disciples came at night and **stole** him **while we were sleeping"**

   b. Gen. sing. fem. aor. mid. dep. ptc.

   ὀψίας δὲ **γενομένης** μόνος **ἦν** ἐκεῖ (Matt. 14:23)
   and **when evening came he was** there alone

    c. Gen. pl. fem. perf. pass. ptc.

ἔρχεται ὁ Ἰησοῦς **τῶν θυρῶν κεκλεισμένων** καὶ ἔστη εἰς τὸ μέσον (John 20:26)

Jesus came, **after the doors had been locked**, and stood among them

3. Dative absolute has a dative substantive as the subject of a dative participle in a subordinate relation to the main clause; rare in the NT.

    a. Dat. sing. masc. pres. mid./pass. dep. and act. ptc.

ἐγένετο δέ **μοι πορευομένῳ** καὶ **ἐγγίζοντι** τῇ Δαμασκῷ περὶ μεσημβρίαν ἐξαίφνης ἐκ τοῦ οὐρανοῦ περιαστράψαν φῶς ἱκανὸν περὶ ἐμέ (Acts 22:6)

and it came to pass, **while I was traveling** and **drawing near** to Damascus about midday, a bright light suddenly shown out of heaven around me

    b. Dat. sing. masc. aor. act. ptc. and gen. sing. masc. pres. mid./pass. dep. ptc.

ἐγένετο δέ **μοι ὑποστρέψαντι** εἰς Ἰερουσαλήμ καὶ **προσευχομένου μου** ἐν τῷ ἱερῷ γενέσθαι με ἐν ἐκστάσει (Acts 22:17)[18]

and it happened **after I returned** to Jerusalem, and **while I was praying** in the temple, I was in a trance

4. Accusative absolute involves an accusative substantive as subject of an accusative participle in a subordinate relationship to the main clause. Acc. sing. fem. aor. act. ptc.

ἐγένετο δὲ ἐν ταῖς ἡμέραις ἐκείναις **ἀσθενήσασαν** αὐτὴν ἀποθανεῖν (Acts 9:37)

and it came to pass in those days **after being sick** she died

B. Causal participles indicate a cause or reason for the main clause.

    1. Nominative case

       a. Nom. sing. masc. pres. act. ptc.

ὥστε ἐχθρὸς ὑμῶν γέγονα **ἀληθεύων** ὑμῖν; (Gal. 4:16)

wherefore did I become your enemy **because I told** you **the truth**?

       b. Nom. sing. masc. aor. pass. ptc.

σπλαγχνισθεὶς δὲ ὁ κύριος τοῦ δούλου ἐκείνου ἀπέλυσεν αὐτόν (Matt. 18:27)

and **because he had pity** [on him] the owner of the servant released him

---

[18] Acts 22:17 text is from GNT, NA, WH & MT: TR has Ἱερουσαλήμ.

c. Nom. sing. masc. perf. act. ptc.

ὅτι κατέβη ὁ διάβολος πρὸς ὑμᾶς ἔχων θυμὸν μέγαν, **εἰδὼς** ὅτι ὀλίγον καιρὸν ἔχει (Rev. 12:12)

for the devil has come down to you having great wrath, **because he knows** that he has a short time

2. Genitive absolute as causal
   a. Gen. pl. masc. pres. act. ptc.

ἐν ᾧ ξενίζονται **μὴ συντρεχόντων ὑμῶν** εἰς τὴν αὐτὴν τῆς ἀσωτίας ἀνάχυσιν (1 Peter 4:4)

in which they are suprised, **because you do not run with [them]** to the same excess of debauchery

   b. Gen. sing. fem. aor. mid. dep. ptc.

εἶτα **γενομένης θλίψεως** ἢ **διωγμοῦ** διὰ τὸν λόγον εὐθὺς σκανδαλίζονται (Mark 4:17)[19]

then **because tribulation** or **persecution has arisen** because of the word immediately they are offended

3. Dative absolute as causal
   Dat. pl. masc. pres. ptc.

καὶ καταγγέλλουσιν ἔθη ἃ οὐκ ἔξεστιν ἡμῖν παραδέχεσθαι οὐδὲ ποιεῖν **Ῥωμαίοις οὖσιν** (Acts 16:21)

and they announce customs, that are not lawful for us to accept or to do, **because we are Romans**

4. Accusative case as causal
   a. Acc. sing. masc. pres. act. ptc.

Διδάσκαλε, ἤνεγκα τὸν υἱόν μου πρός σε, **ἔχοντα** πνεῦμα ἄλαλον (Mark 9:17)

teacher, I brought my son to you **because he has** a mute spirit

   b. Acc. sing. masc. aor. act. ptc.

ἡ γὰρ ἀγάπη τοῦ Χριστοῦ συνέχει ἡμᾶς, **κρίναντας** τοῦτο, ὅτι εἷς ὑπὲρ πάντων ἀπέθανεν, ἄρα οἱ πάντες ἀπέθανον (2 Cor. 5:14)[20]

for the love of Christ impels us, **because we have judged** this, that [since] one died for all, then all died

   c. Acc. pl. masc. perf. pass. ptc.

ἀλλ᾽ οὐκ ὠφέλησεν ὁ λόγος τῆς ἀκοῆς ἐκείνους **μὴ συγκεκερασμένους** τῇ πίστει τοῖς ἀκούσασιν (Heb. 4:2)[21]

but the word that was heard did not profit them, **because they were not united** by faith to the things [they] heard

---

[19] Mark 4:17 text is from GNT, NA & WH: TR & MT have εὐθέως.
[20] 2 Cor. 5:14 text is from GNT, NA & WH: TR & MT have ὅτι εἰ εἷς.
[21] Heb. 4:2 text is from GNT, NA, TR & MT: WH has συνκεκερασμένους.

C. Participle of manner.

   1. Nominative case

      a. Nom. sing. masc. pres. act. ptc.

        ἦλθεν γὰρ Ἰωάννης **μήτε ἐσθίων μήτε πίνων,** καὶ λέγουσιν, δαιμόνιον ἔχει (Matt. 11:18)[22]

        for John came **neither eating nor drinking,** and they say, "he has a demon"

      b. Nom. sing. masc. aor. pass. ptc.

        πίστει κατέλιπεν Αἴγυπτον, **μὴ φοβηθεὶς** τὸν θυμὸν τοῦ βασιλέως (Heb. 11:27)

        by faith he left Egypt, **not fearing** the wrath of the king

      c. Nom. sing. masc. perf. pass. ptc.

        ὁ λόγος ὑμῶν πάντοτε ἐν χάριτι, ἅλατι **ἠρτυμένος** (Col. 4:6)

        [let] your speech [be] always with grace, **seasoned** with salt

      d. Nom. pl. masc. fut. act. ptc.

        αὐτοὶ γὰρ ἀγρυπνοῦσιν ὑπὲρ τῶν ψυχῶν ὑμῶν ὡς λόγον **ἀποδώσοντες** (Heb. 13:17)

        for they care for your souls as **those about to give** an account

   2. Accusative case

      Acc. pl. masc. aor. act. ptc.

      βούλομαι οὖν προσεύχεσθαι τοὺς ἄνδρας ἐν παντὶ τόπῳ, **ἐπαίροντας** ὁσίους χεῖρας χωρὶς ὀργῆς καὶ διαλογισμοῦ (1 Tim. 2:8)

      therefore, I want the men to pray in every place, **holding up** holy hands apart from anger and dispute

D. Redundant participle of speaking is associated with another verb of speaking and is either redundant or equivalent to quotation marks. It is usually in the nominative case.

   1. Nom. sing. masc. pres. act. ptc.

      καὶ προσελθὼν ὁ Ἰησοῦς **ἐλάλησεν** αὐτοῖς, **λέγων,** ἐδόθη μοι πᾶσα ἐξουσία ἐν οὐρανῷ καὶ ἐπὶ τῆς γῆς (Matt. 28:18)[23]

      and when Jesus came **he spoke** to them: "all authority has been given to me in heaven and on earth"

   2. Nom. sing. masc. aor. pass. ptc.

      καὶ **ἀποκριθεὶς ὁ Ἰησοῦς εἶπεν** πρὸς αὐτούς, οὐ χρείαν ἔχουσιν οἱ ὑγιαίνοντες ἰατροῦ (Luke 5:31)

      and **Jesus said** to them, "those who are healthy have no need of a physician"

---

[22] Matt. 11:18 text is from GNT, NA, TR & MT: WH has Ἰωάνης.

[23] Matt. 28:18 text is from GNT, NA & WH: TR & MT have ἐπὶ γῆς.

E. Instrumental participle describes the means by which the action of the main verb takes place. This function is found primarily in the nominative case.
   1. Nom. sing. masc. pres. act. ptc.
      τίς δὲ ἐξ ὑμῶν **μεριμνῶν δύναται** προσθεῖναι ἐπὶ τὴν ἡλικίαν αὐτοῦ πῆχυν ἕνα; (Matt. 6:27)
      but which one of you **by being anxious is able** to add one cubit to his stature?
   2. Nom. sing. masc. aor. act. ptc.
      εἰ μὴ ὀλίγοις ἀρρώστοις **ἐπιθεὶς** τὰς χεῖρας **ἐθεράπευσεν** (Mark 6:5)
      except **he healed** [some] **by laying** his hands on a few sick people

F. Concessive participle indicates a sense of concession.
   1. Nominative case
      a. Nom. sing. masc. pres. act. ptc.
         καὶ **θέλων** αὐτὸν ἀποκτεῖναι, ἐφοβήθη τὸν ὄχλον (Matt. 14:5)
         and **even though he wanted** to kill him, he feared the people
      b. Nom. pl. masc. aor. act. ptc.
         καὶ μηδεμίαν αἰτίαν θανάτου **εὑρόντες** ᾐτήσαντο Πιλᾶτον ἀναιρεθῆναι αὐτόν (Acts 13:28)[24]
         and **even though they found** no cause of death they demanded of Pilate to destroy him
      c. Nom. sing. masc. perf. act. ptc.
         πῶς οὗτος γράμματα οἶδεν **μὴ μεμαθηκώς**; (John 7:15)
         how does this person know letters, **even though he has not learned**?
   2. Genitive absolute participle as concessive
      a. Gen. pl. masc. pres. ptc.
         καὶ **τοσούτων ὄντων** οὐκ ἐσχίσθη τὸ δίκτυον (John 21:11)
         and **even though they were so many** the net was not torn
      b. Gen. pl. neut. aor. pass. dep. ptc.
         ὡς ὤμοσα ἐν τῇ ὀργῇ μου, εἰ εἰσελεύσονται εἰς τὴν κατάπαυσίν μου, **καίτοι τῶν ἔργων** ἀπὸ καταβολῆς κόσμου **γενηθέντων** (Heb. 4:3)
         so I swore in my anger, they shall not enter into my rest, **even though the works were done** from the founding of the world

---

[24] Acts 13:28 text is from GNT, NA & MT: WH has Πειλᾶτον; TR has Πιλᾶτον.

   c. Gen. sing. masc. perf. act. ptc.

τοσαῦτα δὲ **αὐτοῦ** σημεῖα **πεποιηκότος** ἔμπροσθεν αὐτῶν οὐκ
ἐπίστευον εἰς αὐτόν (John 12:37)

but **even though he had performed** so many miracles in their presence,
they did not believe on him

3. Accusative case

   a. Acc. sing. masc. pres. act. ptc.

εἰ ἄρα γε ψηλαφήσειαν αὐτὸν καὶ εὕροιεν, **καί γε** οὐ μακρὰν
ἀπὸ ἑνὸς ἑκάστου ἡμῶν **ὑπάρχοντα** (Acts 17:27)[25]

if perhaps they might grope after him and find [him], **even though
he is** not far away from each one of us

   b. Acc. sing. masc. aor. pass. ptc.

πάντως φονεύς ἐστιν ὁ ἄνθρωπος οὗτος, **ὃν διασωθέντα** ἐκ τῆς
θαλάσσης ἡ δίκη ζῆν οὐκ εἴασεν (Acts 28:4)[26]

by all means this man is a murderer, **whom even though he was
rescued** from the sea the goddess of justice did not permit [him]
to live

   c. Acc. pl. masc. perf. act. and pass. ptc.

διὸ μελλήσω ἀεὶ ὑμᾶς ὑπομιμνῄσκειν περὶ τούτων, **καίπερ
εἰδότας** καὶ **ἐστηριγμένους** ἐν τῇ παρούσῃ ἀληθείᾳ
(2 Peter 1:12)[27]

wherefore I am about to put you always in remembrance concerning
these things, **even though you know** and **have been established** in the
present truth

G. Purpose participles occur only in the present and future tenses in the
nominative case.

1. Nom. sing. masc. pres. act. ptc.

καὶ **ἐπηρώτησεν εἷς** ἐξ αὐτῶν νομικὸς **πειράζων** αὐτόν (Matt. 22:35)

and **one** of them, a lawyer, **questioned [him] to tempt** him

2. Nom. sing. masc. fut. act. ptc.

εἰς Δαμασκὸν **ἐπορευόμην, ἄξων** καὶ τοὺς ἐκεῖσε ὄντας δεδεμένους εἰς
Ἰερουσαλήμ (Acts 22:5)[28]

I was on my way to Damascus **to bring** also those who were there bound
to Jerusalem

---

[25] Acts 17:27 text is from GNT, NA, WH & MT: TR has κάτοιγε.

[26] Acts 28:4 text is from GNT, NA & MT: WH & TR have ζῆν.

[27] 2 Peter 1:12 text is from GNT, NA & WH: TR & MT have οὐκ ἀμελήσω ὑμᾶς ἀεί.

[28] Acts 22:5 text is from GNT, NA, WH & MT: TR has Ἰερουσαλήμ.

H. Conditional participles.
 1. Nominative case
  a. Nom. pl. masc. pres. act. ptc.
   ἔχοντες δὲ διατροφὰς καὶ σκεπάσματα, τούτοις ἀρκεσθησόμεθα
   (1 Tim. 6:8)
   but **if we have** food and shelter, we will be content with these things
  b. Nom. sing. masc. aor. act. and pass. ptc.
   τί γὰρ ὠφελεῖται ἄνθρωπος, **κερδήσας** τὸν κόσμον ὅλον ἑαυτὸν
   δὲ **ἀπολέσας** ἢ **ζημιωθείς**; (Luke 9:25)
   for what is a person benefited, **if he gains** the whole world, but
   loses himself or **suffers damage**?
 2. Genitive absolute as conditional participle
  Gen. sing. masc. pres. act. ptc.
   πάλιν ἀνακάμψω πρὸς ὑμᾶς, **τοῦ θεοῦ θέλοντος** (Acts 18:21)[29]
   again I will return to you, **if God wills**

I. Complementary participle completing the meaning of the main verb normally
   in the nominative case.
 1. Nom. pl. masc. pres. mid./pass. dep. ptc.
   οὐ παυόμεθα ὑπὲρ ὑμῶν **προσευχόμενοι** καὶ **αἰτούμενοι** ἵνα
   πληρωθῆτε τὴν ἐπίγνωσιν τοῦ θελήματος αὐτοῦ (Col. 1:9)
   we do not cease praying for you and **asking** that you may be filled
   with the knowledge of his will
 2. Nom. sing. masc. pres. act. ptc.
   καὶ ἐγένετο ὅτε ἐτέλεσεν ὁ Ἰησοῦς **διατάσσων** τοῖς δώδεκα
   μαθηταῖς αὐτοῦ (Matt. 11:1)
   and it happened when **Jesus finished commanding** his twelve disciples

IV. **Verbal participles.** All participles are verbal, but the verbal idea is not always
   prominent. The following classifications indicate the verbal action or state.

A. The conjunctive participle (or participle of attendant circumstances) indicates
   an action that accompanies the action of the main verb and is both translated
   as a finite verb and connected by "and" to the main verb. The participle so
   closely identifies with the main verb as to take on the same mood and often
   the same tense as the main verb. This is primarily a feature of the present
   and aorist nominative participles.

---

[29] Acts 18:21 text is from GNT, NA & WH: TR & MT have πάλιν δέ.

1. Conjunctive participle with aorist indicative
   a. Nom. sing. masc. pres. act. ptc.

   τότε **ἥψατο** τῶν ὀφθαλμῶν αὐτῶν **λέγων**, κατὰ τὴν πίστιν ὑμῶν γενηθήτω ὑμῖν (Matt. 9:29)

   then **he touched** their eyes **and said**, "let it happen to you according to your faith"
   b. Nom. sing. masc. aor. act. ptc.

   καὶ λαβὼν τοὺς πέντε ἄρτους καὶ τοὺς δύο ἰχθύας, **ἀναβλέψας** εἰς τὸν οὐρανὸν **εὐλόγησεν** (Mark 6:41)

   and when he had taken the five loaves and the two fish, **he looked up** to heaven **and blessed**
2. Conjunctive participle with imperfect indicative
   a. Nom. sing. fem. pres. act. ptc.

   καὶ **ἤρχετο** πρὸς αὐτὸν **λέγουσα**, ἐκδίκησόν με ἀπὸ τοῦ ἀντιδίκου μου (Luke 18:3)

   and **she was repeatedly coming** to him **and saying**, "obtain justice for me from my adversary"
   b. Nom. sing. masc. aor. act. ptc.

   πατάξας δὲ τὴν πλευρὰν τοῦ Πέτρου **ἤγειρεν** αὐτόν (Acts 12:7)

   and **he hit** the side of Peter **and aroused** him
3. Conjunctive participle with present indicative
   a. Nom. sing. masc. pres. act. ptc.

   καὶ πρωΐ, σήμερον χειμών, **πυρράζει** γὰρ **στυγνάζων** ὁ οὐρανός (Matt. 16:3)

   and in the morning [λέγετε, you say] "today [ἔσται, will be] stormy weather, for **the sky is gloomy and red**"
   b. Nom. sing. masc. aor. act. ptc.

   ὁ δὲ ἀρχιερεὺς **διαρρήξας** τοὺς χιτῶνας αὐτοῦ **λέγει**, τί ἔτι χρείαν ἔχομεν μαρτύρων; (Mark 14:63)

   and **the high priest ripped** his clothing **in two and said**, "why do we have any more need of witnesses?"
4. Conjunctive participle with future indicative
   a. Nom. pl. masc. pres. act. ptc.

   καὶ ἐξ ὑμῶν αὐτῶν **ἀναστήσονται** ἄνδρες **λαλοῦντες** διεστραμμένα (Acts 20:30)

   and from among you yourselves **men will rise up and say** perverted things

b. Nom. sing. masc. aor. act. ptc.

ἀναστὰς πορεύσομαι πρὸς τὸν πατέρα μου, καὶ ἐρῶ αὐτῷ,
Πάτερ, ἥμαρτον εἰς τὸν οὐρανὸν καὶ ἐνώπιόν σου (Luke 15:18)

I will arise and go to my father, and I will say to him, "father, I have sinned against heaven and before you"

5. Conjunctive participle with imperative

a. Nom. pl. masc. pres. mid./pass. dep. ptc.

ἐξ ἡμέραι εἰσὶν ἐν αἷς δεῖ ἐργάζεσθαι, ἐν αὐταῖς οὖν
ἐρχόμενοι θεραπεύεσθε καὶ μὴ τῇ ἡμέρᾳ τοῦ σαββάτου
(Luke 13:14)[30]

there are six days in which one must work; therefore, during these [days] **come and be healed** but not on the Sabbath day

b. Nom. sing. masc. aor. act. ptc.

ἀναστὰς βάπτισαι καὶ ἀπόλουσαι τὰς ἁμαρτίας σου (Acts 22:15)

arise and be baptized and wash away your sins

6. Conjunctive participle with subjunctive

a. Nom. sing. fem. pres. mid./pass. dep. ptc.

διά γε τὸ παρέχειν μοι κόπον τὴν χήραν ταύτην ἐκδικήσω αὐτήν,
ἵνα μὴ εἰς τέλος **ἐρχομένη ὑπωπιάζῃ** με (Luke 18:5)

yet because this widow causes me trouble I will obtain justice for her lest **she** perpetually **comes and harasses** me

b. Nom. sing. masc. aor. act. ptc.

ἐπὰν δὲ εὕρητε, ἀπαγγείλατέ μοι, ὅπως **κἀγὼ ἐλθὼν προσκυνήσω**
αὐτῷ (Matt. 2:8)

and when you find [αὐτόν, him] report back to me, so that **I also may come and worship** him

7. Conjunctive participle with infinitive

a. Nom. sing. masc. aor. act. ptc.

οὐκ εἰμὶ ἱκανὸς **κύψας λῦσαι** τὸν ἱμάντα τῶν ὑποδημάτων αὐτοῦ
(Mark 1:7)

I am not worthy **to stoop down and loose** the thong of his sandals

b. Acc. pl. masc. aor. act. ptc.

καὶ κατένευσαν τοῖς μετόχοις ἐν τῷ ἑτέρῳ πλοίῳ **τοῦ ἐλθόντας**
συλλαβέσθαι αὐτοῖς (Luke 5:7)[31]

and they signaled to their partners in the other ship **that they should come and help** them

---

[30] Luke 13:14 text is from GNT, NA & WH: TR & MT have ἐν ταύταις οὖν.
[31] Luke 5:7 text is from GNT, NA & WH: TR & MT have τοῖς ἐν τῷ ἑτέρῳ πλοίῳ.

B. Periphrastic participles use the finite form of εἰμι (sometimes ὑπάρχω, ἔχω, and γίνομαι) and the present and perfect tense participles to indicate an emphatic statement in the given tense of the participle.

   1. Present tense participles

     a. Present tense of εἰμι

       (1) 1 pers. sing. pres. indic. (stative present)

          καὶ ἐγενόμην νεκρός καὶ ἰδοὺ **ζῶν εἰμι** εἰς τοὺς αἰῶνας τῶν αἰώνων (Rev. 1:18)

          and I was dead and, behold, **I am alive** forever and ever

       (2) 3 pers. sing. pres. indic. (gnomic present)

          οὐκ **ἔστιν** αὕτη ἡ σοφία ἄνωθεν **κατερχομένη** (James 3:15)

          this wisdom is not coming down from above

       (3) 1 pers. pl. pres. indic. (progressive present)

          οὐ γάρ **ἐσμεν** ὡς οἱ πολλοὶ **καπηλεύοντες** τὸν λόγον τοῦ θεοῦ (2 Cor. 2:17)

          for **we are not corrupting** the word of God as many [are]

       (4) 3 pers. pl. pres. indic. (elliptical progressive present)

          ἰδοὺ **ἄνδρες τρεῖς ζητοῦντες** σε (Acts 10:19)

          behold, **three men** [εἰσιν, **are**] **looking for** you

     b. Future tense of εἰμι emphasizing progressive or stative nature of the future statement

       (1) 2 pers. sing. fut. indic. (progressive future)

          ἀπὸ τοῦ νῦν ἀνθρώπους **ἔσῃ ζωγρῶν** (Luke 5:10)

          from now on **you will be catching men**

       (2) 3 pers. sing. fut. indic. (progressive future)

          ἀπὸ τοῦ νῦν δὲ **ἔσται** ὁ υἱὸς τοῦ ἀνθρώπου **καθήμενος** ἐκ δεξιῶν τῆς δυνάμεως τοῦ θεοῦ (Luke 22:69)[32]

          but from now on **the son of man shall be sitting** on the right hand of the power of God

       (3) 2 pers. pl. fut. indic. (progressive future)

          καὶ **ἔσεσθε μισούμενοι** ὑπὸ πάντων διὰ τὸ ὄνομά μου (Luke 21:17)

          and **you shall be hated** by all because of my name

       (4) 3 pers. pl. fut. indic. (progressive future)

          ἔσονται δύο **ἀλήθουσαι** ἐπὶ τὸ αὐτό (Luke 17:35)[33]

          two [women] shall be grinding at the same place

---

[32] Luke 22:69 text is from GNT, NA & WH: TR & MT omit δέ.

[33] Luke 17:35 text is from GNT, NA & WH: TR & MT have δύο ἔσονται.

c. Imperfect tense of εἰμί indicating the progressive or stative nature of the statement.
  (1) 1 pers. sing. impf. indic.
      καθ' ἡμέραν ἤμην πρὸς ὑμᾶς ἐν τῷ ἱερῷ διδάσκων (Mark 14:49)
      I was teaching daily in the temple with you
  (2) 3 pers. sing. impf. indic.
      τῇ νυκτὶ ἐκείνῃ ἦν ὁ Πέτρος κοιμώμενοι μεταξὺ δύο στρατιωτῶν (Acts 12:6)
      in that night **Peter was sleeping** between two soldiers
  (3) 3 pers. pl. impf. indic.
      ἦσαν δέ τινες τῶν γραμματέων ἐκεῖ καθήμενοι καὶ διαλογιζόμενοι ἐν ταῖς καρδίαις αὐτῶν (Mark 2:6)
      but **some** of the scribes **were sitting** there and **pondering** in their hearts
d. Imperative of εἰμί
  (1) 2 pers. sing. pres. imper.
      ἴσθι εὐνοῶν τῷ ἀντιδίκῳ σου ταχύ (Matt. 5:25)
      agree with your adversary quickly
  (2) 3 pers. pl. pres. imper. (elliptical)
      ἔστωσαν ὑμῶν αἱ ὀσφύες περιεζωσμέναι καὶ οἱ λύχνοι καιόμενοι (Luke 12:35)
      let your loins be fastened with a belt and [**ἔστωσαν, let**] **your lamps [be] burning**
e. Present infinitive of εἰμί
  καὶ ἐγένετο ἐν τῷ εἶναι αὐτὸν ἐν τόπῳ τινὶ προσευχόμενον (Luke 11:1)
  and it happened **while he was praying** in a certain place
2. Perfect tense periphrastic participles emphasize completed action or the existence of the results of the action.
  a. Present indic. of εἰμί
    (1) 1 pers. sing. pres. indic.
        εἶπεν δὲ ὁ Παῦλος, ἐπὶ τοῦ βήματος Καίσαρος ἑστώς εἰμι (Acts 25:10)
        but Paul said, "**I stand** before the judgment seat of Caesar"
    (2) 3 pers. sing. pres. indic.
        ἃ οὐκ ἔστιν γεγραμμένα ἐν τῷ βιβλίῳ τούτῳ (John 20:30)
        which things are not written in this book

(3) 1 pers. pl. pres. indic.
ἐν ᾧ θελήματι **ἡγιασμένοι ἐσμεν** (Heb. 10:10)
by which will **we are sanctified**

(4) 2 pers. pl. pres. indic.
χάριτί **ἐστε σεσῳσμένοι** (Eph. 2:5)[34]
you have been saved by grace

(5) 3 pers. pl. pres. indic.
ὑμῶν δὲ καὶ αἱ τρίχες τῆς κεφαλῆς πᾶσαι **ἠριθμημέναι εἰσίν**
(Matt. 10:30)
but even **all the hairs of your head have been numbered**

b. Present subj. of εἰμι

(1) 3 pers. sing. pres. subj.
οὐ δύναται ἄνθρωπος λαμβάνειν οὐδὲν ἐὰν μὴ **ᾖ δεδομένον**
αὐτῷ ἐκ τοῦ οὐρανοῦ (John 3:27)
a person is unable to receive anything unless **it has been given** to
him from heaven

(2) 1 pers. pl. pres. subj.
ἵνα μὴ **πεποιθότες ὦμεν** ἐφ᾽ ἑαυτοῖς, ἀλλ᾽ ἐπὶ τῷ θεῷ τῷ
ἐγείροντι τοὺς νεκρούς (2 Cor. 1:9)
that **we should not have trusted** in ourselves, but in God who raises
the dead

(3) 2 pers. pl. pres. subj.
ἵνα καθὼς ἔλεγον, **παρεσκευασμένοι ἦτε** (2 Cor. 9:3)
that even as I said, **"you may be prepared"**

(4) 3 pers. pl. pres. subj.
ἵνα **ὦσιν** καὶ **αὐτοὶ ἡγιασμένοι** ἐν ἀληθείᾳ (John 17:19)
that **they themselves** also **may be sanctified** by truth

c. Imperfect subj. indicating a pluperfect sense

(1) 3 pers. sing. impf. indic.
καὶ **ἦν** ἡ **ἐπιγραφὴ** τῆς αἰτίας αὐτοῦ **ἐπιγεγραμμένη**, ὁ
βασιλεὺς τῶν Ἰουδαίων (Mark 15:26)
and **the inscription** of his accusation **had been written**: "the
king of the Jews"

(2) 3 pers. pl. impf. indic.
κἀκεῖθεν ἀπέπλευσαν εἰς Ἀντιόχειαν, ὅθεν **ἦσαν**
παραδεδομένοι τῇ χάριτι τοῦ θεοῦ (Acts 14:26)
and from there they sailed to Antioch, where **they had been**
commended to the grace of God

---

[34] Eph. 2:5 text is from GNT, NA & MT: WH & TR have σεσωσμένοι.

(3) 1 pers. pl. impf. indic.

ὅτε ἦμεν νήπιοι, ὑπὸ τὰ στοιχεῖα τοῦ κόσμου **ἤμεθα δεδουλωμένοι** (Gal. 4:3)[35]

when we were infants, **we had been subjected** under the fundamental principles of the world

d. Future perfect

3 pers. sing. fut. indic.

καὶ ὅσα ἐὰν λύσητε ἐπὶ τῆς γῆς **ἔσται λελυμένα** ἐν οὐρανῷ (Matt. 18:18)[36]

and whatever you permit on the earth **shall have been permitted** in heaven

C. Special verbal functions.

1. Supplemental participles make an assertion about the direct object of the sentence, whether the object is in the genitive, dative, or accusative case. The assertion is in the same case as the direct object. This function usually follows verbs of perception: hearing, finding, making, having, and seeing.

a. Genitive object after ἀκούω

(1) Gen. sing. masc. pres. act. ptc.

ἤκουσαν οἱ Φαρισαῖοι τοῦ ὄχλου γογγύζοντος περὶ αὐτοῦ ταῦτα (John 7:32)

the Pharisees heard the crowd murmuring these things about him

(2) Gen. pl. masc. pres. act. ptc.

ὅτι **ἤκουον εἷς ἕκαστος** τῇ ἰδίᾳ διαλέκτῳ **λαλούντων αὐτῶν** (Acts 2:6)

for **each person was hearing them speaking** in his own dialect

b. Dative object after βλέπω

Dat. sing. masc. pres. act. ptc.

καὶ **ἐμβλέψας τῷ Ἰησοῦ περιπατοῦντι** λέγει, Ἴδε ὁ ἀμνὸς τοῦ θεοῦ (John 1:36)

and **looking at Jesus walking** he said, "behold the lamb of God"

c. Accusative object

(1) Acc. sing. neut. pres. mid./pass. dep. ptc.

καὶ **ἤλπιζέν τι σημεῖον ἰδεῖν** ὑπ᾽ αὐτοῦ **γινόμενον** (Luke 23:8)

and he was hoping **to see some sign performed** by him

---

[35] Gal. 4:3 text is from GNT, NA & WH: TR & MT have ἦμεν δεδουλωμένοι.
[36] Matt. 18:18 text is from GNT, NA & WH: TR & MT have ἐν τῷ οὐρανῷ.

(2) Acc. sing. masc. aor. act. ptc.

εἶπεν δὲ αὐτοῖς, **ἐθεώρουν τὸν σατανᾶν** ὡς ἀστραπὴν ἐκ τοῦ οὐρανοῦ **πεσόντα** (Luke 10:18)

he said to them, "**I was watching Satan fall** out of the sky as lightning"

(3) Acc. sing. fem. perf. pass. ptc.

εἶδον τὴν συκῆν **ἐξηραμμένην** ἐκ ῥιζῶν (Mark 11:20)

they saw the fig tree withered from the roots

2. Participle of indirect discourse. The genitive or accusative noun or pronoun may function as the subject of a genitive or accusative participle after verbs of saying or hearing.

a. Genitive participle of indirect discourse

Gen. sing. masc. pres. act. ptc.

ἔφη, ἐγὼ **φωνὴ βοῶντος** ἐν τῇ ἐρήμῳ, εὐθύνατε τὴν ὁδὸν κυρίου (John 1:23)

he said, "I [εἰμι, am] **the voice of one crying** in the desert, 'prepare the way of the Lord'"

b. Accusative participle of indirect discourse

(1) Acc. pl. masc. pres. act. ptc.

ἀκούομεν γάρ **τινας περιπατοῦντας** ἐν ὑμῖν ἀτάκτως μηδὲν **ἐργαζομένους** ἀλλὰ **περιεργαζομένους** (2 Thess. 3:11)

for **we hear some are walking** disorderly among you, **working** not at all, but **are busybodies**

(2) Acc. sing. masc. perf. act. ptc.

πᾶν πνεῦμα ὃ ὁμολογεῖ Ἰησοῦν Χριστὸν ἐν σαρκὶ **ἐληλυθότα** ἐκ τοῦ θεοῦ ἐστιν (1 John 4:2)

every spirit that confesses Jesus Christ has come in the flesh is from God

3. Imperatival participle may be used independently like a finite verb.

a. Nom. pl. masc. pres. act. ptc.

τῇ ἐλπίδι **χαίροντες**, τῇ θλίψει **ὑπομένοντες**, τῇ προσευχῇ **προσκαρτεροῦντες** (Rom. 12:12)

rejoice in hope, **endure** tribulation, **be busily engaged** in prayer

b. Nom. pl. masc. aor. mid. ptc.

καὶ **ἐνδυσάμενοι** τὸν νέον τὸν ἀνακαινούμενον εἰς ἐπίγνωσιν (Col. 3:10)

and **put on** the new person that is renewed in knowledge

4. Independent or absolute participle is used as a finite verb when no other finite verb is present.
   a. Nom. pl. masc. pres. mid./pass. dep. ptc.
      ἀλλὰ καὶ **καυχώμενοι** ἐν τῷ θεῷ διὰ τοῦ κυρίου ἡμῶν Ἰησοῦ Χριστοῦ (Rom. 5:11)
      but **we** also **rejoice** in God through our Lord Jesus Christ
   b. Nom. sing. masc. aor. mid. ptc.
      μᾶλλον **ἑλόμενος** συγκακουχεῖσθαι τῷ λαῷ τοῦ θεοῦ ἢ πρόσκαιρον ἔχειν ἁμαρτίας ἀπόλαυσιν (Heb. 11:25)[37]
      he chose rather to suffer with the people of God than to have temporary enjoyment of sin

V. **Voice and the participle.** Emphasis in this section will be placed on the passive voice rather than on the active or middle voices.

   A. Active voice.
      1. Simple active
         Nom. sing. masc. aor. act. ptc.
         καὶ **ἐξελθὼν** ἐκεῖθεν ὁ Ἰησοῦς ἀνεχώρησεν εἰς τὰ μέρη Τύρου καὶ Σιδῶνος (Matt. 15:21)
         and **when Jesus went out** from there, **he departed** into the parts of Tyre and Sidon
      2. Stative active
         Dat. pl. masc. aor. act. ptc.
         εἰ οὖν τὴν ἴσην δωρεὰν ἔδωκεν αὐτοῖς ὁ θεὸς ὡς καὶ ἡμῖν, **πιστεύσασιν** ἐπὶ τὸν κύριον Ἰησοῦν Χριστόν (Acts 11:17)
         if then God gave the equal gift to them as also to us, **when they believed** in the Lord Jesus Christ
      3. Causative active
         Nom. sing. masc. aor. act. ptc.
         ὁ γὰρ Ἡρῴδης **κρατήσας** τὸν Ἰωάννην ἔδησεν αὐτόν (Matt. 14:3)[38]
         for **Herod caused John to be arrested** and bound him

   B. Middle voice.
      1. Middle reflexive
         a. Nom. sing. masc. pres. mid./pass. ptc.
            ἦν δὲ Σίμων Πέτρος **ἑστὼς** καὶ **θερμαινόμενος** (John 18:25)
            now **Simon Peter was** standing and **warming himself**

---

[37] Heb. 11:25 text is from GNT, NA, TR & MT: WH has συνκακουχεῖσθαι.
[38] Matt. 14:3 text is from GNT & NA: WH has Ἰωάνην; TR & MT have Ἡρώδης.

b. Nom. pl. masc. aor. mid. ptc.

ἀποθέμενοι οὖν πᾶσαν κακίαν καὶ πάντα δόλον καὶ ὑποκρίσεις
(1 Peter 2:1)

therefore, **put off from yourselves** all ill-will and all deceit and outward show

2. Middle with active meaning but not deponent

   a. Nom. sing. masc. pres. mid./pass. ptc.

      διανοίγων καὶ **παρατιθέμενος** ὅτι τὸν Χριστὸν ἔδει παθεῖν καὶ
      ἀναστῆναι ἐκ νεκρῶν (Acts 17:3)

      explaining and **placing before [them]** that Christ must suffer and rise from the dead

   b. Nom. sing. masc. aor. mid. ptc.

      καὶ **περιβλεψάμενος** ὁ Ἰησοῦς λέγει τοῖς μαθηταῖς αὐτοῦ
      (Mark 10:23)

      and **when Jesus looked around** he spoke to his disciples

3. Middle with active meaning different from the active voice meaning

   a. Gen. pl. neut. pres. mid./pass. ptc.

      ἀρχομένων δὲ **τούτων** γίνεσθαι ἀνακύψατε καὶ ἐπάρατε τὰς
      κεφαλὰς ὑμῶν, διότι ἐγγίζει ἡ ἀπολύτρωσις ὑμῶν (Luke 21:28)

      but **when these things begin** to take place look up and lift up your heads, for your redemption is approaching

   b. Nom. sing. masc. aor. mid. ptc.

      καὶ εἶπεν ὁ Ἰησοῦς, τίς ὁ **ἀψάμενός** μου; (Luke 8:45)

      and Jesus said, **"who [ἐστιν, is] the one who touched** me?"

4. Reciprocal middle

   Nom. pl. masc. pres. mid./pass. ptc.

   διαμεριζόμενοι δὲ τὰ ἱμάτια αὐτοῦ ἔβαλον κλήρους (Luke 23:34)[39]

   and **while they were dividing** his clothing **among themselves** they cast lots

C. Passive voice.

   1. Passive deponent. The present and perfect tenses have the same form for middle and passive, whereas the aorist has a distinct passive form.

      a. Nom. sing. masc. pres. mid./pass. dep. ptc.

         ἐκ σοῦ γὰρ ἐξελεύσεται **ἡγούμενος**, ὅστις ποιμανεῖ τὸν λαόν μου
         τὸν Ἰσραήλ (Matt. 2:6)

         for **a ruler** shall come out of you, who shall shepherd my people Israel

---

[39] Luke 23:34 text is from GNT, NA & WH: TR & MT have κλῆρον.

b. Nom. sing. masc. aor. pass. dep. ptc.

ἀποκριθεὶς δὲ ὁ ἄγγελος εἶπεν ταῖς γυναιξίν, μὴ φοβεῖσθε ὑμεῖς
(Matt. 28:5)

and the angel **answered** and said to the women, "do not fear"

c. Nom. sing. masc. perf. pass. dep. ptc.

ἐπιποθῶν σε ἰδεῖν, **μεμνημένος** σου τῶν δακρύων, ἵνα χαρᾶς
πληρωθῶ (2 Tim. 1:4)

longing to see you, **remembering** your tears, that I may be filled with joy

2. Agent of the passive voice may be unidentified, or unimportant within the context, or an intransitive verb.

a. Acc. sing. neut. pres. mid./pass. ptc.

πᾶν τὸ ἐν μακέλλῳ **πωλούμενον** ἐσθίετε μηδὲν ἀνακρίνοντες διὰ
τὴν συνείδησιν (1 Cor. 10:25)

eat **anything that is sold** in a market, questioning nothing because
of conscience

b. Gen. sing. fem. aor. pass. ptc.

διετίας δὲ **πληρωθείσης** ἔλαβεν διάδοχον ὁ Φῆλιξ Πόρκιον Φῆστον
(Acts 24:27)

but **when two years were completed** Felix received Porcius Festus
[as his] successor

c. Nom. sing. masc. perf. pass. ptc.

Ἰησοῦν ζητεῖτε τὸν Ναζαρηνὸν **τὸν ἐσταυρωμένον**· ἠγέρθη, οὐκ
ἔστιν ὧδε (Mark 16:6)

you are looking for Jesus the Nazarene **who has been crucified**; he has
risen, he is not here

3. Theological passive, God is implied as the agent

a. Nom. sing. masc. pres. pass. ptc.

καὶ ἰδοὺ ἵππος λευκός, καὶ ὁ καθήμενος ἐπ᾽ αὐτόν, **καλούμενος**
πιστὸς καὶ ἀληθινός (Rev. 19:11)

and there was a white horse, and the one sitting on him [ἦν, **was**]
called faithful and true

b. Nom. pl. masc. aor. pass. ptc.

οἱ δὲ **καταξιωθέντες** τοῦ αἰῶνος ἐκείνου τυχεῖν καὶ τῆς
ἀναστάσεως τῆς ἐκ νεκρῶν (Luke 20:35)

but **those who were considered worthy** to attain that age and the
resurrection that [οὔσης, is] from the dead

c. Nom. sing. masc. perf. pass. ptc.

εἶπον ὅτι οὐκ εἰμὶ ἐγὼ ὁ Χριστός, ἀλλ᾽ ὅτι **ἀπεσταλμένος** εἰμι
ἔμπροσθεν ἐκείνου (John 3:28)

I said, "I am not the Christ, but **I have been sent** before him"

4. Passive agent is assumed as known from the context
   a. Nom. sing. masc. pres. pass. ptc.
      ὁ δὲ στυγνάσας ἐπὶ τῷ λόγῳ ἀπῆλθεν **λυπούμενος**, ἦν γὰρ ἔχων κτήματα πολλά (Mark 10:22)
      but because he was sad at the saying he went away **grieved**, for he had many possessions
   b. Acc. pl. neut. aor. pass. ptc.
      ὅταν ποιήσητε **πάντα τὰ διαταχθέντα** ὑμῖν (Luke 17:10)
      when you have performed **all the things commanded** to you
   c. Acc. sing. fem. perf. pass. ptc.
      οὗτοι μισήσουσιν τὴν πόρνην, καὶ **ἠρημωμένην** ποιήσουσιν αὐτὴν καὶ γυμνήν (Rev. 17:16)
      these shall hate the prostitute, and they shall make her **ruined** and naked
5. Passive agent may be implied as being parental
   a. Nom. sing. masc. pres. pass. ptc.
      καὶ ἰδοὺ ἀνὴρ ὀνόματι **καλούμενος** Ζακχαῖος (Luke 19:21)
      and there was a man [whose] name **was called** Zachaeus
   b. Nom. sing. masc. aor. pass. ptc.
      ἀλλ᾽ ὥσπερ τότε ὁ κατὰ σάρκα **γεννηθεὶς** ἐδίωκεν τὸν κατὰ πνεῦμα οὕτως καὶ νῦν (Gal. 4:29)
      but as then **the one who was born** according to the flesh was persecuting the one [γεννηθέντα, who was born] according to the spirit, so also now
   c. Nom. sing. masc. perf. pass. ptc.
      εἰμι ἀνὴρ Ἰουδαῖος, **γεγεννημένος** ἐν Ταρσῷ τῆς Κιλικίας, **ἀνατεθραμμένος** δὲ ἐν τῇ πόλει ταύτῃ, παρὰ τοὺς πόδας Γαμαλιήλ (Acts 22:3)
      I am a Jewish man, **born** in Tarsus of Cilicia, but **brought up** in this city at the feet of Gamaliel
6. Passive agent indicated by the dative case
   a. Nom. sing. masc. pres. pass. ptc.
      δικαιούμενοι δωρεὰν **τῇ αὐτοῦ χάριτι** διὰ τῆς ἀπολυτρώσεως τῆς ἐν Χριστῷ Ἰησοῦ (Rom. 3:24)
      being justified free gratis **by his grace** through the redemption that [οὔσης, is] in Christ Jesus
   b. Nom. pl. masc. aor. pass. ptc.
      φυλάσσεσθε, ἵνα μὴ τῇ τῶν ἀθέσμων **πλάνῃ συναπαχθέντες** ἐκπέσητε τοῦ ἰδίου στηριγμοῦ (2 Peter 3:17)
      beware, lest **having been led astray by the error** of the lawless you should fall from your own firm hold

c. Nom. sing. masc. perf. pass. ptc.

καὶ νῦν ἰδοὺ **δεδεμένος** ἐγὼ **τῷ πνεύματι** πορεύομαι εἰς
Ἰερουσαλήμ (Acts 20:22)[40]

and now, behold, **having been bound by the Spirit** I am going to
Jerusalem

7. The aorist passive is sometimes used with an active meaning. This is true
of the present and perfect participles as well, but as the middle and passive
forms are identical, this feature is considered under the middle voice.

a. Nom. sing. masc. aor. pass. ptc.

ὁ δὲ **ἐγερθεὶς παρέλαβεν** τὸ παιδίον καὶ τὴν μητέρα αὐτοῦ νυκτός,
καὶ ἀνεχώρησεν εἰς Αἴγυπτον (Matt. 2:14)

and **he arose and took** the child and his mother by night and departed
to Egypt

b. Nom. sing. masc. aor. pass. ptc.

τότε **σταθεὶς ὁ Παῦλος** ἐν μέσῳ αὐτῶν εἶπεν (Acts 27:21)

then **Paul stood** among them and said

8. The present passive participle is sometimes used when translation from one
language to another is indicated.

a. Nom. sing. fem. pres. pass. ptc.

ἐν Ἰόππῃ δέ τις ἦν μαθήτρια ὀνόματι Ταβιθά, ἣ **διερμηνευομένη**
λέγεται Δορκάς (Acts 9:36)

and in Joppa was a certain disciple named Tabitha, which **being
translated** means Dorcas

b. Nom. sing. masc. pres. pass. ptc.

πρῶτον μὲν **ἑρμηνευόμενος** βασιλεὺς δικαιοσύνης, ἔπειτα δὲ καὶ
βασιλεὺς Σαλήμ, ὅ ἐστιν βασιλεὺς εἰρήνης (Heb. 7:2)

first **being translated** king of righteousness, and then also king of Salem,
which means king of peace

9. The passive voice by nature does not have a direct object. However,
there are occasions when an accusative case is associated with the passive
participle. These instances are called accusatives of respect or
reference.

a. Nom. sing. masc. pres. pass. ptc.

κοινωνείτω δὲ ὁ **κατηχούμενος** τὸν **λόγον** τῷ κατηχοῦντι ἐν πᾶσιν
ἀγαθοῖς (Gal. 6:6)

but let **the one who is being taught with respect to the word** share
in all good things with the one who is teaching

---

[40] Acts 20:22 text is from GNT, NA & WH: TR & MT have ἐγὼ δεδεμένος; TR has Ἰερουσαλήμ.

b. Nom. pl. masc. aor. pass. ptc.

καὶ πᾶς ὁ λαὸς ἀκούσας καὶ οἱ τελῶναι ἐδικαίωσαν τὸν θεόν, βαπτισθέντες τὸ βάπτισμα Ἰωάννου (Luke 7:29)[41]

and when all the people and the tax collectors heard, they acknowledged God as just and **were baptized with respect to** John's **baptism**

c. Nom. pl. masc. perf. pass. ptc.

οὕτως καὶ οὗτοι ἀνθίστανται τῇ ἀληθείᾳ, **ἄνθρωποι κατεφθαρμένοι τὸν νοῦν** (2 Tim. 3:8)

so also these resist the truth, **people utterly depraved with respect to the mind**

10. The passive agent is indicated by certain prepositions.

a. With διά

(1) Dat. pl. masc. pres. act. ptc.

εἴτε βασιλεῖ ὡς ὑπερέχοντι, εἴτε ἡγεμόσιν ὡς δι' αὐτοῦ πεμπομένοις (1 Peter 2:13-14)

whether to the king as being superior, or to rulers, as **being sent by him**

(2) Nom. sing. neut. aor. pass. ptc.

ὅπως πληρωθῇ τὸ ῥηθὲν διὰ τῶν προφητῶν (Matt. 2:23)

so that **the word spoken by the prophets** should be fulfilled

(3) Nom. sing. neut. perf. pass. ptc.

ἀλλὰ τοῦτό ἐστιν τὸ εἰρημένον διὰ τοῦ προφήτου (Acts 2:16)

but this is **that which has been spoken by the prophet**

b. With ἐκ

(1) Nom. sing. masc. pres. pass. ptc.

καὶ τίς ὁ εὐφραίνων με εἰ μὴ ὁ λυπούμενος ἐξ ἐμοῦ; (2 Cor. 2:2)[42]

and who [ἐστιν, is] the one who cheers me, except **the one who is being grieved by me**

(2) Nom. pl. masc. aor. pass. ptc.

δικαιωθέντες οὖν ἐκ πίστεως εἰρήνην ἔχομεν πρὸς τὸν θεὸν διὰ τοῦ κυρίου ἡμῶν Ἰησοῦ Χριστοῦ (Rom. 5:1)

therefore, **having been justified by faith,** we have peace with God through our Lord Jesus Christ

[41] Luke 7:29 text is from GNT, NA, TR & MT: WH has Ἰωάνου.
[42] 2 Cor. 2:2 text is from GNT, NA & WH: TR & MT have τίς ἐστιν.

(3) Nom. sing. neut. perf. pass. ptc.

συμβουλεύω σοι ἀγοράσαι παρ' ἐμοῦ **χρυσίον πεπυρωμένον ἐκ πυρός** (Rev. 3:18)

I counsel you to purchase from me **gold purified by fire**

c. With ἐν

(1) Nom. pl. masc. pres. pass. ptc.

τοὺς ἐν δυνάμει θεοῦ φρουρουμένους διὰ πίστεως (1 Peter 1:5)

who are protected by the power of God through faith

(2) Nom. pl. masc. aor. pass. ptc.

πολλῷ οὖν μᾶλλον **δικαιωθέντες νῦν ἐν τῷ αἵματι αὐτοῦ** σωθησόμεθα δι' αὐτοῦ ἀπὸ τῆς ὀργῆς (Rom. 5:9)

therefore, by much more, **having now been justified by his blood**, we shall be saved by him from wrath

(3) Nom. sing. fem. perf. pass. ptc.

ἵνα γένηται ἡ προσφορὰ τῶν ἐθνῶν εὐπρόσδεκτος, **ἡγιασμένη ἐν πνεύματι ἁγίῳ** (Rom. 15:16)

that the gift of the Gentiles might be acceptable, **having been sanctified by the Holy Spirit**

d. With ὑπό

(1) Nom. pl. masc. pres. pass. ptc.

καὶ ἔσεσθε μισούμενοι ὑπὸ πάντων διὰ τὸ ὄνομά μου (Mark 13:13)

and **you shall be hated by all** because of my name

(2) Nom. sing. masc. aor. pass. ptc.

ἐπερωτηθεὶς δὲ **ὑπὸ τῶν Φαρισαίων** πότε ἔρχεται ἡ βασιλεία τοῦ θεοῦ (Luke 17:20)

and **when he had been asked by the Pharisees**, "when is the kingdom of God coming?"

(3) Nom. sing. masc. perf. pass. ptc.

μὴ κατακλιθῇς εἰς τὴν πρωτοκλισίαν, μήποτε **ἐντιμότερός σου ἦ κεκλημένος ὑπ' αὐτοῦ** (Luke 14:8)

do not sit in the most prominent place, lest **a more distinguished person than you should have been invited by him**

(4) Voc. pl. masc. perf. pass. ptc.

ἡμεῖς δὲ ὀφείλομεν εὐχαριστεῖν τῷ θεῷ πάντοτε περὶ ὑμῶν, ἀδελφοὶ **ἠγαπημένοι ὑπὸ κυρίου** (2 Thess. 2:13)

but we ought to thank God always concerning you, brothers **beloved by the Lord**

D. Voiceless participles of εἰμι are used as adjectives, adverbs, substantives, appositional, and verbs.
  1. Adjectival participles with predicate adjectives
    a. Nom. sing. masc. pres. ptc.
      ὁ δὲ θεὸς **πλούσιος ὢν** ἐν ἐλέει (Eph. 2:4)
      but God **who is rich** in mercy
    b. Gen. pl. masc. pres. ptc.
      συνίστησιν δὲ τὴν ἑαυτοῦ ἀγάπην εἰς ἡμᾶς ὁ θεὸς ὅτι ἔτι
      ἁμαρτωλῶν ὄντων ἡμῶν Χριστὸς ὑπὲρ ἡμῶν ἀπέθανεν (Rom. 5:8)
      but God commended his love to us that, **while we were** yet **sinners**, Christ died for us
    c. Dat. pl. masc. pres. ptc.
      πάντα συνεργεῖ εἰς ἀγαθόν, **τοῖς κατὰ πρόθεσιν κλητοῖς οὖσιν** (Rom. 8:28)
      he works all things for good, **for those who are called** according to [his] purpose
    d. Acc. sing. masc. pres. ptc.
      Ἰησοῦν, **πιστὸν ὄντα** τῷ ποιήσαντι αὐτόν (Heb. 3:1-2)
      Jesus, **who was faithful** to the one who appointed him
  2. Adverbial participles
    a. Nom. sing. masc. pres. ptc. as concessive
      καίπερ ὢν υἱὸς, ἔμαθεν ἀφ' ὧν ἔπαθεν τὴν ὑπακοήν (Heb. 5:8)
      even though he was a son he learned patience from the things he suffered
    b. Gen. sing. masc. pres. ptc. as gen. causal absolute
      ὁ γὰρ Ἰησοῦς ἐξένευσεν **ὄχλου ὄντος** ἐν τῷ τόπῳ (John 5:13)
      for Jesus had withdrawn, **because a crowd was** in the place
    c. Dat. pl. masc. pres. ptc. as causal
      καὶ καταγγέλλουσιν ἔθη ἃ οὐκ ἔξεστιν ἡμῖν παραδέχεσθαι οὐδὲ ποιεῖν **Ῥωμαίοις οὖσιν** (Acts 16:21)
      and they announce customs that are unlawful for us to receive and to observe **because we are Romans**
    d. Acc. sing. masc. pres. ptc. as causal
      μάλιστα **γνώστην ὄντα** σε πάντων τῶν κατὰ Ἰουδαίους ἐθῶν τε καὶ ζητημάτων (Acts 26:3)
      especially **since you are acquainted** with all the customs and questions among the Jews

3. Substantive participles
   a. Nom. sing. masc. pres. ptc.

   ὁ ὢν ἐκ τῆς γῆς ἐκ τῆς γῆς ἐστιν καὶ ἐκ τῆς γῆς λαλεῖ
   (John 3:31)

   the one who is of the earth **is** of the earth and **speaks** of the earth

   b. Gen. pl. masc. pres. ptc.

   ὑπὲρ βασιλέων καὶ **πάντων τῶν** ἐν ὑπεροχῇ **ὄντων** (1 Tim. 2:2)

   for kings and **all those who are** prominent

   c. Dat. sing. masc. pres. ptc.

   λέγω γὰρ διὰ τῆς χάριτος τῆς δοθείσης μοι **παντὶ τῷ ὄντι** ἐν
   ὑμῖν (Rom. 12:3)

   for I speak **to everyone who is** among you through the grace that is
   given to me

   d. Acc. pl. masc. pres. ptc.

   ἔγνω κύριος **τοὺς ὄντας αὐτοῦ** (2 Tim. 2:19)

   the Lord knows **those who belong to him**

4. Appositional participles
   a. Nom. sing. masc. pres. ptc.

   εὐχαριστοῦμέν σοι, κύριε ὁ θεὸς ὁ παντοκράτωρ, ὁ **ὢν** καὶ ὁ ἦν
   (Rev. 11:17)

   we thank you, Lord **God** omnipotent, **who is** and who was

   b. Acc. pl. masc. pres. ptc.

   καὶ λαβὼν περιέτεμεν αὐτὸν διὰ τοὺς Ἰουδαίους τοὺς ὄντας
   ἐν τοῖς τόποις ἐκείνοις (Acts 16:3)

   and he took and circumcised him **because of the Jews who were**
   in those places

   c. Dat. sing. fem. pres. ptc.

   τῇ ἐκκλησίᾳ τοῦ θεοῦ τῇ οὔσῃ ἐν Κορίνθῳ (2 Cor. 1:1)

   to the church of God **that is** in Corinth

5. Verbal temporal participle as contemporaneous with the main verb
   a. Nom. sing. masc. pres. ptc.

   μνήσθητε ὡς ἐλάλησεν ὑμῖν ἔτι **ὢν** ἐν τῇ Γαλιαλίᾳ (Luke 24:6)

   remember how **he spoke** to you **while he was** yet in Galilee

   b. Gen. sing. masc. pres. ptc.

   ἄχρι γὰρ νόμου ἁμαρτία ἦν ἐν κόσμῳ, ἁμαρτία δὲ οὐκ
   ἐλλογεῖται μὴ ὄντος νόμου (Rom. 5:13)

   for until law, sin was in the world, but **sin is not put to [one's]**
   account when law does not exist

  c. Dat. sing. masc. pres. ptc.
      ὁ θεὸς τῆς δόξης **ὤφθη** τῷ πατρὶ ἡμῶλν Ἀβραὰμ **ὄντι** ἐν τῇ
      Μεσοποταμίᾳ πρὶν ἢ κατοικῆσαι αὐτόν ἐν Χαρράν (Acts 7:2)
      the God of glory **appeared** to our father Abraham **when he was** in
      Mesopotamia before he lived in Charron
  d. Acc. sing. masc. pres. ptc.
      ἕνεκα τούτων με Ἰουδαῖοι συλλαβόμενοι **ὄντα** ἐν τῷ ἱερῷ
      ἐπειρῶντο διαχειρίσασθαι (Acts 26:21)[43]
      on account of these things **the Jews** seized me **while I was** in the
      temple and attempted to kill [με, me]

VII. **Tense and the participle.** The participle occurs in four tenses: present, aorist,
     perfect, and future, in that order of descending frequency. The meaning of the
     participle is determined by the context.

  A. Present tense participles function essentially with the same kinds of options
      as are found with the present tense indicative. However, only one example
      of each possibility will be included in this section.
      1. Historical present
          Nom. sing. masc. pres. act. ptc.
          καὶ **ἀποθνῄσκων** οὐκ **ἀφῆκεν** σπέρμα (Mark 12:20)
          and **when he died he left** no descendants
      2. Customary present
          Nom. sing. masc. pres. act. ptc.
          ἰδοὺ ἐξῆλθεν ὁ **σπείρων** σπεῖραι (Mark 4:3)
          behold, **the sower** went out to sow
      3. Gnomic present indicating a state of affairs as existing perpetually,
          a timeless fact
          Nom. sing. masc. pres. act. ptc.
          καθὼς ἀπέστειλέν με ὁ **ζῶν πατήρ**, κἀγὼ ζῶ διὰ τὸν πατέρα
          (John 6:57)
          even as **the living father** sent me, and I live because of the father
      4. Stative present
          Nom. sing. masc. pres. act. ptc.
          ἑκατοντάρχου δέ τινος δοῦλος **κακῶς ἔχων** ἤμελλεν τελευτᾶν
          (Luke 7:2)[44]
          now the servant of a certain captain **being ill** was about to die

---

[43] Acts 26:21 text is from GNT & NA: WH has συλλαβόμενοι ἐν τῷ ἱερῷ; TR & MT have οἱ Ἰουδαῖοι συλλαβόμενοι ἐν
τῷ ἱερῷ.

[44] Luke 7:2 text is from GNT, NA & WH: TR & MT have τελευτᾶν.

5. Aorist present, the action of the ptc. is identical with the main verb.
   Nom. sing. masc. pres. act. ptc.
   διδάσκαλε, ταῦτα **λέγων** καὶ ἡμᾶς **ὑβρίζεις** (Luke 11:45)
   teacher, **when you say** these things **you insult** us
6. Progressive present
   Nom. sing. masc. pres. act. ptc.
   ἀμὴν λέγω ὑμῖν ὅτι εἷς ἐξ ὑμῶν παραδώσει με, **ὁ ἐσθίων** μετ᾽ ἐμοῦ
   (Mark 14:18)
   truly I tell you that one of you shall betray me, **one who is eating** with me
7. Iterative present, repeated action at intervals
   Nom. sing. masc. pres. act. ptc.
   καὶ ἀπῆλθεν καθ᾽ ὅλην τὴν πόλιν **κηρύσσων** ὅσα ἐποίησεν αὐτῷ
   ὁ Ἰησοῦς (Luke 8:39)
   and he went away through the entire city **repeatedly proclaiming** what
   Jesus did for him
8. Futuristic present
   Nom. sing. masc. pres. mid./pass. dep. ptc.
   εἶπεν αὐτῷ, Σὺ εἶ **ὁ ἐρχόμενος** ἢ ἕτερον προσδοκῶμεν; (Matt. 11:3)
   he said to him, "Are you **the coming one** or should we look for another?"
9. Present of duration, or past action still in progress
   Nom. pl. masc. pres. pass. ptc.
   ὑπήντησαν αὐτῷ **δύο δαιμονιζόμενοι** ἐκ τῶν μνημείων ἐξερχόμενοι
   (Matt. 8:28)
   two demonized people met him as they were coming out of the tombs
10. Tendential participle, an action contemplated, attempted, or planned,
    but not carried out
    Gen. pl. masc. pres. act. ptc.
    ταῦτα ἔγραψα ὑμῖν **περὶ τῶν πλανώντων** ὑμᾶς (1 John 2:26)
    I wrote these things to you **concerning those who are attempting to
    deceive** you
11. Perfective present participle
    Dat. pl. masc. pres. pass. ptc.
    εἴτε ἡγεμόσιν ὡς δι᾽ αὐτοῦ **πεμπομένοις** (1 Peter 2:14)
    whether to governors as **having been sent** by him
12. Explanatory present participle may be used to interpret or translate
    some event, name, place, or custom.
    Nom. sing. masc. pres. pass. ptc.
    ἐξ ἧς ἐγεννήθη Ἰησοῦς **ὁ λεγόμενος** Χριστός (Matt. 1:16)
    Jesus **who is called** Christ was born of her

B. Aorist tense participles indicate undefined action, undefined as to progress or completion.
1. Historical aorist participle
Nom. sing. masc. aor. pass. ptc.
χρηματισθεὶς δὲ κατ' ὄναρ ἀνεχώρησεν εἰς τὰ μέρη τῆς Γαλιλαίας (Matt. 2:22)
and **when he was warned** in a dream he departed into the parts of Galilee
2. Perfective aorist participle
Nom. sing. fem. aor. pass. ptc.
καὶ τίς ἡ σοφία ἡ **δοθεῖσα** τούτῳ (Mark 6:2)
and what [ἐστιν, is] the wisdom **that has been given** to him
3. Consummative aorist participle
Nom. sing. fem. aor. pass. ptc.
ἡ δὲ ἁμαρτία **ἀποτελεσθεῖσα** ἀποκύει θάνατον (James 1:15)
but sin **when it is finished** brings forth death
4. Aorist participle with pluperfect sense
Gen. pl. neut. aor. pass. ptc.
καὶ πάντες οἱ ἀκούσαντες ἐθαύμασαν **περὶ τῶν λαληθέντων** ὑπὸ τῶν ποιμένων πρὸς αὐτούς (Luke 2:18)
and all those who heard wondered **concerning those things that had been spoken** to them by the shepherds
5. Inceptive aorist participle emphasizing the beginning of the action
Nom. sing. masc. aor. act. ptc.
καὶ **πέμψας** αὐτοὺς εἰς Βηθλέεμ εἶπεν (Matt. 2:8)[45]
and **as he sent** them into Bethlehem he said

C. Perfect tense participles.
1. Intensive perfect participle indicating existing results
Nom. pl. masc. perf. act. ptc.
ἐξανέστησαν δέ **τινες** τῶν ἀπὸ τῆς αἱρέσεως τῶν Φαρισαίων **πεπιστευκότες** (Acts 15:5)
and **some** of those [ὄντων, who were] from the sect of the Pharisees **who had believed** rose up
2. Consummative perfect participle emphasizing completed action
Nom. sing. masc. perf. act. ptc.
ἐξῆλθεν ὁ **τεθνηκὼς** δεδεμένος τοὺς πόδας καὶ τὰς χεῖρας κειρίαις (John 11:44)
the one who had died came out, bound hands and feet with grave clothes

---

[45] Matt. 2:8 text is from GNT, NA & MT: WH & TR have Βηθλεέμ.

3. Perfect participle with present sense
   Nom. sing. masc. perf. act. ptc.
   ὤφθη δὲ αὐτῷ ἄγγελος κυρίου **ἑστὼς** ἐκ δεχιῶν τοῦ θυσιαστηρίου
   τοῦ θυμιάματος (Luke 1:11)
   and an angel of the Lord appeared to him **standing** at the right side
   of the altar of incense
4. Aoristic perfect participle indicating a simple past action
   Nom. sing. masc. perf. act. ptc.
   προσελθὼν δὲ καὶ ὁ τὸ ἓν τάλαντον **εἰληφὼς** εἶπεν (Matt. 25:24)
   and when **he who** also **received** the one talent approached, he said

D. Future tense participles are found only thirteen times in the NT. Thus, the
   variety of functions is limited to the following.
   1. Simple future participle
      Acc. pl. neut. fut. act. ptc.
      πορεύομαι εἰς Ἰερουσαλήμ, τὰ ἐν αὐτῇ **συναντήσοντά** μοι μὴ εἰδώς
      (Acts 20:22)[46]
      I am going to Jerusalem, not knowing **the things that will happen** to me
      in it
   2. Predictive future participle
      Nom. sing. masc. fut. act. ptc.
      ᾔδει γὰρ ἐξ ἀρχῆς ὁ Ἰησοῦς τίνες εἰσὶν οἱ μὴ πιστεύοντες καὶ τίς
      ἐστιν ὁ **παραδώσων** αὐτόν (John 6:64)
      for Jesus knew from the beginning who they were who did not believe
      and who is **the one who will betray** him

Select Bibliography for Participles

Argyle, A. W. "The Genitive Absolute in Biblical Greek." *Expository Times* 69 (October
    1957–September 1958): 285.
Ballantine, William G. "Attributive Aorist Participles in Protasis, in the New
    Testament" *Bibliotheca Sacra* (April 1889): 342-50.
_____. "Predicate Participles with Verbs in the Aorist." *Bibliotheca Sacra*
    (October 1884): 787-99.
Barrett, C. K. "The Imperative Participle." *Expository Times* 59 (October
    1947–September 1948): 165-66.

---

[46] Acts 20:22 text is from GNT, NA & MT: WH has ἐμοί; TR has Ἰερουσαλήμ.

Boyer, James L. "The Classification of Participles: A Statistical Study." *Grace Theological Journal* 5, no. 2 (1984): 163-79.

Daube, David. "The Participle and Imperative in 1 Peter." In *The First Epistle of Peter*, edited by E. G. Selwyn. 2d ed. Grand Rapids: Baker, 1981.

Gallagher, R. E. "The Present Periphrastic in the New Testament." Th.D diss., Dallas Theological Seminary, 1965.

Gillis, C. O. "Greek Participles in the Doctrinal Epistles of Paul." Doctoral diss., Southwestern Baptist Theological Seminary, 1937.

Greenlee, J. Harold. "New Testament Participles." *Bible Translator* 5 (1954): 98-101.

Hamblin, Robert L. "An Analysis of First Peter with Special Reference to the Greek Participle." Th.D. diss., Southwestern Baptist Theological Seminary, 1959.

Hartman, Lars. *Testimonium Linguae: Participial Constructions in the Synoptic Gospels.* Copenhagen: Ejnar Munksgaard, 1963.

Healey, Phyllis, and Alan Healey. "Greek Circumstantial Participles: Tracking Participants with Participles in the Greek New Testament." *OPTAT* 4, no. 3 (1990): 177-259.

Lee, G. M. "The Past Participle of Subsequent Action." *Novum Testamentum* 3 (July 1975): 199.

Meecham, H. G. "The Present Participle of Antecedent Action." *Expository Times* 64 (1953): 285-86.

_____. "The Use of the Participle for the Imperative in the New Testament." *Expository Times* 58 (October 1946–September 1947): 207-8.

Salom A. P. "The Imperatival Use of the Participle in the New Testament." *Australian Biblical Review* 11, no. 1-4 (1963): 41-49.

Scomp, Henry A. "The Case Absolute in the New Testament." *Bibliotheca Sacra* (January 1902): 76-84; (April 1902): 325-40.

Turner, C. H. "Notes and Studies. Auxiliary and Quasi-Auxiliary Verbs." *Journal of Theological Studies* 28, no. 2 (1927): 349-62.

Williams, C. B. *The Participle in the Book of Acts.* Chicago: Univ. of Chicago, 1909.

SCRIPTURE INDEX

Matthew

1:1	66
1:2	44, 77
1:6	37
1:16	50, 66, 421
1:18	82
1:19	23
1:20	156, 215, 239
1:21	79, 83, 292
1:24	48
2:1	50
2:6	44, 101, 412
2:7	62
2:8	85, 405, 422
2:12	6
2:13	44, 356
2:14	415
2:16	35
2:19-20	117
2:20	358
2:22	422
2:23	416
3:4	56
3:6	168
3:10	68
3:11	237
3:13	44, 61
3:14	286, 302
3:17	49, 249
4:1	44
4:3	89
4:6	348
4:10	49, 297
4:13	34
4:14	131
4:19	70
4:21	24, 38
4:24	3, 29
4:25	40
5:6	43
5:7	35
5:8	146, 293
5:14	60
5:16	2, 50, 54

Matthew

5:17	51
5:18	142
5:19	11
5:21	357
5:25	328, 407
5:26	321, 326
5:29	84
5:31	351
5:34	46, 328
5:34-35	66, 109
5:36	282
5:38	190
5:41	346
5:42	339
5:43	37
5:44	226
5:45	46, 65, 69, 265
5:46	90
6:2	284, 337
6:4	322
6:9	120, 167
6:9-13	359
6:10	354
6:19	160
6:21	27
6:24	15
6:25	103, 136, 147
6:26	100
6:27	401
6:29	204
6:30	16
6:34	27, 36
7:6	297
7:7	269
7:9	103
7:12	60
7:16	293
7:17	5
7:24	63
7:25	271
7:26	63, 396
8:2	267
8:4	348
8:6	271
8:8	323
8:9	354

Matthew

8:18	221
8:19	64
8:20	77, 341
8:23	239
8:28	245, 421
8:33	80
8:34	3
9:6	373
9:8	154
9:10	150
9:14	282
9:18	21, 77
9:21	90, 333
9:22	251
9:27	126, 152
9:29	132, 404
9:31	34
10:8	160
10:14	138
10:17	194
10:18	148
10:24	162
10:25	31
10:26	31, 277
10:27	31
10:30	79, 408
10:37	227, 237
10:40	393
11:1	306, 370, 403
11:3	421
11:11	140
11:18	400
11:19	193
11:20	4, 19
11:24	150
11:25	166
11:27	244
11:29	346
12:24	47
12:30	107
12:32	101
12:31	144
12:33	13
12:36	126
12:37	293
12:40	156
12:45	14

Matthew

12:49	176
12:50	115
13:2	314
13:4	371
13:8	2
13:17	4, 80, 281
13:19	394
13:22	9
13:28	320
13:32	18
13:38	60
13:39	52
13:45	150
14:2	275
14:3	411
14:5	401
14:7	217
14:16	372
14:21	232
14:23	20, 186, 397
14:24	276
14:31	200
15:4	152, 358
15:14	293
15:18	74
15:20	6, 152, 368
15:21	411
15:22	167
15:25	164
15:28	163
15:32	108
16:3	28, 155, 404
16:9	102
16:16	236, 384
16:19	296
16:22	294
16:23	287
16:24	349
16:27	216, 284
16:28	132
17:1	41, 282
17:2	9
17:5	307
17:13	120, 221
17:17	27

Matthew

17:20	310
17:27	186, 190
18:1	82
18:3	171
18:4	18
18:9	16
18:13	81
18:14	335
18:15	308
18:18	409
18:21	200
18:22	25
18:27	398
18:32	251
18:34	121
18:35	195
19:5	276, 297
19:12	202, 259
19:18	97
19:21	29
19:26	186
19:27	239, 277
19:28	208, 267
19:30	294
20:2	51
20:4	252
20:8	232, 239
20:12	305, 392
20:13	142
20:15	58, 254
20:20	129
20:26	10
20:28	97, 155
21:13	123
21:15	121
21:16	102
21:19	65
21:21	91, 324
21:24	291
21:25	27, 248
21:31	201
21:34	370
21:40	251
22:4	391
22:13	291
22:14	15
22:16	7
22:20	247
22:29	268

Matthew

22:31	263
22:32	46
22:35	402
22:38	17
22:42	247
23:2	308
23:5	152, 224, 371
23:15	281
23:23	303
23:27	286
23:29	239
23:31	391
23:33	184, 320
23:34	201
23:37	240
23:39	326
24:4	330
24:6	291
24:9	4
24:13	389
24:21	231
24:24	7
24:28	180
24:35	342
24:30	134
24:39	92
24:43	90, 264
25:2	15
25:4	58
25:10	304
25:11	166
25:15	178
25:23	120, 165
25:24	423
25:26	6
25:31	93, 329
25:34	390
25:35-36	302
25:40	19
25:44	239
26:5	328
26:24	264
26:28	220
26:34	23, 371
26:35	74
26:39	347
26:50	211
26:63	90

Matthew	
26:67	53
26:69	64, 272, 299
26:70	230
26:73	79
27:1	85
27:14	379
27:20	306
27:22	158, 159
27:23	347
27:31	160
27:42	291
27:44	75
27:48	150
27:51	27
27:54	275
27:55	145
27:57	151
27:63	251, 308
27:65	345
28:5	413
28:6	276, 302, 346
28:7	283
28:9	348
28:10	351
28:11	177
28:13	397
28:14	213, 292
28:18	400
28:20	118, 231, 374

Mark	
1:1	127
1:7	405
1:10	158
1:13	217
1:15	120, 208
1:17	29, 158, 265
1:27	2
1:35	74
2:2	85
2:6	303, 407
2:8	206
2:12	379
2:14	346
2:17	282

Mark	
2:19	103
2:21	141
2:26	186, 214
2:27	310
3:10	4, 266, 333
3:11	181
3:13	283
3:14	21, 79
3:21	238
3:22	188
3:24	257
3:34	124, 176
4:1	19, 268
4:2	300
4:3	420
4:4	220
4:6	107
4:17	399
4:23	349
4:26-27	328, 334
4:36	204, 283
4:38	164
4:39	345
5:1	196
5:3	9
5:7	159, 166
5:8	125
5:13	121, 214
5:16	388
5:23	30
5:30	158, 201
5:32	394
5:34	125
5:40	129
6:2	422
6:3	270
6:5	401
6:7	22
6:9	334
6:10	327
6:22	93
6:24	332
6:31	8, 240
6:35	8
6:39	127
6:41	197, 404
6:48	133
6:56	133

Mark	
7:4	334
7:6	237
7:10	345, 351
7:15	196, 289
7:23	24
7:25	243
7:27	157
7:34	354
7:37	369
8:1-2	118
8:2	127
8:3	292
8:12	294
8:14	310
8:20	310
8:27	117, 248
8:30	108
8:31	382
8:35	172
9:1	327, 332
9:17	399
9:23	38, 393
9:25	33, 109
9:26	370
9:33	299
9:35	7
9:39	213
10:7	249, 298
10:9	351
10:17	5, 322
10:18	13, 14
10:22	414
10:23	25, 412
10:24	25
10:27	15
10:32	394
10:35	125
10:45	190
11:5	301
11:13	209
11:14	361
11:16	195
11:17	98, 263
11:19	92, 181
11:20	410
11:25	75, 264
11:33	236
12:7	237, 277
12:9	15

Mark			Mark			Luke	
12:13	245		16:4	26		4:1	8
12:20	420		16:6	124, 175,		4:4	212
12:23	305			279, 307,		4:14	214
12:29	21, 305			413		4:23	292
12:30	3		16:7	358		4:24	14
12:34	194		16:11	238		4:26	168, 223
12:37	241		16:13	252		4:30	195
12:44	202, 390		16:15	345		4:36	255
13:1	176		16:18	30, 325		4:38	238
13:5	104					4:42	106, 232
13:7	355		Luke			5:1	220
13:12	116		1:7	148		5:3	128
13:13	228, 295,		1:11	423		5:7	405
	417		1:17	78		5:10	192, 406
13:17	393		1:20	295		5:17	206
13:20	307		1:21	60, 206		5:23	373
13:25	295		1:23	120		5:26	301
13:31	117, 290		1:26	34		5:31	400
13:35	183		1:32	67		5:32	97
14:4	248		1:33	210		5:35	181, 251
14:12	283		1:38	177, 361		5:37	175, 251
14:14	180, 327		1:41	44		6:11	365
14:18	421		1:53	393		6:13	193
14:28	218		1:59	302		6:19	116
14:32	92		1:60	100		6:23	4
14:36	166		1:62	362		6:31	341, 358
14:37	156		1:80	35		6:32	90
14:40	336		2:8	57, 241		6:35	275, 276,
14:41	347		2:15	144			293
14:42	340		2:17	385		6:37	336
14:49	407		2:18	422		6:42	319
14:55	143		2:25	250		6:47	133
14:56	98, 214		2:27	395		6:48	372
14:58	195		2:29	164, 283		6:49	55
14:63	404		2:35	173, 241		7:2	420
14:64	139		2:36	203, 274		7:7	82
14:70	218		2:40	276		7:12	47, 140
15:2	118		2:48	304		7:13	212
15:5	102		2:49	99, 263,		7:14	238
15:10	315			315		7:22	359
15:18	348		3:3	197		7:29	416
15:24	246, 269		3:4	203		7:30	228
15:26	408		3:7	186, 377		7:31	247
15:27	202		3:8	13		7:32	43, 150,
15:32	350		3:13	219			255
15:38	191		3:15	364		7:46	303
15:41	32, 389		3:16	272, 373		7:47	5, 20(2)
15:43	186		3:21	376		8:5	371
16:3	259		3:22	189		8:18	106

Luke

8:22	51
8:24	166
8:27	67
8:28	18, 46
8:29	315
8:39	216, 421
8:42	88, 277
8:45	388, 412
9:14	22, 161
9:18	299, 387
9:25	403
9:26	159
9:29	375
9:36	19
9:41	163, 183
9:46	9
9:48	11
9:57	93, 327
9:60	358
10:4	331, 342
10:7	76
10:8	326
10:18	298, 410
10:23	121
10:30	65
10:35	326
10:39	32
10:40	31
11:1	374, 407
11:2	181
11:3	359
11:5	164
11:8	175
11:9	119, 358
11:18	210
11:20	174
11:27	305
11:40	26, 165
11:44	287
11:45	421
11:51	179
12:4	194
12:8	143, 208
12:12	56
12:19	165, 355
12:24	136
12:30	249
12:32	345
12:34	179, 293

Luke

12:35	349(2), 407
12:37	251
12:45	333
12:48	139
12:52	296
12:53	209
12:54-55	329
12:58	108, 373
13:2	312
13:9	174
13:14	379, 405
13:15	147
13:16	98
13:25	173, 333, 338, 380
13:29	119
13:34	160, 166, 229, 266
14:1	207
14:7	224, 395
14:8	228, 328, 337, 417
14:8-9	333
14:13	325
14:14	206, 232, 329, 337
14:23	312
14:29	333
14:30	368
14:31	148
14:32	224
14:33	59
15:4	93, 326, 395
15:6	42
15:10	212
15:17	47, 152
15:18	231, 296, 405
15:29	284, 339
15:31	254, 285
16:1	394
16:2	284
16:5-6	287
16:13	81, 100, 282
16:16	310
16:17	47, 64, 367

Luke

16:24	134
16:26	85, 106, 328
16:27-28	322
16:28	322
16:30	336
17:2	221
17:8	326
17:10	300, 414
17:12	185
17:20	417
17:22	133, 182, 290
17:25	193
17:28	25
17:31	104
17:35	406
18:2	245
18:3	404
18:5	405
18:9	395
18:10	302
18:12	281
18:13	49
18:16	277
18:18	165
18:19	12
18:30	384
18:31	151
18:36	364
18:40	369
18:43	301
19:2	414
19:3	194
19:5	164
19:7	153, 188, 219
19:8	75
19:10	394
19:17	29, 349
19:22	314
19:47	369
19:48	320
20:6	378
20:10	297
20:11	73
20:13	236, 319
20:17	275
20:21	280

Luke

20:26	306
20:33	157
20:35	132, 413
20:38	77
20:46	349
21:5	151
21:7	183
21:9	285
21:17	274, 406
21:21	346(2), 350
21:24	278, 295
21:25	67
21:26	391
21:28	412
21:31	325
21:37	277
21:38	301
22:7	207
22:10	177
22:11	143, 180
22:15	152
22:19	226
22:27	204, 389
22:28	386
22:31	166
22:41	88, 161
22:61	132
22:69	406
22:70	52
23:8	24, 409
23:15	15
23:19	316
23:24	25
23:27	47, 130
23:28	126
23:30	268
23:31	319
23:33	178
23:34	412
23:40	101
23:41	15
23:43	292
24:1	22
24:5	217
24:6	419
24:11	239
24:13	161
24:21	375
24:23	374

Luke

24:25	163
24:26	262
24:29	225
24:35	87
24:49	335

John

1:1	49
1:6	68
1:9	33
1:11	196
1:12	69
1:14	304
1:15	230
1:17	42
1:19	43
1:22	391
1:23	410
1:29	37, 176
1:31	266
1:33	158
1:36	409
1:47	26
2:1	276
2:2	52
2:3-10	283
2:3	283
2:4	283
2:5	283
2:7	283
2:8	283
2:9	87, 262
2:9-10	283
2:12	52
2:15	397
2:16	104
2:19	290, 347
2:25	246
3:16	45, 85
3:18	104
3:19	86
3:26	176, 281, 312
3:27	408
3:28	413
3:30	252
3:31	45, 419
4:1	17, 81
4:6	67

John

4:9	137
4:10	307
4:11	48
4:12	136
4:14	74
4:15	347
4:18	312
4:22	281
4:24	122
4:25	124
4:27	68
4:31	206
4:32	53
4:37	387
4:38	312
4:40	50
4:41	162
4:43	50
4:52	30
4:53	3
5:7	222, 238, 280
5:9	122
5:11	13
5:13	135, 418
5:14	153
5:24	171
5:30	58, 253
5:35	384
5:37	383
5:46	251
5:47	252
6:2	116
6:10	161
6:28	320
6:30	83, 84
6:33	144
6:36	313
6:39	105
6:51	60, 122, 388
6:57	61, 383, 420
6:63	120
6:64	31, 386, 423
6:65	329
7:15	107, 401
7:16	57

John

7:19	248
7:28	73
7:32	409
7:35	141
7:37	346
7:44	300
7:47	103, 263
7:48	263
7:49	116
7:52	176
8:12	66
8:13	256
8:14	79
8:16	92
8:17	21, 58, 253
8:19	172
8:23	200
8:25	247
8:28	288
8:42	59, 66, 89, 172, 275, 300
8:46	196
8:56	124
8:57	262
9:1	13
9:3	84
9:4	92, 182, 391
9:5	65, 287
9:7	359
9:16	5
9:22	269
9:25	90
9:28	252
10:3	132
10:7	141
10:10	16, 51
10:11	2, 121, 226
10:14	58
10:16	74, 250
10:18	256
10:22	117
10:26	58, 253
10:28	332
10:30	42, 126
10:33	285

John

11:12	264
11:15	240, 272
11:22	173
11:24	32
11:27	52
11:34	176
11:36	183
11:38	239, 257
11:43	164
11:44	422
11:56	255
12:3	141
12:6	275
12:8	265
12:9	288
12:14	240
12:15	209
12:23	335
12:28	164
12:32	91, 258
12:36	123
12:37	230, 402
13:1	200
13:9	154
13:10	100
13:12	309
13:13	125
13:17	273
13:27	252
13:28	224, 390
13:33	20
13:35	253
14:9	388
14:10	262
14:12	73, 249
14:23	262
14:24	254
14:26	125
14:27	2
14:28	307
14:30	4
15:3	273
15:5	209, 232
15:13	17
15:15	261
15:19	264, 274
15:20	254
15:24	313
15:27	285

John

16:4	299
16:5	189, 223, 395
16:7	106, 286
16:9	197, 240
16:13	187
16:17	284
16:20	198
16:24	329
16:27	262, 311
16:33	331
17:5	222, 371
17:10	58, 254
17:11	165
17:14	97, 253
17:17	253
17:18	73, 308
17:19	226, 408
17:20	76
17:23	329
17:25	249
17:26	328
18:1	179
18:2	220, 389
18:4-5	287
18:15	6
18:16	265
18:17	129
18:18	315
18:20	208
18:23	231, 263
18:25	411
18:31	348
18:36	337
19:3	52
19:11	299
19:12	324
19:16	76
19:20	29
19:21	52
19:24	105
19:25	219
19:31	251
20:1	36
20:4	18
20:9	102
20:12	153, 204, 223
20:16	167

John

20:17	353
20:19	198
20:24	202
20:26	398
20:27	176
20:29	80
20:30	407
21:2	201
21:3	236
21:6	194
21:8	135, 150
21:10	308
21:11	401
21:18	181, 261, 272, 300
21:25	384

Acts

1:1	18, 33, 79, 163
1:3	54, 61, 372, 387
1:6	55
1:7	156
1:10	87
1:16	137
1:20	351
1:22	50
2:3	385
2:4	6
2:6	409
2:8	183, 207
2:16	416
2:20	197
2:22	145
2:23	41, 383
2:24	377
2:26	153
2:38	350
2:39	149, 198
2:40	354
2:45	172
3:2	12, 158, 301
3:7	140
3:10	140, 212
3:14	39
3:16	195
3:17	304

Acts

3:19	83
3:24	26, 78
4:1	118, 130
4:2	379
4:5	211
4:8	167
4:10	8, 205
4:12	389
4:13	40
4:17	335
4:19	132
4:21	212
4:25	141
4:33	80
5:4	151
5:14	269
5:15	245
5:23	26
5:25	289
5:28	135
5:31	249
5:34	149
5:36	257
5:39	11
5:41	267
6:1	135, 206
6:2	286, 367
6:7	47, 298
6:10	368, 374
7:2	420
7:3	325
7:4	244, 286
7:10	210
7:21	257
7:33	313
7:35	247
7:51	146, 288
7:55	157
7:58	137, 162, 220
8:1	210
8:10	11, 17
8:15	85
8:19	330
8:24	314, 347
8:29	356
8:31	184, 362, 363

Acts

8:32	211
8:34	247
8:40	231, 372
9:4	162
9:10	177
9:16	143, 227
9:17	140, 168, 335
9:18	298
9:21	315, 386
9:27	183
9:36	287, 415
9:37	398
9:40	304
10:1	12
10:9	162
10:14	108
10:16	27
10:17	206
10:19	406
10:21	284
10:22	187
10:26	240
10:28	375
10:31	164
10:38	5, 54, 192
10:40	12, 147
10:41	392
10:43	249
11:2	268
11:5	271
11:10	27
11:15	371
11:17	247, 262, 411
11:21	66
11:23	152
11:27	120
11:28	369, 380
12:1	193
12:5	271
12:6	27, 407
12:7	404
12:9	98, 388
12:11	24
12:14	222
12:18	174, 204
13:11	230, 281

Acts
13:16	167
13:28	401
13:31	188
13:38	166, 377
13:46	139
13:48	316
13:50	383
14:3	385
14:4	178
14:15	273
14:18	397
14:22	239
14:23	315
14:26	74, 408
14:27	141, 144
15:2	43, 65, 68
15:3	265
15:4	42
15:5	422
15:13	379
15:22	42, 386
15:23	41, 42
15:25-26	146
15:27	242
15:29	138, 348
15:30	53
15:32	123
16:3	419
16:12	246, 272
16:13	265, 301
16:14	392
16:15	12
16:17	250
16:21	153, 399, 418
16:30	335
16:36	250
16:37	83, 236, 350
17:3	412
17:4	3, 34
17:12	43
17:15	29, 88
17:18	362
17:21	17
17:22	18
17:24	126

Acts
17:27	175, 194 362, 363, 402
17:28	48, 208
17:29	46
18:2	246
18:3	189
18:8	300
18:9	342
18:12	210
18:14	307
18:19	73
18:21	403
18:27	374
18:28	381
19:3	46
19:10	370, 381
19:13	159, 280
19:19	231
19:26	288
19:28	135
19:32	315
19:40	376
20:6	218
20:9	194
20:10	203
20:11	211
20:17	129
20:18	192
20:19	207
20:22	415, 423
20:25	293
20:26	26
20:30	241, 404
20:36	225
21:13	28, 198
21:16	246
21:18	225
21:19	22, 187
21:24	355
21:26	226
21:33	246
21:35	229
21:37	282
21:38	222
22:3	414
22:5	402
22:6	222, 398
22:9	225

Acts
22:11	228
22:16	405
22:17	398
22:18	208
22:20	303, 315
22:22	298, 347
22:25	367
22:27	179
22:28	80, 142
23:1	143, 250
23:3	163, 385
23:5	314
23:6	271
23:15	371
23:18	53
23:21	231, 338
23:30	373
24:1	214
24:2	133
24:4	237
24:8	291
24:15	279, 378
24:18	186
24:19	192, 363(2)
24:22	215
24:27	387, 413
25:9	44
25:10	29, 289, 407
25:12	314
25:13	135, 246
25:14	302
25:19	225, 245
25:20	301
25:26	214
26:3	418
26:5	304
26:8	189, 219
26:11	302
26:13	227
26:14	268
26:16	81
26:18	199, 392
26:21	420
26:27	146
26:28	285
26:30	52
26:32	267, 376
27:7	216

Acts

27:11	270
27:12	184
27:14	238
27:15	298
27:20	17
27:21	107, 164, 415
27:34	222, 253
27:39	364
27:44	209
28:4	402
28:11	306
28:17	301
28:18	372
28:19	132, 375
28:22	279
28:24	53
28:25	195
28:26	321
28:28	356
28:31	221

Romans

1:1	13
1:2	55
1:3	62
1:4	137
1:5	117
1:6	141
1:8	3, 279
1:9	59, 87
1:10	184
1:13	229
1:14	78, 81
1:24	208
1:25	137
2:1	64, 167
2:3	163
2:4	285
2:5	215
2:12	69
2:19	76, 158
2:21	64
2:25	129, 339
3:4	173, 349
3:5	103
3:10	278
3:20	69
3:21	144

Romans

3:24	414
3:26	199
3:27	69
3:29	128
3:30	50
4:1	68
4:3	198
4:10	183
4:13	278
4:17	396
4:18	215, 220, 276
4:21	267
4:24	395
5:1	416
5:2	311
5:3	77
5:8	12, 418
5:9	417
5:10	270
5:11	411
5:12	212
5:13	70, 419
5:16	202
5:21	79
6:1	331
6:2	151
6:4	136
6:5	77, 138, 272
6:8	119
6:13	69
6:14	97, 229, 298
6:15	104
6:20	8
6:23	122
7:2	270
7:3	148
7:7	262, 266, 361
7:14	16, 276
7:18	368
7:22	36
7:24	246
8:1	76, 82
8:8	146
8:14	270
8:16	241

Romans

8:17	336
8:21	136
8:23	129, 240
8:27	226
8:28	12, 199, 418
8:32	175
8:33	49
8:34	46
8:35	130
9:1	279, 280
9:7	68
9:8	46
9:12	18
9:15	173
9:17	323
9:20	263
9:21	178, 241
9:26	124
9:29	307
9:30	54
10:4	121
10:6	54
10:9	157, 293
10:11	34
10:13	47, 173
10:14	232
11:2	149
11:4	257
11:6	87, 123
11:8	156
11:10	347, 351, 352
11:22	176
11:25	194
11:30	152
11:33	88, 127
12:1	14
12:2	356
12:3	3, 369, 418
12:6	13
12:9	16
12:12	410
12:14-15	372
12:16	104, 258
12:20	324
12:21	354
13:4	199

Romans

13:8	314
13:9	297
13:10	16, 278
13:11	28, 76, 92, 236
13:12	334
13:14	359
14:4	6
14:5	178, 354
14:11	267, 280
14:13	109, 319
14:15	252
14:19	76
14:20	357
14:23	122, 314
15:4	253
15:5	255
15:6	341
15:8	377
15:9	155
15:10	356
15:11	346
15:13	371
15:16	417
15:19	380, 381
15:20	179, 330
15:30	223
15:31	191, 390
15:32	334
15:33	126
16:1	331
16:1-2	323
16:2	139, 326
16:4	288
16:5	3
16:17	309
16:22	280, 389
16:25	147
16:27	6, 149

1 Corinthians

1:1	124
1:2	62
1:4	45
1:5	266
1:6-7	107
1:9	46
1:10	57, 78, 105, 328

1 Corinthians

1:12	128
1:13	103
1:16	75
1:18	37
1:29	106
2:5	128, 339
2:6	140
2:8	90, 98, 172
2:11	37, 133
2:12	322
3:1	271
3:3	187
3:6	265
3:8	42
3:10	350
3:13	9
3:15	236, 244
3:18	10
4:1	239
4:3	337
4:4	270
4:5	192
4:7	262
4:8	175, 306
4:16	237
4:17	160
5:2	201, 236, 289, 306
5:3	311
5:8	207
6:1	213, 224
6:3	290
6:6	217
6:11	299
6:12	244, 286, 296
6:13	147
6:19	116, 258
6:20	141
7:1	376
7:8	15
7:9	348
7:11	10, 81, 382
7:14	174
7:20	243
7:27	311
7:28	285

1 Corinthians

7:29	339
7:32	38
7:36	347
8:4	313
8:5	289
8:6	243
8:12	200
8:13	83, 197
9:1	205
9:2	175
9:4	103
9:7	182, 247
9:8	263
9:16	277, 331
10:8	109
10:12	328, 348, 370
10:13	296
10:16	99, 138
10:17	21
10:25	413
10:27	108
10:28	396
10:29	85, 229
11:3	369
11:6	353
11:7	122
11:13	242
11:15	119
11:18	161
11:20	242
11:23	50
11:25	330
11:27	139
11:32	338
11:34	88, 173, 322
12:5	56
12:8	177
12:11	19
12:13	80
12:15	86, 202
12:17	28, 121
12:22	11
12:27	203
12:31	18
13:1	330
13:8	82
13:11	182, 301

1 Corinthians

13:12	292, 294, 306
13:13	18, 70
14:10	362
14:11	294
14:15	148
14:16	172, 253
14:17	177
14:20	148
14:23	98, 263
14:28	352
14:29	351
14:31	216
14:34	353
14:37	123
15:2	247
15:8	89
15:8-9	73
15:9	7, 11, 18, 124
15:10	10, 45, 67
15:15	46
15:17	89, 121
15:23	129
15:25	4
15:36	281
15:37	363, 385
15:39	122, 240
15:55	165
15:56	60
16:3	326
16:5	83, 283, 325
16:6	327
16:9	311
16:10	28
16:11	322
16:16	320, 338
16:19	20, 280

2 Corinthians

1:1	48, 148, 419
1:2	66
1:3	39
1:7	295
1:9	213, 258, 408

2 Corinthians

1:11	237
1:12	223
1:23	268
2:2	416
2:3	253
2:7	184
2:11	228, 236
2:13	196
2:14	188, 205
2:15	204, 287
2:17	289, 406
3:1	75
3:2	228
3:3	151, 187
3:5	258
3:8	183
3:14	36
3:15	27
3:17	60
4:1	307
4:2	267
4:3	289
4:4	243
4:6	387
4:7	201
4:13	57
4:16	36
5:1	284
5:2	142
5:4	262
5:13	309
5:14	130, 399
5:15	40, 392
5:16	312
5:17	86
5:20	280
6:9	177
6:14	149
6:15	217
6:17	354
6:18	115, 273, 292
7:1	259, 319
7:8-9	263
7:9	108, 199
7:12	174
7:13	193
7:14	123
8:5	144

2 Corinthians

8:9	9, 252, 306
8:14	198
8:15	5
8:17	309
8:22	305, 309
8:23	227
9:2	50
9:3	408
9:4	187, 324
9:7	202, 282
9:9	266
9:11	238
10:4	224
10:7	128, 129
10:8	324
10:9	174, 195
10:13	230
10:14	204
10:17	352
11:2	136
11:7	160
11:12	290
11:15	276
11:16	342, 381
11:21	173
11:25	305
11:26	68
12:2	232
12:5	103
12:8	191, 227
12:9	25
12:10	180, 340
12:11	229
12:12	204
12:14	223
12:15	226
12:17	312
12:18	98, 231
12:20	104, 338
12:21	213
13:2	292
13:3	199
13:5	259
13:7	339
13:9	93, 325
13:11	56

Galatians
1:1	101
1:2	126
1:4	39
1:7	79
1:10	299
1:11	62
1:13	215
1:15	128
1:16	150, 341
1:21	44
1:22	54
1:23	62
2:1	195, 304
2:3	225, 292
2:5	225, 304
2:6	192
2:7	159
2:10	320
2:14	288
2:16	197, 337
2:19	147
2:20	38
2:21	82
3:1	6, 163
3:5	154
3:8	121
3:11	15
3:14	44
3:22	69
3:23	60, 157
3:24	10
3:25	135
3:27	268, 304
4:1	123
4:3	316, 409
4:4	120
4:9	143
4:16	398
4:21	64
4:25	36, 274
4:26	44
4:29	414
4:31	273
5:3	86
5:4	285, 308
5:6	101
5:8	201
5:13	255
5:14	38

Galatians
5:17	327
5:18	151, 162
5:24	48, 310
5:25	341
5:26	9
6:1	91, 337
6:2	255, 352
6:4	346
6:6	415
6:8	154
6:9	146
6:10	87
6:12	285
6:13	281
6:14	364
6:17	20, 352

Ephesians
1:4	268
1:6	205
1:13	156, 270
1:19	394
1:21	206
1:22	55, 227
2:3	302
2:4	418
2:5	145, 408
2:11	138
2:12	138
2:13	28
2:14	119, 389
2:18	162
2:20	131
3:1	131
3:2	175
3:3	19
3:5	2
3:16	378
3:17	157
3:18	40
4:1	139
4:6	7
4:11	53
4:14	109
4:20	99, 119
4:21	207
4:22	372
4:24	375
4:25	255

Ephesians
4:30	270
4:31	359
5:6	145, 350
5:8	182
5:18	355
5:25	79, 238
5:26	130
5:27	8
5:28	258
5:29	310
5:31	154
5:33	84, 331
6:1	53, 125
6:2	115, 275
6:3	143, 272
6:11	353
6:14	131
6:16	384
6:23	149

Philippians
1:7	381
1:9	78, 340
1:9-10	339
1:19	40
1:21	61
1:22	137
1:26	57
1:27	139
1:29	368
2:2	340
2:10	128
2:13	80, 386
2:15	9, 14
2:16	99
2:26	303
2:28	339
3:1	167, 177
3:5	216
3:9	254
3:11	184
3:12	81, 269
3:18	300
4:5	28, 350
	356
4:7	205
4:10	182
4:11	205
4:12	205

Philippians
4:15	164
4:16	305
4:17	99
4:18	189
4:21	225, 239

Colossians
1:5	62
1:7	32
1:9	403
1:13	128
1:15	33
1:18	49
1:21	387
1:24-5	305
1:28	14
1:29	104
2:4	108
2:5	91
2:10	47
2:17	243, 390
2:21	109, 331
3:1	269
3:3	153
3:10	410
3:11	180
3:13	28
3:15	9
3:18	125
3:19	52
3:20	215
3:21	105, 340
4:3	220
4:4	87
4:6	400
4:9	202
4:12	47, 207, 338
4:16	219
4:17	309

1 Thessalonians
1:2	282
1:5	55
1:6	140
1:8	20, 130, 312
1:9	51
2:4	63, 146
2:7	256
2:8	59
2:9	197
2:10	28, 64
2:13	27
2:17	155
3:3	269, 377
3:4	300
3:11	41, 52
3:12	48
3:13	199, 230
4:1	38
4:6	61
4:10	44
4:12	107
4:14	119
4:15	63, 321
4:17	291
4:18	86, 250
5:2	87, 313
5:6	105
5:9-10	63
5:10	82
5:23	361
5:27	159

2 Thessalonians
1:3	256
1:5	140, 226
1:8	63
1:11	84, 323
2:3	104, 107
2:5	98
2:6	256
2:10	187, 190
2:13	119, 168, 227, 417
2:15	82
2:16	67
3:3	191
3:7	183
3:10	92
3:11	108, 284, 410
3:12	188
3:16	195

1 Timothy
1:3	106
1:8	332
1:12	13
1:16	63
1:18	166, 267, 341
1:19	244
1:20	338
2:2	340, 419
2:4	157
2:5	138, 248
2:7	197
2:8	400
2:10	286
2:15	331
3:4	132
3:7	36, 193
3:12	133, 356
3:15	320, 324
3:16	24
4:4	14
4:5	269
4:6	5
4:8	224, 225
4:10	213
4:12	107
4:15	249
4:16	257
5:1	70
5:3	26
5:5	134
5:9	69, 218
5:16	355
5:17	355
5:18	8, 284
5:19	214, 353
5:22	154
6:2	352
6:8	249, 403
6:9	7
6:10	275
6:12	2, 159
6:14	381
6:16	101
6:19	198, 258

2 Timothy
1:4	413
1:5	146
1:6	276

2 Timothy

1:8	336
1:8-9	40
1:9	63
1:11	309
1:12	313, 379
1:14	390
2:2	297
2:5	91, 324
2:6	132
2:10	323
2:12	286
2:13	10
2:15	154
2:19	419
2:20	178
2:22	216
3:5	353
3:7	109
3:8	146, 222, 416
3:11	305
3:14	306, 352
3:16	14
4:3	383
4:4	210
4:7	265, 311
4:8	20
4:11	199, 274
4:16	364
4:21	144

Titus

1:4	146
1:5	216, 332
1:6	14
1:7	51
1:11	189
1:12	26, 238
1:15	393
2:2	287
2:4	321, 330
2:5	337
2:7	221, 257
2:8	155, 200
2:13	80
2:15	345
3:3	255, 273
3:4	117
3:6	188

Titus

3:7	5
3:13	320
3:14	6
3:15	237

Philemon

1	39
3	126
11	78
15	322
16	156
19	57, 320
20	361
21	118

Hebrews

1:1	51
1:4	136
1:5	24, 248, 271
1:6	352
1:7	157
1:9	160, 249
1:10	130
1:12	88, 241, 290
1:13	173
1:14	396
2:3	229
2:7	151
2:9	30
2:11	157
2:12	154
2:13	124, 295
2:14	56, 241
2:17	123
3:1	39, 165
3:1-2	12, 418
3:3	17
3:11	88, 90
3:12	142, 185, 245
3:13	230, 338
3:18	369, 375, 380
4:1	336
4:2	73, 289, 399
4:3	294, 401

Hebrews

4:4	35
4:8	300
4:11	251
4:12	17, 386
4:16	331
5:3	220
5:5	224, 272
5:8	192, 418
5:11	151
5:12	123
5:13	142
6:3	91, 296
6:10	99
6:11	381
6:12	78
6:13	86, 214, 299
7:2	193, 415
7:3	197
7:7	228
7:10	182
7:11	375
7:20-21	53
7:21	271
7:24	196
7:25	200
8:1	134
8:2	2
8:3	250
8:10	198, 292
8:11	16
8:12	272, 336
9:2	11
9:3	218
9:7	51
9:8	374
9:17	181, 212
9:22	161
9:23	219
9:25	215
9:26	192
9:27	24
9:28	203
10:1	56, 247
10:2	172
10:3	129
10:4	155
10:9	21
10:10	408

Hebrews

10:11	102, 242
10:16	162
10:18	102
10:30	266
10:31	385
10:36	332
11:3	145, 378, 379
11:4	8, 219
11:6	368, 395
11:7	109, 138
11:9	57, 241
11:13	107
11:17	145
11:18	86
11:25	411
11:27	400
11:30	211
11:33	142
12:2	190
12:4	224
12:5	167
12:9	299
12:10	211
12:11	225, 393
12:14	100, 232
12:16	191
12:22	150
12:26	25
13:8	56
13:9	379
13:12	30, 231
13:14	279
13:17	236, 400
13:18	117
13:20-21	361, 363
13:22	117

James

1:1	51
1:4	8
1:5	89
1:6	69
1:7	55
1:12	10
1:14	396
1:15	422
1:18	145
1:19	61

James

1:21	32
1:27	39, 373
2:3	25
2:8	236
2:11	104
2:12	378
2:13	393
2:14	48, 49
2:15	10
2:15-16	324
2:18	291
2:21	49
2:24	348
3:2	249
3:4	19
3:6	122
3:10	56
3:14	116
3:15	406
3:16	180
3:17	20, 26, 136
4:5	51
4:8	165
4:9	354
4:11	346
4:12	63
4:14	278
4:15	191, 324
5:4	311
5:9	313
5:12	99, 159, 179
5:14	353
5:15	91

1 Peter

1:1	67
1:4-5	64
1:5	417
1:13	62, 254
1:15	10, 62, 396
1:16	297
1:17	156
1:18	145
1:20	134
1:21	40, 397
1:25	76

1 Peter

2:1	412
2:5	14
2:6	100
2:7	83
2:10	99, 182
2:12	13
2:13-14	416
2:14	421
2:20	264
2:22	101
2:25	303
3:9	190
3:13	388
3:14	8, 336, 363, 364, 377
3:15	25, 160
3:18	15, 221
4:4	399
4:5	29
4:8	67
4:10	259
4:11	171
4:12	356
4:14	37
4:17	61, 376
4:18	39
4:19	355
5:1	376
5:6	356
5:7	221, 286
5:12	158, 188, 309, 381

2 Peter

1:3	88
1:5	55
1:11	161
1:12	62, 402
1:13	250
1:15	57
1:17	122
1:18	55
1:19	385
1:21	182
2:1	395
2:9	201
2:11	218
2:19	123

2 Peter
2:21	367
3:2	377, 384
3:4	186, 284
3:7	289
3:8	219, 352
3:9	376
3:13	215, 243
3:14	378
3:15	353
3:17	414

1 John
1:1	130, 313
1:2	242
1:3	57
1:5	50, 59, 100
1:7	45, 50
1:9	84
2:1	84, 167
2:2	34, 58, 76, 143, 254
2:12	65
2:20	15, 192
2:23	101
2:25	49
2:26	391, 421
3:2	8, 45, 102, 293
3:4	59
3:7	251
3:10	45, 116
3:16	48
3:17	286
3:21	106
3:22	326
4:2	410
4:3	25
4:4	54
4:7	165
4:8	59
4:9	33, 392
4:10	74
4:17	120
4:18	24, 32
4:21	250
5:1	60, 394
5:4	125

1 John
5:14	332
5:16	159
5:18	268
5:20	2, 146

2 John
1	149
4	143
6	84, 323, 330

3 John
1	3, 34
6	139
11	16, 35
12	56

Jude
2	364
3	384
4	245
5	35
7	240
9	45
10	313
11	142
16	281

Revelation
1:3	394
1:4	33, 193
1:5	396
1:7	179, 213
1:10	267
1:17	223, 271
1:18	288, 406
1:20	33
2:5	24
2:7	392
2:10	134
2:11	33, 144, 337
2:13	180
2:16	217
2:19	4
2:25	174
2:26	390
3:3	184, 330

Revelation
3:4	184, 243
3:5	100, 268, 294
3:7	389
3:8	265
3:14	171
3:15	272, 284
3:18	218, 334, 340, 417
3:20	280
4:1	216, 218
4:8	278, 388
4:9	181, 391
5:1	390
5:4	11, 373
5:5	351
5:7	314
5:9	286
5:12	41
6:3	33
6:6	330, 357
6:12	34
6:13	228
6:14	237
6:15	134
6:16	191
6:17	377
7:2	6, 368
7:3	322
7:12	127, 171
7:13	262
7:14	314, 386
7:15	134, 143
7:16	101
8:4	35, 231
8:10	202, 209
9:5	106, 323
9:8	277
9:11	238
9:12	22
9:14	385
9:17	186
10:1	136
10:3	88
10:4	321
10:6	392
10:7	325
10:11	367
11:2	26, 36

Revelation

11:6	105, 327
11:7	325
11:13	35
11:14	33
11:17	305, 419
11:18	376
12:5	223
12:11	119
12:12	125, 196, 288, 390, 399
12:16	244
12:17	211
13:3	130
13:7	217
13:9	75
13:14	393
14:4	174
14:7	354, 392
14:11	131, 284
14:15	129
14:20	119, 230
15:1	308
15:3	237
15:4	271
15:8	139, 200
16:7	179
16:15	40, 155, 388
16:19	34
17:2	187
17:12	287
17:14	290
17:16	414
17:18	274
18:2	2
18:7	321
18:17	194
18:20	165
18:23	274, 321
19:8	335
19:9	388
19:11	11, 413
19:17	21
19:19	217
20:4	196, 209, 308
20:6	291
20:10	384

Revelation

20:14	21
21:3	119, 217, 275
21:4	278
21:7	276
21:10	192
21:19	150, 387
21:21	203
21:23	99
21:25	98, 321, 336
22:3	265
22:4	267
22:6	145
22:10	27
22:14	297
22:20	387

SUBJECT INDEX

Accusative Case 153, 239, 243, 245, 248,
    249, 252, 255, 258, 259
    Absolute 398
    Adverbial 160
    Apposition 156, 394
    Cognate 159
    Direct object 153, 239, 243, 245, 255,
        259, 393
    Double 160
    Manner 160
    Measure 161
    Oaths 159
    Object complement 69, 157, 387
    Predicate 158, 386
    Prepositions with 161, 240, 243, 255,
        259, 395
    Reference 159
    Subject of infin. 157, 239, 245, 395
    Supplementary ptc. 157, 239
    Time 156
Active Voice 264, 330, 351, 363, 374, 411
    Causative 265, 352
    Simple 264, 330, 351, 363, 374, 411
    Stative 265, 330, 352, 363, 374
Adjectives 1, 98, 105
    Adverbial 19
    Anarthrous 5, 13
    Articular 1, 32, 39
    Attributive 1
        First 1, 32
        Second 2, 33
        Third 2, 34
    Comparative 16
    Elative 19
    Forms of 1
    Functions of 1
    Irregular 3
    Numerals 20, 33, 35, 87, 88
        Adverbial 20
        Attributive 21, 32
        Cardinal 22, 64, 66
        Ordinals 20
        Substantive 21, 35
    Predicate 7
        Accusative 13
    Prepositive 5
    Substantive 15, 35
    Superlative 18
Adverbs 23, 99

Anarthrous 27
Articular 36
Attributive 26
    First 36
    Second 36, 81
Comparative 28
Conjunctive 30
Crasis 74
Forms of 23
Functions of 23
    Negative 99, 105
Predicate 27
Prepositions 30
Special Uses 29
Substantive 26, 36
Superlative 29
Temporal 107
Aorist Tense 303, 342, 358, 365, 379, 422
    Indicative mood 303
        Constative 303
        Culminative 306
        Dramatic 307
        Effective 306
        Elliptical 310
        Epistolary 309
        Futuristic 308
        Gnomic 310
        Historical 303
        Ingressive 305
        Perfect sense 309
        Pluperfect sense 309
        Potential 307
        Proleptic 308
    Infinitives 379
    Imperative mood 359
    Optative mood 365
Apollonius' Canon 45, 66
    Participles 422
    Subjunctive 342
Articles 31
    Absence of 65
    Adjectives 32
        Attributive 32
            First 32
            Second 33
            Third 34
        Numerals 32
            First Attributive 32
            Second Attributive 33

Substantive 35
Adverbs 36
    First Attributive 36
    Second Attributive 36
    Substantive 36
Anaphoric 49
Apollonius' Canon 45, 66
Articles with articles 37
Colwell's Rule 52, 66
Conjunctions with 38
Distributive 51
Forms of 31
Functions of 32
Generic 50
Granville Sharp's Rule 38, 66, 80, 396
Indefinite 21, 64
Infinites with 60
Kataphoric 50
Nonuse of 65
Nouns with 43, 66
Numerals 32
Participles with 61
Particles with 53
Prepositions with 54
Pronominal 48
Pronouns with 47, 52, 54
Repetition of 51
Qualitative substantives 68
Verbs with 59
Case
    Accusative 13, 153, 393
    Dative 144, 391
    Genitive 127, 390
    Nominative 118, 387
    Vocative 163
Clauses
    Causal 86, 398
    Conditional 89, 263, 324, 403
        First Class 89, 263
        Second Class 89, 264
        Third Class 90, 324
    Concessive 90, 324, 401
    Declarative 261
    Dependent 322
    Direct Discourse 87
    Explanatory 83
    Imperatival 84, 103, 320, 372
    Independent 319
    Indirect Discourse 87, 368, 369
    Interrogative 84, 98, 183, 246, 262
    Local 92, 327

Purpose 83, 84, 85, 322, 370, 402
Relative 92, 325
Result 84, 85, 88, 327, 370
Temporal 81, 87, 91, 325, 326, 370,
    397
Conjunctions 73, 98, 103, 107
    Accenting 75
    Adverbial 79
    Adversative 77, 80
    Appositional 80
    Causal 86, 88, 398
    Comparative 81, 87
    Concessive 90
    Conditional 88
    Connective 78
    Coordinating 77
    Crasis 73
    Direct discourse 87
    Disjunctive 81
    Elision 74
    Emphatic 80, 83
    Enclitic 80
    Explanatory 83
    Forms of 73
    Functions of 77
    Illative 83
    Imperatival 84
    Inferential 82
    Indirect discourse 85, 86, 89
    Interrogative 89
    Local 92
    Postpositive 75, 80, 82, 83
    Purpose 83, 84, 85
    Recitative 86
    Relative 92
    Result 84, 85, 88
    Subordinating 83
    Temporal 81, 87, 92
Crasis 74, 90
Dative Case 144, 238, 245, 247, 249, 252
    255, 257, 258
    Absolute 152, 239, 398
    Accompaniment 149
    Advantage 147, 239, 258, 392
    Adverbial 146
    Agency 151
    Apposition 146, 243, 392
    Association 149
    Cause 152
    Cognate 152
    Comparison 150

Destination 149
Direct object 145, 239, 245, 255, 392
Disadvantage 148, 239, 393
Indirect object 144, 238, 391
Instrumental 145
Interest 147
Location 150
Manner 152
Material 150
Means 145
Place 150
Possession 148, 239
Predicate 152
Prepositions with 153, 239, 243, 245, 255, 258, 392
Recipient 149
Reference 151
Respect 151
Sphere 148
Elision 74, 185
Ellipsis 8, 28, 59, 128, 287, 294, 302, 310, 328
Enclitics 85
Finite Verbs 261
Imperative Mood 345
Indicative Mood 261
Optative Mood 361
Subjunctive Mood 319
Future Tense 290, 423
Assurance 292
Elliptical 294
Emphatic Negative 294
Futuristic 290
Gnomic 293
Imperatival 297
Iterative 290
Periphrastic 295
Predictive 290
Prescriptive 297
Progressive 290
Promise 292
Purpose 296
Simple 291
Stative 290
Strong negation 294
Volitive 296
Genitive case 127, 236, 244, 247, 249, 252, 255, 256, 258
Absolute 135, 237, 397
Adverbial 134
Agency 140

Apposition 131, 390
Attributive 136
Comparison 136, 237
Complement 138, 237
Content 135
Descriptive 130, 391
Direction 141
Direct object 131, 237
Material 141
Objective 129, 237, 391
Partitive 133, 390
Possession 128, 255, 258, 390
Predicate 136, 237
Prepositions with 142, 237, 243, 244, 255, 258, 390
Price 141
Purpose 141
Quality 136
Reference 142
Relationship 129, 236, 243, 255, 258, 391
Separation 138
Source 140
Subjective 130, 237, 24, 391
Value 141
Granville Sharp's Rule 38, 66, 80
Imperative Mood 345
Challenge 348
Command 345
Demand 347
Elliptical 349
Exclamatory 348
Exhortation 346
Greeting 348
Indirect 349
Invitation 346
Periphrastic 348
Permission 347
Prohibitive 345
Request 346
Tense 357
Third Person 349
Voice 351
Voiceless εἰμι 356
Warning 348
Imperfect Tense 298
Aoristic 301
Customary 300
Descriptive 298
Elliptical 302
Impersonal 303

Inceptive 301
Iterative 300
Periphrastic 303
Pluperfect sense 302
Potential 299
Stative 299
Tendential 302
Indicative Mood 261
 Conditional 263
 Declarative 261
 Interrogative 262
 Tense 278
  Aorist 303
  Future 290
  Imperfect 298
  Perfect 310
  Pluperfect 314
  Present 279
 Voice 264
 Voiceless ἐμι 271
Infinitives 367
 Accusative Subject 157, 380, 395
 Adverbial 370
 Articular 60
 Complement 368, 372
 Imperatival 372
 Indirect Discourse 368
 Periphrastic 374
 Prepositions with 370
 Purpose 370
 Result 370
 Substantive 367
 Temporal 370
 Tense 378
 Voice 374
 Voiceless εἶναι 378
Middle voice 266, 331, 352, 364, 374, 411
 Active sense 267, 332, 375
 Deponent 266, 331, 352, 364, 375
 Different sense 268, 333, 353, 376
 Intensive 268, 335, 376
 Passive sense 335
 Reciprocal 269, 412
 Reflexive 268, 334, 353, 375, 411
Moods 261
 Imperative 345
 Indicative 261
 Optative 361
 Subjunctive 319
Negatives 97
 Adjectives 100, 107

Adverbs 101, 108
Conjunctions 100, 105, 109
Emphatic 100
Forms of 97
Functions of 97
Imperatives with 103
Indicatives with 103
Infinitives with 106
Interrogative 98, 103
Optatives with 104
Participles with 107
Subjunctives with 104
Temporal 102, 107
Nominative Case 118, 235, 243, 244, 246, 249, 251
 Address 125, 390
 Adverbial 127
 Appositional 124, 388
 Hanging 126, 389
 Independent 126
 Subject 118, 235, 387
 Predicate 52, 122
Nouns 67, 111
 Anarthrous 67
 Appositional 124
 Articular 38, 43
 Attributive 168
 Case 115, 118
  Accusative 153
  Dative 144
  Genitive 127
  Nominative 118
  Vocative 163
 Collective 116
 Common 44, 111
 Coordinate 117
 Declension 111
  First 111
  Second 112
  Third 113
 Distributive 116
 Forms of 111
 Gender 115
 Indeclinable 44, 67
 Indefinite 68
 Monadic 67
 Number 115
 Predicate 52, 122
 Proper 43, 111
 Qualitative 68
Numerals 20, 33, 35, 87, 88

Adverbial 20
Attributive 21, 32
Cardinal 22, 64, 66
Ordinal 20
Substantive 21, 35
Optative Mood 361
  Emphatic wish/prayer 361
  Potential 362
  Tense 364
  Voice 363
  Voiceless εἰμι 364
  Volitive 361
  Wish/prayer 361
Participles 383
  Address 63
  Adjectival 61, 383
    Attributive 61, 383
      First 61, 383
      Second 61, 384
      Anarthrous 385
    Predicate 386
  Adverbial 397
    Accusative absolute 398
    Anarthrous 385
    Causal 398
    Complementary 403
    Concessive 401
    Conditional 403
    Dative absolute 398
    Genitive absolute 397, 401
    Independent nominative 411
    Instrumental 401
    Manner 400
    Nominative absolute 411
    Purpose 402
    Redundant 400
    Temporal 397
  Appositional 63, 383, 384, 388, 394
  Articular 39
  Conjunctive 404
  Imperatival 410
  Indirect discourse 410
  Predicate 386
  Substantival 62, 387
    Accusative 393
    Address 390
    Dative 391
    Genitive 390
    Hanging nom. 388
    Nominative 387
    Periphrastic 288, 406

  Vocative 163
  Supplemental 157, 409
  Tense 420
  Verbal 403
    Conjunctive 404
    Imperatival 410
    Indirect discourse 410
    Periphrastic 288, 406
    Supplemental 157, 409
  Voice 411
  Voiceless εἰμι 418
Particles 171
  Articular 52
  Crasis 74
  ἀμήν 171
  ἄν 172
  ἄρα 174
  γε 174
  ἴδε 175
  ἰδού 176
  μέν 177
  ναί 179
  ὅπου 179
  ὅταν 180
  ὅτε 181
  ποτε 182
  πότε 183
  πῶς 183
  πώς 184
Passive voice 269, 335, 354, 364, 376,
    412
  Active sense 338, 354, 377
  Agent unexpressed 271, 337, 354, 376
  Agent with dative 270, 338, 356, 378
  Agent with preposition 269, 337, 354,
    377, 416
  Deponent 271, 336, 354, 376, 412
  Middle sense 339, 356
  Theological 269, 335, 354, 364, 376,
    413
Perfect Tense 310, 380, 422
  Aoristic sense 314
  Consummative 311
  Gnomic 314
  Indicative mood 310
  Intensive 311
  Iterative 312
  Periphrastic 289, 295
  Present sense 313
Periphrastic participles 288

Future 295, 406
Future perfect 295, 409
Imperative 349, 407
Imperfect 303, 407
Infinitive 374, 407
Perfect 289, 407
Present 288, 406
Subjunctive 329, 408
Pluperfect tense 314
Consummative 315
Imperfect sense 314
Intensive 315
Periphrastic 315
Prepositions 185
Articles with 53
Ellision 185
Idiomatic phrases 66
Improper 189, 229
ἔμπροσθεν 143, 230
ἐνώπιον 143, 231
ἔξω 231
ἕως 144, 231, 371
πρίν 371
χωρίς 144, 232
Proper 185, 190
ἀντί 186, 187, 190
ἀπό 142, 186, 187, 188, 191
ἄχρι(ς) 143, 229
διά 142, 162, 188, 195, 371, 378
ἐκ 142, 189, 200
ἐπί 143, 153, 162, 186, 187, 188, 208
εἰς 161, 196, 370
ἐν 153, 203, 371, 377
κατά 143, 161, 186, 187, 214
μετά 143, 162, 186, 187, 188, 216, 371
παρά 143, 153, 162, 186, 188, 189
περί 143, 162, 220
πρό 144, 222, 371
πρός 153, 162, 222, 370
σύν 153, 225
ὑπέρ 143, 162, 226
ὑπό 143, 162, 186, 187, 227
Present tense 278, 340, 357, 364, 378, 420
Indicative mood 278

Imperative mood 357
Aoristic 279
Conative 285
Customary 281
Descriptive 279
Durative 284
Elliptical 287
Explanatory 287
Futuristic 283
Gnomic 282
Habitual 281
Historical 282
Impersonal 285
Indirect discourse 288
Iterative 280, 341
Perfective 284
Periphrastic 288
Progressive 279, 341
Stative 286
Tendential 285
Infinitive 379
Optative mood 364
Participles 420
Subjunctive mood 340
Pronouns 235
Articles with 54
Crasis 73
Demonstrative 54, 73, 248
Indefinite 64, 244
Intensive 55, 240
Interrogative 246
Personal 54, 73, 235
Explicit 271
Implicit 271
Possessive 56, 252
Reciprocal 254
Reflexive 58, 256
Relative 104, 242
Subjunctive mood 319
Comparative 328
Concessive 324
Conditional 324
Deliberative 319
Dependent 322
Elliptical 328
Emphatic negation 321
Hortatory 319
Imperatival 320
Independent 319
Local 327
Negative result 327

    Periphrastic 329
    Prohibitive 321
    Purpose 322
    Relative 325
    Substantive 323
    Temporal 325, 326
    Tense 340
    Voice 330
    Voiceless εἰμι 339
    Warning 328
Tense 271, 339, 356, 364, 378, 418
    Aorist 303, 342, 358, 365, 379, 422
    Future 290, 380, 423
    Imperfect 298
    Perfect 310, 380, 422
    Pluperfect 314
    Present 279, 340, 357, 364, 379, 420
    Subjunctive 340
Vocative case 52, 163
    Apposition 166
    Attributive 168
    Emphatic 163, 166
    Predicate 167
Voice
    Active 264, 330, 351, 363, 374, 411
    Middle 266, 331, 352, 364, 374, 411
    Passive 269, 335, 354, 364, 376, 412
    Voiceless 271, 339, 356, 364, 378,
       418